Also by Samuel Flagg Bemis

Jay's Treaty, a Study in Commerce and Diplomacy (New York: The Macmillan Co.; 1923).

Pinckney's Treaty, a Study of America's Advantage from Europe's Distress (Baltimore: The Johns Hopkins Press; 1926, 1941).

American Secretaries of State and Their Diplomacy, editor and contributor (10 volumes; New York: Alfred A. Knopf; 1927- 9).

The Hussey-Cumberland Mission and American Independence (Princeton: The Princeton Press; 1931).

The Diplomacy of the American Revolution (New York: D. Appleton-Century Co.; printed for the American Historical Association; 1935; second edition, 1937).

Guide to the Diplomatic History of the United States, 1775–1921, with Grace Gardner Griffin (Washington: Government Printing Office; published for the Library of Congress; 1935).

Diplomatic History of the United States (New York: Henry Holt and Co.; 1936; revised editions, 1942, 1950, 1955).

The Rayneval Memoranda of 1782 (Worcester: American Antiquarian Society; 1938).

La Política Internacional de los Estados Unidos. Interpretaciones (Lancaster, Pa.: printed for the Carnegie Endowment for International Peace; 1939).

Early Diplomatic Missions from Buenos Aires to the United States, 1811–1824 (Worcester: American Antiquarian Society; 1939).

The Latin American Policy of the United States, an Historical Interpretation (New York: published for the Yale Institute of International Studies by Harcourt, Brace and Co.; 1943; Spanish translation: Fondo de Cultura Económica; Mexico, 1943).

John Quincy Adams and the Foundations of American Foreign Policy (New York: Alfred A. Knopf; 1949).

JOHN QUINCY ADAMS

AND

THE UNION

JOHN QUINCY ADAMS

AND

THE UNION

BY

SAMUEL FLAGG BEMIS

NEW YORK ALFRED A. KNOPF
1970

L. C. catalog card number: 55–9271

THIS IS A BORZOI BOOK,
PUBLISHED BY ALFRED A. KNOPF, INC.

PUBLISHED FEBRUARY 20, 1956
SECOND PRINTING, JUNE 1965
THIRD PRINTING, MAY 1970

Manufactured in the United States of America

TO

THE FUTURE BIOGRAPHERS

OF

JOHN QUINCY ADAMS

Till the sad breaking of that Parlament
Broke him, as that dishonest victory
At Chæronea, *fatal to liberty,*
Kill'd with report that Old man eloquent. . . .
                    MILTON: *To the Lady Margaret Ley*

Preface

SEVERAL YEARS AGO appeared a book on what I called John Quincy Adams's First Career, as America's greatest diplomatist and inspired continental-ist.[1] Uncertainty whether I might be able to complete the whole biography had led me to bring it out as an independent book standing by itself, but I then intimated that someday there might be another volume. Here it is: *John Quincy Adams and the Union.*

The present book covers his spectacular Second Career: as Minority President with visions for a consolidated Union of Liberty with Power, then in Congress as a crusader in crescendo for human rights against the expansion of slavery—abolitionist at heart but constitutionalist in practice —until he fell at the climax of his life a dying gladiator on the floor of the House of Representatives. This second volume is the other half of John Quincy Adams's biography, written against a background of the rising sectional controversy over slavery and state rights. My two volumes, on John Quincy Adams's two careers, thus fit together—with some slight unavoidable overlapping in the field of foreign relations—to make a basic, I will not say a definitive, biography. An introductory chapter to the present volume on his Second Career reminds the reader of the background of Adams's First Career.

As biographer I have tried to look behind the statesman to see more of the man himself, his compulsive psychology, his social and family relationships, his religious feeling and attitude toward life on this earth and hereafter. As historian I find myself looking over his shoulder, with the aid of modern scholarship, backwards and forwards in time beyond his controversial publications into the political and moral problems that beset "this Union"—his constant sturdy phrase for the Republic—in the period of its continental growing-pains when it was taking shape as a nation.

Monologue and dialogue used in the narrative are strictly authentic even though some of the forms sound a little stilted to the modern ear, but I have ventured where desirable to turn indirect into direct discourse, adapting the tense thereto where necessary. I have also spelled out the ampersand and other symbols, but have generally preserved the original spelling and punctuation in all quotations, of manuscript or printed material, from Adams papers or others. As explained in the Preface to the earlier volume, hereafter cited as Volume I, I consider John Quincy Adams's extraordinary Diary generally reliable for statements of fact and for dates, but subjectively colored in expressions of opinion where it must be judged according to the canons of historical criticism.

The existing, inadequate biographies of John Quincy Adams are also

[1] *John Quincy Adams and the Foundations of American Foreign Policy* (New York: Alfred A. Knopf; 1949).

mentioned in the Preface to Volume I. Since that publication my attention has been called to a typescript, among the Adams Papers in the Massachusetts Historical Society, of an incomplete biography of John Quincy
Adams by Brooks Adams, constructed largely of excerpts from his Diary
and correspondence, embellished by historical excursions of the grandson
author. Interesting as is this appreciation by a family historian, I have
preferred to follow my own judgment. My present, and final, volume is
based directly on the Adams family papers, printed and unprinted, and
indirectly on a host of other papers of American statesmen, politicians,
and personalities as already largely exploited by biographers and historians. The Adams Manuscripts, hitherto not considerably used by any
scholar outside the family, consist of the diaries, letters, and other unpublished writings of John Adams, John Quincy Adams, and Charles Francis
Adams, together with incoming correspondence. They cover a vital century of American history, and are now being made conveniently available
in microfilm to all historians at libraries strategically located throughout
the United States. These reproductions, supplemented by a program of
extensive publication, will assist future scholars in correcting, refining,
and rounding out the historical picture here presented of the second Adams and his struggles with himself and his times. I hope my work will be
helpful to them.

No definitive archival numeration having yet been established for the
Adams Papers, I have cited documents from them merely as Adams MSS.

The works of John Quincy Adams printed during his lifetime and before 1860 are listed in Joseph Sabin: *A Dictionary of Books Relating to
America, from its Discovery to the Present Time* (24 vols., New York,
1868–1934). A curious modern supplement to Sabin (so far as Adams
printed material is concerned) is: *A Bibliography of John Adams and
John Quincy Adams*, compiled by John W. Cronin and W. Harvey Wise,
Jr. (Washington: Presidential Bibliography Series No. 2; Riverford Publishing Co.; 1935). It is apparently run off from Library of Congress catalogs without perfect discrimination between different individuals bearing
the name of John Quincy Adams. Much more complete will be the Bibliography of the Adams Family now being compiled in the editorial office
of the Adams Papers by Mr. Lyman Butterfield, the Editor, who generously allowed me to consult his cards. It is earnestly to be hoped that this
useful aid will soon be completed and printed. Miss Grace Gardner Griffin's *Annual Writings on American History*, published by the American
Historical Association since 1918 (before that since 1903 by The Macmillan Company and the Yale University Press successively), is an adequate
detailed bibliography of American history and biography from 1903 to
1950. For foreign relations of Adams's lifetime I have relied much on the
standard Bemis and Griffin: *Guide to the Diplomatic History of the United
States, 1775–1921* (Washington: Library of Congress; Government Printing Office; 1935). Now that we have the *Harvard Guide to American His-*

tory (Cambridge, 1954), it would be a supererogation to attach a general bibliography to my volume.

Of the many historical works on the period perhaps the most helpful have been the three volumes of Charles M. Wiltse's life of Calhoun: *John C. Calhoun, Nationalist, 1782–1828; John C. Calhoun, Nullifier, 1829–1839;* and *John C. Calhoun, Sectionalist, 1840–1853* (Indianapolis and New York, 1944, 1949, and 1951). Whether one accepts all of the author's interpretations or not, this distinguished work constitutes the most recent and best political history of the quarter century 1825–50, as well as being the most scholarly biography of the eminent Southern statesman.

The assistance and co-operation of many individuals and institutions made possible the preparation of this volume. First I should like to mention the people responsible for the safekeeping of the Adams Papers. The late Mr. Henry Adams, 2d, of the Adams Manuscript Trust, devoted many hours of his time to searching out miscellaneous items from that voluminous collection now reposing in the Massachusetts Historical Society; and I am indebted to the trustees here mentioned in order of the contemporary descending generations, Charles Francis Adams, Thomas Boylston Adams, and John Quincy Adams, for placing these papers unreservedly at my disposal. Mr. John Adams, President of the Massachusetts Historical Society, Dr. Stewart Mitchell, Director, and Dr. Stephen T. Riley, Librarian, have offered me continuous courtesies, as did Mrs. Wilhcmina Harris of the Adams National Historic Site in Quincy.

My learned friend and colleague Professor David M. Potter read typescript for the entire work, and I have greatly benefited from his criticism of historical content and literary style. Dr. Richard H. Brown, a special student of the period, read the chapters while in preparation, and I am indebted to him for calling various points to my attention. Mr. Lyman Butterfield has also read the whole typescript and made useful suggestions. To Mr. Alfred A. Knopf I am similarly indebted out of his vast experience in publication. The late Professor George H. Blakeslee gave me the benefit of his special competence for the history of the Antimasonic movement. Dr. Catherine M. Fennelly checked the citations to printed titles and quotations from printed material; similarly Dr. Riley checked quotations and citations of manuscript collections in the Massachusetts Historical Society, including the Adams Papers. Among the many individuals who have extended helping eyes, ears, and hands as well as critical comments along the way are: my wife, Ruth Steele Bemis, Miss Helen Boatfield, Dr. Meredith Colket, Jr., Professor Charles Everett, Professor Ralph H. Gabriel, Dr. Henry H. Hart, Dr. John A. Logan, Jr., Mr. Kenneth C. Parker, and Miss Maud F. Steele. A succession of Yale undergraduate office "bursary" assistants have been helpful: Messrs. Richard D. Johnson, '49; George P. Bohan, Jr., '50; Michael O. Pettee, '51; Eugene R. Gonzales, ex-'52; Arthur J. Carlton, '54; Verne Carroll, ex-'55; and Norman R. Allenby, '55. The late Mrs. Geneva M. Walsh typed and retyped my copy several times; Mrs. Edith Macy, Mrs. Alice N. Wheeler, and Mrs. Beatrice G. Bennetto carried on from where Mrs. Walsh left off.

Further I wish to make acknowledgments to the directors, librarians, and professional staffs of the following institutions and libraries: American Antiquarian Society, Baker Library of Dartmouth College, Boston Athenæum, Boston Public Library, Grosvenor Library of Buffalo, Buffalo Historical Society, Cincinnati Public Library, Cleveland Public Library, Public Library of the District of Columbia, Thomas Crane Memorial Library of Quincy, Massachusetts; Houghton and Widener Libraries of Harvard University; Princeton University Library, Library of Congress, Massachusetts Historical Society, National Archives, New York Public Library, New York State Library at Albany, Rochester Public Library, Pennsylvania Historical Society, Philadelphia Public Library, Sterling Memorial Library, and Law School Library, at Yale University; Smithsonian Institution; and Tracy Memorial Library and Colby Junior College Library, at New London, New Hampshire.

A grant-in-aid from the Henry L. Stimson Fund for Research in World Affairs assisted me in meeting expenses of typing, photostating, travel, etc. A Guggenheim Fellowship for the year 1954–5 enabled me to take a full sabbatical year for completion of the work. These are the only financial aids received from any source other than the emolument of my Sterling professorship at Yale University.

I suppose I must make the conventional statement that despite all this help I alone have to answer for the mistakes and shortcomings of my work. I hope they are not too many.

S. F. B.

NOTE TO SECOND PRINTING
[1965]

I have taken advantage of this new printing to make corrections at the following pages and lines: p. xi, line 39; p. 4, line 4; p. 12, lines 6, 9; p. 13, line 26; p. 48, line 16; p. 90, n. 63, line 1; p. 95, lines 17, 18; p. 122, line 9; p. 179, entire; p. 216, line 1; p. 221, lines 14, 15; p. 252, n. 29, line 7; p. 308, line 21; p. 324, n. 56, line 6; p. 339, n. 45, line 8; p. 402, lines 20–22; p. 406, lines 35, 36; p. 426, line 6; p. 447, line 12; p. 464, n. 45, line 2; p. 473, line 19; p. 497, line 4; p. 498, line 7; p. 523, line 4; p. 529, n. 19, line 21; p. 539, n. 52, lines 1–2.

S. F. B.

May, 1965

CONTENTS

CONTENTS

ILLUSTRATIONS

JOHN QUINCY ADAMS

AND

THE UNION

Abbreviations used in footnotes

AHA	American Historical Association
AHR	*American Historical Review*
ASP	*American State Papers*
ASPFR	*American State Papers. Class I. Foreign Relations* (6 vols., Washington, 1832–59)
HAHR	*Hispanic American Historical Review*
LC	Library of Congress
Memoirs	*Memoirs of John Quincy Adams, Comprising Portions of His Diary from 1795 to 1848.* Edited by Charles Francis Adams (12 vols., Philadelphia, 1874–7)
Diary	Diary of John Quincy Adams, in Adams MSS., Massachusetts Historical Society
Diary of CFA	Diary of Charles Francis Adams, in Adams MSS., Massachusetts Historical Society
MHS	Massachusetts Historical Society
MVHR	*Mississippi Valley Historical Review*
Miller: *Treaties*	*Treaties and Other International Acts of the United States of America.* Edited by Hunter Miller (8 vols., Washington, 1931–48)
Writings	*Writings of John Quincy Adams.* Edited by Worthington C. Ford (7 vols., New York, 1913–17)
Vol. I	*John Quincy Adams and the Foundations of American Foreign Policy* (New York: Alfred A. Knopf; 1949)
AA	Abigail Adams
CFA	Charles Francis Adams
GWA	George Washington Adams
JA	John Adams
JA, 2d	John Adams, son of John Quincy Adams, and grandson of John Adams
JQA	John Quincy Adams
LCA	Louisa Catherine (Mrs. John Quincy) Adams
TBA	Thomas Boylston Adams

CHAPTER I
Destiny of a Family
(1767 – 1826)

. then shall I see you become a usefull Member
of Society, a Friend to your Country and a guardian
of her Laws and Liberties—for such is the example
you have before you.

ABIGAIL ADAMS TO HER FIFTEEN-YEAR-OLD SON
JOHN QUINCY ADAMS, NOVEMBER 13, 1782 [1]

IN THE United States many a young man has shaped his career deliberately toward the White House. It is the constitutional privilege of every native-born boy. Thousands of them have had the necessary competence and character for the office. Of every ten thousand youths who have started out to be President, perhaps nine thousand nine hundred and ninety-nine have never reached their cherished goal. Consciousness of the privilege, awareness of the opportunity, determination to grasp it, qualifications for leadership, these are not enough. Whatever the faith or endeavor, however tireless the effort, the boy grown man must successfully ride the unmeasurable tides of politics and all that politics means, in popular psychology, in personal management, in society, in economics, in history, and in the human heart.

Most Presidents have never looked forward from boyhood to the office. Nevertheless there have been at least five young Americans who set out to become President and became President: John Quincy Adams once; Martin Van Buren [2] once; Theodore Roosevelt once and again; Woodrow Wilson twice; and Franklin D. Roosevelt four times in succession.

There is only one case in which the boy's parents planned it that way. That was John Quincy Adams. His father and mother raised their boy to be a statesman. Their cup would not be full, nor his own unwearying toil and ambition be satisfied, until he became President like his father. He gladly accepted their guidance and tutelage. The Presidency early be-

---

[1] Adams MSS.

[2] "He [Henry Fellows, former law student with Van Buren] told us, during the winter [of 1824–5], many characteristic anecdotes of Mr. Van Buren, all showing that Mr. Van Buren, in early youth, cherished high political aspirations." *Autobiography of Thurlow Weed* (Boston, 1883), p. 162.

came his psychological gyroscope, built into his character by these beloved patriots.[3] To him it was the destiny of a family.

John Adams and his wife, Abigail Smith Adams, looked upon their first son on July 11, 1767, in the upstairs bedchamber of a modern New England farmhouse in Braintree (now Quincy) on the shore of Massachusetts Bay. His ancestors on both sides went straight back to the English founders of the colony. As the child was coming into the world one of his maternal great-grandparents, respected member of the colonial legislature, was leaving it. So the young parents named their son John Quincy Adams.[4]

Any son of John and Abigail Adams was also a son of the American Revolution. That epic conflict dominated the most impressionable years of John Quincy Adams's life. As a child in Boston at the side of his revolutionist kinsman Sam Adams he saw the British redcoats parade the streets and the colonial militia drilling on the Common. A boy tugging at his mother's hand, he watched from a distance the Battle of Bunker Hill. The cannons' flash and distant smoke drifting over the Back Bay left an indelible impression in his mind and heart. So did the letters of his patriot father from the Continental Congress at Philadelphia, telling of such excitements as the Declaration of Independence.

John Quincy Adams received his earliest education mostly at the hands of his mother, one of the most accomplished women of Revolutionary times. She taught him to read and write and was his earliest guide to good books. The village school at Braintree had closed when the schoolmaster went away to war. The boy then continued reading under the suggestions of his absent father, faithful guidance of his ever present mother, and the more systematic tutelage of his father's law clerk, John Thaxter. Before he was ten years old he knew something of the best English classics, Shakespeare and Milton, and of course the King James translation of the Holy Bible. All his life he continued an inveterate student in the fields of history, political economy, belles-lettres, and philosophy, extending his readings in the French, Dutch, German, and Italian languages. John Adams as a busy diplomatist managed to keep up with his son's maturing studies. Their exchanges of letters on history, politics, and philosophy, particularly in their later lives, reflect a remarkable American image in the Age of Emancipation,[5] revolutionary aftermath in the Old World and

---

[3] Here I am using, of course, the metaphor and language of current social scientists. See David Riesman, Nathan Glazer, and Ruel Denney: *The Lonely Crowd* (New Haven, 1950).

[4] See the first volume of this biography: *John Quincy Adams and the Foundations of American Foreign Policy* (New York: Alfred A. Knopf; 1949). Hereafter referred to simply as Vol. I.

[5] This phrase was used in Vol. I to indicate the first fifty years of American history including the Revolution and the foundations of American nationality, and also the period of the French Revolution and Napoleonic Wars and their aftermath.

the New of the European Enlightenment of the eighteenth century. And Abigail Adams remained until her last days the intellectual companion of these two statesmen, husband and son.

While John Quincy Adams was in his tender years and folks still called him Johnny, his parents resolved that he should accompany his father to France. That was when the Continental Congress sent John Adams abroad on his famous diplomatic missions during the War for Independence. It was a Spartan decision for Abigail to let her two sons [6] set forth with their father over dangerous seas, but she did not flinch; no Adams ever flinched his duty. It was a wonderful opportunity for the promising boy to improve his natural talents, to learn French, to study in good schools, to carry forward his education by travel and association under high auspices.

Abigail told her little son as he set forth the first time for Europe in 1778 that he might one day become guardian of his country's laws and liberties. "These are times in which a Genious would wish to live," she wrote him in France in 1780: "It is not in the still calm of life, or the repose of a pacific station, that great characters are formed . . . Great necessities call out great virtues, when a mind is raised and animated by scenes that engage the Heart, then those qualitics which would otherways lay dormant, wake into Life, and form the character of the Hero and the Statesman." [7]

Master John, as next they called him, made the best of eight years in Europe. His father put him into a good school at Paris, where he quickly learned French and Latin and the ordinary subjects. Next he went to the University of Leiden. He came to know his father's colleagues, including Dr. Franklin, and later Thomas Jefferson. At Paris and The Hague he mingled in polite and sophisticated society. He went on a year's travel to distant St. Petersburg as private secretary to Francis Dana, on the latter's fruitless mission to Russia, returning by Scandinavia, Hanover, and the Netherlands. After independence he visited England, where his father became first Minister of the United States to the Court of St. James's.

While still in Paris he began his famous Diary,[8] a monumental source of American political history for the next sixty years as well as for his own biography.

He saw the best and got the best out of Europe, but Old World attrac-

---

[6] On the first mission, 1777–8, John Quincy Adams's younger brother Charles went along. He got too homesick to go again.

[7] Abigail Adams to JQA, January 12, 1780. Adams MSS.

[8] Published in part—i.e., any passage that could be construed to be of historical value, as contrasted with strictly personal notes—by his son Charles Francis Adams, as *Memoirs of John Quincy Adams, Comprising Portions of His Diary from 1795 to 1848* (12 vols., Philadelphia, 1874–7). Hereafter referred to as *Memoirs*. Charles Francis Adams, Jr., grandson of John Quincy Adams, published earlier portions of the Diary under the title of *Life in a New England Town: 1787, 1788. Diary of John Quincy Adams while a Student in the Office of Theophilus Parsons at Newburyport* (Boston, 1903).

tions could not bind this son of the American Revolution to that alien scene and its monarchical courts. Abigail and the other three children had joined her Minister husband, but the youth decided to go back home to finish his education at Harvard College. Despite his Puritan background, his serious purpose, and his perfect acceptance of his parents' all-embracing tutelage, he remained a bright and normal youth. He gradu-ated from Harvard in 1787, studied law for two years with Judge The-ophilus Parsons at Newburyport, fell in and out of love there—not without long-lasting inner scars—and settled down to practice in Boston in the year 1790. His father was then Vice President of the United States.

President George Washington first noticed young Adams on the occa-sion of a visit to Newburyport in 1789. The law student drafted the wel-coming address of the citizens of that town. From then on he managed to keep himself in the General's eye. What guidance for a young man and patriot: parents like John and Abigail Adams, boyhood friends and men-tors such as Benjamin Franklin and Thomas Jefferson, a patron like George Washington!

As a young lawyer with few clients John Quincy Adams grew impatient with a dry and tedious profession. He first won public attention as anony-mous author of newspaper articles defending President Washington's pol-icy of neutrality against the intrigues of the Citizen Genet, Minister of the French Republic in Philadelphia at the outset of the war between revolu-tionary France and England. It was easy for Washington to penetrate the anonymity of the Vice President's son. He promptly nominated him Min-ister of the United States to the Netherlands, at the age of twenty-six, in the year 1794. It was one of the best-qualified appointments that could be conceived: young Adams knew French and Dutch, knew the courts of Europe, knew international law; besides that, he thought as Washington thought.

The Hague at that time was a good listening-post for the vast European theater of the Wars of the French Revolution, and John Quincy Adams's diplomatic reports, public and private, confirmed President Washington and his successor John Adams in the policy of neutrality and isolation. Some of the younger Adams's thoughts and phrases found their way into the Farewell Address.

From his next post at Berlin, John Quincy Adams helped his father, President John Adams, to stiffen against the partisan counsels of his Fed-eralist advisers and to decide on peace instead of war with France during the crisis in Talleyrand's time, 1798–1800. After the election of Thomas Jefferson, President Adams recalled his son from the diplomatic service, lest the new Republican President get a chance to dismiss him. (In all likelihood Jefferson would have kept him on.)

During this first tour of diplomatic duty in Europe, Adams had married in London, July 27, 1797, Louisa Catherine Johnson, second of the seven daughters of the United States Consul in that capital, Joshua Johnson of

Maryland, and of his wife, Catherine Nuth Johnson, an Englishwoman. Louisa Adams accompanied him in his subsequent diplomatic wanderings, was the tender and affectionate mother of their three sons, faithful companion of all his later political adventures and vicissitudes. To her the Adams family owes its continuance in direct descent from the Presidents; it also inherited from her a gentle mother's kindness—and fortitude —if character can be inherited.

At Boston again, John Quincy Adams, paterfamilias, bent his body over the grindstone of the law, seeking to re-establish his practice and find a livelihood for his growing family. Soon he got into politics as a member of the general court. The Federalist legislature elected him as United States Senator in 1803. He served until 1807, when he split with his party over Jefferson's Embargo. Politics stopped at the water's edge with Senator Adams. He had never been much of a party man, anyway. His outlook was broadly national. He remembered how his father, President of the United States during the French crisis, had stood forth, not as a leader of a party but as "a man of the whole nation." Ambitiously charting his future, he wrote in his Diary as early as 1802: "I would fain be the man of my whole country." [9]

William Plumer of New Hampshire was a colleague of John Quincy Adams in those still youthful years in the United States Senate, and a life-long friend. He has left this contemporary impression of the man in a letter to William Plumer, Jr., then a student at Harvard College:

"With John Q. Adams I am intimate. He is a man of much information, a bookworm, very industrious. A man of handsome natural and acquired abilities far exceeding his age. He is a very correct and animated speaker. A man of strong passions and of course subject to strong prejudices, but a man of strict undeviating integrity. He is free and independent. On some subjects he appears eccentric." [10]

President James Madison appointed John Quincy Adams as United States Minister to Russia in 1809, and he went over to the Republicans. But until 1817, all his activities being those of representative of the United States Government abroad, he had nothing to do with domestic politics.

As Minister at St. Petersburg during the last phase of the Napoleonic Wars, Adams reported the rout of Napoleon's invasion and the collapse of his French Empire. After that he served as Minister Plenipotentiary and technically chief of the American Commission that made the Peace of Ghent with Great Britain; when the wars were over, he became Minister at London (1815–17). To a striking degree he had followed the historical footsteps of his father in Europe. He had gone as far as he could in the role of a diplomat abroad. John Adams, writing to him from Quincy,

[9] *Memoirs*, I, 249.
[10] William Plumer to William W. Plumer, Jr., at Cambridge, Washington, April 8, 1806. Papers of William Plumer, Letterbook, 1804–7. LC.

warned that he could not afford further delay in Europe: "A man should be in his own country." In 1817 President James Monroe, seeking for a loyal and competent Northern and Eastern man, of neutral political complexion, to balance his Cabinet, called the younger Adams home to become Secretary of State, an office which he filled with singular success and distinction from 1817 to 1825.

John Quincy Adams was now in full maturity of years and personal powers. Physically he was short of stature—five feet seven inches tall—and heavy for his height—one hundred and seventy-seven pounds; with bald head, smooth round face, and steady black eyes. In a letter to an old friend and protégé, he acknowledged in his old age to have had a frigid manner. He further confessed that as he grew older and more experienced in politics he tended to develop a cold heart too.[11] He had a scholar's carelessness about his clothes and a politician's regard for neat republican simplicity in manner.

Psychologically he was a man of inner tensions and constant worries, healthfully released in his Diary. From his youth he was given to introspection and self-analysis. As he got older, at the time of life we are to consider, he indulged in sharp, almost ulcerous judgments of people he did not like, but was warm-hearted and admiring toward men of good will—toward him. The harsh expressions he limited to the Diary, fortunately, in those days of duels. He had about as much sense of humor as his great patron, George Washington, and that was precious little.[12] Inclined to be self-righteous, he nevertheless could stop to look at himself as he fancied others saw him; then he showed as little charity toward John Quincy Adams as he did toward his rivals, Henry Clay for example. He beheld himself dogmatical, wrathy, overbearing in manner, harsh in look and expression, forgetful of the courtesies of society, "cankered by prejudice."

Socially John Quincy Adams would liven up with responsive people over the nuts and wine. Thurlow Weed recalled in his old age a memorable dinner given in the late thirties by Roswell Colt, widely known New York socialite, reputed to have the most famous table of that time, and one of the best wine cellars. Ex-President Adams, Governor Seward, and other notables were present. Madeira was the prevailing beverage, except for a single glass of hock taken with oysters on the half-shell, one glass of sherry after soup, and champagne with the meats. After the cloth was removed, the host proudly brought forth fourteen different Madeiras. To the surprise and delight of everybody John Quincy Adams identified correctly eleven out of the fourteen as unannounced they came his way

---

[11] JQA to Christopher Hughes, September 26, 1833. Clipping from *Michigan Alumnus*, undated, in Papers of JQA, Box "JQA, 1804–34," LC.

[12] ". . . there is nothing that I relish like a good joke, though a bad hand at cracking one myself." JQA to Abigail Brooks Adams (wife of CFA), Washington, December 23, 1829. Adams MSS.

around the table.[13] Doubtless he could not have hung up such a score unless he kept in practice.

With congenial and cultivated company Mr. Adams mellowed like Madeira as the years advanced. As a dinner host to congressional colleagues he could hold forth out of shop on Egyptian hieroglyphics or Hebrew chronology. Distinguished foreign visitors like Tocqueville and Beaumont hung on his explanations of the workings or misworkings of democracy in America.[14] The diarist Philip Hone, congenial host to so many of the nation's élite at New York, tells of a dinner he attended in 1841 where John Quincy Adams was the "fiddle of the party," talking a great deal, gay, witty, instructive, entertaining, the privilege of a lifetime to listen to.[15]

While Adams was at Philadelphia in 1831 on committee business for the House of Representatives, Dr. Philip Syng Physick called on him for a medical check-up. The eminent physician found no real trouble. He asked about diet, questioned him about what he drank and how much.

"I usually take one, sometimes two and occasionally three glasses of Maderia wine after dinner," was the dignified patient's carefully measured response.

Dr. Physick was thunderstruck. "I advise you," he admonished, "to abstain from wine altogether and from all fermented liquors." [16]

Maybe Mr. Adams cut down his intake a bit, maybe not: his Diary does not tell us.

Intellectually Adams was a man of scholarly interests and attainments: a prodigious reader, a thinker with an analytical and expository rather than an imaginative mind. He had a strong interest in natural science, and was a real lover of classical arts and the humanities: painting and sculpture but not music; history, philosophy, literature, particularly poetry, and drama in the heroic tradition, but not mere lyrics nor the new romanticism. Tacitus was his favorite historian, Shakespeare his poet.

Morally he was a man of Christian conscience, a believer and a steady churchgoer though not an actual member of any church until after he became President. Toward the Unitarian congregation in his home town of Quincy he showed a smack of Trinitarian orthodoxy. His private life was impeccable. He was a devoted husband if occasionally an irascible spouse.[17] He loved his children but was severely pedagogical toward them; he wanted so hard for them to be successful and eminent men—statesmen, Adamses, Presidents of the United States.

[13] *Memoir of Thurlow Weed,* by his grandson, Thurlow Weed Barnes (Boston, 1884), p. 484.

[14] George W. Pierson: *Tocqueville and Beaumont in America* (New York, 1938), pp. 417–21. Journal of Edward Everett, January 30, 1834. MS., MHS.

[15] *The Diary of Philip Hone 1828–1851.* Edited, with an Introduction, by Bayard Tuckerman (2 vols., New York, 1889), II, 64–5.

[16] Diary, April 25, 1831.

[17] *Memoirs,* II, 282–3; VI, 46.

In politics John Quincy Adams was tempted to temporize on difficult issues of the day, but his conscience was bound to catch up with him sooner or later: witness his attitude toward the slavery controversy.

His political creed was Independence and Union: Independence in foreign affairs, Union at home. "*Union* is to me what the *balance* is to you," he wrote his father from St. Petersburg on the eve of the War of 1812, "and as without the balance of powers there can be no good government among mankind in any state, so without Union there can be no good government among the people of North America in the state in which God has been pleased to place them." [18] Union and strength at home were necessary for independence and respect abroad. And as we shall see in this volume, Union was necessary for internal improvement of the nation, physically and morally. "This Union" was an ever recurring phrase in his voluminous letters and other writings.

During his diplomatic career, both in the service abroad and in the Department of State in Washington, Adams more than any other single man helped lay the classic foundations of American foreign policy. If the United States has produced a greater diplomatist it would be difficult to name him. During that period people generally regarded the office of Secretary of State as the traditional stepping-stone to the Presidency. If John Quincy Adams were not conscious of that fact—and how could he have been otherwise?—his mother made him so. As he was leaving London to take up his new post at Washington, she wrote that people were already beginning to mention him as "*worthy to preside over the Counsels of a great Nation.*" [19]

Final elevation of John Quincy Adams to the Presidency was not due so much to his parental background and training, as it was to political time and chance, to the breakdown of party politics during the Era of Good Feelings that followed the War of 1812.

[18] JQA to JA, St. Petersburg, October 31, 1811. *Writings of John Quincy Adams,* W. C. Ford, ed. (New York, 1913–17), IV, 267. Hereafter referred to as *Writings.* For the sake of clarity I have slightly altered this quotation. What John Quincy Adams actually wrote, influenced by French grammatical construction, was: "*Union* is to me what the *balance* is to you, and as without this there can be no good government among mankind in any state, so without that there can be no good government among the people of North America in the state in which God has been pleased to place them."

[19] Abigail Adams to JQA, Quincy, March 12, 1817. Adams MSS.

CHAPTER II
The Presidential Campaign of 1824
(1820 – 1824)

If chance will have me king, why, chance may crown me,

Without my stir.

Macbeth, Act I, Scene iii

THE ADMINISTRATION of James Monroe, 1817–25, reflected the halcyon years of the new Era of Good Feelings, a unique period of one-party government in the history of the United States. During Monroe's long and faithful stewardship only two real disturbances interrupted the general harmony, and these involved no divisions in the National Republican Party: the economic depression of 1819, delayed aftermath of the War of 1812; and the Missouri question, dramatic flare-up of the latent sectional conflict over slavery. In those days no one, least of all John Quincy Adams, thought that government could cure an economic depression. Necessarily painful as was the phenomenon, it wore itself out against the recuperative forces of a youthful expanding economy. For a few months the Missouri question flashed and hovered over the nation, but sensible minds, North and South and West, none more sane and cool than the President himself, succeeded in composing it, distrustful as they may have been of the permanence of the compromise. Subsidence of the storm left a profound tranquillity throughout the country. Nobody had ever seen anything like it before, even in Washington's time, nor have Americans seen the like of it since.

Only in such a quiet time could a man like John Quincy Adams ever be elected President. He led no party, controlled no political machine, nor did he have the personal magnetism or other qualities necessary to build one. All he had to stand on politically was his distinguished lineage, his character, his large experience with affairs at home and abroad, and his undoubted competence for public office. No man has ever been better fitted, as professional public servant, for the Presidency. No man has had less aptitude or inclination for the organization and command of political cohorts.

1

There was at this time no accepted way to nominate a candidate for the Presidency. The nearest approach to a national nominating system had been a caucus of party representatives in Congress to agree upon a man and present him to the electors of the several states.[1] John Quincy Adams as United States Senator had participated in such a caucus in 1807. At that time he thought there was less likelihood of intrigue in this method than in any other. That was the way that President Monroe had been nominated for a second term in 1820, by a congressional caucus, although Monroe's acceptability was so general that no caucus was really necessary; he had no opponent. In the ensuing election all the electors except William Plumer, Sr., of New Hampshire voted for him. A persistent tradition had it for a long time that the only reason why this lone elector did not cast his ballot for Monroe was to prevent any other man from equaling the unanimity of Washington's election and re-election in 1788 and 1792. Really Plumer cast his vote in 1820 for his friend John Quincy Adams—over the latter's express disapproval—in order to register Adams before the people for 1824.[2]

A congressional caucus could not represent, even indirectly, the rank and file of the party. All the members of the House of Representatives and one third of the Senate had been elected two years before any Presidential election; another third of the Senators had been chosen four years before; the remaining third six years previously. The voters had nothing directly to do with selection of United States Senators anyway—the state legislatures chose them. Seldom in any case would a candidate for Congress have appealed to his fellow citizens to elect him in order that he might support two years or more later a particular favorite for nomination to the first office in the land. After 1820 the caucus system was breaking down before a newly enfranchised electorate, but no generally acceptable substitute had been devised to take its place.

In the absence of a country-wide system, nominations fell to heterogeneous and often irresponsible groups. A caucus of party members of a state legislature—even these representatives were somewhat archaic before the question; a group of judges, lawyers, jurymen, and spectators got together at a court session; a public mass meeting, spontaneous or prearranged; even a crowded barroom in a Western town,[3] or any body of men, or a newspaper, might recommend a man as candidate for the Presidency.

Generally by election time the party members of the state legislature

---

[1] Charles S. Sydnor has analyzed the meagerness of political organization and the significance of the caucus system in "The One-Party Period of American History," in *AHR*, LI (No. 3, April 1946), 439–51. See also Everett S. Brown: "The Presidential Election of 1824–1825," *Political Science Quarterly*, XL (No. 3, September 1925), 384–403. The most recent and by far the best picture of the period is George Dangerfield's brilliant book: *The Era of Good Feelings* (New York, 1952).

[2] C. O. Paullin explained "The Electoral Vote for John Quincy Adams in 1820," in *AHR*, XXI (No. 2, January 1916), 318–19.

[3] Amos Lane to JQA, Lawrenceburgh, Indiana, June 11, 1824, tells of one such instance. Adams MSS.

would put before the people for their vote a ticket of Presidential electors corresponding more or less to a public demand as registered in these various ways; but this was only in the states where electors were chosen by a general ticket at large; [4] where they were selected by districts,[5] the electors would present themselves to the suffrages of their countrymen in their respective localities. In six states [6] the state legislatures—that is, old expiring legislatures—appointed the electors after they had been nominated by legislative caucuses. As for the electors themselves, once chosen, they usually voted the way they had pledged themselves to do, but not always, and sometimes they might not even be pledged—this was more often the case in the election of the Vice President.

This varied practice of nomination, and cumbersome method, made it difficult to forecast a Presidential election, particularly when there were no opposing parties as was the case when Monroe's second Administration was gliding to a successful end amidst a contest of persons, rather than parties or issues, to succeed him in the White House.

John Quincy Adams's principal rivals in the Presidential campaign of 1824 were conspicuous and ambitious public servants all within the Republican Party: General Andrew Jackson of Tennessee, the national hero; William H. Crawford of Georgia, Secretary of the Treasury; Henry Clay of Kentucky, blithe and popular Speaker of the House of Representatives; and John C. Calhoun, the South Carolina nationalist, Secretary of War. Two of them were colleagues of Adams in President Monroe's Cabinet; of these two Calhoun was a personal friend whom Adams would have liked to turn into a political ally in the South.

2

If one excepts William Plumer, Sr.'s solitary electoral vote for John Quincy Adams in 1820, the first gun in the Presidential campaign for Monroe's succession was a stray shot fired as early as the autumn of 1821. A majority of the members of the legislature of South Carolina, not then in session, recommended a favorite son, William Lowndes, one of the original Expansionists of 1812, president of the Bank of the United States. He had no substantial following outside the state, and died October 27, 1822. The principal effect of Lowndes's nomination was to alert the supporters of Calhoun. Soon after the opening of Congress a small group of unrecorded Southern and Northern members got together and asked the Secretary of War to be a candidate, doubtless without surprising him at all. Not until November 1823 did a caucus of Republicans in the South Carolina legislature actually nominate Calhoun.

[4] New Hampshire, Rhode Island, Connecticut, New Jersey, Pennsylvania, Virginia, North Carolina, Alabama, Mississippi, Ohio, Indiana.
[5] Maine, Massachusetts, Maryland, Kentucky, Tennessee, Missouri, Illinois.
[6] Vermont, New York, South Carolina, Georgia, Louisiana, Delaware.

Meanwhile in January 1822 the Nashville *Gazette* put forth the name of Andrew Jackson. It took like wildfire. In August the general assembly of the State of Tennessee adjourned for a moment while its members in caucus adopted a resolution submitting the name of the General to the people of the United States at the "approaching" election to the chief magistracy. The election was still more than two years away, but already it was the principal political preoccupation of the times. Popular meetings in Nashville, Louisville, Pittsburgh, and elsewhere throughout the West enthusiastically endorsed Jackson's nomination. Later the members of the legislature of Alabama also nominated the General, and those of Mississippi, by the speaker's curious interpretation of a tie vote, recommended both Jackson and Adams.

Andrew Jackson did not actively seek the Presidency. "I have no desire, nor do I expect ever to be called to fill the Presidential chair," he declared, "but should this be the case, contrary to my wishes or expectations, I am determined it shall be without any exertion on my part." [7] And so it was. But his friends made great exertions for him, and he had the good fortune to fall into competent hands at the beginning of the campaign.

The General's friends—a word then widely used to include supporters and workers whatever their motives—sent him to the United States Senate in 1823 in order to station his commanding presence on the immediate field of battle. He was a good Republican. He represented no particular issue. At this time he did not oppose the Bank of the United States. He voted for Clay's protective tariff of 1824; it was necessary for national security to make the country independent of foreign imports in time of war. He favored internal improvements, at least for national military preparedness,[8] but he congratulated President Monroe on his veto of the Cumberland Road bill: [9] it reached too far within the reserved sovereignty of the states. Such sentiments appealed to the Old Republican school.

The inarticulate masses of the nation, becoming fully enfranchised after the examples of the new Western states, the laboring population of the Eastern cities as well as the frontier farmers of the interior country, presented a new and protean force in American political life. To them the personality of the Old Hero was a weightier factor than internal improvements or the protective tariff, the rising political issues of the day. John Quincy Adams, who actually had venerated Andrew Jackson for his

[7] John Spencer Bassett: *Life of Andrew Jackson* (2 vols., New York, 1911) I, 328–9.

[8] Ibid., II, 482.

[9] The Cumberland Road was the first national highway to be projected in the United States. The purpose was to connect the Eastern seaboard with the Old Northwest. Various acts of Congress since 1802 had set aside funds for it. Actual construction began in 1811 at Cumberland, Maryland. By 1818 it had reached Wheeling, Virginia—on the way to Zanesville, Ohio. In 1822 Congress had passed a bill to establish tollgates along the highway, the tolls to be used to maintain the road. President Monroe vetoed the bill as an interference with state rights.

patriotic services to the nation, and had defended him publicly and in the Cabinet, greatly underestimated the General's strength and determination as a candidate for the Presidency, once nominated, and that of the democratic movement that lay gropingly behind him.

William H. Crawford, rather than Andrew Jackson, seemed the most formidable political contender. After the legislature of his own state of Georgia had put forth his name, the Secretary of the Treasury relied on the congressional caucus to drive his rivals from the general field, for he could have no hope of a popular nomination. Crawford's chief virtue, according to Adams, was a certain firmness, or insistence on things. The public life of this politician had been one long effort to build up a patronage to make members of Congress and local leaders everywhere look to him as the dispenser of federal offices. He unblushingly made use of the appointments in the Treasury Department and sought to control as many other Presidential appointments as he could. He was author of the famous four-year tenure-of-office act of 1820. Such a law conscientiously administered could make for efficiency in the civil service.[10] Actually it enabled Crawford to scrutinize the political complexion of all office-holders within his command who must come up for appointment sometime before the election of 1824. What with the federal land offices, customs surveyors, appraisers and collectors in every port, bank examiners, and bookkeepers in Washington, there were more workers under the Treasury throughout the country than were to be found in any other department unless it were the Post Office. Directors of doubtful Western banks in which the Secretary of the Treasury could deposit moneys from public land sales also became ardent Crawford partisans.[11]

In the Cabinet, Crawford generally opposed whatever his most eminent rival, Adams, advocated, and also worked against Calhoun, whom he feared as his most dangerous Southern opponent. In Congress his cohorts used the weapons of economy and reform to pare down the appropriations of the War Department. In every conceivable way Crawford sought to harass Calhoun as "first outwork" of John Quincy Adams's bailiwick.[12] Adams, infuriated at Crawford's obstructive tactics, offered Calhoun an alliance in the Cabinet for the discussion of all Administration measures,[13] but the young South Carolina nationalist did not definitely accept it; he wanted to be free to go his own way if it should turn immediately toward the White House.

Adams's Diary is one long complaint of Crawford's ambiguous and unworthy conduct and electioneering at public expense, of the man's unbri-

[10] Carl Russell Fish: *The Civil Service and the Patronage* (New York, 1905), pp. 65–70.

[11] *Memoirs*, V, 483–4.

[12] Charles M. Wiltse: *John C. Calhoun, Nationalist, 1782–1828* (Indianapolis, 1944), pp. 149–50 and Chapter XVI.

[13] *Memoirs*, V, 314–16, 332–3. March 3, 19, 1821.

dled ambition, his disguised warfare against Monroe's Government—"a worm preying upon the vitals of the Administration within its own body"—,[14] his connivance at fraud in the collection of public revenue, even collusion with slave-smugglers. Crawford had been seven years working uphill in this manner, Adams told himself in 1822, and had three years more to get to the summit: "What chance against him will a man have who neither can nor will use such means?" [15]

One might set all this down as due to puritanical jealousy, if the New Englander were the only man who detested Crawford. The fact is that all of Crawford's colleagues were aware of his ignoble devices. Even the President, who observed a scrupulous neutrality among the Gentlemen of the Administration who were rivals for his succession, finally came to resent the Secretary of the Treasury's efforts to bend him to his will and to create the impression of invincible control over Presidential as well as congressional patronage.

At this period of his life Monroe was not given to unjust commentary, and rarely indulged in personal criticism, but in the case of Crawford he left judgments which by their very temperateness impugn the Georgia politician's good faith and loyalty to the Chief Executive. At the loss of some dignity to himself, the President kept Crawford in his Cabinet in order to prevent a public quarrel within the party. Sometime during the last months of his Administration he had a personal row with the Secretary of the Treasury. "You damned, infernal old scoundrel!" Crawford had called the President of the United States when Monroe refused to make more appointments at his behest. Monroe grabbed some fire-tongs and threatened to ring for servants to throw him out of the White House. The choleric Crawford, calming down, denied any intention to insult! He left the house under his own locomotion. That was the last time the two men met,[16] but Monroe kept him in office until the end. He wanted to preserve at least the outward appearance of Good Feelings as long as he should remain Chief Magistrate of the Union.

Crawford suffered a paralytic stroke in September 1823, from which he slowly recovered during 1824, but never to be his old self. Nevertheless his supporters in Congress convened a meeting at the Capitol, February 24, to recommend a candidate of the Republican Party for the Presidency. Only sixty-six members responded to the call. Sixty-four of them voted for nomination of their leader. The rump caucus was a failure. But so tenacious was the stricken chieftain's hold on his henchmen—and on life itself—that he remained a factor in the campaign. That is to say, he kept decisive Southern votes from Clay, Jackson, and Calhoun.

14 *Memoirs,* V, 315.

15 *Memoirs,* V, 483.

16 Southard heard about the altercation from Monroe's lips a few minutes after the interview. He told President Adams about it on December 14, 1825, and said that the interview occurred "last winter." *Memoirs,* VII, 80–1.

Crawford's obstinate vitality, which his healthier rivals watched attentively, made it likely that none of the other candidates would obtain a majority of electoral votes, and that therefore the election would have to be decided in the House of Representatives voting by states from among the three candidates having the highest pluralities in the electoral college. In such a decision the vote of the sparsely populated new states of Illinois and Missouri, each with only one representative, or of the two smallest of the original thirteen states, Delaware, one member, or Rhode Island, two members, would count as much as Massachusetts with her thirteen members, or Pennsylvania with her twenty-eight, or New York with her thirty-six.

Henry Clay was first formally presented by a caucus of the members of the Kentucky legislature in November 1822—as if he were not already a candidate. Caucuses of the legislatures of Missouri, Louisiana, and Ohio followed suit. These state nominations indicated that however the West and even the South might be divided they were opposed to the selection of a man by a group of professional politicians assembled in a congressional caucus. So were the Northern states. So were all the candidates, except Crawford.

For Henry Clay, Adams had more respect than for Crawford. It was easier to understand a man who was attacking Monroe's Government in order to supplant it, as Clay had been doing in the House of Representatives, than it was to comprehend a person like Crawford who participated in the Administration in order to undermine it and thereby succeed it. Even Adams, principal victim of the Kentuckian's attacks, had to acknowledge that this "political gamester" had qualities of genius and statesmanship, notably in his devotion to a system of internal improvements.[17] Having repaired his personal fortune by two years' law practice, during which time he took occasion to keep as much as possible in the public eye, Clay returned to the House of Representatives in 1823, straightway to be elected Speaker again. In that conspicuous place he was able to control the appointment of committees in his efforts to build up a new opposition party under his own leadership.

Clay's great difficulty was lack of a real issue, after the victory of John Quincy Adams's foreign policy. For none of the rival aspirants really opposed the things that Clay stood for: a national bank, protective tariff, and a broad and national program of internal improvements for the general welfare to be paid for by the whole country. The voice most resembling opposition to this program came rather furtively from Crawford, who professed an old-school Jeffersonianism which questioned the constitutionality of such works without an amendment to the organic law. Crawford had Jefferson's private support in the Presidential campaign.[18]

17 *Memoirs*, V, 325–6.
18 Jefferson to Gallatin, October 29, 1822. P. L. Ford, ed.: *The Writings of Thomas Jefferson* (10 vols., New York, 1892–9), X, 235–6. "Mr. Jefferson is said to

John C. Calhoun at forty-two was the youngest and most eager contestant. He had given his friend Adams indirectly to understand, through the medium of Senator Ninian Edwards of Illinois, that he had "no views to himself" for the next Presidency.[19] Adams took the statement as a commitment to support himself. When Calhoun's ambition became obvious, he sought to give out the impression that he would not have entered the race against his Massachusetts colleague if he thought the latter had any real chance to be elected; it was only to beat Crawford, whose principles and character he detested, that he had come out himself. Calhoun's personal correspondence, and that of others with whom he talked, have revealed the hollowness of this pretense.[20] Adams's old friendship for his colleague from South Carolina broke down under the weight of the campaign and his suspicions that Calhoun's ambitions had got the better of his sincerity, to the extent of double-dealing.

3

John Quincy Adams wanted to be President of the United States as much as Henry Clay or William H. Crawford or John C. Calhoun. "A man must fulfill his destiny," he wrote to himself. Now at the height of his career as a diplomatist, he had no desire to retire into a life of "reading indolence." He must have *"an object of pursuit."* So he mused even before the re-election of Monroe in 1820.[21] He did not wish to appear to pursue the Presidency. But he had been accustomed since youth to look upon that office as a family inheritance. In his tall pride he desired it to come to him as it had come to Washington: unsolicited, unconnived for, without commitments or bargains with any man, a prize for which he, the son of President John Adams and Abigail, would not lift a finger or make a nod. "If my country wants my services, she must ask for them." [22]

At first he was very firm, but in the end he was far from adamant.

---

be careful when talking about the presidential election but is in favor of Crawford." Interview of Samuel Whitcomb with Thomas Jefferson, Charlottesville, Va., May 31, 1824. MS., MHS.

[19] Wiltse: *John C. Calhoun, Nationalist*, pp. 228, 238.

[20] On Calhoun's views, see, in addition to J. Franklin Jameson's edition of the *Correspondence of John C. Calhoun*, in *Annual Report* 1899 AHA, Vol. II (Washington, 1900): A. R. Newsome, ed.: "Correspondence of John C. Calhoun, George McDuffie and Charles Fisher, relating to the Presidential Campaign of 1824," *N.C. Historical Review*, VII (No. 4, October 1930), 477–504; Thomas Robson Hay, II: "John C. Calhoun and the Presidential Campaign of 1824," ibid., XII (No. 1, January 1935), 20–44, and "John C. Calhoun and the Presidential Campaign of 1824: Some Unpublished Calhoun Letters," *AHR*, XL (Nos. 1 and 2, October 1934 and January 1935), 82–96, 287–300; and Everett Somerville Brown, ed.: *The Missouri Compromises and Presidential Politics 1820–1825 from the Letters of William Plumer, Jr.* (St. Louis: Missouri Historical Society; 1926).

[21] *Memoirs*, V, 139. June 4, 1820.

[22] JQA to P. P. C. Degrand, Washington, November 16, 1818. Adams MSS.

"Don't you think it would be advisable to expose Clay's conduct and motives in the newspapers?" Adams's friend and protégé Alexander H. Everett asked the Secretary of State one day in 1818, a few months after he had taken office. "Aren't you determined to do something to promote your own future election to the Presidency to succeed Mr. Monroe?"

"Absolutely nothing."

"The others are not so scrupulous," the younger man urged. "You won't be on an equal footing with them."

"That's not my fault," the Secretary affirmed. "My business is to serve the public to the best of my abilities in the station assigned to me, and not to intrigue for further advancement. I have never, by the most distant hint to anyone, expressed a wish for any public office, and I shall not now begin to ask for that which of all others ought to be most freely and spontaneously bestowed." [23]

Fine words these, and he meant them—at that moment. But he was no man to hide his talents under a bushel. At least he was not unwilling to have his friend Joseph E. Hall, editor of the *Port Folio*, in Philadelphia, publish in 1819 an anonymous sketch of his life and public services to 1808, originally prepared by Adams himself and later touched up by his father, John Adams, in Quincy. It was reprinted in 1824 as a campaign biography, brought up to date in the form of a series of letters to the *Baltimore American* written by "Tell," who was certainly well prepared with information not readily available from any other source than John Quincy Adams himself.[24]

Joseph Hopkinson, distinguished Philadelphia lawyer and member of the committee of foreign affairs of the House of Representatives, was one of those who first urged Adams to come out for the Presidency, to co-operate with some nationwide organization of workers in order to counteract the organized efforts of his adversaries. To him Adams gave the same answer: "I will take not one step to advance or promote pretensions to the Presidency." In his Diary he was equally firm, and pious: "If that office is to be the prize of cabal and intrigue, of purchasing newspapers, bribing by appointments, or bargaining for foreign missions, I have no ticket in that lottery. . . . My time is now not sufficient to discharge the duties of my office; any part of it which I should spend in efforts to make

[23] *Memoirs*, IV, 64. March 18, 1818.

[24] *Sketch of the Life of John Quincy Adams: taken from the Port Folio of April, 1819, to which are added the Letters of Tell originally addressed to the Editor of the Baltimore American. Respectfully submitted to the serious consideration of those Free-holders of Virginia, who desire to exercise the high privilege of voting for a President of the United States at the approaching Election 1824.* (No place of publication listed, 1824.) See also *Port Folio*, Series V, Vol. VII (April 1819), 305–14. For JQA's correspondence with Skelton Jones, for whom he first prepared the sketch in 1809, see *Writings*, III, 292–305; with Hall, ibid., VI, 311–12. John Adams's editorial alterations were well advised: for example, he deleted the self-righteous sentence: "As far as I know myself, my motives of conduct are pure and disinterested."

partizans or to pull down competitors would be an abandonment of public for personal aims." [25]

In vain Hopkinson worked on Mrs. Adams to get her husband to groom himself for the highest office in the land, to mingle more in society, not to be too fastidious and reserved toward people, not to dampen and depress the kind feelings of friends who were trying to help him such as, for example, warm-hearted Robert Walsh, editor of the Philadelphia *National Gazette*.

Adams still kept on sitting and waiting—and hoping—and expecting—to be crowned. His only answer to Hopkinson's friendly admonition was a long and chilly essay entitled "The Macbeth Policy," ending with the quotation from Shakespeare:

> If chance will have me king, why, chance may crown me,
> Without my stir.

"He who asks or accepts the offer of aid to promote his own views," he reminded his friend Hopkinson, "necessarily binds himself to promote the views of him from whom he receives it." [26]

"This won't do," wrote Hopkinson to Mrs. Adams for John Quincy Adams's eye. "Kings are made by politicians and newspapers; and the man who sits down waiting to be crowned either by chance or just right will go bare-headed all his life." [27]

Again and again the Secretary of State affirmed to his friends that the sworn duties of his office left him no time for electioneering.[28]

"I shall not, as at present advised, withhold my name," he declared in January 1821, "but I shall neither solicit the nomination nor take any part whatever in procuring or supporting it." [29]

These professions became increasingly difficult to live up to as the campaign progressed.

4

Adams's first effort to improve his own position was by making use of a time-honored stratagem: to get his principal rivals, all except the detested Crawford, whom he could not decently recommend, sent out of the country on diplomatic appointments.

As early as 1819—before Calhoun's name came into public prominence as a candidate to succeed Monroe—the Secretary of State suggested to his

[25] *Memoirs*, IV, 193; V, 298–9. December 17, 1818, February 25, 1821.

[26] "The Macbeth Policy." *Writings*, VII, 356–62; *Memoirs*, VI, 132–7.

[27] Joseph Hopkinson to Mrs. John Quincy Adams, Philadelphia, January 1, 1823. Adams MSS. *Memoirs*, VI, 130–2. January 1, 11, 1823.

[28] *Memoirs*, V, 242. To John D. Heath, January 7, 1822. *Writings*, VII, 195. JQA to Timothy Fuller, July 31, 1823. JQA to J. A. T. Kilgour, December 15, 1823. Adams MSS.

[29] Affirmation in an interview with Dr. Allison, Vice President of the General Association of Baptist Ministers. *Memoirs*, V, 242. January 22, 1821.

colleague that as a statesman with great expectations a little European experience would do him good. He asked whether he would accept the mission to France in case Gallatin's request for a recall were granted. Calhoun said he could not afford it.[30] (He might have afforded it financially, but he certainly couldn't afford it politically.)

When Henry Clay retired from Congress in 1821 to retrieve his private fortunes, Adams asked him whether it would be consistent with his views to accept a mission abroad if one should open up within the next two or three years. Nothing could have been more pointed. Clay declined with thanks.[31] And the Kentuckian made it very clear that his retirement would be only temporary, that he expected to come back to the House of Representatives as Speaker! Later, when the appointment of missions to South America was under consideration, the Secretary of State repeatedly suggested Clay to President Monroe for Minister to Colombia, or Chile, or Buenos Aires.[32]

"In pursuing a generous policy towards him, as an enemy and a rival," Adams rationalized self-righteously in the unblushing pages of his Diary, "I do some violence to my inclination, and shall be none the better treated by him; but I look to personal considerations only to discard them, and regard only the public interests." [33]

The President, however, kept his fingers crossed as to Clay.

"Has General Jackson occurred to you?" the Secretary asked Monroe as they proceeded to canvass other possibilities.

"Yes," responded Monroe, remembering that Jefferson had warned him about appointing the Old Hero to any mission abroad, "but I am afraid he would get us into a quarrel." [34]

Monroe overcame his hesitation in 1823. Without consulting the General, he appointed him Minister to Mexico.[35] Jackson, too, declined to be removed to a foreign post.

More than once the Secretary of State suggested DeWitt Clinton, another possible rival, to President Monroe for missions abroad.[36]

5

Despite his own forbidding attitude John Quincy Adams was not without a few gratuitous workers feebly organized for his election. But they

[30] *Memoirs*, IV, 477. December 13, 1819.

[31] *Memoirs*, V, 323. March 9, 1821.

[32] *Memoirs*, V, 495–6; VI, 26. April 22, June 20, 1822.

[33] *Memoirs*, VI, 26. June 20, 1822.

[34] *Memoirs*, V, 496. April 22, 1822.

[35] W. R. Manning: *Early Diplomatic Relations between the United States and Mexico* (Baltimore, 1916), p. 36.

[36] Adams said as much to Clinton's friend John W. Taylor, April 17, 1824, apparently as a bid for the support of Clinton in New York. *Memoirs*, VI, 294.

lacked cohesion and discipline, and were isolated in particular states and localities. There was no general leadership.

In Massachusetts there was Peter Paul Francis Degrand,[37] republican émigré of the French Revolution; General Henry Alexander Scammell Dearborn, collector of the port of Boston and son of the Revolutionary General Henry Dearborn, the father being at that time Minister to Portugal; Joseph E. Sprague, postmaster at Salem and aspirant for the collectorship of customs there; John B. Davis of Boston, editor of the *Patriot;* and, later, Benjamin W. Crowninshield, former Secretary of the Navy. They gave initial impulse to the Adams-for-President movement in Boston and Massachusetts by putting up his name at a mass meeting at Faneuil Hall, February 15, 1824, and getting the nomination confirmed by the Republican members of the Massachusetts legislature, June 10. The other New England states followed suit.

In New York State, so vital to Adams's election, another group, not well articulated with the Massachusetts friends, interested themselves in his cause. James Tallmadge of Poughkeepsie, who had gone back to the New York legislature after having made his one bright mark in history by introducing the amendment for restriction of slavery in the proposed new state of Missouri, swung to Adams from Jackson. Micah Sterling, a Federalist member of the United States House of Representatives in the Seventeenth Congress from the Watertown district on the shores of Lake Ontario, came over from Calhoun after the South Carolinian dropped out of the race for first place. James Otis Morse, a country editor in Cherry Valley, was an active political confidant. Two conspicuous liberal supporters were the New York City reformer, Judge Thomas Herttell, pioneer temperance advocate, defender of the legal rights of women, and champion of religious freedom; [38] and Henry Wheaton, youthful journalist and jurist of New York City, subsequently to win renown as a diplomat and international lawyer. Later, two more Calhoun men joined them. John W. Taylor of Ballston Spa, an awkward politician, recently Speaker of the House of Representatives during the one season of Clay's retirement, came over to Adams after the latter had supported him unsuccessfully against the efforts of Crawford and Van Buren to prevent his re-election.[39] Young Thurlow Weed of Rochester, precocious rival to Martin Van Buren, jumped nimbly on the Adams wagon in New York, without invitation; he had not yet so much as corresponded with Adams.[40]

[37] Degrand detailed political trends and personalities in Massachusetts and New England in a numbered series of some 175 personal letters to John Quincy Adams between 1817 and 1825. Adams wrote him only half a dozen noncommittal answers, and stopped replying to him when he realized what he was up to.

[38] Albert Post: *Popular Free Thought in America, 1825–1850* (New York, 1943), p. 129.

[39] Wiltse: *John C. Calhoun, Nationalist,* p. 236.

[40] *Autobiography of Thurlow Weed,* edited by his daughter Harriet A. Weed (Boston and New York, 1883), pp. 157–76.

The most alert and able worker of the New York group was Joseph Blunt, a young lawyer and publicist, afterwards one of the founders of the Republican Party of 1854; he marshaled the forces of Adams against Crawford in the state legislature and contributed polemical articles to the pro-Adams *New York American*, edited by Charles King, son of the Federalist Senator, and Gulian C. Verplanck. These men all enlisted in the Adams campaign, if such it may be called when John Quincy Adams wasn't yet admitting that there was a campaign. Most of them were young. They were politicians. They expected Adams to win, and, like his friends in Massachusetts and Pennsylvania, they looked to his victory to make their own political fortunes.

In Pennsylvania, Joseph Hopkinson, Robert Walsh, and Charles Jared Ingersoll of Philadelphia, and Joel Lewis of Pittsburgh, were eager to work for Adams—if only he would let them. But all that he did was to send to Walsh a record and evaluation of his diplomatic achievements [41] —most useful to the biographer—as basis for another [42] anonymous article, which appeared in the *National Gazette* on October 28, 1824, too late to have much influence on the election.

There were other worthy workers, of more or less activity, always without discipline or direction, who put themselves forward in Virginia, [43] in North Carolina, [44] and elsewhere [45] sporadically throughout the Union.

In Washington, the *National Journal*, established by Peter Force, became a known and avowed Adams paper contending against the supporters of Crawford, Calhoun, Clay, and Jackson, and giving lead to the other pro-Adams newspapers throughout the country. About it and about the Secretary of State in the background assembled another disparate group who began to take a busy but inconspicuous part behind the scenes in the campaign. They included the literary physician and apothecary Dr. Tobias Watkins of Maryland, whom Adams had appointed as secretary to the Florida claims commission. Watkins wrote articles in the *Journal* and echoed the views of his chief in as many other papers as pos-

[41] "JQA Loquitur." Adams MSS. See Vol. I, 394.

[42] For the other campaign biography of 1824, also based on Adams's own notes, see above, note 24.

[43] John Hampden Pleasants, young and importunate editor of the newly established *Virginia Whig*, always asking Adams for money and never getting any, was an uncertain and not very effective supporter. Philip Harrison and William C. Gray of Fredericksburg organized a committee of correspondents to work for Adams's candidacy. Another correspondent in the Old Dominion was J. F. Caldwell, Quaker editor of Lewisburg. None of these Virginians was a man of great influence.

[44] In North Carolina, Adams relied on Governor H. G. Burton.

[45] Among his supporters in South Carolina were David Heath, editor of the Charleston *City Gazette*, and William Crafts, Harvard graduate and emigrant from Boston to the Palmetto State. In Kentucky, Adams's kinsman by marriage, John Pope, was rather doubtful. In Illinois, John Pope's brother, Judge Nathaniel Pope, and Daniel P. Cook, sole member from that state in the House of Representatives, were Adams men.

sible. John Bailey, former secretary to Adams in the Department of State, now a member of Congress from Massachusetts, was also a political intimate. So was William Lee, an old and well-informed friend of the Adams family, whom President Monroe had appointed second auditor of the Treasury [46]—he had a seat within the gates of the enemy! Edward Wyer, Harvard ex-1800, formerly Consul at Riga during Adams's mission in Russia, and later in Hamburg, onetime agent for claims in Santo Domingo, and occasional dispatch-bearer for the Department of State, seems to have been the Secretary of State's confidential leg-man about town. The function of these familiars was to keep Adams informed of what was going on under cover and to hold forth the views of their principal without implicating him in any direct or overt statement.

For all these widely separated groups and individuals there was no central organization to give them encouragement and aliment and to bring direction and unity to their efforts. John Quincy Adams's refusal to make an open campaign at their head when he really wished to be a candidate put him and his friends on the defensive, a weak position, tenable only in this peculiar Era of Good Feelings.

6

There was no campaign by any of the candidates in the sense of going about the country making speeches on the issues of the day. There were no political parties opposing each other in the national election. The candidates for the Presidency—all from within the National Republican Party—did not take positive stands against each other on political grounds. They were all rivals who believed in much the same things, in a contest of personalities.

The campaign took place in the press, and through the speeches of the Presidential electors in those instances where they stood directly before the people by districts, and in the legislatures which chose electors for their states. The candidates or their "friends" would supply the newspapers and local orators with ammunition, proper or improper, to shoot off against the record, politics, person, character, religion, or morals of a rival. Through these means Adams found himself assailed on all sides.

His adversaries did not limit themselves to belittling his diplomatic achievements. They accused him of every personal shortcoming they dared to utter. They said he had an aristocratic reserve and did not un-

[46] In his earlier years he had represented a Boston firm in France, where he made Monroe's acquaintance in 1796, also John Quincy Adams's while traveling in Holland. Lee served as United States Consul in Bordeaux, 1810–16. Monroe made him an auditor in the War Department in 1816, and while President appointed Lee second auditor in the Treasury, in 1817. See William Lee: *John Leigh of Agawam (Ipswich) Massachusetts 1634–1671 and His Descendants of the Name of Lee . . .* (Albany, 1888), pp. 231–72.

bend enough in society. They recalled that he and Mrs. Adams would not make first visits to new members of Congress arriving in Washington, but stood aloof on a European order of etiquette that required a first call upon themselves.[47] They declared he was not easy of official access. He had too quick a temper. Some averred he was not a real Republican, others that he was an apostate to Federalism. Some said he would appoint Federalists to office; others that he would proscribe them. It was declared most ridiculously that he did not pay his just debts, that his aged father was vain and garrulous. One opponent branded him as a Socinian; a defender declared he was an Episcopalian.[48] People in Philadelphia passed on to Louisa, his wife, reports that he was said not to wear a waistcoat, or a collar and tie, that he actually went to church barefoot.[49]

If such trifles annoyed Adams, as his Diary and his private letters so abundantly attest,[50] they need not be dwelt upon here. More serious were the questionings on how he stood on the conspicuous public measures of the day: on internal improvements under national authority, on a protective tariff for the encouragement of domestic manufactures. And how did he stand on the great and dormant issue of slavery?[51]

On the subject of internal improvements John Quincy Adams proceeded to outstrip Henry Clay. It was, as will be seen in chapters to follow, the cardinal measure of his whole political program. On this subject he took pains to let it be known that he was the original proponent of a general nationwide system of internal improvements at national expense, such as Congress had just approved in principle by the adoption of the Survey Act of 1824, and he furnished a copy of his resolution proposed in the Senate on February 23, 1807, to attest the fact. Uncompromisingly he expressed his belief in the constitutionality of such projects, always subject to the territorial rights of the several states, and to indemnification of the proprietary rights of individuals concerned.[52]

John Hampden Pleasants, who had been upholding Adams's candidacy against great local odds in Virginia, suggested that these views might be construed as believing that such constitutional powers *ought* to exist. "It is a question of infinite delicacy here," he wrote from Richmond, the city of refuge for state rights, "and even the Federalists have turned round and become sticklers for constitutional sanctity."

[47] *Memoirs*, IV, 482–91; *Writings*, VI, 565–73.

[48] John Creery to JQA, Baltimore, June 2, 1824. Adams MSS.

[49] *Writings*, VII, 296; *Memoirs*, VI, 54–5.

[50] JQA to P. P. F. Degrand, Washington, November 16, 1818. Adams MSS. JQA to LCA, August 11, 1821. *Writings*, VII, 170.

[51] The Bank of the United States did not come under discussion in 1824.

[52] Daniel Schnebley to JQA, Hagers Town, March 30, June 22, 1824. JQA to Daniel Schnebley, Washington, June 15, June 24, 1824. Adams MSS. See also Hagers Town *Torch Light*, June 8, 1824, and Washington *National Intelligencer*, July 25, 1824. John McLean to JQA, May 5, 1824. JQA to John McLean, May 6, 1824. Adams MSS.

"You and I very well know," Adams promptly replied, "that this would be not only to admit that they *do not* but that they never will possess it. A great majority of the people of this Union now think with me that Congress do possess the power. Why should they beat about the bush for the bird which they have in hand." [53]

Adams would hear more about state rights in Virginia. "Asking one of the States to surrender part of her sovereignty," declared John Randolph of Roanoke, "is like asking a lady to surrender part of her chastity." [54] Adams would hear more from John Randolph, too.

As to the tariff John Quincy Adams was more circumspect. All the other candidates had been in favor of protection. Clay was the chief advocate of the protective tariff of 1824. Crawford believed more in protection by tariff than protection by army and navy. Jackson, who voted for that tariff in the Senate, declared himself for a "judicious" tariff.

Friends of Adams in the manufacturing state of Pennsylvania begged to be assured that he favored a protective tariff for the encouragement of domestic manufactures. [55] Friends in South Carolina and Alabama implored him to come out for a revision of the tariff downward, for the relief of farmers. [56] Adams's own New England as a commercial section had been opposed hitherto to protection, like the agricultural South; but the rapidly multiplying small factories of Massachusetts and Connecticut were beginning to convert the voters of those states. After some slight initial hesitation Adams placed himself on record as favoring a "cautious" protective tariff. There must be "tender and sincere regard to the agricultural interest of the South and the commercial interest of the North"; [57] in short, he declared himself for the "conciliation," rather than the "collision" of conflicting interests. [58] "Cautious" was as wonderful a word as Jackson's "judicious" when applied to the tariff!

On the restlessly sleeping issue of slavery he declined to comment publicly or privately, notwithstanding the importunities of friends North and

---

[53] Jno. Hampden Pleasants to JQA, Richmond, June 19, 1824. JQA to Jno. Hampden Pleasants, Washington, June 25, 1824. Adams MSS.

[54] William Cabell Bruce: *John Randolph of Roanoke 1773–1833* (New York, 1922), II, 203–4.

[55] Degrand to JQA, No. 110, Boston, November 2, 1822. W. Lee to JQA, January 16, 1823. Charles Rich to JQA, January 12, 1824. Robert Walsh, Jr., to JQA, Philadelphia, February 25, 1824. Adams MSS.

[56] Wm. Crafts to JQA, Charleston, S.C., May 31, 1824. J. L. D. Smith to JQA, Florence, Alabama, June 20, July 15, 1824. Adams MSS.

[57] JQA to Robert Walsh, Jr., March 1, 1824. "These are my opinions and I hope you will think I have been sufficiently explicit in avowing them. I am not desirous of obtruding them here or elsewhere. As to the benefit to myself, which I might, as is hinted by you, secure in the South by professing a different sentiment, I must be content to dispense with it." Adams MSS.

[58] *Memoirs*, VI, 451. He told George McDuffie of South Carolina, successor to Calhoun's seat in the House, that he was well satisfied with the tariff of 1824. McDuffie, like Calhoun, was still tinged with nationalism in 1824.

South that he make a statement for or against it. He would not even answer their letters.

7

There had ceased to be a real candidate for the Vice-Presidency. The rump congressional caucus of sixty-eight members which had nominated Crawford for President had endorsed Albert Gallatin for the second place; but when Gallatin returned from Europe he found himself so unknown to the new generation of voters that Crawford's managers easily prevailed upon him to withdraw. The general expectation was that the second office would go to one of the runners-up in the Presidential race, even if it had to be settled in the Senate, as the Presidency most likely would have to be decided in the House of Representatives, for lack of a majority of electoral votes.

Each of the candidates for the Presidency would have been glad to attach one of the others to him as running-mate. Here again Adams took a hand in his campaign. He let it be known that he preferred Jackson for Vice President, although Calhoun would not be unacceptable in the second role, and he did not reject the possibility of Clay. While he refused to tie up with Crawford in any way, he did go so far as to intimate that there would be no changes in the Treasury Department in case he, Adams, were elected.[59] (This was before he learned of the violent altercation between Crawford and President Monroe.) But a state convention at Harrisburg, Pennsylvania, took the Vice-Presidential question from the hands of the politicians by unanimously nominating Jackson for President and Calhoun for Vice President (March 1, 1824). After this blow to his highest ambition, the young South Carolinian, who had so much of the future before him, dropped out of the race for the first prize and accepted candidacy for the second.

In Adams's own New England there persisted until the last a strong feeling among the democratic elements for Jackson as Vice President on a ticket with Adams. Degrand and Dearborn wanted to take advantage of this sentiment and to hold out to Calhoun the office of Secretary of State if and when Adams were elected President.[60] Adams advised against the stratagem: he thought that a vote for Calhoun for Vice President was a vote for Jackson rather than himself for President.[61] Jackson, he was persuaded, would make a much better Vice President than Calhoun! The Vice-Presidency and the Old Hero seemed to Adams ideally made for each other. But some of the politicians in his own section hesitated if only because of what the General had once said about hanging the leaders of

---

[59] *Memoirs*, VI, 269, 274, 289–92, 303, 360.

[60] P. P. F. Degrand to General Dearborn, Boston, January 1824. *Magazine of American History with Notes and Queries*, VIII (New York, 1882), 629–32.

[61] JQA to Timothy Fuller, Boston. Washington, August 1824. Draft, not sent. Adams MSS.

the Hartford Convention. They were afraid that downright expression might have alienated too many Federalist votes.

Adams reassured them. "It was a hasty and undigested sentiment," he told Arthur Livermore of New Hampshire in the presence of the latter's colleague, William Plumer, Jr. "It is hardly fair to hold him responsible for it. You must set off against it the fine sentiments in the same letter, for putting down the monster, party."

Livermore said he was satisfied. "I had only feared," he explained, "that General Jackson's name attached to yours might tend rather to weigh it down than assist it."

"The Vice Presidency is a station where the General can hang no one," responded Adams complacently, "and in which he would need to quarrel with no one. His name and character will serve to restore the forgotten dignity of the place, and it will afford an easy and dignified retirement to his old age." [62]

Neither Jackson nor Calhoun would lend themselves to such a coalition of Adams, Jackson, and Calhoun as that suggested by some of Adams's Boston friends. Jackson was too much in the lead for the first place, and Calhoun too sure of the second.

8

It was plain that John Quincy Adams could not be elected President if New York went against him. As the campaign drew to a close, there seemed a bare possibility that the Empire State, with her thirty-six votes, might decide the election without its going into the House of Representatives, particularly if Pennsylvania, with her twenty-eight electors, should prove to be, as Adams hoped, an "accessory" to New York. But his supporters could not quite control the New York legislature when it came to vote for the Presidential electors of that state. A handful of Clay men held the balance of power between Adams and Crawford in the New York Assembly.

In the midst of this highly uncertain situation Adams's friends anxiously asked him what to do: should they make a deal with the Clay men in order to shut Crawford out altogether and thus secure most if not all of the New York electoral vote for Adams? If the Clay people went over to Crawford in the final vote, it was even possible that Crawford might carry the state.

Faced by the critical situation in Albany, John Quincy Adams's resolves not personally to interfere in the campaign broke down further. In confidential letters to Blunt, Tallmadge, and Sterling he championed the right of the people against the caucus politicians (i.e., the Crawfordites), the right to vote directly for electors. He urged his supporters to work for the passage of a new electoral law, if not possible in the dying old legislature

[62] *Memoirs,* VI, 333. May 15, 1824.

in time for the Presidential election of 1824, then by all means in the recently elected reform legislature which was to convene after the national election. He advised them to delay the final vote on Presidential electors as long as possible, in order to gather support from the reform movement within the state. Particularly he besought them to stand united, not to compromise, to strive for all the electoral votes of New York or nothing, to make sure that New York throw her whole undivided vote effectively into the national scale and thus secure her "natural position" as "the leading state in the Union." [63] In other words, he wanted them to make John Quincy Adams President of the United States.

The New York friends worked loyally at Albany, but they could not swing the vote completely to Adams when the balloting occurred in the joint session of the expiring legislature. By only one vote they failed to carry their ticket. [64] Some sort of concession was necessary. Adams's supporters perforce yielded. With the aid of Thurlow Weed [65] they made an acceptable compromise that secured for their candidate most of the electoral votes of New York. At the final count the choice of state electors for President stood as follows: Adams 25, Clay 7, Crawford 4.

Clay's friends hoped that this deal would give the Kentuckian enough electoral votes to bring him instead of Crawford into the House of Representatives in Washington as the candidate behind Jackson and Adams. So it might have happened if the Clay electors had stood by their original choice. But the Adams group at Albany expected that some of the seven would desert their candidate and vote for Adams when the electoral college met. [66] Actually three of the Clay electors changed their votes—but to Crawford instead of to Adams! The final electoral vote of New York was Adams 26, Crawford 5, Clay 4, Jackson 1. These three votes, lost to Clay and gained by Crawford, were enough to make Crawford third man in the inconclusive, total electoral vote of all the states, and thus to elimi-

[63] JQA to Joseph Blunt, Washington, October 21, November 4, 1824; to James Tallmadge, October 21, 1824; to Micah Sterling, November 4, 1824. Adams MSS.

[64] There were 157 ballots cast, making 79 necessary for a majority, unless three of the ballots, blanks, were not counted. Seven Crawford nominees for electors got 95 votes (thanks to the help of Clay supporters, who could hope that these electors, although chosen on a Crawford ticket, would really vote for Clay in the electoral college); 25 Adams nominees got 78; one Adams nominee got 77. Chairman Erastus Root, a Crawfordite, held that 79 were necessary for a majority, and that consequently the Adams men had failed of election on the first ballot. Thomas Hertell, John W. Taylor, and Joseph Blunt, separately, to JQA, Albany, November 10, 11, 12, 1824. Adams MSS.

[65] In his *Autobiography,* pp. 122–38, Thurlow Weed, at that time a young Rochester journalist (*Rochester Telegraph*) and state bank lobbyist (Bank of Rochester) at Albany, takes credit for arranging the deal which saved New York for Adams and was indispensable to his election as President. At this time Weed was not a confidant of Adams, had had no correspondence with him.

[66] J. W. Taylor, Micah Sterling, James Tallmadge, Henry Wheaton, Thomas Hertell, separately, to JQA, Albany, November 16, 1824. Adams MSS.

nate Clay from the final contest, which took place among Jackson, Adams, and Crawford.

Full returns of the November election gave Jackson 99 electoral votes, Adams 84, Crawford 41, Clay 37.[67] Adams had won only New England and a majority of the electoral votes of New York. Pennsylvania and New Jersey went wholly to Jackson, as if in default of an Adams organization.[68] Only three states went for Crawford: Georgia, Virginia, and Delaware; [69] and three for Clay: Kentucky, Missouri, and Ohio. Jackson captured all the electoral votes in Pennsylvania, New Jersey, Tennessee, North Carolina, South Carolina, Mississippi, Alabama, Indiana; and a majority in Maryland,[70] Louisiana, and Illinois.[71] He also had a heavy plurality of popular votes in those states where the electors were chosen by the people: Jackson 153,544, Adams 108,740, Clay 47,136, Crawford 46,618.

No candidate had the required majority of electoral votes; but if any candidate were the choice of the people in 1824, it was Andrew Jackson.

[67] For tabulation see note at end of chapter.

[68] Joseph Hopkinson in October 1824 convened a group of Adams's friends in Philadelphia, who did some half-hearted last-minute campaigning, but the movement was so belated as to have little effect. Adams got small support in Pennsylvania, where the voters registered as follows: for Jackson electors, 36,100; for Adams electors, 5,440; for Crawford electors, 4,206. The voting was by a general ticket. McMaster: *History*, V, 75–6.

[69] Two electoral votes for Crawford, one for Adams, in Delaware.

[70] Seven votes for Jackson, three for Adams, one for Crawford.

[71] Two votes for Jackson, one for Adams.

The Electoral Vote of 1824 *

States	President				Vice President					
	Andrew Jackson, Tenn.	J. Q. Adams, Mass.	W. H. Crawford, Ga.	H. Clay, Ky.	John C. Calhoun, S.C.	Nathan Sanford, N.Y.	Nathaniel Macon, N.C.	Andrew Jackson, Tenn.	M. Van Buren, N.Y.	H. Clay, Ky.
Maine..........................	..	9	..	..	9	..	..	..	..	..
New Hampshire..................	..	8	..	..	7	..	..	1	..	..
Vermont........................	..	7	..	..	7	..	..	..	..	..
Massachusetts..................	..	15	..	..	15	..	..	..	..	..
Rhode Island...................	..	4	..	..	3	..	..	..	..	..
Connecticut....................	..	8	..	..	..	..	..	8	..	..
New York.......................	1	26	5	4	29	7	..	..	..	..
New Jersey.....................	8	..	..	..	8	..	..	..	..	..
Pennsylvania...................	28	..	..	..	28	..	..	..	..	..
Delaware.......................	..	1	2	..	1	..	..	..	..	2
Maryland.......................	7	3	1	..	10	..	..	1	..	..
Virginia.......................	..	..	24	..	..	..	24	..	..	..
North Carolina.................	15	..	..	..	15	..	..	..	..	..
South Carolina.................	11	..	..	..	11	..	..	..	..	..
Georgia........................	..	..	9	..	..	..	..	..	9	..
Alabama........................	5	..	..	..	5	..	..	..	..	..
Mississippi....................	3	..	..	..	3	..	..	..	..	..
Louisiana......................	3	2	..	..	5	..	..	..	..	..
Kentucky.......................	..	..	..	14	7	7	..	..	..	..
Tennessee......................	11	..	..	..	11	..	..	..	..	..
Missouri.......................	..	..	..	3	..	..	..	3	..	..
Ohio...........................	..	..	..	16	..	16	..	..	..	..
Indiana........................	5	..	..	..	5	..	..	..	..	..
Illinois.......................	2	1	..	..	3	..	..	..	..	..
Total......................	99	84	41	37	182	30	24	13	9	2

* From J. B. McMaster: *History of the People of the United States* (D. Appleton and Company, New York, 1900), V, 76. Copyright, 1900. Reproduced with permission of Appleton-Century-Crofts, Inc.

CHAPTER III

Election by the House of Representatives
(1824 – 1825)

Politics makes strange bedfellows.

OLD AMERICAN APHORISM

THERE WERE two choices before John Quincy Adams after the inconclusive popular election of 1824: to accept the manifest preference of the people among the four candidates and advise his supporters in the House of Representatives to cast their votes for Andrew Jackson, or to push on unrelentingly for his own election. If he followed the people's preference he could adjust himself to another shift in American party politics. It was even possible that Jackson—though he made no promises [1]—would keep him on as Secretary of State; in that case he could continue to lend experience, tone, dignity, and high prestige to what was bound to be a vigorous assertion and vindication of those guiding principles of American foreign policy that he had helped to formulate during his First Career, as a diplomatist. If he ignored the people's preference, as he had a constitutional right to do, and triumphed in the House of Representatives, he would be at best a minority President, inviting opposition on all sides, making himself the enemy instead of the continuing friend of the Hero of New Orleans.

He decided to stick to his constitutional privilege. The Presidency was in his blood. The contest in the House of Representatives would probably be the only opportunity of his lifetime. He would not resign his chances in favor of Andrew Jackson's popular plurality.

1

Prospects for election involved some nice political calculations. John Quincy Adams would have to combine with at least one of his recent rivals against General Jackson. There would be only one man for that role:

---

[1] Jackson told James Buchanan on December 30, 1824, when the latter expressed some anxiety that if Jackson were elected he would keep on Adams as Secretary of State, as follows: "that he thought well of Mr. Adams, but he never said or intimated that he would, or would not, appoint him Secretary of State: that these were secrets he would keep to himself—he would conceal them from the very hairs of his head." Bassett: *Life of Jackson,* I, 358. See below p. 130.

Henry Clay. Adams had all but contemned Clay as leader of an opposition to the Monroe Administration and rival to himself for the succession. If he made friends with Clay now, it would be obvious that he did so for political reasons. And even Clay's support might not surely be enough to clinch the Presidency.

On the part of Clay there were, perhaps, good political reasons for him to prefer Adams. In the first place, the Kentuckian had taken such a conspicuous stand against Jackson in the Florida debates that it would be difficult to reverse his opposition to the General. Furthermore, Clay and Adams were more in accord in political outlook at home and abroad than Clay and Jackson. Jackson had qualified his support of national internal improvements, limiting it to projects essential to military defense of the United States, whilst Adams was an unequivocal advocate of such a program. It was one of the two integral parts of Henry Clay's "American System": the protective tariff, and internal improvements to be financed from mounting tariff revenues. Moreover, there was no longer any difference between Clay and Adams in the field of foreign policy after recognition of the independence of Latin America. But the final and controlling reason for Clay's preference for Adams over Jackson would be the Speaker's own unquenchable ambition. He was out of the race for 1825, but the future was inviting. As a Western man and a natural rival of Jackson for the suffrages of that section, he felt that in the normal give and take of American politics—party lines being still undrawn—he had more of a chance to succeed Adams, an Eastern President, than Jackson, a Western President.

Clay found himself in not too unpleasant a position. Everybody thought he had sole power to make the next President. Friends of Jackson would touch him gently on the shoulder and say: "My dear Sir, all my dependence is upon you, don't disappoint us. You know our partiality was for you next to the hero: and how much we want a Western President." Within the same hour a Crawford man might suggest: "The hopes of the Republican party are concentrated on you; for God's sake preserve it. If you had been returned, instead of Mr. Crawford, every man of us would have supported you to the last hour. We consider him and you as the only genuine Republican candidates." Next a friend of Mr. Adams would come up, with tears in his eyes: "Sir, Mr. Adams has always had the greatest respect for you, and admiration of your talents. There is no station to which you are not equal. Most undoubtedly you are the second choice of New England, and I pray you to consider seriously whether the public good and your own future interests do not point most distinctly to the choice which you ought to make." [2]

Historians have assumed [3] rather generally that Henry Clay, himself cut

---

[2] So Clay wrote playfully to a Kentucky friend, Francis P. Blair, Washington, January 8, 1825. *The Works of Henry Clay*, Calvin Colton, ed. (10 vols., New York, 1904), IV, 109.

[3] Not so, however, John Spencer Bassett in his *Life of Jackson*, I, 363.

out from the Presidency by the popular choice of electors of 1824, nevertheless became President-maker in the House of Representatives in 1825 by his power to throw to the man of his choice the states that had been loyal to his banner: Kentucky, Missouri, and Ohio. It is true that the votes of two of these three states would have sufficed to elect Jackson provided the General could command the delegations in the House from the eleven other states which he had captured in the November elections. He needed only two more to have a majority of thirteen out of twenty-four states. On the other hand, if Clay added the votes of his three states to Adams's seven, the New Englander would have only ten states, less than the required majority of thirteen. To win, Adams would need three more states, which he would have to take away from either Jackson or Crawford. Since Pennsylvania, New Jersey, and apparently Indiana were solid for Jackson, there seemed to be only one Northern state that could possibly be won from its previous choice of electors: Illinois, where the electors had cast two votes for Jackson, and one for Adams. One man would cast the vote of Illinois, Daniel P. Cook, the sole representative, elected in 1822, and not re-elected in 1824. Even if Cook should vote for Adams, he would still need two more states over and above the three that Henry Clay could swing. They would have to be Southern states, states whose electors had voted for Jackson or for Crawford. Already Adams had captured minority electors in Maryland (which went for Jackson), Louisiana (Jackson), and Delaware (Crawford). These three Southern states were likely possibilities.

How fortunate for the Massachusetts man that he had avoided taking any sectional stand during the campaign! How shrewd to have been "cautious" about a protective tariff, pronouncing for one that would conciliate both the manufacturing and the agricultural interests of the country! How discreet to have withheld from public expression the convictions that had been forming in his mind and heart against the evil of slavery!

2

And how about Calhoun's friends in Congress, mostly Southerners, those who had supported him for the first office before he accepted nomination for the Vice-Presidency? Calhoun was running for second place on both Adams and Jackson tickets. Would his following in the House of Representatives be likely to vote for Jackson or Adams for President?

In the New England states the electors who won at the November polls had been pledged to vote for Adams as President but not pledged to anyone for Vice President. There were many Adams men in that section of the country who, like their chief, were admirers of the Old Hero and would have been content to see him elected Vice President. Calhoun therefore suggested to Adams's friends that, whilst he was neutral in any personal contest between Adams and Jackson, he thought it would be better for them to vote for him as candidate for Vice President, lest by supporting Jackson for that second office they give the dangerous impression, just before a possible Presidential contest in the House of Representatives, that Jackson might make a good President! [4]

As has been seen, John Quincy Adams's own preference was for Jackson as Vice President. One of Adams's gratuitous advisers in Washington was a friend of Calhoun, George Sullivan of New Hampshire, who had represented that state before the Supreme Court in the famous Dartmouth College case. He was now lobbying for the State of Massachusetts, seeking to collect claims against the United States arising out of the War of 1812. As Secretary of War it was Calhoun's duty to pass on those claims. So far he had shown himself cold as an icicle [5] to all Sullivan's representations. The Federalist lawyer concluded that the only way to melt Calhoun quickly was to find some political support for him in New England, particularly in the key state of Massachusetts. With the indirect assistance of Attorney General William Wirt,[6] Sullivan intervened in New England politics in an effort to swing the choice of electors for Vice President from Jackson to Calhoun.[7] In Washington the leading Adams paper, the *National Journal*, came out for Calhoun for Vice President, November 6, 1824. At the same time John Quincy Adams significantly ceased to express a strong desire to have Jackson elected Vice President, and adopted a studiously enigmatic attitude.[8]

The Vice-Presidential question suggests another covert intervention of John Quincy Adams, again behind the scenes, in the campaign. If he was not lifting a finger to promote his own candidacy in this instance, he certainly was making a hesitant off-stage nod to the actors. But the truth is that he did not let himself know quite all that his friends were up to. "There are so many *queer* things passing before me that I believe the best present explanation of them is to be found in silence." [9]

Sullivan's electoral artifice brought Adams no support from Calhoun either before or after the latter's easy election as Vice President. It had become all too clear that the South Carolinian would be elected Vice President anyway, even without the help of New England, which actually did cast its electoral votes for him. If Adams wished to win the Presidency in

---

[4] Morgan Dix: *Memoirs of John Adams Dix* (New York, 1883), II, 309–14.

[5] *Memoirs*, VI, 308.

[6] Dutre J. Pearce to P. P. F. Degrand, Providence, R.I., November 30, 1824, enclosing extracts from a letter said to have been written by William Wirt to Henry Wheaton, urging that the electoral votes be cast for Calhoun for Vice President. Degrand to JQA, No. 172, Boston, December 4, 1824. Adams MSS.

[7] George Sullivan to Joseph E. Sprague, Washington, "Saturday Morning" [October 1824], enclosed in Sprague to JQA, Salem, October 28, 1824; and Sullivan to Sprague, January 9, 1825. Adams MSS.

[8] *Memoirs*, VI, 417, 438. JQA to Joseph E. Sprague, November 2, 14, 1824. Adams MSS.

[9] JQA to Joseph E. Sprague, Washington, January 24, 1825. Adams MSS.

the House of Representatives against the people's preference for Jackson, he would now have to look elsewhere in the South than to Calhoun.

3

Nearly two months remained for political canvassing and bargaining after final results of the election of 1824 became known in Washington. John Quincy Adams, hitherto by his own words a solitary man, a "silent animal," [10] suddenly became an unusually gregarious person. Never at any other time in his life did he make so many visits to Washington hotels and boarding-houses, calling on delegations in the House of Representatives and their friends. He did not neglect a single chance of trying to win over a state to his support. All this visiting and conferring went on behind the festivities attending the nation's fervent reception to General Lafayette on his farewell visit to America.

Visitors equally interested in the coming contest came to talk to Adams too. Day after day members of Congress and other politicians filled his office in the Department of State, a stone's throw from the White House. First was Robert P. Letcher, a member of the House from Kentucky, intimate friend of Henry Clay; they lodged in the same quarters and took their meals together. Letcher had seized time by the forelock and called on the Secretary at the Department of State on December 10, six days before the returns had come in from Louisiana, last state to be heard from. Adams returned the call on December 12, after the inconclusive popular count was in from all the states. Letcher talked at length on Kentucky politics and the preference of his constituents for a candidate "next to Mr. Clay." [11] He visited Adams again at his office on December 17, ostensibly to discuss the petty claim of a constituent against the United States Government. Soon he brought the conversation around to the Presidential question.

"What are your sentiments toward Clay?" Letcher asked quite bluntly.

"I harbor no hostility against him," Adams replied. "Whatever of difference there has been between us has arisen entirely from him, not from me." Without disguise Adams adverted to Jonathan Russell's attack on him three years before [12] and his belief that Clay had been back of it. "But having completely repelled that attack," he added quickly, "I feel no animosity against any person concerned in it."

"Clay's friends think he has been wrong in his letter against you concerning that affair," Letcher admitted. "It was written in a moment of excitement. I am sure Clay now feels no hostility toward you. He has spoken respectfully of you and is a man of sincerity."

[10] Diary, July 15, 1820.

[11] Clay himself later came in and spoke of the projected grant of money by Congress to General Lafayette. *Memoirs,* VI, 440.

[12] The affair of the Fisheries and the Mississippi. See Vol. I, Chapter XXIV.

Adams got the drift, all right. It was what his confidential informant Edward Wyer had already told him: that Clay would willingly support him if he could thereby serve himself. What Letcher wanted Adams to understand was that if Clay's friends could *know* that he would have a prominent share in the Administration, it might induce them to vote for Adams, even in the face of their instructions from the Kentucky legislature to vote for Jackson. Letcher did not profess any authority from Clay; his interview with Adams was entirely confidential, he explained. The Secretary of State, whose diplomatic training required a show of full powers before beginning a negotiation, answered in general terms.[13] He then turned his attention temporarily from Kentucky to Indiana, hoping to find the delegation from that state sympathetic to him.

Indiana had given her five electoral votes to Jackson. The popular vote on a general ticket was Jackson 7,343, Clay 5,315, Adams 1,542, a clear majority for Jackson. The state was immovable in its allegiance to the victor of New Orleans. Nevertheless Adams went to Queen's Hotel and had a talk with one of Indiana's representatives, Jonathan Jennings, about appointment of printers in that state for the publication of the federal laws.[14] In doing so he broke a rule of his not to make a change in the printing patronage unless desired by a majority of the state's delegation in Congress.[15] Jennings appeared to be satisfied with the interview.[16] But he was only one of three Congressmen from Indiana who would determine the state's vote. At the final test Indiana did not budge from Andrew Jackson's side.

Just before Christmas, Senator James Barbour of Virginia, former Governor of the Old Dominion, dropped in on Adams. "Our first choice is

[13] *Memoirs*, VI, 446–7. December 17, 1824.
[14] *Memoirs*, VI, 448. December 19, 1824.
[15] *Memoirs*, V, 394. November 13, 1821.
[16] *Memoirs*, VI, 448. December 19, 1824.

The following tabulation shows the changes in the three Indiana newspapers chosen by the Secretary of State for the printing of federal laws:

Eighteenth Congress	*Eighteenth Congress*	*Nineteenth Congress*
1st Session, Dec. 1, 1823– May 26, 1824	2d Session, Dec. 2, 1824– March 3, 1825	1st Session, Dec. 5, 1825– March 4, 1826
Indiana Gazette, Corydon	*Indiana Journal,* Indianapolis	*Indiana Journal,* Indianapolis
Evansville Gazette, Evansville	*Evansville Gazette,* Evansville	*Western Sun and General Advertiser,* Vincennes
Brookville Enquirer, Brookville	*Brookville Enquirer,* Brookville	*Franklin Repository* (formerly *Brookville Enquirer*), Brookville

See Sen. Doc. 88, 19th Cong., 1st Sess., pp. 36, 40, 44.

The dropping of the *Evansville Gazette* occurred after March 4, 1825, when Clay was Secretary of State and Adams President, but that does not eliminate possible political motives.

Mr. Crawford," he declared, "but you are more popular there than General Jackson or even than Mr. Clay, one of our native sons."

The two men canvassed Crawford's chances.

"How do you feel about the tariff and internal improvements?" Barbour asked, bringing up Virginia's most touchy subjects—except for the unmentionable one of slavery.

"*Conciliation,* not *collision,*" Adams answered, "is the ultimate principle of my system with reference to the great interests of the country. I am satisfied with the tariff as now established. If any change in it should be desired I should incline rather to reduce than to increase it. As to internal improvements my opinions have been published in most of the newspapers. . . ."

He had long since made it clear that he favored a national program of internal improvements and considered such a measure constitutional. "Since the Act of Congress establishing the Cumberland Road, there has been no constitutional question worth disputing about."

Adams got the impression that Barbour was quite content.[17] He had at least a hope that Virginia might come his way if the voting ran to more than one ballot, but when the one and only ballot was taken later in the House, Virginia's vote went to Crawford, the preference of her electors.

Letcher of Kentucky, doubtless having talked with Clay, came back to sound out Adams again. "It is important to obtain an election in the House of Representatives at the first ballot," he said. "It is obtainable by securing the votes of Kentucky, Ohio, Indiana, Illinois, Missouri, and Louisiana."

"However desirable that might be," Adams replied, "it would be utterly impracticable. I have no expectation," he reminded the Kentucky Congressman suggestively, "of receiving even the vote of your own state."

A resolution of the Kentucky legislature had in effect instructed the state's delegation to cast its ballot for Jackson! But that did not bind them constitutionally.

Letcher canvassed the Kentucky delegation, one by one, and disclosed that a majority of them were still uncommitted. Kentucky was in a good bargaining position.

Adams pondered over the curious desire of Clay's friends that he, John Quincy Adams, should be elected President on the first ballot! In talking with Letcher he was playing with fire, and he knew it. "*Incedo super ignes* [I am treading coals of fire]," he wrote guardedly in his Diary.[18]

Letcher spoke to Adams again at President Monroe's New Year's reception. The two men went to the Department of State and continued their talk. Letcher now offered assurances that his delegation in the House had made up their own minds to vote for Adams, whatever the advice of the legislature might be. "But the difference between Mr. Clay and you," he intimated, "gives concern to some of the members of the delegation. . . .

---

[17] *Memoirs,* VI, 450–2. December 22, 1824.
[18] *Memoirs,* VI, 452–3. December 23, 1824.

I wish you could have some conversation with Mr. Clay on the subject."

"I will do so very readily," responded Adams, "whenever it may suit the convenience of Mr. Clay." [19]

Later in the day Adams and Clay sat beside each other at a dinner in honor of General Lafayette.

"I would be glad to have some confidential conversation with you upon public affairs," Clay managed to say.

"Whenever it suits your convenience," Adams answered.

At the outset of the campaign he had resolved so highly not to intervene personally. Friends like Hopkinson and Degrand and others had begged him to step forth and take an honorable hand in it. He had refused to come out openly but he had interfered behind the scenes, belatedly. As a result he had come out second best at the polls when an open campaign capably organized and vigorously fought might have won him the election. Now at the last moment should he hold back and let the Presidency go by default to Jackson, whose friends were actively working to hold the General's own states and get the necessary two more? Should he let Nature take its course, unaided? Or should he extend to himself a further helping hand?

"There is in my prospects and anticipations," he meditated at the beginning of the new year 1825, "a solemnity and moment never before experienced, and to which *unaided nature is inadequate*." [20]

4

"I said, I will be wise; but it was far from me." This was the text of the Reverend Mr. Robert Little's sermon in the Unitarian Church, to which John Quincy Adams listened attentively on Sunday morning, January 9, 1825. That afternoon he heard Reverend Daniel Baker preach at the Second Presbyterian Church on Hebrews, xi, 1: "Now faith is the substance of things hoped for, the evidence of things not seen." Adams thought the learning and morality of the morning sermon more satisfactory and instructive than the afternoon preachment. Between sermons he went to call on John W. Taylor and Albert H. Tracy, Representatives in Congress from the State of New York. He speculated with them about the "approaching event" for which he had such hopes, but inconclusive support. They could give him no certain materials for judgment, even in New York. In the evening Henry Clay called according to appointment. He brought stronger expectations.

"The time is drawing near," Clay began, "when the choice must be made in the House of Representatives from the three candidates presented by the electoral colleges. I have been much urged and solicited with regard to the part which I should take in that transaction. Not five

[19] *Memoirs*, VI, 456–7.   [20] *Memoirs*, VI, 457–8. Italics inserted.

minutes after I landed at my lodgings a friend of Mr. Crawford applied to me in a manner so gross that it disgusted me. Some of your friends, also, disclaiming, indeed, any authority from you, have repeatedly applied to me, directly or indirectly, urging considerations personal to myself, as motives for my cause. I have thought it best to reserve for some time my determination to myself: first, to give a decent time for my own funeral solemnities as a candidate; and, secondly, to prepare and predispose all my friends to a state of neutrality between the three candidates who would be before the House, so that they might be free ultimately to take that course which might be most conducive to the public interest."

All three candidates and all their friends professed to be working solely for the public interest! What candidate, what worker, has ever admitted otherwise?

Adams listened attentively as Clay went on:

"The time has now come when I may be explicit in my communication with you. For that purpose I have asked this confidential interview. I wish you to satisfy me, so far as you may think proper, with regard to some principles of great public importance, but without any personal considerations for myself. In the question to come before the House between General Jackson, Mr. Crawford, and yourself, I have no hesitation in saying that my preference will be for you."

There is no doubt that John Quincy Adams, from his previous talks with Letcher, knew what was expected of him. The confidential interview continued. What the two men further said we do not know, but Clay concluded, without explicit assurances, that he could have any situation in the new Cabinet that he wanted.[21] Adams's Diary breaks off exasperatingly at this point. He left a blank space to write up later. It remains blank to this day. The scrupulous editor of his *Memoirs* explains that the extreme pressure of business and visits (which was certainly enormous at this time) prevented the diarist from filling [22] it in—and this one of the most important conversations that he ever had in his life! When John Quincy Adams dropped his Diary in such an important matter as this, he let his conscience slip.[23] *Incedo super ignes!* The road to the President's

[21] Henry Clay to James Brown, January 23, 1825. Cited by Florence Weston: *The Presidential Election of 1828* (Washington, 1938), p. 18.

[22] *Memoirs*, VI, 464–5.

[23] "A man who commits to paper from day to day the employment of his time, the places he frequents, the persons with whom he converses, the actions with which he is occupied, will have a perpetual guard over himself. His record is a second conscience. He will fly from worthless associates and from dishonest deeds, to avoid the alternative of becoming a self-accuser or of falsifying by the suppressio veri [*sic*] his own testimony to his own actions. I will appeal to yourself whether your interruptions in your diary, according as you have kept or neglected it have not been most frequently owing to a sense of shame, an unwillingness to put upon the record time worse than wasted, and actions of which you was ashamed." JQA to GWA, No. 7/70, Boston, November 28, 1827. Throughout his life Adams refrained from putting into writing his conversation with Clay, even when asked to do so for the record of pos-

Mansion was strewn with live coals, and he had to make his way over them. He would try to be wise, but wisdom might be too far from him.

Another interview followed, at Clay's request, on January 29. The Kentuckian talked a couple of hours on prospects and probabilities of the Presidential election. He spoke with the greatest freedom of men and things, intimated doubts and prepossessions about some of the individual friends that surrounded Adams, was particularly anxious that Daniel Webster and Louis McLane be conciliated. So Adams noted in his Diary, but again the record is meager of what Clay said in detail. Adams on his part listened with due consideration.

"My own situation is critical and difficult," Clay declared as he came to an end. "The newspapers are attacking me with fury for having come out for you. Jackson's partisans, particularly those of the Calhoun interest, are largely throwing out threats of violence. . . . This morning I received an anonymous letter from Philadelphia threatening organized opposition and civil war if Jackson is not chosen."

Just like Ingham and McDuffie's talk to Cook,[24] Adams said to himself. Samuel D. Ingham of Philadelphia and George McDuffie of South Carolina, Jackson men, members of the House of Representatives, had been working on Adams's loyal lame duck, Daniel P. Cook, who as sole member from Illinois would cast that state's vote in the coming Presidential ballot. They knew he wanted to be Governor of the Territory of Arkansas. Ingham had intimated to him he would get the appointment if he voted for Jackson.[25] Ingham and McDuffie got Cook into a Washington hotel room in the presence of J. C. Isaacs of Tennessee, another Jackson man.

"It's time for you to make your stand," McDuffie said aggressively. "If you do so you can settle the question in Jackson's favor. There is no doubt that an arrangement has been made between Mr. Clay and Mr. Adams to transfer Clay's influence to him, Clay to be made Secretary of State for doing so. It is in your power to defeat it."

Cook professed not to be sure his vote would settle the matter, anyway. "If my taking a stand in favor of General Jackson," he said, "is to be at all produced by the suggestion you make of a coalition of the corrupt character mentioned, between Mr. Adams and Mr. Clay, I should certainly require satisfactory evidence of its existence. . . . In that case Mr. Adams and Mr. Clay would be unworthy of public confidence."

"Of course," acknowledged McDuffie, "it's difficult to prove such a thing, but I don't doubt its existence."

"I shall keep myself at liberty to act as the interests of the country may require," was Cook's unexceptionable reply.

---

terity. See Albert H. Tracy to JQA, Buffalo, N.Y., December 10, 1838 (unanswered). Adams MSS.

[24] *Memoirs*, VI, 483. January 29, 1825.

[25] *Memoirs*, VI, 496.

"If the western votes in Congress defeat Jackson," McDuffie warned, prophetically, "there will be a tremendous storm in the west, not to be withstood, and Mr. Adams will not be able to sustain his administration. There will be such an opposition to him that he will certainly go out at the end of four years."

"Adams's election," added Ingham, "will produce two parties in this country. The elements for opposition are such that he cannot resist them."[26]

Cook managed to get out of the hotel without making any promises. When the time came, he threw Illinois's vote to Adams, the last act of his legislative career. Later, in 1827, President Adams and Secretary of State Clay gave him a confidential diplomatic junket to Cuba paid for out of the contingent secret-service fund.[27]

Next appeared John Scott of Missouri. He was another Representative whose sole decision would determine the vote of his state. Announced by Letcher, he too came around to see the Secretary of State. Crowninshield, Secretary of the Navy, had mentioned that Scott was affronted because his recommendations for appointments in Missouri had been slighted. Wyer, too, had reported that Scott was sore.

Scott's complaint was that several years ago Adams had appointed one newspaper, politically hostile to Scott, to print the laws of the United States in Missouri. He handed Adams a list of three papers which he wished to have designated for such favors. They proved to be the same three which had already been printing the laws for the last two sessions.[28] Adams, following his standing rule, certainly contemplated no change. "Neither in this instance, nor in any other," he assured the disgruntled Missourian, "have I ever acted with any intentions unfriendly toward you." It seemed easy to appease Scott. But this was not all.

"An application has been made to the President," Scott complained, "for the removal of my brother as Judge in the Territory of Arkansas, because he killed his colleague on the bench in a duel."

Adams was the only one of the three remaining contestants for the Presidency who never had to fight a duel. Perhaps this was because he confined his frank appreciations of people to his Diary. He abhorred dueling in principle. But he kept his composure as to Scott's duelist brother.

"There has been such an application," he acknowledged, "made as long since as last summer. But as the President has not acted on it hitherto, I think he will not."

Scott then proceeded to speak of the approaching election.

"I have made up my mind to vote with the other Western delegations,"

[26] Memorandum of D. P. Cook, Washington, Saturday, January 21, 1825, written out at JQA's request. Adams MSS.

[27] See Vol. I, 541–2.

[28] Compare the lists in Sen. Doc. 88, 19th Cong., 1st Sess., pp. 32, 36, 40.

he said, intimating that he would thereby incur great opposition in his own state. "I am entirely devoted to Mr. Clay, and I hope he will be a member of the next Administration."

"With regard to the formation of an Administration," replied Adams, who then had not yet been elected President, "you would not expect me to enter into details, but *if I should be elected by the suffrages of the West, I should naturally look to the West for much of the support that I should need.*" [29]

Scott went away in good humor. Next day he came back.

"I am under some apprehension, from what I said yesterday," he explained, "that you might consider me disposed to prescribe conditions or make bargains."

"I didn't understand it that way," Adams said comfortably. "I received nothing you said yesterday in that sense."

"I did not mean to speak positively," asserted Scott. "I had not entirely made up my mind how I should vote, and have not now. My prevailing impression is that I shall act with my friends."

"Scott means to vote with the strongest side," Adams said to himself.[30]

When the time came, Scott voted for Adams, the way Clay told him to do. As President, John Quincy Adams took no step to unseat Judge Andrew Scott; in fact, when the jurist's four-year term ran out, President Adams renominated him to the Senate, but that body very properly refused to confirm the nomination. According to the laws of the Territory of Arkansas, no participant in a duel could hold office.

Federalist friends of Daniel Webster wanted to know what his future would be if they voted for Adams in the House of Representatives.

"It is his ambition to go as Minister to England," suggested William Plumer, Jr., of New Hampshire.

"I think it may be gratified hereafter," said Adams, "but not immediately." [31]

There was still some doubt as to how the Maryland and New York delegations might throw the votes of their states respectively in the House of Representatives.

Maryland had given Jackson seven electoral votes, Adams three, and Crawford one. Her delegation in the House of Representatives was about evenly divided between Adams and Jackson. Federalists were worried lest John Quincy Adams as President proscribe eminent members of their party—like Webster—from appointment.

John Reed, a Federalist member of Congress from Cape Cod, Massachusetts, called on Adams to speak about Daniel Webster; about Louis McLane, a Jeffersonian Republican from Delaware, tinctured by some

[29] Italics inserted.
[30] *Memoirs,* VI, 443, 473–5. December 14, 1824; January 21, 22, 1825.
[31] *Memoirs,* VI, 315–16, 474.

Federalist principles, who had supported Crawford; and about Federalists generally.

"I am favorable to you," declared Reed, "but Webster is specially apprehensive that you will exclude the Federalists from office."

"I shall exclude no person for political opinions or for personal opposition to me," the candidate assured him. "My great object will be to break up the remnant of old party distinctions and bring the whole people together in sentiment as much as possible." [32]

Under these circumstances Henry R. Warfield, lame-duck Congressman of Maryland, wrote to Webster stating that the vote of the state might depend on him. He too wanted to know how Adams felt about appointing Federalists. Mr. John Lee, a former Representative from Maryland, once a Federalist but elected to the Eighteenth Congress as a Republican, further talked to Webster anxiously about the same thing.

Webster does not record whether he himself had anything to do with inspiring these inquiries. He drafted an answer to Warfield, which he read to John Quincy Adams before delivering. In his reply to Warfield, Webster disclaimed any authority to speak for Adams, but gave it as his firm opinion that Mr. Adams would administer the Government on liberal principles, not excluding Federalists, as such, from his regard, and that it was just and reasonable to expect that this would be shown "by some one clear and distinct case." [33]

"If that refers to the formation of an Administration," declared Adams, "it would imply more than I can confirm."

"It does not," assured Webster, "but to an appointment, perhaps of a judge."

"I approve altogether of the general spirit of the answer," declared Adams, "and should consider it as one of the objects nearest to my heart to bring the whole people of the Union to harmonize together. I must say, however, candidly that I believe either General Jackson or Mr. Crawford would pursue precisely the same principle, and that no Administration could possibly succeed upon any other." [34]

Daniel Webster took his leave.

William C. Bradley of Vermont reported to Adams rumors that Jackson's friends and Crawford's were huddling together. Some of the Connecticut members, originally for Crawford, were now inclining to Jackson, he said. One of them, Noyes Barber of Groton, was willing to vote for Adams, except for a fear that if elected he would turn out one Richard Law, Collector of the Port of New London, and other revenue officers who were known to have voted for Crawford. The vote of Connecticut might depend on Barber.

[32] *Memoirs*, VI, 474.
[33] Fish: *Civil Service and the Patronage*, p. 71. [Daniel Webster to Henry R. Warfield], H[ouse] of R[epresentatives], February 5, 1825. Copy. Adams MSS.
[34] *Memoirs*, VI, 492–3. February 3, 1825.

"I shall turn out no person for his conduct or opinions in relation to the election," Adams assured Bradley.[35]

The city was now swarming with strangers eager to take advantage of the political situation. Adams's office was so full of visitors that he could not remember all their names, much less write them all down as usual in his journal.

Warfield wanted to see him again. After church on Sunday the 6th of February the Secretary of State went out of his way to call on Webster. "Let Mr. Warfield know that I will be glad to see him at any time to-morrow morning before noon," he informed the Massachusetts Congress-man.

Warfield came. He said he had not yet decided how to cast his vote. "My friends, Mr. Charles Carroll, of Carrollton, and Mr. Taney, of Balti-more, have urged me to vote for General Jackson, under an impression that if you should be elected, the Administration would be conducted on the principle of proscribing the Federalist Party."

"I can assure you," promised Adams, "that I will never be at the head of any Administration of proscription to any party—political or geographi-cal."

Mr. Warfield went away seemingly content.[36] When the time came, Maryland voted for Adams. Webster never did get a political pay-off: as will be seen, the London post went to another, an older Federalist, Rufus King.

5

The second Wednesday in February, the day for the ballot by the House of Representatives, was less than forty-eight hours away. On the surface of things the capital city was all taken up with General Lafayette. On Monday evening there was a gala performance in his honor at the Wash-ington Theater. President Monroe was there with the Nation's Guest, and the Secretary of State, also General Jackson, and Crawford, with perhaps a hundred members of Congress in attendance.[37] John Quincy Adams managed to keep his attention on the play as he watched the last appear-ance of his favorite actor, the aging Cooper, in *Damon and Pythias*; but his mind must have wandered, like those of the others present, to the impending vote in the House of Representatives. How would the New York delegation cast the vote of that state?

Although he had obtained a heavy majority of the electoral votes of New York, he was not sure how the state's vote would go for President. Seventeen of the New York members were known to have been for Ad-ams in November 1824. Two were said to be for Jackson, fifteen perhaps for Crawford. If the two Jackson men should go over to Crawford, and

[35] *Memoirs*, VI, 475.
[36] *Memoirs*, VI, 497–500. February 7, 1825.
[37] *Memoirs*, VI, 500.

every Crawford man stand firm, a tie was possible within the state's delegation. And how Adams needed the vote of New York!

Already he had tried to win the support of Governor Clinton's partisans in Congress. In so striving he had to set aside his low opinion of Clinton and the latter's inordinate ambition for office; knowing this weakness of the man, he had catered to it.[38] During the recent gubernatorial campaign in New York, Adams had confidentially instructed his own lieutenants to support the Empire-Builder as the people's candidate for Governor regularly nominated by a state convention at Utica.[39] He had told Clinton's friend John W. Taylor that several times he had recommended the Governor for important missions abroad. Ever so circumspectly he now intimated that he thought well enough of Clinton to take him into an Administration under certain circumstances: "it is for him to determine how far it might be for his interest to maintain towards me the attitude of a competitor or otherwise." [40]

Clinton's influence, even if secured, might not be enough to swing the state's delegation. Adams continued to worry.[41] One of the Crawford electors from New York was doubtful: Stephen Van Rensselaer, an old Federalist, brother-in-law of Alexander Hamilton. Van Buren was laboring to hold him in line for the Georgian; Henry Clay and Daniel Webster were plying him for Adams. They said that election or no election would depend on his vote. They pictured the danger to propertied interests, including his own rich holdings, if public disorder should ensue. John Quincy Adams personally told Van Rensselaer what he had assured Webster, that he would not proscribe the Federalists from office,[42] as Monroe had done.

According to Van Buren's *Autobiography*, which historically is as significant for what it does not say as for what it says, General Van Rensselaer wobbled back and forth right up to the time when in the House of Representatives he had to pick up a ballot and vote. At the last moment he dropped his head on his desk and made a brief appeal to his Maker, as was his custom in great crises. Opening his eyes he saw a ticket on the floor beneath him bearing the name of John Quincy Adams. Taking this sign for divine guidance he picked up the paper and dropped it in the delegation's ballot box. "In this way," Little Van remembered ruefully, "it was that Mr. Adams was made President." [43]

[38] For JQA's real opinion of Clinton, see remarks in *Memoirs*, VII, 438–9, on occasion of Clinton's death in 1828.

[39] JQA to Joseph Blunt, October 21, 1824. Adams MSS.

[40] *Memoirs*, VI, 444. December 15, 1824.

[41] *Memoirs*, VI, 484, 498.

[42] *Memoirs*, VI, 493. February 4, 1825.

[43] Bassett: *Life of Jackson*, I, 365, has made the most of this. John C. Fitzpatrick edited *The Autobiography of Martin Van Buren* in *Annual Report* 1918 AHA, Vol. II (Washington, 1920). Van Buren explains (p. 152) that Van Rensselaer vouchsafed this information to him "an evening or two after the election."

As a wealthy Patroon in New York, Van Rensselaer needed no recompense from John Quincy Adams. Presumably he received his just reward in heaven. He had to wait until January 26, 1839.

6

On a cold and snowy winter afternoon, Wednesday, February 9, 1825, the House of Representatives by a bare majority of thirteen states elected John Quincy Adams on the first ballot. They were: Missouri, Ohio, and Kentucky (Clay's three states); Louisiana, Maryland, and Illinois (which Adams took away from Jackson); New York; and of course the six New England states. Of Jackson's original eleven states, won in the electoral vote of 1824, only seven stood by him at the call. Crawford's four states— Georgia, North Carolina, Virginia, and Delaware—held fast. Even if Crawford had thrown his support to Jackson, as Adams feared he might do,[44] it would not have elected the Tennessean, given the defection to Adams of Illinois, Maryland, and Louisiana.

In the darkening Senate chamber Rufus King, John Quincy Adams's diplomatic friend of early London days, heard what had taken place in the House. Hurriedly he dipped his pen and wrote a note to the man he preferred as President, at least to "black Candidates" and "Southern Masters": "I send you and your venerable father my affectionate congratulations." [45]

The President-elect's memory flashed back through a half-century of American independence, back to Braintree, to Paris, The Hague, London, Philadelphia, Washington, whence father and mother had bent his steps so steadily toward "the cabinet or the field" as he wandered all over the world. Truly they, not he, were to be congratulated. It was they who had planned it that way. He enclosed King's note in a quick missive to his father in Quincy, and added: "I can only offer you my congratulations and ask your blessings and prayers. Your affectionate and dutiful son, John Quincy Adams." [46]

Massachusetts was eagerly awaiting the outcome of the balloting. The town of Quincy had voted unanimously in the November elections for their second most illustrious citizen, the son of John Adams still living; so did Weymouth, the birthplace of Abigail Adams; in Milton where Abigail's parents, the Smiths, had lived, only three votes had been cast against John Quincy Adams for President. The whole state had gone heavily for him. In Boston, people were besieging the post office, the newspapers,

[44] *Memoirs*, VI, 474. Years later Adams recalled that he knew in 1825 he would have the votes of thirteen states on the first ballot, or at least fifteen on the second. JQA to CFA, December 12, 1833. Adams MSS. See note at end of chapter for tabulation of vote by states in the House of Representatives.

[45] Charles R. King: *The Life and Correspondence of Rufus King* . . . (New York, 1900), VI, 36, 507, 588.

[46] *Memoirs*, VI, 504.

every avenue of intelligence, waiting for the results of the final election. It came with the mail shortly after midnight, on Sunday, February 13. Despite that early Sabbath hour, the crowd turned the night into day.

Someone got the news out to Quincy before three o'clock in the morning. When a kinsman, E. W. Cruft, called to pay his respects to John Adams at an early hour, he found the ex-President very calm, firm, and dignified, his mind as bright as ever.[47]

With welling pride and love the aged patriot wrote to his son the President-elect: "Never did I feel so much solemnity as upon this occasion. The multitude of my thoughts and the intensity of my feelings are too much for a mind like mine, in its ninetieth year. May the blessing of God Almighty continue to protect you to the end of your life, as it has heretofore protected you in so remarkable a manner from your cradle! I offer the same prayer for your lady and your family—and am Your affectionate father, John Adams." [48]

How Abigail Adams would have loved to see her first son now become, like his father before him, "guardian of his country's laws and liberties"!

The election had a tonic effect on the declining strength of the venerable statesman. His good spirits seemed to recover the lost energies of his body. He began to raise himself up in bed. He told stories. He laughed heartily. He ate well. He smoked his cigar after dinner.[49] He looked forward to riding about town with his eminent son when he came home the next autumn. And that he did in due time. The old man's last Christmas, 1825, was a happy one, thinking of his son in the White House, and pleased at a promising grandson coming into manhood, to carry on the destiny of the family.[50]

John Quincy Adams was not so pleased as his father. He had stood for the people against the politicians, against King Caucus. Yet he knew it was the politicians, not the people, who had elected him over Andrew Jackson. They had reversed the verdict of the people in Illinois, Louisiana, and Maryland, and he had not been without a hand in the business. It was not a triumph to be proud of. He could not glory in his victory as a minority candidate. It was unsatisfactory to his pride.[51]

Characteristically he rationalized his position. It was absolutely constitutional! Under the imperfect electoral provisions of the Constitution he was helpless. The verdict could not be undone.

He did not really want to undo it.

[47] Edward Cruft to the Hon. Mr. Lloyd, Boston, February 16, 1825. Adams MSS.
[48] *Memoirs*, VI, 504. *Sic*.
[49] Dr. Benjamin Waterhouse to JQA, July 4, 1825. Adams MSS.
[50] JA to CFA, Quincy, December 19, 1825. Adams MSS.
[51] *Memoirs*, VII, 98.

7

At first Andrew Jackson took the decision of the House calmly enough, like the gentleman he was, one of nature's more fiery noblemen. With other celebrities and distinguished visitors to the city he attended the White House "drawing-room" that evening.

It was the last reception which President and Mrs. James Monroe would give in their official station. Nearly everybody of consequence was there, except the infirm Crawford. John C. Calhoun, the new Vice President, attended, studiously watching, already building up his political plans for the future. So did Henry Clay, the reputed President-maker, still at middle age the dashing Harry of the West, his thin and genial face wreathed with understanding smiles, attentive as ever to the ladies, one belle after another on his arm. Daniel Webster, the reverberating orator with deep-set eyes and rumbling virile voice, was in conspicuous attendance. As the most distinguished member from the President-elect's own state he was chairman of a committee appointed by the House of Representatives officially to notify the successful candidate of his election; Adams told him that he would receive the committee the following day at his home on F Street. Samuel F. B. Morse, the portrait-painter and later inventor of the telegraph, was present. So was Edward George Geoffrey Smith Stanley, a member of the House of Commons traveling in America; as Earl of Derby he would a later day be head of the British Government.

The lion of the evening, one might have guessed, would be the victor John Quincy Adams, or perhaps General Lafayette, the Nation's Guest. On the contrary, the cynosure of all eyes was the defeated candidate Andrew Jackson, the darling of the people, the one who had the greatest number of popular ballots in the November elections as well as a plurality of electoral votes, the frontier General who had whipped the British veterans at New Orleans. To get a glimpse of him, as well as of the other luminaries of Washington, people pushed through the feeble barrier of the marshal who guarded the door, sweeping in guests unwanted as well as wanted. They swirled through the parlors so thick that one lost one's own guidance and had to drift along with the human eddies. Handsome General Winfield Scott had eight hundred dollars picked out of the pocket of his resplendent uniform.[52]

Watchful bystanders were curious to see what would happen when the General and the Secretary of State came face to face at the last Presidential levee of the Era of Good Feelings. Morse, sensitive reader of human visage and carriage, had his eye on John Quincy Adams. The subject

[52] Gaillard Hunt, ed.: *The First Forty Years of Washington Society Portrayed by the Family Letters of Mrs. Samuel Harrison (Margaret Bayard) Smith* (New York, 1906), pp. 182–6. Hereafter referred to as *First Forty Years*.

seemed to be in high spirits, shaking off his habitual reserve while trying to suppress any unseemly show of gratification at the events of the day.[53]

Presently the rival candidates met, the people's favorite and the constitutional choice of the House of Representatives. The General had a lady on his arm at the moment. At first both hesitated a little. Then Jackson stepped forward.

"How do you do, Mr. Adams," said the tall old Indian-fighter politely.[54] "I give you my left hand, for the right, as you see, is devoted to the fair. I hope you are very well, Sir."

"Very well, Sir," responded Adams not without a trace of phlegm. "I hope General Jackson is well." [55]

Promptly they lost contact in the press of the crowd.

Stanley, the Englishman, looked on the evening and on John Quincy Adams without much sympathy for Republican manners or politics. "I never saw a more sinister expression of countenance," he avowed in his travel journal, "than that of Mr. Adams—his figure is short and thick, and his air is that of low cunning and dissimulation, which I believe has not been much belied by the course of his political career." [56]

From this description one might almost think that Adams was nothing less than the American Machiavelli, and not a very attractive-looking one at that. But Stanley had the candor to add that part of this appearance might be attributed to a rheumy disorder: the constant watering of the President-elect's eyes compelled him whenever he raised them for a moment to look at the person to whom he was speaking, again to drop them instantly. Most English officials had not thought too highly of John Quincy Adams anyway, or of his father John Adams before him. Cordially enough disposed toward harmonious relations with England, the Adamses had too clear a sight where American independence, rights, and interests were concerned. Englishmen did not think any more charitably of Andrew Jackson either, the implacable executioner of Arbuthnot and Ambrister during the Indian wars of the Florida border. If they did not properly appreciate the Hero of New Orleans, how could they feel happily toward a man like John Quincy Adams who as Secretary of State had so stoutly defended the General's action?

[53] Edward Lind Morse, ed.: *Samuel F. B. Morse, His Letters and Journals* (2 vols., Boston, 1914), I, 262–3.

[54] "Altogether placidly and courteously" are Adams's words in briefly noting down the encounter, in *Memoirs*, VI, 502.

[55] Bassett: *Life of Jackson*, I, 365–6.

[56] Derby, Edward George Geoffrey Smith Stanley, 14th Earl of: *Journal of a Tour in America, 1824–1825* (London, 1930), p. 313.

8

Next day at noon Webster and the committee of notification [57] waited upon the President-elect at his F Street home and announced that the House of Representatives, "proceeding in the manner prescribed by the Constitution," did the previous day choose him to be President of the United States for the next four years commencing on the fourth day of March next.

The sweat rolled down John Quincy Adams's face as he listened to the notification. He trembled from head to foot.[58] Too agitated to speak, he was forehanded with a prepared acknowledgment. The only previous occasion on which the House of Representatives had been called upon to choose a President was Jefferson's election over Aaron Burr in 1801. Jefferson had then returned a written answer to the House. Following that precedent, Adams had drafted a reply, which he put in the hands of Webster.

He then contrasted his position with that of his predecessors who had been honored with majorities in the electoral colleges. He paid his respect to the worth, talents, and services of the three distinguished fellow citizens who had contested with him the election, two of them in the House of Representatives, noting particularly that one had received a larger minority of the primary electoral suffrages than his own. If there were any immediate opportunity for the people to form and to express a nearer approach to unanimity, he declared, he would not hesitate to decline the office and to submit the decision again to the people. But the Constitution itself had not so disposed of the contingency which would arise in the event of his refusal. "I shall therefore repair to the post assigned me by the call of my country, signified through her constitutional organs. . . ."

The next three weeks flew by filled with political conferences. The results of these confabulations and the construction of the new Administration will appear in the next chapter. As inauguration day drew closer, the future minority President became nervous and sleepless. The pressure of business in the Department of State, always heavy at the close of a session of Congress, redoubled as his own service of eight years rapidly approached its close. The bustle of approaching preparation for his new condition of life, the multitude of visitors, well-wishers and office-seekers, not to mention the merely curious, the melancholy state of his wife's health, all combined to obsess him with anxieties of an approaching crisis. Finally, after two wholly wakeful nights, he began the 4th of March 1825

[57] The two other members were Joseph Vance of Ohio, and William S. Archer of Virginia.

[58] So described by "one of the committee" to Mrs. Margaret Bayard Smith: *First Forty Years*, p. 186.

with a supplication to Heaven: first for his Country, next for those connected with his good name and personal fortunes.[59]

At about half past eleven in the morning he left his house on F Street, residence of his family for the last seven years. Escorted by several companies of militia and a cavalcade of citizens, he proceeded to the Capitol. In the carriage with him rode Samuel L. Southard, Secretary of the Navy, and William Wirt, the Attorney General; it was an obvious sign that he would continue them in office. President Monroe followed with his own equipage. Arrived at the Capitol, they all went into the Senate chamber. John C. Calhoun, already inducted as Vice President, was presiding. That body promptly adjourned. The Senators, joined by the Justices of the Supreme Court, accompanied the Presidential party to the hall of the House of Representatives, that deep round room that is today the Hall of Statuary. Before such a crowd as could get into this sepulchral vault John Quincy Adams, not yet sworn, began his carefully prepared inaugural address. Visibly agitated, he steadied himself and continued with increasingly distinct voice and emphasis.

There was little of the overrich rhetorical flourish of the former Boylston Professor of Oratory and Rhetoric at Harvard College. It was a sober, sensible appeal for national unity—always the Washingtonian compass of Adams's continental outlook.

The Constitution and the confederated representative democracy of the United States, he commenced, had proved itself for a nation and people now stretching from sea to sea. At the outset, a generation ago, the revolutionary upheaval of Europe had led to party conflict, had finally involved the nation in war. That "time of trial," lasting for a quarter-century, was happily past. During the last ten years the "baneful weed of party strife" had withered away. Men no longer contended for principle under party badges. It was now for individuals, North, South, East, and West, magnanimously to compose their differences—to knit the Union together into a government "at once federal *and national.*" [60]

Reviewing the peaceful successes of Monroe's Administration, he referred to the exploration of the Far-Western inner regions of the transcontinental Union, to the scientific researches and surveys which had prepared for the further application of natural resources to the internal improvement of the country, works by the general Government that would deserve the gratitude of unborn millions of posterity in ages to come. The new President hoped that the practical public blessing of such a program, coupled with a continued process of friendly, patient, and persevering deliberation, would smooth away any lingering constitutional objections.

He closed on a note of humility, conscious of being a minority President: an appeal for indulgence and guidance from Congress, assistance from the executive and subordinate departments, the friendly co-opera-

[59] *Memoirs,* VI, 516–18.
[60] Italics inserted.

tion of the state governments, the candid and liberal support of the people; above all, the favor of an overruling Providence.[61]

Chief Justice John Marshall held up to him a volume of the laws of the land. From it John Quincy Adams read and pronounced the oath prescribed by the Constitution: "I do solemnly swear that I will faithfully execute the Office of President of the United States, and will to the best of my ability, preserve, protect, and defend the Constitution of the United States." Although he was a constant and habitual early-morning reader and student of the Bible, there is no evidence to show that he took the oath on that Book.

General Andrew Jackson stepped forth and grasped the President's hand.[62]

Men marveled that a question notoriously menacing to the peace of republics throughout history, a disputed succession, had been settled so peaceably and, to all outward appearances, with such good will.

[61] Richardson: *Messages and Papers of the Presidents,* II, 292–9.
[62] *Niles' Register,* XXVIII, 19.

54

Vote by States in the House of Representatives, February 9, 1825 [1]

States	Adams	Jackson	Crawford	Vote for
Maine.....................................	7	..	..	Adams
New Hampshire........................	6	..	..	Adams
Vermont................................	5	..	..	Adams
Massachusetts..........................	12	1	..	Adams
Rhode Island...........................	2	..	..	Adams
Connecticut............................	6	..	..	Adams
New York..............................	18	2	14	Adams
New Jersey.............................	1	5	..	Jackson
Pennsylvania...........................	1	25	..	Jackson
Delaware...............................	..	..	1	Crawford
Maryland...............................	5	3	1	Adams
Virginia................................	1	1	19	Crawford
North Carolina.........................	1	2	10	Crawford
South Carolina.........................	..	9	..	Jackson
Georgia................................	..	..	7	Crawford
Alabama...............................	..	3	..	Jackson
Mississippi.............................	..	1	..	Jackson
Louisiana...............................	2	1	..	Adams
Kentucky..............................	8	4	..	Adams
Tennessee..............................	..	9	..	Jackson
Missouri................................	1	..	..	Adams
Ohio...................................	10	2	2	Adams
Indiana.................................	..	3	..	Jackson
Illinois.................................	1	..	..	Adams
Total..............................	87	71	54	

[1] From J. B. McMaster: *History of the People of the United States . . .* (D. Appleton and Company, New York, 1900), V, 81. Copyright, 1900. Reproduced by permission of Appleton-Century-Crofts, Inc.

CHAPTER IV

Liberty Is Power

(1825)

> Liberty, when men act in bodies, is power. Considerate people, before they declare themselves, will observe the use which is made of power.
>
> EDMUND BURKE:
> *Reflections on the French Revolution*

JOHN QUINCY ADAMS's election was not a party victory, not a triumph of political principles, not even a personal success. He had seized on no issues. He had stood on no platform. He had as yet put forth no program. He was not the people's preference. When all was said and done, the expiring House of Representatives, elected back in 1822 and voting in 1825 by states, had made him President according to the letter of the Constitution. As a minority President his only hope was to combine his adversaries and their patronage under his own leadership. Otherwise the majority would unite against him.[1] To carry through his individual concepts of American nationality and continental power he would fain prolong the Era of Good Feelings, harmonizing, conciliating, uniting all personal factions with the blessing of James Monroe, bringing the whole people together in national sentiment and outlook.[2] Like George Washington he did not believe in parties or in sections, the essential realities of American politics—and they did not believe in him.

1

It was in line with the newly elected President's attitude and policy to continue the members of Monroe's Administration, as many as possible, in his own Cabinet, including even the treacherous Crawford. (He had still not heard of Crawford's rude encounter with President Monroe.) [3] The

[1] ". . . I had concluded that the supporters of three of the preceding candidates, Jackson, Crawford, and Calhoun, however inveterate against each other then, would in the main combine against the Administration, and *they* would have constituted a majority." JQA to James Barbour, Meridian Hill, Washington, April 4, 1829. Adams MSS.

[2] "My great object will be to break up the remnant of old party distinctions and bring the whole people together in sentiment as much as possible." Statement of JQA to John Reed. *Memoirs*, VI, 474. January 1, 1825.

[3] *Memoirs*, V, 315. March 3, 1821. "Treachery of the deepest dye is at the bottom of Crawford's character." Ibid., VII, 81, 390.

only new appointments would be the Secretary of State, made necessary by Adams's own elevation, and the Secretary of War, to fill the vacancy created by Calhoun's election to the Vice-Presidency. For first position he would have the active and ambitious Western leader Henry Clay. For Secretary of War he thought of General Andrew Jackson. Gallatin, perhaps, would accept the Treasury, if Crawford did not choose to keep it. DeWitt Clinton, old Federalist, could be sent to London. Thus all sections, all factions, all personal followings, all talents, that had contended against each other during the protracted Presidential campaign, would be united in a truly one-party National Republican Government, under the Man of the Whole Nation.

The obvious flaw in this political strategy was that neither his rivals nor the protégés of their patronage would follow along in his wake. They would not accept him as the Man of the Whole Nation. Only Henry Clay found it to his interest, and expectations, to support the new Administration, but many of his followers did not fall in line.[4]

Vice President Calhoun planned to be the real power behind the White House. Right at the start of Adams's Administration he prepared to build his own ramp to the Presidency. He tried to dictate appointments to the new Cabinet. He would make members of the Government conscious that they owed their appointments not to the President but to the Vice President. He would thus cause them to look to him rather than to John Quincy Adams for leadership, as the Old Federalists in President John Adams's Cabinet had looked to Alexander Hamilton.

The morning after the election George Sullivan, who had been so interested in swinging the New England electors on the Adams ticket from Andrew Jackson to Calhoun for Vice President, came around to have a talk with the President-elect. Callers interrupted them, but Sullivan came back next day.

"The Calhounites say," he reported, "that if Mr. Clay should be appointed Secretary of State, a determined opposition to the Administration will be organized from the outset. The opposition will use the name of General Jackson as its head. Only the New England states will support the Administration, New York being doubtful, and the West much divided, and strongly favoring Jackson, as a Western man. Virginia is already in opposition, and all the South is decidedly adverse. The Calhounites have told me what Administration will satisfy them: namely, Joel R. Poinsett [of South Carolina], as Secretary of State; Langdon Cheves [also of South Carolina], as Secretary of the Treasury; John McLean [Calhoun's old friend, now Postmaster General], to be Secretary of War; and Southard [of New Jersey, to be held over from Monroe's Cabinet], as Secretary of the Navy."

---

[4] JQA to Joseph Blunt, Washington, February 14, 1831; JQA to Robert Walsh, Washington, April 16, 1836. JQA Papers, LC. See also letterbook copies in Adams MSS.

Sullivan did not say whom Calhoun had slated for Attorney General. Was it Sullivan himself?

"With whom did you have these conversations?" Adams snapped, as soon as Sullivan had read the slate.

"With Calhoun himself, and with Poinsett."

So here was the secret of the "queer things" that Adams had sensed going on about him! If he did not heed the notice thus served, the threat was clear: the Southern leader, feeling his star in the ascendant, would back an opposition under Jackson now and try to succeed the Old Hero in 1828.

"I am at least forewarned," thought the President-elect.[5]

Calhoun misjudged Adams, as later he misjudged Jackson.

2

Already Jackson's managers had anticipated the appointment of Clay as Secretary of State with a charge of "corruption and bargain." They prompted a simple-minded Representative in Congress, George Kremer of Pennsylvania, to proclaim it to the public. Kremer did so, anonymously, a couple of weeks before the decision of the House, in a communication to the *Columbian Observer* of Philadelphia,[6] from which the *National Intelligencer* picked it up.[7] Clay instantly challenged the accuser to a duel if he should dare to avow his charge and display himself. Kremer avowed his authorship. Clay avoided any duel on the general assumption that Kremer was too simple-minded and eccentric to summon to the field of personal honor. Kremer on his part showed no disposition to fight.

Descending from the Speaker's chair, Clay demanded an immediate investigation. The House of Representatives promptly elected a committee —excluding at Clay's request any of his own supporters. The investigators reported on the morning of the day scheduled for the Presidential ballot: they could discover no substance for the allegation. Apparently the Jackson men feared that the charge might backfire and alienate some of Clay's friends who otherwise might vote for Jackson in the balloting immediately to follow, for the committee refused to summon witnesses and resort to cross-examination. The purpose of the accusation, which was thus fended off, was to prevent Clay from accepting the post if Adams were elected and offered it to him, or if he did accept it, to saddle him and the new President with a public opprobrium which, however unjustified, would grow more burdensome the more they tried to defend themselves.

Kremer's charge did not frighten Clay into declining the office, following Adams's election. A thinly attended Senate ratified the nomination, 27 to 10. The opposition was more than expected. It confirmed the tend-

5 *Memoirs*, VI, 506–7. February 11, 1825.
6 January 28, 1825.
7 February 1, 3, 5, 1825.

ency of the Crawfordites, now that their leader's infirm health had taken him out of national politics, to unite with a coalition of South Carolina and Pennsylvania politicians behind Jackson in opposition to the new Administration. Back of this coalition were Martin Van Buren and John C. Calhoun, each of whom designed to be Jackson's successor.

President Monroe was the first to be informed by the President-elect of his decision to appoint Henry Clay as Secretary of State.

"I consider it due," Adams explained, "to his talents and services, and to the Western section of the Union, whence he comes, *and to the confidence in me manifested by their delegations.*"

This cool announcement disturbed Monroe. He feared it would have an unfavorable effect for Adams as well as for Clay, particularly in the West. Nevertheless it seemed an accomplished fact, so the outgoing President made no comment.[8]

The reasons for the Kentuckian's appointment are thus explained, and frankly enough. Clay had told Adams that he had decided to vote for him. Before the ballot in the House of Representatives, Adams had told John Scott of Missouri that if he should be elected President by the suffrages of the West, he would naturally look to the West for much of the "support" that he would need.[9] Adams and Clay had talked over general questions of policy in a conversation of which there is no record. So far as we know, Adams had made no specific promise to appoint Clay Secretary of State, and Clay made no proposal—both men later affirmed that there had been none—but it is difficult not to assume that there was an implicit bargain—a gentleman's agreement. After the election Adams appointed Clay as an experienced and talented Western man because they agreed on national policies and because the delegates from the Western states had voted for New England's candidate.

The implicit but certainly not corrupt bargain between Adams and Clay was the least questionable of the several deals, described in the previous chapter, that Adams made to secure election by the House of Representatives.

From all quarters the politicians were now pressing the incoming President with advice as to the formation of his Administration. General Jacob Brown, commander of the army, and other friends of DeWitt Clinton tried to convince him that he ought to appoint the New York Governor his Secretary of State. Adams had to explain that he had just offered the place to Clay.[10] Then make Clinton Secretary of the Treasury, urged Brown. Instead, Adams asked for Clinton's "assistance in the Ad-

---

[8] *Memoirs*, VI, 508–9. February 11–12, 1825. Italics inserted. See also *AHR*, XLII (No. 2, January 1937), 273–6.

[9] See above, p. 43.

[10] The offer was made February 12, 1825. Clay replied that he would have to take time to consult with his friends. He accepted, February 18, 1825. Clay to Francis Brooke, Washington, February 18, 1825. *The Private Correspondence of Henry Clay,* Calvin Colton, ed. (New York, 1855), p. 116.

ministration" as Minister to Great Britain. Clinton declined. Reserving for himself a door to the Presidency in 1828, he was feeling his way over to the opposition [11] of Jackson and Calhoun that had begun to coalesce even before the inauguration.[12]

The new President learned indirectly that Jackson would not accept the War Department.[13] It also became evident that Gallatin could not be expected to take any other office than the State Department—and that only in case his friend Crawford remained in the Administration.[14] When the latter declined to continue, Adams nominated a onetime Crawford man, Senator James Barbour, former Governor of Virginia, for Secretary of War. Barbour was an original state-rights man. In the Virginia House of Delegates, back in 1798, he had protested the Alien and Sedition Acts. "From absolute consolidated Government," he had cried, "Good Lord deliver us." [15] For the Treasury he recalled Richard Rush of Pennsylvania from London. William Wirt stayed on as Attorney General; also remaining was the efficient Postmaster General,[16] John McLean of Ohio. Joel R. Poinsett became Minister to Mexico instead of Secretary of State. Apparently Adams still hoped to bring Calhoun into line behind him without submitting to his dictation; he went out of his way personally to notify the Vice President of this last appointment.[17]

Finally, John Quincy Adams redeemed his promises to the Federalists by sending the aged Rufus King to London as United States Minister to the Court of St. James's, a post which he had filled so capably under President John Adams.[18] Daniel Webster, who aspired to that principal diplomatic mission, could scarcely object openly to the appointment of King, leading Federalist since the death of Alexander Hamilton in 1804. As Minister to France, President Adams continued Senator James Brown of Louisiana, the state whose delegates had helped elect him in the House of Representatives. Other appointments in the diplomatic service

[11] Later, in 1826, when he realized Calhoun and Van Buren had threatened him in New York, and in national politics, Clinton tried to feel his way back again to Adams. J. B. Mower to JQA, New York, June 8, 1826. Adams MSS. See also *Memoirs,* VII, 184–5.

[12] Henry Lee to Andrew Jackson, Buffalo, September 14, 1826. J. S. Bassett: *Correspondence of Andrew Jackson* (Washington, 1928), III, 312–13.

[13] "Frye [brother-in-law of Mrs. JQA] spoke of General Jackson; would take in ill part the offer of the War Department." *Memoirs,* VI, 510.

[14] Henry Adams: *Life of Albert Gallatin,* pp. 608–9.

[15] Dumas Malone in *Dictionary of American Biography.*

[16] Not yet a Cabinet member.

[17] *Memoirs,* VI, 522.

[18] Rufus King had been Minister of the United States to Great Britain under President John Adams from 1796 to 1803, a unique instance of a Minister holding such office successively under two Presidents, father and son. The instance becomes still more pronounced when it is remembered that both John Adams and John Quincy Adams had held that office, not to mention their grandson and son, respectively, who served as Minister to Great Britain 1861–8.

fell to old protégés: Alexander Everett [19] of Boston, brother to Edward Everett, became Minister to Spain, a nomination justified by much experience; and Christopher Hughes, the boresome Baltimore wit, got the post of chargé d'affaires at The Hague.[20]

If the Administration thus constructed did not correspond to Adams's full design for national harmony, it was on as broad a bottom as possible under the circumstances of personal politics that governed the day, but not broad enough to conciliate, to harmonize, and to unite the opposing factions that were now coalescing and tending to become sectional. It did not capture the supporters of Crawford or of Calhoun, or of Jackson.[21] It did not appease the South, which became more and more distrustful of the Minority President as he began to speak out in Washington for strong national measures.

3

President John Quincy Adams's political theory was simple, and robust. Liberty had been *won* in the United States—at least for white persons. It was no longer in danger. The people could be relied on to detect and prevent political absolutism.[22] And the Constitution would prevent democracy, the vital air of the republican atmosphere, from investing the multitude with absolute power to endanger the right of property, as natural a right as the right of life itself.[23] Henceforth liberty was to *be enjoyed*—with the assistance of a strong national government. At this period

[19] Later (1829) to become brother-in-law to the President's daughter-in-law, Abigail Brooks Adams, wife of Charles Francis Adams.

[20] See Vol. I for earlier associations of Alexander Everett and Christopher Hughes with John Quincy Adams in the diplomatic service.

[21] Calhoun gloated at the Northern President's failure to satisfy the South or any of its leaders, either himself, or his rival Crawford, or General Jackson. "The folly (to call it by no other name) of Mr. Adams begins to be manifest to the South. The attempt to secure Mr. C—d, and his partisans in Virginia and the Southern States has wholly failed. They are deadly hostile to him and his administration almost to a man, as far as my information extends; and are now, if I mistake not, in active operation to embarrass and weaken him. From this source springs the Georgia movement [conflict between Georgia and the Federal Government over Indian lands; see Chapter V]; and hence the blending of the Slave with the Indian question, in order, if possible, to consolidate the whole South. Against these movements what can sustain the administration in this quarter? Gen'l Jackson's friends and mine have both been regarded, not as friends but enemies; and though far from having a wish to embarrass the administration [*sic!*], they cannot be its active supporters." Calhoun to General J. G. Swift, of New York City. Confidential. Pendleton, S.C., September 2, 1825. *AHR*, XL (No. 2, January 1935), 297.

[22] George A. Lipsky has classified JQA's expressions in refined detail in his study of *John Quincy Adams: His Theory and Ideas* (New York, 1950).

[23] See JQA's later lecture on *The Social Compact, Exemplified in the Constitution of Massachusetts; with Remarks on the Theories of Divine Right* . . . (Providence: Knowles and Vose; 1842). In a letter to George Bancroft, Quincy, October 25, 1835 (*Bulletin* of the New York Public Library, X [1906], 245–8), JQA set forth his views on government and democracy as follows:

of his life he had little concern for the security of individual liberty in America—except for the dormant slavery problem. He was more anxious about the security of property. "We have not succeeded in providing as well for the protection of property as of personal liberty." [24] He would strengthen property rights by a national bankruptcy statute, just and efficacious to creditor and debtor alike; by continuing a sound national banking system; and by a national judiciary independent in fact as well as in law. The favorite word of John Quincy Adams, as it had been of George Washington, for representing the General Government of the Union, was not *federal* but *National*, always with a capital *N*.

For full enjoyment of both personal liberty and private property the first necessity was Union. The second necessity was a strong national government to administer the resources of a continent for improvement of the general welfare. With Union achieved and preserved, the future of the nation would be a republic coterminous with the continent of North America, filled with a mighty people, marching under one flag, speaking one language, living one way of life and liberty, with capabilities of freedom and power such as associated man had never before witnessed on this earth. [25]

Adams did not believe that the Constitution of 1787 was the perfect instrument to carry the nation and the people forward to such a destiny. Its complicated distribution of powers between two co-ordinate sovereignties—"national," and "municipal" or "state" [26]—kept the Union in continual

---

"Now the Theory of *good* Government which I have imbibed from childhood, which I was taught by the instructions of my father, which I learnt in every stage of the history of mankind, which the French Revolution, at the dawn of my political life, brought up again as a problem in politics to be solved again by *experiment,* and which from that day to this has been tested by a continued succession of experiments by almost every civilized nation in Europe, all terminating in the same results and fixing it upon my mind firm as an oracle of Holy writ, is a Government compounded of the three elements—A Government, instituted for the protection both of persons and of property, to secure alike the rights of persons and the rights of things. The right of property is a natural right as much as the right of life, which is merely personal, but as the earth was given by the Creator to mankind in common, the distribution of property in it is left to be settled among the human race, by physical force or by agreement, compact, covenant. This I take to be the origin of Government. It is founded on persons and on property. And if Democracy is founded exclusively on persons and not on property, I fear it will follow the tendency of its nature and degenerate into ochlocracy and Lynch Law, burning down convents and hanging abolitionists or gamblers, without Judge or Jury, without fear of God to restrain, and without remorse to punish."

[24] JQA to James Lloyd, Washington, October 1, 1822. *Writings,* VII, 312.

[25] JQA to AA and JA, St. Petersburg, June 30, August 31, 1811. See Vol. I, 182.

[26] Such are the terms which JQA used in an analysis, with Montesquieu at his elbow, of the balance of powers under the Constitution of 1787, and the powers of the President thereunder, particularly in regard to diplomatic appointments and treaty-making. These manuscript notes are preserved in a volume of drafts of Presidential messages and papers in the Adams MSS.

jeopardy.[27] But at least one merit of the organic law was the provision for checks and balances among the three branches of the Federal Government, and between the two houses of Congress—so extolled in John Adams's famous exposition of American constitutions. This device provided a substitute for political parties. Political parties, so John Quincy Adams felt, only served by their contentions to paralyze the national progress of a free people. They had no healthy place in American life. They had sprung up as a contemporary reflection of the wars and revolutions in Europe. In his inaugural address he dismissed them as mere "transitory" collisions of party spirit, originating in speculative opinions or in different views of administrative policy. Now happily they had disappeared, after the European upheaval had spent itself.

Before the rise of American political parties President Washington had taken the first bold step "to administration"—Madison's queer accusing verb—the Constitution into a truly national instrument. Alexander Hamilton's Assumption Act of 1790 had transformed the old state war debts into a "national blessing." Now that political parties had all but disappeared, President John Quincy Adams, George Washington's disciple, thought the time had come to take another strong step toward national unity and greatness. He would cement diverging sectional interests indissolubly together (as Washington himself had counseled in the Farewell Address) by a splendid network of national highways and canals, North, South, East, and West. Every speculative scruple as to the constitutionality of such a program would be solved by the practical public benefits thus conferred upon the nation.

Along with this concept of internal improvements would go a broad program of conserving and developing the public domain as a national blessing. A humane policy of Indian removal would transfer the tribes to the west of the Mississippi, educating and civilizing them, perhaps eventually assimilating them into the body of citizenry. As highways and canals approached the West the public lands would rise in value. Scientific administration would distribute and settle them carefully and compactly. Proceeds of land sales, following the extinction of the national debt, to which they were pledged, would "reflow in unfailing stream of improvement from the Atlantic to the Pacific Ocean." Meanwhile the orderly settlement of the national domain would afford an unequaled home market for domestic manufactures. Such was the gist of his annual messages to Congress on the state of the Union. In private correspondence he communicated less conspicuously his views on the tariff. It must be a "cautious" tariff, balancing and conciliating the opposing interests of agriculture and industry, to protect the growing nation against the discriminations of foreign governments and make it self-sufficient in time of war.[28]

[27] JQA to James Lloyd, Washington, October 1, 1822. *Writings*, VII, 311.

[28] JQA to Messrs. Jonathan Nesbit and William Knox, of Baltimore. Washington, July 12, 1828. Adams MSS.

To bring forward and fashion such a tariff would be the duty of the Congress, best representing the several sections and interests of the whole country.[29]

Like George Washington, John Quincy Adams, who took the Farewell Address for political gospel, believed it was a function of the National Government operating under a benign Providence to promote and assist the "general diffusion of knowledge" and its application for the continuing improvement of American citizens and of mankind. It was his duty as President to give leadership and direction to the Government in exercising this strong national function for the greater enjoyment of liberty. In the back of Adams's mind, taking shape deep in his conscience, lurked a final internal improvement—moral improvement. Someday, somehow—perhaps even by martial law—an enlightened people might bring liberty to black persons too.[30] He would not talk about that yet. It was not safe to do so, not safe for him politically, not safe for the nation. First must come the Union great and strong, a Continental Republic stretching from sea to sea.

4

"The first right and the first duty of nations," John Quincy Adams had written as Secretary of State, were "self-dependence and self-improvement." [31]

President Adams's promised national program for internal improvements, physical and moral, to be conceived, established, and even maintained by the General Government, was nothing new. It was really a reversion to Federalism. The necessity for internal improvements beyond the agreement or capacity of any one state had produced the meeting of the Annapolis Convention of 1786 that led to the assembly of the Philadelphia Convention of 1787 and helped produce the Constitution itself. The resulting organic law of the nation had given to the Congress specific powers to lay and collect taxes, to regulate commerce among the several states and with the Indian tribes, to establish post-roads, to raise and support armies and navies, to declare war, to dispose of and make all needful rules and regulations respecting the territory or other property of the United States, to provide for the common defense and general welfare,

---

[29] JQA outlined these policies in his four successive annual messages to the Congress, notably in his first annual message of December 6, 1825. But he did not publicly mention the tariff until his fourth annual message of December 2, 1828. For his views on the tariff see his letters to Edward Ingersoll of Philadelphia, Quincy, September 7, 1828; and to James H. McCulloch, Collector of the Port of Baltimore, October 1, 1828. Adams MSS.

Brooks Adams appraises and extols his grandfather's national policies in the remarkable introduction to Henry Adams: *Degradation of the Democratic Dogma* (New York, 1919).

[30] *Memoirs*, IV, 531; V, 4, 12, 210.

[31] In a commonplace book of JQA, 1823. Adams MSS.

and also to make all laws which should be necessary and proper for carrying these powers into execution. Adams was convinced, and so told the Congress, that these powers both individually and collectively gave the General Government the right to build and maintain internal improvements within the states for the general welfare of the whole nation.

He acknowledged to himself that his program was rooted in an old Federalist background. "The federalism of Washington, Union, and Internal Improvement," he wrote after leaving the White House, "have been the three hinges, upon which my political life and fortunes, good and bad, have turned." [32] What Adams did not acknowledge to the public, or to himself, was that these ideas were not limited to Washington's Federalism, that they stemmed partly from Thomas Jefferson [33] and Albert Gallatin, and agreed also with those of his recent rivals for the Presidency, John C. Calhoun, Henry Clay, and Andrew Jackson.

But they were anathema to the Old Republican state-rights exponents of the South, to whom Jefferson had turned back in the last years of his life at Monticello. John Randolph of Virginia, original and inveterate spokesman of state rights, opposed them, as firmly as he had attacked every other strongly nationalistic measure throughout his career: "If Congress possesses the power to do what is proposed by this bill [in 1824, for a survey, plans, and estimates of national roads and canals all over the Union], they may not only enact a sedition law—for there is precedent— *but they may emancipate every slave in the United States*—and with stronger color of reason than they can exercise the power now contended for. And where will they find the power? They may follow the example of the gentlemen who have preceded me, and hook the power upon the first loop they find in the Constitution; *they might take the preamble— perhaps the war making power. . . ."* [34]

Prophetic sweep of fearful thought! John Quincy Adams in his own mind had seen this very avenue to emancipation. He had not yet made public his inner views on slavery, but at the time of the Missouri debates he had written in his Diary: "If slavery be the destined sword in the hand of the destroying angel which is to sever the ties of this Union, the same sword will cut in sunder the bonds of slavery itself. A dissolution of

[32] JQA to Robert Walsh, Jr., Meridian Hill, Washington, March 18, 1829. Adams MSS.

[33] President Jefferson, anticipating extinction of the national debt (as a result of his dangerous economies in the national defense) had recommended the application of continuing tariff revenues to "the great purposes of the public education, roads, rivers, canals, and such other objects of internal improvement *as it may be thought proper to add to the constitutional enumeration of federal powers."* (Annual Message to the Congress, December 2, 1806. Italics inserted.) In this instance, as contrasted with the Louisiana Purchase, Jefferson had salved his objections to loose construction by advocating a constitutional amendment to give the Federal Government more specific powers; meanwhile a national plan could be worked out in anticipation of the enabling amendment.

[34] *Annals of Congress,* 18th Cong., 1st Sess., I (1823–4), 138. Italics inserted.

the Union for the cause of slavery would be followed by a servile war in the slave-holding States, combined with a war between the two severed portions of the Union. It seems to me that its result must be the extirpation of slavery from this whole continent; and, calamitous and desolating as this course of events in its progress must be, so glorious would be its final issue, that, as God shall judge me, I dare not say that it is not to be desired." [35]

He had not confined these thoughts entirely to his Diary. He had also expressed them to John C. Calhoun, in the days of their friendly intimacy in Monroe's Cabinet.[36]

The survey provided by the Act of 1824 was under way when Adams became President. He proposed to lay it before Congress as soon as completed. It would provide specifications for implementation of his bold pronouncements.

If John Quincy Adams could not bring all his rivals of 1824-5 into his Administration, he would at least put forward the program for internal improvements and point it up nationally. It would help place him before the country as the Man of the Whole Nation.

5

Spring and summer went by in the first year of the Presidency with little political movement apparent in the air. A special session of the new Senate, called by the retiring President to confirm executive appointments and consider new treaties, met in executive session for five days and unanimously rejected the treaty which Adams as Secretary of State had recently negotiated with Colombia for the suppression of the slave trade—another uncomfortable portent of what to expect from the upper chamber of Congress during the regular sessions to come.

As if in respite from the tension of the previous winter the members of Congress had scattered to their homes throughout the Union. The Adams Administration took over the Government with little change in the rank and file of the civil service. About all the new President did was to fill vacancies.[37] In late summer he set off on his annual vacation to visit his aged father, the Sage of Quincy, and to turn over in his mind the national program that he would announce more fully to the country in his first annual message on the state of the Union when the new Congress should assemble the following December.

Refreshed by the New England air of his native shore, the President returned to Washington at the end of October. He immediately set about

[35] *Memoirs,* V, 210. November 29, 1820.
[36] *Memoirs,* IV, 531. February 24, 1820.
[37] He actually removed only twelve persons from office during his whole tenure. Carl Russell Fish: *The Civil Service and the Patronage,* p. 72.

preparing his message. To this "task of deep anxiety" [38] he devoted most of the ensuing month. By the 22d of November he had ready a first draft, recommending the subject of internal improvements in general principle and in definite degree.

Internal improvements must be moral as well as physical, he declared. They must be sustained by the example of character in public life and the active implementation of such institutions as a national university, as George Washington had advocated, "unfolding its portals to the sons of science and holding up the torch of human improvement to eyes that seek the light"; a national astronomical observatory; a national naval academy; by the national sponsorship of research and geographical exploration, particularly to the Pacific Ocean and the North West Coast; and by a new Department of the Interior, to relieve the other departments of the multiplying burdens of home affairs all through the country.

He read the concluding section of his proposed message to the Secretary of the Treasury, Richard Rush. It was the most important recommendation of all, in favor of internal improvements under national authority.

"I approve the whole," said Rush, "although I know it will not be approved by other members of the Administration."

That evening the President worked late into the night, preparing himself for future trials with Congress. In the morning he read to the Cabinet the whole of the first draft of his message, nearly five thousand words. It took an hour and a half. Patiently the several Secretaries heard it through.

Barbour of Virginia, garden-bed of state rights, objected to the concluding recommendations on internal improvements. So did Clay, in part. They set that aside to come back to later. Clay also objected to the pacifical tone of reference to the unsatisfied spoliation claims against France. "The United States would be fully justified in resorting to their own force for redress," admitted the President; "but that force, instead of obtaining redress, is more adapted to aggravate than to repair such wrongs. Our policy will be to persevere until justice be obtained but explicitly without resorting to force or committing any hostility."

"That would be equivalent to a total abandonment of the claims," responded Clay. "I recommend the issue of letters of marque and reprisal—that would not be war," he insisted, "at least I would intimate to Congress that such a measure would be advisable if France continues to disregard the representations of our Minister."

"Reprisals, even special reprisals," objected the Secretary of War, "will be war, or certainly lead to war. . . . Nobody in this country has the remotest idea of going to war over these long-standing claims. Nobody but the claimants is excited about them."

After some discussion the Cabinet postponed to the next day further

[38] *Memoirs,* VII, 66.

consideration of the claims while the President tried to find a middle term of expression.[39] He also agreed to expunge a reference of doubtful expediency to the Greek insurrection.[40]

So far only minor changes had been suggested. But the Cabinet was nervous about the whole message.

"I wish the whole concluding part, respecting internal improvements, could be suppressed," Barbour at last remarked.

Clay thought so, too. "I am for discarding the National University, and perhaps some other objects. Let us not recommend anything so unpopular as not likely to succeed."

"Let us not propose anything so popular as to be carried without recommendation," Barbour added dryly.

"We seem to to be stripping off your draft alternately," remarked Clay good-naturedly, looking at the President.

"It's like the man with two wives," responded the President from the head of the table. He was a reader of Addison's *Spectator*. "One is plucking out his white hairs, the other the black, till none are left."

They adjourned for further deliberation, to meet next day. When they assembled again, Adams, on Rush's request, once more read the entire draft. Barbour withdrew his objections to it as a whole, but both he and Clay picked at disparate portions of the text.

"I wish to strike out the National University and the recommendation for a new executive department," repeated Clay. "Also everything related to the Patent Office, and the final enumeration of all the purposes of internal improvements, for which you assert that Congress has powers."

It looked as though they were going to pull out all the President's bristling proposals.

"I will give up all that relates to the Patent Office," he conceded.

"The University is certainly hopeless," persisted Clay. "There may be something in the Constitutional objection to it. It does not rest on the same principle as internal improvements, or the bank."

"I agree that no absolutely impracticable projects ought to be recommended," the President conceded, "but I look to a practicability of longer range than a simple session of Congress. General Washington recommended a military academy more than ten years before it was obtained. The plant may come late, though the seed be sown early," he added sen-

---

[39] In the message as finally delivered the President intimated that if he could not obtain justice peaceably through the constitutional power of the Executive he might turn the matter over to Congress.

[40] In the final message the President alluded to the necessity of keeping a respectable naval force in the Mediterranean to protect American neutral rights in the Greco-Turkish war. He then added this gratuitous sentence: "The heroic struggles of the Greeks themselves, in which our warmest sympathies as freemen and Christians have been engaged, have continued to be maintained with vicissitudes of success adverse and favorable."

tentiously, "I have not really recommended a University. I have only referred to Washington's recommendations and observed that they have not been carried into effect."

Clay moderated. "The new executive department is of most urgent necessity," he admitted. "No one knows that better than I. But I am sure there would not be twenty votes for it in the House—I don't believe there would be five."

"It is not very material to me," declared the President, "whether I should present these views in the first or the last message that I send in to the Congress. But I feel it is my indispensable duty to suggest them." He paused a moment. "I can never be sure of the future. I may not be destined to send in another message!"

John Quincy Adams seemed to think that this whole program, little of which was popular with the people, hung on the thread of his own life!

The faithful Rush seemed impressed by the President's solemn reflection. "I urge communication at this time," he said very earnestly.

"I too am anxious that almost all of what has been written should go," yielded Clay. After all, John Quincy Adams was President, even though Clay had helped to make him such. "I myself am fully convinced that Congress has the powers," he added, "and I have no doubt but that if they do not exercise them there will be a dissolution of the Union by the mountains." Clay was thinking of his American System—really first proposed by Senator John Quincy Adams back in 1807—a system of national highways and canals supported by abundant revenue from a protective tariff and the sale of public lands, to bind together the whole Union, North, East, South, and West, and to build up national manufactures for consumption by a growing home market. Adams had equivocated on the tariff, but he and Clay saw eye to eye on the rest of the program— and Clay stood before the nation as sponsor of it all.

Barbour, sympathetic to state rights, reluctantly withdrew his objections. Clay approved the general principles though scrupling at some details. Rush approved nearly everything. Southard had said scarcely a word.

"The perilous experiment is to be made," noted the President in his Diary that night. "Let me make it with full deliberation, and be prepared for the consequences."

During these talks the Attorney General, William Wirt, biographer of Patrick Henry, had been absent on government business in Baltimore and Annapolis. Apparently he got wind of what was being proposed. When he returned to the capital he asked to see the message. Adams read to him the vital passages: the concluding part on internal improvements.

"It is excessively bold," was Wirt's first comment. "There is not a line in it which I do not approve. But it would give strong hold to the party in Virginia who represent you as grasping for power. I have been traveling about Virginia, last summer. I found the Administration gaining strength and friends there. But this subject was a great source of clamor. Patrick Henry's prophecy would be said to have come to pass: that we want a great, magnificent Government. It is a noble, spirited thing," he continued tactfully, "but I dread its effects on my popularity in Virginia."

"They will cry down as a partiality for monarchies," he added, "your reference to the voyages of discovery and scientific researches in monarchies. They will bring in the project of a voyage in search of the Northwest Passage as evidence that you are a convert to Captain Symmes."

Wirt argued with the President two or three hours to this effect. Rush happened in while they were talking. He was as earnest for the message as Wirt was against it.[41]

The President decided to make "some" alterations to that part of the draft and (he noted in his Diary) "if it were fitting to be intimidated, to abandon the whole of it."

Since John Qunicy Adams was never a man to be intimidated, scarcely even a man to heed a friendly warning, this meant that he would not abandon it. He went ahead with the perilous experiment. He sent the message to Congress, December 5, 1825. After reviewing the peaceful circumstances of foreign affairs, including the coming Inter-American Congress at Panama, the flourishing condition of the national finances, the state of the nation's defenses, and relations with the Indian tribes, he recommended the establishment of an additional executive Department of the Interior, a national naval academy, a national university, a national astronomical observatory to emulate the "lighthouses of the skies" maintained by European governments for the advancement of science; a uniform national bankruptcy law, uniform national militia law, uniform national system of weights and measures, a more effective national patent law to secure to inventors the rewards of their discoveries, finally a national system of internal improvements.

"Liberty is power," President Adams reminded the Congress. "The nation blessed with the largest portion of liberty must in proportion to its numbers be the most powerful nation upon earth, and the tenure of power by man is, in the moral purposes of his Creator, upon condition that it shall be exercised to ends of beneficence, to improve the condition of himself and his fellow-men. While foreign nations less blessed with that freedom which is power than ourselves are advancing with gigantic strides in the career of public improvement, were we to slumber in indolence or fold up our arms and proclaim to the world that we are palsied by the will of our constituents, would it not be to cast away the bounties of Providence and doom ourselves to perpetual inferiority?"

The words of this peroration echoed and re-echoed forebodingly throughout the Southern states where a large proportion of the white population—not to mention the slaves—was already doomed, so they

[41] For the deliberations of the Cabinet, here summarily reproduced in authentic dialogue, see *Memoirs*, VII, 58–64.

thought, to perpetual economic inferiority. Did President John Quincy Adams mean that a Great Magnificent Government endowed with Power as well as Liberty for national internal improvement both physical and moral would one day become so powerful as to upset the sectional balance and perhaps redeem the coin of freedom by abolishing human slavery? Did these words portend the end of old days and old ways in the South?

CHAPTER V

Problems of a Minority President
(1825 – 1829)

The more *National* and less *Federal* the Government
becomes, the more certainly will the interest of the
great majority of the States be promoted, but with
the same certainty will the interests of the South be
depressed and destroyed.

ROBERT J. TURNBULL OF SOUTH CAROLINA,
IN *The Crisis* (1828)

How could a man who stood at the head of the only political party of
any consequence in the Union be regarded a minority President? The answer is that John Quincy Adams never did really preside over the National
Republican Party. He had been elected by a minority of the popular suffrages in 1824 plus a bare majority of the state delegations in the House
of Representatives in 1825, including such thinly populated states as
Maine, New Hampshire, Vermont, Rhode Island, Illinois, Maryland, Louisiana, and Missouri. From the outset of his Administration the personal
factions that had supported Jackson, Calhoun, and Crawford began to
combine against Adams and Clay to form a new political party, the Democratic Republican Party, as it was called after it had captured control
of the House of Representatives in 1826, or the Democratic Party, whose
partisans later in the decades of their triumphant rule referred to it as
"The Democracy." It was during Adams's Presidency that this major new
party crystallized to overthrow him.

To put through his bold program of Liberty with Power, the Minority
President needed the co-operation of his rivals in the recent contest for
the Presidency, and this he did not have; he required loyal subordinate
party leaders, whom he was unwilling to take on and build up politically;
and he had to have control of both houses of Congress, which he could
not get. In this situation John Quincy Adams was not politician enough
to be, like his father John Adams, a Man of the Whole Country. The
South, particularly, began to turn against him and his national proposals.

1

First test of alignment in the new Congress was election of the Speaker of the House of Representatives. The leading aspirant was John W. Taylor of New York, who had held that office for one term in 1820–1 during Henry Clay's brief retirement to private life. A candidate with a sectional tinge, he was author of the bill prohibiting slavery in the territories of the United States north of 36° 30′ N. Lat., cardinal feature of the Missouri Compromise. During the Missouri debates, before his first election as Speaker, he had seconded the Tallmadge Amendment to prohibit further introduction of slaves into the new state and to emancipate at the age of twenty-five all children born therein of slave parents. He himself had brought forward a similar amendment to the bill for the organization of Arkansas Territory. Taylor was as strong an antislavery man as it was possible to find in Congress. He was also one of that little group in Albany who had secured the majority of electors in the key state of New York in 1824, without whose labors Adams could never have been elected. The new President could scarcely disclaim this loyal friend's pretension to the Speakership. His support of Taylor for Speaker straightway weakened him in the South.

Another possibility was Daniel Webster. Of Federalist antecedents like Adams himself, Webster was, next to the President, the most prominent political leader in New England. He, too, had actively opposed the admission of Missouri as a slave state.[1] Webster's friends wanted to present him for the Speakership. But during the campaign Adams had received a pledge from him not to run against Taylor and to support the New Yorker with all his influence. When Congress convened in December 1825, the President reminded Webster of that pledge. Webster kept his word. He was not too eager for the Speakership anyway.[2] It would hinder him from taking part in debates on the floor, his particular forte. It would also make it difficult for him to argue cases before the Supreme Court, source of his fattest fees. The South would have had reason to distrust Webster even more than Taylor, if only because he was an abler and a more dynamic man.

The evening before the assembly of the Nineteenth Congress, Adams had a long talk in the White House with Taylor about the prospects of his election as Speaker and the composition of the House committees which depended from that office.

"I expect 109 votes," Taylor assured the President. (Total membership of the House of Representatives was 214. A majority of members present was required for election of Speaker.)

[1] Claude Moore Fuess: *Daniel Webster* (Boston, 1930), I, 270–1.
[2] *Memoirs*, VII, 69.

Adams was not so confident. To him the "duplicity" of electors casting votes by ballot was no flattery to human nature. But he was not the man to dampen Taylor's optimism.

"With regard to the committees," he reminded him, "I suppose you cannot displace generally the chairmen who held such positions in the last Congress; but I assume you are disposed to arrange the members so that justice may be done as far as practicable to the Administration." [3]

This was a reasonable suggestion, one of John Quincy Adams's rare manifestations of practical political sense.

Taylor won on the second ballot, with a slender majority of two.[4]

"His election is evidence of the strength of the Administration," Henry Clay assured the President cheerfully. "Many of the Members have strong personal objections to Taylor."

The contest over election of the Speaker was another signal, this time unmistakable, of the rising Opposition. First sign, the previous March, had been the show of votes in the Senate against Henry Clay's confirmation as Secretary of State. That had not been on sectional lines. The absence of a personal roll-call on the vote by ballot for Speaker makes it impossible to register the sectional character of Taylor's victory, but it was evident that the Southern members would not be sympathetic to him.

The new Administration sadly lacked practical direction. Henry Clay was as much of a general manager as there was, but Adams wouldn't consistently heed his suggestions. In the Senate no one seemed to represent the Administration. Vice President John C. Calhoun controlled the committees, until the Senate rules were amended in 1826 to appoint standing committees by ballot for the remainder of the Nineteenth Congress. In the House of Representatives, Daniel Webster ought to have been a natural spokesman. His very appearance on the floor would be an asset for any Administration. But somehow Adams mistrusted the temper of Webster's transcendent talents.[5] Perhaps it was because Webster was the ideological heir of Alexander Hamilton, the opponent of John Adams; perhaps it was jealousy on the President's part; perhaps both. The President's offers to Webster were too unsubstantial to enlist such a self-interested man.[6] The great man from the Granite State—now representing Boston in Massachusetts—did not reject the role of House leader, neither did he accept it wholeheartedly. He was not a person to labor in another's

[3] *Memoirs*, VII, 70.

[4] Taylor got 99 votes. The other candidates were Louis McLane of Delaware, 44 votes; John W. Campbell of Ohio, 42 votes; Andrew Stevenson of Virginia, 5 votes; scattering, 3 votes: total 193. *Register of Debates in Congress*, II, Pt. I, 795; 19th Cong., 1st Sess.; House of Representatives, Monday, December 5, 1825. *Memoirs*, VII, 70.

[5] JQA to CFA, Washington, January 29, 1829. Adams MSS.

[6] "I invited Mr. Webster to come and spend the evening with me whenever it might suit his leisure and convenience." *Memoirs*, VII, 84. December 16, 1825.

vineyard without promise or firm prospect of reward.[7] Adams had not
promised him anything, unless it were to show by some signal act that
he would not proscribe "old Federalists" in making appointments.[8] And
it had been the aged Federalist Rufus King who got the benefit of the
signal act.

A more faithful personal follower in the House was Edward Everett,
Representative from the Middlesex district of Massachusetts. He had
been a friend of the Adams family since boyhood. The pride of Harvard
College, a Greek god in appearance, Everett was one of the outstanding
men in Congress. Though by no means bereft of political artfulness, he
labored under the unprofitable reputation of being a clergyman and a
scholar, therefore not a man of the world. He could hardly wield a party
whip in the lower house, especially when there wasn't any real party over
which to crack it: one party had been no party.

Outside of Congress, President Adams also suffered grievously, by
comparison with his defeated opponent, from a lack of effective political
subalterns. Not that there was no material at hand. P. P. F. Degrand of
Boston and temporarily of Philadelphia, and Joseph Hopkinson of the
City of Brotherly Love, were eager to stand at his elbow, if he would
have found places for them. George Sullivan of New Hampshire aspired
to the role, but he was too close to Calhoun to be trusted. There were also
ambitious young men, like the useful Joseph Blunt of New York, who
asked nothing specifically for themselves but who looked to political careers. Thurlow Weed, already rival to the master Martin Van Buren in
the art of political management, came down from Albany ready to make
Washington his next headquarters. Adams did receive him politely in the
White House, but refused to talk politics, quite in contrast with the affable Secretary of State.[9] Weed went back to Rochester to wait—to wait
in vain—for Henry Clay's star to rise to its zenith.

Instead of availing himself of the services of one or more of these able
politicians, who could have kept at least the two states of New York and
Pennsylvania in line for him, John Quincy Adams pitched on the Washington apothecary, "Dr." Tobias Watkins, to be his political Man Friday.
He appointed him as fourth auditor in the Treasury and made him go-
between for politicians, newspapermen, and office-seekers who wanted to
get the President's ear. Tobias was a clever underling, but at most a
clerkish soul, a denizen of the District of Columbia, with no significant
outside connections.

Like a Massachusetts farmer or fisherman contemplating New England's
dubious weather John Quincy Adams felt the bleakness of the political
climate without being able to do anything about it. He could sense no

---

[7] "Throughout his life," says Fuess, not without restraint, "Webster attached perhaps an undue importance to material possessions." *Daniel Webster,* I, 278.

[8] See above, pp. 44–5.

[9] *Autobiography of Thurlow Weed* (Boston, 1883), p. 181.

promising wind with which to launch the national program that he had proposed after the election of this very Congress.

"If it is possible in any manner to obtain this [program] from Congress," he declared to Daniel Webster at the beginning of the session, "it must be a very short act, expressing in very general terms the objects committed to it—the internal correspondence [a new Home Department; i.e., Department of the Interior], the roads and canals, the Indians and the Patent Office. . . ."

Just how any "short act," such as Adams spoke of, could provide adequately for his new national program is difficult to understand. At most it would be some kind of resolution putting Congress behind the President's pronouncements of policy. This was impossible, because it soon became evident that he could not sway the Senate and that his control over the House was somewhat uncertain.

Webster seemed in no hurry to do anything. He was more interested in a bill to enlarge the membership of the Supreme Court.[10] That would give the President a chance to appoint at least two new justices—perhaps Webster as one of them. This bill never passed Congress during Adams's residence in the White House. It would have given the Minority President too many judicial appointments.[11]

His position was further weakened by friend John Bailey of Massachusetts, formerly clerk in the Department of State, who, against the President's advice,[12] introduced into the House of Representatives an amendment to the Constitution giving the Federal Government power to construct roads and canals for urgent purposes of military, commercial, or mail communication.[13] The President had declared that the Congress had that power; for one of his friends to introduce an amendment to provide it in a limited way was to suggest that the state-rights people were correct and the President was wrong.

Congress paid no attention to the proposed amendment, much less to John Quincy Adams's national program for internal improvements, physical or moral. All that it would do was to pass small bills for particular projects here and there, without general plan or system, and to continue voting funds to keep the Cumberland Road in repair and build it westward from Wheeling to Zanesville, Ohio. It also made land grants to or subscribed unsystematically for stock in various canal companies.[14]

[10] *Memoirs*, VII, 83–4.

[11] Charles Warren: *The Supreme Court in United States History* (Boston, 1932), I, 652–85.

[12] *Memoirs*, VII, 80.

[13] Herman V. Ames: "Proposed Amendments to the Constitution of the United States during the First Century of Its History." *Annual Report* 1896 AHA, II, 262.

[14] $100,000 (1,350 shares) in the Louisville and Portland Canal Company, $150,000 (200 shares) in the Dismal Swamp Canal Company, 10,000 shares in the Chesapeake and Ohio Canal Company, 750 shares in the Chesapeake and Delaware Company.

This was all. The brave new proposals—national bankruptcy law, national university, national astronomical observatory, national naval academy, national research and exploration, and a new Department of the Interior to help administer increasing national business—all remained unacted on in Congress and were the laughing-stock of the opposition press.

It would have been better if President Adams had not mentioned the subject of internal improvements at all. His advocacy only served to recall Patrick Henry's old fear of a Great Magnificent Government that would consolidate federal power into national power and do away with the reserved rights of the states. He raised this specter just as the South was beginning to realize that its "peculiar institution" was in peril. Already there were people in that section such as Calhoun, his recent Cabinet colleague, who could guess the inner secret of John Quincy Adams's heart, his desire to abolish the twin evils of mankind, war and slavery.

Faced with these sectional misgivings and a political opposition that made the most of them, the President's grand concept soon degenerated at the hands of successive Congresses into a miserable system of logrolling and finally gave way to state authority. Toward the end of his term Adams took some satisfaction in the piecemeal legislation that he had signed for local works, such as the Delaware breakwater.[15] It was small comfort for the failure of his national policy of applying the surplus revenue of the Union flowing into internal improvements from a carefully husbanded treasure-trove of public lands.

2

Because John Quincy Adams's friends in Congress did not venture to bring forward any item of his national program, there was at first no definite Administration measure for the Opposition to oppose. The President, however, soon supplied an issue, inspired by Clay, in the field of foreign policy: he sent to the Senate nominations for United States Ministers Plenipotentiary to the Congress of Panama.

The reader of the previous volume will recall how the Senate had rejected the treaties which Adams, as Secretary of State, had signed with Great Britain and with the Republic of Colombia for the suppression of the African slave trade. Old memories of British abuse of visit and search in time of war, and of impressment, had been partially responsible for the failure of these treaties, but Southern sensitivity on slavery had also been a factor. The same feeling united with traditional isolationist sentiment to oppose the nominations of the plenipotentiaries to Panama, expressed in long and dilatory debates. Southern Senators shrank from the prospect of participating in any international congress that might deal with such subjects as the abolition of the African slave trade, or the status

---

15 JQA to CFA, No. 31, Washington, May 28, 1828.

of Cuba, or might discuss diplomatic relations with the Negro Republic of Haiti. The possibility of slavery being discussed at Panama, even indirectly, was alarming to Southern spokesmen. "With nothing connected with slavery," declared Senator Hayne of South Carolina, "can we consent to treat with other nations, and, least of all, ought we to touch the question of the independence of Hayti in conjunction with Revolutionary Governments, whose own history affords an example scarcely less fatal to our repose." [16]

Ultimately the Senate confirmed the Panama nominations by a vote of 27–17, and the House passed the necessary appropriations by a vote of 134–60. This first and only victory of the Administration in Congress proved an empty one, because the meeting at Panama never amounted to much, nor did an American plenipotentiary get there before it adjourned.

The cleavage of votes on this issue of foreign policy revealed the lines of a new political combination between "Southern planters and plain republicans of the North," with Martin Van Buren of New York as architect of the coalition. As an unwritten support for the alliance Van Buren would rely on state rights and the least government possible in Washington. For the South the new party would serve as a bulwark for the protection of slavery.[17]

It is appropriate now to turn from the default of Adams's more imaginative national program to some of the outstanding problems of his Administration, notably those of federal land disposal, Indian removal, and the tariff—perennial subjects that necessarily would have confronted any President who held office at that time.

3

Public land policy was, of course, a broad field for disputation as to what would be best for the national interest in the long run: a systematic, disciplined, and discriminating disposal of the national domain by advancing compact settlement, or a give-away policy to attract quick and easy occupation and an early build-up of productive new states and expanding taxable resources in the West.[18]

Frontier settlers had advanced by 1825 ahead of surveys, even ahead of Indian treaties, to "squat" without title on pioneer locations. All were voters or potential voters. There were also thousands of legal settlers who

[16] *Register of Debates in Congress, 1825–6*, II, Pt. I, 166, as quoted by Bassett: *Life of Jackson*, II, 385. See Vol. I, 544–61.

[17] Wiltse: *John C. Calhoun, Nationalist*, p. 348.

[18] Turner: *Rise of the New West*. See also Shosuke Sato: "History of the Land Question in the United States," *Johns Hopkins University Studies in History and Political Science*, Vol. 4, Fourth Series, Studies VII–VIII–IX (Baltimore, 1886), and Raynor G. Wellington: *Political and Sectional Influence of the Public Lands 1828–1842* (Cambridge, 1914). Benjamin Horace Hibbard has published a methodical and comprehensive *History of Public Land Policies* (New York, 1924).

were actual purchasers on installments under early land laws. Now in default, they faced dispossession, unless Congress came to their relief. Representatives from the new Western states, such as Senator Benton of Missouri, pressed for legislation to give pre-emptive rights to squatters as against other buyers to enable defaulted purchasers to convert their original commitments into smaller holdings fully paid for, to graduate minimum land prices downward, to donate small tracts to actual settlers as homesteads, and to cede the unsold portion of the public lands to the new states in which they were located. Eastern representatives of the populous states of New York and Pennsylvania urged distribution of the proceeds of sales to all the states in proportion to the number of their inhabitants. Senator Rufus King of New York had made a startling proposal that echoed ominously through the Southern states: all moneys received from land sales should be applied to the emancipation of slaves!

President Adams regarded the public lands more as a potential fund to pay off the country's debt and to finance a general system of internal improvements than he did as a national domain to give away to settlers. Orderly settlement would come in the wake of internal improvements, rather than internal improvements follow the quick population of the land.[19] He nevertheless approved and signed the several relief acts passed by Congress during his Administration,[20] and recommended renewal and extension of "beneficent accommodations" to debt-ridden purchasers of public lands, "among the most useful of our fellow citizens." [21]

Having drawn attention to the subject in his messages, Adams preferred to leave the whole question of land policy to Congress and thus to keep his hands off a rising issue that threatened to become sectional. There was a political motive here. It has already been stressed that he could not have been elected by the House of Representatives in 1825 without the vote of at least one Southern state. It was also true that he could not have been elected without the votes of some of the states of the Northwest whose pioneers wanted free land. If he hoped to become a majority President in 1828, he would need electoral votes from both Southern and Western states. He would have to give up his old ideas of a scientific disposal of the public lands. "The best days of our land-sales are past," he rationalized by the end of 1826. "We shall have trouble from that quarter [Benton and the West]." [22]

[19] See Inaugural Address, March 4, 1825, and first annual message, December 6, 1825.

[20] Payson Jackson Treat: *The National Land System, 1785–1820* (New York, 1910), p. 161.

[21] See First and Third Messages.

[22] *Memoirs*, VII, 188.

4

There was an aspect of public land policy that President Adams would not sidestep. It touched vitally his concepts of national authority and good faith. That was the problem of Indian removal, which had to be accomplished before surveys and sales of lands could take place. The problem invited debate over a controversy which went back to the time when Washington's Government took over control of Indian affairs and began making treaties with the various tribes for land cessions. Here national policy came into conflict with a legacy of state treaties made during the Revolution and the period of the Confederation. This was particularly so in the State of Georgia, where theories of state sovereignty were entwining themselves like poison ivy around the Constitution of the United States.

An agreement between Georgia and the Federal Government in 1802 temporarily resolved their initial discord concerning Indian territory. By this contract Georgia ceded all lands hitherto claimed by her west of her own boundary (fixed at that time), to become a part of the federal domain and to be used for all the states.[23] In turn the United States agreed to extinguish Indian title to all lands within the state, "at their own expense, for the use of Georgia, as early as the same can be peaceably obtained, on reasonable terms." The agreement confirmed Georgia's full title to the land within her borders and jurisdiction over it, and obliged the Federal Government to quash the remaining Indian titles.[24] That process proved too slow to suit local settlers. The higher state of organization and culture among the Southern Indians, notably the Cherokees and Creeks, made them more recalcitrant and difficult to remove peaceably than were the tribes of the Northwest. The people of Georgia, anxious to get into the rich cotton lands, pressed their own government irresistibly, and the state officials importuned the authorities in Washington to get on with the promised treaties.

From his previous expressions about the Indians one might expect Adams to have been a firm exponent of national sovereignty over all native tribes within the boundaries of the United States. In his Plymouth Oration of 1802, delivered just after returning from his first tour of diplomatic duty abroad, he had argued for the right of Europeans to encroach upon the possessions of the aborigines in the New World.[25] This was the prevailing theory of international law. During the peace negotiations at Ghent in 1814 Adams and his colleagues had asserted the sover-

[23] Except for 5,000,000 acres to be devoted to the settlement of the Yazoo claims. Ulrich B. Phillips has dealt with this subject and the controversy over the Creek Indians in the early chapters of his study of "Georgia and State Rights" in *Annual Report* 1901 AHA (Washington, 1902), II, 15–66.

[24] *ASP, Public Lands,* I, 125–6.

[25] See Vol. I, 113.

eignty of the United States over the Western tribes, British allies, in American territory north of the Ohio River, against all efforts to detach and form them into a neutral barrier state of their own. In the period after the War of 1812 he had defended General Andrew Jackson's rough campaigns against the Creek Indians in Spanish Florida. As President he was convinced that the United States as a national sovereign over the Indian tribes had the duty of protecting them against violation of their treaty rights with the Federal Government by any one of the states in the Union. In adhering to this conviction his ideas of national honor and sense of fair play soon came into collision with the rapacity of local and sectional interests determined to get hold of the Indian lands by whatever means, however unscrupulous.

Upon his inauguration the President found on his desk the Treaty of Indian Spring, to which the expiring Senate had just advised and consented (March 3, 1825) by a vote of 38 to 4, with very little discussion. Two commissioners of the United States Government, both citizens of the State of Georgia, professed to have negotiated this treaty with "the Chiefs of the Creek Nation, in Council assembled." Actually it was signed with William McIntosh, principal chief or headman of the Lower Creek tribes, and seven lesser chiefs. By this treaty with a rump group of tribes, the "Creek Nation" agreed to exchange all its lands in Georgia for an equal acreage west of the Mississippi River plus a bonus of $400,000, and annuities. The aboriginal inhabitants of the ceded areas were granted approximately eighteen months to evacuate the lands of their ancestors from time immemorial; no state surveys of the lands thus ceded could take place before September 1, 1826.[26]

The commission had pushed through this negotiation against the advice of the local United States Indian agent, Colonel John Crowell. That conscientious officer hastened to Washington to urge the President not to ratify the treaty. It was not fair, he protested: the commissioners had overreached the Indians; McIntosh and the chiefs of minor grade who signed it represented only eight of the forty-six towns of the "Creek Nation." [27] Adams nevertheless signed and ratified the treaty to which the Senate had advised and consented by such an overwhelming vote. He was soon to regret this hasty and ill-considered action.[28]

A few weeks after the signature of the Treaty of Indian Spring a protesting band of Creek warriors set fire to McIntosh's house and killed him as he fled from the flames. Upon receipt of news of this deed the Secretary of War dispatched a special agent, Timothy P. Andrews, with Major General Edmund P. Gaines to inquire into the true state of affairs in the

[26] C. J. Kappler: *Indian Affairs, Laws, and Treaties* (Washington, 1904), II, 214.

[27] *ASP, Indian Affairs,* II, 571–82. *Memoirs,* VI, 528.

[28] "The Senate sanctioned its ratification without giving it an examination," President Adams rationalized a few weeks later, "and I had no practicable alternative but to ratify it accordingly." *Memoirs,* VII, 12. May 20, 1825.

disturbed area. It became apparent to them that the treaty was unjust if not fraudulent. Upon their advice the betrayed majority of the Creeks sent a delegation to Washington to call upon the Great White Father and persuade him to revise it.

Governor Troup of Georgia anticipated this mission of the Indians with objurgations of his own. The treaty must stand, as signed and ratified, he wrote to the President: the sovereign State of Georgia would proceed to survey the ceded land for sale to settlers; it would do so even before September 1, 1826, by virtue of a special article that Troup had presumed to sign with McIntosh before his death.

Adams acted sympathetically to the dispossessed natives. He caused orders, approved in a Cabinet meeting, to be sent to Major General Gaines to prohibit any premature state survey of the Indian lands.[29] The bellicose Governor in his turn demanded Gaines's "immediate recall, arrest, trial, and punishment, under the articles of war." [30] Troup was full of "guns, drums, trumpets, blunderbuss, and thunder," [31] but he stopped short of making a survey before the date set for execution of the treaty.

Meanwhile the delegation of dispossessed Creek Indians appeared at the White House, fantastically attired in a combination of civilized and tribal costume, suggesting their mixed culture, half Indian, half white. Chief spokesman was Opothle Yoholo. His countenance, like the faces of his comrades, reflected a dark and settled gloom.

The President welcomed them and bade them be seated. "We should all meet in friendship," he said.

"We are glad to be here," replied Yoholo, through an interpreter. "Things have happened which have frightened us. We hope now that all will be well."

"That is my desire," the President assured them. "I also have heard of things which displease me much. I expect you will be able to arrange things with the Secretary of War to the satisfaction of all."

There was no doubt that the Treaty of Indian Spring had been a dishonorable affair. The two commissioners who made it, Messrs. Meriwether and Campbell, had acted more as Georgians than as officers of the United States.[32] Adams could not let it stand as it was, no matter what the Georgians thought about him. One of two things must be done: negotiate a new treaty, acceptable to the whole Creek Nation, or call upon Congress to annul the shameful one that had been signed and ratified.

"Above all things," Daniel Webster told Secretary of State Henry Clay and Representative Edward Everett, "don't let the Georgia question go before Congress."

[29] *Memoirs,* VII, 34.
[30] *ASP, Indian Affairs,* II, 815. Phillips, op. cit., p. 58.
[31] *Memoirs,* VII, 49.
[32] *Memoirs,* VII, 87.

"If it goes before Congress," Clay declared immediately, "they will do nothing."

That remark gave the President a momentarily tempting thought.

"But wouldn't this release the Executive from the obligation of doing anything, either?" he asked his Cabinet. "We ask of Congress to annul the treaty, or to furnish means to compel the Indians to execute it. Congress do nothing. We consider the treaty as binding, but the Indians refuse to comply, and remain on the lands after September, 1826. We have no means to compel the Congress, and therefore can do nothing till Congress meet again."

It seemed a neat way of evading the issue, but it would not bring peace in the Southwest.

They decided to try more negotiation with the Indians, this time through General Gaines in Washington. He tried to get Yoholo's delegation to agree in a new treaty to a cession of all their lands within the State of Georgia—nothing less than assent to the terms of the old obnoxious deal. This Yoholo refused to do, but he and his comrades seemed not unwilling to let go everything east of the Chattahoochee River, about two thirds of the territory ceded by the minority chiefs at Indian Spring.

Meanwhile Chilly McIntosh, brother of the assassinated William, arrived at the capital with another minority group of ten or twelve "friendly" Creek Indians. Obviously the Georgians had inspired their visit. The Superintendent of Indian Affairs, Thomas L. McKenney, shepherded the visitors aside into a Pennsylvania Avenue lodging, as if to keep them out of contact with the politicians, but the Georgia delegation in Congress got hold of them and moved them into quarters on Capitol Hill, promising to take care of their expenses. Somebody was furnishing them with plenty of money: about $4,000, said "Governor" Barbour, Secretary of War.[33]

"I would rather take the line of the Chattahoochee," John Forsyth, now a member of Congress from Georgia, told the Secretary of War. "Meriwether has admitted to me that a river makes a very convenient boundary." [34]

Secretary Barbour was a high-minded man. He would have solved the whole Indian question by incorporating the aborigines within the states of the Union and placing them under the same laws that governed other men and women (white, of course), ceasing to make any treaties with them at all.

"Don't you think," the President asked him in Cabinet, "that question would be made of the constitutional power of Congress to change so essentially the character of our relations with the Indian tribes?"

"I have no doubt there would," admitted Barbour, "but it will soon be unavoidably necessary to come to such a system."

"I think it would be impracticable," commented Henry Clay, who in his youth had crossed over the mountains to the dark and bloody ground of

---

[33] *Memoirs*, VII, 76.   [34] *Memoirs*, VII, 79.

Kentucky. "It is impossible to civilize Indians. There never was a full-blooded Indian who took to civilization. It's not in their nature. I believe they are destined to extinction. Although I would not use or countenance inhumanity towards them, I do not think them, as a race, worth preserving. I consider them as essentially inferior to the Anglo-Saxon race which is now taking their place on this continent. They are not an improvable breed. Their disappearance from the human family will be no great loss to the world. As a matter of fact they are rapidly disappearing. In fifty years there will not be any of them left."

Few anthropologists would subscribe to Henry Clay's views on the American Indians. Today there are twice as many Indians in the United States as in his time, mixing rapidly with the whites and taking to civilization very aptly.

Clay's opinions shocked Barbour. But the President feared there was only too much foundation for them. The immediate question was what to do about Georgia and the Creeks, rather than to speculate on the future of a general race problem. The Cabinet decided to have the Secretary of War sound out the Georgia delegation as to whether they would accept the line of the Chattahoochee in a new treaty.[35]

Senator Howell Cobb of Georgia got wind of the proposed offer. If the Government would not insist on the whole territory, he would not accept a settlement. "Georgia will necessarily be driven to support General Jackson," he threatened.

Barbour thought it over. For a moment he hesitated in his humanity.

"If Mr. Clay's ideas of yesterday are correct," he observed to the President next morning, "and the Indians are going to inevitable destruction anyway, what need is there to quarrel for their sakes with our friends? Why should we not yield to Georgia at once?"

"Because we cannot do so without gross injustice," replied John Quincy Adams. "I consider Mr. Clay's observations of yesterday as expressing an opinion founded upon the operation of general causes, but not as an object to which we ought to contribute purposely. As to Georgia's being driven to support General Jackson, I feel little concern or care for that. I have no more confidence in one party there than in another." [36]

The immediate result was the signature at the War Department, January 24, 1826, of a second treaty with the "chiefs of the whole Creek Nation," without participation of the McIntosh delegation. Yoholo and his chieftains also refused to take part in any way. By the new Treaty of Washington the Creeks ceded all their lands in Georgia except the portion lying west of the Chattahoochee River, and the United States guaranteed to them such lands as were not ceded.[37] The Indians had until January 1, 1827 to get out of their ancient homes and hunting grounds.

[35] *Memoirs,* VII, 90.
[36] *Memoirs,* VII, 92.
[37] Phillips, op. cit., p. 59. See map in ibid., facing p. 40.

This guaranty must puzzle the historian today. Particularly must it have vexed any contemporary Georgian student of the contract of 1802 which had confirmed to that state full ownership of all the soil within its borders and jurisdiction over it. That agreement had given to the United States authority only to extinguish the Indian title, not power to guarantee to the Indians ownership of their remaining lands to which their title had not been extinguished.

The President sent the Treaty of Washington to the Senate, January 31, 1826, explaining that it abrogated and replaced the Treaty of Indian Spring, which had been ratified under the mistaken belief that it had been concluded with a large majority instead of an impotent minority of Creek chiefs.

To Barbour the new treaty was only a temporary expedient. He wanted a more permanent solution of the whole problem of Indian policy. But he had given up his first idea of incorporating the aborigines into the several states where they resided. "As a substitute," he told the Cabinet, "I have that of forming them all into a great territorial government west of the Mississippi."

Barbour read to his colleagues a paper he had written on the subject in the form of a letter to the chairman of the committee on Indian affairs in the House of Representatives. It proposed to transplant the Indians, not as tribes but as individuals, west of the Mississippi or west of Lakes Michigan and Huron, where they would live under a territorial government to be maintained by the United States. In due time their tribal organization would be liquidated, and property distributed among individuals, looking toward their complete civilization.[38]

Barbour's plan seemed to the President to be full of benevolence and humanity. It accorded most with his own doubtful feelings that a slow and tutored evolution from a nomad hunter's culture to sedentary life was the only hope for ultimate solution of the Indian question and all its cruel history in the United States.[39] If Barbour's idea was somewhat impractical, none of the Cabinet officers had been able to propose anything more promising. Adams approved it at least in principle, but he wasn't sure it would work. "I fear there is no practicable plan," he confessed in his Di-

[38] ASP, *Indian Affairs*, II, 646–9.

[39] Ex-President Adams in 1840 delivered a lecture in Boston, repeated in New York, Brooklyn, and Baltimore en route to Congress that year, "The Progress of Society from the Hunter State to that of Civilization," in which he explained the development of modern civilization through successive states of nomad hunter, shepherd, tiller of the soil, and husbandman, proceeding thereby from polygamy and polytheism to a unity and fixedness of habitation, to monogamy, and to unity of worship of one God. See Roy Harvey Pearce: *The Savages of America: A Study of the Indian and the Idea of Civilization* (Baltimore, 1953), pp. 156–7, citing Baltimore *Sun*, December 3, 1840, and Charles and Mary Beard: *The Rise of American Civilization*, pp. 153–4. Presumably such an evolution represented Adams's last hopes for the Indians.

ary, "by which they can be organized into one civilized, or half-civilized government." [40]

The Treaty of Washington proved only a stopgap to the trouble with Georgia. It did afford a lull during which the President was able to go to Quincy to attend some of the obsequies following the death of his father and to have his annual autumnal sojourn in Massachusetts. After he returned to the capital, the controversy flared up again, more flagrant than ever. Governor Troup paid no attention to the new treaty. As soon as September 1, 1826—dateline for surveys under the superseded Treaty of Indian Spring—had passed, he sent surveyors into the Indian country to mark out the lands for sale. Creek officials arrested some of them. Thereupon the Governor ordered out a troop of cavalry to protect the surveyors. "Georgia," he pronounced, "is sovereign on her own soil."

President Adams held a Cabinet meeting on the problem. His advisers consulted the Act of March 30, 1802 for regulation of trade and intercourse with the Indians. Plainly it authorized military protection by the United States Government. The Cabinet recommended that troops be ordered to the spot.

John Quincy Adams demurred. "I have no doubt of the right," he told the Gentlemen of the Administration, "but doubt much the expediency of so doing."

Clay at first urged that the Indians be protected by force, then he weakened. "I think civil process will be adequate to the purpose . . . ," he concluded. "Before coming to a conflict of arms I should choose to refer the whole subject to Congress." [41]

Barbour suggested sending a confidential agent to warn the Georgians.

The President prepared a letter for the Secretary of War to send to Troup, seeking to avoid all irritating expressions, and a message to Congress along the lines of Clay's advice.

"Charged by the Constitution with the execution of the laws," the Governor was warned, "the President will feel himself compelled to employ, if necessary, all means under his control to maintain the faith of the nation by carrying the treaty into effect." [42]

"From the first decisive act of hostility, you will be considered and treated as a public enemy . . . ," retorted the fiery Troup, "and, what is more, the unblushing allies of the savages whose cause you have adopted." [43]

The Governor announced his intention to resist any military attack by the United States.[44]

[40] *Memoirs*, VII, 113.
[41] *Memoirs*, VII, 219.
[42] *ASP, Indian Affairs*, II, 864. January 29, 1827.
[43] E. J. Harden: *Life of George M. Troup* (Savannah, 1859), p. 485.
[44] Phillips, op. cit., 63, citing Harden's *Troup*, p. 485.

Adams looked upon his message to Congress (February 5, 1827) as the most momentous he had ever written. Well might he say to himself: "Cast me not away from Thy presence, and take not Thy Holy Spirit from me." [45]

In the first draft of his document he declared that a military conflict between the nation and a state would be a dissolution of the Union. The Cabinet had objected to this stark statement, and the President toned it down. "In the present instance," he finally told the Congress, "it is my duty to say that if the legislative and executive authorities of the State of Georgia should persevere in acts of encroachment upon the territories secured by a solemn treaty to the Indians, *and the laws of the Union remain unaltered,*[46] a superadded obligation even higher than that of human authority will compel the Executive of the United States to enforce the laws and fulfill the duties of the nation by all the force committed for that purpose to his charge. That the arm of military force will be resorted to only in the event of the failure of all other expedients provided by the laws, a pledge has been given by the forbearance to employ it at this time. It is submitted to the wisdom of Congress to determine whether any further act of legislation may be necessary or expedient to meet the emergency which these transactions may produce."

The reaction of Congress to the President's message was to stick to principle and look for practical compromise—that, indeed, is what Adams wanted. The elections of 1826 had already chosen a majority in the House of Representatives opposed to the President. After March 4, 1827 John Quincy Adams would not have any substantial influence in either chamber. The anti-Administration majority would quickly elect (104 to 94) Andrew Stevenson of Virginia over John W. Taylor as Speaker, and he would appoint the committees.[47] But the old lame-duck Congress was still in session. For a few days more the lower house would be favorable to the President. The committee to which the message was referred brought in a report, voluminously documented, declaring that it would be expedient to purchase Indian title to all the lands in Georgia. "Until such a cession is procured, the law of the land, as set forth in the treaty of Washington, ought to be maintained by all necessary and constitutional means."

The less amenable Senate, already veering under Martin Van Buren's adroit management toward Andrew Jackson, the old Indian-fighter, listened to a committee report expressing perfunctory approval of what the President had done so far, with sympathy for Georgia's claims to the lands within her borders. Even if the United States had committed a fraud in connection with the Treaty of Indian Spring, reported Senator Benton, champion of free land for Western settlers, the Federal Government could not interfere with the rights of Georgia fully vested in the state after ratification of that treaty.[48]

[45] *Memoirs*, VII, 221.
[46] Italics inserted.
[47] *Memoirs*, VII, 369.
[48] *ASP, Indian Affairs*, II, 869–72.

In the end still another treaty, signed November 15, 1827, took care of the controversy: the Creeks finally ceded all their lands, and Georgia took them over.[49] It did not settle the underlying issue. Adams's humane Indian policy only served to force Georgia to join the opposition forming under the banner of Andrew Jackson.

Whatever the destiny of the white man to civilize the continent, Adams continued all his life to believe that the Indians had been treated shamefully in the process. "We have done more harm to the Indians since our Revolution," he wrote in 1837, "than had ever been done to them by the French and English nations before. . . . These are crying sins for which we are answerable before a higher jurisdiction. . . ."[50]

5

Defenders of state rights roused themselves against another instrument of national policy, the protective tariff. The tariff of 1824, a legislative compromise, had provided only moderate increases over the schedules of 1816. By increasing the rates on hemp, it marshaled the support of Kentucky and Missouri; by raising duties on raw wool, it won the votes of the Northwestern states and of Vermont. On the other hand it alienated the agricultural South, which bought its manufactured articles cheapest abroad and had England as its best customer for cotton exports. The Southern members of Congress voted generally against the bill, which threatened to subject that section to the economy of the whole Union, more for the benefit of the North and West than that of the South.[51] Around the tariff issue a new school of writers on state rights, such as John Taylor of Caroline,[52] Dr. Thomas Cooper of South Carolina College,[53] Robert J. Turnbull of South Carolina [54]—Southern boll-weevils in the growth of nationalism—had arisen to unmask the economic tyranny of the industrial North over their section and to disguise the tyranny of capitalist slaveholders who feared Liberty with Power, and eventual emancipation of their slaves.

For the first time Southern spokesmen introduced an ominous note in

[49] Kappler: *Indian Treaties*, II, 284–6.

[50] JQA to S. S. Gregory, New York. Washington, November 23, 1837. Adams MSS.

[51] Charles M. Wiltse: *John C. Calhoun, Nullifier, 1829–1839* (Indianapolis, 1949), pp. 41–2.

[52] *The Constitution Construed, and Constitutions Vindicated* (Richmond, 1820); *Tyranny Unmasked* (Washington, 1822); *New Views of the Constitution* (Washington, 1823). See Bernard Drell's able identification of "John Taylor of Caroline and the Preservation of an Old Social Order" in the *Virginia Magazine of History and Biography*, XLVI (No. 4, October 1938), 285–98.

[53] *Consolidation: An Account of Parties in the United States from the Convention of 1787 to the Present Period . . .* (2 vols., Columbia, S.C., 1824–34). *On the Constitution, Two Essays: 1. On the Foundation of Civil Government. 2. On the Constitution of the United States* (Columbia, S.C., 1826).

[54] *The Crisis* (Charleston, 1827).

the debates, a new constitutional argument: it was a violation of state rights; the Constitution had not granted explicitly to the Federal Government the power to lay a *protective* tariff. John Randolph went further than that. "I do not stop here, sir," he declaimed: "I do not stop to argue the constitutionality of this bill; I consider the Constitution a dead letter; I consider it to consist, at this time, of the power of the General Government, and the power of the States—*that* is the Constitution. . . . A fig for the Constitution . . . there is no magic in this word *union*." [55]

By *power* he meant, of course, force. Liberty did not mix with Power in John Randolph's mind. Property and Power, resting on Negro slavery, were the foundation of his Old Republicanism and state rights. [56]

Adams was well aware of the implications of a protective tariff for the South, for the Union, for the Presidency. He looked upon the tariff as a political trap-door. "Beware of Trap doors," he counseled his eldest son as he took seat in the Massachusetts legislature. "Pass by without seeming to notice them." [57] He let his Secretary of the Treasury, Richard Rush, extol the protective tariff, while he kept quiet, at least in public. Henry Martindale, member of Congress from New York, spurred by manufacturing constituents in the Hudson Valley, came to the President and protested that he had never expressed himself on the protective tariff, and urged him to do so in the annual message of 1827. Adams replied that the friends of the Administration thought that the "safest course" was to say nothing, lest he exercise an improper influence over the House. "The report of the Secretary of the Treasury," he added in this oral conference, "will recommend the protection of the manufacturing interest in the most effective manner with my entire approbation." [58]

These were the times for an astute investor to get in on the ground floor of the textile industries of New England. Many a Massachusetts family recouped and expanded its moldering maritime fortunes by buying stocks in the new manufacturing corporations. Some of Adams's friends offered him an opportunity to take up cheaply shares in the new mills at Lowell. He passed by that trap-door, too. [59]

Dissatisfied with the tariff of 1824, the protectionists made another ef-

[55] *Annals of Congress*, 18th Cong., 1st Sess., II (1824), 2360–1, 2368.

[56] Russell Kirk: *Randolph of Roanoke, A Study in Conservative Thought* (Chicago, 1951).

[57] JQA to GWA, December 31, 1826. Adams MSS.

[58] *Memoirs*, VII, 365.

[59] "I wish you to see Colonel [Israel] Thorndike again, to thank him in my name for the very liberal offer which he has made, with regard to the stock in the new Manufacturing Company at Lowell, and to say that I should certainly take as large an interest in the Company as my means would allow but for a consideration which has occurred to me on mature reflection—which is—that in my public capacity, I may be required to perform acts, which may affect deeply the manufacturing interest generally, and in particular the value of this stock. . . ." JQA to GWA, Washington, November 4, 1827. The President had visited Colonel Thorndike in his home at Beverly, Massachusetts, September 26, 1827.

fort. They introduced into the last session of the Nineteenth Congress a woolens bill, raising the rates on both the raw product and the manufactured cloth. The tariff bill of 1826 signalized a spectacular reversal of sectional economy, political attitudes, and personal positions. For example, Daniel Webster, a former New England sectionalist who had voted against the moderate tariff of 1824, now became, by virtue of the influence of the Industrial Revolution that was transforming the economy of Massachusetts, a leading advocate of protection and presently an eloquent champion of strong national government and Union. The bill passed the House of Representatives, but the Senate quickly laid it on the table, by the casting vote of Vice President Calhoun (March 1, 1827). Under Randolph's virulent tutelage, and that of Southern writers on state rights, Calhoun too had reversed his position. The former ardent expansionist and nationalist, who had voted for the tariff of 1824, became, under the deteriorating economy of South Carolina, an inveterate sectionalist and exponent of state rights, the theorist of nullification, and finally the precursor of secession.

The advocates of higher protection persisted. During the summer of 1827, representatives of manufacturers and farmers (mostly sheep-raisers) from the Northern and Middle states met in convention at Harrisburg, Pennsylvania, to frame a new bill to present to the Twentieth Congress. Under the leadership of Hezekiah Niles, editor of *Niles' Register,* and Mathew Carey, Alexander Hamilton's most conspicuous ideological follower, they set forth their cause widely before the people.[60] Their lobbyists descended on Washington. They tried to commit Adams to a higher protective tariff.

The President was cautious, very cautious. "Independence and Union are the ends, internal improvement and domestic industry the means of the American Patriot, and so inseparably connected together that it is impossible but by the pursuit and promotion of the one to secure and perpetuate the other." [61] That was the most he would say. He declined to state just how much protection would fit the means to the end. He refused to advocate a protective tariff for manufactures alone. It was for Congress, representing all sections of the country, to conciliate all interests.[62]

The friends of Jackson now turned against the President a device contrived from his protectionist constituencies. Van Buren and his associates

[60] Edward Stanwood summarizes the controversial literature in his history of *American Tariff Controversies in the Nineteenth Century* (Boston, 1903), I, 261–8. F. W. Taussig's classic *Tariff History of the United States* (New York, 1931) does not nicely evaluate Adams's "cautious" attitude toward the protective tariff, nor Jackson's "judicious" tariff policy.

[61] JQA to Messrs. Jonathan Nesbit and William Knox, acknowledging to the Weavers of Baltimore a "handsome specimen of domestic goods" manufactured in Baltimore and paraded in a Fourth of July procession. Washington, July 12, 1828. Adams MSS.

[62] JQA to James H. McCulloch, Esq., Washington, October 1, 1828. Adams MSS.

did not want to vote against the principle of protection and so lose any hope of effective support in the North and East. Nor did they wish to antagonize the South, so vitally important in the coalition for the defeat of Adams in 1828, by voting for it. Therefore they concocted a tariff so grotesque and unreasonable in its schedules that even the advocates of protection might be expected to vote against it. They lowered the duties on medium-priced woolens, which New England manufacturing interests desired to protect more heavily, while they studiously raised the tariff on molasses and articles for shipbuilding, which New England consumers would like to import free. Then, professedly in the name of protection, they loaded the bill with "abominations"—absurdly high duties on items for which nobody demanded any protection. If unexpectedly this unspeakable bill should actually be passed by Congress, the President would have to sign it or veto it. If he signed it, it would show that he believed such a crazy protective tariff both constitutional and desirable—that would alienate the South. If he vetoed it, he would discontent the North. Whatever happened, the Jacksonians would step in and take over the votes of the South in the next election without losing anything in the areas of genuine protection. As John Randolph said, when they were debating the title of the proposed law in the Senate, "the bill referred to manufactures of no sort or kind except the manufacture of a President of the United States"—namely, Andrew Jackson.[63]

To the surprise of its architects, the bill passed by a narrow margin: 105 to 94 in the House of Representatives, and 26 to 21 in the Senate, over the groans of the South and the grunts of the whole nation. Adams signed it. In his last annual message on the state of the Union, December 1828, he referred to the tariff publicly for the first time, and placed on Congress full responsibility for the recent act.[64]

But if anything more was necessary to finish John Quincy Adams in the South—and even in the Northwest—the Tariff of Abominations did it.

Ostensible issues for which Southern spokesmen resurrected their once abandoned doctrine of state rights were Indian removal and the tariff, but back of these problems lurked a greater anxiety that was to bind the varying regions of that great section of the Union together: protection for slavery and Southern economy and the way of life that rested on it. If

---

[63] This is the standard interpretation. Robert V. Remini: "The Early Political Career of Martin Van Buren, 1782–1828" (Ph.D. thesis, Columbia University, 1951, microfilm in Yale Sterling Memorial Library), pp. 625–49, suggests a newer interpretation: that the bill was intended from the beginning for passage in order to preserve harmony among the New York Republicans, win the doubtful State of Pennsylvania and the Northwest to Jackson's candidacy, and set the troublesome issue of the tariff at rest for the electoral campaign. See also Silas Wright to A. C. Flagg, April 7, 1828. Flagg Papers, New York Public Library.

[64] For Adams's constitutional arguments about nullification, voiced in this message, see below, Chapter XI.

Liberty meant Power, then a Great Magnificent National Government expanding into the West could build up such a majority of free states as to be able to do away with slavery in all the common territories of the United States, could some day amend the Constitution so as to abolish the South's peculiar institution within the states themselves. Such was the sectional basis of opposition to the Minority President.

CHAPTER VI
Life in the White House
(1825–1829)

I never saw a family which had so little of the asso-
ciating disposition. . . .

DIARY OF CHARLES FRANCIS ADAMS,
JUNE 21, 1826 [1]

FIRST OFFICIAL occupants of the Executive Mansion had been John Quincy Adams's own parents, President John Adams and his incomparable wife, Abigail, for a few months in the years 1800–1. They had moved the Government down from Philadelphia to Washington and set up housekeeping in the new building before all the rooms were finished. The famous East Room was then an unplastered apartment where Abigail used to hang her laundry up to dry. John Adams's steady footsteps must still have echoed about the hallways in John Quincy Adams's imagination and his mother's cheerful spirit stirred in his heart as he and his "disassociating" family took up their residence in the house, a second generation of Adamses in the Presidency.

1

The President's House stood conspicuously on Pennsylvania Avenue about a mile from the Capitol, halfway along the dusty road to Georgetown. People were just beginning to call it the White House.[2] The main block of the structure looked in 1825 much as it does now except that the north portico had not yet been added and the building was still unshaded by great trees. But how different the immediate surroundings! Low wings of sheds and stables, long since built over into offices and storerooms, were banked down out of sight of the street; they gave shelter for eight horses, a small dairy, and tools, and served for other purposes. East of the house on Pennsylvania Avenue was the brick building of the State Department,[3] where John Quincy Adams had his office for so many years,

[1] Adams MSS.
[2] There is a great deal of useful but disorderly information about the President's House and its contents in Esther Singleton's *Story of the White House* (2 vols., New York, 1907).
[3] Near where the present Treasury Building now stands.

THE PRESIDENT'S HOUSE, NORTH PORTICO, 1826

FROM PHELPS STOKES COLLECTION IN NEW YORK PUBLIC LIBRARY

THE PRESIDENT'S HOUSE FROM THE RIVER, *circa* 1830

FROM THE COLLECTIONS OF THE LIBRARY OF CONGRESS

and south of that the Treasury Building. Flanking the White House on the west was the War Department, south of that the Navy Department. The four executive buildings, according to the city plan, were at the four corners of a square around the President's House. With their attractive front columns they presented a pleasing appearance in those early years when Latrobe's architectural influence still dominated the environs.

Across the avenue from the President's House was the President's Square, soon to be known as Lafayette Park. Beyond that common was St. John's Episcopal Church, built in 1817 at the northeast corner of H Street and Sixteenth Street. Only three other buildings, private residences, graced the square when John Quincy Adams became President: Commodore Stephen Decatur's mansion, which still stands at the southwest corner of H Street and Jackson Place; Dr. Thomas Ewell's house a few yards to the south, near the present Brookings Institution; and Richard Cutts's residence at H Street and Madison Place, site of the Cosmos Club from 1883 to 1952. From the north portico of the White House one could look out across Pennsylvania Avenue and the square into open country west of Sixteenth Street.

The architect built the mansion to look out over the Potomac. From the front or south portico the occupants enjoyed a broad and gentle rural scene. Beyond some formal gardens a spacious unkempt field of grass two blocks wide, between Seventeenth and Fifteenth Streets, sloped to the riverside a few hundred yards away. A cow or two could be seen grazing there through most seasons of the year—the source of milk and butter for those who lived in the mansion. A few sheep helped to keep the grass down. Seventeenth Street ran down to the water near where the Pan American Union building now stands. From the east, and in back of the President's grounds, Tiber Creek flowed across Fifteenth Street into the river, to form a shallow estuary, subsequently filled in for the present Potomac Park.

A point of firm land, site of the later Washington Monument, rose on the other side of Tiber inlet, also called Goose Creek. From the house this little eminence looked like an island. Behind the point the river's bank ran steeply into deep tidewater. There was a big rock there and an old sycamore tree. It was a good and inconspicuous place to go swimming. The Chief Magistrate of the Republic could peel off his clothes and dive in *au naturel*. At the bottom of Seventeenth Street a little dock jutted out into the widening mouth of the Tiber. From the south portico one could see a canoe or sailboat tied up there and look out across the sunny river to Virginia's shore and the rising hills where now sleep the nation's dead in Arlington National Cemetery.

Amidst these almost pastoral surroundings, in the big gleaming structure devoid of plumbing or any other modern convenience, even running water, John Quincy Adams and his family fitted themselves cautiously into their official residence. The incoming President had a careful inventory made of every piece of furniture lest details of expenditure get confused in the public accounts and audits, the way Monroe's had. Along with the furnishings which Congress allowed him, the new President bought from his rival Crawford a set of silver plate, being careful first to have it weighed and valued by professional appraisers; later he purchased a chest of silver service from the departing Russian Minister, Baron von Tuyll. He added what proved to be politically dangerous installations: a set of chessmen stated to have cost twenty-three dollars and a half, and a billiard table with balls and cues worth sixty-one dollars.[4]

2

The White House family comprised in addition to the President and his lady their two younger sons, John and Charles Francis, and the three orphaned children of Mrs. Adams's sister Nancy: Mary, Johnson, and Thomas Hellen. Mary lived with her Aunt Louisa and the President throughout their stay in the official residence. Her older brother Johnson Hellen decamped one day without notice or explanation, after residing there three years—later he ran away with one of the family housemaids. John Quincy Adams advanced funds against the younger nephew Thomas's patrimony to put him through Exeter and part way through Harvard. He lasted only two years in Cambridge before he was back at the White House, without a job—a problem to the President and to the boy's guardian, Nathaniel Frye, another of Mrs. Adams's numerous brothers-in-law.[5]

Frequent visitors were children of the President's brother Thomas Boylston Adams, whose family had moved into the "Adams Mansion" at Quincy after John Adams's death in 1826. Among these was a favorite niece, Elizabeth, who died a very old lady in Boston in 1903, her last words: "Thank God for Hull's victory!"[6] General Lafayette also lived with the family for several weeks during his stay in Washington in July and August 1825, before embarking for home on the U.S.S. *Brandywine*.

The President's oldest son, George Washington Adams, visited the White House frequently but never lived there. He was a brilliant if nervously erratic young man who had graduated from Harvard in 1823. He studied law in Daniel Webster's Boston office, was admitted to the Massachusetts bar in 1824, and elected to the Massachusetts legislature in

[4] When the Opposition in Congress spotted these items on an inventory furnished by the President's private secretary, it immediately branded them as "gaming tables and gambling furniture." When the President read the printed report of the committee of the House of Representatives which handled the subject, he explained to the chairman that his secretary had been mistaken, that these articles had not been purchased on public account. MacMaster: *History*, V, 503–4. This did not stop his opponents from attempting to make campaign material out of the items in the election year 1828.

[5] Diary of JQA, March 30, 1830. Adams MSS.

[6] Charles Francis Adams, Jr., in *AHR*, XVIII, 521.

1826, first rung in a hopeful career. The President gave George his first legal business, the conduct of his father's personal affairs in Boston. The young lawyer did not prove as meticulous a man of business as his father had been at that phase of his career. He was tardy with statements, imprecise with details, tangled up in his financial accounts, given to irregular habits of work and life that did not fit the rigid self-discipline of a successful Adams. The President and Mrs. Adams were much worried about their oldest boy in Boston.[7]

John Adams, 2d, had missed his diploma at Harvard because of his part in the great student riot of 1823,[8] and nothing that the Secretary of State could do as one of the university's most distinguished alumni could change President Kirkland's mind about that. So the youth came to Washington to study law under his father's tutelage and to become in 1825 the President's private secretary.

Charles Francis Adams was the youngest son. After some private schooling in Washington while his father was Secretary of State, and tutoring in Cambridge, he entered Harvard in the class of 1825. Following graduation at the age of eighteen he spent two years in Washington studying law with his father, then followed his brother George in Daniel Webster's Boston law office. To have both John Quincy Adams and Daniel Webster as preceptors, as did these two Adams brothers, was uncommonly good legal training. Charles was admitted to the Massachusetts bar in January 1829, at the age of twenty-two.

In his own mind and heart John Quincy Adams had destined all three sons for public service and high office, like their father and grandfather before them. He thought that study of the law, supported by wide reading in history and politics, offered the best training for such a career. It could also provide some private competence for protection against the suffrage of a fickle public.

The President was not content to leave the two absent boys unguided as his father John Adams had left him to study law in Newburyport and to set up practice in Boston. To each of them he wrote every week, sometimes oftener, regulating and rationing their work and recreation from morning to night, trying by remote control to shape them into images of their father and grandfather.[9] It proved a heavy burden for all three, for one of them too heavy.

[7] JQA to GWA, March 25, October 28, November 28, December 4, 11, 14, 19, 1827; January 1, 1828. Adams MSS.

[8] Samuel Eliot Morison: *Three Centuries of Harvard 1636–1936* (Cambridge, 1936), p. 231. In 1873 the Harvard Corporation granted posthumous degrees to the expelled senior students, including John Adams, 2d.

[9] "My sons have not only their own honor but that of two preceding generations to sustain." JQA to GWA, Washington, December 19, 1827. Adams MSS.

3

President and Mrs. John Quincy Adams lived up to the social obliga-tions of the White House, but they did no more than was strictly required of them. The President preferred the family circle, his books and writing-table; Louisa did not have the strength for further official entertaining. They were quite content to continue the rule already established by Monroe's time: the First Magistrate gave but did not accept invitations; he received but he did not go out socially in Washington. Their set din-ners given weekly during the social season, which corresponded with the regular session of Congress, to high officials of the Administration, mem-bers of Congress, and the diplomatic corps, reflected the President's social experience and that of Mrs. Adams in the numerous capitals of Europe during a rich diplomatic career, as well as seven years in Washington as Secretary of State. Formal affairs, they lacked sparkle and wit.

In more intimate dinners for occasional company of a few friends [10] he could open up surpassingly to his guests on almost any worth-while sub-ject, particularly literature and the arts and sciences—for example, paint-ing, classical poetry, history, drama and the stage, or such specialties as the vintages and qualities of fine wines.[11] Evenings and talk like this, some contemporary observers generously noted, matched the best that might be found at any "genteel" house and board in England itself! Din-ner talk between him and Henry Clay discussing pleasantly their old con-troversies and their current common problems of state was a treat for youthful ears or old.[12]

To dull people John Quincy Adams was dull indeed.[13] One such person who failed to spark the Yankee President to say anything at all wrote this doggerel that found its way into Louisa's notebook:

> Asked by the Nation's chief to take my tea,
> I hastened to him in surprising glee,
> But when I got there, all my treat, by God,
> Is just to watch His Excellency's Nod.[14]

[10] *Memoirs,* VIII, 95.

[11] "My father was uncommonly eloquent after dinner today and laid himself out more forcibly than usual. When he does so, how immeasurably he rises above all oth-ers. There is no comparison." Diary of CFA, March 31, 1827. See also *Autobiography of Martin Van Buren,* 272.

[12] "We sat very late and on the whole, I consider this as one of the most fortunate occurrences of my life, by which I was admitted behind the scenes and saw these men exhibited in some of their highest respective points." Diary of CFA, October 19, 1828.

[13] "He himself is very dull and his neighbors at table when he gives formal dinners have a hard time of it." So noted Gulian C. Verplanck. Robert W. July: *The Essential New Yorker: Gulian Crommelin Verplanck* (Durham, 1951), p. 124.

[14] Adams MSS.

The Adamses realized that Congress provided for the President's House out of the public money, and that the people, the taxpayers and voters, expected to see and visit their elected President on terms of equality. The White House remained the people's palace, as much as a palace could exist in a republic. Citizens with professed business could call any time; there were at least a dozen of these visitors daily. Members of Congress made it a practice to take distinguished or even merely respectable constituents to meet the Chief Magistrate in his cabinet—that is, study, or "writing-chamber." Almost any personable foreign visitor could present himself at the White House and pay his respects to the President. Strangers "not particularly distinguished" and other ordinary citizens might wait for one of the fortnightly levees. Practically anybody could go to these. According to the custom it was easy enough to get a card, or walk in without a card or invitation of any kind. Even so, it was rare to find there an uncouth person—unless it were among the servants of a foreign minister.[15] There seems to have been no screening or secret-service protection.

People began to arrive in their carriages or in public hacks about eight o'clock in the evening. Few stayed later than ten. Ladies had to have male escorts, but one gentleman could take two of the other sex, and many did. A gentleman with only one lady took her always on his left arm, leaving the right free to fend off the crowd. If he were caring for two fair guests it may have doubled his pleasure but it limited his ability to move about.

After coming in the main north entrance everybody made his way through the great hall to the Oval Room, or official drawing-room. There stood the President and his lady, somewhat apart, their backs to the south or front portico. Those of his personal acquaintance, or persons introduced to him, usually by some member of Congress or high government official, would shake hands. Those not presented would salute and pass along to make their bows also to Mrs. Adams. Then they would push on into two reception rooms, the Green Room and the Yellow Room, on each side of the Oval Room. There they found liveried waiters weaving in and out among the crowd as best they could with trays of coffee, tea, and ice cream, cake, light wines, cordials, and liqueurs. A special treat for the guests sometimes during the winter season was fresh fruits from the West Indies. Some people went to partake of the delicacies, others just to see the President and his wife, the "Gentlemen of the Administration," and the distinguished gathering. Occasionally the President made Mrs. Adams's drawing-room the occasion for first receiving a minor diplomat.[16] To go to the President's levee was the thing to do when in Washington.

---

[15] "Mr. [Secretary of State] Clay spoke of a circular to several of the foreign ministers here, complaining of the conduct of their servants on the drawing-room evenings." *Memoirs*, VII, 223.

[16] *Memoirs*, VII, 108.

At these affairs there was no special *rigeur,* no demand for smallclothes as in previous regimes since George Washington. Most visitors, particularly the ladies, came in ball dress, but there was no music or dancing until the last one or two evenings of the season; therefore many gentlemen wore boots instead of pumps. The President contented himself with the plain dress of a decently attired citizen: frock coat and trousers. Many of those present would not have been able to tell him from other men if they had not seen the crowd moving up to him or had him pointed out. It was easy enough to know who Mrs. Adams was, with her gracious bearing, her ornate headdresses and fashionable gowns; she always looked the part of the First Lady even if she did not really enjoy the role.

Grand gala day for the people and the people's servants in the People's Palace was the New Year's drawing-room or general reception. On that day between noon and three o'clock in the afternoon the President received everybody high and low, friend and foe, who wished to offer the compliments of the season if not good wishes for the coming year. Customarily present were the Vice President, Justices of the Supreme Court, Cabinet officers, members of Congress, top army and navy officers, all with their staffs and families, as well as scores of subordinate civil servants. The President's most outspoken critics and political enemies, with the decent exception of Calhoun during the last year, did not shrink from attending. They would come and wish him a happy New Year and then go back to Capitol Hill or to their newspaper offices and attack him with the idea of putting him out of the White House at the earliest day possible. "In a democracy . . . !"

It was the diplomatic corps that made the most vivid splash of color. With their cocked hats and gilt braid and Old World manners they appealed most to the populace. But the press of people got to be so bothersome that one year the French and Russian Ministers took exception to having to push their way through a vulgar crowd to present themselves to the President and Mrs. Adams. When they stayed away for this reason or remonstrated, John Quincy Adams told them to come early at noon before the crowd or late at three o'clock when the assembly had thinned out, then they wouldn't have any trouble! [17]

So great was the crowd on New Year's Day that all available space on the ground or public floor of the White House had to be thrown open, including the still unfurnished East Room.[18] John Quincy Adams estimated that he saw between two and three thousand people at his first reception on New Year's Day 1826, about twelve hundred to open the year 1827. "Our last New Year's drawing-room," he noted at the close of his

[17] *Memoirs,* VII, 99, 101.
[18] It was still unfurnished in 1825. The President hoped that when members of Congress saw the salon in all its nakedness they would do something about it, but they didn't. *Memoirs,* VII, 101. Wilhelmus Bogart Bryan: *A History of the National Capital* . . . (New York, 1916), II, 179–81.

Administration on January 1, 1829, "was crowded beyond all previous example, and passed quietly off." [19]

Not all of those present on that day, or at Mrs. Adams's fortnightly soirées, were there to wish the President and his family well. For instance, there was Russell Jarvis, editorial scribe of Duff Green's *Daily Telegraph*, whose scurrilous editorials had got under the Adamses' skin. When Jarvis and a group of relatives attended a White House drawing-room the evening of April 2, 1828, John Adams, 2d, remarked in a loud voice that there was a man who, if he had any sense of propriety in the conduct of a gentleman, would not show his face in the house. This led to an attempted nose-pulling in the Rotunda of the Capitol to provoke a duel. It took all the resourcefulness of the President's Cabinet, including Henry Clay, the Administration's most experienced duelist, to prevent a meeting of Jarvis and John.[20]

4

John Quincy Adams never liked to "exhibit himself" to the people.[21] Early in his Administration the Maryland Agricultural Society invited the President and his Cabinet officers to attend the next cattle-show and exhibit of domestic manufactures, near Baltimore. He politely declined. "See thou a man diligent in *his* business," he wrote to the society's secretary. It would cost him four precious days of work. Obviously they wanted to make the President of the United States a part of their exhibition. It would be a precedent for all the cattle-shows throughout the Union. "From cattle-shows to other public meetings for purposes of utility or exposures of public sentiment, the transition is natural and easy." [22]

Most Presidents since him have not discouraged such a transition. Having accomplished it, they have selected times and places to show themselves to the voters throughout the Union. John Quincy Adams never spent a cent of the public funds nor an hour of the public's time for such purposes.

His biggest extravagance was the annual vacation trip to Massachu-

[19] *Memoirs*, VII, 98, 394; VIII, 89.

E. Cooley, M.D.'s *Description of the Etiquette of Washington Exhibiting the Habits and Customs that Prevail in the Intercourse of the Most Distinguished and Fashionable Society at that Place during the Session of Congress* (Philadelphia: L. B. Clarke; 1829) gives a contemporary description of White House receptions of greater historical value than the various reminiscences about Washington society and Presidents and their families written by old men and women years later or based on such. Two of the latter are Mrs. E. F. Ellet's *Court Circles of the Republic* . . . (Hartford, 1869), and the veteran journalist and editor, Benjamin Perley Poore: *Perley's Reminiscences of Sixty Years in the National Metropolis* (2 vols., Philadelphia, 1886).

[20] See "The Case of Russell Jarvis," H.R. Report, No. 260, 20th August, 1st Session. A paper delivered before the Massachusetts Historical Society on "The Scuffle in the Rotunda" will be printed in MHS *Proceedings*.

[21] *Memoirs*, VII, 250.

[22] *Memoirs*, VII, 13.

setts, from August to October. This included always a visit, on the way back, to his old friend Ward N. Boylston [23] who had a model farm and secluded country home at Princeton, Massachusetts, where Mount Wachusett seemed about to come down and enter the front door, carrying with it "a forethought of eternity." [24] Boylston was an old friend of London days, a former Tory long since repatriated in the Bay State, who made the President one of the executors and trustees of his estate. He died in January 1828, leaving Mr. Adams 400 acres of farm land in the town of Weston [25] appraised for tax purposes at $5,366.

Adams made the journeys to and from New England as unostentatiously as possible without announced schedule, traveling by common stage and steamship accommodations and suffering inconveniences like any ordinary traveler. The record of popular encounters or hearty public greetings on these trips is meager. Because he did not know how to handle people he avoided them, to the dismay of those who wished him well. Louisa had long since tried tactfully to suggest that he owed it to his supporters and to the people at large to let them see more of him. There was a wide difference, his wife told him, between *courting* and *shunning* the advances of the public.[26]

On his way back from Quincy in 1827 some people assembled spontaneously at the wharf in Philadelphia to see the President come and go. They gave him three cheers on each occasion. These shadows of good will touched him excessively. He was grateful to his fellow citizens for such rare—if moderate—demonstrations. He thanked Heaven that they had been moved to do it, but he did not know what to say. As the steamboat backed out to swing down the river, he returned the people's salutations with a bow, waved his hand, and said (rather stiffly): "God bless you all!"

People accept benedictions, but they do not glory in them. He could think of nothing to tickle their fancy, nothing to warm their cockles, nothing to draw forth a throaty roar of applause, nothing to leave behind for the growth of a legend. It took Andrew Jackson to do that!

In these little episodes of public life John Quincy Adams could not say

[23] See Vol. I, 132.

[24] Diary of JQA, October 6–8, 1827. Adams MSS.

[25] Will of Ward N. Boylston, probate No. 2353, Dedham County Probate Records, now in Norfolk County Court House, Dedham, Mass. For tax valuation in 1827 of this property, see *The Tax Lists, 1757–1827*, published by the Town of Weston (Boston, 1897) with a Preface by Mary Frances Peirce, p. 380.

For Ward N. Boylston, see Francis Everett Blake: *History of the Town of Princeton . . .* (Princeton, Mass., 1915), I, 278–80. There is an obituary in the Boston *Centinel*, No. 4568, January 19, 1828.

The bequest yielded a very meager income. Diary of JQA, July 28, 1829; Diary of CFA, July 28, 1829; LCA to CFA, Washington, January 24, February 1, 1828. Adams MSS.

The estate of Dr. Stephen T. Riley, librarian of the Massachusetts Historical Society, is now (1956) located on a portion of this former Boylston, later Adams property.

[26] LCA to JQA, Boston, July 16, 1827. Adams MSS.

the easy, human thing to friendly strangers. It just would not come to his lips. A large group that greeted him at Baltimore on this same return trip contained not a few of his political adversaries. Some of these, not to mention his own supporters, were a little boisterous from drink. One said: "Although I am opposed to you, I am glad to see you well and take you by the hand."

"We are all friends *here*," said the President, frigidly enough to sober the man completely and keep him voting for Jackson forever.

"I hope the Constitution may never be broken," said another inebriate, reaching unsteadily for the President's hand.

"I concur heartily in that wish," Adams responded, "and hope that *your* constitution may never be broken." [27]

We may be sure that these replies failed to pick up a single new vote in Baltimore. Nor did an obscure toast which he essayed on his Baltimore visit, adapted from Voltaire's *Le blanc et le noir:* " 'Ebony and Topaz': General Ross's coat of arms and the republican militiaman who gave it." He had to interpret the literary allusion so pedagogically that it became a butt for irony among sophisticates.[28]

Some Baltimoreans said a few cordial words, and many told him they hoped he would be re-elected. Most came up, shook his hand, and passed on. He left them cold while his political supporters stood by and shivered in their shoes. He was glad to get back to his hotel room and to bed by ten o'clock. Adams simply was not a popular man, and he was always conscious of being a minority President, with Andrew Jackson as the people's darling.[29]

---

[27] *Memoirs*, VII, 331–6.

[28] The explanation was as follows: whenever the spirit of evil (Ebony), at continual variance with the spirit of good will (Topaz) in human affairs, should invade the United States, let there be patriots to stop it, as the militiaman's bullet stopped dead the British General Ross (whose sovereign rewarded his family with a heraldic addition to its coat of arms) at Baltimore in 1814! *Niles' Weekly Register*, 3rd Series, IX, No. 8, Baltimore, October 20, 1827. *Diary of Philip Hone*, I, 97. *Memoirs*, VII, 338.

"I can perceive neither sense nor wit in the President's toast unless (which can scarcely be possible) he meant by *Ebony* and *Topaz* to personify the *Slave* and *free* States. Can that be. He is fond of obscure but bitter allusions. Is there nothing in the [story?] that would confirm or destroy this supposition. I am not familiar with it and cannot at the moment make myself so. Look at it but let my suggestion remain with yourself." Martin Van Buren to C. C. Cambreleng [Albany], October 22, 1827. Van Buren MSS, LC.

The John Quincy Adams who copyrighted the two successive American editions of *Voltaire's Philosophical Dictionary*, with notes by Abner Kneeland (Boston, 1836, 1856), was a stranger unknown to the subject of this biography and his family. JQA to Revd. Joseph Emerson, New London, Conn. Quincy, June 17, 1843. Adams MSS.

[29] "Poor Adams used to visit New York during his presidency. The papers, to be sure, announced his arrival; but he was welcomed by no shouts, no crowd thronged around his portals, no huzzas rent the air when he made his appearance, and yet posterity, more just than ourselves, will acknowledge him to have been in all the qualifications which constitute his fitness to fill the office of a ruler of this great republic,

Once an old man came up to him and said: "My wife used to know your family and you. She used to cut your hair when you were a small lad."

"Well," said the President inanely, "I suppose she cuts *yours* now."

The one instance of really spontaneous and hearty applause that John Quincy Adams ever got from a crowd while President was quite unexpected. It was something he could not help. It occurred on the occasion of breaking ground for the Baltimore and Ohio Canal on July 4, 1828. Except for the farewell to Lafayette it was the only public address he made during his tenure of office. It was the nearest to an outright political speech that he had ever made in his life.

He was of course greatly interested in the canal, one of the most important internal improvements of the period. To him it was a worthy subject for an Independence Day celebration. Early that morning the President and his son John joined a group of officials of the canal company at Georgetown. Present were the mayors and committees of the corporations of Washington City, Georgetown, and Alexandria, Virginia, together with the Cabinet officers, foreign ministers, and other invited persons. They proceeded on a small steamboat to the entrance of the existing Potomac Canal, then by canalboats to the head of that waterway. The spot selected for beginning the new works was just within the bounds of the State of Maryland, seemingly the last place in the region in which a crowd could be brought together. Nevertheless about two thousand people had assembled there to see the ceremonies and listen to the President's remarks.

The president of the company made a short introductory speech and then handed a spade to John Quincy Adams. Nobody had prepared the ground. On the first thrust the spade struck a tough hickory root. The President tried three or four times more, without results. This little frustration greatly amused the spectators as they watched in good-natured suspense. It was a hot day. Not to be daunted, the Chief Magistrate threw off his coat and, getting down to business, quickly threw up the first shovelful. Delighted at the great man's earthy triumph, the crowd let out a roar, or, as Adams gratefully recorded, "a general shout burst forth from the surrounding multitude." He then completed his fifteen-minute address, slowly and awkwardly, but without gross or palpable failure. It was an oratorical plea for the use of the powers, physical, moral, and intellectual, of the whole Union to the improvement of its own condition— even to the conquest of physical nature—an argument for the principle of internal improvement,[30] as exemplified by this project: "a great central chain of union between the Atlantic and Western States."

The speaker could not help noting that the incident of spade, shirt-

---

twenty times superior to Jackson." *Diary of Philip Hone 1828–1851*, edited by Allan Nevins (New York, 1927), I, 97.

[30] Text in *National Journal*, V, No. 3195. July 8, 1828.

sleeves, and hickory root struck the eye and fancy of the spectators more than all the flowers of rhetoric of his discourse. It diverted them from the stammering and hesitation of a fatigued mind and body and a deficient memory. Quite by accident he had made a little hit—with the spade, not the speech! [31]

The daily life of any real politician is full of such little common touches that warm the people to him. But this is the only incident of the kind on record during Adams's Presidency.

5

Before John Quincy Adams became President of the United States he had never joined a church. He had grown up in a Congregational parish in Braintree where great freedom of thought prevailed. Old John Adams, a member of that church with his wife, Abigail, boasted of having been the first Unitarian in Massachusetts. The younger Adams graduated from Braintree, so to speak, without a diploma, but in contrast to his father he retained a "smack of orthodoxy" that lasted all his life. He always started the day by reading at dawn—before dawn in the shorter days of the year —a chapter or two from the Holy Scriptures with the aid of Scott's and Hewlett's commentaries. As President he continued his fixed habit of Bible-reading and churchgoing. Principally he attended the Unitarian Church at Sixth and D Streets, N.W., where the learned Robert Little was pastor until his lamented death in August 1827. Often he would go to church twice on Sunday, morning and afternoon—in the afternoon frequently to the Second Presbyterian Church, of which he was a trustee, in the triangle of H Street and New York Avenue, where the Reverend Mr. Daniel Baker held forth. [32]

During many years of service at European courts he had developed sincere respect for the Catholic Church and its clergy. He had often attended Mass in the European capitals. On the first Christmas during his Presidency he went to St. Patrick's Church to hear the Irish cleric John England, Bishop of Charleston, S.C., preach, without notes or apparent preparation, a sermon on the birth of Christ and the influence of Christianity upon the fortunes of mankind. The Bishop's liberal discourse and tolerant attitude opened up so wide a field of thought for Adams that he went again to hear him at the Capitol one Sunday a fortnight later. So crowded was the public service that the President, unannounced, found it hard to get a seat. The sermon proved to be an "altogether conciliatory" discourse, pronounced in "true Christian temper," its theme the compulsion of God's spirit upon the souls of men.

Adams all his life had believed in obedience to the will of God; in-

[31] *Memoirs*, VIII, 49–50.

[32] Bryan: *National Capital*, II, 181–5. The church was torn down toward the middle of the twentieth century.

scrutable though sometimes it seemed to be, he yielded himself to it. One of his favorite texts was: *"it is not in man that walketh to direct his steps."* Bishop England said that indeed Christians must obey the will of God, "once ascertained," that it was not the Pope who had the last word on what that will was, but a council of bishops. This of course was before Pius IX's decree of papal infallibility on matters of faith or morals (1870).

The President was pleased to hear the Bishop disclaim all persecution and admired the ingenuity with which he almost explained away some of the earlier conciliar decrees for the extermination of heretics. Adams never inveighed against the Catholic Church or against Popery as did some of his Calvinist contemporaries. But as a son of the American Revolution, as a son of John Adams, he insisted that man's mind must always be free to understand God and his heart to feel Him. He could not accept constraint of this innate individual human freedom of worship whether from a council of bishops or a congregation of his fellow townsmen.[33]

On another occasion the President listened, again in the House of Representatives, to the earnest and affectionate cantations and prayers of the female Quaker preacher Elizabeth Robeson, speaking as the Spirit moved her.[34]

At one time or another he must have worshipped at nearly every Christian church in Washington. He regarded public worship as a Christian obligation and family duty, not to be neglected with impunity even in reference to worldly prosperity.[35] He believed that Christians of all denominations were only traveling by different roads to the same end.

"Hope in the goodness of God, reliance upon His mercy in affliction, trust in Him to bring light out of darkness and good out of evil, are the comforts and promises which I desire from attendance on public worship. They help to sustain me in the troubles that are thickening upon me, and although every day adds to the gloom and threatening fury of the storm, and not a ray of light is discernible before me, yet do I gather strength and fortitude, and a vague and indefinite confidence of escaping, or of passing unhurt through the furnace that awaits me, from the constant exhortations to trust in the Lord which abound in the Psalms, as well as in the selections of hymns at the churches where I attend." [36]

As he grew old the mysteries of the Christian God and the truth of the Gospels became more and more a subject of anxious reflection resolved, or half-resolved, by common sense rather than by religious inspiration.

---

[33] For Bishop England's sermons, see Diary, December 25, 1825, and *Memoirs*, VII, 101–2. January 8, 1826.

[34] *Memoirs*, VII, 467, 470–1.

[35] "Attendance upon public worship is an obligation of deep morality to every husband and father. It is due to public decency from every Christian in a Christian country. And even in reference to worldly prosperity it cannot be neglected with impunity." JQA to CFA (following the latter's marriage), Washington, January 25, 1830. Adams MSS.

[36] *Memoirs*, VII, 376. December 9, 1827.

Many of his meditations he set down in his Diary. *"For God so loved the world that he gave his only begotten Son, that whosoever believeth in Him should not perish, but have everlasting life."* What did this mean? "What is the meaning of the term *loved,*" the President asked himself, after listening in St. John's Church to an unsatisfactory sermon on this text, the second Sunday in Lent 1828. "What is the world, as here used? If God loved the world, was the gift of his only begotten Son the only way in which that love could be manifested? What is the precise idea conveyed by the terms only begotten Son, as applied to God? How could belief in the Son of God save the believer from perishing and confer upon him everlasting life?"

Adams could not answer these questions, he could not find anybody else who could do so to his satisfaction. But on this earth, he told himself, life is mortal enjoyment disciplined by God's love: "Animated existence is a gift of God demonstrating his goodness; intellectual life given to man is a yet choicer blessing, granted on this planet to man alone."

How about immortal life? To John Quincy Adams everlasting life was the perpetuation in another world of the blessing of animated existence in this world. How this future life should be effected was the mystery imperfectly revealed in the Scriptures—not fully disclosed, however, to the puny understanding of mankind. "We now see it as 'through a glass darkly, but then face to face.'" Existence, duration, he reasoned to himself, were incomprehensible. It was just as easy to believe that existence should be everlasting as that it should not be. "Matter undergoes perpetual mutation, but is never destroyed; why not the same of mind?" Alas, he could not show himself how. His times lacked the aid as they lacked also the despair of modern science and philosophy. He fell back on the Bible: "It is in the gospel that we must seek for proofs of our immortality." [37]

The Bible bothered him with its literal statements. How about the miracles? He did not believe that they were beyond the power of an almighty Creator, but he had come to doubt the *facts* as related in the Scriptures.

"The miracles in the Bible furnish the most powerful of all the objections against its authenticity, both historical and doctrinal; and were it possible to take its sublime morals, its unparalleled conceptions of the nature of God, and its irresistible power over the heart, with the simple narrative of the life and death of Jesus, stripped of all the supernatural agency and all the marvellous incidents connected with it, I should receive it without any of those misgivings of unwilling incredulity as to the miracles, which I find it impossible altogether to cast off." [38]

What about the divinity of Christ? He could not bring himself to believe in it, nor could he cast aside the concept. "Neither this [the Gospel of St. Matthew] nor any other argument that I ever heard, can satisfy my judgment that the doctrine of the Divinity of Christ is *not countenanced*

[37] *Memoirs*, VII, 459.　　　　[38] *Memoirs*, VII, 176.

by the New Testament. As little can I say that it is clearly revealed." [39]
Adams, not venturing beyond the Scriptures on this transcendent question, and still affected by his smack of orthodoxy, left the point in doubt.

And the Trinity? This doctrine made him impatient and had bent him
toward the Unitarians, if not in their great fundamental, at least in their
concept of the fatherhood of God however existing and the brotherhood
of man. "I believe in one God, but His nature is incomprehensible to me,
and of the question between the Unitarians and Trinitarians I have no
precise belief, because no definite understanding." [40] So thought many
Congregationalists who in their uncertainty had become Unitarians.

When Mr. Baker once pressed him on this point, he answered as freely
as he had once expressed himself to the General of the Jesuits at St. Petersburg: "I am not either a Trinitarian or a Unitarian. I believe the nature of Jesus Christ is superhuman; but whether he is God, or only the
first of human beings, is not clearly revealed to me in the Scriptures." [41]

So he went on prayerfully through life doubting and believing: doubtful on points of doctrine that had mystified men for centuries, convinced
of the existence of God and the blessings of Divine Providence, hopeful
about an after-life, looking to the example of Jesus Christ and the simple
Christian ethic and practicing it imperfectly but to the best of his ability.[42] Every night before he went to bed, no matter where he was in his
travels or who was in the room, he said aloud the prayer his mother
taught him as a child: "Now I lay me down to sleep . . ." And he didn't
mumble it either.[43]

---

[39] *Memoirs,* VII, 229.

[40] *Memoirs,* VII, 324.

[41] *Memoirs,* VII, 477. "First" means obviously first in rank.

[42] "I have at all times been a sincere believer in the existence of a Supreme Creator
of the world, of an immortal principle within myself, responsible to that Creator for
my conduct upon earth, and of the divine mission of the crucified Savior, proclaiming
immortal life and preaching peace on earth, good will to men, the natural equality of
all mankind, and the law, 'Thou shalt love thy neighbor as thyself.' Of all these articles
of faith, all resting upon the first, the existence of an omnipotent Spirit, I entertain involuntary and agonizing doubts, which I can neither silence nor expel, and against
which I need for my own comfort to be fortified and sustained by stated and frequent
opportunities of receiving religious admonition and instruction. I feel myself to be a
frequent sinner before God, and I need to be often admonished of it, and exhorted to
virtue. This is administered in all the forms of Christian worship, and I am sure of
receiving it with whatever denomination of Christian worshippers I associate to obtain
it." *Memoirs,* XI, 341. March 19, 1843.

I cannot accept Mr. Brooks Adams's inference throughout his Introductory Note to
The Degradation of the Democratic Dogma (New York, 1919) that Andrew Jackson's
victory in 1828 and the defeat thereby of John Quincy Adams's national program of
internal improvements made him doubt (in 1837) the existence of a Providence. It
was Brooks Adams, not his grandfather John Quincy Adams, who asked the question:
"But, after all, is there a Providence?" (Ibid., p. 25).

[43] See the recollection told in 1882 to young Henry Cabot Lodge by Dr. George
Ellis, who shared a room in a New York hotel with John Quincy Adams when they

6

As President, Adams allowed the Government to rest too heavily upon his shoulder. He busied himself personally with all manner of administrative details that he could have left to other people: reform of army regulations, promotions and pay, review of the findings of courts-martial, the rivalries of officers, including the quarrelsome and unseemly pretensions of Major Generals Winfield Scott and Edmund P. Gaines to outrank each other; the question whether cadets at West Point should have to strip naked for physical examinations; the tympanum and the pediment of the Capitol façade and other features of the architecture and ornamentation of the building. As ever he remained a slave to his cabinet and his desk and to the hordes of people and problems that invaded both.[44]

Day after day, from breakfast time to the dinner hours, there streamed an unending procession of visitors, petitioners, solicitors, politicians, office-hunters, pardon-seekers, inventors, panhandlers, and cranks, as well as heads of departments and federal officers on inevitable government business. They crowded his antechamber. They filed into his office. They consumed his time. They forced him into the evening hours for the writing of state papers and personal correspondence. It was a harassing, wearying, teasing condition of existence. His Diary began to fall into arrears, digests, blanks, so as to threaten "chasms" in the record of his life and defeat its principal purpose of controlling the "chain of events." By the end of the day his strength was wilting, his spirits drooped.

In Adams's time there was scant secretarial service for the President's Mansion. All he had was his own son as private secretary. The President was the only person in the White House who knew and practiced shorthand, and no copyist could read his. He drafted in his own hand the great body of his political and personal correspondence, including thousand-word letters weekly to each of his two sons in Boston. Under the unending labor his writing hand grew shaky, his eyes red and rheumy, and he frequently had to abridge his Diary. But the crowding office visitors and the hours of writing helped him to hold off brooding private cares that had begun to crawl upon him like a "nest of spiders." [45]

---

both were attending the fiftieth anniversary of the New York Historical Society in 1844. Lodge: *Early Memories* (New York, 1913), pp. 271–2.

[44] One of the innumerable executive acts of John Quincy Adams as President was remission of penalties and forfeitures, and proclamation of pardon, for the overloading of the now historically famous sloop *Restoration*, the "Mayflower" of Norwegian-American immigrant annals. Theodore C. Blegen has made the most of Norwegian and American sources for the history of this episode in *John Quincy Adams and the Sloop "Restoration"* (Northfield, Minn.: Norwegian-American Historical Association; 1940).

[45] *Memoirs*, VII, 200, 221, 235.

7

July 4, 1826 was the fiftieth anniversary of the Declaration of Independence. Adams recalled how his mother Abigail in the farmhouse at Quincy had read to the children their father's letters from the Continental Congress at Philadelphia telling how he and old Dr. Franklin and young Mr. Jefferson had been sitting in a committee appointed by the Continental Congress to draw up the Declaration. John Adams had little to do with the drafting and wording of the immortal document—that was Jefferson's composition. But his family were proud of the part he had played; he had led the movement for independence. Their son, the President, could remember one letter almost word for word: "The second day of July, 1776," the father had written his family from Philadelphia, "will be the most memorable epocha in the history of America. I am apt to believe that it will be celebrated by succeeding generations as the great anniversary Festival. It ought to be commemorated, as the day of deliverance, by solemn acts of devotion to God Almighty. It ought to be solemnized with pomp and parade, with shows, games, sports, guns, bells, bonfires and illuminations, from one end of this continent to the other, from this time forward, forevermore." [46]

Custom set the fourth of July, the day of the Declaration, rather than the second, the day of the resolution for independence, as the anniversary festival. Now, in 1826, the fiftieth anniversary was being celebrated from one end of the continent to the other. The United States reached from sea to sea, thanks to Thomas Jefferson with his lucky Louisiana Purchase of 1803, and to John Adams's son with his Anglo-American boundary convention of 1818 and Transcontinental Treaty of 1819 with Spain. The old patriot, stretching out his ninety-first year in his bed at Quincy, hoped to live to see the jubilee of a half-century of independence. For him it would be a momentous epoch in the annals of the human race. Only the future could tell, he wrote to a committee of his fellow citizens in a letter that was read at their ceremonies, whether July 4, 1776 was destined to be "THE BRIGHTEST OR THE BLACKEST PAGE" in human annals. It would be according to the use or the abuse of those political institutions by which the United States should in time to come be shaped by the human mind.[47]

As on July 4, 1826 the second President Adams sat listening in the Cap-

---

[46] *Letters of John Adams, Addressed to his Wife*, edited by his grandson, Charles Francis Adams (2 vols., Boston, 1841), I, 128–9.

[47] JA to Captain John Whitney, Chairman of the Committee of Arrangements for celebrating the approaching anniversary of the Fourth of July in the town of Quincy. Quincy, June 7, 1826. JA to Messrs. Jacob B. Taylor, *et alii*, a Committee of Arrangements of the City Corporation of New York. Quincy, June 10, 1826. *Works of JA*, X, 416–17. The Massachusetts Historical Society published and distributed in 1955 a broadside containing the exchange of letters between Captain Whitney and the first President Adams.

itol at Washington to the commemorative ceremonies, John Adams and Thomas Jefferson lay dying in Quincy and at Monticello. When the elder Adams was told it was the Fourth of July, fiftieth anniversary of independence, he said: "It is a great day. It is a good day!" [48] Already, in response to a request from the townsmen for a toast for the day, he had sent them the immortal words: "Independence Forever!" As if under the inspiration of fifty years of independent freedom, he rested easier. He spoke of members of his family, asked that letters be written to his son the President. In the afternoon about one o'clock his granddaughter Mrs. Clark [49] saw his lips moving. She bent over his head. "Thomas Jefferson still surv—" he managed to say. He recognized his favorite grandson, George Washington Adams, when he arrived from Boston, but could no longer speak. At half past six he died as calmly as an infant slips into slumber.[50]

Jefferson's thread of life had already broken a few hours before: he died at Monticello at about one o'clock. His last words were: "Is it the Fourth?" [51]

The extraordinary coincidence of the deaths on the same day of the two statesmen, old colleagues, old political opponents, continuing friends, struck the attention of people all over the land, and throughout the world. That it fell on the fiftieth anniversary of their greatest achievement made men marvel all the more. It was even more dramatic that each in his last hours should have had that great day, that good day, uppermost in mind.[52] That they were united in death on such a day of earthly jubilee made John Quincy Adams fondly imagine that their joint supplication would be for the perpetual Union of their country. "The time, the manner, the coincidence with the decease of Jefferson," he noted in his Diary, "are visible and palpable marks of Divine favor." [53]

Jefferson's death was known in Washington on the 6th. Two days later letters of the 3d and early morning of the 4th from Quincy brought word to the White House that the President's father was rapidly sinking. The news was really unexpected; John Quincy Adams was looking forward to another annual vacation visit with the old statesman. At dawn the following morning, July 9, he and his son John, leaving Mrs. Adams and Charles

---

[48] *Memoirs*, VII, 129–33.

[49] Susan B. Clark, daughter of JQA's deceased brother Charles Adams.

[50] GWA to JQA, Quincy, July 5, 1826. Adams MSS.

[51] Sarah N. Randolph: *Domestic Life of Thomas Jefferson* (New York, 1871), p. 425.

[52] After James Monroe died on the Fourth of July 1831, Henry Clay wrote to JQA that it would no longer be fashionable for an ex-President to make his final exit on any other day but the Fourth of July: "That *your* fourth may be far distant I most sincerely wish." Ashland, July 26, 1831. Adams MSS.

[53] *Memoirs*, VII, 125, July 9, 1826. Lyman H. Butterfield has suggested the national significance of "The Jubilee of Independence, July 4, 1826" in *Virginia Magazine of History and Biography*, XXI (No. 2, April 1953), 119–40.

Francis at the White House, started for Quincy. At Merrill's Tavern, Waterloo, halfway to Baltimore, at eleven o'clock, the innkeeper delivered to him the word that his father was gone. Proceeding from Baltimore by steamboat and stage, they reached Boston the evening of the 12th, four days from Washington, and arrived at Quincy next morning.

As John Quincy entered his father's empty bedchamber the painful instant struck him like an arrow to the heart. In this room they had sat so often during the last two yearly visits; here the son had taken what proved to be his last leave. Gone was the ineffable charm that had always made the house an abode of enchantment at every home-coming. Yet his attachment to the place, and to the whole region round about, was stronger than ever. He knew that there was where he wanted to end his own days.

The funeral had already been held on the 7th of July, before a throng of two thousand people. Peter Whitney, pastor at Quincy, had delivered a sermon from the First Book of Chronicles, xxix, 28: "He died in a good old age, full of days and honor." At least that is the way the son recorded it in his Diary. The actual text, of course, is: "He died in a good old age, full of days, riches, and honor, and Solomon his son reigned in his stead"!

The surviving President was even more affected when he took his seat in the family pew at the old church the next Sunday. Here was the scene of the earliest devotions of his childhood. The memory of his father and mother, of their tender and affectionate care for him, of the times of peril in which they lived, their hopes and fears for their country, welled up into his mind and heart. His eyes flooded with tears. He looked around the church. Where were they with whom he used to meet in bygone days; where were the snows of yesteryear? Mr. Wibird, the minister who had baptized him, the deacons whom he remembered, the old folks of that time, they were all gone. Those who were then middle-aged had followed their elders to the grave. Five or six persons who had been children like himself during the American Revolution, now with their gray hairs and furrowed cheeks, sat in the house of worship, two or three of them with their families of a succeeding generation. It was another race of men who filled the church fifty years after the Declaration of Independence.

When the next Sunday President Kirkland came over from Harvard to preach a sermon in memory of John Adams, and made some direct references to mother Abigail, John Quincy Adams felt his heart would burst: he had never known that human speech could so affect a man.

For nearly two centuries his fathers had belonged to this congregation, this brotherhood, now the Unitarian Church of Quincy. He himself had never become a member. The tumult of the world, a sense of his own unworthiness to participate in communion, continual residence elsewhere, all this changing about had made him keep putting off joining the church. Now that he was resolved to return at the end of his public service and be gathered to his fathers here in his home town, he decided to join formally, and informed Mr. Whitney of his desire to make public profession of his

faith and hope as a Christian. On October 1 the pastor asked each of
those present who wished to express a belief in the divine mission of
Christ, and who had a fixed purpose to live according to the rules of his
gospel, to rise. One by one they stood up, including the President. Mr.
Whitney then proceeded with the solemnity of communion. John Quincy
Adams had become a professed Christian.[54]

During the month of August he attended numerous memorial services
in honor of John Adams and Thomas Jefferson: Edward Everett spoke at
Charlestown; Horace Mann discoursed at Dedham; the Reverend Mr.
Storrs at Braintree; Samuel L. Knapp held forth to a public gathering at
Chauncey Place, in Boston; Joseph E. Sprague of Salem spoke at the Old
North Church; and Daniel Webster gave a notable oration in Fanueil
Hall lasting two hours and a half, during which everybody sat mute.[55]
The orator's rhythmic eloquence rolled melodiously through columns and
arches draped for the first time in mourning black: "The tears which flow,
and the honors that are paid, when the founders of the Republic die, give
hope that the Republic itself may be immortal." [56]

Other orators all over the land did justice to the two fathers of American independence. The most lasting words of memorial to the second President of the United States and his famous spouse are on the tablet in
honor of John and Abigail Adams which his son the sixth President later
caused to be affixed to the wall of the new church in Quincy at the right
of the pulpit under a bust of the patriot by Horatio Greenough.[57]

John Adams's will left his eldest son the Mansion House in Quincy and
103 acres of land attached to it along the Plymouth-Boston road, on condition that John Quincy Adams pay into the estate the sum of $12,000; [58]
and his family pictures, papers, letters, manuscripts, and library of books
(some of which were in trust for the town of Quincy), providing that
John Quincy pay to his brother Thomas Boylston Adams one half the
value of the library. Eight acres across the main road were detached and
left to the town—as sites for a new Church Temple and a Classical School
to be built from benefactions already made by the testator.[59] The estate
was then divided into fourteen parts to be distributed equally to John
Adams's two sons, his eleven grandchildren, and one niece, Louisa Catherine Smith,[60] who had been brought up in the family. The portion that
each received of the estate as finally liquidated amounted to about $3,000.

[54] *Memoirs*, VII, 147–9.

[55] The circumstances of John Adams's death and details of the various memorial
services are recounted at length in *Memoirs*, VII, 124–50.

[56] *The Works of Daniel Webster* (11th edition; Boston, 1858), I, 113.

[57] See reproduction of inscription at end of this chapter.

[58] $10,000 for the house and land, and $1,000 each for two designated "rocky
pastures."

[59] See pp. 188–9, below.

[60] She was a daughter of Abigail Adams's brother William. The dates of her life
were 1773–1857.

Thomas Boylston Adams's portion and those of his children were to be held in trust by the executors, Josiah Quincy and John Quincy Adams, until the children came of age.[61]

President Adams decided to take up the option on the place where he had passed the happiest years of his life. He had to go in debt to do it, but he had three years in which to pay the money, with interest, to the estate. Soon he went much further into debt to purchase all the other lands that had belonged to his father.[62] He planned to come to the old home as a place of retirement, a safe and pleasant retreat, at least in the summer, where he could pursue his literary occupations as long and as much as he pleased.

It was a weary retreat back to the labors of Washington. On the 6th of October 1826 he left the dwelling-house where his father had resided principally for forty years, and altogether for the last twenty-five. He departed with the "anxious and consoling hope" of returning within three short years to occupy it for the rest of his allotted time in exercises of filial reverence and affection, of usefulness to his children, of benevolence to the neighborhood of his own and his father's nativity, and of ultimate improvement of the condition of his country. Among other things he hoped to prepare a biography of his father, and to write, as Cicero had planned to do in his old age, a history of the Republic. He would do this as soon as his tour of duty in the White House was over. He had no real expectation of being elected for a second term.

8

The years of the Presidency were burdensome to Mrs. Adams, and her troubles added to those of her husband and children. Entering the White House meant for her a change of life in more ways than one, a long period of ill health and increasing melancholy. After the first year she no longer accompanied her husband on his annual trips north, but visited his relatives in New York State on separate trips of her own. She withdrew more and more from people and dwelt in the White House a melancholy invalid mournfully reviewing her life and marriage.

The union with John Quincy Adams, though one of mutual affection and respect, had not been a first romance for either of them. Each had been in love before, and frustrated: he in his youthful passion for Mary Frazier,[63] she in a girlhood attachment for David Sterrett which she buried secretly in her heart. For her, marriage meant a family, children. For him it meant a surcease from celibacy, an anchorage for his career in a

---

[61] A copy of the will, dated September 19, 1819, in the eighty-fourth year of John Adams's life, is in the Adams MSS. See also *Memoirs*, VII, 130.

[62] See below, p. 191.

[63] Vol. I, 24–5.

JOHN ADAMS, AGED 90

FROM "LIFE MASKS OF NOTED AMERICANS OF 1825"
BY JOHN H. I. BROWERE
COURTESY NEW YORK STATE HISTORICAL ASSOCIATION

MRS. JOHN QUINCY (LOUISA JOHNSON) ADAMS

FROM A PORTRAIT ATTRIBUTED TO CHARLES BIRD KING, UNDATED.
PHOTOGRAPH FROM THE ADAMS-CLEMENT COLLECTION IN THE
SMITHSONIAN INSTITUTION

steadier life and responsibilities, a satisfactory and honorable condition of life, the perpetuation of the Adams family and its destiny. He rarely discussed his political ambitions with her, or consulted her. And she continually grieved that she was, as she fancied, a political liability to him.

Their marriage nevertheless had survived its trials and dissensions. They differed greatly in sentiment, taste, personality, in matters of domestic economy. They disagreed, too, about the education of their sons: she inclined to be easygoing, not pressing them on to higher grades and distinctions; he anxious, vigilant, stern, and spurring. Both had frail tempers. He was irascible,[64] by his own confession often harsh; she indulged in female sarcasm, sometimes gratuitously so. He was matter-of-fact and negligent of the niceties of social intercourse; she was romantic, flighty, self-pitying in her invalidism, almost enjoying [65] ill health, sometimes using it to get her way; given to hysterical fainting fits that never failed to bring the family scurrying to her side.[66]

John Quincy Adams adjusted himself with reasonable equanimity and at least outward composure to his personal problems. He knew he had a loving wife, a careful, tender mother if too indulgent, in his eyes, with the children—so he recorded fourteen years outward bound on the marital voyage. Again at the quarter-century mark: "The happiest and most eventful portion of my life is in the lapse of those twenty-five years." [67]

Then followed the term in the White House. Louisa's mind began to roam back to the halcyon years of her parents' family in London, when the young diplomat appeared in his queer Dutch-cut clothes at the Consul's home on Tower Hill, and first admired her elder sister Nancy, a plump, auburn-haired Hebe whose daughter Mary Hellen now lived in the White House and made eyes at Louisa's sons. She recalled John Quincy's strange, almost reluctant courtship in London, how her mother had to speak to the young man about his dalliance. Incidents of their engagement came to mind that revealed an unnecessary harshness of character that from the beginning cast a damp on her natural spirits. Then came the painful, dubious waiting for her betrothed to come back from

[64] "It is a painful thing to state but it is nevertheless the fact," Mrs. Adams admonished her son Charles Francis on the occasion of his engagement to Abigail Brooks, "that as it regards women the Adams family are one and all peculiarly harsh and severe in their characters. There seems to exist no sympathy, no tenderness for the weakness of the sex or for that incapacity of occasional exertion which is a part of their nature arising from the peculiarities of their constitutions. . . ." LCA to CFA, Saratoga, August 19, 1827. Adams MSS.

[65] "I take pleasure in the idea that I am gradually sinking into that state which leads to a happier and better world." LCA to CFA, Washington, March 7, 1828. Adams MSS.

[66] "A more pitiable set I do not think I know than my father and mother," declared the uncharitable Charles Francis Adams to himself, and rejoiced as soon as circumstances made him independent from them. CFA Diary, June 1, 13, 1829. Adams MSS.

[67] *Memoirs*, II, 282–3; VI, 46. July 26, 1811, July 26, 1822.

The Hague to marry her, while her Maryland father, always distrustful of Yankees, urged him on so that he and the rest of the family could remove to America. Before that could take place the Consul failed in business, on the eve of their wedding, a disaster that blasted innocent expectations of a five-thousand-pound dowry. Her father's creditors and former servants beset her honeymoon with their cries and imprecations. It looked to the world, and must have looked to John Quincy Adams, so she had thought ever since, as if her family had tricked him into a marriage. This thought was a lifelong obsession, although her husband never left the slightest word to justify it.

She recalled her gruelling illness as they traveled to Prussia, the recurring physical distresses, the miscarriages, the birth of the first child, George, in the Prussian capital in 1801, the jealous discovery, on the way to America, of her husband's earlier attachment for the beautiful Mary Frazier, now long since married and dead. She remembered the first shocks of the astonishing life and manners of Quincy: the great Noah's Ark of the Adams Mansion, and the strange Yankee friends who frequented it—Dr. Tufts! Deacon French! Mr. Cranch! Old Uncle Peter! and Captain Beale! even the church with its severe formularies and pious people forever snuffling through the nose!

Louisa felt that, except for the "old gentleman," John Adams, she had never fitted into the Adams family nor measured up to their expectations as the wife of a man obviously marked for great deeds of intellectual brightness.[68] There had followed some not unpleasant gossipy months in a home of her own in Boston, where her second boy, John, was born and named for his patriot grandfather. Then came the years when John Quincy Adams was Senator and they lived in Washington with her sister Nancy and her husband, Walter Hellen—Nancy too was dead these many years and Walter married again, to Louisa's youngest sister, Adelaide, who also had left him a widower; the return of the Adamses to Boston and Cambridge, and the birth of her last baby, Charles Francis, darling of her later motherhood; diplomatic stations in St. Petersburg, the death of her babe there, her only daughter; Ghent, London, including the long sledge ride with young Charles across Europe from St. Petersburg to Paris on the eve of Napoleon's Hundred Days; long years once more in Washington when her husband served as Secretary of State, his life more and more absorbed in diplomacy and politics, until those occupations seemed all there was left to it. The man's untiring ambition, spurred on by his parents, to be President. His dreadful restraint towards those closest to him.[69] And now life in the President's House, the hateful social duties, the pressure of politics, the great cases of books stacked in her hus-

[68] "Adventures of a Nobody," written by LCA to CFA, Washington, July 1, 1840. Adams MSS.

[69] Fragment of a Journal in LCA's handwriting, St. Petersburg, August 14 [1812]. Adams MSS.

band's chamber that made her so low-spirited and uncomfortable every time she had to walk past them.[70] Louisa could not escape the clutch of gloomy thoughts that pursued her like phantoms through the shadows of the White House and lurked behind her as she looked out over the sunny Potomac. She came to regret her marriage, and sat down to write a history of its failure for the edification of her sons after she should leave this world of troubles and self-torment.[71]

9

A major anxiety to both the President and Mrs. Adams during these difficult years was the unstable health and conduct of their eldest son, George, who took after his mother more than his father. When he was eight his parents had left George Washington Adams and his brother John, two years younger, in the board and care of uncles and aunts in Massachusetts, under the general supervision of his patriot grandparents, while they went on the long diplomatic mission to Russia. George was a boy of gentle disposition, starved for love and understanding. Experiences of human affection would send him into transports of joy; indifference would throw him into the depths of dejection. He reveled in romantic fiction, particularly Walter Scott, enjoyed amidst the delightful scenes of nature that surrounded Mount Monadnock. In macabre balance to these joys of youth he developed a singular taste for mental excitement that

[70] LCA to CFA, Washington, September 16, 1827. Adams MSS.

[71] MS. "Story of My Life." This morbid document, commenced in July 1825, never got beyond the period of the residence in Prussia. The last sentence reads: "At this time I heard of Mr. Adams's attachment to Miss Frazer [*sic*], and I had another cause added to the misfortunes for regretting the marriage. I had made [it] as it appeared impossible for him to view me in any other light than as a person who had known all these impediments [her father's impending failure] and who determined for the sake of what is called a settlement to marry him at the expence of honour, truth and happiness." Adams MSS.

These putative impediments over which Louisa began to brood in 1825 must have been ancient history in their married life. John Quincy Adams never seems to have made anything of them, or even mentioned them himself. They are not reflected in an extensive journal on family, social, and political happenings which Louisa kept from time to time during the years 1820–4 and sent largely to her father-in-law, John Adams, for his perusal. The later (1840) retrospective manuscript "Adventures of a Nobody" represents her husband as a man of "fine qualities, easy temper, quiet home habits and indefatigable power of application." It looks as though at this critical period of her life from forty-nine to fifty-four years of age, which coincided with the years in the White House, Mrs. Adams in a wave of melancholy and self-pity reverted back over the more normally balanced portion of her married life and its problems to the less complicated felicities of her girlhood.

The historian Henry Adams compiled from Louisa Catherine (Johnson) Adams's journals, autobiographical fragments, and letters a somewhat expurgated digest of her life. This unique account, copied down in Henry Adams's copper-plate hand, is now in Houghton Library of Harvard University, bound under the gilt-lettered title: "Biographical Notes on Louisa Johnson Adams."

called up the most painful impressions and shook the inmost feelings, and for narratives of crime, tales of terrible depravity, mysterious horror, and supernatural power.[72]

At twelve he discovered Shakespeare: "key to all future literary enjoyment." Four years later the two brothers joined the family in England, where John Quincy Adams was Minister to the Court of St. James's. George went to Dr. Nicholas's private school at Ealing and prepared for Harvard under his father's tutelage. All the while he read drama and poetry, including fifteen volumes of the *Bibliothèque du Théâtre Français*, with the works of Corneille and Racine. He began to scribble poems and dramas. A visit to the Continent and the Paris theaters further fired his passion for poetry and plays. A fragmentary letterbook for a few weeks in 1817 reveals an adolescent freshman at Harvard speedily recovering from a stately case of puppy love after a dream in which the stern and forbidding visage of his father appeared behind his beloved and he heard the words: "Remember, George, who you are, what you are doing!" [73]

At Harvard he got a more disciplined education in the classics and went in for dramatics.[74] In his third year he participated normally enough in the great student riot of 1819, convinced that he was gloriously resisting tyranny like his grandfather in 1776.[75] In competition for the Boylston Prize he won first place over Ralph Waldo Emerson. As a young lawyer in Boston, after studying in Daniel Webster's office, he planned to write a great work on poetic literature, and mapped out time for readings.[76] He delivered, in the tradition of his fathers, the Fourth-of-July oration to the townspeople of Quincy, where he had spent so many months with his grandparents—this was in 1824, while John Adams was still living.[77] But his inner conflicts produced such irresolution as to destroy all discipline for either work or play. Clients steered shy of the dreamy youth.[78]

On visits to Washington, George fell in love with his coquettish cousin Mary Hellen in the White House. They became engaged, expecting to wait five or six years until his prospects would warrant marriage;[79] but she cooled off right away when he wrote her from Boston only once a month.[80] His brother John, on the spot as his father's private secretary,

[72] Autobiographical fragment by GWA in January 1826. Adams MSS. See below, p. 183, n. 27.

[73] GWA to Thomas O. Bracket, Quincy, September 25, 1817. Adams MSS.

[74] Minutes of an abortive Dramatic Club at Harvard. Letterbook of GWA, September–October, 1817. Adams MSS.

[75] Harriet Welsh to LCA, Boston, January 16, 1819. Adams MSS.

[76] Notebook of Compositions by GWA. Adams MSS.

[77] George Washington Adams: *An Oration Delivered at Quincy, on the Fifth of July, 1824* (Boston, 1824).

[78] Letters of CFA to LCA. Adams MSS.

[79] Diary of JQA, July 30, 1823.

[80] Diary of CFA, August 10, 1829. Adams MSS.

soon replaced him. After this his cousin Abigail Adams of Quincy delighted his soul in moments of conversation, but she would have nothing seriously to do with him, nor would any of the eligible young ladies of Boston. The disillusioned young lawyer and poet was now ecstatically happy, now deep in the blues,[81] languishing in health and resolution.

In the summer of 1827 George's debilitated condition brought him down with an abscess and fever. His mother threw off her own ills and journeyed as fast as she could from Washington to his bedside. With her affection and nursing he quickly revived: "the same old exaggerated conceited timid enthusiastic negligent cold and eccentric being that he has been ever since he was born." But it was evident that he was in badly run-down condition, in spirit as well as body. He seemed to be ashamed of his nervous irritability, mortified at his personal shortcomings, apprehensive of censure, "constantly acting like one divested of understanding." [82] Old Dr. Welsh and the family friend Mr. Ward Boylston felt strongly that he should be relieved of all cares and business.

Louisa wrote her husband, about to set forth for Quincy and Boston, concerning the young man's serious condition. "You must not appear to know anything of what I have written," she warned, "for I verily believe that it would deprive him of his reason, if he thought I had done so." Among other larger worries George feared his father might not approve the political opinions he was forming. She reminded the President that their son had reached a period in life when he was certainly in every respect his own master. "Our influence can only be obtained by kindness blended with firmness to prevent his taking some rash step which may destroy all his future prospects." [83] Yet she continued herself to write and warn the young man.

When John Quincy Adams got to Boston on his annual vacation, he went thoroughly into George's tangled affairs, tried to be a companion, loaned him money to pay off his debts, once more extracted promises, still hoped for the best.[84] Returned to Washington after a few weeks, he directed to his errant son a steady stream of exhortation, admonition, prodding, and advice: programs for self-discipline, early rising, hard work. Keep busy all day, he urged. Be temperate. Take regular exercise. Chew tobacco to tone the stomach. Observe the Sabbath; it will improve both the mind and the heart. Hold to a program of reading. Keep a diary; it is the "time-piece of life," a "second conscience." He even insisted that George send sample stretches of diary to Washington, and sent Presiden-

[81] GWA to LCA, July 19, 1825. Adams MSS.

[82] LCA to JQA, Boston, July 6, 1827. Adams MSS.

[83] LCA to JQA, New York, July 26, 1827. Adams MSS. George had accompanied his mother as far as New York City on her return to Washington.

[84] "George's health is as it was, and is likely to be—depending entirely upon himself. He is to me dutiful and affectionate, and wants nothing but a firm purpose to be all that I could wish." JQA to LCA, Lebanon. Boston, September 4, 1827. Adams MSS.

tial samples in return.[85] The mother also tried to reach him with her advice through letters directed to his younger brother.

The more the President tried to impose self-discipline on his irresponsible son, and the more the mother pleaded with him for his remissness, the more ashamed George became of his relapses, the less he wanted to see of his loving parents, either one of whom would have died to save him.

The attachment of John Adams, 2d, and Mary Hellen could not be staved off, though the President at first refused his consent if only because the son was in no position to support a wife. The wedding in the White House was quiet and relatively private, February 25, 1828.[86] The last addition to the White House family was a much cherished granddaughter, born December 2, 1828, and christened Mary Louisa.

10

Mrs. Adams's precarious health, the problems of the boys, and the political worries and vicissitudes of the day, together with the climate and heat of Washington combined to make Adams an unhappy President much of the time. They fretted his health, they wore down his spirits. Even the printed portions of the Diary—the *Memoirs*—give enough testimony of increasing melancholy. After the Opposition had captured both houses of Congress, he began to lay his plans for retirement to Quincy to lead the quiet life of a frugal gentleman farmer and American scholar and historian. Only two years more to wait! "My own career is closed. My hopes such as are left me, are centered upon my children." [87]

He developed all manner of small aches, pains, and nervous symptoms. He had soreness and pain in his right side that bothered him when he swam and threatened to bring on deadly cramps.[88] He complained of chronic costiveness, indigestion, catarrh. He could not sleep well. He had no appetite. He couldn't perspire enough in the hot weather, and developed a sort of erysipelas. His spirit flagged. He became skilled in word pictures of his miseries, self-bolstered by the expression of stoic fortitude to ride them out. He dwelt upon his "uncontrollable dejection of spirits, insensibility to the almost unparalleled blessings with which I have been favored; a sluggish carelessness of life, an imaginary wish that it were terminated, with a clinging to it as close as it ever was in the days of most

[85] JQA to GWA, October 28, November 4, 12, 18, 28, December 4, 11, 14, 19, 30, 1827; January 1, 1828. Adams MSS.

[86] Diary, October 18, November 20, 27, 1827; February 25, 1828. See *National Intelligencer*, XXIX, No. 4165, March 1, 1828.

[87] *Memoirs*, VII, 273.

[88] *Memoirs*, VII, 35–8, 302–3.

animated hopes." [89] These were the very symptoms against which he was trying to brace his hypochondriacal son George in distant Boston.

Young Dr. Hunt gave him the standard advice. How many hard-working, anxious men of sixty have heard it from then to now, often from physicians who do not practice what they preach: ease up, take a good long vacation! "Go and pass the remainder of the summer in the North," the good doctor advised the President. "Doff the world aside and bid it pass. Cast off as much as possible all cares public and private. Vegetate yourself into a healthier condition." [90]

Adams grasped readily at such a prescription. An eleven weeks' visit alone to Quincy in 1827 gave him days of "idleness" and "dissipation" at the old homestead. He saw much of his sons and relatives, visited friends, went seabathing, enjoyed excursions, dinners, fishing parties below Boston Light, picnics.[91] He returned to Washington greatly refreshed in body and mind for the "toil and distemper" of his office.[92] But before long he had to steel himself against the most alarming and insidious symptom of all: an aversion to work, to that steady habit of labor with the pen that hitherto had sustained him against all his trials.[93] His mental and physical ailments crept back upon him: "My eyes complain of inflammation, and my heart is sick." "I wrote this evening with a heavy heart." [94]

The state of his mind reflected itself in undue notice of trivial things and seeing in them allegories, signs, symbols, portents. When his chronometer stopped he drew his old moral: Lean not on friendship, nor on time.[95] "The year begins in gloom," he wrote on January 1, 1829. "My wife had a sleepless and painful night. The dawn was overcast, and, as I began to write, *my shaded lamp went out, self-extinguished.*" As the obscure light of day spread itself mournfully through the umbrageous White House chamber, he reached trustfully for his Bible: "May the light of this lamp never forsake me!" [96]

11

From these troubles of mind and heart Adams sought relief and respite by burying himself in the multifarious details and self-imposed minor labors of his office, and in reading the classics. When office visitors and state work had not soaked up his time too much, he read Tacitus, "who always instructs and charms," Plutarch, Cicero, Milton. He exchanged

[89] *Memoirs*, VII, 284, 288, 311.
[90] *Memoirs*, VII, 312.
[91] *Memoirs*, VII, 328.
[92] JQA Diary. September 30, 1827.
[93] *Memoirs*, VII, 339.
[94] *Memoirs*, VII, 457, 501.
[95] *Memoirs*, VII, 346. October 26, 1827.
[96] *Memoirs*, VIII, 89. Italics inserted.

long literary letters with his son Charles. He turned to study and experimentation with horticulture and silviculture. He developed programs of determined physical exercise.

He lengthened the customary early morning walk to the Capitol building around Capitol Square and back. In the shorter days of the year he started before dawn at the cock's crow and returned to the White House in time to see the rising sun from the East Room. Generally the round trip took him an hour and fifteen minutes. He raced with himself for records and got his time down to sixty minutes flat. An alternate brisk morning walk was to College Hill (Georgetown University) and back, about the same distance.

Adams took joy in the simple charms of nature, the rising and setting of the sun, the verdure of the spring and blossoming of the flowers, the song and flight of birds. He loved to leave the White House while it was still dark in order to see the sky brighten and to return with the first dazzling beams of the king of day rejoicing in the east, to pass from the gloom and silence and solitude of night to the brisk and joyous feathered chorus of the morn. Of all the birds his favorite was Chanticleer, the clarion call that echoed and re-echoed in rival vauntings to the dawn, embodiment of vigilance, of generous tenderness and gallantry, of stout fidelity and unconquerable courage. He carried on his finger a signet ring made from a basket seal which his wife gave him, with the figure of a cock upon it and the motto "Watch," closing word of the thirteenth chapter of St. Mark's Gospel.[97]

In the last year of the Presidency, Adams varied his walking with horseback-riding about the District, as much as twelve or fourteen miles at a time. When he set forth on his trip to Quincy in 1828, after some lapse from this exercise, he and his son John brought along saddle horses as well as a coach. They took turns at riding both on the way to Massachusetts and return, with proper benefit.

There was no swimming pool in the White House then, but there was the broad and still clean Potomac. In the morning just before sunrise, John Quincy Adams, in warm weather clad in pea-jacket and pantaloons, towel in hand,[98] would make his way rapidly down Seventeenth Street across the Tiber to the big rock by the sycamore tree on the riverbank. Stripped to his birthday suit, the President would dive off, come up spouting water into the first slanting rays of the summer sun, thrash out and play about like a porpoise. Nobody was there to watch him frisk in the river at that time of day, any more than to see him rounding Capitol Square before sunrise in the winter air.

Not even a mischievous urchin was abroad at that hour to tie up his

[97] JQA to CFA, Washington, December 31, 1827; JQA to GWA, Washington, December 19, 1827, May 30, 1828. See title page and front binding stamp of this volume.

[98] *Autobiography of Thurlow Weed,* p. 179.

clothes. There seems to be no support for the legend that the unbashful journalist, that female pest Anne Royall, got up early one summer morning, shadowed the President down to the river, sat on his clothes, and would not go away until he promised her an interview!

He was a strong swimmer. The summer before his election he swam the Potomac in one hour where it was a mile wide. He was then fifty-eight. What biographer could do it at the same age? Adams prepared to swim across the river again at the same place on June 13, 1825 with his son John, accompanied by his valet, Antoine Giusta. They planned to cross in an old boat and swim back with Antoine following them. John thought the craft too leaky, not very safe. He undressed at the rock, saying that he would wait and swim out to meet his father and the servant halfway when they came back.

The boat looked all right to the President; he did not inspect it carefully. He gave his watch to John to keep on dry land, took off his shoes, made a bundle of his coat and waistcoat, stepped into the craft and pushed off. Antoine, completely stripped, did the paddling. Before they had got halfway across, the boat leaked itself half full, and they had nothing with which to bail it out. At midstream a squall suddenly came upon them downriver from the northwest, blowing like a huge bellows. The boat began to dance about dangerously, and waves to come over the gunwales. The President jumped overboard, followed by Antoine. The boat filled up and drifted out of reach. The two men struck out for the opposite shore. Antoine managed it easily, but the loose sleeves of John Quincy Adams's shirt filled out with water and pulled him down like fifty-pound weights. Gasping and struggling, he finally got ashore. On the way he handed his hat to the unencumbered Antoine, who faithfully took it to safety.

The President wrung out his shirt and pantaloons, and waited for John to swim across the river. Then they basked naked in the sun by the riverbank while Antoine somehow managed to clothe himself enough to go back over the Long Bridge and pick up the watch and surviving clothes and summon a horse and carriage to fetch President and son from the Virginia side. They finally got home, half dressed, after being away for five hours and a half. Nobody seems to have missed them. He listed his losses of personal apparel: one old summer coat, one white waistcoat, two napkins, two white handkerchiefs, and one shoe.[99]

The accident warned him to be more careful in the future. He decided to cut out stunts, but not his morning baths. He kept up his swimming whenever in Washington, until well over seventy years old. No trained lifeguards watched the President as he swam at dawn. No bodyguard, not even a secret-service man, accompanied him as he went to and fro about the Capital City whatever the hour of day or night. He frequently

[99] *Memoirs*, VII, 27–9.

walked home alone from church or from a meeting of the Columbian Institute, sometimes late in the evening.

On the White House grounds was a considerable vegetable garden with fruit trees and berries, and an experienced gardener, Owsley by name, to care for them. The President began to take great personal interest in the vegetables, berries, and fruits. Their shapes and colors delighted him through all the growing seasons of the year: plums that flowered with balls of snow, the pink peach bloom, "Owsley's double-blossom peaches," white jonquils and blue periwinkles; marjoram, mint, sage, tansy, and tarragon; the esculent vegetables with their blossoms—deep-red-colored beet, white-flowered carrot, and yellow parsnip, horse-radish with its enormous green leaves, Jerusalem artichoke, tall and slender-stemmed. Rue, sage, and hyssop he watched coming into bloom, the red and black currants heavily ripening, the blossoming flowers of Holyoke's bladder senna, and the beautiful petals of the flowering catalpas floating over a garden border of colorful thyme.

Strolling in the White House gardens the President ruminated in tranquillity over honeybees in the poppy flowers and wasps in the wormwood.[100] Even the weeds pleased him: shepherd's-purse, the lamium or archangel plant that covered the ground, and the self-planted wild cherries. Pleasure in these growing things tempted him to give up his walks abroad for exercise, tedious and irksome, in order to indulge the more in attractions of the garden.

Delight in the White House garden led him to appreciate the joys of trees and shrubs in his walks and horseback rides about the city. He observed the approach of spring in Capitol Square: oval cups opening into leaves at the ends of fresh twigs of the horse-chestnut trees, showing heads of white blossoms on snowy medlars; the roseate hue of bursting peach blossom; the scarlet maple disclosing its first leaves; the rusty hue of cedar; and claw-pointed leaves of holly taking on new gloss.[101]

With the plants he suffered the adversities of nature: hailstorms which broke and lacerated so cruelly the tender leaves of young sprouts, withering heat of the sun, and devouring insects, all so merciless to the infancy of shoots as delicate as that of new-born animals; trees wounded by storm and lightning; the hard bite of late spring frost.[102]

A resolution of the House of Representatives in 1826 looking toward the cultivation of mulberry trees for silkworms and the domestic manufacture of silk quickened Adams's interest in silviculture and led him to embark upon a new and congenial hobby: the domestication of wild trees and shrubs. It quickly took the place of his former interest in weights and measures that had furnished such an important contribution to the history

[100] *Memoirs*, VII, 288–93, 489–91.
[101] *Memoirs*, VII, 488.
[102] *Memoirs*, VII, 529; VIII, 23.

of American science. The White House grounds were big enough for his purposes. He added seedling beds to the vegetable and flower gardens until the whole took up all of two acres. In his excursions about the District and his trips back and forth to Massachusetts he collected acorns, nuts, seeds, vines, and shoots; others were gifts from friends at home or abroad. These he planted with his own hands and nursed with Owsley's aid; oaks of all sorts, including Spanish cork; walnuts; shagbark, black, and pignut; persimmons, willows, tulip trees, chestnuts and catalpas, honey locusts. Added to the wild things were all kinds of domestic fruit: apples, pears, cherries red and wild, peaches, apricots, plums—the best fruit garden in Washington.

Around the garden he planted a border of oaks, hoping the grown trees would outlast many succeeding Presidents. He charted the seedling beds. He watched for them to sprout. He measured their growth fondly. He started nurseries in Quincy and urged his sons George and Charles to carry on after him. He consulted London's *Encyclopedia of Gardens* and studiously read the horticultural treatises of the French botanists Duhamel and Michaux—the latter had an expert knowledge of North American flora and silva. Almost desperately he studied the natural history of trees and the domestication of exotics. It sustained his enervated health and braced his wilting spirits.[103]

Plants and trees gave him some peace of mind, but his White House hobby was less of a help to science than his earlier interests in weights and measures.[104] Nevertheless his conclusion that some wild things seemed to do better in their native habitat than under domestic cultivation meets the approval of modern mycologists. He did succeed in establishing by wide construction of an enabling act of Congress, and at small expense, a government plantation of 30,000 acres at Santa Rosa, near the Pensacola Naval Station, in Florida; set out with 100,000 live-oak trees for future naval shipbuilding; but the Jackson regime that succeeded him abandoned it in the name of retrenchment and reform, just as it began to flourish. Its history affords an interesting precedent for government forestry.[105]

12

The President was seated at his writing-table one Sunday evening in March 1828. Suddenly the board began to shake under his hand, the floor to tremble beneath his feet, the window sash and shutters to rattle before him. The room felt like a steamboat in motion. There was a sensation of heaving like the moment before the lurch of a ship at sea. It lasted about two minutes. He recognized it for an earthquake. People felt it simultane-

---

[103] *Memoirs*, VII, 290–1.

[104] See Vol. I, 258–9.

[105] Jenks Cameron gives it an early chapter in *The Development of Government Forest Control in the United States* (Baltimore, 1928).

ously in western New York, in Pennsylvania from Philadelphia to Pittsburgh, in Virginia from Richmond to the Shenandoah Valley, and on
westward to Lexington, Kentucky. Adams had never experienced the
phenomenon. He paused in his writing to see how it felt: "The Agitation
of the Moment might have been animated with hope, or appalled by fear,
according to the humour in which it found me. I did reflect that the spot
upon which I was seated was peculiarly adapted to Earthquakes, and I
said to myself:

> 'If Storms and Earthquakes mar not Heaven's design
> Why then a Borgia or a Catiline?' [106]

Was it another sign, another portent? The Borgias and the Catilines
were abroad in the land. The spot where he sat, and the whole frontier
West through which the disturbance noisily rumbled and shook, were indeed susceptible to earthquakes of more kinds than one. All through that
region and to the south there was a political heaving to be noticed everywhere, the moment before the anticipated lurch of the Ship of State
that would throw John Quincy Adams out of the White House. The Presidential campaign was already under way. From the Mississippi to the Sus-
quehanna the earth was shaking under the tramping cohorts of General
Andrew Jackson.

[106] JQA to GWA, Washington, March 12, 1828. *Memoirs,* VII, 471. *National Journal,* VI, No. 3176, March 22, 1828.

The memorial tablet to John and Abigail Adams on the wall of the church at Quincy, to the right hand of the pulpit and in front of John Quincy Adams's pew, reads as follows:

LIBERTATEM AMICITIAM FIDEM RETINEBIS

D. O. M.

Beneath these Walls
Are deposited the Mortal Remains of

JOHN ADAMS,

Son of John and Susanna [Boylston] Adams,
Second President of the United States.

Born $\frac{19}{30}$ October 1735.

On the fourth of July 1776
He pledged his Life, Fortune and Sacred Honour
To the INDEPENDENCE OF HIS COUNTRY.
On the third of September 1783
He affixed his Seal to the definitive treaty with Great Britain
Which acknowledged that Independence,
And consummated the Redemption of his Pledge.
On the fourth of July 1826
He was summoned
To the Independence of Immortality,
And to the JUDGMENT OF HIS GOD.
This House will bear witness to his Piety:
This Town, his Birth-Place, to his Munificence:
History to his Patriotism:
Posterity to the Depth and Compass of his Mind.

At his Side
Sleeps till the Trump shall Sound

ABIGAIL,

His beloved and only Wife,
Daughter of William and Elizabeth [Quincy] Smith.
In every Relation of Life a Pattern
Of Filial, Conjugal, Maternal and Social Virtue.
Born November 8 1744,
Deceased 28 October 1818,
Aged 74.

Married 25 October 1764.
During an Union of more than Half a Century
They survived, in Harmony of Sentiment, Principle and Affection
The Tempests of Civil Commotion;
Meeting undaunted, and surmounting
The Terrors and Trials of that Revolution
Which secured the Freedom of their Country;
Improved the Condition of their Times;
And brightened the Prospects of Futurity
To the Race of Man upon Earth.

PILGRIM,

From Lives thus spent thy earthly Duties learn;
From Fancy's Dreams to active Virtue turn:
Let Freedom, Friendship, Faith, thy Soul engage,
And serve like them thy Country and thy Age.

CHAPTER VII

The Triumph of Andrew Jackson
(1825–1829)

The next election yet depends upon the chapter of
accidents; but behind that is a wise, unerring hand.

DIARY OF JOHN QUINCY ADAMS,
NOVEMBER 6, 1826 [1]

LONG before the election of 1828 the Presidential Question, as it was universally referred to, had narrowed to a choice between John Quincy Adams, Minority President, and General Andrew Jackson, the Hero of New Orleans. It was still a contest of men, for Jackson had not taken direct issue with President Adams over any of the measures which the Opposition had attacked in Congress, not even the American System, or state rights. Back of Jackson was a group of new men on the make, who aspired to shoulder the established élite out of their old aristocracy of status and wealth that had given a patrician leadership to public thought and action.[2] They wanted to elect a man in order to fashion a party under their control. The current social malaise, rather than any real revolutionary tension, would assist them to stir up new winds [3] to help them on their way. The man would come first; after that they would make the issues.

It was like Roosevelt a hundred years later. Once elected, Jackson in his century, like Roosevelt in his, would promptly take the politicians in tow. Those Presidents themselves raised the issues; they took their own

---

[1] *Memoirs*, VII, 171.

[2] Merle Curti: *The Growth of American Thought* (New York, 1943), pp. 213–92.

[3] Carl Russell Fish: *Rise of the Common Man, 1830–1850. A History of American Life*, VI (New York, 1929). See also Arthur B. Darling: "Jacksonian Democracy in Massachusetts, 1824–1848," *AHR*, XXIX (No. 2, January 1924), 271–87.

"The literature of Jacksonian democracy abounds in epithets but is lacking in philosophy." Herbert W. Schneider: *A History of American Philosophy* (New York, 1946), p. 117. A considerable amount of anthological or semi-anthological publication recently displays a contemporary drift of theory of have-nots opposed to haves, but does little to explain the political combination that brought Jackson into the White House in 1829. See, for example, Joseph Dorfman: *The Economic Mind in American Civilization, 1606–1865* (2 vols., New York, 1946), II, 601–95, and Joseph L. Blau, ed.: *Social Theories of Jacksonian Democracy, Representative Writings of the Period 1825–1850* (New York, 1947).

Richard H. Brown's study, "Southern Planters and Plain Republicans of the North: Martin Van Buren's Formula for National Politics" (Yale Ph.D. thesis, 1955) is the best political analysis of the election of Andrew Jackson to the Presidency.

places in history, and we must not judge them altogether by their lack of political tenets before election.[4] Thus did Andrew Jackson and Franklin D. Roosevelt supplant John Quincy Adams and Herbert Hoover to become dynamic national figures. Thus did an old political and social élite give way, in each instance, to a new leadership.

Behind the rivalry of men and élites there was an unspoken issue which made the election of 1828 also a sectional contest.

1

Jackson's principles, so far as known, had not varied notably from those of Adams. His discreet sympathies for the patriotic Federalists—as distinct from the Hartford Convention Federalists—were as strong as Adams's.[5] At no time so far had Andrew Jackson stood forth as a champion of the underprivileged. He was himself a rich cotton-planter. In Tennessee politics he had been a friend to creditor rather than to debtor interests, a supporter of sound money, an opponent of stay laws or relief legislation. On the larger scene, whether at New Orleans in 1815, or in the later Indian campaigns of the Southwest, or in the United States Senate in Washington, he was an ardent nationalist rather than a champion of state rights, a continental expansionist like his early admirer John Quincy Adams. All over the nation he appealed to fellow citizens, many of them recently enfranchised by white manhood suffrage, not as spokesman of the common man so much as a virile example of the self-made man, a personal revelation of the possibilities of democracy in America.

Master strategist for the Jackson group was Martin Van Buren of New York. His ambition was to take the place of the nationalist Calhoun as heir presumptive to Jackson in 1833. His first stratagem was to line up the slavery capitalists of the South with Republican apostles of democracy of the Middle States in the name of state rights behind Andrew Jackson as their bellwether. A strange alliance for slaveholders and conservators of the *status quo* who feared Liberty with Power! For at heart Van Buren was a political reformer, secretly opposed to slavery like John Quincy Adams. But the South would not find that out till later.

Adams was quick to recognize the "wise, unerring hand" (of Van Buren) that pulled the wires behind the scenes.

Tacticians of the new combination were the politicians in Congress; the shocktroopers before the people were journalists and pamphleteers. Among them were Senators John H. Eaton and Hugh L. White of the General's native state; Major W. B. Lewis and Judge John Overton, also

[4] Along this line of thought, compare Arthur M. Schlesinger, Jr.: *The Age of Jackson* (Boston, 1945), pp. 17, 43.

[5] James Parton: *Life of Andrew Jackson* (New York, 1861), III, 134. See also Jackson to James Monroe, January 6, March 4, 1817. Bassett: *Correspondence of Jackson*, II, 272–3, 277–82.

of Tennessee; literary polemicists such as Francis P. Blair of Kentucky
and Henry Clay's former friend Amos Kendall, Massachusetts-born editor of the Frankfort *Argus of the West;* and Senator Thomas Hart Benton of Missouri, Jackson's quondam adversary and Adams's long-standing
opponent. In the East were political aspirants like James Buchanan of
Pennsylvania, David Henshaw, the Boston druggist and banker, and Isaac
Hill, editor of the *New Hampshire Patriot* of Concord. Their mission in
the long campaign was to attack and discredit the President in every possible way, not excluding his person and character. Early in his Administration he began to feel their slings and arrows.

2

It is a sorrowful task for biographers of John Quincy Adams and Andrew Jackson to record the personal break that took place between the
two great Americans following Adams's election by the House of Representatives.

Adams had always admired the General. He esteemed him as a fellow
continentalist. He had defended him at home and abroad for his vigorous
action during the incursion into Florida in 1818. He had applauded him
as a national hero. In his own home he had feted him in 1824 at a grand
ball on the anniversary of the Battle of New Orleans.

Jackson, too, had a high respect for Adams as an able, honest, and virtuous man. He had been the first to step forward and grasp his successful
rival's hand at the inauguration. But after that the two saw no more of
each other. Jackson later explained that when Clay's appointment confirmed rumors of corruption and bargain he withdrew from all personal
intercourse with Mr. Adams.[6] It is likely that the estrangement developed
more gradually, because Jackson departed for Tennessee soon after the
installation of the new Administration and did not return to Washington
for four years. At any rate, the two never had anything to do with each
other personally after March 1825.

Jackson's disappointment in the election vented itself more on Henry
Clay, "Judas of the West," than it did on Adams. Clay's campaign description of Jackson as a "military chieftain" had nettled the General. Already before the appointment of the new Secretary of State, Jackson had
begun to resent this "political gambler," who, so he believed, had cheated
the people, and Jackson himself, out of the election. In a private letter,
published just before the Senate's vote on Clay's confirmation, the Old
Hero proudly acquitted himself in his military character, and went on to
say, tellingly, that no one had ever beheld *him* seeking through art or
management to entice any representative in Congress from a conscientious responsibility to the wishes of his constituents: "No midnight taper

    [6] Jackson to Major Henry Lee, Hermitage, October 7, 1825. Bassett: *Correspond-
ence of Jackson,* III, 291–2.

burnt by me; no secret conclaves were held, nor cabals entered into to persuade any one to a violation of pledges given, or of instructions received." [7]

Jackson warmed to this theme as he accepted the shouting plaudits of his admirers along the way home from Washington in the spring of 1825.[8] At Nashville he reminded them that he had never sought the nomination in the first place nor had he intervened in any way to influence the electoral decision of the House of Representatives. In a Fourth-of-July address at Franklin he declared that the high distinction of the Presidency disappeared when it was attained through any other channel than that of the people. This must have touched John Quincy Adams to the quick, for it was just what he himself had believed, before the election—and after the election, too.

In October 1825 the Tennessee legislature again nominated the state's favorite son for the Presidency, to put him before the people long in advance of the election of 1828. Accepting the role, Jackson dramatically resigned his seat in the United States Senate in order, he professed, to be able the more properly to advocate amendments to the Constitution that might be said to benefit him personally in the campaign ahead: such as to place the election more directly in the hands of the people, and to prevent the President from appointing members of Congress (like Henry Clay) to high executive office with corresponding patronage.

Jackson soon convinced himself that there had been a corrupt bargain between Adams and Clay, and that he had proof of it. The proof was, in his distorted memory, that Clay's supporters first made to his friends and to him personally the same offer that later they made to Adams, and that he had refused it. Did this not show their readiness to do business with whoever would pay the price? He began to say as much in private letters and conversations, which inevitably got into print. One Carter Beverley, following a visit to Jackson's home, wrote an anonymous letter reporting the master of the Hermitage to have said to a company of guests: "Mr. Clay's friends made a proposition to my friends that if they would promise for me not to put Mr. Adams into the seat of Secretary of State, Clay and his friends would, in one hour, make me the President." [9]

Duff Green in the *United States' Telegraph* of Washington endorsed the Beverley letter and said Jackson had told him the same thing two years before; he called upon the General to sustain the charge before the people.[10] Clay immediately asserted that General Jackson could never have

[7] Andrew Jackson to Samuel Swartwout, Washington, February 22, May 16, 1825. Published March 12 in *Niles' Weekly Register*, XXVIII, 20–1. Bassett: *Correspondence of Jackson*, III, 278–85.

[8] R. Carlyle Buley: *The Old Northwest: Pioneer Period, 1825–1840* (Indian Historical Society, 1950), II, 160–2.

[9] Reprinted, under Beverley's name, in *Niles' Weekly Register*, XXXII, 162. May 5, 1827. Translated here into the first person.

[10] *United States' Telegraph*, III, No. 827. April 26, 1827.

said any such thing. Who were my friends, asked the Kentuckian, who made such a proposal to the General? Jackson named James Buchanan.[11]

Called upon by Jackson, Buchanan had to explain that he had not been an agent of Clay or any other man: he had acted on his own responsibility. Jackson, he declared, had told him, in response to the suggestion that the General pledge himself not to reappoint Adams as Secretary of State (thus inviting a bargain with Clay), that he thought well of Mr. Adams, but he had never said or intimated that he would, or would not, appoint him Secretary of State, that these were secrets he would keep to himself: "he would conceal them from the very hairs of his head." [12]

The Old Hero had no knowledge of the canons of historical criticism, and for the rest of his life he went about believing that Clay's friends had proposed the bargain to him before they turned to Adams.

The charge of "corruption and bargain" between Adams and Clay would not down, no matter how much Clay denied it.[13] Adams on his part did not dignify it with a reply as long as he remained President; but promptly thereafter, "in the presence of our country and of heaven," he pronounced the charge "totally unfounded." [14] He challenged anyone to name a man better fitted to have been appointed to the office of Secretary of State than Clay, by pre-eminent talents, splendid services, ardent patriotism, all-embracing public spirit, fervid eloquence in behalf of the liberties of mankind, and long experience in the affairs of the Union, foreign and domestic. Clay responded with a grateful letter to Adams for having eradicated forever the calumny. "So far was I [Clay continued], in voting for you as President, from being influenced by any personal or selfish consideration, that I felt and I stated, at the time, that, if I knew and *disapproved* every member of your Cabinet, I should still greatly prefer you to General Jackson. All that I have since seen and known in respect to both of you has tended to strengthen and confirm that preference." [15]

Methinks they did protest too much. There was, as we know, an implicit

[11] Andrew Jackson to Mr. Carter Beverley, June 5, 1827. *Niles' Weekly Register,* XXXII, 317. Henry Clay's speech at Lexington, July 12, 1827, is printed in ibid., XXXII, 375–80, August 4, 1827.

[12] Buchanan's letter to the editor of the *Lancaster* (Pa.) *Journal,* August 8, 1827, was reprinted in *Niles' Weekly Register,* XXXII, 415–16. August 18, 1827. McMaster: *History,* V, 504–10, gives a short cut to these newspaper citations. For correspondence in greater fullness see Bassett: *Correspondence of Jackson,* III, 348–63.

[13] See Clay's "Address to his Constituents," of March 26, 1825; his Lewisburg address of August 30, 1826 on "The Election of 1825"; and his Lexington address of July 12, 1827 on "Bargain and Corruption." *Works of Henry Clay,* Calvin Colton, ed. (New York, 1904), VI, 299–319, 322–5; VII, 341–55.

[14] In a statement dated March 11, 1829, directed to a Committee of Citizens of Essex and Middlesex Counties, New Jersey, acknowledging expressions of respect and regret at the result of the recent election, and extolling Samuel Southard of New Jersey, and other members of his Administration. Printed on satin. Adams MSS.

[15] Clay to JQA, April 16, 1829. Adams MSS.

bargain, a gentleman's agreement, but, we repeat, nothing corrupt, nothing unconstitutional, if nothing to be proud of. Both John Quincy Adams and Henry Clay lived to regret that the appointment had been offered and accepted. The facts, so circumstantial, spoke for themselves: there was Adams in the White House, there was Clay in the Department of State; there was Andrew Jackson left out in the West although he had held a plurality of the people's votes in 1824; and there were those states that had switched from the people's preference at the November polls in 1824 to cast their ballots for John Quincy Adams in the House of Representatives in February 1825.

Adams's appointment of Clay put the Administration on the defensive from the earliest moments of its existence, helped build up an opposition which frustrated the President's national policies, assisted Jackson's election in 1828, and deprived Clay of the cherished Presidency. It altered the course of American politics for a generation.

3

Already the reader has seen, in a previous chapter, the reaction of the rising opposition to President Adams's program of Liberty with Power. While the master strategist Van Buren was aligning his combination of Northern republicans and planters of the South behind Jackson against the nationalist measures of Adams, the political tacticians began to assail the President's front in every possible exposure, always in such a way as to command the greatest popular attention, now that nearly every man—that is, every white man—had the vote. In Congress they kept alive the charge of corruption and bargain by proposing and debating amendments to the Constitution to make it impossible in the future to betray the people's real preference: [16] no second term for President; no appointment of members of Congress to federal office (except judicial) during the terms of their election and for two years thereafter—appointments that Jackson later as President made in profusion. None of these measures could command the two-thirds majority necessary to put them before the state legislatures, but in their crusade for the people's mandate the Jackson men used every parliamentary trick.

They passed resolutions and calls for reports meant to harass the executive departments with exasperating and duplicating labors. To portray Adams as a corrupter of civil service, they brought forth in the Senate (May 1826) the report of a select committee on executive patronage, and six bills pretending to reduce it.[17] It all served the purpose of spectacular political propaganda and helped to elect in 1826, for the first time in American history, a majority in both houses of Congress hostile to the

---

[16] Thomas Hart Benton: *Thirty Years' View*, I, 78–87.
[17] Fish: *Civil Service and the Patronage*, pp. 73–5.

Administration. What Adams had contemned as a faction had now become a real Opposition to the Minority President.

In the new Congress the tacticians transferred their activity back to the House of Representatives. They moved a series of resolutions on Retrenchment and Reform in order to picture the prodigal extravagance of the President and to show up his wanton waste of public funds. John Randolph of Roanoke was parliamentary fugleman of the new maneuver. However eccentric his character and bizarre his habits, the original Old Republican of Virginia was a man of genius, almost as well read in the classics as the President himself, a far greater orator, and a man of political principles quite the opposite of John Quincy Adams's theory of the Constitution and the Union.[18]

After Randolph's extraordinary remarks in the Senate that had led to the duel between him and Clay,[19] the Virginia legislature refused to return him again to that more august chamber, but his constituents of the hustings had elected him to the House. Personally and politically he was Adams's implacable and rancorous enemy. The Nemesis of the South never closed his eyes even for one careless instant to the dreadful implications for his section of the President's concept of Liberty with Power, and internal improvements both physical *and moral.* Nor could he ever forget a fancied humiliation to his family from the Adamses in his youth, when, many years before, John Adams's coachman had snapped his whip over the head of Randolph's half-brother in the streets of Philadelphia as the boy ran up too close to see the Vice President's coach go by.[20]

Randolph began to pitch his shrill attacks on John Quincy Adams the moment the New Englander had assumed national political prominence.

"The cub," he had pronounced, after Adams entered Monroe's Cabinet, "is a greater bear than the old one." When the second Adams became President, Randolph declared: "This is the last four years of the Administration of the father renewed in the person of the son." Randolph exulted in his new opportunity: "I bore some humble part in putting down the dynasty of John the First, and by the Grace of God, I hope to aid in putting down the dynasty of John the Second." He saw his chance to blow the last of the dynasty sky-high: "Yes, Sir, sky-high." Up rose the voice of Mr. Randolph, recorded Adams's friend Josiah Quincy, who heard the speech, "as if to follow Mr. Adams in his aerial flight." [21]

John Quincy Adams hid his appraisal of Randolph in the depths of his Diary and his family correspondence: "the image and superscription of a

[18] Russell Kirk has presented a perspicuous analysis of the political ideas of *Randolph of Roanoke: a Study in Conservative Thought* (Chicago, 1951).

[19] Vol. I, 553.

[20] Henry Adams: *John Randolph* (Boston, 1883), p. 19.

[21] William Cabell Bruce: *John Randolph of Roanoke, 1773–1833* (New York, 1922), I, 507–9, 542–5.

great man stamped upon base metal." [22] Citing a list of famous orators for his son Charles Francis to study: Cicero; Burke, Chatham, Pitt, Canning, in English history; and also, in American history, Ames, Dexter, Bayard, Harper, Wirt, Pinkney, Webster, Clay, he did not fail to include John Randolph of Roanoke, but in these words: "Even in the mind of that fragment physical, moral and intellectual of a man, overspread as it is with stinking weeds and stinging nettles, an occasional sweetbriar shoots up and sheds its fragrance round him. But the metempsycosis is no fable. Surely John Randolph sat for that picture when nineteen hundred years ago Ovid wrote the lines:

'Ghastly pale in face, and thin in frame, . . .
His breast alive with bile, and poison dripping from his tongue.' " [23]

Whipped on by the mad genius of the man of Roanoke, the Opposition sounded and re-sounded the charge of corruption and bargain against the President and Secretary of State, and cried out for Retrenchment and Reform of the corrupt and extravagant Adams Administration. They dwelt on the allegedly vast patronage that these men were building up to perpetuate themselves in power. They took them to task for paying off political supporters with junkets out of the State Department's contingent fund.[24] They accused the President of making West Point a rich man's academy. They said he was a Federalist, that he had never voted for the

---

[22] *Memoirs*, VIII, 64.

[23] JQA to CFA, No. 33, Washington, June 13, 1828. Adams MSS. I have slightly changed the order of the words in the sentence before the last quotation, but certainly not their appositeness or strict sense. The above translation I have provided from the Latin lines quoted by JQA. See *Documents Relating to New England Federalism;* Henry Adams, ed. (Boston, 1905), p. 232. Bruce: *John Randolph of Roanoke,* II, 741, took the trouble to look up the lines and point out what Adams left out, indicated below in brackets:

> Palor sedet in ore; macies [est] in corpore toto,
> [Nusquam recta acies, livent rubigine dentes.]
> [With shifty glance, teeth yellowed with decay;]
> Pectora felle virent: lingua est sufusa veneno.

The first part of the omitted line, notes Bruce, would have fitted Randolph, but not the second.

[24] Daniel P. Cook, lame-duck Congressman who cast Illinois's vote for Adams in the House of Representatives after the state had gone for Jackson in the November elections of 1824, was sent on a secret mission to confer with the Governor General of Cuba, in 1827, about preserving the *status quo* of the island. See Vol. I, 541-2.

Less plausible was the appointment of John Hampden Pleasants, editor of the pro-Adams *Virginia Whig* of Richmond, Virginia, sent as a dispatch-bearer to Buenos Aires via England. He received $1,950, the usual sum. Illness prevented him from completing his errand. He hired a substitute (who delivered the dispatches) and returned from England without ever reaching Buenos Aires. It should be remembered that England was often a way station between South America and the United States, when no direct passage was obtainable. Pleasants had often importuned Adams for money out of the President's own pocket.

Louisiana Purchase;[25] they attacked him in the next breath for being an apostate to the Federalists. They declared he had ceded Texas away to Spain—Henry Clay himself had said so, so had Don Luis de Onís in his *Memoir*. They brought up the old libel that at Ghent he had tried to swap the navigation of the Mississippi for fishing privileges in British North American waters.[26] Some of them called him to account for spending White House appropriations for the old billiard table and the set of chessmen, even though he had corrected his statement of expenses so as to show that he had paid for these out of his own pocket; others, realizing the pettiness of the complaint, ridiculed it as second-hand furniture—too shabby for the Executive Mansion. They went over his old accounts as Minister abroad, long since accepted and settled by President Monroe's Secretary of the Treasury, none other than William H. Crawford. They pictured him, not to mention his father before him, as a lifelong pólitician grown plump at the public crib. They added up all the pay he had ever received from public services from the time he left Boston in 1809 on his mission to Russia until he returned to become Secretary of State in 1817: total, $104,804.76—about $12,500 per year! And they repeated over and over again the canards that their shocktroopers had planted in the public mind.[27] The debates in Congress lent a fierce sanction to the propaganda of the Opposition in pamphlets, newspapers, handbills, stump speeches, down to the dialogues of dramshops, all over the land.

"If, after such an appeal as has been made to the People," concluded Randolph, "and a majority has been brought into this and the other House of Congress, this Administration shall be able to triumph, it will prove that there is a rottenness in our institutions, which ought to render them unworthy of any man's regard." [28]

This was moderate language for John Randolph. He had displayed an unusual decorum since Henry Clay had brought him to account.

4

Whatever the attacks of the Opposition, no serious scholar can doubt that the Government of the United States during the Administration of John Quincy Adams operated on a high plane of civil service and economy. The merit and standards of his appointments contrast with the spoils system which his successor would revive and perfect in the name of Retrenchment and Reform.

[25] Adams arrived in Washington one day too late to vote in favor of the Louisiana treaties. He announced that he would have voted in favor of ratification. He voted for the appropriation for the purchase. He voted against the Louisiana territorial acts pending amendments that he proposed to the Constitution. See Vol. I, 119–21.

[26] See Vol. I, 212–14, 316–24.

[27] *Register of Debates in Congress*, IV (1827–8), Pt. 1, 1064–1458. See particularly p. 1198.

[28] Ibid., p. 1334.

Immediately after his inauguration Adams's friends in various quarters urged him to sweep out all the offices at his disposal and pleasure to make room for his own supporters. A provoking case was that of one Sterret, naval officer at the Port of New Orleans, who planned a public demonstration against the home-coming of William Leigh Brent, the Louisiana member of Congress whose vote had turned the ballot of that state from Jackson to Adams in the election of 1825. Brent begged the President to get rid of this "noisy and clamorous reviler" right away. Clay, too, suggested removal, and advised a general policy.

"With regard to the conduct of persons holding office at the pleasure of the President," urged the new Secretary of State, "the course of the Administration should be to avoid, on the one hand, political persecution, and on the other, an appearance of pusillanimity."

"If I remove Sterret by a mere executive fiat," objected Adams, going into the matter at some length, "he would consider himself injured, and immediately demand the cause of his removal." How the newspapers then would howl up and down the land! "To answer that it is the pleasure of the President would be harsh and odious—*inconsistent with the principle upon which I have commenced this Administration.* . . . And where is it possible to draw the line? Of the custom house officers throughout the Union, four-fifths, in all probability, were opposed to my election. . . . If I depart from this [rule] in one instance, I shall be called upon by my friends to do the same in many. An invidious and inquisitorial scrutiny into the personal dispositions of public officers will creep through the whole Union, and the most selfish and sordid passions will be kindled into activity to distort the conduct and misrepresent the feelings of men whose places may become the prize of slander upon them." [29]

Adams had intervened behind the scenes to get himself elected by the House of Representatives, but he would do nothing to build up a political machine to keep himself in power. He would not even reward his friends. Clay dropped the subject, at least for the time being. He saw that the President was not a practical politician who would appoint only his political friends to office.[30] What could one do for a President like this?

The Four-Year Law governing the tenure of federal office steadily made available numerous government jobs to bestow on those who had worked for Adams's election. But Adams declined to supplant the incumbents when their four-year terms expired with appointments of his own fresh choice. He kept them on unless official or moral misconduct were proved against them. And he did not regard opposition to himself politically as official or moral misconduct. He did not believe in the Four-Year

[29] *Memoirs*, VI, 546–7. Italics inserted.

[30] "I think the principle ought to be adhered to of appointing only friends to office. Such I believe is the general conviction of the Cabinet." J. D. Learned to Henry Clay, April 14, 1827. Florence Weston: *Presidential Election of 1828*, p. 60.

Law, anyway. It had been only a device of Crawford's to gather up patronage.

During his Administration Adams made only twelve actual removals from office,[31] mostly in the customs service and post offices, and all for good reasons of fraud or malfeasance.

Perhaps the most glaring of these cases was that of the collector at Philadelphia, John Steele, who connived with the tottering firm of the China importer Edward Thomson to let a huge consignment of tea out of the customs warehouse before the duty was paid. When Thomson went bankrupt and his private creditors got hold of his tea, the Government lost nearly a million dollars. Richard Bache, the Postmaster at Philadelphia, also became involved in fraud and had to be dismissed. To make it worse, Bache's successor and brother-in-law, Thomas Sergeant,[32] was too close to the Opposition; he did not clear up the delinquencies with promptness and efficiency.

Historians have uniformly attributed to rigid principle John Quincy Adams's refusal to put out his opponents from federal offices and put in his friends. It is true that in his own utterances there is nothing to gainsay this puritan stand, and much to support it: the Diary seems to establish it completely; so also do his personal letters. But we may wonder whether his motives were altogether so quixotic as commonly believed. He may have hoped that good principle would be good politics, too. By the mere art of not removing his rivals' appointees from office he might make them Adams men, looking to him as the Man of the Whole Nation. If this were the Minority President's stratagem, he was a sorely mistaken man. It failed to win over the patronage of his inveterate rivals, and it taxed, almost overtaxed, the loyalty of his own friends.

It was one thing to let civil servants keep their offices even though they were known to be opposed politically to the Administration; it was another matter not to appoint one's friends where new vacancies occurred through resignation, death, or removal for good cause. Adams's attitude in this respect invoked dismay in his own camp. Clay kept calling it to his attention: "The friends of the Administration have to contend not only against their enemies, but against the Administration itself, which leaves its power in the hands of its own enemies."[33] It did not make sense to a politician.

"In this state," wrote an anonymous friend from South Carolina, "the whole influence of the Administration is arrayed against the Administration."[34]

[31] Fish: *Civil Service and the Patronage*, p. 72.

[32] Brother to JQA's trusted friend John Sergeant, one of the two ministers plenipotentiary to the Congress of Panama. See Vol. I, 556–61. McLean, Postmaster General, had recommended Thomas Sergeant's appointment as a mitigation of the loss to Bache himself! *Memoirs*, VII, 509, and index to same. (Vol. XII).

[33] *Memoirs*, VII, 163.

[34] "Amicus" to JQA, Charleston, S.C., August 17, 1826. Adams MSS.

In Pennsylvania, too, friends of the Administration were cooling off. Daniel Webster, on a visit to Philadelphia in the spring of 1827, urged the President to pay more attention to his old friend Robert Walsh, independent editor of the *National Gazette;* and to give a federal judgeship to Joseph Hopkinson.[35] So annoyed was the President by all this "electioneering" that he resolved to bypass Philadelphia altogether on his trip north to Quincy, and only with the greatest of tact was his wife, Louisa, able to persuade him that he owed it to his friends and supporters at least to stop and greet them.[36] The President did appoint his highly qualified friend Hopkinson to a federal judgeship when a vacancy finally occurred in the eastern district of Pennsylvania, but only after the unexceptionable recommendation of Judge Bushrod Washington.[37]

The officious Peter Paul Francis Degrand, Boston broker and politician who had so importunately bespoken Adams's confidence and patronage, suddenly took an interest in Pennsylvania politics. He visited Philadelphia, after his business failure in Boston, and started a new series of political letters to the President. He wanted his friend to appoint him a director of the Bank of the United States, which Adams refused to do if only because Degrand was a broker. "Barnes,[38] Binns,[39] and other friends," pleaded this self-styled tribune of the people, "are amazed at the cold-hearted support, or rather hostility, of your own servants. I am almost tempted to ask the question: who is President of the United States? Is it J. Q. Adams, or is it the deputy-collector at Philadelphia?"[40]

Degrand renewed his plaints and pleas in an interview at Quincy: "Such conduct from the officers of Government toward friends and supporters of the Administration makes it their interest, as individuals, to go over to the enemy."

"Well, Mr. Degrand," the President retorted phlegmatically, "do so."

"No," protested Degrand, "I certainly shall not do so." But he continued to complain about the Philadelphia deputy collector. "An officer disposed to be partial," he explained, "may in many ways favor his friends and annoy his adversaries without coming exactly within the verge of responsible official misconduct."

Adams knew this to be true, but he did not see anything he should do about it. "I cannot dismiss an officer for that which could not be charged to official misconduct; and as to the political preferences of public officers

---

[35] Daniel Webster to JQA, Philadelphia, March 27, 1827. Adams MSS.

[36] LCA to JQA, Boston, July 16, 17, 18, 1827. Adams MSS.

[37] He commissioned Hopkinson in October 1828, just before the Presidential election of that year, and the Opposition Senate confirmed the nomination in March 1829. JQA to Joseph Hopkinson, October 23, 1828, and February 23, 1829. Adams MSS.

[38] Joseph Barnes was Presiding Judge of the Pennsylvania District Court for the City and County of Philadelphia.

[39] John Binns was editor of the Philadelphia *Democratic Press.*

[40] P. P. F. Degrand to JQA, Philadelphia, July 13, September 5, 1827. Adams MSS.

in relation to the Presidency, I can take no cognizance of them." [41] He completely disgusted Degrand [42] by appointing a Jackson man postmaster at Philadelphia the very year of the national election.

The coterie of Adams workers in New York politics got little for their decisive labors in the electoral contest of 1824. Tallmadge, Sterling, Morse, Herttell, Taylor, Thurlow Weed, those who had held the line in Albany against Van Buren's maneuvers for Crawford, all went unrewarded. It has already been noted that when Thurlow Weed called at the White House promptly after the election, the President received him only politely. Joseph Blunt, most enthusiastic and forward of the New York group, also went to Washington and suggested the employment of young men in the party, new blood: he asked nothing for himself, but recommended the appointment of Charles King as Collector for the Port of New York "in the event of a vacancy." [43] The faithful Blunt went home empty-handed, never did get an appointment. Charles King, despite his old friendship with John Quincy Adams's family, and editorship of the pro-Administration *New York American,* didn't get anything either.

In a series of friendly letters during the following months and years Blunt made it clear to the President that he was losing ground in New York by refusing to do anything for his supporters and leaving the impression that only those opposed to him would get any consideration. "The effect of this was to drive your friends into private life or to compel them to conceal their preferences . . . they are losing their spirit, and, I fear, will soon . . . retire altogether from the political arena." [44] Adams's reply was forbidding: "I write no letters upon what is called politics— that is electioneering. But I listen with interest to whatever any friends say upon topics of public concern." [45]

George Sullivan, Charles King, and Joseph Blunt protested when the President, in appointing a federal judge for the New Jersey district, passed over the name of Richard Stockton, district attorney, whose family had put a lot of money into a newspaper, the *New Jersey Patriot,* established for the express purpose of sustaining the Administration. The President's long reply can be summed up in one sentence from it which offered

---

[41] *Memoirs,* VII, 316–17. "His conversation was painful to me and mortifying to him; but what I said to him was due to candor, and he recovered his good humor before he went away." Ibid.

[42] "The objection is not to the individual. But our friends say: 'If the Administration prefer promoting those we have to fight, let them fight their own Battles themselves! We have hard work enough to carry the State without the weapons furnished against ourselves by the General Government.'" P. P. F. Degrand to JQA, Philadelphia, April 23, 1828. Adams MSS.

[43] *Memoirs,* VI, 522.

[44] For example: Joseph Blunt to JQA, New York, October 29, 1825, March 27, 1827, November 6, 14, 1828. Adams MSS.

[45] JQA to Joseph Blunt, Washington, March 20, 1827. Adams MSS.

little consolation: "Such a system [of political rewards] would be repugnant to every feeling of my soul."[46]

Most conspicuous example of Adams's refusal to remove a civil servant who was opposed to him was that of Calhoun's friend John McLean of Ohio, Postmaster General, originally appointed by President Monroe. This officer had by his position a vast influence over petty appointments in every city, town, and village of the land. He had brought the postal service to the highest level of efficiency ever attained, and Adams had reappointed him on the basis of his unexampled merit and qualifications. McLean hated Clay and had no real respect for Adams. Despite protestations of loyalty he did not hesitate to closet himself with Opposition leaders. Soon the President began to sense the Postmaster General's exertions in favor of Calhoun and Jackson. Clay and Barbour both complained bitterly, but it was difficult to prefer a specific charge. Toward the end of his term the President became abundantly convinced of McLean's duplicity and treachery, convinced also that it was too late to remove him, even though there was by then good reason: for example, McLean's recommendation, in collusion with Ingham and Dallas, of the shuffling Thomas Sergeant, whom Adams appointed as postmaster at Philadelphia. By the summer of 1828 the damage was done, and there was little chance that the hostile Senate would confirm any Presidential nomination of a successor to McLean. It was better to let him stay on than to fire him in the midst of the campaign. McLean's complete immunity from attack or criticism by the Opposition, either in Congress or in the newspapers, is sufficient proof, out of those days, of where his real loyalties lay.[47]

It is a wonder that Adams had any political friends left. Some, like Edward Everett, doubtless bowed to his high statements of principle. A cold sense of duty kept others in line to uphold the privileges of the established élite against the new pretenders.[48] The rest, who had taken such a position against Jackson that they could expect no reward from him, kept up desperately the campaign against the "military chieftain." Few of

---

[46] George Sullivan to JQA, September 13 [1827]. JQA to George Sullivan, Quincy, September 22, 1827. See also *Memoirs*, VII, 313–14.

[47] See *Memoirs*, VII, 56, 180, 275, 343, 349, 355, 364, 509, 531–8, 540–1.

[48] Young Charles Francis Adams, finding himself at the Fourth-of-July celebration in New York City in 1826, in the midst of his father's political friends, commented in his diary: "I was very kindly distinguished by many of my father's friends who really seemed to feel an attachment to him amounting even to enthusiasm. But perhaps the wine produced as much of this as anything else. My father has unfortunately such a cold manner of meeting this sort of feeling that I am surprised at the appearance of it any time among his supporters. These mostly should be and are more impelled by a sense of his merit in the performance of his duty than by any art of personal popularity." Diary of CFA, July 4, 1826. Adams MSS. Charles Francis Adams's pleasure trip from Washington to New York was interrupted by news of his grandfather John Adams's death, received on July 9. The President had already reached New York on his way to Quincy on July 8.

them loved the President. "We do not entertain for him one personal kind feeling," wrote Ezekiel Webster to his brother Daniel, "nor cannot unless we disembowel ourselves like a trussed turkey of all that is human nature within us." [49] It was more the friends of the warmhearted Harry of the West who defended the Adams Administration and John Quincy Adams himself against the invective of the Opposition.

5

As in the previous election, neither candidate did any formal campaigning. To keep the Old Hero fixed in the public eye, Jackson's managers inspired and staged a spectacular ceremony at New Orleans, in commemoration of his great military victory of January 8, 1815, and he delivered some speeches carefully constructed by ghost writers.[50] After that he waited at the Hermitage for his countrymen to call him to the White House, while John Quincy Adams lingered in that official residence for the verdict of the people to turn him out. Adams made only one public appearance that could conceivably be connected with the campaign: that was the Fourth-of-July speech 1828, dedicated to the theme of internal improvements, when he opened construction work on the Chesapeake and Ohio Canal.[51] It was rather in state legislatures, state and county conventions, and mass meetings throughout the land that the supporters of either candidate presented their man and their broadsides to the voters, or proclaimed his merits and damned his rival through the local press.

In the debates in Congress the advantage had lain altogether with Jackson's political tacticians. They attacked and the Administration defended. In the press it was otherwise. There Adams and Clay and their friends could and did assume the offensive.

The two most conspicuous party journals of the day were both in Washington and conducted by very able men: the Administration newspaper already mentioned, the *Daily National Journal,* edited by scholarly Peter Force; and Duff Green's *United States' Telegraph.* The *Journal* was a more dignified sheet than its rival the *Telegraph.* It ran weekly news sum-

[49] Parton: *Jackson,* III, 3, 166.

Adams acknowledged to his youngest son that he did not possess the "art" of attaching others to himself with "intense affection," but affirmed that his temper was neither "vindictive nor malicious"; as their old friend Dr. Benjamin Waterhouse had said, it "failed more by over-indulgence than by asperity." "You and all my children know that although my speech is sometimes harsh, my temper is not bad. That it carries anger as the flint bears fire. That it is positive, stubborn, exceedingly tenacious of what it knows or believes to be right, but not captious, fretful or difficult to live with. . . ." JQA to CFA, Meridian Hill, Washington, March 23, 1829. Adams MSS.

[50] Bassett: *Life of Jackson,* II, 401–3.

[51] Above, p. 102.

maries, foreign and domestic, occasionally featured literary and philosophical articles, and paid some attention to the arts and sciences. John Quincy Adams and Henry Clay influenced its policy and inspired its editorials, even contributed some of them. It enjoyed the lucrative favor of printing the federal laws and acts. Clay seems to have been more directly in touch with Force and his editorial colleague Agg than the President. Sometimes the Secretary of State would send in copy in his own handwriting "to be printed in tomorrow's Journal." [52]

The *Journal's* motto was: "For our Country and our Country's Friends." It identified the Administration with the whole nation. At first it disdained the Opposition as a combination of personal factions, based on men not principles. It stressed the general prosperity that blessed the country in those good times. It called for national unity and an end of personal politics. It supported without reservation the "broad measures" and "correct principles" of the Administration: the American System, public-land policy, Indian policy, foreign policy. It upheld the constitutionality of internal improvements and protective tariff. But soon it found itself on the defensive, desperately so after the Opposition captured both houses of Congress in the congressional elections of 1826.

Heaviest of the *Journal's* labors was to defend Adams and Clay against the refrain of bargain and corruption. These charges, involving the honor and character of his patrons, incited Force to hit below the belt. After having renounced any desire to indulge in personalities and particularly any reflections on "female character," [53] he reprinted an electioneering pamphlet by one Thomas L. Arnold, candidate for Congress in Tennessee, presenting slanderous comments on Jackson's irregular marriage.

"General Jackson," said Arnold, "spent the prime of his life in gambling, in cock-fighting, in horse-racing, and has all his life been a most bloody duelist; and to cap all his frailties he tore from a husband the wife of his bosom, to whom he had been for some years united in the holy state of matrimony. Robards, the wretched man whose wife was taken from him, did not very long survive the disgraceful transaction; but during the time that he did live, General Jackson lived with his wife in a way that would have subjected any other to an indictment in the County Court for 'open and notorious lewdness.'. . . I heard one of the General's prominent friends boasting of it, as an act of gallantry, and said that *'the General had driven Robards off like a dog and taken his wife.'* If General Jackson should be elected President, what effect, think you, fellow-citizens, will it have upon the American youth?" [54]

[52] Newman F. McGirr: "The Activities of Peter Force," *Records of the Columbia Historical Society,* Vols. XLII, XLIII.

[53] *Daily National Journal,* III, No. 815. April 12, 1827.

[54] *Daily National Journal,* III, No. 809. Monday, March 26, 1827. The *Richmond Whig,* a pro-Adams paper edited by the sycophantic and materialistic John Hampden Pleasants was the first to reprint the Arnold Circular, March 16, 1827. The *Journal*

When Thomas Ritchie's *Richmond Enquirer* taxed the *Journal* with departing from its promise not to bring women into the Presidential Question, Force explained that he had reprinted the circular because it had initial reference to the tariff question, and anyway it wasn't Mrs. Jackson's character that was reflected on: it was the General's! [55]

Against such tactics the *United States' Telegraph* could more than hold its own for Jackson. When the followers of Calhoun and Jackson were coalescing into a political opposition against John Quincy Adams during the first year of his Administration, they had secured control of that newspaper. Then they brought on from Missouri the capable and none too scrupulous political writer Duff Green, owner of the pro-Jackson *St. Louis Enquirer,* and turned the *Telegraph* over to him, with personal loans,[56] and with the Senate's official printing, which was beyond the control of the Administration. After the congressional elections of 1826 Green received the printing of the House of Representatives too. Duff Green was the Charlie Michelson [57] of his century—the ablest newspaperman that political managers could hire to smear their adversaries. For diatribe the *National Journal* could not hold a candle to the Jackson-Calhoun mouthpiece.[58]

Principal purpose and reason for existence of the *Telegraph* was to castigate and vilify the Administration and Adams's program of Liberty with Power. "Power is always stealing from the many to the few" was the motto at its masthead. There was little else in the paper but polemics. It printed speeches of politicians who attacked the President and his Secretary of State. It refused to print those who supported him—unless perchance an extract as a text to refute or demolish. Truth was not of the essence.

When Green got to Washington he began at the top. He caricatured

---

took it from the *Whig.* For explanation and defense of Jackson's marriage see the statement and affidavits published by the Jackson Corresponding Committee of Nashville, and reprinted in the *National Journal,* March 29, 1827.

[55] *Daily National Journal,* III, No. 875. June 22, 1827.

[56] Bassett prints a memorandum from the Jackson Papers of "Loans to Duff Green." Eaton endorsed a note of Green for $3,000: and the following persons agreed to be responsible in turn to Eaton for $2,000, in the following amounts each: J. Hamilton, Jr., of South Carolina, $300; G. Kremer, $300; Geo. Pater, $300; John S. Barbour, $300; James K. Polk, $100; J. C. Isacks, $100; S. D. Ingham, $150; S. D. Miller, $150; John Branch, William King, and Samuel Carson, $300. Bassett: *Correspondence of Jackson,* III, 301–2.

[57] Charles Michelson was the newspaperman whom the Democratic National Committee hired in 1929 at a salary of $10,000 as its publicity director, with the principal task, it was asserted, of discrediting President Herbert Hoover.

[58] Later, after Van Buren's triumph over Calhoun in the struggle within the party for the succession to Jackson, Duff Green remained Calhoun's fiery partisan. The Jackson forces brought on Frank Blair from Kentucky and established a new paper, the Washington *Globe,* as the mouthpiece of Jackson's Kitchen Cabinet. Green then became spokesman of the Calhoun opposition to Jackson.

the President and his Secretary of State: "The Yankee short and thin; the Orator tall and slim." The phosphorescent columns of the *Telegraph* gleamed with abuse and scurrility of Adams as a dangerous and designing politician, an avowed enemy to the rights of free men,[59] and of Henry Clay as his corrupt collaborator. One of the attacks that the President most resented and which the *Telegraph* printed was *An Exposition of the Political Conduct and Principles of John Quincy Adams,* a pamphlet anonymously written by Samuel D. Ingham, "Showing by Historical Documents, and Incontestable Facts, that he was educated as a Monarchist, has always been hostile to Popular Government, and particularly to its great Bulwark the right of Suffrage, and that he affected to become a Republican only to pervert and degrade the Democratic Party; and to pave the way for such a change in the Constitution as would establish the United States an Aristocratical and Hereditary Government." [60]

"Prince of slanderers" was the title Adams gave in his Diary to Duff Green. It was an exalted honor compared to the "skunks of party slander" that he reserved for his enemies in Congress: "Ingham, Wickliffe, Hamilton, Randolph, Floyd, Smyth, and Carson, have been for the last fortnight squirting round the House of Representatives, thence to issue and perfume the atmosphere of the Union." [61]

Duff Green rang, continually and persistently, all the changes on the thriving charge of bargain and corruption. Among other variations and repetitions he suggested that Clay threw his vote to Adams in 1825 because of his pecuniary embarrassments, which compelled him to look to the office of Secretary of State and its emolument to sustain his private credit.[62] He asserted that Clay had corruptly voted for Adams in the House of Representatives after once having borne false witness against him (affair of Jonathan Russell).[63] He held up the Administration, rather than the Opposition, as the coalition, a coalition of political gangsters.

"By power and money," so he had John Quincy Adams declaim, "we may yet retain the throne and continue the succession. How fortunate that I did help myself to that double outfit, double salary, double expenses and double contingencies, for the Ghent business. With that and the contingent fund, we'll buy up rogues and honest men." [64]

The *Telegraph* opened its columns to contributors, anonymous or otherwise, who could say anything against John Quincy Adams or his friends, and printed selections of this kind that it could extract from other Opposition papers throughout the country. They repeated all the charges

[59] *United States' Telegraph,* II, Nos. 143, 144, 145, September 1, 4, 6, 1827.
[60] Also printed by Duff Green, 1827, and widely distributed in pamphlet form. Another edition printed by *Northern Sentinel,* Burlington, Vermont, 1827.
[61] *Memoirs,* VII, 431.
[62] *United States' Telegraph,* III, 22. February 19, 1828.
[63] See Vol. I, 498–509.
[64] *United States' Telegraph,* II, No. 147, September 11, 1827.

sounded on the floor of Congress and added others: that Adams was a friend of the extension of slavery, and an enemy of Christ's religion—a Unitarian.[65]

Duff Green reprinted with glee the famous "Adams Catechism" of the *Boston Statesman* "for the use of 'noble families,'" holding up the late John Adams as an aristocrat and monarchist:

"Q. What should such a family, having obtained a restoration to power, do in order to keep it? A. . . . turn monarchist and aristocrat again." [66]

Among the reprints in the *Telegraph* was the ridiculous story, from the Philadelphia *Mercury*, about Thomas Boylston, the "former Tory" (after whom John Quincy Adams's brother was named), and his alleged bequest of half a million dollars to President Adams as heir to his prejudices and passions for England! "It is rumored that it is the intention of Mr. Adams to *return to England* there to purchase a PATENT OF NOBILITY." [67]

Responding to the reflections on Mrs. Jackson, Duff Green ridiculed Mrs. John Quincy Adams's high tone and associations with royalty.[68] He hinted darkly that there was more he could do in retaliation for the assaults on Mrs. Jackson's reputation, but for the time being he would chivalrously forbear.

Jackson's unfurbished reply to all this was a very elastic warning for such a determined man:

"The course of my friends, ought now to be as heretofore on the defensive; should the Administration continue their systematic course of slander, it will be well now and then to throw a fire brand into their camp by the statement of a few facts, but female character never should be introduced or touched by my friends, unless a continuation of attack should continue to be made against Mrs. J. and then only, by way of *just retaliation* upon the *known guilty*. My great wish is, that it may be altogether *avoided*, if *possible*, by my friends. I *never war against females* and it is only the base and cowardly that do—your course, has hitherto been approved by my friends, and must continue to be approved, so

---

[65] Ibid., III, Nos. 6, 9, January 12, 19, 1828.

[66] Ibid., III, No. 23, February 21, 1828.

[67] Ibid., III, No. 15, February 2, 1828.

[68] Mrs. Adams denied such implications in an obviously autobiographical article, first printed in the *Saturday Evening Post*, reprinted in the *United States' Telegraph*, II, 230, June 20, 1827, with editorial comment on "Female Character"; and later in *Mrs. Colvin's Monthly Messenger*. Duff Green wrote as follows to Jackson, July 8, 1827: "I saw the necessity of bringing home the matter to Mrs. Adams's own family and by threats of retaliation drove the *Journal* to condemn itself. This you have no doubt seen and understood. The effect here was like electricity. The whole Adams corps was thrown into consternation. They did not doubt that I would execute my threat, and I was denounced in the most bitter terms for assailing female character by those very men, who had rolled the slanders on Mrs. Jackson under their tongues as the sweetest morsel that had been dressed up by Peter Force and Co., during the whole campaign." Bassett: *Life of Jackson*, II, 394–5.

long as you adopt truth and principle for your guide, never departing from either." [69]

The General's ire was more for Clay than Adams. If he could have proved Clay guilty of those misleading reflections on his beloved Rachel, he would have sought him out and shot him dead.[70]

The biographer has to record that although John Quincy Adams had no part in inspiring these aspersions on Jackson's marriage, he never reproved those who concocted them, or tried to suppress such slanders.

The General and his friends were unable to keep the slandermongering from Mrs. Jackson's eyes. Already in declining health, she drooped and died, just after the election.[71] This tragedy completed the estrangement between the two patriots.

From the master journalists in Washington the partisan editors took their opposing cues throughout the whole country. Here the Administration had a certain advantage. Henry Clay as Secretary of State had at his disposal the assignment of public printing in the District of Columbia and in each of the several states and territories. He placed it to favor pro-Administration journals and, one may suspect, suggested leads for political innuendo. As if this advantage were not enough, Daniel Webster and others urged John Quincy Adams to subsidize new sheets to be set up in strategic sections, as the Jacksonians were doing, particularly in Pennsylvania and Kentucky. Congressman John Bailey of Massachusetts, formerly clerk in the Department of State during Adams's Secretaryship, told the President that five or ten thousand dollars rightly employed with newspapers, pamphlets, and handbills in Kentucky could win the Governorship of that state in the early autumn elections.

Kentucky, with state elections coming in August before the congressional elections in November, had the same significance in national politics then that Maine has now.

John Quincy Adams's reply to this suggestion was quick and emphatic. "The Presidency of the United States is an office neither to be sought nor declined," he reminded Bailey. "To pay money for securing it is, in my opinion, incorrect in principle. This is my first reason for declining [to make] such a contribution. A second reason is that I could not even command a sum of five thousand dollars, without borrowing it; and a third is, that if once I depart from the principle and give money, there is no rule, either of expediency or morality, which would enable me to limit the amount of expenditure. . . ."

[69] Andrew Jackson to Duff Green, Hermitage, August 13, 1827. Bassett: *Correspondence of Jackson*, III, 377.

[70] A letter of Andrew Jackson to Sam Houston, Hermitage, December 15, 1826, entitles us to think this. Bassett: *Correspondence of Jackson*, III, 325.

[71] Ibid., III, xvi.

Bailey seemed surprised. "Mr. Webster told me you have a large sum—fifty or sixty thousand dollars—lying dead in a bank in Boston."

Patiently and candidly the President explained to Bailey: "The expenses of my family and the support of my three sons absorb very nearly the whole of my public salary. All my real estate in Boston and Quincy is mortgaged for the payment of my debts. The income of my whole private estate is less than six thousand dollars a year. Finally, upon my going out of office in one year from this time, destitute of all means of acquiring property, it will only be by sacrificing what I now possess that I shall be able to support my family." [72]

It cannot be said that the established Adams newspapers were less resourceful or cleaner than the mushrooming Jackson press. One of Clay's friends, and a correspondent of the President, was Charles Hammond, editor of the *Cincinnati Gazette,* which had supported Adams ever since 1825. On his anti-Jackson propaganda there were no restraints. He established a special publication in 1828, *Truth's Advocate and Monthly Anti-Jackson Expositor,* to sing Adams's virtues and detail Jackson's wickedness and "adultery." Jackson believed Hammond the source of an infamous whispering campaign about the General's pious mother, already fifty years in her tomb: that she had been a prostitute intermarried with a Negro, and his eldest brother sold as a slave in Carolina! [73] In Philadelphia, John Binns of the *Democratic Press* accused Jackson of arbitrary execution of six militiamen whom he had court-martialed for desertion at the end of the New Orleans campaign. He printed posters and handbills adorned with six black coffins, the better to picture the General's bloody deeds to voters liable to militia service. In Boston the *Massachusetts Journal,* sponsored by a committee of Adams's friends including General H. A. S. Dearborn, Thomas Handasyd Perkins, and Abbott Lawrence, pilloried Jackson for all his "faults and crimes": he had not a single redeeming quality, only the bravery of a ruffian and the warlike cunning of an Indian chief, a professed duelist, a confederate of Aaron Burr, the "Tennessee Slanderer," the "Great Western Bluebeard," destroyer of family ties, a "man of blood," whose very "touch was pollution." [74]

On the other hand the General had his front-line workers in every state. There was, for example, Thomas Ritchie's powerful *Richmond Enquirer,* which tried to reconcile Jackson's campaign with state rights and the unconstitutionality of a protective tariff. And in New York, Major M. M. Noah made the *National Advocate* a Jackson vehicle, not unfriendly to the protective tariff. In Adams's home state the *Boston States-*

---

[72] *Memoirs,* VII, 469–70. March 8, 1828.

[73] Andrew Jackson to Brigadier General Richard K. Call, Hermitage, August 16, 1828. Bassett: *Correspondence of Jackson,* III, 426.

[74] A Jackson committee in Boston in 1828 published some of these choice morsels as an antidote to their own poison in *Political Extracts from a Leading Adams Paper, the Massachusetts Journal.* There is a copy in the Boston Athenæum.

man, Nathaniel Greene owner and editor, reviled the President as unremittingly as any anti-Jackson expositor could do in the Old Northwest. The vilest canard of the Jackson publications was a story apparently furnished by Adams's old enemy Jonathan Russell,[75] which first appeared in a note to a short campaign biography of Jackson published by Isaac Hill, editor of the *New Hampshire Patriot:* that John Quincy Adams while Minister to Russia had "pimped" the person of a beautiful Boston girl, a nursemaid in his household, Martha Godfrey by name, to the lust of Czar Alexander I. Absurd as this charge was, it seemed necessary for the President to supply Edward Everett with an explanation that was presented on the floor of the House of Representatives.[76]

6

The most significant issue in the Presidential campaign of 1828 was the hidden issue. For back of all the personal charges, back of all debate on Indian removal, on public-land disposal, internal improvement, and the tariff, back of the contest between the American System and state rights, which was also a contest between industrial capital and agricultural capital, lay the issue of slavery. Only occasionally did men such as John Randolph bring it into view.

Neither Presidential candidate said anything about the hidden issue for fear of arousing opposition among his party supporters in the other section of the country: Jackson did not want to antagonize the "plain Republicans of the North" by openly defending slavery; Adams did not wish gratuitously to alienate the Southern planters by denouncing the evil. But silence did not signify the same thing for both men. Jackson did not have to tell the South where he stood on slavery. He had bought and sold slaves all his life. If only because he was a wealthy planter and slaveowner the South would vote for him, and for Calhoun for re-election to the Vice-Presidency, as men of their own way of life. Silence on Ad-

[75] "The author of this pamphlet and imputation was Jonathan Russell. . . ." *Memoirs,* VIII, 217. April 12, 1830.

[76] For the canard, see *Brief Sketch of the Life, Character and Services of Major General Andrew Jackson,* by a Citizen of New England (Concord, N.H.: Printed by Manahan, Hoag, and Co. for Isaac Hill; 1828).

For the explanation, see *Register of Debates,* IV, Part I, 1827–8, pp. 1312–14. February 1, 1828.

For Hill's defense of this atrocity, see *New Hampshire Patriot,* XX, No. 983. February 4, 1828. See also *Boston Statesman,* VIII, No. 7. February 9, 1828.

The real facts from which this story was trumped up were as follows. The Russian post office had intercepted a gossipy letter from Martha Godfrey to friends at home telling of the Emperor's reputed amours and gallantries. This epistle greatly diverted the Emperor and Empress, who expressed a curiosity to see the credulous nursemaid. So Mr. and Mrs. Adams arranged for Martha to visit the Palace with their small son Charles, who passed some ten minutes together in the presence of the two sovereigns. *Memoirs,* VII, 415–16.

ams's part did not mean that he approved the institution as did Jackson. The Southern politicians sensed his disapproval clearly enough; if they did not sense it they had Calhoun to tell them—from his personal talks with Adams as a colleague in President Monroe's Cabinet at the time of the Missouri Compromise. The hidden issue silently transformed the Presidential Question of 1828 into an underlying sectional contest, personified by two Northern men, John Quincy Adams and Richard Rush, running against two Southern men, Andrew Jackson and John C. Calhoun.

7

Adams did express himself, cautiously and off the record, on the Antimasonic issue that came up late in the campaign, particularly in the State of New York. There will be more to say about this subject in a later chapter. Suffice it to mention here that in the midst of the excitement caused by the abduction and murder of William Morgan, attributed to the Masons, an Antimasonic National Republican, Oliver Heartwell of Canandaigua, wrote Adams to ask him frankly whether he was a Mason.

Here was an interesting question. The Antimasonic movement promised to galvanize the rather flaccid Adams support into something really dynamic. In New York the astute Thurlow Weed was making the most of it, hoping to exploit it for Adams in the coming national election. It could do no harm for the President to declare he was not a Mason, and it might do some good: it would clinch the Antimasonic vote in the two important states of New York and Pennsylvania, both of which he needed to win the election. But he must be careful not to condemn good Masons, for there were thousands of Masons all over the nation, National Republicans or lingering Federalists, who would vote for Adams and the American System. He must be careful not to throw them into the arms of their brother Andrew Jackson, a long-standing member of the order. It would be safe to say something against kidnapping and murder, but he must be careful not to oppose the Masons as such—not yet. Adams's studious answer was designed to get the Antimasonic voters and keep in his fold such Masons as had favored his program.

"I state that I am not, never was, and never shall be a Free-Mason," the President wrote to Heartwell. He declared, however, that he was unwilling to add in any manner to the excitement caused by the mysterious abduction and "probable murder" of William Morgan. Therefore he asked that no publicity be given to his letter. Then he went on further to express himself, studiously: "The deep and solemn feeling which pervades the community on this occasion is founded on the purest principles of human virtue and human rights. In the just and lawful pursuit of a signal vindication of the Laws of Nature and of the land, violated in his [Morgan's] person, which has been undertaken and is just in progress, with the authority and cooperation of your Legislature, I hope and trust that the fellow-citizens of the sufferer will temper with the spirit of Justice the reparation of his wrongs, and in the infliction of every penalty carefully abstain from visiting upon the innocent the misdeeds of the guilty." [77]

When his letter got published he did not scold anyone. To offset its appeal to Antimasons his adversaries circulated in the counties of western New York a handbill with a deposition under judicial oath by someone who professed to have been present with him on two occasions at meetings of a Masonic lodge in Pittsfield, Massachusetts, though he had never entered a house in that town in his life. The Boston *Centinel* also falsely asserted during the campaign that the President was a Mason.[78]

8

As the election drew near, it was clear that the result would hinge on New York and Pennsylvania. Granted that Jackson would capture all the slave states south of the Potomac, and Adams might get the votes of New England, New Jersey, Delaware, and Maryland, and even those north of the Ohio River—the last by no means likely—he could not win without all the electoral votes of the two great middle states. Except for the gesture against kidnapping and murder (very bad sins) the Puritan President had done absolutely nothing to build himself up politically in those states, nor anywhere else for that matter. He stood unvociferously on his rejected program of Liberty with Power.

Not so with Jackson's managers. They had the South behind them; Jackson himself was a Southerner as much as a Westerner. They had the West behind them; Jackson was a Westerner, a border captain, a man of direct action, a nationalist, a friend of the people.[79] They controlled the Old Northwest; Jackson had voted for the tariff of 1824, and believed in internal improvements at least for national defense.[80] They had a majority of the voters of Pennsylvania and New York behind them, too; Jackson was a Democrat. By November the Jackson campaign had melded into one refrain loudly declaimed throughout the whole Union, louder in Pennsylvania and New York than anywhere else: "Jackson and Reform," "Hurrah for Jackson!" It was General Andrew Jackson, darling of the people, versus John Quincy Adams, personification of the old élite.

A spirit of defeatism gripped the Adams forces. After the Opposition captured both houses of Congress, in the mid-term balloting of 1826, no

[77] JQA to Oliver Heartwell, Canandaigua, N.Y. Washington, April 19, 1828. Adams MSS. Printed from *Albany Argus,* August 6, 1828, and in *Niles' Weekly Register,* XXXV, No. 885, August 30, 1828.

[78] JQA to the People of the Commonwealth of Massachusetts [Autumn 1833] in John Quincy Adams: *Letters on the Masonic Institution* (Boston: Press of T. R. Marvin; 1847), pp. 235–6.

[79] Hattie Mabel Anderson: "The Jackson Men in Missouri in 1828," *Missouri Historical Review,* XXXIV (1940), 301–34.

[80] Buley: *Old Northwest,* II, 162–3.

one in the Government had any expectations of winning the Presidential election, least of all John Quincy Adams. Henry Clay repeatedly tried to resign, but hung on out of loyalty to the President and party, doubtless with hopes for 1832. As the storm came on, other members of the Cabinet wanted to leave the sinking ship. Both Rush and Barbour actively bespoke diplomatic posts for themselves. In March 1828 the President appointed Barbour to the Court of St. James's, thereby disappointing Daniel Webster again, and placed General Peter B. Porter in the Department of War. Rush was hopelessly drafted to be Adams's running-mate as National Republican candidate for Vice President. Southard became a candidate for the United States Senate from his home state of New Jersey. "I cannot blame them," John Quincy Adams sighed. "The majority of the people in their respective States are inveterately opposed to the Administration; and there is scarcely any condition so mortifying as that of being in a minority home." So he noted in his Diary, and turned to the reading of Milton's *Paradise Regained*.[81] As for himself, perhaps in the quiet of Quincy he would find peace in the library of his paternal mansion, looking out upon his garden and seedling beds, amid the shades of his patriotic ancestors.

The election took place in different states on different days between October 31 and November 5, 1828. Jackson and Calhoun made a clean sweep of Pennsylvania and everything west and south of Maryland. Adams and Rush captured the New England states, New Jersey, Delaware, six out of eleven electoral votes in Maryland, but only sixteen out of New York's thirty-six—these came principally from the Antimasonic districts.

Whether measured by electoral votes, 178 [82] to 83, or popular votes,[83] 647,276 to 508,064, Jackson had won an earth-shaking triumph, based on the vote of the solid South, plus the Northwest, Pennsylvania, and New York.

Adams read the returns as a sectional victory for the South. "Sectional feeling was more powerful than personal attachment." [84] Looking back upon his defeated Administration from the perspective of 1837, following Van Buren's election to the Presidency, he declared for the record of history:

"When I came to the Presidency the principle of internal improvement, was swelling the tide of public prosperity, till the Sable Genius of the South saw the signs of his own inevitable downfall in the unparalleled progress of the general welfare of the North, and fell to cursing the tariff

[81] *Memoirs*, VII, 474; VIII, 79.

[82] Calhoun received 171 electoral votes for Vice President, because Georgia's 7 votes went to his South Carolina rival, William Smith.

[83] In South Carolina and Delaware there was no popular vote; there the legislature selected the electors.

[84] JQA to James Barbour, E.E. and M.P. of the U.S., London. Meridian Hill, April 4, 1829. Adams MSS.

and internal improvement and raised the standard of Free trade, Nullification and State Rights. I fell, and with me fell, I fear never to rise again, certainly never to rise again in my day the system of internal improvement by National means and National Energies. The great object of my Life therefore as applied to the Administration of the Government of the United States, has *failed*. The American Union as a moral person in the family of Nations, is to live from hand to mouth, to cast away, instead of using for the improvement of its own condition, the bounties of Providence, and to raise to the summit of Power a succession of Presidents the consummation of whose glory will be to growl and snarl with impotent fury against a money broker's shop, to rivet into perpetuity the clanking chain of the Slave, and to waste in boundless bribery to the West the invaluable inheritance of the Public Lands." [85]

Jackson's election was only in part a sectional triumph for the forces of slavery. The defenders of slavery would soon learn that they could not count on the Old Hero to support them in any action against the Union.

[85] JQA to the Reverend Charles W. Upham, Salem, Massachusetts. Washington, February 2, 1837. See Edward H. Tatum, Jr., ed.: "Ten Unpublished Letters of John Quincy Adams, 1796–1837," *Huntington Library Quarterly,* IV (No. 3, April 1941), 381–4. A holograph copy of this letter was in the autograph collection of the late John Marshall Holcombe, Jr., of Farmington, Conn., who kindly allowed me to read it. Letterbook copy in Adams MSS.

CHAPTER VIII
Meridian Hill
(1828 – 1829)

❁

The sun of my political life sets in the deepest
gloom. But that of my country shines unclouded.

JOHN QUINCY ADAMS'S DIARY,
DECEMBER 3, 1828 [1]

THE LITTLE MAGICIAN of American politics, Martin Van Buren, had
courted successfully the vested interests of the slavery capitalists. A
combination of plain Republicans of the North and Southern planters
had elected Andrew Jackson President of the United States. Molded
into a new political party, they proceeded to put an end to John Quincy
Adams's Washingtonian—not to mention Hamiltonian—concepts of Liberty with Power. To the Democrats liberty meant the least government
possible in Washington.

1

The new President-elect, white-haired and thin, bereaved by the death
of his beloved Rachel, came over the mountains from Tennessee and
slipped into Washington with a minimum of parade or show. He put up
at Gadsby's Tavern, immediately to be belabored by a swarm of office-
seekers. Then the people began to converge on the capital of the Republic. They were coming to see "their" President inaugurated. In
stagecoaches, in provisioners' wagons, in rowboats across the river, on
horseback, on muleback, on foot, they thronged from the country round
about. Never had such a crowd filled the little city by the Potomac. They
took up all the lodgings, they ate up all the food, they spread like locusts
into Georgetown and over the river into Alexandria.

Some twenty thousand spectators massed around the Capitol to see the
Old Hero walk humble and bareheaded up the Hill to take the oath of
office from Chief Justice John Marshall. Not a shadow of military restraint
contained the populace as it pressed about the North Portico. Tranquil
and silent the people stood there, straining to hear Andrew Jackson's

[1] *Memoirs*, VIII, 78.

weak voice as he read the inaugural address. Not until he made his final bow did the multitude press up the steps in a struggle to seize the new President's hand. With some difficulty he escaped through the Capitol and got away on a waiting horse before they closed in impenetrably.

Down the Hill the crowd chased madly after him. It swelled and swept on, up Pennsylvania Avenue toward the White House. Countrymen, gentlemen, farmers and shopkeepers, boys, women and children, black and white, mounted and on foot, in wagons and in carts, pushed ahead upon the People's Palace.

During the ceremony on Capitol Hill the majesty of the people had inspired reflective minds with respect. At the White House it broke down. A mob of all ages pushed in from the street in muddy boots, romping, shouting, scrambling, outdoing the office-seekers in their fight to get up front. Not even a police officer was in sight to keep order, to protect public property, to secure the person of the new Chief Magistrate. The crowd all but trampled the General to death before some friends were able to form a living barrier behind which he escaped through the south entrance to make his way back to Gadsby's. People stood roughshod on the damask upholstery the better to see what was going on. They clung to draperies, tearing and pulling them down. In their rush for the tables they broke the costly chinaware and shattered bowls of cut glass. To prevent a real disaster amidst this suffocating confusion someone had presence of mind to have tubs and pails of punch and lemonade, with cake and ice cream, put outside here and there on the lawn. Decamping through the doors and out the windows, the swarm of humanity dispersed itself uproariously and safely about the refreshments.

"Ladies and gentlemen only had been expected at this levée, not the people en masse," wrote Margaret Bayard Smith, to whom we owe the best account of that inaugural day. "But it was the People's day, and the People's President and the People would rule. God grant that one day or other, the People, do not put down all rule and rulers." [2]

Nothing like Jackson's first inaugural reception has happened before or since in American history.

2

John Quincy Adams was conspicuous by his absence from the inaugural of his successor. Since coming to Washington, General Jackson had personally ignored his vanquished foe. Duff Green in the *United States' Telegraph* attributed this signal lack of courtesy to Adams's personal association with the slanders about Mrs. Jackson in the *National Journal*. "It is not true," Adams averred in his Diary. "I have not been privy to any publication in any newspaper against either himself or his wife." [3] We

[2] *First Forty Years of Washington Society*, p. 296.
[3] *Memoirs*, VIII, 102. February 28, 1829.

have already noticed that he took no step to stop such publications or publicly to deplore them.

Having received no communication of any kind from his elected successor, Adams had sent word by the United States Marshal for the District of Columbia, Tench Ringgold, that he would be ready to remove with his family from the White House in time for the General to receive his "visits of congratulation" there on the 4th of March. Jackson politely returned his thanks, and suggested that the outgoing President's family be in no hurry at all, but stay as long as suited their convenience, even a month. It was finally agreed that the President's House would be vacated in time for the inaugural reception.[4]

The state of Mrs. Adams's health did not permit a departure for Quincy until the spring was advanced and the roads dry for more comfortable traveling, so the ex-President rented temporarily from Commodore David Porter his house on Meridian Hill. Conveniently constructed for two family residences, it allowed separate quarters for son John's little family, near the parents and grandparents.[5] This country place, about a mile and a half from the White House, sat astride the original center line of the District of Columbia. The "meridian line" of 76° 53' W. Long. ran due north and south through both the portals of the White House and the entrance to the Porter mansion.[6] There the retiring President joined his family on the evening of the 3d of March after walking back to the White House from the Capitol, whither he had been to sign final bills of the expiring Twentieth Congress. That same morning he had put to the members of his Cabinet in their last meeting a final question: whether he should attend Jackson's inauguration. All except Richard Rush, defeated candidate for Vice President, advised against it.[7]

John Adams and his son John Quincy Adams are the only two Presidents who have declined to play a personal role in the installation of their successors. In the case of the younger Adams it is difficult to see how, given the unfortunate situation, he could have done otherwise.

3

John Quincy Adams's comments on the election of Andrew Jackson varied according to his intimacy with the person whom he was addressing. Whatever the blow to his own fortunes, he did not despair of the Republic—not quite yet. Outwardly he kept his face and even showed optimism.

---

[4] *Memoirs*, VIII, 99–102.

[5] LCA to CFA, Meridian Hill, March 29, 1829. Adams MSS.

[6] F. A. Emery: "Mount Pleasant and Meridian Hill"; *Columbia Historical Society Records*, XXXIII–XXXIV (Washington, 1932), pp. 196–7. D. B. Warden: *A Chronological and Statistical Description of the District of Columbia, the Seat of the General Government of the United States* . . . (Paris, 1816), p. 28.

[7] *Memoirs*, VIII, 104.

The country had been in such good shape, so prosperous during his recent Administration, that things simply couldn't easily go wrong. On the surface, he wished Jackson well.[8]

To his sons in Boston his appreciations of the new Government were less restrained. His sarcastic remarks on the make-up of the new Administration reflect a satisfying comparison with his own Presidential appointments. Elevation of the faithless McLean to the Supreme Court and appointment as Postmaster General of William T. Barry, defeated by a Clay man in the recent gubernatorial contest in Kentucky, called out his contempt for previous professions of reform. "The General Post Office . . . and all the Post offices are to be subjected to its [executive] patronage. Memorable reform. The next step will be to turn it into a Police Department, and to take the fingering of all the letters into Executive hands. . . . The composition of the Cabinet is not satisfactory to the Heroite party itself. . . . The dictation of Caucuses and Central Committees, the conflicting puppets of Van Buren and Calhoun . . . feed the ravin of hungry and prostituted partizans."

"Under such auspices . . ." concluded the disappointed nationalist, "commenced the present Administration. Its day will be the day of small things. There will be neither lofty meditations, nor comprehensive foresight, nor magnanimous purpose, nor the look for the benizons of future ages, presiding at the helm of State. Much mischief I do not apprehend. The gigantic growth of the Country will be checked, but I hope and trust will ultimately shoot forth with double vigour from its bonds." [9]

In his Diary he was pessimistic for himself and optimistic for his country: "The sun of my political life sets in the deepest gloom. But that of my country shines unclouded." [10]

He was sure—almost sure—he was done for politically. He planned to go into complete retirement, to withdraw from all connection with public affairs.[11] But he never absolutely pledged himself to anybody so to do. The Presidential gyroscope did not altogether stop spinning.

4

The ex-President's relations with Henry Clay in the hour of defeat evoke our historical and biographical curiosity. A minority President overwhelmingly defeated for re-election in the heyday of national prosperity could scarcely expect—whatever his intentions for the future—to

[8] JQA to Jeremiah Condy, Charleston, S.C. Washington, January 24, 1829. JQA to James Barbour, E.E. and M.P. of the United States, London. Meridian Hill, April 4, 1829. Adams MSS.

[9] JQA to CFA, Meridian Hill, March 8, 1829. See also JQA to William Plumer, Epping, N.H. Meridian Hill, March 16, 1829. Adams MSS.

[10] *Memoirs*, VIII, 78. December 3, 1828.

[11] *Memoirs*, VIII, 80–1. December 9, 1828.

lead an opposition party to a return to power. Leadership of the National Republicans must pass into other hands. The resilient Henry Clay was the natural candidate. He had baptized the American System. He was unequivocal champion of the protective tariff as well as internal improvement. He was a Western leader who could look North and South as well. He had supported Adams in 1825. As Secretary of State he had shown a gentle, courteous, and faithful, almost pathetic loyalty to the Minority President and his sinking Administration.[12] The defeated Adams could not deny Clay his turn in the future. But he did not lay on hands.

Before he left the Presidency, Adams offered his Secretary of State a place on the Supreme Court. That would have put him out of politics. Clay politely declined. It is uncertain whether the Senate would have ratified such a nomination. The Kentuckian left no doubt that he expected to head the party. Shortly after Christmas 1828 Clay asked Edward Everett whether he might depend on the support of the Eastern states in the next election; if he could, he said, he thought he could be sure of the Western states.[13] A few days later he had a talk with Adams himself on the problems before the country.

"The South threatens disunion," he declared. "The Western states are grasping after all the public lands. Ninian Edwards, Governor of Illinois, wants me to take the lead from Senator T. H. Benton of Missouri, who commenced this inroad on the public lands."

"It is impossible for me to divest myself of a deep interest in whatever should affect the welfare of the country," Adams averred, "but after the third of March I shall consider my public career closed. From that time I shall take as little part in public concerns as possible. I shall have enough to do to defend and vindicate my own reputation from the double persecution under which I have fallen." [14]

It looked like a resignation to Clay of the leadership of the National Republican Party. To be sure, the words "as little . . . as possible" could be taken a number of ways.

Clay suggested that in future political struggles the Republicans apply the "epithet" of Federalist to opponents of the tariff and internal improvements [15] who were beginning to call themselves the Democratic Party. Apparently he had in mind the looser bond of federalism as compared with nationalism. Adams had no wish to revive old party distinctions, nor could he see how the term *Federalist* could be applied to the Jacksonians, who had made state rights the "cornerstone" of their party— in Van Buren's later word.[16] "The old federalists were generally friendly to those interests [protective tariff and internal improvement]," he re-

---

[12] Dangerfield: *Era of Good Feelings,* p. 350.
[13] *Memoirs,* VIII, 86. December 27, 1828.
[14] *Memoirs,* VIII, 88. December 31, 1828.
[15] Clay to JQA, Ashland, April 12, 1829. Adams MSS.
[16] *Autobiography of Martin Van Buren,* p. 214.

minded Clay from Meridian Hill. "Washington was pre-eminently so. The remains of the federal party now are divided upon those questions, as they are upon all others of present political interest. They have now no public principle peculiar to themselves."

"I have no wish to fortify myself by the support of any party whatever," Adams told Clay.[17]

He continued to regard himself as the Man of the Whole Nation.

5

During the first days and weeks at Meridian Hill the ex-President had plenty of visitors, principally old friends and associates. Members of his Cabinet came to take leave as they set forth for their home states. The diplomatic corps appeared severally to pay their last compliments. Republican members of both houses in Congress, sadly departing civil servants, pastors of local churches, naval officers who appreciated his interest in seapower, artistic and literary folk, one by one they came up the hill to visit him. The four volunteer companies of infantry of the District came to wish him future health and happiness. Persico, the sculptor, who had executed the Capitol pediment, designed by President Adams, called a number of times to paint miniatures and to take a model for a final bust.

The dignitaries of the new Administration paid little attention to their defeated enemy. These were the same people who had been on terms of friendly acquaintance with him in previous months and repeatedly shared the hospitalities of the White House. Of course they were following the ostensible lead of their chieftain. Only Van Buren, the ablest of the new leaders, appeared at Meridian Hill—after having consulted Jackson. It would be a good example for other members of his Administration, allowed the new President, who thought that they should treat Mr. Adams at least with respect. Van Buren went along with the *locum tenens* of the State Department, James A. Hamilton, on one of the latter's visits to take over some unfinished confidential negotiations with the Ottoman Porte. The interview was civil enough, not uncordial. "He pursues enmity," thought Adams, "as though it might be one day his interest to seek friendship."[18]

Actually Van Buren made a serious effort to re-establish friendly personal relations between the two patriots who once had respected each other so greatly. He even got the General to promise to shake hands with Mr. Adams on some likely occasion. An opportunity soon came when President and ex-President attended the funeral of Philip Doddridge, a member of the House of Representatives from Virginia, but Jackson, despite prompting from his Secretary of State, could not bring himself to

[17] JQA to Henry Clay, Meridian Hill, April 21, 1829. Clay Papers, XV, 265, LC. Letterbook copy in Adams MSS. *Works of Henry Clay,* IV, 226–7.

[18] *Memoirs,* VIII, 129. April 4, 1829.

the point. "I approached Mr. Adams with a *bona fide* intention to offer him my hand," the onetime Indian-fighter later explained with a smile, "but the old gentleman, observing the movement, assumed so pugnacious a look that I was afraid he would strike me if I came nearer." [19]

6

Perhaps Adams's unbending demeanor was due in part to Jackson's assault on the civil service. "We do not know what line of policy General Jackson will take," wrote Duff Green shortly before election. "We take it for granted, however, that he will reward his friends and punish his enemies." [20]

The new President did not follow the example of his predecessor and keep in office men opposed to his Administration. He cleaned them out to make room for his own clamoring supporters. To the victors belonged the spoils! A ruthless scythe swept through the ranks of public servants everywhere, cutting down every man of doubtful allegiance. Terror seized old-timers who had no place to go, no other means of subsistence. Old friends and familiar workers for Adams were the first to feel the ax. One of the former was Richard Cutts, second comptroller, and an old landmark in Washington society, official and private. William Lee, political handyman and scribe, and Dr. Tobias Watkins, petty confidant and legman of the recent Administration, lost their choice berths in the Treasury. Philip R. Fendall, another political amanuensis, was dropped from the Department of State to make room for a Jackson journalist.

Tragedies were daily occurring among the civil servants displaced by the results of the election. The uncertainty of his situation and that of his family threatened to drive crazy many an old government officer who still held on to his job. Henshaw, a Jackson partisan whom Adams had left undisturbed in the Treasury Department, began to doubt whether his new chief felt him sufficiently loyal. In despair he cut his throat from ear to ear. One Linneus Smith, a competent person still left unmolested in the Department of State, became so worried that he went ravingly distracted.[21] The plight of the persons actually displaced to make way for the new élite was increasingly pitiful.

In their places Jackson put his own publicity men: the journalists Amos Kendall of Kentucky, Major Lewis of Tennessee, Isaac Hill of New Hampshire. Altogether he appointed to federal offices about fifty newspapermen who had supported him in the recent campaign: "writers and pub-

[19] *Autobiography of Martin Van Buren,* p. 270.
[20] *United States' Telegraph,* III, No. 128, November 3, 1828.
[21] *Memoirs,* VIII, 144. April 25, 1829. Fish: *Civil Service and the Patronage,* p. 130. Van Buren kept on the Chief Clerk, Daniel Brent (who served 1817–33), as indispensable to the continuity of business. In 1833 he resigned to accept the consulship at Paris.

lishers of scurrilous newspapers," in the words of John Quincy Adams's Diary, "electioneering skunks." [22] One or two were so malodorous that the new Senate would not confirm the nominations: for example, Isaac Hill, who had published Jonathan Russell's slander on Mr. and Mrs. Adams concerning Martha Godfrey at the Court of Alexander I, and Henry Lee, one of Jackson's ghost-writers, notorious for his personal irregularities. Everywhere the new politicians pushed the old officeholders out into the cold.

One of President Adams's intimate helpers escaped the first purge. He was Antoine Giusta, personal valet, whom he had picked up in Amsterdam as a deserter from Napoleon's army in 1814. Antoine had married an English woman who worked in the Adams household when her employer was Minister of the United States in London. Both had been in his service since then, but he was not able to continue them in his private employment after leaving the White House. He readily gave them a good character when they found an opportunity to continue with the new President. The General said he did not mind if once in a while they went to visit their old master; [23] later he gave Antoine to understand that he and his wife must keep away from the Adamses.[24] After a couple of years both left Jackson's establishment, because, explained Adams, they could not "abide" his Negro slaves and violent temper.[25]

Separation from these two friendly domestics was only one of the personal tribulations that followed the election. What hurt him more than the loss of ten elections, so he said, was the faithlessness of trusted Tobias Watkins, fourth auditor of the Treasury.[26] Unbeknownst to his patron, this familiar had got to gambling, and reached into his official trust to float his personal debts. The Democrats had caught him red-handed. Jackson had the grim satisfaction of having him indicted by a federal grand jury, tried, convicted, and put in jail. Then he had a sign hung over the miscreant's cell: "Criminal's Apartment." Adams, of course, could not defend the rascal,[27] but he resented the "outward flourish of indignation" by which Jackson "glutted his personal revenge" upon the wretched apothecary.[28]

President Jackson's lieutenants eventually uncovered seven other cases of embezzlement in the Treasury Department, mostly collectors of cus-

[22] *Memoirs*, VIII, 215.

[23] *Memoirs*, VIII, 103, 108–9.

[24] LCA to CFA, Washington, November 15, 1829. Adams MSS.

[25] After leaving Jackson's employ Antoine and his wife opened up an oyster and coffee house and within five or six years saved enough money to retire comfortably to a cottage and garden of their own. They remained in friendly contact with their former employers. Diary, November 28, 1840. Adams MSS.

[26] *Memoirs*, VIII, 141.

[27] The scholarly Carl Russell Fish thought the defalcation more technical than criminal. *Civil Service and the Patronage*, p. 128.

[28] *Memoirs*, VIII, 290.

toms distant from the capital, from Portsmouth, New Hampshire, to St. Marks, Florida. They had stolen a total of $280,000.[29] Adams suffered as much over these defalcations as Jackson did later when similar, bigger thieves turned up in his Administration. For instance, there was Samuel Swartwout, who went to Washington in March 1829 to see what he could pick up in the general scramble for plunder. The Old Hero gave him the juiciest plum of all: collectorship of the Port of New York. This "king of defaulters" stole more money under Jackson, and got away with it to Europe, than all the miscreants of the Adams Administration put together. And he was only one of many.[30] Not even the high standards of civil service under Adams nor the party discipline of his successor could keep the Treasury safe from official looters.

Soon the victors were in full possession of the green pastures, and the vanquished had drifted from the scene—at least until the next session of Congress. At Meridian Hill, Adams found himself withdrawn as completely as if he had been a thousand miles from the nation's capital.[31] However painful and mortifying his defeat, he welcomed the relief from responsibility, the quiet of the countryside. He would have been tranquil in his temporary retreat, except for old adversaries, onetime friends, who he thought had taken the occasion to pounce upon him in his downfall [32] by reviving an old controversy between him and the Essex Junto back in the time of Jefferson's Administration. It is to these former contentions that we must now turn our attention as we follow the ex-President through a period of enforced retirement from the political seethings of the day.

[29] Claude G. Bowers: *Party Battles of the Jackson Period* (Cambridge, 1922), p. 75.

[30] Bowers, above noted, might have consulted Fish: *Civil Service and the Patronage,* pp. 134–9. Leonard White's recent works on *The Jeffersonians* and *The Jacksonians* treat authoritatively these questions.

[31] JQA to William Plumer, Meridian Hill, April 16, 1829. Adams MSS.

[32] JQA to CFA, Washington, January 15, 1821. Adams MSS.

CHAPTER IX

The Thirteen Confederates
(1829 – 1830)

. . . the inhabitants of this mighty empire are fellow-citizens of one republic . . . never to be dissolved. . . .

JOHN QUINCY ADAMS'S REPLY TO
THE *Appeal* OF THE MASSACHUSETTS
FEDERALISTS, 1829 [1]

THE MINORITY PRESIDENT repudiated by his countrymen at the close of
his constitutional term did not seem so much worried about future political contention and leadership as he was immediately concerned to justify
his own record in the shifting struggles of the past. During the campaign
of 1828 his onetime friend and colleague of Embargo days in the Senate,
William B. Giles of Virginia, now a bitter political enemy, had succeeded
in entangling him in an unnecessary and unprofitable quarrel with certain
Federalist leaders of Massachusetts. The ensuing controversy illustrates
the compulsive psychology of John Quincy Adams and the emotional
overtones that always accompanied it.

1

The reader of the first volume of this biography will recall that the Federalist Party of Massachusetts had sent Adams to the United States Senate in 1803 after his return from his first tour of diplomatic duty in
Europe, only to be dismayed by the independent attitude which he manifested, particularly his approval of the Louisiana Purchase. He finally
parted company with the party on a vital question of foreign policy when
he voted for the Embargo that President Jefferson rushed through Congress with no chance for deliberation. Federalist charges of Jefferson's
complicity with Napoleon in instituting the Embargo soon made Senator
Adams uneasy. The Embargo certainly fitted in neatly with Napoleon's
Continental System against England, but Adams suspected that certain

[1] Printed posthumously, as edited by his grandson Henry Adams, in *Documents
Relating to New England Federalism, 1800–1815* (Boston, 1877), p. 329. Hereinafter
cited as *New England Federalism*.

Federalist leaders, the Essex Junto, were conniving with Great Britain rather than that Jefferson was concerting with Napoleon. His suspicions had been aroused by an intriguing letter which he had seen from the Governor General of Canada, Sir James H. Craig, circulated in Massachusetts in 1807 when war seemed certain after the *Chesapeake-Leopard* outrage.[2] This led him to confer confidentially with several Republican colleagues in the Senate: with Giles of Virginia, and Representative Wilson Cary Nicholas of the same state; and with Senator Jonathan Robinson of Vermont. They urged him to have a talk with President Jefferson. An interview took place on March 15, 1808.[3]

Young Adams told the President about the Craig letter. Both men silently drew the obvious inference of an unpatriotic—to say the least—collusion between Massachusetts separatists and the British Government opposed to Jefferson's foreign—and domestic—policy. Jefferson on his part assured Adams that he had never had any negotiation with France on the subject of the Embargo, nor any understanding whatever with Napoleon.[4] That was enough for Adams. In a long public letter to his Federalist friend Harrison Gray Otis of Boston he frankly put the interest of the Union, the nation's interest, above that of his own section, in supporting the President.[5]

The communication failed to convince the Massachusetts Federalists, and the legislature of the state in effect recalled Adams by electing and instructing his successor over a year ahead of time. Thus rebuked, he immediately resigned his seat.

Although Adams, in defiance of his Federalist colleagues and constituents, had voted for the Embargo as a means of supporting the President in a national question of peace or war, he soon realized how ineffective and risky the measure really was. Returned to private life in Massachusetts he warned his Republican friends in Congress, including Giles, that the Embargo if continued might drive the New England Federalists to extremities.[6] He had in mind Timothy Pickering's conspiracy of 1804 to set up a separate confederacy of the Northern states after Jefferson's addition of Louisiana to the Union. Adams's advice helped to carry through Congress repeal of the hated Embargo and substitution of a new bill, presented by Giles, the famous Non-Intercourse Act of March 2, 1809.[7]

---

[2] The time element would seem to make it impossible to associate this letter with the secret and separate reconnaissances to Massachusetts of John Henry and John Howe in 1808 and 1809 for the Governor General of Canada and the Lieutenant Governor of Nova Scotia respectively.

[3] Vol. I, 142–7.

[4] *Memoirs*, I, 512, 518–23.

[5] See *Interesting Correspondence between His Excellency Governour Sullivan and Col. Pickering* . . . (Boston, 1808). John Quincy Adams to Harrison Gray Otis, March 31, 1808. *Writings*, III, 220–2.

[6] *Writings*, III, 238–88.

[7] Vol. I, 148–50.

Adams's confidential interview with Jefferson of March 15, 1808 and his private letters of advice to Republican Senators had never been made known to the public, although his split with the Federalist Party was of course a matter of historical record. All this old controversy seemed, like the subsequent Hartford Convention, "hidden in the receptacle of things lost upon earth" when seventeen years later President Adams sent Congress his first annual message, on Liberty with Power.

To Giles, Adams's bold national program signalized a converted Republican's reversion to his old Federalist allegiance, completion of a two-fold apostasy. He resolved to write some "political disquisitions" stressing the personal "inducements" that had prompted Adams's conversion from Federalism to Republicanism and to trace his shifty political career since then. Picturing himself as the original father-confessor of John Quincy Adams's first change of political heart, Giles appealed to the aged Jefferson for an account of the interview of March 15, 1808, which, he promised, he would publish only with permission. "Without hearing directly from you in relation to the present crisis in our political affairs, I take it for granted that you view it with the same regrets and alarms that I do."[8]

Giles expected that any statement from Jefferson would cause Adams to be pressed for further explanations. His purpose, of course, was to show that Adams had risen to the Presidency by betraying both parties, and all his friends both North and South.

Jefferson responded with two letters. The first, of December 25, 1825, gave an infirm recollection of the interview of March 15, 1808, all mixed up with memories of the later War of 1812. It ended by stressing Senator Adams's patriotic motives and the personal disinterestedness of his support of the Embargo when the safety of his country was brought into question.

Jefferson wrote again to Giles the next day, December 26. "I wrote you a letter yesterday," he began, "of which you will be free to make what use you please. This [second letter] will contain matters not intended for the public eye." It reflected Jefferson's "deep affliction" at the rapid usurpation by the "federal branch" of the Government of the rights reserved by the Constitution to the states, illustrated among other instances by the doctrines of President Adams's recent message to Congress. As if in a final confession of political faith, Jefferson penned a statement of state rights against Adams's implications of Liberty with Power. The author of the Kentucky Resolutions of 1799 characteristically counseled patience and forbearance and reliance on the future chapter of accidents, but barely stopped short of secession as an ultimate remedy: not until the evil of an accumulation of national usurpations would overweigh the evil of separation from the Union should such a final step be taken. To solve the immediate issue of internal improvements under federal authority—

[8] *New England Federalism,* pp. 20–2.

on which his own record had been none too consistent—he urged an amendment to the Constitution.[9] In the last months of his life Jefferson had gone back to his first principles of strict construction. His letter to Giles was a constitutional argument for the South in the new sectional struggle. Let it be repeated it was not intended for the public eye: it was for Giles only.

After Jefferson's death Giles published the *confidential* letter of December 26, 1825 in order to marshal the final political testament of that great man behind state rights,[10] but held back Jefferson's unrestricted letter of December 25 in praise of Adams's personal disinterestedness and patriotism. Somehow it became known that such a letter existed. During the campaign of 1828 Archibald Stuart, a Virginian veteran of the Revolution and staunch supporter of Adams, appealed to Jefferson's grandson, Thomas J. Randolph, for a copy of it. Randolph complied, and Stuart published the letter.[11]

2

Whatever one might think of Giles's betrayal of Jefferson's confidence [12] soon after the latter's death, neither of the letters need have called forth any statement from Adams. He did let the confidential political letter, published by Giles in 1827, pass without comment. There was no call to argue with the shade of Thomas Jefferson on state rights: Adams had already stated his position and staked his political fate on the constitutionality of internal improvements. As to the vindication of Adams's patriotic character, which Jefferson gave leave to publish but which Giles had not chosen to make known,[13] it would have been sufficient, now that it was published, to let it stand without further comment.

Adams nevertheless authorized the *National Intelligencer* to make a statement, October 21, 1828, in his name. After pointing out at some length the tricks that Jefferson's memory had played upon him—something obvious to any informed reader—this declaration went on to explain Adams's letters of 1808 about the Embargo, written to Giles and other Republican members of Congress, as "the solicited advice of friend to friend—both ardent friends to the Administration and to their coun-

---

[9] Thomas Jefferson to William B. Giles, Monticello, December 25, 26, 1825. *New England Federalism*, pp. 11–13.

[10] *Richmond Enquirer*, III, No. 35, September 7, 1827. See *New England Federalism*, pp. 6–9.

[11] Archibald Stuart to Thomas J. Randolph, Charlottesville, October 11, 1828. Thomas Jefferson Randolph to Archibald Stuart, October 11, 1828. Ibid., pp. 10–12.

[12] Giles concealed this bad faith at the time of publication by suppressing the opening lines of the second letter: "I wrote you a letter yesterday, of which you will be free to make what use you please. This will contain matters not intended for the public eye." Ibid., p. 6, n. 1.

[13] Giles explained his failure to publish Jefferson's letter of December 25, 1825, so laudatory to Adams, as due to his charitable disposition not to display the failings in detail of a very old man harassed by current troubles (presumably debts).

try." He had counseled the substitution of non-intercourse for Embargo lest the latter measure lead to violent resistance to the Government.

"In that event," President Adams recalled himself to have warned his Republican friends in Congress, "he had no doubt that the leaders of that [Federalist] Party would secure the cooperation with them of Great Britain; *that their objective was, and had been for several years, a dissolution of the Union, and the establishment of a separate confederation,* he knew from unequivocal evidence, although not provable in a court of law; and that, in the case of a civil war, the aid of Great Britain to effect that purpose would be as surely resorted to, as it would be indispensably necessary to the design." [14]

Giles was delighted at Adams's outburst. The Minority President had practically charged his old Federalist associates with treason! How could a Federalist vote for him now in 1828? And think of the moral effect of the President's charges on the Massachusetts Federalist survivors of Embargo days and of the Hartford Convention! They would be certain to call him publicly to account before their countrymen.

"Mr. Adams's 'Washington *exposé,*'" Giles wrote gleefully to that palladium of state rights, the *Richmond Enquirer,* "must lead to the development of a transaction which will necessarily tend to the *utter ruin of its author.*" [15] Giles himself could not find in his own past correspondence any old letter from Adams that justified the latter's description of the political objectives of "certain" Federalist leaders in 1808, and he doubted whether Adams had written anything to anyone else that would support it.

3

Immediately after the election of November 1828, thirteen prominent Federalists of Massachusetts, headed by Harrison Gray Otis, in a signed public statement called on John Quincy Adams to name the Federalist leaders who had plotted to set up a Northern Confederacy in alliance with Great Britain. What was the nature, they demanded, of the "unequivocal evidence" that he had to prove such a conspiracy? Who were the conspirators?

Most of the thirteen signatories were old personal friends. Otis had been an intimate of Adams's youth. Thomas Handasyd Perkins and Daniel Sargent had been members with young John Quincy Adams of the convivial Crackbrain Club of 1792.[16] Perkins had actively supported Adams in the campaign of 1828. Benjamin Pickman had come to the financial rescue of Adams and his father upon the failure in 1803 of Bird, Savage, and Bird, their London bankers. C. C. Parsons was son of his old law pre-

[14] Ibid., pp. 23–6. Italics inserted. JQA used the italicized words in a letter to William Branch Giles, Boston, November 15, 1808. *Writings,* III, 251.

[15] October 24, 1828. *New England Federalism,* pp. 27–42. Italics inserted.

[16] Vol. I, 26.

ceptor at Newburyport, Theophilus Parsons. Franklin Dexter was son of his old friend Samuel Dexter. Israel Thorndike was the industrialist who had entertained President Adams in his home at Beverly in September 1827. Otis, Perkins, Sargent, Thorndike, and William Sullivan, another signer, had been members of the powerful "Central Committee" that ruled the Federalist Party in the Old Bay State. Two of them, Otis and Prescott, had been delegates to the Hartford Convention. Three of them, Otis, Prescott, and Sullivan, had constituted the abortive Massachusetts "embassy" to carry the petitions of the Convention to Washington in 1815. The Thirteen represented the cream of surviving Federalism.

"A charge of this nature," they jointly declared, referring to the statement authorized by Adams of October 21, 1828, "coming as it does from the First Magistrate of the Nation, acquires an importance which we cannot affect to disregard; and it is one which we ought not to leave unanswered. We are, therefore, constrained, by a regard to our deceased friends and to our posterity, as well as by a sense of what is due to our own honour, most solemnly to declare that we have never known nor suspected that *the party* which prevailed in Massachusetts in the year 1808, or any other party in this State ever entertained the design to produce a dissolution of the Union, or the establishment of a separate confederation." [17]

For themselves they disclaimed any design to produce an effect on any current political party or question, neither was it their purpose to vindicate the measures publicly adopted or avowed in the past by the Federalist leaders, whoever they were, against whom Adams had made his charges. That their challenge, as distinct from Giles's earlier provocation, was devoid of political purpose is evident by the fact that it was not issued until after the election. Their motive was distinctly personal.

Adams received the document the day after he read the final election returns.[18] It was more of a shock than his expected defeat in the Presidential campaign. What a bitter home-coming was being prepared for the return of the native! Repudiated by the nation, he was now to be dishonored among his own people.[19]

[17] Messrs. H. G. Otis, Israel Thorndike, T. H. Perkins, William Prescott, Daniel Sargent, John Lowell, William Sullivan, Charles Jackson, Warren Dutton, Benjamin Pickman, Henry Cabot, C. C. Parsons, and Franklin Dexter to JQA, Boston, November 26, 1828. *New England Federalism*, pp. 43–5. Italics inserted.

[18] *Memoirs*, VIII, 79. December 3, 1828.

[19] "I hear from other quarters," Adams noted in his Diary, "that some of the principal old federalists have determined to break off all personal intercourse with me; so that I shall go into retirement with I know not how many bitter controversies upon my hands." *Memoirs*, VIII, 79. December 5, 1828.

"The desire to know the first movements of a man who has filled a great place is natural, and therefore I send you the rumor of the day, that Mr. A. will remain in this district after the expiration of his term,—his friends say because the state of Mrs. A's health will not bear the rigors of a northern winter,—his enemies, that he waits for the

The defeated President set about preparing an answer to the "Thirteen Confederates," his name for them, which reflects an image of conspiracy to destroy him. With the greatest of care he drafted and redrafted his reply. He showed it to Edward Everett, who tactfully reminded him about the "polite" nature of the Federalists' letter. He asked each member of his expiring Cabinet to criticize the paper: Clay, Rush, Wirt, Southard. He talked to them more about this trouble than he did about the election. Each approved the document weakly, with a minimum of comment—all except perhaps Rush, who wondered whether it were wise for the President to make any answer at all while in office.[20]

Adams's *Reply to the Massachusetts Federalists,* dated December 30, 1828, was designed to vindicate himself before the bar of public opinion and at the same time to remonstrate equably with old friends not to continue a controversy that might do ultimate hurt to men whose reputations rested contentedly in their graves. In the first place, he denied the Thirteen to be representatives of the rank and file of the Federalist Party. Having taken this position, he refused to disclose names of any of the Federalist leaders who were connected with the alleged plot of 1808 to dissolve the Union and establish a separate confederacy. He was willing to satisfy each correspondent individually on that question, he declared, but he rejected their joint right to demand from him names of other people who might hold him legally responsible. The truth was that, as he acknowledged five years later to Benjamin Pickman, none of the living Thirteen had been party to the old "conspiracy." [21] The "unequivocal evidence" had to do not so much with them as with their forebears, and not so much with the year 1807 as with the years 1803–4.

Actually Adams's evidence was mostly hearsay related to him in confidence by men no longer living, such as Rufus King and Uriah Tracy. As testimony sufficient to guide honorable human conduct if not to satisfy a court of law, Adams cited a general design of "certain leaders of the Federalist Party" to secede and form a Northern Confederacy. It went back to the winter following the Louisiana Purchase and Jefferson's attack on the federal judges. The alleged conspirators had even fixed their minds on a military leader, presumably Alexander Hamilton. In all this there was no "overt act of treason," he admitted, but there was a policy on foot, then and thereafter down to the time of the Hartford Convention, to deny the constitutionality of laws of the Federal Government and to resist them by state authority. To Adams this could mean nothing less than disunion and establishment of a separate confederacy. Skillfully he threw over the old Federalist leaders the current malodor of nullification.

Adams's published *Reply* contained a warning to his fellow country-

storm to abate which seems to be brewing in the North East." Thomas H. Benton to Martin Van Buren, December 3, 1828. Van Buren MSS, LC.

[20] *Memoirs,* VIII, 83.

[21] JQA to Benjamin Pickman, Quincy, October 4, 1834. Adams MSS.

men, more explicit than that of his last annual message to Congress of December 2, 1828 on the state of the Union,[22] against the Jeffersonian dogma of nullification which John C. Calhoun was perfecting as an answer of the South to the tariff.

"I . . . hold it as a principle, without exception," Adams declared, "that, whenever the constituted authorities of a State authorize resistance to any act of Congress, or pronounce it unconstitutional, they do thereby declare themselves and their State *quoad hoc* out of the pale of the Union. . . . the *people* of a State . . . have delegated no such power to their legislatures or their judges; and, if there be such a right, it is the right of an individual to commit suicide,—the right of an inhabitant of a populous city to set fire to his own dwelling-house. These are my views. But to those who think that each State is a sovereign judge, not only of its own rights, but of the extent of powers conferred upon the general government by the people of the whole Union; and that each State, giving its own construction to the constitutional powers of Congress, may array its separate sovereignty against every act of that body transcending this estimate of their powers,—to say of men holding these principles, that, for the ten years from 1804 to 1814, they were intending a dissolution of the Union, and the formation of a new confederacy, is charging them with nothing more than with acting up to their principles."

Adams tried to close his public letter on a personal friendly note. "Gentlemen," he concluded, "I have waived every scruple, perhaps even the proprieties of my situation, to give you this answer, in consideration of that long and sincere friendship for some of you which can cease to beat only with the last pulsation of my heart. But I cannot consent to a controversy with you. Here if you please, let our *joint* correspondence rest." Gently he reserved the possibility of making fuller disclosures in his own good time.[23] He signed himself appealingly: "Your friend and fellow-citizen." After all, he would have to go back to Massachusetts to live with these people!

The kindly close and the mild reminder that the writer might be more severe if pressed further did not end the affair. The Thirteen Confederates came back with a public *Appeal to the Citizens of the United States,* January 28, 1829.

John Quincy Adams, the Thirteen now averred, had brought the State of Massachusetts into disrepute by his charges of a plot against the Union. He had not been able to produce "unequivocal evidence" to support this "secret denunciation of his ancient friends." In his high office he had put himself in the predicament of an unjust accuser. Stung by his references to the Hartford Convention, they went on to justify that assembly, something which, in their first letter, they had said they would not discuss or justify, something no longer possible to vindicate unless to Southern nullifiers, to the apostles of slavery itself.

[22] See below, p. 224.   [23] *New England Federalism,* pp. 46–62.

In their first public letter the Thirteen had professed to speak for the old Federalist Party in Massachusetts. Now they were speaking in the name of the State of Massachusetts—which had just cast its vote for Adams in the Presidential election! Soon, reflected Adams, they would presume to be the voice of the whole nation: finally, like Anacharsis Clootz, they would be orators for the whole human race.[24]

4

By blending his answer to the Thirteen with the cause of Union, Adams had thrown his adversaries back on the Hartford Convention. It were well to have let the matter rest there. But the defeated President was worried how the people of Massachusetts would treat him when he got back home, after the Federalist leaders—that is, the inner core of proper Bostonians—had excluded him from their society.[25] His inner compulsions pushed him defensively on. He must unhorse his former friends before they rode him down. Before he left the White House he began labor on a rejoinder to the second publication of the Massachusetts Federalists.

It was difficult to get conclusive proofs of any plot of 1807–8 and the plotters about which he had heard indirectly and in confidence so many years ago. Avidly he searched for more evidence. He requested his son Charles in Boston to collect pamphlets and prints. He reviewed his correspondence files. He consulted his Diary. He wrote to long-standing friends who had not yet deserted him: to Ezekiel Bacon of Utica, a surviving congressional correspondent of 1808–9; to Charles King of New York, son of Rufus King, intimate of Timothy Pickering and the Essex Junto, friend of Alexander Hamilton; to honest Robert Walsh of Philadelphia; to old William Plumer of New Hampshire, historical annalist of the *Journal and Proceedings of the United States Senate*, once a colleague from New Hampshire when Adams sat in that body, a fellow deserter from the Federalist Party. He addressed himself to Thomas Jefferson Randolph, grandson of Jefferson and custodian of his papers, and to ex-President James Madison. He appealed to them all for further verification of the plottings of the Essex Junto. All except Plumer were reticent, though cordial. They were not able, or not willing, as with Charles King and his brothers, to divulge anything. They wanted to keep out of the quarrel. But from the elder Plumer soon came some frank and unexpected revelations.

Plumer had been an advocate of New England separatism as an answer to Jeffersonian Democracy and the Louisiana Purchase, and had lived to regret it as the greatest political mistake in his life.[26] As if to make amends in the tranquillity of his old age for such a grave error of earlier years, he

24 *Ibid.*, p. 211.
25 CFA to LCA, November 15, December 20, 1828. Adams MSS.
26 See Papers of William Plumer, Autobiography and Letterbooks, in LC.

now opened himself to his lifelong friend. He had known all about the plan in 1803–4, he acknowledged, to establish a confederacy of the Northern and Eastern states to escape the rising power of the growing West and the clutch of the slaveholding South. The separatists had planned to have a meeting in Boston in the autumn of 1804. Alexander Hamilton had consented to attend the meeting, but his death had canceled the proposed conclave. Plumer himself at that time had favored it; later he became convinced of his folly, and when the project was revived in 1808 and 1809 and during the War of 1812 he used every effort in his power to defeat it.[27] The plot lived on after 1804, said Plumer, though he thought that a majority of the Federalist leaders were opposed to it.

Plumer gave the President complete liberty to make such use of his statement as he thought proper. In a separate, confidential letter of the same date, he mentioned the names of some of the members of Congress who had first broached the separatist plan to him: Senator Uriah Tracy of Connecticut, Roger Griswold, Representative from Connecticut, and Samuel Hunt, Representative from New Hampshire. He listed others supposed to be in the plot: James Hillhouse, the junior Senator from Connecticut, and Timothy Pickering.[28] All these were now dead, except Pickering, who died on January 29, 1829.

This new evidence surprised and comforted Adams. He had never known or suspected that his old senatorial colleague had any relations with the plotters. He turned over to Jonathan Elliot, editor of the *Washington City Gazette*, such of the revelations as Plumer authorized to be published, and supplementary papers, to be added to a reprint of the Thirteen Confederates' *Appeal.*[29] He sent copies of the resulting pamphlet to his two sons in Boston so that they could be masters of the facts as they observed public reaction to the controversy. *They* would see that their father "never deserted his party, never denounced his friends, never charged any man with treason, and never ceased to exercise every faculty of his soul to preserve and maintain the Union, the Constitution, and laws of his Country." It was rather the Federalists who had deserted their country in 1807 and after.[30]

First reaction to the Plumer letter was a summons from James A. Hamilton. This son of Alexander Hamilton was Van Buren's man Friday. He

---

[27] William Plumer to JQA, Epping, N.H., December 20, 1828. *New England Federalism*, pp. 144–6.

[28] William Plumer to JQA, Epping, N.H., January 16, 1829. Adams MSS.

[29] *Memoirs*, VIII, 96–8. See *Correspondence between John Quincy Adams, Esquire, President of the United States, and Several Citizens of Massachusetts Concerning the Charge of a Design to Dissolve the Union Alleged to Have Existed in that State, to which are Now Added Additional Papers, Illustrative of the Subject* (Washington: printed and sold by J. Elliot; 1829).

[30] JQA to CFA, No. 46, Washington, February 20, 1829. JQA to GWA, No. 10/104, Washington, February 24, 1829. Adams MSS.

had arrived in Washington to administer the Department of State until his patron could wind up his responsibilities as newly elected Governor of New York and take up Cabinet duties under Jackson. In a letter sealed with the impression of a bulldog and the motto "take heed," [31] Hamilton demanded to know whether anything in Adams's reply to the Confederates, or in Plumer's letter, implicated his father in a separatist conspiracy.[32] Adams promptly replied, stating very explicitly that he understood that although Alexander Hamilton was aware of the plot of 1804 he was opposed to it and that if he had gone to the Boston meeting it would have been with the desire of dissuading his friends from their plans.[33] This satisfied James Hamilton completely, who proceeded to publish the exchange of letters. He added an extract from a speech by DeWitt Clinton in the New York Senate, January 31, 1809, saying the same thing about Alexander Hamilton's relation to the separatist project of 1804—that he disapproved it.[34] Some friendly interviews followed at Meridian Hill. The Adamses and the Hamiltons, steady political opponents that they had been personally, always had at least one magnificent end in common: that was a strong Union with a government of national power for the general welfare.

5

In the quiet of his hilltop retreat Adams worked zealously on his proposed Reply to the Appeal of the Massachusetts Federalists. He gave to it the freshest hours of the morning. He went over it sheet by sheet with Philip R. Fendall, who was now preparing to write, perhaps with the collaboration or at least the assistance of his former chief, a History of the United States up to and including the recent Administration. Fendall softened up some of Adams's asperities.

Steadily the Reply to the Appeal lengthened. It became almost a history of party controversy in the United States, going back to the old issues of his father's Presidency: Hamilton's quarrel with John Adams; the split in the Federalist Party that brought Thomas Jefferson into power; the Louisiana Purchase and Jefferson's attack on the judiciary that served

[31] JQA to GWA, Meridian Hill, March 13, 1829. Adams MSS.

[32] James A. Hamilton to JQA, and JQA to JAH, Washington, March 6, 1829. Adams MSS.

[33] This conviction rested on a conversation which Adams recalled having had with Rufus King during several days' sojourn in New York in April 1804. *New England Federalism*, pp. 147–8.

Adams's published Diary notes that he had conversations with Rufus King on public affairs in New York on April 8 and 10, 1804, but it does not record what was said. *Memoirs*, I, 313. His unprinted Diary mentions a call and walk with Mr. King on April 11, but does not reveal any conversation. Adams MSS.

[34] *Memoirs*, VIII, 118.

to foment the separatism of the Essex Junto and the subsequent movement of New England Federalism toward disunion; the maritime issues
with England culminating in the War of 1812 and the defeatist Hartford
Convention happily frustrated by the Peace of Ghent.

Adams wrote down the names of the conspirators, certainly enough to
have answered the Thirteen Confederates, if that were really what they
wanted. The arch-plotter was Timothy Pickering. Included were George
Cabot [35] and Theophilus Parsons of Massachusetts; James Hillhouse of
New Haven; and William Plumer of New Hampshire before he saw the
light. He could also have named Uriah Tracy and Roger Griswold of
Connecticut, but for the confidence imposed in Plumer's last letter.[36] But
with all his urge of suspicions he could not quite prove that Harrison Gray
Otis was an advocate of separation. Protesting communicants privy to the
plot were Alexander Hamilton, Rufus King, and perhaps Senator James A.
Bayard of Delaware. Reporters to the British Government were Minister
George Rose and John Henry, emissary of the Governor General of Can-
ada in 1808, who later took another tack and sold his records to President
Madison.

The private papers of Timothy Pickering, Gouverneur Morris, Rufus
King, William Plumer, and the archives of the British Government, not
then available to Adams, have long since corroborated the conspiracy of
"certain Federalist leaders" for nullification and disunion *in the year
1804*, if not in 1808.[37] In the event of Aaron Burr's election as Governor of

---

[35] Cabot in his letter of February 14, 1804 to Pickering said he did not desire a
separation "at this monent": it would not be "practicable" without "the intervention
of some cause which should be very generally felt and distinctly understood as charge-
able to the misconduct of our Southern masters! Such, for example, as a war with
Great Britain, manifestly provoked by our rulers. . . ." John Quincy Adams could not
have known of this letter in Pickering's papers, later printed in H. C. Lodge's life of
George Cabot and reprinted in 1877 by Henry Adams in *New England Federalism*,
pp. 346–9.

[36] *Life of William Plumer, by His Son, William Plumer, Jr., with a Sketch of the
Author's Life*, by A. P. Peabody (Boston, 1856), pp. 290–2. Adams remembered
talking in the Senate with Tracy about the project of 1804.

In the Letterbook of William Plumer, Vol. VIII, there is this note, in Plumer's
handwriting, after the copy of his open letter of December 20, 1828 to JQA, and before his confidential letter of the same date to the same person. This "Private Note
Not Sent to the President" reads: "The persons with whom I had the numerous conversations alluded to were:

Simeon Olcott, Senator	from New Hampshire
Samuel Hunt, Representative	" " "
Uriah Tracy, Senator	from Connecticut
James Hillhouse, Senator	" "
Roger Griswold, Representative	" "
Calvin Goddard, Representative	" "

Papers of William Plumer, LC.

[37] The late John T. Morse, Jr., a biographer of *John Quincy Adams* (Cambridge:
American Statesman Series; 1882) and grandson of Charles Jackson, one of the Thir-

New York they hoped to add that state and perhaps Pennsylvania to the proposed new confederacy. They gambled on Burr to lead the way.

It was to prevent such a consummation that Alexander Hamilton accepted Burr's challenge and laid down his life at Weehawken Heights in July 1804. As he put it in the final sentence of his famous letter to posterity, written on the eve of the fatal duel: "The ability to be in the future useful, whether *in resisting mischief* or effecting good, in those crises of our political affairs which seem likely to happen, would probably be inseparable with a conformity with public prejudice in this particular." [38]

Although Adams had disavowed to Hamilton's son James any understanding that his patriot father was other than opposed to the plot of 1804, his mind kept coming back to these last words. He couldn't help wondering whether Hamilton, disapproving as he did of the separatist project, would not have yielded after all to ambition had he lived to attend the projected Boston meeting:

"I would hope, and may not disbelieve, that Mr. Hamilton's attachment to the Union was of that stubborn, inflexible character which, under no circumstances, would have found him arrayed in arms against it. But, in the events of Mr. Hamilton's life, a comparison of his conduct with his opinions, in more than one instance, exhibits him in that class of human characters whose sense of rectitude itself is swayed by the impulses of the heart, and the purity of whose virtue is tempered by the baser metal of the ruling passion." [39]

Such misgivings were unjust to the nobler and ruling elements of Hamilton's character, never better expressed than in his farewell to the world.

Adams's manuscript also contained other severe *obiter dicta* on the demagoguery and atheism of Thomas Jefferson, friend of his boyhood, the President to whom he had confided his suspicions of New England Federalists in 1808.[40] It will be more convenient to present in detail in a later chapter Adams's feelings about Jefferson.

Fortunately the ex-President tempered his personal obsessions by showing his manuscript to some trusted friends—to his cousin Judge Cranch,

---

teen Confederates, declared in a note (ibid., p. 220): ". . . a thorough study of the whole subject has convinced me that Mr. Adams was unquestionably and completely right, and I have no escape from saying so. His adversaries had the excuse of honesty in political error—an excuse which the greatest and wisest men must often fall back upon in times of hot party warfare."

Professor Samuel Eliot Morison, a great-grandson of Harrison Gray Otis, and his biographer, points out that separatist sentiment in Federalist circles of New England was no worse than the threat of nullification or secession in any other state or section during the nationally unsettled period before the Civil War. He shows that Otis himself never actually favored disunion. *The Life and Letters of Harrison Gray Otis* (2 vols., Boston, 1913), I, 268–70; II, 158–9, 172–3.

[38] Italics inserted.
[39] *New England Federalism*, pp. 169–70.
[40] Ibid., p. 154.

to the William Plumers, father and son, to Robert Walsh, to the Everett brothers—and asking their advice. The Plumers felt that he might go ahead with it, but the others counseled him not to publish the rejoinder no matter how telling, certainly not without some judicious expurgation. Adams's son Charles had thought it better to let the unprofitable contest blow over without being revived by the "testiness" of his father's "sarcasm." [41] The friends consulted did not give their reasons for going slow on publication. But they are evident enough. The gratuitous reflections on Jefferson and Hamilton were too harsh, too prejudiced, too subjective. The passages on Otis were too challenging. The main argument would have been too painful a reminder to good Unionist friends of his, like Nathan Dane of Beverly, who had gone to Hartford in 1814 but who would not sign the *Appeal* of the Thirteen Confederates in 1828.[42] Publication would have brought New England's historic precedent for nullification—perhaps even secession—too conspicuously into public attention contemporaneously with nullification in South Carolina.

There was perhaps another reason for not publishing the long manuscript. For the first time Adams would have come out openly in condemnation of slavery. To the "sable power of slavery" he ascribed the recrudescence of state rights that had defeated his national program of internal improvements physical and moral. To that sinister influence he attributed Giles's attempt to enlist Jefferson against the policies of the Adams Administration. It was slavery that had brought about the gloomy sunset of his political life. But to take a public stand against slavery at this time might shut him out from ever witnessing another sunrise through White House windows. He finally decided not to publish.[43] Ten years afterward he had forgiven his erring friends: "Their policy, which I encountered and exposed, has long been buried fathoms deep, never to rise again." [44]

Half a century later, long after the moldering relics of the Essex Junto and the Hartford Convention had whitened bare in the sepulcher of history, John Quincy Adams's gifted grandson the historian Henry Adams published the manuscript for the first time with sustaining documents then available. The printed text contained some 84,000 words [45]—all the manuscript except some of the bitterest paragraphs on Otis. The expurgated passages which Henry Adams felt it wise to delete assumed that Otis was the real author of the *Appeal*—as documents discovered as late

[41] CFA to LCA, Boston, November 15, December 20, 1828. Adams MSS.

[42] JQA to Alexander H. Everett, Quincy, September 18, 1831. Adams MSS. For Dane, see Chapter XII, below.

[43] *New England Federalism,* p. 139.

[44] *Memoirs,* X, 469.

[45] *Reply to the Appeal of the Massachusetts Federalists* in *New England Federalism,* pp. 107–329. For sustaining documents, principally from the Pickering MSS. in MHS, see pp. 330–46.

as 1954 would seem to indicate [46]—as well as of the Hartford Convention, that immedicable sore of his career, the ominous example to separatists outside of New England. "Stand forth, Harrison Gray Otis, before the people of this Union, our common Country," Adams had challenged. "The question is between you and me. The question is between the Hartford Convention and the Union." [47]

The postponed contribution to the literature of American political controversy closes with a pæan of praise and thanksgiving for the frustration of New England separatism in the War of 1812 and the continuing preservation of the Union after the gladsome Peace of Ghent:

"Under the beneficent guidance of this overruling power, the projected New England confederacy and the war with Great Britain, two of the greatest calamities which have ever befallen this Union, have been turned into two of the most effective instruments for its preservation. The Hartford Convention is a perpetual *momento mori* to every deliberate projector of disunion throughout this confederate republic. . . . Fourteen years have elapsed since the peace with Great Britain was concluded, and since that day no portion of this great confederation has been more faithfully devoted to the Union, none more candid and liberal in support of the administration of the general government, than New England. During the same time, a steady system of gradual increase and improvement of the navy has been in constant operation, and has been adding from year to year to the strength, the dignity, and the security of the nation. And may that Being in whose hands are the destinies of men continue thus to protect and preserve that great bond by which the inhabitants of this

[46] In 1954 the Massachusetts Historical Society acquired the Wendell Papers from a descendant of Charles Jackson, one of the Thirteen Confederates of 1828. This collection includes a bundle of papers containing drafts of the *Appeal*, and informal notes relating thereto. An undated letter of H. G. Otis to Jackson says that preparation of the *Appeal* was put into the hands of "Mr. L.[Lowell] and myself. . . . We have to meet and correct in sub-committee then in whole—then to contract for printing, etc." A postscript to one of the drafts reads:
"Bubble bubble, toil and trouble
When shall we five meet again?"
Initials and signatures to the papers indicate that the five members of the drafting committee were: H. G. Otis, William Sullivan, Charles Jackson, John Lowell, and William Prescott.

[47] MS. copy of the Reply to the Appeal, pp. 152–3, 188–91, 226–8. Adams MSS. In 1834–5 there was a touching exchange of correspondence between John Quincy Adams and his old friend Benjamin Pickman of Salem, one of the Thirteen. Feeling himself in the twilight of life, Pickman in the friendliest of terms solemnly adjured Adams to do the Federalists the justice of presenting evidence on who the alleged plotters and traitors were. In equally friendly vein Adams assured Pickman that neither he nor any of the thirteen signers were among them. As evidence for the old conspirators he cited DeWitt Clinton's speech in the New York Senate of January 21, 1809 and Plumer's letter to JQA of December 20, 1828, above mentioned. Benjamin Pickman to JQA, Salem, September 27, 1834, January 20, 1835. JQA to Benjamin Pickman, Quincy, October 4, 1834, and January 20, 1835. Adams MSS.

mighty empire are fellow-citizens of one republic . . . never to be dissolved. . . ." [48]

With this posthumous invocation to Union we may end the chapter. John Quincy Adams had blown off a lot of steam on Meridian Hill, but fortunately the public knew nothing about it.

[48] *New England Federalism,* pp. 328–9.

CHAPTER X

The Trials of Job
(1829 – 1831)

It is in affliction itself that the splendor of God's
mercy shines, from its very depths, in the heart of
its inconsolable bitterness.

SIMONE WEIL: *Waiting for God* [1]

THE WARM sun of a late Washington spring had dried the mud on the
highways. At last the weather seemed settled. Mrs. Adams was perhaps a
little stronger, at least no worse. Her husband's health had firmed with
the controversial occupation of his writing table and respite from official
responsibilities. The Reply to the Thirteen Confederates was almost finished. It was time for him and his family to start for home and see what
awaited them from his former friends in Boston.[2] He sent for his son
George to come from Massachusetts and help manage their trip.[3] Charles
Francis, the third son, would get the Big House in Quincy ready to receive
them. John Adams, 2d would remain in Washington, where he planned to
build a new house for his own family.

On the fourth Sunday in April, John Quincy Adams walked to the Second Presbyterian Church, perhaps for the last time. His friend Dr. James
Laurie was in the pulpit. President Jackson was in the congregation. The
minister read for the scripture lesson of the day the fourteenth chapter of
Job with such power and energy as to make the familiar words sound almost new. "Man that is born of woman is of few days and full of trouble."

The minister's manner as he read the trials of Job impressed the former
President exceedingly.[4] Sitting there in the pew he reviewed the ups and
downs of his own life. What did the future hold for him after the hour
of defeat, for himself and for his family?

Outside, the horse-chestnut trees were fresh and green after late flurries
of snow. The song of mating birds came flutelike through the branches.

---

[1] New York: G. P. Putnam's Sons; 1951, p. 88. Quoted with permission of the
publisher.
[2] *Memoirs*, VIII, 149. April 30, 1829.
[3] JQA to GWA, Meridian Hill, April 20, 1829. Adams MSS.
[4] Diary, April 26, 1829.

To many of those within the church the festival of nature gaily restoring herself out of earth's bounty must have contrasted painfully with the trials of a government renewing itself periodically from the people's favor.

Dr. Laurie came to the last verse: "But his flesh upon him shall have pain, and his soul within him shall mourn." Quietly the pastor closed the Book. Facing John Quincy Adams and Andrew Jackson, he began his sermon.

1

In Boston things had not been mending in the personal affairs of George Washington Adams. The President's earnest exhortations, whether by letters from the White House or in long heart-to-heart conferences, had failed to hold the young man to a stable course. Business fell into arrears or went unattended. Accounts dropped behind. The favored steward did not give his father's affairs the attention due to any client. He delayed making quarterly statements, or made none at all. He failed to answer letters asking for them. He grew more and more careless about his own affairs. He squandered the money loaned him to save selling his books and the few shares of bank stock built up from his grandfather's legacy. He had got into debt once more, "for books." Should he sell his library? It was worth perhaps $2,500. Again he appealed to his father.

Coming to his aid once more, John Quincy Adams "bought" the young man's books for $2,000. To make it seem like a real sale he instructed George to send a list of them, so that the father might pick out certain volumes for his own name plates, allowing George to hold the others as "agent."

Six months later the President had not received the list of books.[5]

John Quincy Adams was a loving if not an overindulgent parent. But the more he did for his eldest son, the more there was to do and the less disposition on George's part to requite it over preachments and advice.[6] It was the same old story, familiar from the day of the prodigal son to that of the modern psychiatrist. The irresponsible youth expects help without wanting to help himself. The loving father is willing to help and help, but he continues to give advice and admonishment and to expect gratitude and affection in return.

George was again in evil days when, during the last weeks of the hopeless electoral campaign of 1828, his father came back to Massachusetts.

---

[5] JQA to GWA, No. 5/93, July 10, 1828. Adams MSS.

[6] "And now let me once more implore you by every consideration that can operate upon your heart, by all that you have dear in this world, and especially by your filial gratitude and affection, never more to burden yourself with shameless expenses and senseless debts. As to Books! debts for BOOKS! of what earthly use to you are, or can be books, with such a life as you have led? The very possession of books is a perpetual sarcasm upon your prostitution of your time to licentiousness. You are surprised to find yourself indebted for your necessary expenses, even for your board!" JQA to GWA, January 21, 1828. Adams MSS.

He was deep in debt. He couldn't even pay his board with Dr. Welsh. His brother Charles wrote to their mother that George was living like a pig.[7] One Henry Wood was pressing him for payment of a thousand-dollar note. More intimate talks followed between father and son. We can only surmise their nature.[8] Back in Washington, at Christmastide, he sent George a check to take up Wood's note. Once more he admonished him to profit by bitter experience.[9]

It was useless. George was soon back in his old loose habits and in more trouble. He had become involved with a chambermaid, one Eliza Dolph, in the Welsh household. In December 1828 she gave birth to a child and part of the borrowed money was being used to take care of this problem. He had already addressed a confidential letter to his brother Charles Francis explaining the predicament: if he should die within the year 1828, he said, he wished his debts to be paid and the balance be secured for her, to be forfeited in case of ill conduct. This paper he put in a trunk with his most personal effects, and told his brother there was an important document to look for in case anything happened to himself.[10]

When his father's letter arrived asking him to come to Washington to help take home his fond and ailing mother, George Washington Adams was broke, forlorn, worried, panicky, teetering on the edge of reason. He dreaded to face his parents, who were waiting to receive him with utmost kindness, confidence, and affection.[11] The strain of the impending trip was more than he could stand. He began to have hallucinations.

7 CFA to LCA, Boston, March 28, 1829. Adams MSS.

8 The Diary is unaccountably vacant for the period from August 6, when the President arrived at Philadelphia en route for Quincy, until December 1, 1828, following his return to Washington. Perhaps it is because troubles were coming so thick and fast that it was too discouraging to set them down. Even if he had been able to keep up the journal there would be no note in it on such matters. He did not write the Diary for public posterity, but rather for the eyes of his children and his children's children, and one would not expect to find there any confidences relating to one of them for the others later to read. It is in the letters of John Quincy Adams to the unfortunate George and in the correspondence of George and younger brother Charles Francis with their father and mother in Washington that the sad story unfolds. Only fragments of George's journals, correspondence, and papers, have been preserved. See note 27. Whether JQA knew about Eliza Dolph is uncertain. His own papers do not refer to the affair, which was made public in the unofficial *Report of a Trial: Miles Farmer versus Dr. Humphrey Storer . . . reported by the Plaintiff* (Boston: printed for the Reporter; 1831). See the editorial notes in *Diary of Charles Francis Adams*, edited by Aida DiPace Donald and David Donald (Cambridge: Belknap Press of Harvard University Press; 1964), II, 376 *et passim*.

9 "In the hope that bitter experience will have more effect upon your future conduct than all the counsels and warnings that I have lavished upon you, I remain, your still and ever affectionate father." JQA to GWA, No. 12/75, Washington, December 22, 1827. Adams MSS.

10 Diary of CFA, Wednesday, May 13, 1829. Adams MSS.

11 "George will be received with the utmost kindness, confidence and affection by all." LCA to CFA, Meridian Hill, April 16, 1829. Adams MSS.

Birds seemed to be speaking to him. Two nights before he departed he fancied that somebody was trying to break into his room. He got up and looked around the chamber, could find nobody, but could not rid himself of the impression.

He took the stage from Boston Wednesday morning, April 29. Arriving at Providence, he immediately boarded the palatial new steamboat *Benjamin Franklin*,[12] Captain E. S. Bunker, for New York. To passengers that afternoon he seemed rational and cheerful, but in the evening he complained of a severe headache and wished the motion of the boat would only get strong enough to make him really seasick. There was a missionary on board, with some Indians in his charge; George gave him a donation. Tobias Watkins was there too, on his way from Boston to Washington to face arrest.

As the evening wore on, George felt worse. The ship's engines seemed to be talking to him. "Let it be, let it be," they kept saying. "Let it be, let it be." The wheels churned round and round in his head: "Let it be." He went to bed, but got up repeatedly. Then he awakened a passenger and asked if he had been circulating rumors against him among the other passengers. When this person said no, George went with a candle from berth to berth, peering at the occupants. Finally he went back to his own bed. About three o'clock in the morning, Thursday, April 30, he got up again and asked the captain to stop the ship and set him on shore.

The boat was then in the lower reaches of Long Island Sound, making about sixteen miles an hour.

"Why do you wish to be set ashore?" asked Captain Bunker.

"There is a combination among the passengers against me," declared the miserable man. "I heard them talking and laughing at me."

A few minutes later he fell into conversation with Mr. John Stevens of Boston, a warm Jackson partisan hurrying to Washington to get a job. About ten minutes after he left Stevens the latter, walking on the upper deck, noticed George's hat near the stern. It was then about an hour or more before sunrise, the stars still showing above the horizon like sparks at sea. A search was made immediately. All that was to be found was George's cloak, not far from the hat. There was no other trace of the owner.[13]

2

The news reached Washington on Saturday, May 2, by way of a notice in the *Baltimore American* of that morning. Louisa's brother-in-law Nathaniel Frye brought it to Meridian Hill about one o'clock in the after-

[12] For descriptions of this floating palace of the day see *Columbian Centinel* of Boston, Nos. 4634, 4635, 4636. September 6, 10, 13, 1828.

[13] These are the facts as set down finally in JQA's Diary chiefly from information furnished by a young man by the name of Keep, who had struck up an acquaintance with George on the ship. John Quincy Adams wrote to Stevens asking for more particulars, and received a reply, but the letters are apparently not preserved.

noon. Then another kinsman, Judge Cranch, of the District of Columbia court, called and confirmed the news. He delivered letters from Charles King and George Sullivan in New York, and one from the firm of Davis and Brooks, undertakers, that had taken charge of George's baggage.

Now the lesson of the previous Sunday out of the Book of Job, which had lingered in John Quincy Adams's mind all through the week, bore upon him and his wife with crushing reality.[14] Their suffering was so deep and prostrating as to threaten their own reason. They regarded the death of their eldest son as the punishment of Heaven for their mistaken zeal in continuing to discipline and urge the man for his own welfare "to exertion foreign to his nature." [15]

First upon their hearts was the irreparable loss of a beloved son. All her life Louisa would recall with anguish the ecstasy with which she had clasped her first-born to her breast in those bleak days in Berlin twenty-eight years before. She repented having left him and his brother so long in other hands during the tender years of youth.[16] It rent the father's heart to think of his son, "as he was, all goodness and affection." [17] They no longer dared to look ahead. So completely had they been wrapped up in the future of this brilliant son, heir apparent to the patriotic career of the Adams family, that all prospects of delight for the remainder of their lives seemed destroyed.[18]

By his death George brought his parents together as nothing else could do, not even his birth. They prayed for each other continually, seeking the mercy of Heaven for deserved chastisements, imploring divine help in holding fast to their Christian faith, seeking for fuller revelation of God's will and purpose in this affliction.[19] The mother was so fearful that her heart might betray its own agony in the language of reproach or blame and thereby add to her husband's misery that she begged him not to believe anything she might say in her wanderings.[20] His sufferings were almost beyond control.

The husband who sometimes had seemed so harsh in his outward manner was now tenderness itself, a ministering angel always at Louisa's side.[21] At her request he recited before the family the service for the dead from the Episcopal Book of Common Prayer—his wife's religion out of Old England. In her invalid chamber he read to her from books of travel and novels, trying to distract her unstanched grief.

Alone, John Quincy Adams poured out his heart in prayer during long

[14] Diary, Sunday, May 3, 1829.
[15] Diary, May 4, 1829. LCA to CFA, Meridian Hill, July 5, 1829. Adams MSS.
[16] Statement of LCA, April 12, 1847, "the birthday of my first-born son." Adams MSS.
[17] Diary, May 6, 1829.
[18] Diary, May 5, 7, 1829.
[19] Diary, May 4, 5, 1829.
[20] Notebook of LCA. Undated. Adams MSS.
[21] LCA to CFA, Meridian Hill, May 7, 1829. Adams MSS.

wanderings through the Rock Creek woods and about the District. "May we humble ourselves in the dust," he petitioned to the Throne of Grace, "and be conscious that thy chastisements have been deserved." Not a day seemed to pass without some new affliction.[22]

On one of these walks, deep in anguish of soul, he looked up and saw a glorious rainbow spread before him in the sky. It touched his heart as an admonition to trust in the goodness and mercy of God.[23] If nature's radiant promise did not dissipate his grief, it at least gave direction to his perturbed mind. Desperately he took up his former occupations and exercises. To preserve himself from utter despondency he began work on some notes on political parties in the United States which he had promised Philip R. Fendall as an aid to the latter's projected history of the Adams Administration.[24] Day by day the manuscript lengthened under his hand until it assumed the proportions of a history itself.

John Adams, 2d, and his cousin William Steuben Smith [25] went to New York and brought back George's trunk and such effects as were left on the steamboat. The father and mother continued with their plans for the journey to Massachusetts. But she had little enthusiasm for the trip. In her weakened condition she dreaded the fatigues of travel; even more she shrank from the family and social contacts she would have to face when she got to Quincy. At the last moment she said she would stay in Washington, at least for the time being, with her daughter-in-law and the baby granddaughter. John Quincy Adams and his son John set out for the north without her, John to come back to his family in the course of a month or six weeks, his father to remain in Quincy until the autumn in an effort to bring his neglected personal affairs there into some semblance of order.

On the steamboat *Swan* between Brunswick and New York the grieving father picked up the *Morning Herald* of New York and read that his son's body had been found. It had drifted in with the tide on City Island, above the East River at the western end of the Sound. George Sullivan, Charles King, and other friends gave particulars when he arrived in New York. A coroner's inquest had already been held and the body placed in a tomb at East Chester. John Quincy Adams and John went there from New York, accompanied by a group of friends. He descended into the crypt and saw the coffin, but could not bring himself to have the cover unscrewed and look at the remains. The local Episcopalian pastor held a brief funeral service in the churchyard before the tomb in the presence of the Adams

---

[22] Among these he counted the disclosure of Watkins's malfeasance and the failure and ruin of the sons John and Thomas of his old friend Dr. Thomas Welsh of Boston. Diary, May 5, 16, 1829. John Welsh went to a debtor's prison. Diary of CFA, July 6, 1829. Adams MSS.

[23] Diary, May 4, 1829.

[24] Diary, May 14, 20, 26, 1829.

[25] John Quincy Adams's nephew and Louisa's brother-in-law.

party and people of the vicinity. After that they returned to New York and arranged to have the body sent on to Quincy in the late autumn. The coroner handed over to them the articles found on the drowned man: some bills and change, a watch, a cypher-seal, a silver pencil, comb, snuff-box, and penknife, and some sleeve-buttons that the father could not recognize nor identify. The hands of the watch were stopped at 3:40.[26]

In Boston, Charles Francis Adams had gone through his brother's effects. He found the last message and destroyed it together with most of the "schoolboy effusions" and all other papers that he considered useless or that might grieve the family.[27]

Shortly after George's death there appeared in the *New Bedford Mercury* a poem by him entitled *The Spark at Sea*.[28] John Quincy Adams read it reprinted in the *National Journal* of Washington, May 21, 1829:

> There is a little spark at sea
> Which grows 'mid darkness brilliantly,
> But when the moon looks clear and bright,
> Emits a pale and feeble light,
> And when the tempest shakes the wave
> It glimmers o'er the seaman's grave.
>
>   *   *   *
>
> Such friendship's beaming light appears
> Through the long line of coming years

[26] Diary, June 13, 14, 1829. JQA to LCA, New York, June 13, 15, 1829. Adams MSS.

[27] George had one large notebook of several hundred pages of which he had used only the first fifty-six for an autobiographical fragment which he wrote at the beginning of the year 1826. It deals with his boyhood and youth until he entered Harvard College. Charles later made economical use of the blank pages for his own Journal (see the year 1843). There is another large notebook with a few pages of George's compositions, lucubrations, and plans for work. They are a source for the characterization given of him in Chapter VII, pp. 115–18.

"The debts to my father were so large that the balance [of George's property] will amount to little, and that would be too much to put into the hands of a weak young girl, to say the least of it. Indeed his wish was that it should be secured from her and forfeited in case of ill conduct. I shall do what I can in pursuit of the spirit of the request, though I confess [*sic*] the whole to be a foolish effusion of a thoughtless moment. I destroyed the paper, it being in itself of no value, and apparently laid aside among a parcel of old papers, not thought of again. But I will attempt to find her out, and preserve her, if possible, from destruction." Diary of CFA, May 13, 1829. See also May 4, 1829.

George left debts to the amount of about $1,000, which his father paid. Charles's comments upon the fate of his brother, after the first shock, were cool: it was "not untimely." He declined to go to New York when the body was found. "Poor fellow, he had wound himself nearly up in his own net." Diary of CFA, May 28, July 15, 29, 1829. JQA to CFA, January 8, 1830. Adams MSS.

[28] George had given it to his friend Russell Freeman, who had it published in the New Bedford paper. Later in the year Freeman gave the original copy to the father. Diary of JQA, December 14, 1829.

In sorrow's cloud it shines afar,
A feeble but a constant star.
And like that little spark at sea
Burns brightest in adversity.

The Adams family had the custom of writing affectionate verse to each
other. Louisa copied George's tender words into her album of family
poems and treasured them in her sorrows. Long after her son stepped out
toward a spark at sea to seek a home beyond his earthly fears, she wrote
verses to his memory:

So long in memory shalt thou live
In that fond heart enshrined.
And God in pity will forgive
This weak and erring mind.[29]

3

John Quincy Adams alighted at his paternal mansion in Quincy in June
1829, resolved to make his home there for his short remaining years.[30]
The Adams Mansion had been, was then, and still is, the show-place of
Quincy. It stood only half a mile from the ancient New England farm-
houses at the foot of Penn's Hill, birthplaces of the two Presidents.[31]
What a contrast between the appearance of the Big House as John and
Abigail Adams had enjoyed it in the heyday of their retirement and its
looks when the son came back in his turn from the Presidency! Major
Leonard Vassall, wealthy Boston merchant and owner of plantations in
the West Indies, had built the house in 1731, nearly a century before
in the early years of the reign of King George II, for a country home in
Braintree. Though of queer proportions, it was an impressive residence
for those days, with brick end-walls west and east, and two principal stories and guest chambers above them under a mansard roof. From the
road—now long since known as Adams Street—one entered the south door
over a flagstone walk across a wide lawn. To the left of the front hall,
with its staircase of carved spindles, was the famous West Room, paneled
in darkly glowing mahogany that the Major had imported from the island
of Santo Domingo. Opposite was the dining-room, elegantly finished, upstairs two spacious family sleeping-chambers.

[29] Poem entitled "Poor George
              To him that is gone forever"
              LCA
              12 Feb. 1831.
[30] *Memoirs*, VIII, 154.
[31] On the old Plymouth road, now Nos. 133 and 141 Franklin Street, Quincy. Today they are the property of the City of Quincy under custody of the Quincy Historical Society and the Daughters of the American Revolution. See Vol. I, 4.

George Washington Adams
2nd January 1822.

SILHOUETTE OF GEORGE WASHINGTON ADAMS, 1822

FROM COLLECTION GIVEN BY ELIZABETH COOMBS ADAMS TO THE
ADAMS PAPERS, MASSACHUSETTS HISTORICAL SOCIETY.
PHOTOGRAPH BY GEORGE M. CUSHING, JR.

THE ADAMS MANSION, 1822

FROM A DRAWING BY MISS SARAH APTHORP. PHOTOGRAPH BY GEORGE M. CUSHING, JR.
COURTESY OF OLD HOUSE, ADAMS NATIONAL HISTORIC SITE, NATIONAL PARK SERVICE,
DEPARTMENT OF THE INTERIOR

The height of the original building in relation to its limited breadth and shallow depth front to rear had made it seem like a "wren's house" to Abigail when she returned from Europe with John to enter it for the first time in 1788. He had just purchased it in England from one of the Vassall Tory descendants for six hundred pounds, including seventy-five acres of farm land. The second President and his lady were only able to use it for vacations until they left the White House in 1801. Then they made it over to suit their own taste. They opened windows through the solid brick wall of the West Room. To lighten up things still more they painted white the rich mahogany! They added on a two-story ell for servants' quarters, with a kitchen. They made a new west door to open on a pebbled path running between formal rows of roses through a carefully landscaped garden ending at a New England stone wall before the setting sun. On the front, a lengthened porch with lattices, and a second flag walk from another front door, both leading to a white picket fence along the street. Greatest change of all, they doubled the length and size of the house by extending it eastward, with doors piercing the other brick wall to a long drawing room, with a fine and spacious study-chamber upstairs.[32]

John and Abigail Adams had filled up the Big House—or the Old House, as the family later came also to call it—with their inherited antiques, with pictures and portraits, mementos of the Revolution, of their travels, of the Presidency, and furniture brought back from Europe. During his last years, when the patriot widower lived there alone, with his wife's spinster niece Louisa Smith looking after him, he had not been able to keep the home in good repair. Steadily the petty improvisations and neglect of extreme age had impoverished the appearance of everything. A farmer, Isaac Farrar, and his wife, who occupied a small tenement house to the rear of the grounds, worked the arable part of the estate with little interest in the condition of the mansion, much less after the patriarch's death in 1826.

House and grounds continued to run down, despite John Quincy's visits. His brother Thomas, who occupied the premises from 1826 to 1829, had done nothing to improve the looks of things. Liquidation of the estate had stripped the dwelling of most of its contents. There was hardly enough furniture left for one to pass the night there comfortably. Foot-

---

[32] The devoted descendant, Henry Adams, 2d, described in careful detail *The Birthplaces of Presidents John Adams and John Quincy Adams in Quincy, Massachusetts,* and *The Adams Mansion, the Home of John Adams and John Quincy Adams, Presidents of the United States* (Adams Memorial Society, Quincy, Massachusetts, 1934, 1936). His own funeral services took place in the Long Room of the mansion on April 30, 1951.

The Adams Memorial Society maintained the house after the death in 1927 of the last resident, John Quincy Adams's grandson Brooks Adams, son of Charles Francis Adams. Since 1946 it has been a National Historic Site in the custody of the National Park Service.

steps echoed from uncarpeted floors through empty, naked rooms. The ceilings were cracked and showed stains from drippings of a leaky roof. The cavernous fireplaces breathed forth a damp and sooty air. Outside, the place looked "worse than Mr. Clay's farm." [33] Garden and nursery were a desolate sight. Of the shoots that had come up from the vacationing President's experimental plantings during two previous summers a scant third remained. Scarcely one was left in the seedling bed. Great weeds lay like serpents coiled around surviving saplings, strangling them to death. Only three or four white oaks were to be seen and not a single Spanish cork. But the horse-chestnuts that the President had brought from Washington were still living. [34]

To the fastidious Charles Francis Adams, inspecting the place before his father's arrival, it seemed rather hopeless. For more than one reason he was glad he did not have to live there, and could look forward to the brand-new house which Mr. Brooks was building in Boston for him and his bride-to-be. [35]

The aging heir to the Adams Mansion was not unduly dismayed. He and John took dinner with brother Thomas and came back to pass the night at home. Next day they set up bachelor's hall there, and engaged Louisa Smith as a housekeeper. Charles Francis, now his father's legal agent in Boston, came out frequently to stay overnight, and Lieutenant Thomas B. Adams, Jr., a nephew on furlough, at his uncle's intercession, from his army station at Fort Pickens, South Carolina, passed much of the summer there, helping out with paper work. The ex-President promised his brother to put another nephew, John Quincy Adams 2d, through Exeter to prepare him for Harvard. [36]

"Almighty God," he prayed that first night, "bestow upon me a spirit of gratitude, of humility, of cheerfulness, and of resignation. Of gratitude, for the numberless blessings which thou hast given me to enjoy and which thou art yet heaping upon me from hour to hour; of humility, to be conscious of my own infirmities and unworthiness; of cheerfulness, to be contented with the favours thou art pleased to bestow; and of resignation to the dispensations of thy will. Bless and preserve the partner of my life, the children thou hast given us, my kindred, friends, and country, and finally all my fellow-beings of the human race. Grant me health, peace of mind, the will and power to employ the remaining days which thou hast allotted me on earth to purposes approved by thee and tributary to the well-being of others, and to my own preparation for appearing in thy presence to give an account of the deeds done in the body. 'It is not

[33] JQA to LCA, Quincy, July 14, 1829. Adams MSS.
[34] Diary, June 22, 1829.
[35] Diary of CFA, June 1, 1829.
[36] Diary, November 8, 1829. JQA to CFA, No. 11, Washington, February 5, 1830. JQA to TBA, Washington, February 6, 1830. Adams MSS.

in man that walketh to direct his steps.' Be thou, Oh merciful God, my guide. Give me discernment and perseverance in life, fortitude in death, and the hope and fruition of a blessed immortality." [37]

John Quincy Adams's emotions choked in tears when he took his place in the family pew of the village church, the new "Temple." His fellow townsmen had just built it from funds that John Adams had donated to the town of Quincy for a church and school. It was a "gracious, neat and elegant building" constructed on simple lines from Quincy granite taken from the quarry given by John Adams. Friends and neighbors had already removed the old patriot's remains and those of his wife Abigail from the family vault in the churchyard and interred them in a special stone crypt beneath the church, granted to their son out of grateful memory and paid for by the parish.[38] As he listened to the service his soul was "humbled to the dust," his heart "distressed almost to convulsion." [39] The reading of the 284th hymn helped to soothe his agitation:

> In every joy that crowns my days,
>   In every pain I bear,
> My heart shall find delight in praise,
>   Or seek relief in prayer.
>
> When gladness wings my favour'd hour
>   Thy love my thoughts shall fill;
> Resigned when storms or sorrow lower;
>   My soul shall meet thy will.[40]

He consigned his aching, contrite heart to the will of God.

So extensive were the repairs necessary to put the Old House in condition that John Quincy Adams thought seriously of building a new stone residence that would conform to and overlook the Temple and new Classical School still to be built from accumulating funds left by John Adams

[37] Diary, June 18, 1829.

[38] D. M. Wilson has edited the commemorative services of *The "Chappel of Ease" and Church of Statesmen* that were held upon the 250th anniversary of the gathering of the *First Church of Christ in Quincy* (Cambridge: printed for the [Unitarian Church of Quincy] Society; 1890). It contains excellent photographs of the Stone Temple, exterior and interior, the memorial tablets, Adams residences and other historic houses, noteworthy pastors, members of the Adams family, and other personalities.

[39] Diary, Sunday, June 21, 1829.

[40] I am indebted to Mr. William C. Edwards, historian of the Unitarian Church at Quincy, and to Dr. Stephen T. Riley, Librarian of the Massachusetts Historical Society, for identification of this hymn, by Helen Maria Williams (1762–1827), published in Jeremy Belknap's hymnal: *Sacred Poetry, Consisting of Psalms and Hymns Adapted to Christian Devotion* (Boston: Thomas Wells; 1817), p. 229. Another edition was published by the same house in 1820.

for the purpose. The five or six thousand volumes of his own collection, plus the books and papers of his father which he was keeping in custody for the town of Quincy, would not be safe in the existing house.

Louisa protested against any such idea. Let him build two frame houses, she begged, one in the locality of each of his surviving sons, so that each could inherit and live in it if he wished.[41] It was soon evident that he did not have the means to do either. He fell back on the concept of a small stone office and study in the garden of the Big House, safe for books and papers. As he measured up his assets he found that even this was quite impossible. So he settled for putting this priceless collection, the best library possessed by an individual in America, not excluding that of Thomas Jefferson,[42] in his bedchamber and elsewhere in and about the wooden house. Josiah Adams, the local carpenter, began to encompass him around with board shelving, forcing him to a remote bedroom for his daily desk work. As the books came out from Boston, where they had been stored in the Athenæum, the ex-President unpacked them and put them on the shelves, still unsorted and uncatalogued.

Abandoning the idea of a new house, or of a fireproof library outside in the garden, Adams started in to make the Big House livable at least for a summer home. He got out some pieces of furniture that he had brought back from England in 1817 and stored in Boston, and Charles picked up some second-hand articles, shipping them down with the cases of books by sloop to Greenleaf's wharf. He narrowed the four-foot fireplaces and put in Franklin stoves to save wood, and "Rumfordized" the kitchen. It would be a place that Louisa could live in not uncomfortably whenever she came. She could add the refinements later. It could be a winter home too, if she could stand the climate.

The personal stone library for Adams's books was a dream that finally materialized at the hand of his son in 1870 in the garden of the Adams Mansion.[43] Meanwhile John Adams's gift of books to the town was placed in the Quincy Town Hall, only to suffer there irreparably from indifferent care. The Adams Academy, with a schoolmaster versed in the Latin, Greek, and Hebrew languages, was finally completed in 1871 and opened in September 1872.[44] A room was provided there for John Adams's collec-

[41] LCA to JQA, Meridian Hill, July 17, 1829. Adams MSS.

[42] Henry Adams, 2d, with Introduction by Worthington C. Ford: *Catalogue of the Books of John Quincy Adams* . . . (Boston: printed for the Athenæum; 1938), p. 15.

"No such library exists in the hands of any other individual in the United States, but I have never had the enjoyment of it." Diary, October 17, 1829.

[43] Henry Adams, 2d: *The Adams Mansion*, pp. 39–40.

[44] In 1907 the Adams Academy closed for lack of funds to maintain it under new conditions. At that time it was valued at $190,000. Since then it has been used at various times to house civic groups, young women's clubs, Boy Scouts, G.A.R., American Legion, Quincy Red Cross, and Quincy Historical Society. In 1951 it was being used by the Quincy Department of Veterans' Service. The income from the original

tion together with other books for a public library. Later a place was found for them in four gallery alcoves of the Quincy public library in Crane Memorial Hall. But John Adams's books proved to be more useful to needs of the erudite scholar [45] than for popular reading. In ten years only two persons consulted them. With the consent of the town fathers they eventually (1893) went to the Boston Public Library. Today they constitute one of the most prized possessions of that noble institution.[46]

People in Quincy were as friendly as ever. The ex-President quickly took up the habits of exercise and recreation which had become a part of his life for so many summers there. One could see him working with a spade in garden and nursery, steadily pastinating the soil an hour a day. As soon as the water warmed up he went to swim with his nephews several times a week at Daniel Greenleaf's wharf, where Black's Creek [47] flows into Quincy Bay: a routine of a quarter of a mile from the upper wharf to the lower wharf, sixteen minutes for the round trip of half a mile: 238 strokes to go down, and 293 to come back,[48] tolerably good for a man who had passed his sixty-second birthday and did not feel himself long for this world! [49]

For mental occupation he applied himself to putting his father's papers in order and began work on a biography of John Adams. First it was necessary to trace the "short and simple annals" of ancestors in Massachusetts: "They are records of humble life, but there is nothing in them of which a descendant need be ashamed." [50] He read much on the background of New England history and that of the English colonies in America and on English political history in the eighteenth century, and began to write a page of text each day. But by the end of the summer he had barely scratched the surface.

If everybody in Quincy welcomed him back to the town of his birth it was quite different in Boston, the home of the "leading Federalists." There Adams felt a chill in the social atmosphere. In contrast to his visits of previous summers there was no welcome, there were no gatherings, no dinners with the solid men of Boston and of Essex County, no testimonials of confidence. The American Academy of Arts and Sciences dropped him as president, an honor he had enjoyed for the last twelve years

---

John Adams Fund is now used to buy books for the Junior and Senior High School libraries in Quincy and thus promotes the donor's wishes to assist in the educational advancement of the boys and girls of Quincy.

[45] Charles Francis Adams, Jr.: *Three Episodes of Massachusetts History* (Boston, 1892), II, 940–3.

[46] Miss Eleanor Gow, Reference Librarian of the Thomas Crane Public Library of Quincy, has placed me, and the reader, in her debt by compiling notes out of the reports of that library, on which the above statements are based.

[47] Formerly called Mt. Wollaston River.

[48] Diary, June 27–August 3, 1829.

[49] *Memoirs*, VIII, 154. July 11, 1829.

[50] Diary, August 10, 1829.

though absent in Washington.[51] The Athenæum tried to cancel his original proprietor's membership.[52]

Harrison Gray Otis, leader of the Thirteen Confederates, had been elected Mayor of Boston with the backing of the Jacksonian Democrats, truly as great a revolution as ever took place in local American politics.[53] In his function as Mayor he dutifully invited the ex-President to attend the city fathers' Fourth-of-July ceremony in Faneuil Hall,[54] but he added no personal civility. Adams declined the perfunctory invitation, as was quite fitting in his bereavement, but he went into the city later in the month on personal business and to visit the Brooks family in Medford, principally that he might not seem to stay away on purpose. On one of his trips to Boston a month later he met Otis, who saluted him by name "in passing" on the street.[55]

4

In Washington at Meridian Hill, Louisa and her son's family suddenly found the Porter Mansion sold over their heads and themselves obliged to secure a new dwelling by August 1. She had to seek shelter in John's new house before it was completed.[56] After casting about for possible rentals, or purchases, she decided to join her husband for the remainder of the summer in Quincy, "our proper residence," and be on hand for Charles's wedding the first week in September.[57] On August 15 Mrs. Adams, son John and his wife Mary, and the baby, all set out for the cooler clime of Massachusetts. They arranged that John would escort them as far as Philadelphia or even New York, and that Charles would come to New York to bring the ladies on to his father's house.

Charles took the carriage and horses to Providence, and arrived in New York on the *Benjamin Franklin*—the same ship from which his brother George had ended his life—to find his family at the City Hotel. His mother collapsed when she heard the name of the boat he had come in, and that she might have to go on in. The baby also became alarmingly ill, and it was finally agreed that it would be best for the family to return to Washington. Charles went back alone to Quincy to his distressed father,[58] who was the sole representative of the family to attend his wedding at Medford on September 3, 1829 to Abby Brooks, daughter of Peter Chardon Brooks, wealthy insurance man of Boston and Medford.

[51] *Memoirs*, VIII, 247.

[52] JQA to Proprietors of Boston Athenæum, Quincy, September 7, November 6, 1829. F. C. Gray, Secretary of Boston Athenæum, to JQA, Boston, November 7, 1829. Adams MSS.

[53] CFA to LCA, Boston, December 20, 1828. Adams MSS.

[54] Diary, July 4, 1829.

[55] Diary, August 29, 1829.

[56] LCA to JQA, Meridian Hill, July 12, 17, August 2, 5, 1829. Adams MSS.

[57] LCA to CFA, Meridian Hill, July 5, 1829. Adams MSS.

[58] Diary of CFA, August 18–24, 1829.

John Quincy Adams could only look forward to Louisa's coming back with him to the paternal residence another summer.[59] He could not return to Washington before he had set his affairs in partial order and looked after the final interment of George's remains.

It was fortunate that he found himself at home in Quincy during these months. He was needed for the administration of continuing responsibilities in connection with his father's estate. Friend Boylston's will also proved to be long and detailed in its bequests and trusts, including benefactions to Harvard University. Adams was guardian for the education of two of Ward Boylston's grandsons. He further charged himself with carrying out the intent of his father's earlier gifts to the town of Quincy, including the church and school fund and the gift of books for a library. He saw to it personally that an inscription and memorial tablet to his father and mother, with a bust of John Adams by Horatio Greenough, were properly carved and placed on the wall of the Temple before the family pew.[60] And he made sure that their names were correctly chiseled on the granite slab that covered the vault below. Then there was the laborious problem of surveying the lands of his deceased father and his own holdings by purchase from the estate.

John Adams had bought extensive tracts of land in and about Quincy during the early part of his life, picking them up at cheap prices. They proved more than he could hold. During his financial troubles that followed the failure of Bird, Savage and Bird of London in 1803, John Quincy had raised money on his own Boston real estate and kept the paternal holdings in the family by purchasing one quarter of the lands for an appraised price of $12,812. John Adams late in life gave another quarter of his property to his son Thomas Boylston Adams and in 1819 he made over a third quarter to John Quincy in return for a personal annuity of $1,000. He bequeathed 211 acres more of land (in addition to two tracts of cedar swamp) to the town for the church and library building fund already mentioned. After his father's death the President bought for about $20,000 the land remaining to the estate and other holdings round about it.[61] He also purchased for $12,000 the Big House and lots stipulated for him at that price in John Adams's will.

Back home John Quincy Adams found himself land-poor, with nine hundred acres more or less in Quincy and Weston. These parcels were so numerous and so varied that he hardly knew what belonged to him and what was still a part of the estate. Some of them he had never even seen. He set about a survey, tramping daylong with the surveyor over hill and down dale, through field and orchard, meadow, bog, and marsh, and back to familiar scenes.[62] On one of these occasions they ended up at the place

[59] JQA to LCA, October 6–11, 1829. Adams MSS.
[60] See above, p. 125.
[61] Diary, October 13, 1829.
[62] JQA to LCA, Quincy, October 20, 1829. Adams MSS.

where the boy Johnny and his mother Abigail more than half a century before had climbed over the stone wall to ascend Penn's Hill and watch the Battle of Bunker Hill.[63]

What emotions must have risen in his mind and heart as, trudging over his paternal acres, he came to such a spot! So devoted was he to those scenes of his childhood and memories of his beloved parents that it was with difficulty that his friend Noah Curtis prevailed on him to sell half an acre for a house lot. When neighbor Harvey Field offered six dollars for an old oak near the road he declined to part with the ancient tree because he used to pick up acorns under it as a boy.[64]

Toward the end of November George's remains arrived by sea from New York. The last sad duty had to be performed. Neighbor William C. Greenleaf, who had been helping Mr. Adams as a copyist and cataloguer, accompanied him and the pastor, Mr. Whitney, to the churchyard. After a short prayer they saw the coffin placed in the family sepulcher.

That evening John Quincy Adams breathed another prayer to himself: "May I cherish the hope that this afflictive dispensation comes not as the first stroke of the destroying Angel, but as the discipline of a chastising hand?" He poured out his grief in his Diary:

"In this journal was recorded on the 12th of April 1801 the birth of this my first born son. Desired how long, how anxiously! Granted to fervent prayers after frequent disappointments. With what earnestness of hope, with what anguish of fear have we followed the course of his short career! How small a portion of his life was passed under the paternal roof! With what exquisite delight I have hailed the gleams of prosperous fortune which so rarely illumined his path, and how have I grieved in spirit at the afflictions with which it was so thickly beset. His heart so full of the kindliest affections! A soul so abstracted from the business of earthly concerns, that it could not endure the contemplation of its own infirmities. Heavenly Father, let it have mercy before thee, and in the day of retribution let not my errors be visited upon my child!"[65]

It was time to get back to Washington. On the 2d of December he set forth anxiously to join Louisa and the family of son John, who had renounced all political ambition for a business career in the District of Columbia.

The destiny of a family now rested on the youngest son.[66] Charles Fran-

---

[63] Vol. I, 6.

[64] Diary, November 6, 1829.

[65] Diary, November 24, 1829.

[66] "I had this morning much conversation with my father upon the prospects of the family. John has decided to desert the state. Poor George is now no more, and I am the only one who remains to keep the name and the family in our branch at least from destruction." "Evening, A long conversation with my father. Family pride. A strong instance in himself, much exceeding even what I suspected. I feel at times depressed by it, for now the dependence upon me is perfectly prominent. And beyond

cis Adams thought of the family, marveled about his father's new adjustment to life: "He is beyond ambition. I am just aiming at it. Life is therefore seen by us in different phases." [67]

John Quincy Adams rejoined his wife, Louisa, at John's home just as Congress opened in December 1829. To his great relief he found them all well. John's house, built with help of the parents, stood on the west side of Sixteenth Street, between I and K Streets, less than two blocks north of the President's Square. Louisa had equipped it with such furniture as they personally possessed upon removing from the White House and from Meridian Hill. They were near the government offices, the churches, the residences that were springing up in that quarter, in walking distance of all Washington.

Settling down as a private citizen for another winter in the national capital Adams, racked in body and sore in spirit, summed up what the last twelve months had done to him:

"At the close of the year the only sentiment that I feel to be proper is of humble gratitude to God for the blessings with which it has been favored. Its chastisements have been most afflictive, but I have experienced mercy with judgment. The loss of power and of popular favor I could have endured with fortitude, and relief from the slavery of public office was more than a compensation for all the privations incident to the loss of place. Its vanities I despised, and its flatteries never gave me a moment of enjoyment. But my beloved son! Mysterious Heaven! let me bow in submission to thy will! Let me no longer yield to a desponding or distressful spirit. Grant me fortitude, patience, perseverance, and active energy, and let thy will be done!" [68]

5

The ex-President soon picked up his old Washington routine of exercise and study. The beloved classics now stood him in good stead. Like Cicero after a life of political turbulence he took delight in turning to the studies and meditations of his youth. On leaving the White House he had resolved to peruse in the original every surviving passage of the great Roman.

At Meridian Hill overlooking the Potomac he had seen his own country and life reflected in the letters of the immortal Latinist from his retreat at Tusculum. Andrew Jackson conqueror of the British at New Orleans had taken the place of John Quincy Adams in the Republic of the Western World even as Julius Cæsar conquerer of Britain had displaced

---

me there is little hope, though in my father, that little centers in the person of his nephew John Quincy." "Family pride does strongly centre in him now. It has become an absorbing passion." From Diary of CFA, July 4, 14, 20, 1829. Adams MSS.

[67] Diary of CFA, July 29, 1829.

[68] *Memoirs*, VIII, 159–60. December 30, 1829.

Marcus Tullius Cicero in the ancient Roman Republic. And Cicero's lamentations for his dead daughter Tullia paralleled Adams's anguish for his lost son George.

"Every one of the letters of Cicero," he wrote to Charles from Sixteenth Street, "is a picture of the state of the writer's mind when it was written. It is like an evocation of shades to read them. I see him approach me like the image of a Fantasmagoria—he seems opening his lips to speak to me and passes off, but his words as if they had fallen upon my ears are left deeply stamped upon the memory. I watch with his sleepless nights. I hear his solitary sighs. I feel the agitation of his pulse, not for himself, but for his son, for his Tullia, for his country. There is sometimes so much in it of painful reality that I close the book. No tragedy was ever half so pathetic. My morning always ends with a hearty execration of Cæsar, and with what is perhaps not so right, a sensation of relief at the 23 stabs of the Ides of March, and the fall at the feet of Pompey's statue. . . ." [69]

At the time of George's death he had started reading the Bible again and once more went through it from Genesis to Revelation. He also finished his notes on Political Parties in the United States and gave them to Philip R. Fendall [70] for his projected history and justification of the recent Administration, never actually written.[71] Further to keep his mind usefully occupied and strengthened in adversity against "decaying" faculties, he agreed to do some articles for Joseph Blunt's *American Annual Register:* one on the recent Russo-Turkish War, which had ended in the Treaty of Adrianople and the independence of Greece; [72] and a later one on contemporary England.[73] To Adams, Russia's advance toward the Mediterranean balanced British power to the advantage of the United States. He thought the Turks ought to be driven out of Europe, and Russia possessed of Constantinople. This made Baron Krüdener, the Russian Minister at Washington, eager to furnish him with a wealth of his own opinion and memories, as well as with such Russian prints as he could lay his hands on, including an imperfect file of the *Journal de St. Petersbourg,* official

[69] JQA to CFA, Washington, February 21, 1830. Adams MSS.

[70] Diary, May 25, 1830.

[71] There is a copy of these notes in the Adams MSS. Fendall's copy eventually fell into the hands of a dealer. Charles True Adams, no direct descendant, purchased it and published it in 1941: *Parties in the United States*, by John Quincy Adams (New York: Greenberg, Publisher, 1941). Charles Wiltse, biographer of Calhoun, has written a brilliant review of this publication in *Journal of Politics*, IV (No. 3, August 1942), 407–14. The work traverses in somewhat more moderate language the background covered by the Reply to the Appeal of the Massachusetts Federalists discussed in the previous chapter.

[72] See Vol. III for 1827 and 1828 (New York, 1830), Chapters X to XV inclusive, and Vol. V for 1829 and 1830 (New York, 1831), Chapter XXI. Correspondence between Joseph Blunt and JQA, 1829–31. Adams MSS. JQA's holographs in JQA Papers, Box 1804–34, LC.

[73] *American Annual Register* for 1829–30, pp. 419–68; for 1830–1, pp. 235–93. JQA to Robert Walsh, Washington, April 16, 1836. JQA Papers, LC.

voice of Russia to the outside world. For three months the ex-President devoted six hours a day to the Near Eastern Question. The result was not as sympathetic to British policy as his later publication on the Anglo-Chinese War (1841).[74]

Some interesting reflections on the requirements of historical writing came out of these efforts. Paucity of materials in Washington had reduced his sources of information to a collection of secondary fragments, "a Joseph's coat of many colors over an uncompleted body." "Nor can I so well put into it the heart, with the system of arteries and veins, through which might run one stream of pure political and religious morality, little exposed to the surface, but felt in every pulsation. Thus should history be written; and, lastly, a rapid style, enlivened by sagacity and inspirited with meditation, should give to the whole the attraction of interest to grapple the attention of the reader. *Multum abludit imago.*" [75]

The last sentence plus the epigram doubtless referred to Gibbon, whom John Quincy Adams was rereading for a background of the Near East.[76]

Adams had the linguistic equipment, the erudition, the industry, the analytical mind of a historian, and at least a critical instinct. But when put to the test his historical writings were either polemical, self-justificatory, or unavoidably biased by the destiny of a family. Realizing this, he would leave them either unfinished or unpublished. Emerson said that John Quincy Adams was not a "literary gentleman" but rather a "bruiser" who loved the political mêlée.[77]

To have anybody think he was not a literary gentleman would have insulted Adams. That was precisely what he wanted to be, what he believed himself to be now that he had the time to read and write again.

Company was not wanting in Washington. As a private citizen he could come and go as he pleased, where he pleased. It did not please him to attend the Jackson Day Dinner on January 8, 1830, when unexpectedly invited to do so. It was enough to say that the conditions of his family did not permit him to be present. Many of his old political associates called on him, and he on some of them. After the opening of the Twenty-first Congress, Clay, Wirt, Everett, J. W. Taylor, and others conferred cautiously with him. Members of the diplomatic corps came to pay their private respects. Senators and Representatives of both parties, army and naval officers, explorers and literary people, judges and clergymen, called on him. On his walks about town he conversed with Jared Sparks the historian and with Chief Justice John Marshall. He speculated with them

[74] See below, p. 458, n. 26.

[75] *Memoirs,* VIII, 196.

[76] "I never can read this author without indignation. Yet his irony, his bitter indifference, and his art of insinuation may be studied to advantage. His keenest sarcasms upon Christianity and the Bible are in distant allusions. His philosophy is shallow, and always infected with anti-religious acrimony." *Memoirs,* VIII, 163.

[77] *Journals of Ralph Waldo Emerson:* E. W. Emerson and W. E. Forbes, editors (Boston, 1911), VI, 349–50.

about the ownership of private correspondence—Sparks was then preparing to edit the private as well as the public letters of George Washington. It was Marshall's sidewalk opinion that title to correspondence would rest with the receiver rather than the writer, qualified by the confidence of the latter.[78]

Old familiars like William Lee and Philip Fendall kept him abreast of current political gossip.

He noted, not without cynical complacency, the consternation of some of the recently hopeful Democratic party leaders at the weak construction of President Jackson's first Cabinet and its personal tensions. The "Eaton malaria" gave him sardonic amusement as it settled like a gleaming miasma about the heads of the new Administration. The President and his widowed Secretary of State socially accepted the easy spouse of the Secretary of War, Peggy O'Neale Timberlake Eaton, without embarrassment and entertained her at all the official receptions and dinners and other state functions. But the wives of most of the Cabinet members would not speak to her or recognize her. Jackson noticed that resentfully. Anyone who wanted to get the favor of "the Old Horse-Racer himself" would do well to pay attention to her, thought the ex-President. Most diplomats at Washington, like Baron Krüdener and Charles Vaughan, the British Minister, were quick to do that, if only in the line of duty. It became a court war, like the ancient struggle between the Caps and the Hats. "I confine myself to my Russian and Turkish war," Adams journalized.[79]

The situation of an ex-President did not permit him to listen to the debates in Congress, but he followed its proceedings with sustained interest. He went to the House of Representatives to hear Edward Everett deliver the anniversary address to the Columbian Institute. While President, John Quincy Adams had been elected president of that organization, earliest learned society of Washington, 1816–38, forerunner of the National Institution and the Smithsonian.[80] Upon his retirement the membership had re-elected him. The Institute was now speckled with some of the new Jacksonian élite. There he greeted Vice President Calhoun and various members of Jackson's Cabinet, ignoring Ingham, who had defamed him so in the recent campaign; when the Secretary of the Treasury advanced as if to accost him, Adams barely turned an eye upon his old enemy. The culprit "slunk back" into his seat.[81]

It was the historic debate between Senator Robert Y. Hayne of South Carolina and Daniel Webster that attracted the ex-President's attention

---

[78] *Memoirs*, VIII, 187.

[79] *Memoirs*, VIII, 159, 197, 203.

[80] Richard Rathbun: *The Columbian Institute for the Promotion of Arts and Sciences* (Smithsonian Institution, United States National Museum, Bulletin No. 101; Washington, 1917).

[81] *Memoirs*, VIII, 171.

most signally. It seems best to take up the nullification movement more particularly, in another chapter. It struck at the heart of John Quincy Adams's body politic: the Union.

6

Like most of his predecessors, Adams in retirement found it difficult to make both ends meet; at the same time to keep up his home in Quincy and provide for the future. When he left the White House he was worth about $100,000, mostly invested in sundry pieces of real estate in Quincy, Boston, and Washington, and in government bonds, United States Bank stock, and shares in various insurance, turnpike, and bridge companies, and a few friendly mortgages.[82] As Secretary of State and President, Adams was a generous man, whether in handouts to unfortunate individuals, or in substantial assistance to good causes, notably churches and educational institutions.[83] Such benefactions ate into his capital and income at a time when he could not well afford it. He also made mortgage loans to his brother Thomas of Quincy. His basic difficulty, however, came from a most ill-advised business investment that he had suddenly entered into in 1823 while Secretary of State: the Columbian Mills.

Mrs. Adams's cousin George Johnson had been proprietor of some grist and flour mills on Rock Creek in the District of Columbia, which existed at the foot of the present-day Adams Mill Road where the motor drive crosses the Creek in the National Zoological Gardens.[84] The business consisted in buying wheat and corn carted in from surrounding areas,

[82] Memorandum book, with drafts of will in JQA's handwriting, and statements of his estate, 1829–32. Adams MSS.

[83] One such gift was $1,000 toward an astronomical observatory at Harvard, later returned because the contingent fund was not raised.

Another was $3,000 to the new church at Quincy. Diary, September 17, 1833.

In 1824 and 1825 he loaned upwards of $13,000 to the Columbian College in the District of Columbia. Later loans brought the peak of indebtedness of that institution to him up to $20,000. In 1842, according to the records of the college, he accepted $8,796.23 in full payment. JQA to Reverend Elon Galusha, Treasurer of Columbian College in the District of Columbia. Quincy, August 19, 1826. See also *Historical Sketch of George Washington University*, by Charles Herbert Stockton in General Alumni Catalogue of The George Washington University, 1917. A facsimile of JQA's receipt of March 5, 1842 is reproduced on page 8 of the memorial publication: *A University in the Nation's Capital* (Washington: The George Washington University; 1947).

Perhaps it is not too much to say that John Quincy Adams's loans and gifts to the Columbian College, now George Washington University, saved it from extinction in the year of its greatest struggles for existence.

[84] Allen C. Clark locates and describes "The Old Mills" in and about the District of Columbia in *Records of the Columbia Historical Society*, XXXI–XXXII (Washington, 1930). He explains that Benjamin Stoddert likely built this mill, before 1800. Johnson bought it from Jonathan Shoemaker, in 1809. The buildings were removed from the tax lists in 1867. No vestige of them now remains.

grinding it into flour and meal, selling part in Washington, and shipping the rest by schooner down the Potomac from Georgetown to Atlantic coastal ports. Johnson claimed to have put $60,000 into the property. After that he had to mortgage everything to the Bank of Columbia for a loan of $20,000 payable with interest in installments over five years. In July 1823 the bank was about to foreclose and Johnson had no means of raising funds. He appealed to John Quincy Adams to take over the business and keep him on as manager with an option to buy half ownership back for a sum equal to what Adams would put up: $20,000 plus $10,000 to get things into shape and buy wheat for the season's grinding.[85]

The venture was a leap in the dark for Adams. It involved his whole financial future and that of his family. Yet within a week's time, with only the most cursory inspection of a property and business that he knew nothing about and could never personally manage, he agreed to purchase the Columbian Mills,[86] with the provision that George Johnson would buy back not half but all or nothing in the future. To take over the property he transferred $9,000 United States six-per-cent stock (i.e., bonds) to the Bank of Columbia together with a mortgage on his F Street Washington dwelling-house! He actually seems to have believed that this was a "gracious offer of Providence" that would support him and his family in retirement and give him ease for the literary occupations that he looked forward to, perhaps as soon as 1825. It also promised employment later for his second son, John Adams, 2d. It suggests that at that time he intended to spend his future years in the District of Columbia, come what might in the nation's politics. This was before the death of his father and when he had not yet made up his mind to return to Quincy. If he were not elected President and ceased to be Secretary of State he would at least be a millowner with grain to grind and time to write.

Adams remained a troubled millowner all the rest of his life. Even before the deeds were conveyed difficulties began to crop up. More repairs proved necessary than Johnson had counted on. The assistant miller did not put in an appearance. Business was dull as the summer advanced. They ground only a hundred barrels of flour a week instead of an anticipated hundred a day. Accounts were in a tangle. Only with great delay and difficulty did John Adams, 2d, succeed in clearing them up and putting in a reliable set of books.[87] Affairs dragged heavily from month to month. At the end of the first year there were no profits in sight. By spring 1824 there were seven hundred barrels of flour on hand, not to mention green corn meal heating up in the warehouse, with no buyers.

Flash floods from summer thunderstorms poured down the creek tear-

---

[85] The late Henry Adams, 2d, gathered for me these details and others, mentioned below, from the MS. Diary of JQA.

[86] "He is a singular man with regard to the management of his property. Investments with him are chance things." Diary of CFA, September 4, 1829.

[87] Correspondence of JQA and JA, 2d, 1829–33. Adams MSS.

ing out works and washing out roads. Scanty local crops held up milling when sales were good. Competing flour and meal came in from the West by the new Baltimore and Ohio Railroad to put one flour mill after another out of business in the District of Columbia and throw Georgetown into decay. George Johnson was a complete disappointment and failure as a manager. His services had to be terminated. After Adams left the White House his son took over all responsibility. By hard work and constant attention to business John succeeded in getting the business barely solvent. Meanwhile interest had to be paid on the loans and the obligations renewed from year to year on the ex-President's credit.

The wretched mills preyed "like gangrene" on his spirits when Adams rejoined his wife and second son's family in Washington in the winter of 1829–30. Loaded with bereavement, his face swollen with a painful neuralgia that kept him from sleeping nights, he would wander out to Rock Creek by day, watch the wheels turn round and round, grinding away the savings of a lifetime and the inheritance of his children, shaking the structure under his feet with the unsteady vibrations of their unprofitable revolutions. As he watched, he saw himself settling into the position of a typical American ex-President, barely ahead of the sheriff, like Thomas Jefferson and James Monroe.[88]

Still another blow greater than the loss of earthly rank or things was in store for the American Job. No sooner had son John got the mills operating at least temporarily on a sound basis than his health began to fail. He lingered on for two years, often in acute pain, weaker and weaker. The father implored him to leave Washington and its sickly climate, to bring his family to Quincy, where he could manage the paternal estate, with expectations of inheritance.[89] It was already too late. John Quincy Adams hurried to his son's deathbed from Quincy only to find him at midnight in a state of coma a few hours before he breathed his last, October 23, 1834.

John had devoted himself with unbounded filial affection to the fallen fortunes of his father. He had been steward, housekeeper, secretary, social companion, and kindest friend. "A more honest soul, or more tender heart never breathed on the face of this earth." [90] His death numbed the father almost to a state of collapse. Louisa's grief at the loss of the second son was again boundless. She remembered him through the years in her prayers and poems. One was entitled "John's Grave":

> Softly tread! For herein lies
> The young, the beautiful, the wise. . . .

After John's death and the liquidation of his estate Mr. and Mrs. Adams took Mary and the two granddaughters into their family and moved

[88] Diary, May 14, 1830.
[89] JQA to JA, 2d, Quincy, July 23, 1834. Adams MSS.
[90] Diary, October 23, 1834.

into the house at 1333–5 F Street where he had resided as Secretary of State.[91] By mustering his resources John Quincy Adams managed to pay off the last of the $30,000 mill debt, plus other debts of his son that had been put into the enterprise.[92]

John had brought his father's summer amanuensis, William Greenleaf, from Quincy to help run the mills. Without close supervision Greenleaf proved incapable. The works had to close down from time to time, impossible to lease, or sell without total loss. Eventually Adams's friend and kinsman Nathaniel Frye, Louisa's brother-in-law, took over the management of his Washington property. He was now financially strapped, land-poor in Quincy, almost insolvent in Washington, finding it difficult to meet current expenses and pay interest on his debts. It was at this period, 1836–9, that his old friend and former valet Antoine Giusta came to his aid with loans on personal notes, renewed conveniently until the former President had paid them off with interest.[93]

Under Frye's competent stewardship the Columbian Mills, relieved of interest burdens, afforded some scant income during Adams's last years.[94] Together with the rentals from Washington property and his mortgaged real estate in Boston, and his remaining investments under the capable management of his only surviving son Charles, and occasional small lecture fees, he and Louisa were able to keep income above outgo, to pay taxes on the family estate in Quincy, and eventually to leave his lands and debts together with a few liquid securities to his wife, daughter-in-law and granddaughter (John's widow and daughter), and surviving son.

7

What with his reading and writing, his walks and his rides about Washington, and his interest in the deterioration of current politics under his rival's succession, Adams kept so well occupied as to have less leisure to meditate upon his mounting afflictions. The tone of his health gradually improved. His spirits slowly revived. His Diary began to lose some of its recent dullness.[95] His unyielding hold on life strengthened. Emerson later recorded that someone asked Adams toward the end of his life for his rules for preservation of health and faculties in old age. He replied that there were three rules: (1) Regularity, (2) Regularity, (3) Regularity.[96]

Regular occupation of body and mind, imposed by self-discipline and Christian prayer, raised him from depression and despair and enabled him in unshaken faith to survive the trials of Job.

[91] Vol. I, 275. *Memoirs*, X, 46, November 30, 1838.
[92] JQA to CFA, Washington, October 24, 1834. Adams MSS. Diary, March 5, 1835.
[93] JQA to CFA, March 3, 23, 1837. JQA to Antoine Giusta, Quincy, June 21, 1839. Adams MSS.
[94] Diary, July 28, 1840 [Washington].
[95] *Memoirs*, VIII, 202.
[96] Emerson: *Journals*, VIII, 353.

Slowly he began to surmount the cluster of woes that threatened to palsy the remainder of his days. By the end of 1829, following the marriage of his son Charles, some light had begun to shine through the dark clouds that had shadowed his life after the people had retired him from the Presidency.[97]

[97] See the cheerful letter of JQA to Abigail Brooks (Mrs. Charles Francis) Adams, Washington, December 23, 1829. Adams MSS.

CHAPTER XI

Life Begins at Sixty-three
(1830 – 1831)

I have two fixed ideas. . . . The first is the compar-
ative uselessness of men above forty years of age.
. . . My second fixed idea is the uselessness of men
above sixty years of age and the incalculable benefit it would be in commercial, political, and in professional life if, as a matter of course, men stopped
work at this age.

SIR WILLIAM OSLER, *æt.* 55:
FAREWELL ADDRESS AT JOHNS HOPKINS
UNIVERSITY, FEBRUARY 22, 1905

WOULD John Quincy Adams have subscribed to Sir William Osler's dictum, invoked for the life of a teacher: study until twenty-five, investigation until forty, active professor until sixty—after that retirement under a
double allowance? Roughly speaking, he had followed some such schedule in his own life: a student in Europe and Massachusetts until twenty-
eight, including three years devoted to the beginning of law practice;
from twenty-eight until fifty an investigator into international politics
during his career as a diplomat in Europe, with the interval of five years
in the United States Senate; then active practice as Secretary of State
and President from fifty until sixty-two.

When he left the White House he appeared to be definitely out of
politics—though on no double allowance! When he and Louisa went back
to Quincy after their tragic year 1829, it was to make the Big House eventually their permanent home, with perhaps occasional winters in Washington as long as their son John with his family continued to reside there
and run the Columbian Mills. Loaded with incessant physical *douleurs*
and anxious introspections he did not allot to himself many more years
on this earth, nor was he sure that it would be worth while to linger and
ruminate over the wreckage of his national engines for Liberty with
Power.

1

"My grand climacteric is turned," John Quincy Adams recorded on his sixty-third birthday, "and I enter upon the sixty-fourth year of my age. In turning back to the notice of the last year's anniversary, the thought presses upon me of how little has since been effected of that preparation which even then formed an essential part of my duty." [1]

The duty, of course, seemed now nothing more than the assembly of his father's papers and the writing of his biography, perhaps even a history of the United States.

In retirement amidst his nut trees and his berry bushes he read Cicero's dissertation on death penned at Tusculum before his fatal return to politics. He meditated on it at the most favorable moment of his life to let the argument sink in. But something stirred within him against Cicero's logic. "I have no plausible motive for wishing to live," he admitted, "when everything that I foresee and believe of futurity makes death desirable, and when I have the clearest indications that it is near at hand. [But] I should belie my conscience should I not acknowledge that the love of life and the horror of dissolution is as strong in me as it ever was at any period of my existence." [2]

Somehow Adams, dedicated to rural retirement, quiet reading, and filial literary endeavor, could not believe that he was done at sixty-three.

For the summer of 1830 Louisa, Mary Hellen Adams, and the three-year-old granddaughter journeyed along with the ex-President to the Old Mansion in Quincy, which he had made ready for them the year before. A week of travel north by carriage, stage, and inland waterways exhausted Mrs. Adams and granddaughter. From New York to Providence they proceeded on the steamboat *President,* in charge of the same Captain Bunker who had commanded the *Benjamin Franklin* when their beloved George had left this world. Off Point Judith in heavy swells they met the *Franklin* on her way into Long Island Sound. The sight of the sister ship wallowing in the open seas trailing a funereal plume of black smoke pressed heavily on Louisa's mournful spirits, and left her husband in a disposition scarcely more cheerful. [3] She arrived at Quincy so ill as not to want to see anybody, and remained painfully confined to the mansion all the first part of the summer.

Despite his wife's prostration, the paternal home afforded a center of reunion for the Adamses. John managed to join them for a short vacation in July, and in September John Quincy Adams held a second granddaughter to be baptized by Mr. Whitney in the new stone Temple: Georgiana Frances Adams. The younger son Charles and his bride of the previous autumn, Abby Brooks, came out frequently from Boston for days at a

---

[1] Diary, July 11, 1830.   [2] *Memoirs,* VIII, 235.
[3] Diary, June 2, 1830.

time. From now on, as successive summers followed one another, Adams's family roots sank deeper and deeper into his native soil.

He devoted his time that summer principally to three occupations: Cicero and the Bible, his nursery and garden, and his Diary. Up by habit at four or five o'clock, taking to early morning lamplight as the summer wore on and the days shortened, he reread each day three chapters from the New Testament with commentary, then passed to Cicero, ten to fifteen sections of the orations before breakfast. He got through the Bible again on August 18, begun in May of the previous year; by October 24 he finished the last fragment of Cicero, whose entire writings he had started the previous December to read through in the original.[4]

The Bible gave continued solace and steady daily direction to the end of his life. He read it not as a professional critic but as a teacher of his own duties and the rights of others, a monitor for public counsel, and "a guide through the darksome journey of life." [5] Cicero afforded hours of high enjoyment, as well as a feeling of exalted community with his own American career. The old Roman's stamp of style and feeling shows through many a passage of Adams's letters and Diary and throughout his controversial writings. His letters to his son Charles on books and men and measures take on something of the tone of Cicero's letters *De Officiis* to his son Marcus.

After the morning meal he customarily spent from one to two hours in the garden with spade or hoe, or in "barren observations upon vegetation," then three or more hours of reading or writing miscellaneously in his library. At intervals he and his son Charles would occupy themselves with John Adams's voluminous manuscripts, but little writing got done that summer. At two o'clock the family usually sat down to dinner; in sultry weather the elder statesman napped until five and teatime. In the cool of the evening he rode about the village at the side of his daughter-in-law greeting the neighbors. At nine o'clock came the supper bell, afterward a long evening of journalizing or conversation with friends and family before bedtime.

Such was the schedule set down in his Diary. Once in a while he varied the routine to indulge in a friendly clambake or "chowder dinner" at Squantum shore. More often he went swimming from Daniel Greenleaf's wharf, usually accompanied by one of his sons or nephews, or a younger neighbor. Sometimes the elderly man went alone and might be seen by distant eyes beneath a white nightcap to protect his bald head from the sun's blaze. Exercise in Northern sea water seemed very tiring, and bodily labor in the garden at first produced twinges of lumbago and rheumatism to call forth discouraging reflections on age, but he kept up both activities all summer.

---

[4] *Memoirs*, VIII, 248.

[5] JQA to Reverend L. D. Dewey, New York. Quincy, September [no day given], 1846. Adams MSS.

"*Serit arbores quæ alteri seculo prosint.*" [6] John Quincy Adams, who had wrought in Washington to bring forth laws and works for the Republic's future centuries, was now content to plant acorns and walnuts for tall trees to shade future generations of Adamses to follow him in Quincy and in the nation.

Quiet contact with growing useful things gave increasing pleasure to his retirement. He loved to grow and pick good New England vegetables, his peas, string beans, green corn, potatoes, cabbages, cucumbers, beets, parsnips, turnips, squashes, and rhubarb. He delighted in his apple trees and his pears, peaches, and plums. And the berries that gave color and taste to the Yankee diet: blackberries, strawberries, raspberries, and whortleberries, the last an imported species of European blueberry that could never compete with the wild New England variety. John Quincy Adams should have known that!

Between house and garden towered a big shagbark. A squirrel had established himself there, waiting for the nuts to ripen. The retired President delighted to watch his furry friend balancing in the branches, descending to scamper along the garden fence, coming closer and closer, chattering immitigable protest at his landlord's respites from labor. Behind the garden was a poultry hatch. There the new owner of the paternal seat experimented none too successfully with black hens of Norman breed setting on nineteen eggs to the clutch.[7]

Was it not Cicero who said that the pleasures of agriculture afford the nearest approach to the life of a sage?

The summer was one of the hottest on record, long dry and sunny spells alternating with cold northeast rainstorms. The sexagenarian native returning to the soil of his fathers found that he did not pick up as usual in health and strength. Digging, swimming, tramping with his brother across the marshes did not seem to restore his strength as in former years. A persistent catarrh weakened him with long coughing spells every morning. When in early autumn he stopped the strenuous sea baths his ailments soon disappeared and he felt fresher and stronger, relieved also from bouts of despondency. He began to take interest again in what was going on outside of Quincy.

In September occurred the bicentennial celebration of the settlement of Boston. It would have been too shocking for that event to take place without there being present a representative of the only Massachusetts family that had furnished a President, two Presidents, to the United States. The committee in charge could not but send a special invitation to John Quincy Adams. Three of the Thirteen Confederates of 1829 presided over the ceremony: Harrison Gray Otis, Mayor of Boston; William Sullivan, Chief Marshal of the day; and Adams's onetime friend of the

[6] Cæcilius in Cicero's *Tusculans*, I, 14–31. See also *De Senectute*, 7. *Memoirs*, VIII, 234.

[7] Diary, July 28–30, 1830.

youthful years in Boston,[8] Thomas Handasyd Perkins. They came forward and offered their hands. He "accepted" the "salutation."

He took his assigned place in the procession down Tremont, Court, and State Streets to the Long Wharf and back to the Old South Meeting House, where his friend President Josiah Quincy of Harvard delivered the oration. Afterward, following fireworks on the Common, he attended an evening party at Lieutenant Governor Winthrop's house. There he met again some of the people who had greeted him earlier in the day, also acquaintances from Washington, and numerous old Boston friends: the Everetts, the Bulfinches, Coolidges, Crowninshields, Silsbees—and many other persons that he did not even know.[9] Even the crusty Boston Federalists, after initial experience with their newly accepted hero Andrew Jackson, were beginning slowly, very slowly, to thaw out again toward John Quincy Adams. Earlier in the year Harvard University, the last stronghold of Federalism, had elected him to the Board of Overseers, perhaps through the influence of President Quincy.[10]

2

A week or ten days before the bicentennial ceremony of September 17, 1830, the *Boston Daily Courier* printed an anonymous paragraph proposing the former President as next representative from the Plymouth district, to which the Federalists had recently gerrymandered the town of Quincy. The *Courier's* suggestion was, as young Charles Francis Adams put it, a nomination with a sneer.[11] Its editor, Joseph Tucker Buckingham, was a supporter of Henry Clay; the *Courier* was the strongest Clay organ in Boston. His sole motive was to get Adams out of Clay's way for the next nomination of the National Republicans for President. What better scheme than to get the new sage of Quincy sent by his district to the House of Representatives!

Already a loyal movement had gotten under way to send Adams to Congress, if he would go, as a good representative, free from all clannish partisanship and local prejudices, to throw off the "incubus of Jacksonianism."[12] At the Boston Bicentennial the Reverend Joseph Richardson, in-

---

[8] Vol. I, 26.

[9] *Memoirs*, VIII, 237–8.

[10] *Memoirs*, VIII, 180.

[11] See CFA's pseudonymous communication by "A Looker-On" in *Boston Patriot and Mercantile Advertiser*, XXIX, No. 4, September 2, 1831; and Diary of CFA, September 1, 1831. Adams MSS. Buckingham's hostile attitude toward Adams was sufficiently revealed in the columns of the *Courier* (Vol. VIII, Nos. 2314, 2316, 2319, 2322, 2323, 2329, 2342, September 1, 3, 7, 10, 12, 19, October 4, 1831) as soon as John Quincy Adams's name was mentioned conspicuously for the Antimasonic and National Republican nominations for the Presidency for 1832.

[12] Solomon Lincoln, Jr., to John Brazer Davis, Hingham, October 1, 1830. "Letters to John Brazer Davis, 1819–1831," MHS *Proceedings*, XLIX (1915–16), 234–6.

cumbent Representative of the district, and John Davis of the Norfolk district—both National Republicans—took Adams aside and said they would call upon him next day for a conference. Edward Everett, National Republican from the Middlesex district, openly asked him what he thought of going to Congress. "Mr. Richardson has declined a renomination," he explained.

Richardson himself so declared the next day in company with Davis. "I come personally to inquire," he said, "if you will serve, if elected, as member for the district."

"I observed about ten days since," admitted Adams, "a nomination to that effect in a paper the editor of which, without any cause known to me, has been uniformly hostile to me. I don't know from whom the nomination came, but I believe it was made in no spirit friendly to me. I don't suppose it is serious, or that any person has a thought of holding me up for election."

"If you will serve," Richardson assured Adams, "I believe the election can be carried by a large majority. The *Old Colony Memorial* and the *Hingham Gazette*, the only two newspapers printed in the district, and another paper published in the adjoining district and taken by some of my constituents, will support the nomination. If you decline, it is not possible that the district will unite upon any other person, and there will be no election."

The constitution of Massachusetts required an absolute majority of votes cast to elect a representative to Congress. It seemed that no candidate from the Plymouth district was likely to get such a majority in 1831, that therefore it might go unrepresented. Such was often the case in Massachusetts; for this reason during the next session the state would be missing three of its members in Congress for a large part of the session, two for all of it, as Adams and his colleagues would point out to the Governor.[13] This predicament was a serious handicap to Massachusetts during the debates of 1832 on the new apportionment bill following the census of 1830, as a result of which the state lost permanently one representative.[14]

An ex-President of the Republic descending to the forum again! Ex-

[13] G. N. Briggs, John Reed, George Grennell, Jr., Joseph G. Kendall, R. Choate, John Quincy Adams, J. C. Bates, H. A. S. Dearborn, N. Appleton, Edward Everett [all the members of the Massachusetts delegation in the House of Representatives except John Davis] to Governor Levi Lincoln, Washington, December 5, 1831. JQA to Governor Levi Lincoln, Private, Washington, December 7, 1831. Adams MSS.

[14] JQA leading the crippled Massachusetts delegation in Congress made a valiant fight for a smaller population ratio, which would have retained Massachusetts's old number of representatives. *Memoirs*, VIII, 460–73. Adams's speech of February 8, 1832 was printed in *Daily National Intelligencer*, XX, No. 5946, February 28, 1832. *Register of Debates*, VIII, Part II, 1831–2, pp. 1699, 1762, 1775, 1779, 1814, 1816, 1820. For results of the apportionment law of 1832 see JQA's "Address to the People of Massachusetts," 1833, in John Quincy Adams: *Letters on the Masonic Institution* (Boston, 1847), p. 264.

posing himself to the heat of debate, to the previous question, and all the devices of the *lex parliamentaria* in the hands of a willful majority; to the Speaker's refusal to recognize him, to his power to declare out of order, to the power of the House to compel a member to come before the bar for censure, or even to expel him! No wonder the anonymous paragrapher had not ventured to communicate such an unthinkable suggestion to any of the old pro-Adams newspapers. It was quite contrary to the established pattern of the life of a retired Chief Magistrate. The founding fathers— Washington, John Adams, Jefferson, Madison, Monroe—had all retired to their rural estates to become hosts to distinguished visitors, to be serene and disinterested advisers on transcendent issues, ornaments of the nation, elder statesmen, republican sages. The precedent already was fixed as strongly as the unwritten law against a third term in the White House. John Quincy Adams following the example of his illustrious predecessors, including his own father, had prepared a similar retreat from the Presidency, although he didn't know how he was going to manage financially the luxury of being a sage.

Richardson seemed to divine Adams's thoughts. "I think," he said, "that the service of an ex-President of the United States in the House of Representatives would elevate the representative character instead of degrading it."

"In that respect," Adams affirmed, "I have no scruple whatever. No person could be degraded by serving the people as a Representative in Congress. Nor, in my opinion, would an ex-President of the United States be degraded by serving as a Selectman of his town, if elected thereto by the people. But age and infirmity have their privileges. I have not the slightest desire to be elected to Congress. I cannot consent to be a candidate for election."

"I don't know how the election will turn," he intimated, "and, if chosen, it might depend upon circumstances whether I should deem it my duty to accept or decline. The state of my health, the degree of opposition to the choice, the character of the candidate in opposition, might each or all contribute to my determination."

"That is sufficient," concluded the Reverend Mr. Richardson. "I will go to work."

Richardson worked fast. A few days later Deacon Spear reminded Adams that the election would take place the first Monday in November. "Do you consider yourself an inhabitant of Quincy?" he asked pointedly.

"Certainly," the ex-President assured him. "If I am not an inhabitant of Quincy, I am an inhabitant nowhere."

"That's all I want to know," responded the good deacon. He went on to hint that the Jackson men—both Federal and Democratic—would try to upset the election.

Presently the *Hingham Gazette* proposed Adams's name, supported by two commendations from readers.

"Will you accept the office if elected?" John Bailey asked him bluntly. "I want to be able to answer people who ask me."

"I won't go so far as that," Adams declared demurely. "To say I would accept would be so near to asking for a vote. I want the people to act spontaneously."

"If you decline," protested Bailey, "there is no prospect they can agree upon a candidate." [15]

One unhappy experience as Minority President was enough for a lifetime of elective office. Adams was determined not to go to Congress unless it be as the overwhelming choice of his district. And, of course, he would never seek office, or work for it, no, never!

His family was opposed to the whole idea of launching himself again on the faithless wave of politics. Sapient twenty-three-year-old son Charles was rather presumptuous with his advice, which was unflattering, to say the least. He thought it would be beneficial to *neither* of them always to be struggling before the public without rest or intermission. Poor young Charles! His parents, to whom he owed so much for his start in life, were getting to be such a "load of care!" [16]

Nothing would hold back the old contender any longer. Whether he would admit it or not, Adams's heart seemed set on some sort of political comeback, big or little, as the future might reveal.

A National Republican convention of delegates from thirteen towns of the Plymouth district met in the town of Halifax on October 12, 1830. Jackson men tried to prevent the nomination by invading the convention, but the Adams delegates withdrew to a separate meeting and agreed unanimously to present Adams's name for election to the Twenty-second Congress, beginning in December 1831. The Jacksonians under designation of Republicans nominated a candidate to oppose him, one Arad Thompson.[17]

The election took place November 1, 1830. Reading the last returns in a newspaper of November 6, the Quincy candidate noticed the results from twenty-two towns:

[15] *Memoirs*, VIII, 237–41.

[16] Diary of CFA, November 16, 1830.

"October 3: I copied a letter for my father, and held some subsequent conversation with him upon the project of electing him to Congress. He does not disappoint me as I wish he had done. His is not the highest kind of greatness, and much as he may try to conceal his feeling under the cloak of patriotic inclination, my eye is a little too deep to be blinded by the outside. I regret the decision on his account; I regret it upon my own. To neither of us can it prove beneficial to be always struggling before the public without rest or intermission."

"October 4: . . . My father did not seem in very good humour, probably from the course which I felt it my duty to take about the election. This matter is not an agreeable one to him nor is it so to me, but I feel as if he ought not to take any course without having the whole ground laid out before him. The precedent is important to the whole nation. . . ." Ibid., 1830. Adams MSS.

[17] *Memoirs*, VIII, 242–5.

John Quincy Adams	1,817
Arad Thompson	373
William Baylies (Federalist)	279

"I am a member-elect of the Twenty-Second Congress," the reviving warrior recorded jubilantly that evening in his Diary.[18]

Despite the opposition of Jacksonites and Federalists he had received three fourths of all votes cast. The "spontaneous" victory was sweet balm for the agonies of mind he had been through since his defeat for re-election to the Presidency: the attacks of the Massachusetts Federalists when he seemed down and out, domestic calamity, social ostracism in his own state—abandoned by all the world, like Richard Cœur de Lion, it had seemed to him. So elated he now felt that he did not dare to tell a soul, any more than he had cared to reveal to anyone his feelings in the days of political rout and personal sufferings. "My election as President of the United States was not half so gratifying to my inmost soul," he wrote in his Diary. "No election or appointment conferred upon me ever gave me so much pleasure. I say this to record my sentiments; but no stranger intermeddleth with my joys, and the dearest of my friends have no sympathy with my sensations." [19]

That was the way John Quincy Adams really felt about it. As his family continued to show little enthusiasm, and some of his friends questioned the wisdom of his going to Congress after having been President, he rationalized the step to them as an act of patriotic self-sacrifice. He had not wanted to go back into politics, he declared. There was little pleasure, honor, perhaps not much profitable service to his country to be expected. It might mean slights, mortifications, loss of reputation, self-exposure to infirmities of temper unsuited to the trials he would encounter—even dangers to his life (he had received an anonymous threat that he would meet a Brutus if he went to the Capitol). It was a Call, of duty.[20] No personal considerations could set it aside. "For myself, taught in the school of Cicero, I shall say: *'Defendi rempublicam adolescens; non deseram senex.'* [21] The People of the District in which I reside when they called upon me to represent them in the Congress of the United States consulted not my inclinations. To those of them who enquired whether I would serve if elected, my answer was that I saw no warrantable ground upon which I could withhold my services if demanded."

He even construed precedents from his predecessors to justify his new political departure. Had not Washington accepted a military commission from President John Adams? Had not ex-Presidents John Adams, James Madison, and James Monroe served "in conventions of fundamental leg-

---

[18] *Memoirs*, VIII, 245.
[19] *Memoirs*, VIII, 245–7.
[20] JQA to CFA, Washington, January 15, November 22, 1831. Adams MSS.
[21] "I will not desert in my old age the Republic that I defended in my youth."

CHARLES FRANCIS ADAMS, AGED 22

PORTRAIT, 1829, ATTRIBUTED TO CHARLES BIRD KING. PHOTO-
GRAPH BY GEORGE M. CUSHING, JR. COURTESY OF OLD HOUSE,
ADAMS NATIONAL HISTORIC SITE, NATIONAL PARK SERVICE,
DEPARTMENT OF THE INTERIOR

islation [i.e., constitutional conventions] in their respective states"? Did not Jefferson become "rector of his own University"? One of his motives in accepting the Call, he reasoned, was to set a further example to future ex-Presidents for useful service to the Republic.[22]

There was another reason why the Call must have been welcome. As we have seen, he was land-poor; his son, who had charge of his affairs in Boston, regarded him as on the verge of ruin. Charles felt a double concern: for his parents' security, and for his own patrimony.[23] By the time John Quincy Adams had got his financial affairs untangled in the summer of 1832 he found that he owed $42,000,[24] including notes for a total of $13,000 that he would have to pay or renew at heavy interest. He hardly knew where to turn to raise a dollar. He really needed the pay of eight dollars a day that a member received for each session of Congress plus forty cents a mile traveling allowance.[25]

3

The Old House in Quincy was still only a summer home. Regardless of the election to Congress, the Adamses had planned to go back to Washington for another winter with their son John and family. Louisa wanted to escape the rigors of the New England climate and to get away from the rubbings and spongings of Yankee relatives. She always liked Washington better than Quincy. John Quincy wished to keep an eye on the uncertain business of the Columbian Mills; he wished even more to watch the political arena from a ringside seat. Both wanted to be with John and Mary and the grandchildren. Within a month of the election they left for the capital, even though the opening of the Twenty-second Congress was still a year away. A few days before Christmas 1830 they settled down for the coming season at their son's new house on Sixteenth Street.

In Washington that winter Adams followed his customary routine of

---

[22] JQA to Samuel L. Southard, Quincy, December 6, 1830. Adams MSS.

[23] Diary of CFA, December 3, 1830, July 18, 1831. "Should the worst come to worst I can now reasonably hope to be no great charge to him. Until then, however, it is but fair that I should derive a little benefit to my children [none born yet!] from my father's property and not let it all sink in the gulf which he and John are forming for it." Ibid., September 5, 1831. Adams MSS.

[24] $21,000 was to beneficiaries of John Adams's estate. The remainder, presumably, was on account of the Columbian Mills. It is detailed in an untitled memorandum book containing drafts of JQA's will.

[25] LCA wrote to JA, 2d, Quincy, August 29, 1832, that JQA did not know where to turn for a dollar and had just got a tax bill for $500. "Your father is very well, but much depressed by the examination of his affairs upon which he finds himself burthened with a small debt of 40,000 dollars on which he is paying interest. It is a sad state of things but it is better that we should all know the truth." LCA to JA, 2d, Quincy, October 20, 1832. Adams MSS.

early morning rising and walks about the city. Distinguished visitors, members of the diplomatic corps, and National Republican politicians were frequent callers at the Sixteenth Street home, and he called on them freely at their homes and boarding-houses. On New Year's Day 1831 over three hundred persons came to pay their compliments. Among them were the Secretary of State Martin Van Buren, and Senator Edward Livingston of Louisiana, presently to succeed to that office.[26] Adams could now dine out as well as receive guests. He thoroughly enjoyed the flow of company, the variety of conversation, social, artistic, literary, and on foreign affairs. And there was always the seething politics of the national capital, now more and more agitated by the renewed conflict over state rights and by the open warfare that had at last broken out between President Jackson and Vice President Calhoun.

4

On the way down from Massachusetts, John Quincy Adams had paid a call on ex-President James Monroe, then sojourning at the home of his daughter and son-in-law, Samuel L. Gouverneur, in New York. Monroe in the last year of his life, feeble and emaciated, almost poverty-stricken, his country estate in Virginia up for sale, was worrying about some correspondence that the quarrel between Jackson and Calhoun had imposed upon him. It concerned the censorious attitude that Calhoun as Secretary of War in Monroe's Cabinet had taken toward General Jackson's invasion of Spanish Florida in 1818.

Friends of Jackson and Van Buren had learned through Crawford at least as early as 1828 that Calhoun, far from defending the General's conduct, had wanted to disavow it to Spain, even to have him court-martialed for violation of orders. For political reasons—to keep the South united as much as possible for Jackson's election—they had remained quiet for the time being, holding their knowledge to plant a mine under Calhoun to touch off later, as soon as they were ready to destroy him as Jackson's successor. In April 1830 they exploded it, in the shape of a letter from William H. Crawford, recalling that, in President Monroe's Cabinet discussions of 1818, Calhoun had favored "reprimanding" General Jackson.

Once anybody had opposed Jackson it was difficult to remain a friend afterward! The President immediately demanded an explanation from Calhoun. "He will either have to deny the truth of the statement, in Mr. Crawford's letter," the Old Hero wrote, "or be in a delicate situation if he admits the fact." [27]

---

[26] *Memoirs*, VIII, 261.
[27] Andrew Jackson to Colonel James A. Hamilton, Washington, May 18, 1830. Bassett: *Correspondence of Jackson*, IV, 137.

Calhoun's labored reply and subsequent correspondence [28] did not satisfy Jackson, who believed that President Monroe had given him secret and confidential orders in 1818, cautiously conveyed in a letter from the General's friend in Washington, Representative John Rhea of Tennessee, sanctioning the incursion into Florida, and that Secretary of War Calhoun knew it at that time. Calhoun admitted that he had seen such a letter *from* Jackson, but declared it had never been answered, directly or indirectly. Both Crawford and Calhoun appealed to the venerable Monroe to testify whether this was so. Monroe denied that he had ever read Jackson's confidential request at the time it was received, much less answered it. By then the almost senile Rhea could not remember much of anything, but on President Jackson's insistent briefing he declared he had written the letter at Monroe's suggestion.[29]

Both Crawford and Calhoun, Adams's old rivals, now turned to the other members of Monroe's Cabinet for corroboration. What did they remember about the discussions? Did they know about any Rhea letter? In the summer of 1830 Crawford had got a corroborative statement from B. W. Crowninshield, Monroe's Secretary of the Navy, only later to find that Crowninshield had not been present at those Cabinet meetings, had not even been in Washington at the time! John Quincy Adams, who had been there, as Secretary of State, replied to Crawford from Quincy that he had no recollection of "such a production" as Jackson's request for secret instructions through Rhea.[30]

After ex-President Adams returned to Washington in 1830, Vice President Calhoun addressed a series of letters to him asking about the Rhea letter, requesting a copy of Adams's letter of the previous summer to Crawford, and any further record of the Cabinet deliberations of 1818. The newly elected member from the Plymouth district knew what was back of all this controversy. Crawford still nursed his old rancorous feud

[28] Calhoun to Jackson, May 29, 1830. *Works* of Calhoun, VI, 362–85; *Niles' Register*, XL, 11–45, March 5, 12, 19, 1831.

[29] See Vol. I, 313–16. This subject belongs more to the biographies of Jackson and Calhoun than to that of John Quincy Adams. Both Bassett (for Jackson) and Wiltse (for Calhoun) have treated the subject fully and are not far apart in their opinion that it was part of a political intrigue in 1830–1 to thrust aside Calhoun in favor of Van Buren for succession to the Presidency. Richard R. Stenberg, after reviewing the evidence, concludes that Jackson invented the Rhea letter as a device to discredit Calhoun. "Jackson's 'Rhea Letter' Hoax," *Journal of Southern History*, II (1936, No. 4), 480–96.

Calhoun wrote a public statement to sustain his side of the controversy, published in Duff Green's *United States' Telegraph*, Vol. VI, Nos. 20, 21, 24, February 15, 17, 24, 1831. See also *Niles' Register*, XL, 11–24, and *Works* of Calhoun, VI, 349–445. Jackson prepared a reply but did not publish it while President. Thomas Hart Benton later printed it in his *Thirty Years' View*, I, 167–80.

[30] *Memoirs*, VIII, 274–5, 297; W. H. Crawford to JQA, July 5, 1830; JQA to Crawford, Quincy, July 30, 1830; Adams MSS. JQA to J. C. Calhoun, January 14, 1831. *Niles' Register*, XL, 24.

with Calhoun; the Georgian was glad to lend himself vindictively to the new and bitter conflict between Van Buren and Calhoun for the succession, in which the Red Fox of Kinderhook now had Jackson's active alliance. All three of the parties at war with each other, Jackson, Crawford, Calhoun, were Adams's enemies too, open or covert.

As Crawford and Calhoun desperately appealed to him to sustain each against the other, Adams tried to put aside all personal considerations. He realized that he was walking between red-hot plowshares, and was mindful where he put his foot. He declined to tell either anything that the other had said about Jackson in Florida. But he could not say he knew anything of secret instructions or any letter of old "Johnny" Rhea to General Jackson back in 1818.[31] And it was common knowledge that he himself had justified Jackson's conduct in those bygone days, notably in his famous instruction of November 28, 1818 to Minister George W. Erving in Spain, the "great gun from Washington to Madrid." [32] What was not publicly known was that, in Monroe's Cabinet, Adams had successfully championed Jackson's aggressive conduct against censorship of all the "gentlemen of the Administration," including Crawford as well as Calhoun, and the President himself.[33]

Net result of the whole controversy would be complete isolation of Calhoun from the Jackson Administration and the ruin of his ardent hopes for succession to the Presidency in 1832 or 1836. As will be seen at a later place this excommunication threw Calhoun into open leadership of the nullification movement and into indirect debate with John Quincy Adams on the question of state rights versus national authority.

Calhoun acknowledged John Quincy Adams's decency during the quarrel with Jackson by personally calling on him at the Sixteenth Street residence.[34] Adams returned the call. The two rivals, who had grown so far apart in politics since their union in Monroe's Cabinet, now at opposite poles of political philosophy, resumed their social relations. "I meet Mr. Calhoun's advances to me because I cannot reject them," Adams recorded in his Diary. "But I once had confidence in the qualities of his heart. It is not totally destroyed, but so impaired that it can never be fully restored. Mr. Calhoun's friendships and enmities are regulated exclusively by his interests. . . . Calhoun veers round in his politics . . . and makes his in-

[31] *Memoirs,* VIII, 273–5, 296, 305, 307. J. C. Calhoun to JQA, Washington, January 12, 1831, *Works* of Calhoun, VI, 429–33; to JQA, January 29, 1831, Adams MSS.; to JQA, February 3, 1831, J. F. Jameson: *Correspondence of John C. Calhoun* in *Annual Report* 1899 AHA, II, 285–7; to JQA, February (*sic*), received February 12, 1831, Adams MSS.; JQA to J. C. Calhoun, January 14, 1831, *Niles' Register,* XL, 24; JQA to J. C. Calhoun, January 31, February 4, 12, April 12, 1831; Adams MSS. *Memoirs,* VIII, 404–5.

[32] Vol. I, 328.

[33] *Memoirs,* IV, 108–14.

[34] Young Richard Peters, acting under the inspiration of Calhoun's friend Virgil Maxcy, served as an intermediary for this reconciliation. *Memoirs,* VIII, 323, 332.

tellect the pander to his will." But he preserved a certain respect for Calhoun that he could never feel for the despised Crawford, who now made his memory "tributary to the course of events." [35]

Calhoun's eclipse in the Jackson Administration meant also a blackout for the journalist Duff Green and his Washington *United States' Telegraph* as an official mouthpiece. Jackson brought on Frank Blair from Kentucky and set him up as editor of a new organ, the Washington *Globe,* for a decade afterward the most powerful journal in the United States.

Adams could hold himself a neutral and cautious spectator of these personal feuds of his enemies, as he had been a tranquil and neutral observer of the political combinations, rivalries, and wars of Europe. But where Calhoun's burning ambition turned from national to sectional leadership and mischief to the Union, he would no longer be quiet, as succeeding chapters will show.

5

Adams's personal attitude toward his old rival, the living Calhoun, contrasts agreeably with deprecation of his boyhood friend, the deceased Jefferson. During these years of leisure his ever active critical eye fell upon the first published collection of Jefferson's writings, a four-volume edition edited by the grandson Thomas Jefferson Randolph, published in 1829 at Charlottesville, Virginia, and in London, England, under the title: *Memoir, Correspondence, and Miscellanies, from the Papers of Thomas Jefferson.*[36] The rancorous appraisal of Jefferson which Adams recently had written into his unpublished "Reply to the Massachusetts Federalists" and his unprinted "Parties in the United States" now found additional expression in his Diary as he read the memoirs and correspondence of the author of the Declaration of Independence. Personal pique stemming from Jefferson's letters to Giles in 1825 and Adams's uncomfortable controversy with the Massachusetts Federalists sharpened these appreciations.[37] They also reflect the specter of nullification that was now hovering over the Union, for which Adams held Jefferson fundamentally responsible.

Adams had to admit that the Declaration of Independence was one of the best-composed state papers he ever saw, but thought that Jefferson's original draft was too "declaratory, argumentative, and overloaded with crudities." Some of these had persisted in the final document itself, but fortunately Congress, in revising and rewording the draft, had struck out

[35] *Memoirs,* VIII, 323, 331.

[36] Charlottesville, Va.: F. Carr and Company; 1829. London: H. Colburn and R. Bentley; 1829. A later American edition was published in 1830 by Gray and Bowen of Boston, and G., C., and H. Carvill, of New York. Hereafter referred to in this chapter as *Writings of Jefferson.*

[37] See above, Chapter IX.

some inadvisable matter, including the "fanatic paragraph" against the slave trade and slavery—"indiscreet beyond measure and not a little unjust."

Historical inaccuracies and faulty memory, attested in Jefferson's earlier state papers of the Revolution, and in an autobiographical fragment written at the age of seventy-seven, were the least of Adams's indictments. He noted a twofold levity characteristic of "a disbeliever in a future state and of the double-dealer in the present," and typical of a man "whose duties to his neighbor were under no stronger guarantee than the laws of the land and the opinion of the world." (As a matter of fact, Jefferson was no more of a free-thinker than Adams's own father. John Adams was an avowed original Unitarian, Jefferson a Deist who hoped that every young man in the United States would grow up to be a Unitarian.)

Adams thought Jefferson guilty of intellectual and physical cowardice. The Virginian statesman avowed a persevering opinion against Negro slavery, but dared not let it loose until after his death. (Adams himself had not yet publicly acknowledged his long-standing repugnance to slavery.) Jefferson ran away ignominiously, so the diarist critic remarked, when Tarleton's forces occupied Monticello. (Who would have remained there and let himself be captured?) In the darkest moment of the Revolution, Jefferson refused to stand again for Governor of Virginia. He declined diplomatic appointments abroad while the war still continued, because of fear of himself or members of his family being captured by the enemy while crossing the seas. "These are dangers which high-souled men engaged in a sacred cause should not flinch from," observed Adams, remembering the voyages that he had taken with his father during the Revolution. He felt that Jefferson glossed over unsavory features of his life, or omitted them altogether. "He says nothing of his adventure with Mrs. Walker,[38] nor of the correspondence to which it gave rise." [39] (A less prejudiced reader might well ask why was it necessary to print this all over again.) Particularly egregious to Adams seemed Jefferson's denial of any political understanding with the Federalists through Senator Bayard of Delaware [40] to break the deadlock with Burr in the contest for the Presidency in the House of Representatives in 1800. (Such a reproof, even though secreted in intimate pages of a personal diary, came with poor grace from a man who himself had made bargain after bargain with members of the House of Representatives for election to the same high office!) [41] The elderly John Quincy Adams in his notes did not refer to

[38] Jefferson had acknowledged having made improper but fruitless advances to the wife of his friend John Walker. She repulsed them. Dumas Malone appraises the evidence in *Jefferson the Virginian* (Boston, 1948), pp. 447–51.

[39] *Memoirs*, VIII, 271.

[40] For this political deal see Charles A. Beard: *Economic Origins of Jeffersonian Democracy* (New York, 1915), pp. 401–14.

[41] *Memoirs*, VIII, 270–310.

Jefferson's affectionate message to his "dear friend" John Adams at the death of Abigail, a letter to disarm any ordinary mortal.[42]

Adams protested to his friend Alexander H. Everett, editor of the *North American Review*, at the too abundant "liberality" which Andrew Ritchie had bestowed upon his review of the Randolph edition of Jefferson's correspondence in that quarterly. Jefferson had grown up under the influence of an "infidel school"—Bolingbroke, Hume, Voltaire, Diderot—"and the rest of that gang." [43]

Contemporary critics of Jefferson's writings in England [44] were more generous than Adams. The *Westminster Review* went so far as to hail the *Memoirs and Correspondence* as one of the most important publications ever presented to the world, and lauded Jefferson, whose principles of government were taking a "deeper and deeper hold on the American people," as "undoubtedly the greatest public benefactor that has yet appeared in the nineteenth century." [45] Alluding to Jefferson's letters to John Adams from 1812 to 1825, the English reviewer said: "We know of nothing more beautiful in the records of the retirement of illustrious men."

" 'Judge not, that ye be not judged!' " So Adams had said in his unpublished "Reply to the Appeal of the Massachusetts Federalists," when making his severe comments on his father's old friend and colleague, the author of the Declaration of Independence. His invocation of the scriptural word was only rhetorical.

His later uncharitable judgment on Jefferson, like the "Reply to the Appeal," did not see the light of day for nearly half a century. Henry Adams, who digested his grandfather's papers for the *History of the United States during the Administrations of Jefferson and Madison*, was far juster to the great American than was the son of John Adams. But few historians today would deny that Jefferson's Kentucky Resolution of 1799 planted the seed of nullification.

Between these savage comments on Jefferson's character, John Quincy Adams read *Childe Harold* and *Don Juan* and other works of Byron,

---

[42] *Writings of Jefferson*, T. J. Randolph, ed. (Charlottesville, 1829), IV, 309–10.

[43] *North American Review*, Vol. XXX (No. lxvii, April 1830), 511–51. "Mr. Jefferson's *infidelity*—his *anti-judicialism* and his *nullification*," Adams reminded Everett at great length, "were three great and portentous errors. I did hope that the cause of the Cross, the cause of *Justice*, and the cause of the American Union, would have found in the North American Review a head and heart capable of defending them against the insidious, and therefore most formidable assault of his posthumous correspondence." JQA to Alexander H. Everett, Washington, May 24, 1830. *AHR*, XI (No. 2), 338–9.

[44] The reviewer in the *Eclectic Review*, 3rd series, III (London, January 1830), 64–72, and IV (July 1830), 139–53, rather grudgingly admitted Jefferson's greatness, particularly to Americans. More appreciative, if diffuse, was the *Edinburgh Review*, LI (April–July 1830), 496–526.

[45] *Westminster Review*, XIII (No. XXVI, October 1830), 312–35.

wrote hymns, and made poetical paraphrases of the Psalms. A veritable frenzy of versification seized upon him, "melancholy madness, without inspiration"—unless from "ale and viler liquors." [46] He walked about the District of Columbia putting stanzas together, writing them down when he got home, reading them to his patient wife, polishing them. In this way he composed, during a period of two months, the epic of *Dermot MacMorrogh*, in his own opinion the greatest measure of his poetical power. It was an original "tale" of the conquest of Ireland, with a "clear and palpable moral" for Irish freedom. The poem swelled to ponderous length, until he got waterlogged with it as once he got swamped in the middle of the Potomac River. Concluded in Washington in April 1831, the work enjoyed three small editions. [47] No modern reader would ever wade through the "epic."

Versification of the Psalms, on which he spent snatches of time daily for several years, filled up many pages of his notebooks. Fortunately few of these paraphrases were printed, [48] for who can improve on the King James translation of the Psalms? Adams himself had to concede that he was not a poet. But he kept on writing verses big and little. Some of the nicest were the little ones that graced many a sweet young lady's album.

6

Mr. and Mrs. Adams left Washington in the spring of 1831. That summer at Quincy was one of the pleasantest that they would spend there. Louisa enjoyed better health all through the season. John Quincy resumed his garden hobbies and, with more moderation, his vacation exercises, and felt better for his prudence. He and Louisa waited anxiously on the marital fortunes of son Charles Francis and his young wife Abby. Would the first-born be a girl like John's two children, or a boy to carry on the family's destiny? It was another girl, born in Boston, August 13, 1831, Louisa Catherine Adams.

With his son Charles, John Quincy Adams whiled away more pleasant hours sorting, arranging, and reading his father's papers, and cataloguing the Adams library. But he made little headway on the biography. Instead, he occupied himself in a growing correspondence with leaders of the Antimasonic movement, to be noticed more particularly hereafter. He

---

[46] *Memoirs*, VIII, 339, 351.

[47] *Dermot MacMorrogh, or the Conquest of Ireland; an Historical Tale of the Twelfth Century,* in Four Cantos (Boston: Carter Hendee and Company; 1st ed., 1832; 2d ed., 1832; 3rd ed. by I. N. Whiting and Company; Columbus, Ohio, 1834). For notes on JQA's poetical propensities and habits of versification, see *Memoirs*, VIII, 338–41, 346–9, 352. Also JQA to William Montgomery of Danville, Pennsylvania, Washington, December 27, 1827, Meridian Hill, March 22, 1829; to Robert Walsh, Washington, February 18, 1829. Adams MSS.

[48] Some were printed in William P. Lunt's *The Christian Psalter* (Boston: Charles C. Little and James Brown; 1844).

devoted many days in preparing an address for the Fourth of July at Quincy,[49] others to a long oratorical eulogy of James Monroe, who died on that same Fourth of July 1831.[50] He spent a great deal of time in deliberations of the Phi Beta Kappa chapter of Boston. He attended commencement, the first time since his defeat for re-election to the Presidency of the United States and his ostracism by the Massachusetts Federalists. He sat as judge in the Boylston prize speaking-contest. He met with the Board of Overseers. He marched in the commencement procession.[51] He came into contact again, in Cambridge and Boston, with his associates of yesteryear, even though Mayor Harrison Gray Otis and company kept studiously out of sight [52] at the Monroe elegies in the Old South Church, August 25, 1831.[53] More and more he was winning back his prestige, recapturing the respect of the mercantilist community of Massachusetts over the "mouldering relics of the Hartford Convention."

Despite these activities his spirits began to droop.[54] Life at Quincy was too quiet. He had too little to do. He even thought of buying the *Boston Patriot* as a personal organ and putting in his son as business manager and literary editor.[55] The fact was that his ambition was reviving. He was eager to get back into national politics. He could hardly wait for the Twenty-second Congress to begin, the first week in December. At the end of October he and Louisa set out for the nation's capital.

Adams's journey to Washington was a little triumph for a man who so recently had looked on himself as finished. When he visited briefly a tariff convention in New York, one of the vice presidents, James Tallmadge, came down the aisle to meet him. The audience rose and applauded as he was escorted to a chair beside the president [56]—a tribute that afforded him much pleasure. Political leaders and literary personalities called on him at his lodging. With Albert Gallatin and Dr. Jonathan Wainwright he attended the Literary Convention then in session. They immediately made him presiding officer, and member of a committee to draw up plans for a National Library and Scientific Institution. At Philadelphia he was pres-

---

[49] See next chapter.

[50] On September 27, 1836 John Quincy Adams delivered at Boston another eulogy, on the life and character of James Madison, the text of which was abridged by his son Charles to an address of only two hours and a half! *Memoirs*, IX, 304, 308, 340. These two addresses, printed separately at the time in several editions, may be found in expanded form in: *The Lives of James Madison and James Monroe, Fourth and Fifth Presidents of the United States*. By John Quincy Adams, with historical notices of their administrations (Boston: Phillips Sampson and Company; Buffalo; G. H. Derby and Company; 1850).

[51] *Memoirs*, VIII, 408–10.

[52] Benjamin Waterhouse to JQA, Cambridge, September 24, 1831; LCA to JA, 2d, Quincy, August 30, 1831. Adams MSS.

[53] *Memoirs*, VIII, 401–2.

[54] Diary of CFA, July 19, 1831.

[55] Ibid., September 19, 20, 1831.

[56] *Memoirs*, VIII, 417.

ent at a meeting of the American Philosophical Society, where he admired Audubon's magnificent work on American birds, and other new artistic, literary, and scientific publications.[57]

People still looked up to him, even if Judge Joseph Hopkinson, Charles J. Ingersoll, Robert Walsh, and other friends in Philadelphia and elsewhere questioned the wisdom of his going back into politics.[58] After the new member from the Plymouth district had gone on from New York City, the *New York Whig* commented on the "moral grandeur of the spectacle" of the venerable ex-President taking his humble seat in the lower house of Congress like a true republican. "Where but in our own free land could such an event take place?"[59]

Young Charles Francis still disapproved his father's new departure. More interested in his own political future, he asked his father how to go about it.[60] "Confine your attention to such business as you have," advised John Quincy.[61] The son had sense enough to see that this was wise for him. But he continued to protest to his father, all through the sessions of the Twenty-second Congress, about the latter's mistake of going back into politics. Why didn't he stick to literature? "The nation wants a national Literature."[62]

"I must fulfill my Destiny," John Quincy answered, after submitting to such remonstrance for over a year.[63] Charles was not satisfied: "I cannot help thinking success would be far more certain, if you rejected the idea of *Destiny* altogether!" On reflection, the father agreed that Destiny was perhaps an ill-considered expression. "I must take blame to myself," he admitted, "for all the disasters that befall me."[64]

Charles Francis Adams was one of those precocious young men who in their very early twenties marvel how little their fathers seem to know. As he grew older he came to understand his father's real character and to appreciate his greatness.

So John Quincy Adams at the passing of his grand climacteric found himself again where he wanted to be, back in the breakers of national politics, aware of a personal destiny yet to be experienced, sensing the future of a great Union of Liberty with Power in which he was still to play a part.

[57] *Memoirs*, VIII, 417–26.

[58] C. J. Ingersoll to JQA, Philadelphia, July 29, 1831; JQA to C. J. Ingersoll, Quincy, September 8, 1831. Adams MSS.

[59] *New York Whig*, December 27, 1831. Cited by Gilbert Hobbs Barnes: *The Antislavery Impulse* (New York, 1933), pp. 126, 258.

[60] CFA to JQA, Boston, November 12, 1831. Adams MSS.

[61] JQA to CFA, November 22, 1831. Adams MSS.

[62] CFA to JQA, Boston, November 12, 1831. Adams MSS.

[63] JQA to CFA, Washington, November 25, 1832. Adams MSS.

[64] CFA to JQA, Boston, December 6, 1832; JQA to CFA, Washington, December 11, 1832. Adams MSS.

CHAPTER XII

Union or Disunion

(1829 – 1831)

The powers not delegated to the United States by
the Constitution, nor prohibited by it to the States,
are reserved to the States respectively, or to the
people.

TENTH AMENDMENT TO THE CONSTITUTION
OF THE UNITED STATES

THREE economic developments conspired after the peace settlements at
Ghent and Vienna in 1815 to fix the institution of slavery and the theory
of state rights on the South. They were: (1) release in England, France,
and the Low Countries of the pent-up forces of the Industrial Revolution,
particularly for the manufacture and export of textiles; (2) invention by
Eli Whitney of the cotton gin, making it possible to separate the seeds
from the fiber cheaply enough to warrant manufacture and sale of cotton
textiles on a large scale; (3) Andrew Jackson's conquest of the Indian
tribes in the Southwest, opening up a wide area of black bottom-lands
for the extensive cultivation of cotton in Georgia, Alabama, and Mississippi. A world market for cotton in piping times of peace and new lands
to grow it on made plantation slavery profitable in larger and larger
units.[1] The planters (cotton, tobacco, rice, sugar) continued to be
the dominant power in the South, their interest reinforced by the
constitutional three-fifths representation for their slaves in Congress.[2]
Meanwhile the Industrial Revolution spread to America, creating an economic conflict between the new manufacturing capitalists of the North
with their free labor and the agrarian slavery-capitalists of the South.[3]
On the surface the struggle between the two sections reflected itself po-

[1] Ulrich B. Phillips in *Annual Report* 1912 AHA, p. 150.

[2] William E. Dodd: "Profitable Fields for Investigation in American History, 1850–
1860," *AHR*, XVIII (No. 3, April 1913), 523.

[3] Historians of agriculture and slavery in the South argue that the plantation system was essentially a capitalistic institution depending on land and slaves and a staple
crop. See Lewis Cecil Gray: *History of Agriculture in the Southern States to 1860*
(2 vols., Washington: Carnegie Institution of Washington Publication No. 430; 1933),
I, vi–vii, 302, 470–1; II, 708–9, 940–1. Ulrich B. Phillips: *American Negro Slavery*
(New York, 1918) and *The Course of the South to Secession* (New York, 1939),

litically in the protective tariff. Ever lurking beneath that was the issue of slavery itself.

The tariff question focused on the State of South Carolina.

1

At first the South Carolinians had not challenged the constitutionality of a protective tariff, firmly buttressed as it was in precedent by the votes of that state's own representatives. But as the majority for protection mounted throughout the Union, making it difficult to expect early downward revision of the tariff, local politicians and polemicists of the state followed the lead of Robert J. Turnbull.[4] They convinced themselves that the protective tariff, which kept up the costs of slave labor, and of the white way of life, while the price of cotton went down and down, was unconstitutional—palpably and dangerously so. It was therefore the duty of the state, said Turnbull, echoing the words of Jefferson in the Kentucky Resolutions of 1799, to interpose its authority to arrest the progress of the evil, by nullifying the federal tariff law. He and his converts warned their countrymen that "usurpations" of reserved powers by the Federal Government—such as a tariff for protection instead of a tariff for revenue— might make it necessary for South Carolina to reconsider the value of her place in the Union. The Tariff of Abominations confirmed this argument for the majority of the planters. Despite a persistently strong Union party, it threw South Carolina into the hands of the state-rights people.

Calhoun could not expect to deny the altered interest of his state and retain its support politically. Accordingly he restudied the Constitution to find a way by which a state could interpose its authority for remedying the evil without destroying the Union—if the Union were destroyed Calhoun could never be President of the United States. Prompt result of his new researches was *The South Carolina Exposition and Protest,* covertly written for a committee of the state legislature appointed to consider the tariff of 1828. The committee made Calhoun's draft, after some considerable alteration, into its own report. Although the legislature did not adopt the Report, it caused it to be printed early in 1829 and distributed far and wide. It became a significant document in American political history.

Calhoun's treatise—for such it is—began with an assertion, briefly developed, that the protective tariff, culminating in the Tariff of Abominations, was unconstitutional because it perverted tariff for revenue into a system of protection for manufactures, something not expressly included in the delegated power to lay and collect taxes and regulate commerce

---

looked upon it also as a system of social adjustment and social order (white supremacy).

  [4] Robert J. Turnbull: *The Crisis; or, Essays on the Usurpations of the Federal Government.* By "Brutus" (Charleston, 1827). See Wiltse: *John C. Calhoun, Nationalist,* pp. 375–86.

with foreign nations. The *Exposition* brushed aside all precedents of previous protective-tariff legislation, including those that Calhoun himself
had voted for. It was not precedent, said the committee, that counted: it
was the Constitution itself. Here the Report did little more than rehearse
the arguments and language of the Virginia and Kentucky Resolutions of
1798 and 1799 and of the later Report of the Hartford Convention.

Historians have called the *Exposition* long-winded and metaphysical.
The long-winded part is an argument to show that the tariff of 1828 benefited the Northern industrial states at the expense of the agrarian South,
which could not transform its staple agriculture to meet the new situation
because of its climate and its "peculiar system of labor." Thus the Southern states became the "serfs" of the North. The metaphysical part is not
metaphysical at all. It is factitious; it is ingenious; but it is not metaphysical. Recalling that ratification by three fourths of the states of the United
States was necessary for any amendment to the Constitution, Calhoun
"inferred" that when one state, through the "sovereign" pronouncement
of a state convention, declared that a usurpation by the Federal Government had taken place through an act of Congress "under color" of the
Constitution, the act was void until three fourths of the states should
override the one state's dictum by an amendment to the Constitution.
Meanwhile the state could nullify an obnoxious federal law within its
own sovereign limits.

Believers in this ingenious theory discounted the possibility that the
Federal Government might dare enforce the law in question against nullification by a state. Had not John Quincy Adams's Administration failed to
do so in the case of Georgia and the Creek Indians? Had not Governor
Troup forced the Federal Government to back down and renegotiate Indian treaties to the satisfaction of Georgia? An equally firm stand by
South Carolina—perhaps by other Southern states too—might compel the
new Administration of Andrew Jackson to back down on any enforcement of the protective tariff. Nullification would be simple, safe, and
sane. To resist it by federal enforcement would be to destroy the Union!

Such was Calhoun's effort to reconcile state rights with the continuation
of the Union of which he hoped to be elected President. The same argument runs through all his subsequent statements on the subject, presently
to be noticed.

2

The nullification movement in South Carolina provoked a dialectical
duel between Calhoun and Adams, now a member of the House. On the
issue which they disputed depended the ultimate fate of the Union.

The *Exposition* of South Carolina was Calhoun's first, concealed shot.
He did not immediately reveal his position behind the rail fences of his
cotton plantation at Fort Hill despite rumors that it was he who had actually written the earlier Report. Perhaps this was because the legislature's

committee did not wish to acknowledge that it had resorted to outside help
in drawing it up. Perhaps it was Calhoun's consciousness of the impropriety of a Vice President of the United States, a candidate for re-election,
constructing an engine by which a state might set at naught laws of the
Union. More likely it was due to his consciousness that authorship of such
a *liberum veto* might damage his chances to rout his rival Van Buren and
succeed Jackson in 1832.[5]

It was doubtless the suggestions in Turnbull's *Crisis* rather than Calhoun's *Exposition* that first aroused John Quincy Adams's concern about
nullification, expressed in his Presidential message to the Congress (December 2, 1828) on the state of the Union. He could not have had Calhoun's document before him when he drafted the message. In this last
annual message he reminded his fellow citizens that the Constitution had
not provided for a conflict between the two powers of state and Federal
Government, any more than virtuous nations of ancient times made laws
for the punishment of parricide. More than once, in moments of excitement, he said, the people and legislatures of one or more states had been
incited to such conflict by allegations that acts of Congress were to be resisted as *unconstitutional*. "If we suppose the case of such conflicting
legislation sustained by the corresponding executive and judicial authorities, patriotism and philanthropy turn their eyes from the condition in
which the parties would be placed, and from that of the people of both,
which must be its victims."

He did not yet [6] go into the question whether a special convention of
the people of a state (as distinct from the regular legislature) summoned
by the legislature for that purpose could declare a law of Congress unconstitutional. But legislature or convention, a state undoubtedly had the
power and means to attempt resistance to the Federal Government. In
plain words the Presidential valedictory was a warning to his countrymen
that support of nullification meant nothing less than civil war.

Adams's Reply to the *Appeal of the Massachusetts Federalists,* which
he began to write during the last weeks of his Administration, was an
answer in his own mind to the *South Carolina Exposition and Protest* as
well as to the Hartford Convention. Nullification meant secession, he had
stated in that unpublished philippic against would-be Federalist nullifiers of the War of 1812. But to recall in 1829 and 1830 the example of the
Hartford Convention even for the purpose of condemning it and its members might give the aid and comfort of New England precedent to current
nullifiers, potential secessionists. Nor would it have been altogether helpful to the cause of Union to make a blow at nullification incidental to a

---

[5] David Franklin Houston published what remains so far the clearest and most
balanced *Critical Study of Nullification in South Carolina* in Volume III of the *Harvard Historical Studies* (New York, 1908). See p. 79 for conjecture as to Calhoun's
motives.

[6] See JQA to Henry Clay, September 7, 1831. Adams MSS.

personal controversy.[7] So the departing President withheld this round of fire behind the stone walls of Quincy and waited for his principal adversary to come out into the open.

Before Calhoun and Adams stepped forth as opposing advocates of state and nation respectively, the issue flared up in a historic scene on the floor of the United States Senate. The Hayne-Webster debate brought to a spectacular boil the long-suppressed seethings of sectional politics.

3

Within Martin Van Buren's political combination of "planters and plain republicans," the slavery capitalists of the South had some reason to expect that Andrew Jackson, rich cotton-planter and slaveholder himself, might support the states in their efforts to remove the Indians from potential cotton fields of the Southwest. They hoped also for his help in resisting protection of Northern manufacturing industries at the expense of Southern agriculture by the Tariff of Abominations. One would be tempted to say protection of Southern slavery capitalists against Northern industrial capitalists, if one did not remember that Northern free-labor votes far outnumbered Northern capitalists, whilst Southern slaves had no vote at all.[8] Free labor at its worst under Northern industrial capitalism was far better than slavery in the cotton fields. The free laborer could not be torn from his family and sold down the river. He could rise in fact to become a member of Congress, or even President of the United States. By virtue of their rapidly increasing population in comparison with the agricultural South, the free laborers of the North by their increasing numbers and votes could eventually overcome the handicap of the three-fifths ratio, and look forward to the increasing restriction of slavery and its final abolition by constitutional amendment.

Southern leaders could rest easy about Jackson's attitude on the score of the aborigines, but they could not be so sure how far the old Indian-fighter would go against the protective tariff. Too many of the "plain republicans," including Calhoun's new rival Martin Van Buren, represented manufacturing states of the Northeast, notably Pennsylvania. Jackson and Van Buren were dependent on such representatives as well as Southern planters to keep their party and leadership in power in Congress. To bolster their traditional weight in the Union against the increasing population of the free states the Democratic champions of state rights turned hopefully to the West. They looked to Illinois, where Governor

[7] "The publication of my pamphlet would have been the signal for raising the standard of a Holy Alliance to glut the revenge of the old Federalists and the rancorous ingratitude of Jackson by treating me as Falstaff treats the body of Percy, stabbing me after death for fear I should revive." JQA to William Plumer, Jr., Quincy, September 30, 1830. Adams MSS.

[8] Kenneth M. Stampp has given thoughtful reminders for "The Historian and Southern Negro Slavery," in *AHR*, LVII (No. 3, April 1952), 613–24.

Ninian Edwards had declared to the state legislature that the sale of public lands from Washington was actually unconstitutional;[9] and particularly to Missouri, whose Senator Thomas Hart Benton was leading advocate of giving away the public lands to actual settlers. They proposed a political marriage between West and South of free trade and free lands. An opportunity to confirm such an alliance in Congress seemed to present itself in January 1830 when Senator Samuel A. Foote of Connecticut introduced a resolution to appoint a committee to inquire into the expediency of further limiting the sale of public lands.

Foote's proposed resolution blew up a thunder-gust from the four winds of the Capitol, South, West, North, and East.[10] The ensuing debate in the Senate held the attention of the nation for several weeks. Benton loosed a whirlwind of arguments against the resolution. The golden-tongued Robert Y. Hayne of South Carolina sprang to defense of the West on the issue of public lands, bidding for Western support for the South against the tariff.[11] Skillfully Daniel Webster of Massachusetts deflected the Southern orator into a defense of state rights and nullification. Then he fell on him with all the weight of the Constitution and Union as expounded by Chief Justice John Marshall and the Supreme Court. For generations schoolboys would repeat the thrilling climax of Webster's peroration: "Liberty and Union, now and forever, one and inseparable."

The debaters glossed over the real canker, the hidden issue of slavery, the "peculiar system of labor" with which Southern agriculture had to adjust itself to new conditions. The expansive new cotton culture had fastened slavery capitalism on the South, and it had fastened Calhoun and state rights to slavery. "I consider the Tariff but as the occasion rather than the real cause of the present unhappy state of things," wrote Calhoun. "The truth can no longer be disguised that the peculiar domestick institution of the Southern States, and the consequent direction, which

---

[9] Message to the legislature of Illinois, December 2, 1828.

[10] "The convocation of the four winds at the Capitol, has blown up a thunder gust, and many left-handed compliments between East, West, North, and South. Mr. Webster has made two speeches recently in the Senate of which I have heard much and you perhaps will hear more. I have seen the first which is good, and expect shortly to see the second, which was the great effort. A quidam by the name of Hayne, and another by the name of Benton have assured the Senate each for the other, that he is more than a match for Mr. Webster, and according to the rule in Boileau's *Art Poétique,* 'Un sot trouve toujours un plus sot qui l'admire,' each of them gives full credit to the other. The only question between them is which of the two is the greatest admirer." JQA to TBA, Washington, February 6, 1830. Adams MSS.

[11] "Benton and Hayne, by a joint and concerted attack upon the Eastern portion of the Union, proposed to break down the union of the Eastern and Western sections, and of [sic] restoring the old joint operation of the West and the South against New England. Benton's object is personal advancement and plunder; Hayne's, personal advancement, by the triumph of South Carolina over the tariff and internal improvement, and Calhoun's succession to the Presidency." *Memoirs,* VIII, 190–1. February 19, 1830.

that and her soil and climate have given to her industry, has placed them in regard to taxation and appropriations in opposite relation to the majority of the Union; against the danger of which, if there be no protective power in the reserved rights of the states, they must in the end be forced to rebel, or submit to have their permanent interests sacrificed, their domestick institutions subverted by Colonization and other schemes and themselves and children reduced to wretchedness." [12]

The famous debate put the constitutional issue squarely before the people: state versus nation. Adams read Webster's final speech, revised and corrected for posterity by the author himself,[13] in the columns of the *National Intelligencer*. "It is defensive of himself and of New England," he noted, "but carries the war effectually into the enemy's territory. It is a remarkable instance of readiness in debate—a reply of at least four hours to a speech of equal length.[14] It demolishes the whole fabric of Hayne's speech." It "pulverized" the false doctrine of nullification, whether from Hartford in New England or from Charleston in South Carolina. "The Otis of the East and the Hotspur of the South preach the same identical doctrine." [15]

The controversialist of 1829 was still thinking of his old Massachusetts adversary in terms of the Hartford Convention. Actually Otis and the other "Confederates" of New England, like all the old Federalists, would follow Webster's banner of Union against current nullifiers in South Carolina, even as spokesmen of that state had reproved the would-be New England nullifiers and separatists of 1808–15.

So impassioned were the debates, so striking the arguments,[16] so eloquent the speakers, so conscious the listeners of the sectional issues involved, with the great question of slavery hiding behind them, that the Senate lost the original motion from view and never voted on it.

After dinner one evening with a distinguished company at Benjamin Ogle Tayloe's [17] new house on Lafayette Square, Adams discussed with Van Buren certain details of Hayne's speech, relating to Jefferson's mem-

---

[12] Calhoun to Virgil Maxcy, Fort Hill, September 11, 1830. Maxcy Papers, LC.

[13] Wiltse: *John C. Calhoun, Nullifier*, p. 61.

[14] *Memoirs*, VIII, 192–3.

[15] JQA to Joseph Blunt, Washington, March 4, 1830. Adams MSS.

[16] "Mr. Webster has maintained the station which you assign to him by two splendid speeches, the first of which only has been published. Messrs. Benton, Hayne, Rowan, Sprague, Holmes, and Barton have also entered deeply into the debate and made speeches much celebrated. The debate is not near its termination, and there is much more eloquence to be wasted, all upon the question whether a committee shall be appointed to enquire into the expediency of suspending the surveys of public lands. There are conditions of the human body when the scratch of a pin produces a mortification and death; and there are tendons in the body the slightest puncture of which ends in a *lock-jaw*." JQA to CFA, Washington, February 21, 1830. Adams MSS.

[17] B. O. Tayloe, a graduate of Harvard of the class of 1815, had served as attaché in the United States Legation in London, in 1817. His house was on a part of the lot where the Cosmos Club later existed until 1952.

ory of the interview of March 15, 1808 about the Embargo.[18] Van Buren professed not yet to have read the debate.

"You will do well to read it," suggested the ex-President. "I think it is the most important one that has taken place since the existence of the Government. The two doctrines are now before the nation. The existence of the Union depends, I fully believe, upon this question." [19]

4

The party leaders in Congress made another effort to cement a political alliance of the South and West on the basis of state rights, free trade, and free lands—a platform that Calhoun could stand on with the support of the South, but which would be impossible for Van Buren with his manufacturing constituencies in Pennsylvania, New York, and New England. Benton and Hayne arranged a grand party dinner at Philadelphia for Jefferson's birthday, April 15, 1830, with a program of prearranged toasts apotheosizing the Sage of Monticello and his political gospel.[20] Their purpose was to commit the Pennsylvania delegation in Congress to such an antitariff alliance by their presence at the dinner.

Jackson saw through the stratagem. He was willing to go a considerable way to satisfy the South on the tariff, but he would not help to set the stage for Calhoun's ascent to the Presidency. With Van Buren's help he resolved to upset the whole maneuver.

The President, Vice President, and Secretary of State were guests at the dinner. The President sat at the toastmaster's right, Calhoun at his left.

As if by prearrangement the Pennsylvania delegation marched out of the hall before the dinner began. One by one the Southern spokesmen raised their glasses to Jefferson and state rights. Then came the time for voluntary toasts from the distinguished guests. All eyes turned to Andrew Jackson. The old soldier drew his racked body to full height, straight as when he faced Pakenham's British army at New Orleans. Up rose the audience with him.[21] With steady hand and flashing eyes the President raised his glass:

"Our Union: it must be preserved!"

The quick-witted Hayne stepped up behind Jackson's chair to suggest that the toast be recorded as: "Our *Federal* Union: it must be preserved!"

---

[18] See above, pp. 162–3.

[19] *Memoirs*, VIII, 200.

[20] Richard R. Stenberg: "The Jefferson Birthday Dinner, 1830," *Journal of Southern History*, IV (No. 3, August 1938), 334–45. See also Bassett: *Life of Jackson*, II, 554–7, and Wiltse: *John C. Calhoun, Nullifier*, pp. 67–73.

[21] Many writers have decorated the scene with capable hands, but none with surer dramatic touch than Margaret L. Coit in her *John C. Calhoun, American Portrait* (Boston, 1950), a canvas of the whole feverish society, as well as a picture of Calhoun.

Depending on how one construed *Federal,* that would make the toast sound delphic both North and South. Jackson made no objection. As a matter of fact, explained Van Buren in his *Autobiography,* this is the way he had originally composed it.

Calhoun responded: "Our Federal Union, next to liberty most dear. May we always remember that it can only be preserved by respecting the rights of the states and distributing equally the benefit and burden of the Union."

It was an anticlimax. Jackson had stolen the show for the Union. Calhoun's chance for the Presidency had vanished in one evening.[22]

The suave Van Buren tried to invoke the balm of conciliation. He closed with the toast: "Mutual forbearance and reciprocal concessions: through their agency the Union was established—the patriotic spirit from which they emanated will forever sustain it."

Jackson's toast fitted Adams's lifelong polity as the sword of Union fitted the scabbard of the Constitution. But one looks in vain in Adams's Diary for tribute to those resolute words, epitome of his own national principles. What he noted was the "Hickory toast, so tough and so tender," and "the Vice toast so brave and blustering." [23] Jackson's words meant no more to Adams than the words of the ancient oracle to Pyrrhus: "*Aio te, Æacida, Romanos vincere posse*" [24]—words that could mean either victory or defeat. In that delphic utterance, concluded the ex-President, each of the two factions could claim the Presidential toast to itself.[25]

The embittered ex-President could not believe that Andrew Jackson really meant to put down the Nullifiers. On the contrary, Old Hickory seemed to encourage them, with his submissive attitude toward internal improvements, the public lands, the Bank of the United States, the Indian wards of the nation, the protective tariff too. Adams firmly believed that under Jackson and Van Buren the Federal Administration was leagued with the nullifying states, and that the laws of the United States were sinking under the weight of the combination,[26] loosening the ligaments of the Union.

[22] Of the great debate and the Jefferson Dinner toast, we have two critical accounts, reflecting each side of the historic question: Bassett's *Life of Andrew Jackson,* II, 545–59, and Wiltse's *John C. Calhoun, Nullifier,* pp. 53–73.

[23] JQA to CFA, Washington, April 28, 1830. Adams MSS.

[24] In Latin those famous words could mean equally well either: (1) I say to you, Pyrrhus: you can conquer the Romans; or (2) I say to you, Pyrrhus: the Romans can conquer you.

[25] *Memoirs,* VIII, 229. May 22, 1830.

[26] JQA to William Plumer, Quincy, September 24, 1830. Adams MSS.

"The Indians, the Public Lands, the Public Debt, the Bank, have been ties to hold the Union together. They are severed or loosened. The Navy will soon be a wreck. The struggle of domestic industry is desperate, the prospect is that it will be sacrificed to the cotton-bagging or the Birmingham and Manchester interest." JQA to Samuel S. Southard, Quincy, June 6, 1830. Adams MSS.

5

Adams's alarm mounted as he watched the progress of nullification sentiment in Georgia and South Carolina. He wanted to wake up the people of New England, New York, Pennsylvania, and the other states of the North and East to the object and end of such false doctrine.[27] His friend and former diplomatic protégé Alexander H. Everett had just bought control of the *North American Review* from Jared Sparks and was planning to edit it in support of "correct principles in taste, politics, morals, and religion." Through his brother Edward Everett he asked John Quincy Adams to be a regular contributor, and to begin with an article on the Hayne-Webster debate, for the July number of 1830. Adams was not unwilling to be an occasional contributor, but he wasn't sure that the *Review* was ready for exposure of the "nefarious conspiracy" now in high tide of successful experiment: it would suit neither one of the "parties militant." "For the sake of the Union and honest politics," he challenged his old friend, "summon to action all the faculties of your mind, and all the virtues of your heart." [28]

The Everetts tactfully accepted Adams's word that such a powerful piece as he had in mind would not suit the *Review*.[29] Edward Everett took upon himself the task of reviewing the Webster-Hayne debate and questions surrounding the subject. He did this in his own way, in the course of which he elicited from ex-President Madison the famous statement, made in the conscientious sunset of his life, repudiating nullification and declaring that the Virginia and Kentucky Resolutions of 1798–9 had never proposed to do anything more than procure concurrent declarations from the other states, so that by the co-operation of measures known to the Constitution they could arrest the evil of the Alien and Sedition Acts—the framers of the Constitution, Madison testified, had considered the Supreme Court of the United States to be the final arbiter of all cases between states and the Federal Government.[30]

In Quincy, Adams sought to inspire others, such as Justice Joseph Story,

[27] JQA to General Peter B. Porter, Washington, April 4, 1830. "How long are these things to last? Till the people of New York and Pennsylvania make in their turn the discovery of their object and end." Adams MSS. See also JQA to Samuel L. Southard, Quincy, June 6, 1830. Adams MSS.

[28] JQA to Alexander Everett, Esq., Boston, Mass. Washington, April 15, 1830. Adams MSS.

[29] "It belongs of course to yourself only to judge how far it suited your views of the political situation in the country to furnish an article upon the debates in the Senate on the public lands." Alexander H. Everett to JQA, Boston, May 4, 1830. Adams MSS.

[30] For Madison's letter to Edward Everett, see *North American Review*, XXXI (No. 69, October 1830), 537–46; and *Writings of James Madison*, IX, 383–403. See also JQA to A. H. Everett, Quincy, September 18, 1831. *AHR*, XI (No. 2, January 1906), 340–3.

holder of the new Dane professorship of law at Harvard University, to teach the doctrine of Union against recrudescence of state rights in the South.[31] As a member of the Supreme Court of the United States since 1810 Story had written the majority of that tribunal's decisions, including some of those with which the name of John Marshall is justly associated. Adams admired greatly John Marshall's nationalism: "he has done more to establish the Constitution of the United States on sound construction than any other man living." [32] The Chief Justice's ailing health became to him a matter of patriotic as well as personal anxiety. He shuddered to think of what might happen if some "shallow-pated wildcat" like the state-righter Philip Barbour of Virginia,[33] "fit for nothing but to tear the Union to rags and tatters," should be appointed to the Court in Marshall's place.[34] Story thought like Marshall. Conservatives like Adams hoped that he might eventually succeed Marshall as Chief Justice.

Professor Story sent Adams at Quincy a copy of Nathan Dane's *Appendix* (published at Boston in 1830) to his voluminous *General Abridgment and Digest of American Law.*[35] The veteran Dane as a member of the Continental Congress had been author of the famous Northwest Ordinance of 1787. In the days before Kent's *Commentaries,* Dane was the leading expounder of American law. Although he did not altogether recant his old Hartford heresy—rather he argued himself out of it—he had declared in this latest work that it was the people of the United States acting as a nation who had ordained and established the Constitution; it was not a compact or contract between the states.

After the Webster-Hayne debate Dane reaffirmed these views in the somewhat prolix *Appendix* to his extensive *Supplement.* He carried the theory of a united American people further back than the Philadelphia Convention and the Constitution of 1787—back to the establishment of the Continental Congress in 1775. Creation of that body was a revolutionary act of the people of all the colonies acting together, confirmed by another act of the people in their national capacity, the Declaration of Independence. "Thus we see from the commencement of the Revolution, on a national scale, the people of the Colonies and States, have conducted their respective *State* concerns, even made their state constitutions in the *acknowledged subordination* to the *delegated* sovereignty of the General Government, vested first in Congress, then in Congress, the President, and Judiciary of the United States." The word *sovereignty,* declared Dane, deserved a popular rather than a strictly constitutional usage when applied to states.[36]

[31] *Memoirs,* VIII, 157, 387.
[32] *Memoirs,* VIII, 315.
[33] Brother of James Barbour, Secretary of War in the Adams Administration.
[34] *Memoirs,* VIII, 315–16.
[35] 8 vols., Boston, 1823, with a ninth volume *Supplement,* 1829.
[36] *Appendix* (9th volume) of Dane's *General Abridgment of American Law, etc.*

Nathan Dane's ideas of the Union suited Adams's thought perfectly.[37] "He shows very forcibly," the ex-President noted in his Diary, "that under our system, no State legislature possesses the power to nullify an act of Congress." [38] "Those who can," he wrote to Story acknowledging receipt of Dane's *Appendix*, "will find great and decisive consequences from that simple historical reminiscence of Mr. Dane that from the beginning the independence and consequently the sovereignty of each State was the child and creature of the Union." [39]

John Quincy Adams spurred Judge Story to teach more national doctrine for the Union.[40]

Opinion in South Carolina became more and more inflamed, "potioned, philtered and back-scourged, into a frenzy of excitement." [41] The state elections of 1830 returned a majority of Nullifiers.[42] The newly elected Governor General James Hamilton, Jr., called upon the legislature to summon a constitutional convention to nullify the tariff of 1828. But the Nullifiers still lacked the two-thirds majority, required by the state constitution, to call a convention. They had to content themselves with a series of six resolutions repeating the language of the Virginia and Kentucky Resolutions, and of the Hartford Convention, asserting the unconstitutionality of the protective tariff, a usurpation by the Federal Government that justified interposition by the State of South Carolina.[43]

The state-rights party in South Carolina took heart from the steady success of Georgia in defying and finally nullifying the Federal Government's protection of Indian tribes within the limits of that state. Andrew Jackson had expressed his belief that Georgia had complete jurisdiction over Indian lands within her boundaries. As soon as he became President he reversed Adams's policy upholding treaty rights of the tribes, and defied decisions of the Supreme Court affirming them. The South Carolinians hoped to have Georgia on their side and also Alabama and Missis-

---

[1830], p. 21. This print, without indication of place or date of publication, is in the collections of the Massachusetts Historical Society.

[37] "Your ground appears to me philosophically, morally, and historically correct." JQA to Nathan Dane, Quincy, October 22, 1830.

[38] Diary of JQA, October 27, 1830. Adams MSS.

[39] JQA to Joseph Story, Quincy, October 23, 1830. Adams MSS.

[40] JQA to Joseph Story, November 4, 1829. Adams MSS. *Memoirs*, VIII, 157, 387.

[41] "South Carolina had been potioned and philtered and back-scourged, like an old lecher, into a frenzy of excitement, and has now a prospect of coming into physical collision with the Government of the Union. As the Government is now administered, there is every prospect that her bullies will succeed, to the sacrifice of the interest of all the rest of the Union, as the bullies of Georgia have succeeded in the project of extirpating the Indians, by the sacrifice of the public faith of the Union and of all our treaties with them." *Memoirs*, VIII, 227. May 13, 1830, after a conversation with the South Carolina Unionist, Joel Poinsett.

[42] Chauncey Samuel Boucher: *The Nullification Controversy in South Carolina* (Chicago, 1916).

[43] *Ibid.*, pp. 103–6.

sippi, which were successfully asserting authority over Indian treaty lands.

Would Jackson defend the Constitution and preserve the Union in another test, over the protective tariff in South Carolina? Adams didn't think so. The Constitution, treaties, and laws of the United States were but chaff before the wind when a President, backed up by both houses of Congress, was in league with a state. "There is no harmony in the Government of the Union. The arm refuses its office; the whole head is sick, and the whole heart faint." [44]

6

The great issue between nation and state was burning in John Quincy Adams's breast when he and Louisa returned to Quincy for the summer of 1831. An opportunity to speak out came when his fellow townsmen invited him to give their Fourth-of-July address for that year, an oration which he prepared and rehearsed with most studious care and practice. He delivered it in the new stone meeting-house, for the first time filled to overflowing, to hear the native son. After a choral song, a prayer by Mr. Whitney, and an anthem on the words of Lord Byron's "Hebrew Melody," the Reverend Mr. Potter, minister of the Episcopal Church, read the Declaration of Independence. Following this the choir sang a versification by Adams of the 149th Psalm. Then the orator of the day stepped forth.

In the Declaration of Independence, John Quincy Adams like Nathan Dane found the beginning of the Union. That great document was a complete refutation of the doctrine of state nullification. "We the Representatives of the *United* States of America, in General Congress assembled, do, in the name and by the authority of the good PEOPLE of these Colonies, solemnly publish and declare that these *United Colonies*, are, and of right ought to be, free and independent States." There was no naming of individual states, only the United States of America. The delegates signed the Declaration not as representatives of any state, but as individual representatives of the whole people. The American people thus crowned themselves with the glory of nationhood.

"The Declaration of Independence," continued Adams, "was a social compact, by which the whole people covenanted with each citizen of the United Colonies, and each citizen with the whole people, that the United Colonies were, and of right ought to be, free and independent states. To this compact, union was as vital as freedom or independence." State sovereignty only cropped up later in the state constitutions, out of the abstractions of Blackstone's *Commentaries*. The people of the United States had never granted sovereignty to the separate states. In ordaining the Constitution of 1787 they had given some powers to the Federal Govern-

[44] *Memoirs*, VIII, 262–3. January 4, 1831.

ment, some to the states, and had kept the rest to themselves, as confirmed by the Tenth Amendment.

The doctrine of nullification, he pointed out to his fellow townsmen and to fellow Americans throughout the Union, rested on the "hallucination" of state sovereignty. Its exponents believed in such a thing as absolute, unlimited power—that is, "sovereignty." They had endowed the individual states with it just as deftly as Blackstone had placed it in Parliament. Here was the theoretical source of the mischief. "It is now the claim for one State of this Union, by virtue of her sovereignty, not only to make, but to unmake the laws of the twenty-four, each equally sovereign with herself." Nothing could be more absurd. There was no such incubus on free men as unlimited absolute power. The real power rested in the American people, who had never harnessed themselves with tyranny under whatever name.

"The States, united, and the States, separate, are both sovereign, but creatures of the people, and possess none but delegated powers. The power of nullifying an act of Congress never has been delegated to any one State, or to any partial combination of States. Any and every attempt at such nullification, by one or more States, less than the number required, *and otherwise than in the forms prescribed for Amendment of the Constitution,* would, however colored, and however varnished, be neither more nor less than treason, skulking under the shelter of despotism." [45]

Fifty-five years after the Declaration of Independence, Adams invoked the astounding growth and success of the nation, its "progressive improvement." He appealed to his listeners—all over the continent—not to spoil it all by accepting poisonous sophistries to which one group after another, including Massachusetts and Connecticut as well as Virginia and Kentucky, had been tempted in earlier periods by temporary, passing grievances. Stripped of all sophistical argumentation, declared Adams, nullification meant nothing less than waging war against the United States.[46] It was a plan "to interpose the arm of State sovereignty between rebellion and the halter, the traitor and the gibbet."

The audience was listening intently, occasionally interrupting with applause. Toward the end of his address the voice of his mother Abigail spoke out to John Quincy from his childhood: "It is not in tranquil ease and enjoyment," he reminded his listeners in Abigail's words, "that the active energies of mankind are displayed. Toils and dangers are the trials of the soul." [47] Breasting these stormy controversies over state rights, he

[45] Italics inserted.

[46] "The doctrine in all its parts is so adverse to my convictions, that I can view it in no other light, than *organized* civil war." JQA to Henry Clay, Quincy, September 7, 1831. *The Private Correspondence of Henry Clay,* Calvin Colton, ed. (New York, 1855), 311–17. This letter is an exegesis of the Quincy oration, by its author. It denies the right of any state to nullify an act of Congress whether by an act of its legislature or by a convention of the people.

[47] See above, p. 5.

prophetically declared to his listeners, would only strengthen the cause of Union.

Before his peroration the speaker paused briefly. His glance embraced the friendly townsmen in the new meeting-house which his father had caused to be built for them out of Quincy granite. Most of those there must have remembered the town's Fourth-of-July ceremonies five years before, the day on which John Adams and Thomas Jefferson died, fiftieth anniversary of American independence. They recalled John Adams's last words to them, his toast for that day: INDEPENDENCE FOREVER.

The son of John and Abigail Adams came to his last paragraph. He had spent much of the previous day in perfecting it.

"In the course of nature, the voice which now addresses you, must soon cease to be heard upon earth. Life and all which it inherits, lose of their value as it draws towards its close. But for most of you, my friends and neighbors, long and many years of futurity are yet in store. May they be years of freedom—years of prosperity—years of happiness, ripening for immortality! But, were the breath which now gives utterance to my feelings, the last vital air I should draw, my expiring words to you and your children should be, INDEPENDENCE AND UNION FOREVER!" [48]

Long-continued plaudits followed the patriotic appeal. The citizens of Quincy streamed out of the Temple into the bright sunlight of a hot summer's day and made their way to the Town Hall, where a festive dinner awaited them. After the repast, and the toasts, they called on their illustrious townsman for something more. He had just spoken to them widely, to the nation. Now he spoke to them intimately, as personal friends. He recalled the Plymouth Colony, "primitive mother of those principles which have made this day a day of glory and joy." Plymouth, part of the congressional district that had just elected him as its representative in the councils of the Union, his "own, his native land." He raised his glass for a last toast: "The root struck from the seed of the *Mayflower*, and the plant ascending from it—salutary, fruitful, perennial. It shall rise to heaven and overspread the earth."

Someone proposed three times three. The roof rang back cheers from the descendants of Plymouth and the old Bay Colony for their eminent neighbor. [49]

Adams's heart glowed within him as he walked home in the blazing sun. It had been a good day. It had been a glorious day. He had done his immortal father proud. To John Adams's polestar of INDEPENDENCE FOREVER he had added the watchword of UNION FOREVER.

Perspicacious young Charles Francis Adams, after listening to the address from the audience, shook his head as he stopped in the shade to think about his father's brashness. "The matter was very good," he admit-

[48] *An Oration Delivered to the Citizens of the Town of Quincy, on the Fourth of July, 1831* . . . (Boston, 1831).

[49] *Memoirs*, VIII, 377.

ted to himself, "but I fear for him lest in his age it should bring upon him the war of words to which through all his life he has been accustomed." [50]

Meeting Justice Joseph Story at a Phi Beta Kappa committee meeting some weeks later, Adams gave him a copy of the oration, together with a copy of a Eulogy to James Monroe which he had delivered in Boston, August 25, 1831. Story had just finished eight lectures at Harvard against the doctrine of nullification and Blackstone's theory of sovereignty. "I propose to publish the lectures next year," he said, "and shall cite you as authority for my doctrine. I am glad you named Massachusetts as one of the States which had countenanced the absurdity of nullification." [51]

A Boston printer struck off two thousand copies of the Quincy address, then quickly two thousand more. He got rid of them in no time. Small parcels went to Southern cities and to parts of the Western country. [52]

John Marshall was among the many friends who acknowledged complimentary copies. The Chief Justice had never heard it suggested that the Declaration of Independence was also a declaration of a previously existing Union. Yet there it lay right on the surface. "That the independence of the states is a graft on the stock of the union of the states, and is nourished by that stock, I firmly believe," he wrote John Quincy Adams: "they exist, flourish and must perish together." Marshall also accepted the justice of Adams's commentary on the doctrine of sovereignty, "the root from which many of the extravagancies of the day, including nullification, unquestionably spring." [53]

7

Adams in the Quincy oration did not connect John C. Calhoun by name with nullification, for the Vice President had not yet avowed his sponsorship of the destructive doctrine. But there could be no doubt whom he had in mind as the most recent exponent of the dogma. Calhoun revealed himself a few days later.

[50] Diary of CFA, July 4, 1831.

[51] *Memoirs*, VIII, 387. July 25, 1831. "From this [Eulogy of James Monroe] as well as from your 4th of July oration I have gathered many useful hints for my own lectures upon constitutional law. I shall avail myself of some of your illustrations."

Some critics charged Adams with having borrowed his expositions of sovereignty from Nathan Dane. (See Salem *Gazette*, XLV, New Series, IX, No. 59, July 26, 1831.) "I did not borrow them from Mr. Dane but from the paper itself, and from personal knowledge of the time. Mr. Dane had the same opinion drawn from the same sources; he no more borrowed it from me than I borrowed it from him, as is well known to Judge Story." JQA to Alexander H. Everett, Quincy, September 18, 1831. Adams MSS.

[52] *Memoirs*, VIII, 388.

[53] John Marshall to JQA, Richmond, August 9, 1831. See also same to same, October 3, 1831. Adams MSS.

"Your views upon the doctrine of nullification were not only very strong, but somewhat original, to me at least, and places that subject, odious as it has become, in a point of view too preposterous to be tolerated." Joseph Kent to JQA, Rose Mount, September 14, 1831. Adams MSS.

JOHN CALDWELL CALHOUN, DEFENDER OF SLAVERY

BUST BY CLARK MILLS, 1850, FROM A PLASTER MODEL, 1845. IN THE
COLLECTION OF THE CORCORAN GALLERY OF ART, WASHINGTON, D.C.

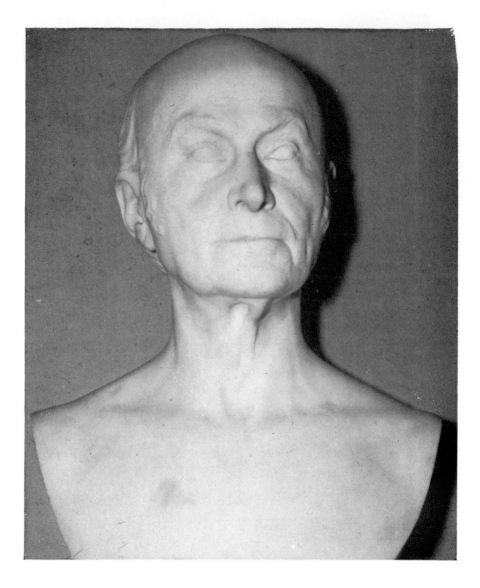

JOHN QUINCY ADAMS, DEFENDER OF FREEDOM

BUST BY HIRAM POWERS, 1837. ON FRONT WALL OF THE UNITARIAN
CHURCH AT QUINCY. PHOTOGRAPH BY CHARLES F. MCGRATH

There was now no reason for the South Carolinian to mask his position. The break with Jackson was complete. He could no longer hope to succeed the Old Hero as President of the United States. In a carefully written statement directed to the whole country, dated at his Fort Hill plantation, July 26, 1831, he expounded publicly "The Relation which the States and General Government Bear to Each Other." Once more he developed, this time openly over his own name, the theory advanced in the *Exposition and Protest of South Carolina,* the doctrine of state rights with the anomalous principle of a "concurrent majority."

As soon as John Quincy Adams heard of Calhoun's open publication, he took occasion [54] to send to his former colleague, "with ever-friendly recollections," a copy of the Fourth-of-July address. He hoped thereby to draw Calhoun on into further dialectical exchanges.[55] On the surface all was amicable. "Opinions indeed can never become national calamities until carried out into action," he declared in a covering letter. "I cannot abandon the hope that councils of peace and harmony may yet preserve the Union." [56]

Calhoun returned Adams's compliment by sending him a copy of the Fort Hill paper. "It is on my part, as well as yours, a subject of pain," he agreed, "that we should differ so widely on a point so fundamental in our political system. . . . Whatever may be the final disposition of the people, I hope the Union will be safe."

During the next year Calhoun followed up his Fort Hill statement with several lengthy documents elaborating the same doctrine.[57] Plainly he intended these later papers as answers to Adams's "dangerous and heretical doctrine" that the Constitution was the collective act of the whole American people rather than a compact between the people of the several states. "Admit its truth," the South Carolinian asseverated, "and the States at once sink into mere geographical divisions,[58]—bearing the same

[54] The occasion was that of sending Calhoun a copy of Adams's eulogy of their former chief James Monroe, delivered in Boston, August 25, 1831.

[55] JQA to A. H. Everett, Quincy, September 18, 1831. Adams MSS. *Memoirs,* VIII, 411.

[56] Alluding to the Fourth-of-July oration, Adams in his letter to Calhoun remarked: "Its more than simple dissonance from sentiments which you was understood and are now known to entertain, restrained me from asking your acceptance of it before—lest it might have been liable to the surmise of motives other than of kindness and respect. Disclaiming at this time all others, I present it with the single [simple] assurance of my regret that upon topics of transcendent importance, our opinions should be so much at variance with each other." JQA to John C. Calhoun, Quincy, September 19, really 9th, 1831. Adams MSS.

[57] "A Report Prepared for the Committee on Federal Relations of the Legislature of South Carolina, at its First Session, in November, 1831"; "An Address to the People of South Carolina," prepared for the members of the legislature at the close of the session of 1831; "A Letter to General Hamilton on the Subject of State Interposition," dated Fort Hill, August 28, 1832.

[58] "We are authorized to hope that a proper organization of the whole [Union],

relation to the whole, as counties do to the States,—possessed of no right, and exercising no power, but such as may be derived from the concession of the majority of the people of the whole Union,—from whom all power would be derived, and to whom, only, allegiance would be due." [59]

Presumably Calhoun had Adams's remark about the traitor and the gibbet in mind when he advised Governor Hamilton that "*he* who would prescribe for our political disease *disunion* on the one side, or *coercion of a State* in the assertion of its rights on the other, *would deserve,* and *will receive, the execrations of this and all future generations.*" [60]

In his open letter to Governor Hamilton, Calhoun stressed more than in previous statements the doctrine of concurrent majority as a peaceful corollary to nullification. It was, he suggested, an important and salutary "modification" of the sovereign powers of the states. [61]

Such far-fetched inference, advanced for the protection of minorities, was really an ingenious device by which the minority could block any majority action: namely, that one state in its sovereign capacity could declare a federal law null and void, to remain of no effect within that state until three fourths of the other states—a number equal to that required for ratifying an amendment to the Constitution—should declare to the contrary. Suppose three fourths of the states, deferring to Calhoun's theory, eventually should make state-nullified acts constitutional, by an amendment of the Constitution. Must the nullifying state then bow to the constitutional will of the three-fourths majority? Not if the state deemed the amendment incompatible with the objects of the Union! "In the case stated," persisted this unique expounder of the Constitution, doubtless having in mind the possibility of emancipation of slavery in the states by constitutional amendment, "should the other members undertake to grant the power nullified, and should the nature of the power be such as to *defeat the object of the association or union,* at least as far as the member nullifying is concerned, it would then become an abuse of power on the part of the principals, and thus present a case *where secession would apply. . . .*" [62]

---

with the auxiliary agency of governments for the respective subdivisions, will afford a happy issue to the experiment." George Washington's Farewell Address. September 17, 1796.

[59] Report for the Committee on Federal Relations of the Legislature of South Carolina, at its Session in November 1831. *The Works of John C. Calhoun,* Vol. VI, *Reports and Public Letters of John C. Calhoun.* Richard C. Crallé, ed. (New York, 1856), p. 106.

[60] Letter to Governor James Hamilton. Ibid., p. 180.

[61] Ibid., pp. 174–6.

[62] The remainder of the sentence is: ". . . secession would apply; but in no other could it be justified, except it be for a failure of the association or union to effect the object for which it was created, independent of any abuse of power." Ibid., p. 169. Italics inserted.

Calhoun had reduced the Union to the absurd, the complete *liberum veto,* perfect anarchy in the members.

The issue could not be clearer between John Quincy Adams defender of freedom and John Caldwell Calhoun defender of slavery: Nation or state, Union or disunion.

CHAPTER XIII
The Adams Tariff
(1831–1832)

❁

The preservation of the Union is to me what the destruction of Carthage was to Cato,—the conclusion
of every discourse.

JOHN QUINCY ADAMS TO BENJAMIN VAUGHAN,
QUINCY, SEPTEMBER 9, 1831 [1]

ON the Fourth of July 1831 John Quincy Adams was still speaking
ex cathedra, for his concept of the Union. Although his fellow citizens
of the Plymouth district already had elected him to the next session of
Congress, he could have scarcely realized, when he delivered that oration,
that he would be called upon to play an active part in the arena of current
politics on the floor of the House of Representatives. Much less could he
have expected to remain a member of that body for the next seventeen
years—the remainder of his long life. He had manifested no intention of
serving indefinitely in the House of Representatives. But soon his compulsion for political contention involved him in the bitter tariff controversy of
the day, surface symptom of a deeper and more threatening sectional conflict over slavery, involving the future of his cherished Union.

1

It was a problem for the Speaker of the House of Representatives, Andrew Stevenson, to know to which committees to assign an ex-President.
The natural place for Adams, with his tested experience as a diplomatist,
would have been chairman of the committee on foreign affairs, but the
rupture of personal relations between him and his successor in the White
House made such an appointment impossible. Speaker Stevenson, perhaps
inspired by Adams's having visited the tariff convention in New York on
the way south, solved his problem by making Adams chairman of the committee on manufactures.

It was a new field for the Plymouth member, and he came to realize how
little he knew about it. He rather resented the burden, and tried to throw

[1] Adams MSS.

it off in the shape of an exchange with Edward Everett for another place—on the committee of foreign affairs. Though Everett was willing enough, the Speaker was obdurate; he claimed that any change, once the assignments had been made, would require a vote of the House. Adams did not care to solicit that indulgence of his new colleagues at the very beginning of the session.[2] So he took on the load, like the patient camel he fancied himself to be.[3]

The views of Jackson and Adams had never been far apart on the tariff, the issue that was to precipitate the great nullification controversy. Both accepted the principle of protection. Jackson had favored a "judicious" tariff, Adams a "cautious" one. Both had advised a "conciliatory" tariff. As President, Adams had declared that it was the duty of Congress, representing all sections of the Union, to adjust and conciliate the national interest to a generally acceptable degree of protection. As ex-President, as a member of Congress, he began by hewing to the same line, more like a Man of the Whole Nation than a party man.

The compelling reason for his conciliatory attitude on the tariff was his dread of nullification, his fear that the Union might not last five years longer under existing tensions.[4] There is a striking analogy between his attitude in the House at this time and his position in the Senate during the Administration of Jefferson in Embargo days. A quarter-century before, Senator Adams had not agreed with his Federalist constituents that the Embargo was unconstitutional, but he knew how determined they were to resist it, some of them to the point of separation from the Union; therefore he had advised his new Republican friends in Congress to repeal or modify the obnoxious measure. Similarly in 1831 Representative Adams of the Plymouth district thought the tariff perfectly constitutional, but whatever the right of the matter, he feared that the Nullifiers of South Carolina had the will, and the means, to resist a law of the Federal Government. He did not applaud Jackson's readiness to enforce the Constitution. The only way to preserve the Union was to compromise again, to keep the states together until there should be a President, *and* a Congress, determined to do their sworn duty. Therefore to avoid civil contention,

---

[2] *Memoirs,* VIII, 436–7. The members of the committee on manufactures were: John Quincy Adams of Massachusetts, chairman; John Strode Barbour, a state-rights Democrat from Virginia; Lewis Condict, a National Republican from New Jersey; Charles Dayan, a National Republican from New York; James Findlay, a Jacksonian Democrat from Ohio; Henry Horn, a Jacksonian Democrat from New York; John T. H. Worthington, a Maryland Democrat.

[3] "Mr. Speaker Stevenson has made me chairman of the Committee of Manufacturers. I believe he took me for a *Jack,* which any Mason or anti-Mason might have told him I am not.

"The camel kneels to receive his burden, and so did Cæsar's horse. I shall rather resemble the horse of Sir Hudibras and kneel to cast my burden off." JQA to CFA, Washington, December 13, 1831. See also same to same, December 15, 1831. Adams MSS.

[4] *Memoirs,* VIII, 479. February 22, 1832. Adams MSS.

most likely civil war, he favored appeasing the Nullifiers by a lower tariff without abandoning the principle of protection.

In blind disgust with the whole Jacksonian program Adams could not see that the Old Hero was determined to preserve the Union,—Jackson's toast at the Jefferson Day dinner should have convinced anybody of that. But like Adams, Andrew Jackson preferred to compromise on the tariff rather than to put the question of Union versus Disunion immediately to the test of armed force. In successive messages to Congress he had urged a judicious reduction of the tariff. Despite a slight reduction in 1830, Congress had not been able to satisfy the South, because the Democratic Party was split, North and South, on the issue of protection, as was the majority of Democrats in Adams's committee on manufactures.

John Quincy Adams himself might have written the tariff passage of Jackson's message on the state of the Union which greeted him and his colleagues at the opening of the Twenty-second Congress in December 1831. The President asked for a reduction of the tariff "in a spirit of concession and conciliation" which had distinguished the friends of Union in all great emergencies, so as to adjust revenue to the wants of Government "with equal justice to all our national interests." Since the national debt was being paid off at a rate that would extinguish it within a year or two, the wants of the Government soon would decrease sharply—unless there were some great program of internal improvements at national expense (such as Adams had always favored).

The House referred the President's recommendation on the tariff to the committee on manufactures. To the committee on ways and means, George McDuffie of South Carolina chairman, it referred another proposal of Jackson, to relieve the people from unnecessary taxation after extinction of the national debt. McDuffie's committee reported that the protective system was utterly ruinous to the planting states, injurious to the Western states, exclusively beneficial to the manufacturing states, and ought to be abandoned with all convenient and practicable dispatch, upon every principle of justice, patriotism, and sound policy. They submitted a bill proposing to reduce the tariff on all protected articles to a flat level of twenty-five per cent for the first year, eighteen and three-fourths per cent for the following year, and twelve and a half per cent thereafter.[5] McDuffie's bill, never acceptable to Jackson, was the Nullifiers' price for Union.

Adams realized from the beginning that he was in no position to bring forth any plan which his heterogeneous committee on manufactures would adopt. With Jackson in control of the Government no proposal for a compromise tariff could succeed that did not originate with the Executive. He therefore accepted the suggestion from the committee on manufactures, at its first meeting, that as chairman he consult with the Secretary of the

[5] Edward Stanwood: *American Tariff Controversies in the Nineteenth Century* (Boston and New York, 1903), I, 374.

Treasury, Louis McLane, to see whether that Department had any specific ideas. When all was said and done, the Adams committee's resulting compromise tariff bill did not stray too far from the Administration's approval.[6] Its purpose was to appease the discontents of the South, without sacrificing too much the manufacturing interests of the North.[7]

The leaders of the National Republican Party, which had now become the Opposition, met at Edward Everett's lodgings to agree on what they should do about the tariff. Both Adams and Clay were there, the latter having been returned to the Senate by Kentucky.

"How do you feel upon turning boy again to go into the House of Representatives?" Clay asked playfully, as he shook hands with his old chief.

"I find the labor light enough," replied the new member, "but the House has not got to business."

On the surface relations seemed affable enough when the two men met in party councils on the tariff, although Clay and his friends had sensed Adams's willingness to be nominated by the Antimasonic *and* National Republican Parties in 1831 for the Presidency in 1832.[8]

"You will find your situation sufficiently laborious," Clay told him, more than once. Adams realized it already. Before his work finished he would ask the House, and ask in vain, to be relieved of some of his burdens.

"There are other points to be considered besides taking off the tariff duties," Clay advised the party steering committee. "One very important one is to change the mode of valuation. Another is to introduce cash payments, as for the public lands. A third is the expediency of increasing duties upon some of the protected articles, so as to make them nearly prohibitory."

Prohibitory duties on protected articles for the express purpose of decreasing revenue was a new idea to Adams.

"In the gracious operation of remitting taxes," he asked Clay, "would there not be an admixture of harshness in extending the protective system, and a danger of increasing the discontent of the Southern states,

---

[6] Ibid., p. 375. *Memoirs*, VIII, 439, 460.

"My friends may make themselves easy with regard to my opinions upon the Tariff.

"First, because they may be assured they will not have the slightest influence upon any individual or any party here.

"Secondly, because they will not be servilely devoted to any individual, or any party here.

"The Independence of the United States, and the Constitution of the United States, were the result of *compromise*. My opinion is that the revision of the Tariff should be the effect of *compromise*. But as that will suit no party here, the result will be—with heaven." JQA to Joseph E. Sprague, Salem. Washington, February 2, 1832. Adams MSS.

[7] *Memoirs*, VIII, 460.

[8] See *National Journal* (Washington), VII, No. 427. November 18, 1831. *Boston Press*, December 2, 1831. Diary, December 5, 1831. *Memoirs*, VIII, 427. For John Quincy Adams and the Antimasonic nomination, see Chapter XV, below.

which are already bitterly complaining of the unequal operation of the duties?"

Clay was not at all worried. "The discontents are almost all, if not entirely all, imaginary or fictitious," he said. "In almost all the Southern states they have, in great measure, subsided."

This easy confidence did not impress Adams. "Here is one great error of Mr. Clay," he said to himself.

Next day in Congress, Thomas R. Mitchell of South Carolina, a free-trader, conferred with Adams. "How much reduction of duties do you want?" asked the Massachusetts Representative. "I want to reduce the revenue down to thirteen millions," Mitchell affirmed. "We cannot do with less than twenty," declared Adams. He had in mind his old program of internal improvements, already hopelessly defeated.

"I have represented you to the South as an anti-tariff man," Mitchell insinuated.

"I am no worshiper of the tariff," acknowledged Adams, "but of internal improvement, for the pursuit of which, by Congress as a system, I claim to have been the first mover." [9] He recalled the resolution that he had presented to the Senate back in 1807.

The Opposition leaders met again the next week. Clay now acted as chairman. He spoke with assurance as the nominee (December 1831) of the National Republican Party for the Presidency in 1832. He had the draft of a tariff bill all ready. It would abolish duties on many articles not of domestic production: for instance, tea, coffee, spices, and indigo.

"The policy of our adversaries," explained the new leader of the party, "is to break down the American System by accumulation of the revenue." To counteract such a stratagem Clay wanted to reduce the revenue immediately at the rate of seven or eight million dollars annually, while retaining, even increasing to prohibitory levels, the tariff on articles that could be grown or manufactured in the United States. Dr. Condict, the only other member present of Adams's committee on manufactures, moved that the Clay bill be introduced into the Senate. How a revenue bill could be initiated in the Senate he did not explain.

Adams thought they ought to go slow. "I have no objection to the introduction of the bill," he declared, "but I ought in candor to say that the Committee on Manufactures, of the House, are already committed upon the principle that the reduction of duties should be prospective, and not to commence until after the extinguishment of the national debt. . . . It must be distinctly understood that I could not support, or vote for, any bill which would conflict with the pledge already given by the committee on manufactures to the Secretary of the Treasury. An immediate remission of duties, with a declared disposition to increase the duties upon the protected articles, would be a defiance not only to the South, as

[9] *Memoirs*, VIII, 443–4. December 26–7, 1831. Diary of Edward Everett, December 21, 1831. MHS.

Mr. Everett has observed. It would be defiance also of the President, of the whole Administration party. It is not possible for this bill to pass against them all combined."

"I do not care who it defies," Clay exclaimed. "To preserve, maintain, and strengthen the American System, I would defy the South, the President, and the devil. If the committee on manufactures has committed itself as you have stated, they have given a very foolish and improvident pledge. There is no necessity for the payment of the debt on the 4th of March, 1833."

Although polite enough to Adams personally, Clay's manner became more and more peremptory as he took hold of the subject.

Adams replied respectfully but warmly. "Without determining whether the President's passion to pay off the national debt by March 4, 1833 is the wisest idea that ever entered the heart of man," he said, "it is one in which I think he ought to be indulged, rather than opposed."

"It is an idea which will take greatly with the people," he continued. "It will be a great and glorious day when the United States is able to say that we owe not a dollar in the world. Payment of the debt will obviate another difficulty which you [turning to Clay] have suggested. There would certainly be no accumulation of revenue within that time. . . . I am much surprised to hear that the chairman of the ways and means committee will report such a bill."

"I shall report the bill," asserted Clay.

"If it gets to the House," responded Adams equivocally, "I shall favor it as far as I can reconcile it with the principles which the committee on manufactures, at my own suggestion, has assumed."

The exchange between the two recent political bedfellows emphasized a parting of their ways. Adams was sure that Clay wanted to make an issue, at the next election, of the American System against extinction of the national debt. Himself a champion of the system long before Henry Clay had coined the phrase, he nevertheless did not want to exploit this issue uncompromisingly to the point of danger to the Union.

He was worried here at the beginning of his new career about this contretemps with Clay. "Do you think anything I said last evening could be offensive to Mr. Clay?" he asked J. W. Taylor of New York next day in the House. "Not a word," assured Taylor. He thought that Clay, rather than the ex-President, might have been the man to ask that question.[10]

This was the first and only party council that Mr. Adams sat in on, and that because of his chairmanship of the committee on manufactures. His colleagues regarded him less and less as a party man.

The report of the committee, as distinct from its bill, represented Adams's opinion more than that of the other members, who nevertheless consented that he should make it. Three features stood forth in this states-

[10] For the above dialogue, see *Memoirs*, VIII, 445–9. December 28, 1831. Diary of Edward Everett, December 29, 1831. MHS.

manlike document: (1) extinction of the national debt; (2) concessions in the tariff to meet reasonable expectations of the Southern states; (3) vigorous prosecution by the General Government of a system of internal improvements. Adams took issue in his Report with the assertion that the interests of the planter and those of the manufacturer were irreconcilable in the same community. He added a bold and prophetic warning to the South. What would be the necessary and unavoidable consequence of dissolution of the tie that bound the Union? [11]

It would be war. To those who denied the power of the Federal Government to protect by the energy and resources of the whole nation a great and comprehensive but not universal interest (i.e., manufactures), Adams reminded his Southern colleagues that there was an interest most deeply their own (i.e., slavery) protected by the Constitution and laws of the United States and *effectively* protected by them alone. "Among the consequences from which a statesman from either portion of this Union cannot avert his eyes in contemplating that which must ensue from its severance, is the condition in which that great interest would be found immediately after the separation should have been consummated." [12]

At first the ex-President worried about his lack of experience in speaking extemporaneously in the debates on the floor of the House. He, a former Harvard professor of rhetoric and oratory, given to set speeches, found himself strangely agitated by the sound of his own voice, forgetting half of what he had thought to say when he rose to his feet. But by the close of his first session he had warmed up enough to crack a bone in his right hand while speaking to the tariff.[13]

The compromise tariff bill that finally emerged from Adams's committee along with his Report eventually passed both houses of Congress and received the signature of President Jackson, July 14, 1832. The times quickly baptized it as the Adams Tariff. As a matter of fact, it was as much an Administration as it was an Adams Tariff. Adams considered that he had played a humble and secondary part in the interest of compromise.[14] Nevertheless he accepted paternity for the half-and-half offspring which nobody seemed to admire.

[11] "It is the decided opinion of many persons here, that if the Tariff is not modified to suit the Southern States, South Carolina will proceed to Nullify the law, next summer. Forsyth and some others have told me, that Virginia and other Southern States will soon be ready to join her [S.C.]. I have replied to such statements, that if S. Carolina *alone* nullifies, it will be an abortive act. If Virginia and the other Southern States go with her, it will be a Separation of the Union. I incline to think it all *Menace*. Mr. Adams thinks otherwise and told his Committee, the other day, that if Mr. Clay's plans were pursued blood would flow." Edward Everett to Alexander H. Everett, January 17, 1832. E. Everett MSS., MHS.

[12] House Rept. No. 481, 22d Cong., 1st Sess.

[13] JQA to LCA, Washington, June 29, 1832. Diary, June 21, 1832. Adams MSS.

[14] "My share in the accomplishment of the compromise ultimately effected was humble and secondary." JQA to Richard Rush, August 3, 1832. Adams MSS.

The Adams Tariff made a substantial concession to the South by reducing the duty on cheap and coarse woolen fabrics, used to clothe slaves, to only five per cent ad valorem. This was Adams's personal contribution to the new law. The low-tariff men and free-traders were bitterly disappointed at its rates, compared with those of the McDuffie bill; the high-tariff advocates, despite the substantial degree of protection remaining,[15] regarded it as a parliamentary disaster.[16] Actually it was the most equitable tariff law that Congress had passed in twenty years,[17] including those that Calhoun and the other Southern quondam nationalists had once voted for with such conviction.

2

During the bill's tortuous progress through Congress, Speaker Stevenson, a Virginia state-rights man, allowed Thomas Ritchie to print in his *Richmond Enquirer* a letter that James Madison had written to Stevenson in November 1830. Actually it had nothing to do with the tariff controversy of 1832. It was in answer to a question of Stevenson whether the words of Article 1, Section 8 of the Constitution "to provide for the common defence and general welfare" gave to Congress a general and substantive power to do things not covered by powers specifically enumerated. Madison's opinion was that this language did not convey any such general power. He presented the same reasoning that had led him as President in 1817 to veto national internal improvements, and later to advise Jackson, through Van Buren, to do so, as that President had done recently in the famous Maysville veto of 1830 to the bill for a national road to connect Tennessee and Kentucky ultimately with the Cumberland Road.[18] Ritchie and Stevenson were avowedly publishing the Madison letter to disprove the "doctrines" of Adams's Report from the committee on manufactures. Just what doctrines they did not say.

While engaged in many other duties Adams found time to write a reply of some five thousand words to the paper of his respected friend Madison. He signed it on his sixty-fifth birthday, July 12, 1832, and the *National Intelligencer* printed it next day. Originally he had intended the document as a final speech on the tariff bill, but the previous question

15 For wool valued at over eight cents a pound it still left a duty of four cents a pound and forty per cent ad valorem (as compared with former duties of fifteen per cent on wool costing less than ten cents a pound, and four cents a pound and fifty per cent ad valorem on wool of higher cost). It actually raised the duty on higher-priced woolen cloth from forty to fifty per cent ad valorem and let that on cotton goods stand unchanged at twenty-five per cent. It reduced the rates on unmanufactured hemp by one third. It lowered the rate on worsteds by twenty-five to ten per cent. There was only a five-per-cent reduction on iron and wrought iron. But the Act of 1832 put 180 articles on the free list as compared with 49 in the tariff of 1828.

16 Stanwood: *American Tariff Controversies*, I, 364–86.

17 Channing: *History of the United States*, V, 427.

18 Bassett: *Life of Jackson*, II, 475–96.

had closed him off. Therefore he printed it after the lower chamber had passed the bill on third reading, but before final enactment. He presented it in the form of a public letter to Speaker Andrew Stevenson, written from the Hall of Representatives.[19]

In this piece of dialectics Adams agreed that the clause "to provide for the common defence and general welfare" did not give powers beyond those stipulated as ways and means to that end. But if Adams's opponents invoked Madison's authority in one direction, they could not reasonably reject it in others, and it was a matter of record that the Architect of the Constitution had pronounced the protective tariff to be constitutional. In this way John Quincy Adams turned Madison's guns, and his own, against the state righters. He brought up other artillery even more annoying. President Thomas Jefferson, despite his constitutional scruples, had stretched the general-welfare clause far more than he, Adams, as Senator had been willing to do, when he signed a law of Congress extending territorial regulations over the inhabitants of Louisiana without their consent. Adams thus invoked the patron saint of state rights, the man who had first used the word *nullification,* in the Kentucky Resolutions of 1799, to sanction a much wider construction of the Constitution than he, or even Madison, had ever been willing to advance.[20]

3

Jackson's friends made one more attempt to effect a personal reconciliation between the President and Adams when the latter was returned to the House. Colonel Richard M. Johnson, then a member of the House from Kentucky and an intimate friend of Jackson, took upon himself the role of intermediary, backed up by Lewis Cass, Secretary of War. It was no fault of Jackson that the effort did not succeed.

Johnson invited Adams to take a friendly walk.

"I think the first advances should come from him," he began. "Mr. Cass, Secretary of War, agrees with me."

[19] "The publication, apparently by your authority, of a private letter from Mr. Madison to you, with the avowed purpose of affixing the brand of heresy upon a principle asserted by me in a document prepared in discharge of a public duty assigned to me by yourself, will, I trust, be a sufficient apology to you and to the public, to warrant my addressing you in this manner, rather than upon the floor of the House."

[20] Charles Francis Adams, Jr., first printed the letter of his grandfather John Quincy Adams "to Andrew Stevenson, Speaker of the House of Representatives," dated "Hall of Representatives U.S., Washington, July 11, 1832," in MHS *Proceedings,* Second Series, XIX (December 1905), 535–53. In extensive remarks introductory to this document, Mr. Adams digested the records of the Twenty-second Congress, the printed *Memoirs* of JQA, the unprinted Diary, and numerous letters to and from JQA, CFA, and LCA, thereby saving me the labor of doing the same for this particular point. The paper was separately printed as: *John Quincy Adams and Speaker Andrew Stevenson of Virginia; an Episode of the Twenty-Second Congress (1832)* (Cambridge: John Wilson and Son; University Press; 1906).

"General Jackson himself suspended personal intercourse between us," responded Adams. "I never knew the reason. At the time I saw in the *Telegraph* an anonymous statement that it was because *he knew* that I had caused or countenanced abusive charges against Mrs. Jackson in the newspapers. It is not a fact. I never caused or countenanced, directly or indirectly, any such publication."

"I have always been sure it was not so," answered Johnson graciously. "General Jackson came here with entirely friendly dispositions toward you, and intending to call on you. His mind has been poisoned by scoundrel office-seekers. He is a warm-tempered, passionate man, and was led to believe that you were the cause of those publications about his wife. But I know his feelings are now as friendly as ever toward you. He told me that at the time of the debate on the Seminole War in the House of Representatives he received more assistance from you, in drawing up the minority report of the military committee, than from all the outside world. I do not speak by authority of General Jackson, but . . . I have no doubt, if a friendly advance from him will be accepted by you, he will make it."

"I have no desire that the interruption of friendly relations between us shall continue," said Adams punctiliously. "I am disposed to receive any friendly advance from General Jackson with kindness."

"Will you accept an invitation to dine with him?"

"No," declared the ex-President. "That is an act of mere ordinary courtesy, usually paid to every member of Congress, which I could not consider as an advance towards reconciliation."

"Will you accept an invitation to a small and select party of friends?"

"That will be liable to the same objection," declared the Representative from the Plymouth district. "It would pass for mere civility to a member of Congress, and be set to the account of my present situation."

"What then do you yourself think proper?"

"It is not for me to prescribe," Adams affirmed stoutly. "I can only say I am willing to receive in a spirit of conciliation any advance that General Jackson may make in that spirit."

Colonel Johnson seemed satisfied with this, but Adams began to worry. It had placed him in a "profoundly delicate" situation. What would people say back in Boston if John Quincy Adams, who had gone over from the Federalists to the Republicans in Jefferson's time, now by a reconciliation with the President seemed to go over from the National Republicans to the Democrats in Jackson's time?

Next day he received a formal note from Johnson saying that General Jackson had expressed great satisfaction at the conversation reported to him, and assurance of personal regard and friendship, and an anxious desire to resume social intercourse. He was perfectly satisfied that Mr. Adams had never countenanced the publications that had been alluded to, and had the highest opinion of him as a man of honor, etc.

Adams did not respond. His thoughts about Jackson were worse than those which, if he had not countenanced, he had at least failed to rebuke in the press during the campaign of 1828. His private statement that "Jackson lived in open adultery with his wife" is perhaps the prize solecism of American diarists.[21] Such uncharitable opinions were not the ex-President's reason for hesitating to resume personal relations with his rival. "A restoration of friendly, social, and personal intercourse between President Jackson and me at this time," concluded the cautious politician of Quincy, "would attract much public notice, and could not fail to expose me to obloquy. The old Federal party, now devoted to Mr. Clay, have already more than once tried their hands at slandering me. They have drawn the sword and brandished it over my head. If I set my foot in the President's house, they will throw away the scabbard. I must, therefore, walk with extreme circumspection: even that will not protect me from their malignity. Something is due to myself; and the path is narrow to avoid on the one hand the charge of an implacable temper, and on the other of eagerness to propitiate the dispenser of power." [22]

This explanation in his Diary was candid enough. He did not want anybody to call him an apostate again.

Adams never softened his opinion of Jackson. When the President came to Cambridge for an honorary degree of Doctor of Laws at commencement in 1833, Adams stayed away. "I *would not* be present to see my darling Harvard disgrace herself by conferring a Doctor's degree upon a barbarian and savage who could scarcely spell his own name." [23] It is a pity to record that Harvard's most distinguished living graduate, himself an active overseer of the university, sulked in his paternal mansion as America's popular hero took the scroll from the hands of President Josiah Quincy.

Never did fair Harvard bestow a degree more honored by the recipient. Jackson, suffering severely from dysentery and hemorrhages of the lungs, continued a triumphant tour through New England, acclaimed alike by Democrats and Federalists, until he collapsed in Concord, New Hampshire, and had to be taken back to Washington. The ex-President, painstakingly recording his own aches and symptoms and measuring the shadows of approaching dissolution, sourly noted in his Diary that the Old Hero displayed his illnesses only to attract public sympathy and attention, *pour le valoir!* [24]

4

In the midst of tariff debates in Congress, Adams had a long conversation with Vice President Calhoun, at the latter's lodgings, on nullification

---

[21] Diary, July 5, 1831.

[22] *Memoirs*, VIII, 484–6. March 2, 3, 1832.

[23] JQA to CFA, No. 14, Washington, January 18, 1843. Adams MSS. *Memoirs*, VIII, 546–7; IX, 4–6. June 18, 1833, July 2, 1833.

[24] *Memoirs*, IX, 5–6.

and the constitutional questions that they had debated at long range from Quincy and Fort Hill. One would give much for a record of this rehearsal of opposite views on a question so vitally involving the fate of the Union. Adams merely mentions it in the fragmentary entries to which he had reduced his Diary during the pressure of affairs that summer.[25] Calhoun must have read Adams's warning to the slaveholders in the tariff committee's report. Doubtless he recalled other conversations between the two over slavery when they were colleagues in President Monroe's Cabinet.[26]

As the two talked quietly together that summer evening in 1832, with heat lightning flashing fitfully in the southern sky, Adams might well have asked his onetime associate, author of the Fort Hill Letter to Governor Hamilton, whether an amendment to the Constitution, ratified by three fourths of the states, abolishing slavery, would, in Calhoun's own words, "defeat the object of the association or Union." [27] Would it really justify a sovereign state in dissolving the "compact" and seceding from the Union, as Calhoun had suggested so strongly in his Letter to the People of South Carolina?

5

Besides the tariff question, Adams also got involved in the other great political issue of the period: the Bank of the United States.

Nicholas Biddle, masterful president of that powerful corporation, was mistrustful of the President's real attitude toward a new charter for the Bank,—the old charter was due to expire in 1836. Relying on the confident attitude of Henry Clay and other opposition politicians who craved a fresh political issue,[28] Biddle decided to precipitate the question into national politics before the Presidential election of 1832 so that in case a charter should be denied, or Jackson should veto a bill for the same, the question could go before the people; in that event he seemed to have no doubt about a favorable outcome. Through Pennsylvania members in each house of Congress the Bank applied for a new charter. The House of Representatives, acting on the motion of Augustus S. Clayton of Georgia, an enemy of the Bank, resolved to appoint a special committee to go to Philadelphia and inquire into its affairs. Adams took some part in the discussion of this resolution, insisting that the committee be given adequate powers to summon persons and papers. Thereupon Speaker Stevenson, also hostile to the Bank, appointed the ex-President one of a committee of seven for this purpose, packing the group with a majority of

[25] "June 24 [1832]—Visit to G. McDuffie and to J. C. Calhoun. Long conversation with Calhoun upon Constitutional questions and nullification."
[26] See Vol. I, 417, 419. Memoirs, IV, 430–1.
[27] See above, p. 238.
[28] Marquis James: The Life of Andrew Jackson (Indianapolis, 1938), pp. 552–66, 583–602.

anti-bank people.[29] It looked like a deliberate effort to overburden Adams. When he asked the House to relieve him meanwhile of his responsibilities with the committee on manufactures, it led to vociferous if perfunctory protests by some members that they could not spare his valuable abilities in so important a matter. Sensing effusive and perhaps sardonic remarks, even a call for yeas and nays, he withdrew his request and took on the additional load.[30]

Ever since his years as Secretary of State, John Quincy Adams had been a staunch believer in the Bank of the United States. To him it did not simply perform useful fiscal functions for the Federal Government, such as custody of deposits of moneys, the transfer of public funds, and assistance in service of the national debt. It was more than that; it was a protector of private property and the sanctity of contract against the paper-money devices of irresponsible debtors working through banks chartered by state legislatures. To him, as to Alexander Hamilton before him, it was an indispensable instrument of Union.

"It is my firm belief," Adams had told President Monroe during the agitation over the Missouri question, "that this Union cannot hold together while every State exercises an unlimited power of making paper money under the pretence of incorporating banks, unless the General Government, by such a bank substantially under its control, and always regulating the national currency, by preserving specie payments inviolate, could preserve the obligations of contracts and give security to property against the frauds of paper swindling." [31]

Whenever a question had come under Adams's authority involving the Bank of the United States he had favored the Bank if possible: for instance, as Secretary of State, and over his general scruples against permitting government employees to receive pay for private services, he once or twice had allowed a diplomatic officer to transact special business for the Bank abroad, for a commission.[32] During his Presidency there was no Bank question; everything had gone smoothly with the institution.

Nicholas Biddle took pains to ingratiate himself with the new and eminent member of Congress. Adams owned a few shares of Bank stock, bought with his earlier savings. On his way back and forth from Washington to Quincy he would occasionally stop at the main office in Philadelphia and collect his dividends. Biddle would attend to these little

[29] The members of the committee were: Augustus S. Clayton of Georgia, chairman, a Jackson Democrat; John Quincy Adams; Churchill C. Cambreling, anti-bank and anti-tariff, Jackson Democrat from New York; George McDuffie of South Carolina, an anti-tariff, nullificationist, pro-bank (initially) Democrat, who split with Jackson over the issue of nullification; Richard M. Johnson of Kentucky, a Democrat who followed Jackson on the Bank issue; Francis Thomas of Maryland, Jacksonian Democrat; John G. Watmough of Pennsylvania, National Republican.

[30] *Register of Debates,* 22d Cong., 1st Sess., pp. 2175–82. *Memoirs,* VIII, 497, 500.

[31] *Memoirs,* IV, 499.

[32] *Memoirs,* IV, 342–5, 345–9.

matters himself. He played host to Mr. and Mrs. Adams in Philadelphia whenever possible. Biddle went out of his way to register his personal approval of Adams's taking a seat in Congress,[33] in contrast to the opinion of their mutual Philadelphia friends John Sergeant and Charles J. Ingersoll, who thought it unbecoming to an ex-President's dignity. A man of fine classical education and good taste in books, Biddle was a congenial friend. He could write flattering letters.[34] He could turn an elegant literary phrase or introduce an apt poetical quotation in letters to Adams. On occasion he appealed pleasingly to the ex-President's judgment on a question of Latin translation or identification of a poetical quotation.

Adams liked the well-educated, the cheerful and good-natured head of the Bank. He liked to get together with him and philosophize upon the aspects of the plancts, the pastimes of the muses, and the virtues and vices of fellow mortals.[35] He frequently accepted his hospitality, but he was not unaware of his urbane friend's principal interest and concern. On the way to Washington in November 1831 he stopped at Biddle's office to collect his dividends, but this time he left all fifteen shares of his stock to be sold. "I might be called upon to take part in public measures concerning the Bank," he explained. "Since I am favorable to it, I want to divest myself of all personal interest in it." [36]

During the first session of the Twenty-second Congress, and thereafter, Mr. and Mrs. Adams remained in friendly, reassuring, and even affectionate correspondence with Biddle.[37] But when Adams went to Philadelphia with the congressional committee of investigation he was careful to avoid all appearance of social contact with the Bank's president.[38]

[33] *Memoirs*, VIII, 251. "You are perfectly right. Right in principle, as I am sure you will be right in practice, right as respects yourself, and right for the example." Nicholas Biddle to JQA, Philadelphia, July 29, 1831. Adams MSS.

[34] "My impression indeed now is, that the fate of the bill [recharter of the Bank] is involved in this [Clayton resolution for investigation], that if you do not raise your voice on this occasion, no other may probably occur. To that voice I have so often listened with pleasure, either in its direct enunciation, or its ideas thro' the press, that I should regret the loss of this opportunity of hearing it." Nicholas Biddle to JQA, Philadelphia, March 4, 1832. Adams MSS.

[35] JQA to Nicholas Biddle, December 12, 1833. Adams MSS.

[36] *Memoirs*, VIII, 425.

Biddle waited for a propitious moment in the market and sold the shares at 130%, charging the usual brokerage of ¼ of one per cent. He sent Adams in Washington a draft for $1,952.60 on the Bank's Boston Branch, and the recipient remitted it to his son Charles to apply to his father's Boston debts. JQA to Nicholas Biddle, Washington, December 3, 1831. Biddle to JQA, December 12, 1831. Adams MSS.

[37] Nicholas Biddle to JQA, Philadelphia, March 4, May 7, 1832; JQA to Nicholas Biddle, Washington, March 7, May 15, November 23, December 21, 1832; Quincy, July 29, 1833. Adams MSS. LCA to Nicholas Biddle, "January" 1827; August 25, 1834; February 23, 1836. Photostats in LC from papers in possession of Charles Biddle in 1926. JQA to Nicholas Biddle, Washington, November 18, 1835. Adams MSS.

[38] "Among the privations most deeply felt by me during my late visit to Philadelphia was the necessary suspension of the friendly and social intercourse which I had

The majority report of the committee, which Clayton delivered to Congress, was what could be expected. According to the scrupulously objective historian of the Bank,[39] the majority consisted of members who showed a total ignorance of banking operations and astonishing incompetence in dealing with the piles of technical documents that had to be examined. They accused the Bank and its president of usurious practices and violations of its charter: in the use of exchange drafts on its different branches instead of notes signed personally by the president (as required by law), in the sale of coins as bullion, in selling stock taken over from the Government, in making donations to public subscriptions for canals and railroads, and in building houses and other structures to sell or rent.

McDuffie, the Nullifier, whom Adams to his surprise found a congenial member of the committee, submitted a minority report exonerating the Bank on all charges, but not strong enough for the ex-President. The latter's talents for scathing analysis showed no decline in a special report that he made, with the concurrence of his National Republican colleague Watmough, to supplement the minority report. He tore the majority's conclusions to shreds, particularly the charge of usury. Nicholas Biddle ordered six thousand extra copies of the *National Intelligencer* in which Adams's Report on the Bank first appeared.[40] But the judicious distribution of these prints had very little effect on the hostility to the Bank which the Jacksonian politicians and editors were working up, and which soon led to Biddle's complete defeat when Jackson vetoed all Congress's bills for recharter.

The only trace of Adams's ever seeking a favor from the Bank was when he overcame personal scruples and recommended his old literary henchman Philip R. Fendall and his long-time political acolyte P. P. F. Degrand for berths in the institution, to be considered "on their own merits, rather than from any friendly feelings for myself." [41] Louisa, his wife, however, was willing to go further. When she learned that Benjamin Lear, attorney for the Washington Branch of the United States Bank, had suddenly died in that city from the cholera, she solicited the place for her son John, then struggling with the burden of the Columbian Mills and failing in his health and eyesight. In case young John Adams would not do because he was no longer a lawyer, although he had studied law with

---

so often enjoyed before. But that as well as the result of all my investigations taught me to estimate you the more." JQA to Nicholas Biddle, May 15, 1832. Adams MSS.

[39] Ralph C. H. Catterall: *The Second Bank of the United States* (Chicago, 1903), p. 230.

[40] Biddle to John G. Watmough, Philadelphia, May 11, 1832. *Correspondence of Nicholas Biddle* . . . , R. C. McGrane, ed. (Boston and New York, 1919), p. 190.

[41] "A friendly regard for both, and the natural disposition to oblige, by good offices, where they may be yielded without impropriety, lead me to overcome some scruples of delicacy, and the perilous hasard of receiving, while a Member of Congress, *favours from the Bank*." JQA to Nicholas Biddle, Quincy, October 23, 1832. Adams MSS.

his father, then she recommended her nephew Johnson Hellen, who seems to have entered that profession.[42] How much her husband knew, at the moment, about this improper solicitation, is not clear, but it is certain that he very soon wrote John urgently advising him to pull up all stakes in Washington—as he himself was then preparing to do—and come home to Massachusetts to make a new start in life.[43] Shortly thereafter in Philadelphia one evening, on the way to the last session of the Twenty-second Congress, he had a long talk with Biddle. There is no record of what was said. We can only surmise that Adams put his foot down on Mrs. Adams's proposition, even if Biddle were disposed to consider it.[44]

When it became apparent that the Administration might withdraw the public deposits from the Bank, Adams assured Biddle that if the subject should ever be discussed in Congress he for one would be disposed to do justice to the Bank.[45] The occasion came in the spring of 1834. Since this was an administrative measure, it was difficult to speak to it in Congress. Adams sought to do so by presenting a resolution of the legislature of Massachusetts opposing the measure, but again the Speaker cut him off by recognizing a previous question. He then published his intended speech in the *Daily National Intelligencer*, April 12, 1834. It was a comprehensive review of the whole Bank question, a defense of the institution and of the integrity of its president, "irreproachable and unreproached," a man whom one could be proud to call a friend. Removal of the deposits, he argued eloquently, was calculated to break the Bank. To put the public funds in chosen (or "pet") state banks would hurl the nation into universal bankruptcy.[46] The future showed that Adams was all too right.

Biddle saw that the masterly speech was widely circulated in a reprint of fifty thousand copies.[47]

---

[42] LCA to Miss Meas [*sic*], Quincy, October 6, 1832. LC photostat of original in possession of Mr. Charles Biddle in 1926. See Papers of JQA in LC. Miss Mease, a kinswoman of Dr. James Mease of Philadelphia, seems to have been a secretarial employee of Biddle.

[43] JQA to JA, 2d, Quincy, October 28, 1832. Adams MSS.

[44] Diary, November 13, 1832. JQA to Biddle, Washington, November 23, 1832. Adams MSS.

[45] JQA to Nicholas Biddle, Washington, November 23, 1832. Adams MSS.

[46] Walter Buckingham Smith: *Economic Aspects of the Second Bank of the United States* (Cambridge, 1953), p. 233, citing *Register of Debates* (1833–4), 22d Cong., 1st Sess., Vol. X, Pt. III, p. 3493.

[47] *Speech [Suppressed by the Previous Question] of Mr. John Quincy Adams, of Massachusetts, on the Removal of the Public Deposites, and its Reasons* (Washington: Gales and Seaton; 1834). *Memoirs*, IX, 116–17, 122–7.

J. Gales, Jr., to JQA, April 13, 1834, and Joseph Hopkinson to JQA, Philadelphia, April 21, 1834, make it evident that Biddle ordered the print.

"I have read, and read again, your admirable speech. For the kind mention which it contains of myself and my friends I have no words to thank you; and the only evidence of my gratitude which is in my power is the silent fullness of a heart which

During Jackson's famous and successful war on the Bank there was never any doubt where Adams stood in Biddle's grateful mind.[48] And Adams had confidence in Nicholas Biddle.[49]

6

Speaking of the obligation of contract, one should take note of John Quincy Adams's opinion on imprisonment for debt, a procedure which cried out for humanitarian reform. There were four or five times as many debtors in the jails as there were convicted criminals. Most of them were poor men, locked up for being unable to pay debts under fifty dollars, sometimes for less than a dollar, and expected to pay board in jail or not get anything to eat. Private charity had to feed the wretches lest they starve. Frequently it cost the creditors more in court expenses and lawyers' fees than the debts were worth. The poorer classes and workingmen's organizations urged the abolition of the state laws that sanctioned this penalty. On the other hand most of the bankers and merchants supported them.[50] So did John Quincy Adams. In November 1831 a committee appointed at a meeting of reformers in Boston, who were petitioning the Massachusetts legislature to abolish imprisonment for debt, addressed him a letter asking for his opinion. Before the opening of Congress he responded from Washington with a considered statement of nearly three thousand words. He was well aware that his opinion would be unpopular.[51]

Human rights, Adams admitted, always came before property rights, but protection of property was one of the great objects of civil society. So was the obligation of contract, represented in the Constitution of the United States—itself a social contract—forbidding any state to pass a law

---

will cease to feel deeply and affectionately this proof of your regard only when it ceases to beat." Nicholas Biddle to JQA, Philadelphia, April 14, 1834. Adams MSS.

[48] ". . . I cannot now suppress the acknowledgment of the great obligations under which I feel myself personally to you, for the part which you have taken in the whole of this late matter, an obligation which is shared by all the gentlemen connected with the institution." Nicholas Biddle to JQA, Philadelphia, May 7, 1832. Adams MSS.

[49] "There is except my own son, not a man living with whom I could open in such unlimited confidence all my impressions of public duty. . . ." JQA to Nicholas Biddle, Washington, November 18, 1835. Adams MSS.

[50] Frank T. Carlton has conveniently summarized the social groups that favored and opposed "Abolition of Imprisonment for Debt in the United States," *Yale Review*, XVII (1908–9), 339–44. Edwin T. Randall has pointed out that there was much more arrest than real "Imprisonment for Debt in America," in *MVHR*, XXXIX (No. 1, June 1952), 77–102. There were many ways for quick release of a debtor who made honest declarations.

[51] "The tide in the affairs of men, when it has once begun to ebb, will go down. This free and bold expression of my opinion, which I disdain to withhold, will hasten my downward course, and nothing can redeem it. Let me fulfil my destiny, and, so far as may be possible, sustain my character." *Memoirs*, VIII, 427.

impairing the obligation. Abolition of imprisonment for debt, he conceded, would not necessarily be an impairment of obligation, but it would remove one of the principal sanctions between debtor and creditor. The chief objection, he conceived, was that abolition of imprisonment for debt would deprive the poor and friendless of one of their great privileges, that of pledging freedom of persons for credit that otherwise would be impossible to get!

The farthest Adams would go unreservedly was to leave the question to the courts, with the recommendation that if they should sustain the liability of person for debt, in no case should a creditor be able to imprison a citizen upon the mere allegation of defaulted debt, without even requiring the creditor to sustain the fact by oath. On this point he would have no hesitation in saying to the legislature of Massachusetts: " 'Oh, reform it altogether.' "[52]

Adams was sadly behind his times in this particular humanitarian reform. Kentucky had already abolished the practice in 1821, New York in 1831; all the states in the Union were to follow suit by 1868, his own state of Massachuetts not until 1855. To even the most reactionary twentieth-century American, John Quincy Adams's position on this question seems almost medieval. But he voted for the uniform national bankruptcy law of August 18, 1841, providing for both voluntary and involuntary bankruptcy for individuals, without application to corporations, and voted against its repeal when Congress took the law off the statute books in 1843.[53]

7

Adams's first session in the House of Representatives had proved a *tour de force*. Midsummer's heat lay heavy on the returning Plymouth member as he left the nation's capital. Louisa had already gone to Quincy in May. A cholera epidemic had smitten the Atlantic seaboard. In New York City the sickness was taking a hundred lives a day. All steamboat service on Long Island was suspended—the *Benjamin Franklin* lay tied up in Taunton River. Adams took a boat from Hoboken up the Hudson to Kingston, and thence proceeded by stage across country: Litchfield, Hartford, Woodstock, Framingham, Boston, Quincy—three long days of bumping over dusty roads.[54] As he looked back on what had happened, he felt as though he had been standing on his head six months in a trance.[55] But he was content. "The tariff bill," he reported to Louisa, "acts as a universal anodyne." Even Henry Clay's "partizans" were claiming it for their

[52] JQA to Messrs. W. F. Otis, Nathaniel Bowen, George W. Bryant, Boston. Washington, November 16, 1831. Adams MSS. *Memoirs*, VIII, 426–8.

[53] Charles Warren: *Bankruptcy in United States History* (Cambridge, 1935), pp. 60–86. *Congressional Globe*, X, 350; XII, 163.

[54] JQA to JA, 2d, Quincy, July 27, 1832. Adams MSS.

[55] JQA to LCA, "June" 1832; to Richard Rush, August 3, 1832. Adams MSS.

own.[56] As Man of the Whole Nation he had tried to keep the Union hanging together a little while longer without giving up the principle of protection. He was pleased that some of his friends like Charles J. Ingersoll who had doubted the wisdom of his going to Congress were beginning to congratulate him nevertheless on his achievements. George Sullivan wrote that J. Watson Webb, the Democratic editor of New York, said many adherents of the Jackson Administration were in favor of a change: "Tell Mr. Adams [said he] that if he is nominated [i.e., by the Antimasons] he shall have all the support I can give him." The nomination, suggested Sullivan, ought to come from the middle states and be put in motion at Baltimore.[57] Of this there will be more to say in a later chapter. Professing such hints to be a joke, Adams answered that if he were wise he would make the last session of Congress the "euthenasia" of his political life. "One short campaign more seems however to be in prospect before me, and then, if so long I live, I shall have attained the age at which all our principal men have withdrawn from the stage." [58]

Louisa saw that politics, disgusting as they were to her, made her husband happy, and she was glad. "Your father," she wrote to John in Washington after John Quincy had returned safely to Massachusetts once more, "is in high spirits dabbling as usual in public affairs while *fancying he has nothing* to do with them. His mind must be occupied with something, and why not this?" [59]

The Presidential gyroscope was still spinning.

[56] Charles Francis Adams, Jr.: *John Quincy Adams and Speaker Andrew Stevenson.*
"It was ridiculous eno' to hear men, who but three years ago, were abusing Mr. Adams with all their might, & compassing the continent to get him out of office, now suddenly impressed with the belief, that he is the only man who can save the union." Edward Everett to Alexander Everett, March 18, 1832. E. Everett MSS., MHS.

[57] George Sullivan to JQA, West Point, "July" 1831. "P.S. I shall probably go to Baltimore next week. If you write me address me here—." Adams MSS. Sullivan was doubtless referring to the Antimasonic Convention scheduled to meet in Baltimore in September. See below, pp. 292–3.

[58] JQA to George Sullivan, Quincy, August 4, 1832. Adams MSS.

[59] LCA to JA, 2d, Quincy, August 22, 1832. Adams MSS.

CHAPTER XIV
Jackson and Adams on Nullification
(1832–1833)

> We declared ourselves a nation by a joint, not by
> several acts. . . .
>
> PRESIDENT ANDREW JACKSON'S
PROCLAMATION AGAINST NULLIFICATION
IN SOUTH CAROLINA, DECEMBER 10, 1832

> The Constitution of the United States thus became
>
> the Act of the *whole* People. . . .
>
> JOHN QUINCY ADAMS'S ANONYMOUS EXEGESIS
OF THE UNION, DECEMBER 10, 1832 [1]

THE READER of the previous chapters and of the preceding volume has seen John Quincy Adams and Andrew Jackson standing forth as two great patriots of the times: Adams the man of books and letters, the cultured linguist and diplomatist, a republican at ease in the courts of Europe—the scholar statesman; Jackson, the frontiersman of sword and pistol, whose word unschooled had all the force of pith and will—the soldier, the man of action. In those uncertain years when heavy pressures of the Industrial Revolution were weighing down expediency on principle, each of these Americans nourished his countrymen with the courage of the Union against the forces of sectionalism: Adams for a Union of Liberty with Power, Jackson for a Union with the least government necessary but powerful always to defend the nation from without and within. How close these two sons of the American Revolution were in their love of the Union, how far apart in practice and in personality! Witness now the reaction of each to nullification in South Carolina: President Jackson's bold public pronouncement and preparation for action, and ex-President Adams's theoretical support of the Union and querulous distrust of Jackson's determination to enforce the Constitution.

[1] See note 9 below.

1

The compromise of the "Adams Tariff" between the industrial capitalists of the North and the slavery capitalists of the South only encouraged
the planters of South Carolina to demand the abolition of all protection
for manufacturers. After the elections of 1832 in the Palmetto State, where
only ten per cent of the population were qualified to vote,[2] returned an
overwhelming majority of Nullifiers, the legislature by the necessary two-
thirds majority summoned a constitutional convention. The convention
then ordained (November 24, 1832) all previous protective tariffs, and
specifically those of 1828 and 1832, to be null, void, and of no law, not
binding upon the state, its officers and citizens. In the name of the people
of South Carolina it declared their determination to maintain the ordinance at every hazard and not to submit to the use of force by the Federal
Government to reduce the state to obedience. The legislature passed laws
to enforce nullification, and imposed ironclad test oaths, with heavy penalties for all citizens who might disobey the state law. It sent copies of the
Nullification Ordinance to all the sister states.

Calhoun in a new Address, not to the people of the United States—
whom he did not recognize as such—but to "the people of Maine, New
Hampshire, Massachusetts, Rhode Island, Connecticut, Vermont, New
York, New Jersey, Pennsylvania, Delaware, Maryland, Virginia, North
Carolina, Georgia, Kentucky, Tennessee, Ohio, Louisiana, Indiana, Mississippi, Illinois, Alabama, and Missouri," called for a general constitutional
convention of all the states to settle the great emergency.[3] Set aside as
Vice President by the Jacksonians in the election of 1832, Calhoun resigned his office before his term expired, to reappear in the upper chamber of Congress as newly elected Senator from South Carolina, spokesman
and defender of nullification.

The federal tariff law stood nullified only so far as South Carolina
theory was concerned. Federal collectors still collected the imposts. And
none of the other states, not even Georgia—which had such good reason
to be beholden to Jackson—responded to the call of South Carolina. None
failed to condemn nullification.[4] Meanwhile Governor Hamilton urged
the legislature to pass laws for the raising of a state army of twelve
thousand men to prevent the General Government from coercing the
commonwealth. Both Nullifiers and Unionists began drilling companies
in the fields of South Carolina and streets of Charleston.

[2] Wiltse: *Calhoun, Nullifier*, pp. 148, 155.

[3] *Works of J. C. Calhoun*, VI, *Reports and Public Letters*, 193–209. November
1832.

[4] Virginia's sympathetic but noncommittal answer was that she stood by her resolutions of 1798 and 1799. The Georgia and Alabama legislatures passed resolutions
calling for a convention of the states to amend the Constitution so as to settle the
question. Houston: *Nullification in South Carolina*, p. 119.

Again all eyes turned to Andrew Jackson. Again the question was: what will the President do?

To John Quincy Adams, back in Washington for the second session of the Twenty-second Congress, South Carolina was acting like a bully, trying to hold up the Union at the point of a gun. "They must rule or they must ruin." He was sure that Jackson would do nothing. The President, he strongly suspected, though irreparably at odds with Calhoun, was in combination with the Nullifiers. He would pay their price by sacrificing the tariff to them, as he had sacrificed the Indians. The protection of manufactures, as much as was still left by the Adams Tariff, internal improvements, the American System, all were doomed. "Calhoun is to be put down by abandoning the protective system." [5]

The President's annual message on the state of the Union only seemed to confirm Adams's worst fears. The tariff of 1828, explained the Chief Magistrate, had filled the nation's coffers to overflowing. All except a few millions of fixed debt was paid off. There was no need for all of the diminished revenue to be anticipated by the new (Adams) tariff law. In this happy state of affairs, he urged Congress to do away with tariff "inequalities" that were causing discontent among such a large portion of the people in one section of the country, some of whom even held the imposts to be unjust and unconstitutional. Therefore let the duties gradually be lowered to a uniform level for revenue only to suit the reduced wants of the Government, except for protection of articles essential to national independence and safety in time of war. He further advised an inquiry into the Bank of the United States to see whether that institution, suspected by many, was a safe depository for the people's money. He came back again to the unfortunate Indians, and suggested liberal inducements for their removal across the Mississippi, particularly the remaining Cherokees in Georgia. Rather grudgingly he approved a continuation of the existing naval establishment. He recommended that public lands be no longer considered as a source of revenue now that the national debt, to which they had been pledged, was extinguished. Bowing to the influence of "another great national interest" (the new Western states), he recommended a policy of easy land disposal to encourage rapid settlement by independent farmers, "the best part of the population," everywhere "the basis of society and the true friends of liberty." Let the right to the soil and future disposal of public lands accordingly be surrendered "in convenient time" to the states respectively in which they lay. As to any national system of internal improvements (to which the American System would have constructively devoted a surplus revenue), Jackson urged that Congress in "all doubtful cases" await a constitutional amendment.

The message seemed to throw a veil over the great issue that weighed

[5] JQA to Richard Rush, York, Pennsylvania. Washington, November 30, 1832. Adams MSS.

on all minds. Alluding briefly to opposition to the revenue laws "in one quarter" that threatened the integrity of the Union, the President hoped that the "judicial authorities of the General Government," acting under existing laws and aided by the prudence of their own officers and the people's patriotism, would be able to overcome whatever obstacles might be thrown in their way. If not, then later he would suggest to Congress further views and other measures.

Finally Jackson sounded a note of new and fixed policy based on established reforms. In regard to most of our great interests we at last found ourselves, after salutary experience as a nation, fixing definitely upon a permanent system of policy best calculated to promote the happiness and liberty of the people: that was, in short, the least federal government possible.

Adams now really did begin to despair of the Republic. Jackson seemed to be going much further than compromise, than appeasement itself, to satisfy the Nullifiers. He was surrendering everything that Adams had stood for as President in his program of Liberty with Power: reasonable protection of manufacturers, internal improvements, the Bank, faith to the Indians, a stronger navy, all were to be swept away so that there would be nothing left to nullify. It was a vicious bargain between South and West that Jackson was proposing, at the expense of the Eastern and Central states. It was "the most deadly blow at the Union that ever was struck." It meant nothing less than a revolution in the administration of the Government of the United States. Jackson had only awaited his reelection to proclaim it.[6]

The President and his political advisers certainly did intend to reduce federal activities to a minimum, leaving every possible power to the states. They had reverted to a Madisonian—if not a Jeffersonian—concept of state rights. They would have preferred to settle with the Nullifiers on that basis. None of them, except the President, was determined to take action against South Carolina. But Andrew Jackson never had any intention of truckling to nullification. His personal letters written from November 1832 to January 1833 leave no doubt of a passionate fidelity to the Union: "I would die for the Union." When it became evident that the Nullifiers were preparing to resist the Union by force, Jackson issued his famous public proclamation of December 10, 1832.

After patiently explaining the absurdity [7] of their doctrine, the President paternally warned fellow citizens of his "native state" against resisting the laws of the Union. Sharply he admonished them not to "lend

[6] JQA to Benjamin F. Hallett, Boston. Washington, December 17, 1832. To Samuel L. Southard, Governor of New Jersey, December 19, 1832. Adams MSS.

[7] "To shew the absurdity—Congress have the right to admit new states. When territories they are subject to the laws of the Union. The day after admission they have the right to secede and dissolve it." Andrew Jackson to Martin Van Buren, December 25, 1832. Bassett: *Life of Jackson,* II, 579–80.

themselves thereby to an act of disunion, under penalty of *treason.*" His language was pointed and unequivocal: "I consider, then, the power to annul a law of the United States, assumed by one State, *incompatible with the existence of the Union, contradicted expressly by the letter of the Constitution, unauthorized by its spirit, inconsistent with every principle on which it was founded, and destructive of the object for which it was founded.*"

Despite the unmistakable italics John Quincy Adams could scarcely believe what he read. It was good Washingtonian doctrine. It reflected his own Fourth-of-July oration at Quincy. Charles Francis Adams, reading the Proclamation in Boston, fancied that the writer of it had studied the Quincy address carefully.[8] Jackson was actually saying that in their national capacity the people of the several states had created the Union and made the Constitution. Edward Livingston of Louisiana, Secretary of State, who is generally credited with the expository part of Jackson's Proclamation, seemed to have thought about the Union like George Washington, John Quincy Adams, Nathan Dane, Joseph Story, and John Marshall.

"In our colonial state . . . and before the declaration of independence," declared Jackson, "we were known in our aggregate character as *the United States of America.* That decisive and important step was taken jointly. We declared ourselves a nation by a joint, not by several acts, and when the terms of our Confederation were reduced to form it was in that of a solemn league of several States, by which they agreed they would collectively form one nation for the purpose of conducting some certain domestic concerns and all foreign relations. . . . But the defects of the Confederation need not be detailed. Under its operation we could scarcely be called a nation. . . . This state of things could not be endured, and our present happy Constitution was formed . . . [to make] a more perfect Union. . . ." President Jackson actually called it "the National Constitution."

The very day that the President's Proclamation appeared the ex-President had just sent in to a New York publisher some anonymous remarks as preface to a source book on American history which was to contain the Declaration of Independence, the Constitution of the United States, and Washington's Farewell Address. "The Declaration [of Independence]," explained the anonymous Adams, "was issued *in the name and by the authority of the whole People.* But after constituting the thirteen Colonies free and independent States, the People of the Union did not immediately proceed to form *a Government* for the whole." Instead they attempted a mere Confederation which by its "imbecility" brought the Union to the verge of dissolution. Then the whole People, acting through delegates of the several states to the Philadelphia Convention, drew up a new Constitution, solemnly adopted by the conventions of the People of each and

8 CFA to JQA, Boston, December 17, 1832. Adams MSS.

every one of the thirteen states. "The Constitution of the United States thus became the Act of the *whole* People"—attested by its opening words: "We the People of the United States."

So striking was the similarity of political theory between Adams's anonymous exegesis [9] of the Union and Jackson's famous Proclamation that the uninformed might guess the same man to have written the two documents. The publisher was so impressed that, without consulting Adams, he added the Proclamation to the source book. Andrew Jackson's theory of the Union seemed to agree almost perfectly with that of John Quincy Adams.

The astonished ex-President could come to only one conclusion when he read the Proclamation: Andrew Jackson did not mean what he said! [10]

Adams believed that Jackson was only bluffing. The big danger was not in South Carolina: it was in Washington, in a Congress that, acting under the President's advice, would abandon the substance of the Union. In vain Adams tried to get the House of Representatives to call upon the President for the text of the Proclamation, in order that the Chief Executive might point out to Congress and to the country its inconsistency with the message. Presently Jackson disarmed that tactic by presenting the Proclamation, with relevant documents from South Carolina, to Congress of his own accord.

Jackson now began making troop dispositions and looking to the offers of volunteers that came in from the various states. He was resolved if necessary to take the field personally against any insurrection. The country was falling in line with him. In Boston, Daniel Webster made a famous speech to a great public meeting in Faneuil Hall [11] called to uphold the President. Even the "mouldering relics of the Hartford Convention" put themselves behind the Union. Harrison Gray Otis declared the Hartford resolutions of 1814 had been only a cry of distress, never a note of defiance. Another of the Thirteen Confederates, Franklin Dexter, supported still a third, Thomas Handasyd Perkins, in resolutions against the Nullifiers of 1832.[12]

Adams was quite affected by this demonstration of loyalty to the Union by the old Federalists. He was glad he had never published his Reply to the *Appeal of the Massachusetts Federalists*.[13]

---

[9] *The Declaration of Independence; The Constitution of the United States; the Farewell Address . . . the Proclamation of Andrew Jackson . . . to which are prefixed prefatory remarks by one of the most distinguished statesmen of the United States* (New York: Octavius Longworth; 1833).

[10] JQA to CFA, Washington, December 11, 1832; to George Sullivan, December 11, 1832; to Samuel Southard, December 19, 1832. Adams MSS.

[11] Adams had not at first thought a public meeting of protest necessary in Boston. "The danger is all here," he wrote to his son from Washington. JQA to CFA, December 11, 1832. Adams MSS.

[12] CFA to JQA, Boston, December 17, 1832. Adams MSS.

[13] JQA to CFA, Washington, December 25, 1832. Adams MSS.

As a showdown approached, the Nullifiers began to lose heart.[14] Cooler heads prevailed in Charleston. They managed to put off actual resistance until it could be seen whether Congress would repeal the Adams Tariff. News from South Carolina made Adams concede that the Proclamation had fortified the Union party there.[15]

Friends of Union in South Carolina, and all over the United States, felt still stronger, and the Nullifiers weaker, when Andrew Jackson sent to Congress a special message (January 16, 1833) asking for all means necessary to enforce the laws of the United States. The Administration brought forth a bill for the collection of the revenue. In weeks of hectic debate and national excitement Congress devoted itself to the "Force Bill" and to bills for the further reduction of the tariff.

2

In the House of Representatives at the opening of the second session in December 1832 Speaker Stevenson made a change in the personnel of the committee on manufactures that left only two men who favored continuing the protective system even to the moderate degree of the Adams Tariff. "Admiral" Michael Hoffman of New York, a strong Administration man, chairman of the committee on naval affairs, had proved too much of a small-navy advocate to suit the President; so the Speaker switched him to Adams's committee, displacing Charles Dayan, also of New York, a protectionist. In his new assignment Hoffman served as an active checkmate to Chairman Adams.

The House referred the tariff part of the President's message not to Adams's committee but to the committee on ways and means. Under its new chairman, Gulian C. Verplanck, that committee brought in a bill quite in line with the new policy of the Administration, calling for reduction of the tariff in two years to about half its present rates. This would leave practically no protection. The House went off into a prolonged debate on the Verplanck bill.

As Adams listened to the debate, he wondered how the Government would have enough money to deal with an insurrection in South Carolina or a war with Buenos Aires (then threatening over the Falkland Islands question) if existing duties were done away with. He suggested that the House ask the Secretary of the Treasury whether the Government was financially prepared for such contingencies, but the idea met little support and he did not press it.[16] Obviously he had intended only to embarrass the Verplanck bill.

The more he heard all this talk about discrimination against the South

---

[14] Houston: *Nullification in South Carolina*, pp. 122–6. Bassett: *Life of Jackson*, II, 571–4.
[15] JQA to CFA, Washington, December 25, 1832. Adams MSS.
[16] *Memoirs*, VIII, 506–8.

by protection of Northern manufactures, the more impatient the New Englander became at any disposition to appease that section still further. Augustus Smith Clayton of Georgia had asserted that the planters' slaves were in effect the slaves of the North too. "Our slaves," he declared, "sail the Northern ships and run the Northern spindles. . . . *Our slaves are our machinery,* and we have as good a right to profit by them as do the Northern men to profit by the machinery they employ." [17]

All Adams's instincts revolted at this putting of enslaved human beings on the same cold basis as machines. For the first time real eloquence poured forth from his heart in an extemporaneous speech on the floor of the House. No longer did he grope for words. No longer did the sound of his own voice frustrate him. He suddenly became a compelling speaker.[18]

Adams moved to strike out the enacting clause of the Verplanck bill. Swiftly he gave his reasons. For one thing, the bill was in response to bullying threats of the Nullifiers. The other states, particularly the North and East, should not yield to it. The manufacturing interests were as much entitled to protection as any other great interest of the Union. Actually they did not have as much. Look at the special protection which the South and Southwest enjoyed under the Constitution and the laws of the United States! Look at the three-fifths ratio of the Constitution for additional representation of slaveholding states in the House of Representatives. It gave them twenty members that they would not have had without it. "I am for adhering to that bargain because it is a bargain," he affirmed, "not that I would agree to it if the bargain were to be made over and over again."

Another special protection for the owners of "Southern machinery," he pointed out, was the constitutional provision, "so contrary to the motives and feelings of the people of the North," for the rendition of fugitive slaves. He recited the circumlocution of the Constitution on this subject. There was also the federal army that served to protect the people of the South and Southwest particularly against the Indians, and to enforce the guarantee of the Constitution that protected each state against domestic violence. Again he reverted to Clayton's unfortunate figure of speech, "our machinery." "That 'machinery,' " he observed, "sometimes exerts a self-moving power." [19]

Adams had touched the South's rawest nerve. Only two summers before, Nat Turner's rebellion in Southampton County, Virginia, just over the line from North Carolina, had caused the butchery of fifty-one whites,

[17] *Register of Debates,* 22d Cong., 2d Sess., p. 1583, February 2, 1833. Italics inserted.

[18] "Little did I imagine that my *chiffon* of a speech upon the Southern Machinery would have been the most popular thing I ever did or said." JQA to CFA, Washington, March 13, 1833. Adams MSS.

[19] *Register of Debates,* 22d Cong., 2d Sess., pp. 1609–15. February 4, 1833.

including eighteen women and twenty-four children. It horrified the whole nation from Quincy [20] to New Orleans, and left the South throbbing with continual fear. Immediately after receiving news of the uprising the steely-faced Calhoun ordered thirty lashes laid on a runaway slave brought back to his model plantation. All over the South the slaveowners looked to their whips.[21] They looked also to the United States Army and Navy for quick protection in case of further active responses of the Negro to his enslavement. Only the United States marines from Norfolk prevented the Nat Turner rebellion from spreading into North Carolina. The House had this terrible picture before it when Adams stated: "My constituents possess as much right to say to the people of the South, 'We will not submit to the protection of your interests,' as the people of the South have the right to address such language to them."

William Drayton of South Carolina jumped to his feet: "The member from Massachusetts . . ." he declared hotly, "has thrown a firebrand into the Hall."

"It is not I who have thrown the 'firebrand,'" Adams told his fellow members three days later. "The Nullification Ordinance is the firebrand." He quoted to the House the boasts of William Campbell Preston, one of the leaders of the nullification movement in South Carolina: " 'The protective system reels under our blows. Last summer the fear of that resistance [to the tariff law], which we had announced, drove them into a reduction [the Adams Tariff], a cheat, it is true, that benefits them, not us. Still, it was an attempt to appease us, and now, before one tittle of the reduction has gone into effect, comes upon the back of our late proceedings, another offer of eight millions more. Let us go on then and we shall get the whole debt.' " [22]

Adams did not want to go on. He opposed any new tariff bill, any further concession.

3

Senator Henry Clay was listening in the House of Representatives when Adams made his "firebrand" speech about the self-propelling "machinery" of the South.[23] Before the Presidential election of 1832 Clay had stood for the American System come hell or high water. Since then Jackson had chastened him with a stinging defeat at the polls. Clay walked back through the Rotunda thinking deeply. He was no longer in a position to defy the South, the President, and the devil. It was John Quincy Adams who was hurling defiance at all three. He must find a new combination for public favor. Clay, increasingly worried about the sectional

---

[20] "The news from Virginia is momentous indeed! It is too horrible. God send it may soon be set to rights." LCA to JA, 2d, Quincy, August 30, 1831. Adams MSS.

[21] Wiltse: *Calhoun, Nullifier,* p. 119.

[22] *Register of Debates,* 22d Cong., 2d Sess., pp. 1639–51. February 7, 1833.

[23] JQA to CFA, Washington, March 13, 1833. Adams MSS.

cleavage, decided to present himself as advocate of Compromise, Peace, and Union, the role that Adams had essayed the year before without success.

Clay's dramatic about-face in the interest of domestic harmony was as unexpected as if, in a later age, Woodrow Wilson had accepted the Lodge reservations to the League of Nations in order to get that international covenant through the Senate. The great champion of the American System abandoned it altogether. He offered a tariff bill that all but capitulated to the Nullifiers. It provided for reduction by successive steps every two years down to a uniform level of twenty per cent by 1842 on all dutiable articles, thus giving ten years to protected manufactures to absorb the shock. As a sop to New England, Clay's bill increased the protection on coarse woolen fabrics—slave cloth—from five to fifty per cent before the step-downs began.[24] Even at the eventual twenty-per-cent level these textiles would enjoy more protection than they would have in the Adams Tariff of 1832.

Faced with the President's Force Bill, the Nullifiers compromised with their principle that any degree of protection in a tariff was unconstitutional. Calhoun had presumed too much when he advanced nullification as a peaceful remedy. With Andrew Jackson in the White House for another four years, he could not rely on a block of other Southern states to support South Carolina. He could not even count on the united resistance of his own state—there was too resolute a Union party there. Before the South would coalesce in rebellion it would be necessary to wait for a broader and more vital issue than the protective tariff. Calhoun drew in his horns.

Clay's compromise tariff quickly took the place of the Verplanck bill for an immediate tariff for revenue only. As soon as it was apparent that the Senate would accept the new measure, it passed the House of Representatives initially almost overnight (February 26, 1833) by a vote of 119 to 85, John Quincy Adams in the negative.[25] In the Senate the vote was 29 to 16 (March 1), Calhoun and Clay in the affirmative, Daniel Webster and Nathaniel Silsbee of Massachusetts opposed.

The Force Bill led the way through the Senate (February 20, 1833) over the walkout of Calhoun and Miller of South Carolina and eight other Senators from North Carolina, Kentucky, Georgia, Mississippi, and Alabama—no vote was recorded for Henry Clay. The bill did not pass the House until after the Compromise Tariff—namely, on the same day,

[24] Stanwood: *American Tariff Controversies*, I, 397–401. JQA to Henry Middleton, March 25, 1833; to Thomas B. Wales, March 21, 1833. Adams MSS.

[25] "I did not vote for the compromise Bill, nor did I believe that it would ever go into effect. I was fully convinced and then said that a revisal of it would be found necessary at this very session of Congress, nor did I believe that it would produce the excess of revenue which would require a further reduction. Nor have I more faith in the compromise now than I had at the time when it passed." JQA to Charles Augustus Davis of New York, Washington, February 20, 1834. Adams MSS.

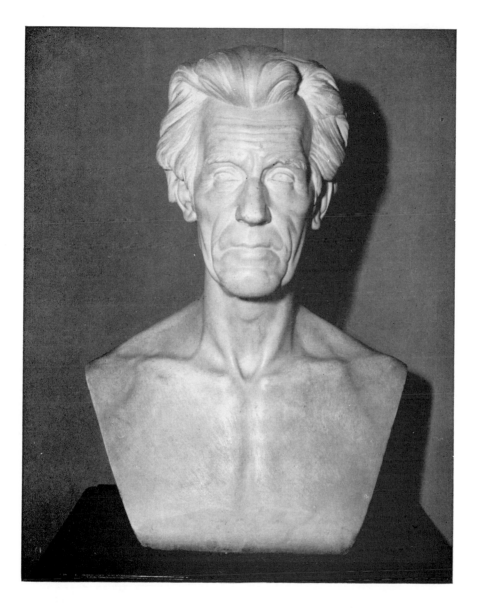

ANDREW JACKSON, DEFENDER OF THE UNION

SCULPTOR UNKNOWN. BUST OWNED BY DR. ISAAC M. CLINE OF NEW
ORLEANS, NOW IN LOUISIANA STATE MUSEUM. COURTESY OF DR. ISAAC M.
CLINE AND FAMILY. PHOTOGRAPH BY LEON TRICE

March 1, 1833, by a vote of 149 to 48. With great satisfaction Jackson signed the twin measures at the close of his first term.

Adams voted unhesitatingly for the Force Bill. In his opinion that was the only piece of legislation necessary to solve the South Carolina crisis. In his mind Jackson had lost the glory of exterminating the Nullifiers by not already having seized the opportunity to put them down.[26]

The legislature of South Carolina now called another constitutional convention. Solemnly its members repealed the nullification ordinance of 1832. With equal gravity they passed an ordinance nullifying the Force Act. That was that.

Who had triumphed? Adams thought the Nullifiers had won. The tantrums of South Carolina had scared Congress into a repeal of the Adams Tariff just as a hysterical dowager might rule the other members of her family with fainting fits.[27] (He should know the force of this simile.) In Adams's metaphor, nullification in 1832 was only chickenpox. The real, virulent, confluent smallpox would break out later from the feverishly pulsing virus of slavery. To yield to the hysteria of 1832 would only feed the virus.

Calhoun and his cohorts loudly claimed that theirs was the victory, won by unflinching defense of liberty, of the Constitution, of Union!

Certainly Adams had not won anything from the affray. To his inner disgust,[28] it was Henry Clay, and not the author of the Adams compromise tariff of 1832, who now seemed to stand forth before the country as the Man of the Whole Nation, the Great Pacificator. But when the smoke drifted away from the crisis of 1833, as from the battlefield of New Orleans on the 8th of January 1815, it was Andrew Jackson who still commanded the field of Union.

---

[26] "If the Annual Message had been in the Spirit of the Proclamation, South Carolina Nullification would have been exterminated, and Andrew Jackson would have had all the glory of putting it down. His popularity would have been ten times more overwhelming than it ever has been, and if he could *after that* have borne his faculties meekly like Washington, he might have been a benefactor to his Country. As it is, halting between Washington, Federalism and Nullification, he has lost the opportunity of acquiring honour to himself, or of strengthening the foundations of the Union." JQA to William Ellis, of Dedham, Massachusetts. Washington, March 15, 1833. Adams MSS.

[27] JQA to Robert Walsh, Quincy, September 19, 1833. Adams MSS.

[28] "Before last December I know that for about two years National Republicans meant—Henry Clay, High Tariff, and the American System. But now—Where is High Tariff? Where is the American System? Where is Henry Clay? The tariff's with the world beyond the flood—Henry Clay? You shall find him on a Negro plantation, south of the Potomack. The American System? I have written its epitaph. I mourn over it as over my own child, for I and not Henry Clay was its father. . . ." JQA to CFA, Washington, March 26, 1833. See also JQA to William Ellis, of Dedham, Massachusetts, Washington, March 15, 1833. Adams MSS.

4

When "Admiral" Hoffman succeeded in blocking any expression—at least of majority opinion—of the House committee on manufactures, Adams had set about preparing a major speech in favor of protection. A siege of illness, together with his occupations on the bank committee, prevented him from delivering it on the floor of the House before the passage of Clay's Compromise Tariff. He therefore proposed it to the committee on manufactures for a report. Hoffman sensed its content and blocked it in committee. The fresh-water Admiral proposed instead to report no progress, to ask the House for dismissal. When the majority of the committee so decided, Adams put forward a minority report. On February 28, 1833 he moved that it be laid on the table with order to print. Hoffman tried also to block that, but a vote carried it 93 to 58.[29]

Adams regarded this prolix document as one of the greatest papers he had ever written. Really it was a political tract against nullification and against the President's message which pandered, he believed, to the Nullifiers. Since nullification was already dead, it was too late to repeat the old arguments against that doctrine—in fact, Adams himself couldn't have improved on Jackson's Proclamation in that respect. One of the outstanding paragraphs, smothered by the twelve thousand words of the minority report, read as follows:

"The subscribers [30] believe that this great confederated Union is an union of the people, an union of the States, an union of great national interests; an union of all classes, conditions, and occupations of men; an union co-extensive with our territorial dominions; an union for successive ages, without limitation of time."

The greater part of the paper was an expostulation against the "revolutionary" doctrine of the President's annual message to Congress of December 1832: "the development of an entire system for the future Government of the Union . . . unheard of, incompatible with the foundations of our political existence"—as laid down by George Washington.

Adams seized on Jackson's flattering phrase describing independent farmers as "the best part of the population"—which the President had really applied to Western settlers—and stretched it arbitrarily to mean the wealthy slaveholding planters. Such a concept, he averred, was the fundamental axiom of a landed aristocracy. It was on behalf of this feudal class that Jackson was sacrificing the rest of the Union, including the free labor of the North. From such a "revolutionary" system flowed fateful results. First was abandonment of all appropriations for national internal

---

[29] *Register of Debates*, 22d Cong., 2d Sess., pp. 1865, 1902–3. JQA to CFA, Washington, March 13, 1833. To William Plumer, Jr., Washington, April 6, 1833. Adams MSS.

[30] Lewis Condict also signed the Minority Report, but Adams wrote it all.

improvements, despite specific powers of the Constitution, itself a "great organized engine of improvement physical, moral, political." It also signalized destruction of all protection to domestic manufacturers, involving masses of free laborers who were as much entitled to the nation's protection as were "the best part of our population." Again, it meant nullification of all future revenue from the nation's public domain, in favor of a "privileged class of citizens," cultivators of the soil. Finally, the President had hurled a hurtful denunciation at the Bank of the United States, damaging to its solidity and to the value of the stock that the Government owned in it.

The author of the Report went to as great a length as the *Exposition and Protest of South Carolina* to show that the national services and protection, including the army and navy, and the constitutional guarantee of a republican form of government against domestic violence, were far more valuable to the South, endangered as it was by Indian hostilities and the ever dreaded menace of servile rebellion, than they were to the North. In this way he attempted to show that the free labor of the North was actually subsidizing the slaveowners of the South.

"Now," said Adams, "the subscribers [to the Report] cannot suppress the mortification and alarm with which, at the very moment when the arm of one of the States of this Union was thus raised, proclaiming with a voice of thunder her inflexible purpose to strike a vital blow at the right [of the people] . . . that, at this peculiar moment, the Chief Magistrate of the United States should have addressed to the legislative councils a message, recommending not only a gradual withdrawal of *all* that protection, but a whole system of administration for the future government of the Union, adapted to that principle of withdrawn and nullified protection. . . ."

Adams regarded this document as his epitaph to the American System, and his own political testament.[31] He got it printed in the newspapers before it was buried in the House Reports of the Twenty-second Congress, second session, and in the Appendix to the *Register of Debates*. Charles Francis Adams had an edition of five thousand copies printed in pamphlet form at Boston.[32] Studious readers paid some attention to it in Boston, New York, Philadelphia, and Baltimore.[33] Adams's constituents of the Plymouth district must have found it satisfactory. On April 1, 1833 they re-elected him to the next, Twenty-third Congress by a majority of over three fourths of all votes cast.[34] But the salvo that he launched against President Jackson in 1833 overshot its mark. It was too heavy, too wearily tautological, too much of an anticlimax to the nullification controversy.

[31] JQA to CFA, Washington, March 26, 1833. Adams MSS.

[32] *Report of the Minority of the Committee on Manufactures, Submitted to the House of Representatives of the United States*, February 28, 1833, by J. Q. Adams and Lewis Condict (Boston: Eastburn; 1833).

[33] JQA to CFA, Washington, March 26, 1833. Adams MSS.

[34] *Memoirs*, VIII, 539.

Adams must have realized this. "The faggot-fire of Nullification has burnt itself out," he wrote from his Quincy retreat to Robert Walsh at Philadelphia after adjournment of the Twenty-second Congress, "and I always thought there was more blaze in it than fuel. But the moral disease of this Union will disclose itself in a great variety of symptoms before it assumes its final type. The South has ruled and rules and will rule us by her *Machinery;* and she is now rallying her forces to the standard of slavery." [35]

Rheumatics and Antimasonry by now had driven John C. Calhoun and Nullification temporarily out of John Quincy Adams's mind.[36] He was soon deep in the Antimasonic controversy.

[35] September 19, 1833. Adams MSS.
[36] JQA to Robert Walsh, Quincy, September 19, 1833. Adams MSS.

CHAPTER XV

Zealous Antimason
(1831 – 1835)

I am a zealous Antimason—

JOHN QUINCY ADAMS TO EDWARD INGERSOLL QUINCY,
SEPTEMBER 21, 1831 [1]

IT has not been previously told how John Quincy Adams ever became mixed up with the Antimasonic movement. Until we follow through this chapter of his political life we cannot understand the fullness of his ambition, nor indeed the man himself.

Adams's indictment of Masonry rested on what he regarded as the antisocial and immoral nature of the secret promises, obligations, and penalties that the Order imposed on its initiates. It is therefore necessary at the outset to set forth these oaths, windmills against which the old contender was to break another lance.

1

In the oath for the first degree of Masonry, the Entered Apprentice's Obligation, the neophyte swore as follows:

I, A.B., do, of my own free will and accord, in the presence of God, and of this right worshipful lodge, erected to God, and dedicated to holy St. John, hereby and hereon most solemnly and sincerely promise and swear,

That I will always hail, forever conceal, and never reveal, any of the secret or secrets of Masons or Masonry, which at this time, or any time hereafter, shall be communicated to me as such, except it be to a true and lawful brother, or within the body of a just and regular lodge, him or them whom I shall thus find to be, after strict trial and due examination. . . .

All this I solemnly and sincerely swear, with a full and hearty resolution to perform the same, without any evasion, equivocation or mental reservation, under no less penalty than to have my throat cut

---

[1] John Quincy Adams: *Letters on the Masonic Institution* (Boston: Press of T. R. Marvin; 1847), p. 14. Hereinafter cited as JQA: *Masonic Institution*. See p. 303, note 124, below.

across from ear to ear, my tongue plucked out by the roots, and buried in the rough sands of the sea, a cable's length from shore, where the tide ebbs and flows twice in twenty-four hours. So help me God, and keep me steadfast in this my obligation of an Entered Apprentice. K. once.[2]

The second degree, or Fellow Crafts Obligation, required similar promises under equally gruesome penalties:

. . . under no less penalty than to have my heart taken from under my naked left breast, and carried to the valley of Jehoshaphat, there to be thrown into the fields to become a prey to the wolves of the desert, and the vultures of the air. So help me God, etc. Kiss [the Bible] twice.

The third degree, or Master Mason's Obligation, after enjoining never to reveal the secrets of Masonry, laid down the following:

. . . I furthermore promise and swear, that I will attend a brother barefoot, if necessity requires, to warn him of approaching danger; that on my knees I will remember him in my prayers; that I will take him by the right hand and support him with the left in all his just and lawful undertakings; that I will keep his secrets as safely deposited in my breast as they are in his own, treason and murder only excepted and those at my option; that I will obey all true signs, tokens, and summonses, sent me by the hand of a Master Mason, or from the door of a just and regular Master Mason's lodge, if within the length of my cable tow.

All this I most solemnly and sincerely promise and swear, with a full and hearty resolution to perform the same, without any evasion, equivocation or mental reservation, under no less penalty than to have my body cut across, my bowels taken out and burnt to ashes, and those ashes scattered to the four winds of heaven; to have my body dissected into four equal parts, and those parts hung on the cardinal points of the compass, there to hang and remain as a terror to all those, who shall presume to violate the sacred obligation of a Master Mason. Kiss [the Bible] thrice.

The standing penalties of the first three degrees of Masonry went back by fable, and by jumble of Old Testament phraseology and suggestion, to a mythical trio, Jubelo, Jubela, and Jubelum, pictured as having betrayed Hiram Abiff, master of a legendary lodge of Masons[3] at the building of King Solomon's Temple. In remorse for his treachery each of the

---

[2] Kiss the Bible once.

[3] JQA searching the Old Testament found in the seventh chapter of the First Book of Kings a reference to Hiram of Tyre, the widow's son, who worked at building the Temple of Solomon, not as a mason, but as one "cunning to work all works in brass."

three culprits had invoked upon himself one of the successive penalties which were executed, so the fable went, by the King of Tyre.

Members of the Royal Arch Masons, an order "erected to God, and dedicated to Zerubbabel," vowed, under similar dire penalties, to employ companion Royal Arch Masons in preference to any other person of equal qualifications, and to assist each other, *whether right or wrong*, in any difficulty.

The Knights Templar, in another advanced degree, pledged to the protection of innocent maidens, destitute widows, helpless orphans, and the Christian religion, swore to keep secret the mysteries and to fulfill duties of Masonry under no less penalty than having their heads struck off and placed on the highest spire in Christendom.

Those Masons who chose to take the rites of the Fifth Libation drank wine from a human skull in testimony to the mortality of the body and the immortality of the soul. Each of them repeated after his lodge Master a vow to take upon himself in all future life the sins of him from whose skull he drank, in addition to his own, should he ever violate or transgress any obligation of Masonry or its orders of knighthood.

Such were the oaths, obligations, and penalties of Freemasonry [4]—as they took shape at the beginning of the Order in London in the early eighteenth century.[5] They remained the basis of the institution, but interpolations could and did creep into the texts as new chapters appeared in different localities across the ocean. For example, in certain lodges in New York and Vermont the words "treason and murder excepted" were changed, unbeknownst to the generality of the Order, to "treason and murder not excepted" in the rites for the third degree and Royal Arch degree.[6]

Taken literally, these oaths, promises, and sanctions were fearful indeed, governing a secret society that might act contrary to law and the common obligations of all citizens under the Constitution, creating a self-preferring citizenry within the commonwealth. Taken literally, the bloody sanctions were cruel and inhuman, long since outlawed by civilized peoples.

Few initiates had taken this rigmarole literally or too seriously. Some of

[4] Synonymous with Masonry. So called because originally the Order sprang from persons made "free"—that is, honorable members of the chartered Society of Stonemasons of London of the seventeenth century, from which Freemasonry (i.e., Masonry) descended.

[5] The above-quoted excerpts are taken from the texts furnished by Colonel William L. Stone to John Quincy Adams and printed in the appendix to JQA: *Masonic Institution*. See William L. Stone: *Letters on Masonry and Antimasonry Addressed to the Honorable John Quincy Adams* (New York, 1832), p. 67, and Appendix. Hereinafter cited as Stone: *Masonry and Antimasonry*. See also David Bernard: *Light on Freemasonry* . . . (Utica, 1829). Bernard was one of the leaders of the conventions of seceding Masons at Le Roy, New York, in 1828, and thoroughly familiar with the texts.

[6] Stone: *Masonry and Antimasonry*, pp. 74–5.

the brethren enjoyed the ceremonies. Some felt a bit sheepish. Most of them seem to have regarded their rites as seriocomic, much like the earnest tomfoolery of college fraternity initiations in our days. Others didn't worry about the literal meaning of the oaths because the master explained that they bound no member contrary to the law. Others were sustained by the example of many patriotic Americans who had been Masons. Dr. Joseph Warren, the ideal of Adams's boyhood, had been a Mason. So had his great patron, hero of his manhood, George Washington. So had Benjamin Franklin and Lafayette. So had Patrick Henry. Andrew Jackson was a Mason. So was Henry Clay. John Quincy Adams's own father, John Adams, once had some good things to say for Masons and Masonry, though he never thought it worth while to join the Order.[7]

In the United States people had generally considered Masonry as a useful auxiliary to Christianity and republican liberty, at least a harmless fraternity—until the sudden abduction and tragic disappearance of William Morgan of Batavia, New York, in September 1826, in the middle of John Quincy Adams's Administration.

2

William Morgan was a disgruntled Mason who had entered copyright on a book in which he was about to publish the secrets of the Order, including the oaths, obligations, and penalties of the first three degrees set forth above in abridged form. A band of Masons from lodges in the western counties of the state kidnapped him and planned to take him to the remote interior of Canada where he could do no mischief to the institution. On the way to Canada they incarcerated him temporarily in an empty powder-magazine of the disused Fort Niagara. At this point there seems to have been a hitch in the plot, when some of the Canadian confrères refused to escort Morgan over the frontier. Thus frustrated, a group of the conspirators rowed him out into the Niagara River and sank him roped and weighted with irons to the bottom of the stream near where it flows sluggishly, as if exhausted by its great leap over the Falls, into Lake Ontario. The body was never found. The deed took place probably on the night of September 18, 1826. Contemporary trials, confessions, jury verdicts, and jail sentences left no doubt about the "abduction."[8] It has also been established historically, though not juridically, beyond any reasonable doubt that Morgan was murdered.[9]

---

[7] JQA to a reviewer of Sheppard's *Defence of the Masonic Institution*. JQA: *Masonic Institution*, pp. 2–14.

[8] John C. Palmer: *The Morgan Affair and Antimasonry* (Washington: Masonic Service Association of the United States; 1924); Stanley Upton Mock: *The Morgan Episode in American Freemasonry* (East Aurora, N.Y., 1930). Both of these accounts are Masonic histories.

[9] The late Professor George H. Blakeslee sifted the evidence and came to this conclusion in a still unprinted doctoral thesis on "The History of the Antimasonic Party"

Morgan's disappearance did not prevent the publication of his book in 1827 with the aid of a surviving partner whom the Masonic conspirators were unable to intimidate. It included the ritual of the first three degrees substantially as given above though with more detail and verbiage.[10]

At no time did the Masonic Order as such condemn or help bring the criminals to justice. On the contrary, Masonic sheriffs, Masonic judges, and Masonic jurors conspired to prevent indictments, to frustrate prosecutions, to block verdicts wherever possible. Masonic encampments voted funds for the relief of their "western sufferers," and assisted some of the conspirators to flee from justice, even to get out of the country.

Morgan's tragic fate and the attitude of Masonry toward it led to a popular uprising such as the nation had never witnessed since the foundation of the Union. It turned the office of Freemasonry as viewed by a substantial proportion of the people from that of a handmaiden to Christianity and republican liberty to that of a secret and impious conspiracy against the rights of freemen and the majesty of the law. The Antimasonic excitement first flamed up in the emotionally "Burned-over District" of western New York, seedbed of radical religious movements and utopian social experiments, forcing-frame of humanitarian efforts for national propagation: such as evangelical revivals, temperance, woman suffrage, and (as will appear in a later chapter) the antislavery crusade.[11] It spread through the rural areas of the Northern states. It crystallized politically into the first third-party in the history of the United States.

Under the direction of young and dynamic leaders such as Thurlow Weed and William H. Seward of New York, and Thaddeus Stevens of Pennsylvania, the new party bade fair to take over and make over the tired National Republican Party. Its constituents were most numerous in New York and the five states contiguous to it, besides Rhode Island, and in the distant territory of Michigan settled by New England stock that had lingered long enough in the Burned-over District on their way west to get singed. When Adams took his seat in the Twenty-second Congress in December 1831, there were eighteen Antimasonic members in the House of Representatives who, like himself, were not taken into the councils of the National Republican Opposition. Adams, the nominee of the National Republicans of his district, also had the undivided support of the Antimasons who had helped to send him to Congress.[12]

(Harvard, 1903), which he kindly placed at my disposal. I have relied heavily on this scholarly account of the Morgan affair and the Antimasonic Party, both for facts and for guidance to printed documentary sources.

[10] *Illustrations of Masonry, by One of the Fraternity Who Has Devoted Thirty Years to the Subject* (New York, 1827).

[11] Whitney R. Cross has written a notable study of *The Burned-over District; the Social and Intellectual History of Enthusiastic Religion in Western New York, 1800–1850* (Ithaca, N.Y., 1950).

[12] The Antimasonic Convention of the Plymouth district "recommended" "un-

Most spectacular showing of the new party had been in the New York state elections of 1830. There the National Republicans had accepted the Antimasonic candidates for Governor and Lieutenant Governor, and the coalition nearly carried the state.[13] In those states where the party still remained unorganized, as in New Hampshire, Maine, Delaware, Maryland, Indiana, and Illinois, there was a great deal of moral Antimasonic sentiment. Political Antimasonry was an agrarian movement[14] of the Northern states, largely fermented by New England and Quaker conscience. But "moral Antimasonry" as distinct from the political party had its isolated spokesmen, even its journals, in the South, in Kentucky, Tennessee, Virginia, and Alabama.[15] In all the states where the crusade had any appeal it was predominantly to a rural "yeoman" constituency.

National party nominating conventions[16] as an established institution in American political history took shape with the Antimasonic Convention that met at Philadelphia, September 11 and 12, 1831. The delegates assembled for the purpose of declaring principles and organizing a national party. They did not yet speak out on national issues such as the American System. Rather they adopted a platform drafted by the youthful Seward, an appeal to the people to overcome the evils of Freemasonry through exercise of the elective franchise. To this end they called a second national convention to meet at Baltimore, September 26, 1831 for the purpose of nominating candidates for President and Vice President.

The strength of the third party was not to be measured by the handful of political offices that they held in states and nation, but rather by their weight in the balance of power. Before them glittered the possibility of a coalition with the National Republicans to be effected by adopting the American System in turn for acceptance of Antimasonic candidates for the Presidency and Vice-Presidency and for members of Congress. To

divided support" to John Quincy Adams for Congress. Boston *Free Press,* IV, No. 43, 44, October 22, 29, 1830. This was equivalent to a formal nomination.

[13] The Antimasons lost the election by only 8,000 votes: 128,000 for Throop, the Democratic candidate, to 120,000 for Granger, Antimason. Apparently there was enough Masonic influence left among National Republicans to swing the election to the Democrats, rather than see an Antimason become Governor of the state. At the last moment the *Albany Daily Advertiser,* state organ of the National Republican Party, suddenly shifted its support from Granger to Throop, a change supposed to have been dictated by certain prominent upstate National Republicans.

[14] Charles McCarthy: *The Antimasonic Party: A Study of Political Antimasonry in the United States, 1827–1840. Annual Report* 1902 AHA, I, 365–559. Hereinafter cited as McCarthy: *Antimasonic Party.*

[15] Blakeslee: Chapter VII, p. 3.

[16] The secret Federalist Party conventions of 1808 and 1812 were more in the nature of caucuses than public conventions with openly selected delegates. See John S. Murdock: "The First National Nominating Convention [1812]," *AHR,* I (No. 4, July 1912), 680–3, and Samuel E. Morison: "The First National Nominating Convention, 1808," *AHR,* XVII (No. 4, July 1912), 744–63.

studious politicians it appeared that this young, enthusiastic, crusading party might be able to name the next President and throw Andrew Jackson out of office.

Undoubtedly such was the new party's appeal to politicians like Weed,[17] Seward, and Stevens. They saw a chance to rejuvenate and bring back to power a party debilitated by the defeat of 1828. Nor was its significance lost on Adams and on older political leaders, including members of his onetime Cabinet: [18] Richard Rush, William Wirt, John McLean—and Henry Clay, to whom leadership of the National Republican Party had passed after Adams's downfall, almost with the latter's consent if not his blessing. By this time poor William Morgan had all but passed from public attention amidst the clash of opposing systems and strife of rival politicians contending for prizes of office and power.

3

Many Antimasons, as well as National Republicans, hoped that Henry Clay would renounce his Masonry and thus make himself an acceptable candidate to both parties so that they could unite on general principles against Jackson. Clay had long since ceased to attend lodge meetings and was at most a tepid member, but he did not think it good policy to come out against the Order. Thurlow Weed, political genius of the new party; Benjamin F. Hallett, Antimasonic leader in Massachusetts; and Willim L. Stone, unregenerate Federalist editor of the *Weekly Commercial Advertiser* of New York, a contrite high Mason who stepped forth in 1831 as a mediator between the Order and the crusade against it, all worked on Clay to make an unequivocal disavowal that would satisfy the Antimasons. The most he would commit himself to was this statement: "While I do not, and never did, care about Masonry, I shall abstain from making myself any party to that strife. I tell them that Masonry or Anti-Masonry has legitimately, in my opinion, nothing to do with politics; that I never acted, in public or private life, under any Masonic influence; that I have long ceased to be a member of any lodge; that I voted for Mr. Adams, no Mason, against General Jackson, a Mason, etc." [19]

The Antimasons had to look about for another candidate. If they could get a non-Mason of the right stature, maybe the National Republicans would accept him at their convention in December 1831 to lead the fight

[17] Glyndon G. Van Deusen: *Thurlow Weed: Wizard of the Lobby* (Boston, 1947), pp. 38–69.

[18] Samuel L. Southard, Adams's Secretary of the Navy, seems to have been the only member of his Cabinet who was not interested in the Presidential Question of 1832. He aspired only to be governor of New Jersey, or at most United States Senator.

[19] Clay to Francis Brooke, Ashland, June 23, 1831. Colton: *Works of Henry Clay*, IV, 303–4.

against the Democracy. Some of the leaders glanced at Calhoun, who privately condemned Masonry in no uncertain words,[20] but Calhoun would not do: he was too much of a Southerner—a Nullifier—and Antimasonry was essentially a Northern movement.[21] Antimasonic committees in Pennsylvania and Massachusetts then approached Richard Rush, asking him specifically for his views on Masonry. Rush was a widely popular National Republican. He had an impressive record as a statesman: successful Minister to the Court of St. James's during Monroe's Administration, a highly competent Secretary of the Treasury under Adams, a conspicuous supporter of the American System. As candidate for the Vice-Presidency he had been Adams's running-mate in the disastrous campaign of 1828.

Rush responded to these inquiries in two long public letters, May 4 and June 30, 1831. Confessing that he had once been an Entered Apprentice, he declared that he had withdrawn from the Order by letter in 1826 before the murder of Morgan was known to him, after attending only one lodge meeting. He branded the institution as subversive of the law, suborner of a free press, the greatest danger of the day to American liberties. The murder of Morgan was a public crime, he charged, for which the Order was basically responsible: "It is no case for county courts. It is for the nation. That is the proper tribunal." [22]

Richard Rush seemed to have placed himself in the lead for the Antimasonic nomination for election in 1832. There was only one other non-Mason who towered above him in stature, who might have an even greater appeal to the National Republicans as well as to the Antimasons. That was ex-President John Quincy Adams, who felt himself to be not a party man but the Man of the Whole Nation.

[20] John C. Calhoun to Christopher Van Deventer, May 25, August 5, 1831. *Letters of John C. Calhoun*, J. F. Jameson, ed., *Annual Report* 1899 AHA, II, 293, 296.

[21] Anonymous memorandum of a conversation with Calhoun, December 4, 1831, ibid., 305–6.

"The free, the cold, clear, intelligent North is the field for the growth of our cause. Let us not jeopardize it by transferring its main stalk into the South Carolina sands." W. H. Seward to Thurlow Weed [1831]. Frederick W. Seward: *William H. Seward: An Autobiography from 1801–1834, with a Memoir of His Life, and Selections from His Letters, 1831–1846*, I (New York, 1891), 195. Hereinafter cited as Seward: *Autobiography*.

Wiltse: *Calhoun, Nullifier*, pp. 121–2, suggests that the Antimasons might have accepted Calhoun if sure that at least the entire South would sustain the views expressed in the Fort Hill Address on Nullification (q.v., above, p. 237).

[22] Richard Rush to William McIlwain, John Kauffet, Hugh McDonald, and Thomas C. Hambly, Anti-Masonic Committee of Correspondence, for York County, Pennsylvania; York, Pa., May 4, 1831; Rush to Timothy Fuller, president, Stephen P. Gardner, Abner Phelps, Epaphras Hoyt, and Micah H. Ruggles, vice presidents of the Massachusetts State Antimasonic Convention; York, Pa., June 30, 1831. *A Collection of Letters on Freemasonry in Chronological Order* (Boston, 1849), pp. 6–43, particularly p. 14.

4

It must be recorded that the expression of Adams's sympathy for the Antimasonic uprising was rather tardy and not unconnected with political considerations. So it had been with his belated support ten years earlier of the movement for suppression of the African slave trade.[23] When Secretary of State Henry Clay suggested to the President that he recall Minister Joel Poinsett from Mexico because of his Masonic intrigues (which he had used to further the Administration's plan to purchase Texas), Adams declined to do so.[24] He did nothing about a petition from the Le Roy (New York) Convention of seceding Masons in 1827 protesting against the use of Fort Niagara for the unlawful detention of William Morgan.[25] Adams at first did his best to steer clear of the controversy between Masons and Antimasons,[26] but, as has been seen, took occasion during the election campaign of 1828 to deny his membership in the Order. The heavy vote for him in western New York that year, as opposed to Jackson, must have impressed him with the political significance of the Antimasonic movement.

In the bitter months after March 4, 1829 Adams was too immersed in his controversy with the Thirteen Confederates to pay attention to the Antimasons, too deep in family grief, too preoccupied in rehabilitating the paternal estate at Quincy and in straightening out his personal affairs. He considered himself definitively out of politics. The only expression we have from him during this period is a statement made to one Bache of Pawtucket, Rhode Island, declining to subscribe for an Antimasonic newspaper that the latter proposed to set up in that community: "I told him that until lately I had thought not unfavorably of the masonic institution, nor yet very favorably, but that having now become a subject of party discension [sic] I thought it mischievous and hoped it would be voluntarily given up; but that I was not disposed to countenance any persecution against it or against any of its members. I declined patronizing his proposed paper." [27]

Adams's neutrality [28] toward the Masonic controversy commenced to

[23] Vol. I, 415, 427–8.

[24] President JQA to Henry Clay, Secretary of State, Quincy, August 31, 1827. JQA Papers 1802–46, in LC.

[25] Stone: *Masonry and Antimasonry*, p. 328.

After some debate Congress, in May 1827, had referred the subject to the Executive, as having charge of the army. See *Register of Debates in Congress*, IV, Pt. 2 (May 12, 1828), pp. 2644–8; *Niles' Register*, XXXIV, 198; and Weed: *Autobiography*, 256.

[26] JQA to Rev. George Allen at Shrewsbury, Massachusetts. Quincy, August 11, 1834. Adams MSS.

[27] Diary, June 24, 1829.

[28] JQA to Rev. George Allen, Shrewsbury, Massachusetts. Quincy, August 11, 1834. Adams MSS.

break down as little by little he recovered his interest in national politics. He came to perceive in the summer of 1830 that the Antimasonic spirit would operate against Clay, certainly in New York, perhaps elsewhere.[29] He began to flirt with the Antimasons. In a letter declining to subscribe to another Antimasonic newspaper, to be published in Boston, he declared that the Masonic oath ought to be "suppressed," that Freemasons throughout the Union ought themselves to renounce all secrecy in their proceedings. "The secret that is written in blood should be revealed." But he left the duty of combating Masonry to younger men. He intimated that Antimasonic activity ought to be focused more on the Order itself rather than on individuals.[30] Such a letter certainly would not discourage Antimasons who might wish to vote for Adams for any office.

By the time of his election to Congress in November 1830 the Antimasonry movement had begun to involve Massachusetts and Quincy. The legislature was deciding contested elections to Congress[31] in every instance in favor of the Masonic candidate, whether he had a plurality of popular votes or not.[32] The "brawl" between Masons and Antimasons was a sign, Adams concluded, of politically squally weather ahead.[33] The showing made by the new party in the New York elections of 1830 convinced him that Antimasonry was a real force immediately to be reckoned with in American politics: "The Spirit is up and will not soon be [down]."[34]

One thing seemed more and more certain to the ex-President in Congress as the months sped by and the election of 1832 approached. The candidate of the National Republicans to contest the re-election of Jackson must be acceptable to the Antimasons, who seemed to hold the balance of power. He could not be a Mason. That, at least in Adams's estimation, let out Henry Clay.

In the spring of 1831 he attended, upon the invitation of Dr. Abner Phelps, an Antimasonic Convention in Faneuil Hall, Boston.[35] It was first signal to the world where his sympathies lay. In the same manner he had first raised a new flag back in Embargo days by attending a Republican mass meeting in remonstrance against the *Chesapeake-Leopard* outrage. Son Charles Francis Adams, twenty-four years old, disapproved of his father's new opinions. "They will be imputed to selfish motives," he

[29] Conversation of JQA with Alexander H. Everett, June 22, 1830. *Memoirs*, VIII, 232–3.

[30] JQA to Stephen Bates, Boston. Quincy, July 16, 1830. Adams MSS.

[31] Massachusetts law for the election of members of the national House of Representatives required a majority of votes in the district for election. Failing this, the legislature made the choice between the two runners-up.

[32] JQA to Richard Rush, Quincy, June 17, 1831. Adams MSS.

[33] Diary, November 12, 15, 1830.

[34] Diary, November 28, 1830.

[35] Diary, May 20, 1831.

warned. His father would do better, thought the young man, to occupy himself more effectively with the ordering of John Adams's papers for publication.[36]

Once Adams had taken the first step, he rationalized it characteristically. He would have to meet imputations of his motives. But he would not flinch from his patriotic duty.[37] Anybody worth his salt, he knew, who engaged in political controversy would have to meet these charges:

"No man can escape them; and a man susceptible of being intimidated by them is not fit for any useful agency in public affairs. I have for nearly five years abstained from taking part in the Masonic controversy as much as possible, but upon such questions there is a time when it becomes the duty of a good citizen to take his side. In the conflict between Freemasonry and its adversaries, I apprehend the time is approaching when my duty to my country will require a free and open avowal of my opinions; and, whatever may be the consequences, I shall not flinch from it. The danger is not imaginary, nor, I hope, underrated by me."[38]

This was a bit self-righteous, but we must remember that it is what he told himself rather than proclaimed to other people.

In the summer of 1831 Adams and his friend Richard Rush had some intimate and confidential correspondence. It was occasioned by Rush's public letter in support of Antimasonry. Rush recalled that Adams himself in their last conversation in Washington had helped inspire his stand.[39] "I certainly perceived that you had no veneration for Masonry, or horror of Antimasonry."[40] The purpose of his public statements, Rush explained, was to convince their friend Henry Clay of the force of Antimasonry, to make him denounce Masonry in order to capture the support of the Antimasons as well as the National Republicans; otherwise he would certainly lose the election. This much Rush had conveyed to Clay himself directly, and through Edward Ingersoll of Philadelphia.[41] Adams remembered the Washington conversation perfectly. As to Clay, he now

[36] "But that is only my opinion. . . . It is clear my father and I disagree." CFA Diary, May 22, 23, 1831. "I tried as mildly as possible to put a rein over indiscretions, which it must be confessed he will commit at times." Ibid., May 31, 1831.

[37] *Memoirs*, VIII, 364–5.

[38] *Memoirs*, VIII, 364. May 31, 1831.

[39] Probably May 23, 1830, as noted in *Memoirs*, VIII, 222, although JQA did not mention that they talked specifically about Antimasonry. "I told him I thought he was right in the intention to remove [from Washington as his home to Pennsylvania], and hoped he would be instrumental in saving the Union, which I believed depended entirely upon the accomplishment of a great change in her political partialities. This is the forlorn-hope of the Union."

[40] Richard Rush to JQA, York, Pa., May 11, 1831. Adams MSS.

[41] Rush enclosed a confidential copy of his letter to Ingersoll, June 9, 1831, in his to JQA of June 11, 1831. Adams MSS. See also Glyndon G. Van Deusen: *The Life of Henry Clay* (Boston, 1937), pp. 240–5.

declared to Rush, it was evident he would not abjure the Order: the National Republican Party, at least in New England, was the party of "Clay Masonry."

The greatest abomination of Masonry, Adams went on to say, was the secret oaths, promises, and penalties which led to crimes like the Morgan murder and consequent obstruction of justice. Hitherto he had abstained from taking part in the controversy in the hope that the fraternity would itself see the necessity for reform. But in vain. "Your letter," he assured Rush, "is a Trumpet blown in Zion." [42]

"The ballot boxes alone, can rid us of it," Rush responded after he learned from Ingersoll that Clay would not come out against the Order. He had been importuned to be a candidate for the Antimasonic nomination, but hesitated only on account of the feelings he had cherished toward Clay.[43] He had wished they would ask "someone else." On July 9, 1831 he informed Adams that he had "unequivocally refused" to be a candidate for the nomination.

In pressing Rush to reconsider, Adams used the strongest word in his vocabulary.[44] "It may become your indispensable *duty*," he urged.

Rush still refused to change his mind.[45] In a third public letter, this time to the Massachusetts Antimasons, he explained that he did not want his motives to be misinterpreted, on the eve of the Baltimore Convention, as due to personal ambition. In a long statement he blasted the Masonic institution once more as the greatest political evil of the day and pledged himself to the "cause" of Antimasonry.[46]

Rush's letters to Adams leave little doubt that the real reason for his refusal was his unwillingness to oppose his old colleague Clay, with whom he had served so loyally in Adams's Administration, and his hope that Adams himself might raise the new standard.

Dr. Phelps and an Antimasonic deputation invited Adams to give his Fourth-of-July oration [47] of 1831 to the Antimasons at the Old South Church in Boston instead of Quincy. But he was already committed to give his oration at Quincy, and was further unwilling to introduce any political partiality into such an address, on the anniversary of his father's death as well as of the independence of the United States. "My opinions concur with those of the Antimasons," he assured the commit-

[42] JQA to Richard Rush, Quincy, May 23, 1831. Adams MSS.

[43] Richard Rush to John Quincy Adams, York, Pa., July 2, 9, 1831. Adams MSS.

[44] JQA to Richard Rush, Quincy, July 23, 1831. Adams MSS.

[45] Richard Rush to JQA, York, Pa., July 31, 1831. Adams mentions receipt of the letter on August 6, 1831. Diary.

[46] Richard Rush to Amos Ellmaker, John Bear, Samuel Wagner, J. F. Charles, Adams Bare, H. G. Long, Samuel Parke, E. C. Reigart, George Heckbert, Z. McLenegan, T. H. Burrowes, George Mayer, H. Mehaffy, in behalf of themselves and the Antimasonic citizens of Lancaster County, Pennsylvania; York, Pa., August 13, 1831. *Collection of Letters on Freemasonry*, pp. 44–54.

[47] Above, pp. 233–5.

tee. "If it should be necessary for me to take part publicly in this controversy I should prefer any other day for putting on the harness to the
Fourth of July." [48]

Now that Rush was out of the race, would the Antimasons name a candidate at Baltimore in November whom the National Republicans could
also nominate in their convention a few weeks later in the same city?
Could a Man of the Whole Nation be found to hold the balance of power
offered by the Antimasonic movement? Such a man would have to be
known at large as an avowed Antimason. People were beginning to talk
about John Quincy Adams. [49] Everybody knew he was no Mason, but was
he an Antimason? So far he had listened more than he had talked about
Antimasonry.

Timothy Fuller, another leading Antimason, spoke to Adams on the
street in Boston. "I have been questioned," explained Fuller, "how far
your attendance at the Antimasonic Convention in Boston might be considered as pledging you in opposition to the election of Mr. Clay as
President of the United States."

"Mr. Clay did not enter into my consideration at all," responded Adams. "I do not propose to take any part in the next presidential election.
I don't know whether the Antimasons will support Mr. Clay or not. . . .
If they should fix upon another candidate than Mr. Clay, it would be an
incident in no wise essential to the principle. The dissolution of the Masonic institution in the United States I believe to be more important to us
and our posterity than the question whether Mr. Clay or General Jackson
shall be the President chosen at the next election."

"I am satisfied with your answer," Fuller declared. [50]

After the Fourth of July, Adams went into Boston to hear Fuller make
an Antimasonic address at Faneuil Hall and to listen to the reading of
Richard Rush's letter directed to the Antimasons of Massachusetts. The
hall was not crowded. Few of his Boston acquaintances were there, not
one of the aristocracy, the old Federalists, of whom many were Masons.
It was obviously a lower-middle-class constituency of little zest; there
were no party songs, no transparencies, to make the spirit rise. "The application of a blister upon the public bosom is wanting." [51]

He had some talk with his old protégé John Bailey, [52] recently a member of Congress, now state senator, and delegate to the coming Antimasonic Convention at Baltimore.

"I think Mr. Clay is in secret Masonic communication with the Masons
his supporters," he insinuated. "If the Anti-Masons do not propose to
support Mr. Clay, it is of the last importance to them to communicate
with each other in the different States upon the candidate to be assumed
by them, before their contemplated meeting at Baltimore; else they will

48 *Memoirs*, VIII, 367. June 6, 1831.
49 Diary, April 20, 1831.
50 *Memoirs*, VIII, 368–9. June 10, 1831.
51 *Memoirs*, VIII, 379.
52 Above, pp. 75, 209.

certainly disagree there." He suggested that, "without a second thought" they should take up Rush.[53]

"I hope you will be their candidate," vouchsafed Bailey loyally.

"I have not the slightest desire to be so," replied the elder statesman, "and wish not even to be thought of." [54]

In his own mind he was not sure of support. "There is a combination of parties against me," he jotted morosely in his Diary, "including almost the whole population of the country, of which my former supporters are the most inveterate—the Clay Masons and the so-called National Republicans." [55]

That summer of 1832, in a series of meetings of Phi Beta Kappa, John Quincy Adams and Judge Joseph Story led a movement to amend the constitution of the society so as to abolish all secret oaths and proceedings. There was much debate about this reform. Adams gave as his reason the popular excitement that was abroad in the land. "That is the very reason for retaining secrecy," stoutly asserted Theophilus Parsons, a professor in Harvard Law School, son of Adams's old law tutor. The reformers prevailed. Thanks to Adams, Phi Beta Kappa has not been a secret society ever since.[56]

Richard Rush's unyielding refusal to be nominated opened the field to John Quincy Adams, if Henry Clay would not disavow Masonry.

5

All over the Northeastern states Adams's name was being mentioned for President.[57] It seemed time for him to make some kind of public statement against Masonry, something that would condemn the evils of the Order but would not at the same time serve to drive good Masons out of the National Republican Party into the arms of their brother Andrew Jackson. For John Quincy Adams could not get anywhere without the nomination and support of the National Republicans as well as that of the Antimasons.

An opportunity was at hand to publish his views conveniently and discreetly. Back in the time of the X Y Z affair in 1798 the Grand Lodge of Massachusetts had been one of the many groups, along with grand juries, militia companies, and other assemblies of citizens, to send President John Adams patriotic expressions of support in the crisis with France. The first President Adams had responded in complimentary terms. Recently one John H. Sheppard had used extracts from John Adams's old letter in an oration on "The Defense of Masonry" delivered to the Lincoln Lodge in Wiscasset, Maine. He quoted the elder Adams as saying that although he had never happened to have the "felicity" of having been in-

[53] *Memoirs*, VIII, 379–80.
[54] Ibid.
[55] *Memoirs*, VIII, 389. July 28, 1831.
[56] *Memoirs*, VIII, 384–97, *passim.*
[57] *Memoirs*, VIII, 392–3. August 3, 1831.

itiated into the Masonic fraternity, some of his best and most patriotic friends had been Masons, including "the immortal Warren," and Jeremiah Gridley, his old preceptor in law: "Such examples as these and a greater still in my venerable predecessor (Washington) would have been sufficient to induce me to hold the institution and fraternity in esteem and honour *as favorable to the support of civil authority,* if I had not known *their love of the fine arts, their delight in hospitality, and devotion to humanity. . . ."* [58]

A writer on the Antimasonic Boston *Free Press,* Stephen T. Bates, enclosed the above passage in a letter to John Quincy Adams inquiring, as a reviewer of Sheppard's oration, now published in pamphlet form, whether the text of the whole letter might put a different construction on the excerpt.

John Quincy Adams did not have to make any further answer to this question than to say that he did not have the original in his possession. Nevertheless he went out of his way to make a studiously balanced statement as if calculated to condemn evils of Masonry without antagonizing Masons among his National Republican friends. He declared that of course his father could have had no knowledge in his day of the "unrefuted charges of unlawful *oaths,* of horrible and disgusting *penalties,* and *secrets,* the divulging of which had been punished by a murder unsurpassed in human atrocity." John Adams could not have foreseen that the bloody avengers, Morgan's murderers, would have gone unarrested for five long years, probably forever, thanks to the "contumacy of witnesses setting justice aside in her own sanctuary. . . . To speak of the Masonic Institution as favorable to the support of civil authority at this day, and in this country, would be a mockery of the common sense and sensibility of mankind."

"You are at liberty to make what use of this Letter you please," Adams concluded suggestively and hopefully, "giving notice if you publish it, that it is in answer to a Letter of enquiry received by me." [59] "You will have seen by the Newspapers that the Masons have stumped me out," he wrote to Rush, "by an impudent attempt to make my father one of their Champions." [60]

At last Adams was on record, albeit in a very cautious way. He had

---

[58] Stephen Bates to JQA, Boston, August 17, 1831. Adams MSS. Quotations above, including parenthesis and underlining, are from Bates's MS. copy of the passage. I have not been able to discover in the Adams MSS. the original address from the Grand Lodge of Massachusetts to John Adams, nor any letterbook copy of John Adams's reply to it. Sheppard printed in full, in reply to John Quincy Adams, the letter of President Adams dated Philadelphia, June 22, 1798. See *Boston Courier,* VIII, No. 2333, September 23, 1831. Bates sent to JQA a copy of the John Adams letter (acknowledged by JQA, September 2, 1831), but I have not been able to find even this copy in the Adams MSS.

[59] JQA to Stephen Bates, Quincy, August 22, 1831. Adams MSS.

[60] JQA to Richard Rush, Quincy, September 17, 1831. Adams MSS.

made it clear that the Antimasons could call him to their banner at Baltimore if they wished. Even then he was in friendly correspondence with his former Secretary of State: on the nature of the Union and the danger of Nullification and the future of the National Republican Party [61]—not on Masonry and Antimasonry. Politics makes and unmakes strange bedfellows. Young Charles Francis Adams questioned his father's complete disinterestedness.[62]

The Kentucky legislature was expected to send Henry Clay back to the Senate, but the National Republicans had made a poor showing in the state and congressional elections of 1831. What with the Antimasonic opposition, Clay's Massachusetts friends, who had nominated him for the Presidency in a legislative caucus, were beginning to have misgivings.

"What do you think we should do?" Joseph E. Sprague, National Republican of Salem, asked Adams confidentially.

"Your legislative caucus nomination of Mr. Clay for the Presidency last winter," pointed out Adams, "has put it out of your power to choose what you will do."

"That was altogether the act of General Dearborn," Sprague declared.

"Further," scolded Adams, "you have kicked and buffeted the Anti-Masonic party until it is impossible for them to support Mr. Clay, and you cannot fail to lose by that operation from sixty to seventy Electoral votes. . . . You are acting under an influence of which you are not aware. Are you a Mason?"

"I am an Antimason," Sprague affirmed.

"Then I do not see how you can support Mr. Clay. He is now the head of the United Masonic and so-called National Republican Party."

"Mr. Clay must be withdrawn," the Salem politician agreed. "Since the Kentucky elections it is clear he cannot succeed. I should like to bring forth Mr. Madison and you."

Adams made no remark on this point, although he understood it perfectly. "I have spoken with perfect confidence to you . . . ," he reminded his interlocutor, "supposing what you have said to have been on your own account alone. I have never been consulted upon the movements of the Party since March 3, 1829. But if you wish my opinions for any other than yourself I am willing to give them, upon condition of knowing by whom, and for whom they are asked." [63]

Obviously Adams was ready to advise the National Republicans to drop Henry Clay if they could find a way of doing so. One way would be for the Antimasons to nominate a man who might heal the breach over Masonry, a man whom the National Republicans could also nominate, a Man of the Whole Nation. Dr. Abner Phelps and George Odiorne [64] came out

[61] JQA to Henry Clay, Quincy, September 7, 1831. Adams MSS.
[62] Diary, August 25–9, 1831. Diary of CFA, August 25, 1831.
[63] *Memoirs*, VIII, 400–1. August 25, 1831.
[64] Antimasonic leader and father of James T. Odiorne, who wrote: *Opinions on*

from Boston to ask Adams if he would be the candidate, notwithstanding the efforts of Charles Francis Adams to dissuade them.[65] Phelps showed a letter from an Antimasonic correspondent in Pittsburgh asking about the former President's views on Masonry.

"My sentiments are sufficiently known to you," responded the first citizen of Quincy. "I have authorized Mr. Bates to publish a letter from me, which will leave no doubt of my views on the mind of any man who reads it. I supposed it would be published before now. I don't know why it hasn't been."

Adams then read aloud from his letterbook the letter to Bates.

"As to the nomination," he continued, "I neither desire it nor even the office of President of the United States itself. I will give no pledge nor make any promise to any man, or body of men, to obtain it. *Nor shall I feel myself called upon to decline a nomination, either by a single individual, or by any body of men. I see no necessity of declining any nomination which any one might please to make.* I have no reason to believe that the Antimasons have thought of me anywhere, and I regret that Mr. Rush has declined the nomination offered to him, because I believe it would have been unanimous. Now I am very apprehensive it won't be. If they propose my name, my only entreaty is that they shall not press it one instant after ascertaining that any other name would be likely to receive a more unanimous vote." [66]

Phelps and Odiorne got the idea all right. Adams was willing for them to toss his hat into the ring. They declared themselves perfectly satisfied. They departed. Four days later Adams's letter to Bates appeared in the Boston *Free Press*.[67]

Next visitor was Joseph Blunt, Adams's faithful and unrequited political supporter in New York City. He had been making a trip through Rhode Island to Massachusetts, talking with Antimasonic leaders. Ostensibly he came to Quincy to inquire about an article Adams was writing for the *American Annual Register*. Quickly he got down to politics. "Since the results of the Kentucky elections," he said, "the National Republicans are satisfied there is no prospect for Mr. Clay for the Presidency. It is advisable to fix upon some other candidate." He mentioned Daniel Webster and

---

Speculative Masonry, Relative to its Origin, Nature and Tendency. A Compilation, Embracing Recent and Important Documents on the Subject, and Exhibiting the Views of the Most Distinguished Writers respecting it. (Boston: Perkins & Marvin; 1830.)

65 ". . . his family felt," said Charles, "and I felt," he added by way of peculiar emphasis, "as if it was hard that the last days of his Life should be molested by attacks more bitter even than any he had yet experienced. That this would be a war of great violence and its result would undoubtedly be defeat. I therefore dissuaded him [Phelps] from making a nomination. . . ." Diary of CFA, August 25, 1831.

66 *Memoirs*, VIII, 403–4. August 27, 1831. Italics inserted.

67 August 31, 1831. Joseph T. Buckingham's pro-Masonic *Boston Courier* reproduced it next day, September 1, 1831.

Chief Justice Marshall, both of whom had pronounced against the institution of Masonry. (Actually Webster was firmly devoted to Clay.[68]) "I suppose if there should be a nomination of you by the Antimasonic Party at Baltimore, your name would come up also before the [National Republican] Convention to meet next December." Blunt was already designated as a delegate to that convention.

"Until a very few days ago," asserted Adams, "the Antimasons have not thought of me anywhere. Now I apprehend it's too late. I am apprehensive they will not agree, and that their party will fall off to different candidates, to the ruin of their cause." [69]

To none of these interviewers, Antimasons or National Republicans, did Adams use the words "our party." He regarded himself above party lines.

Finally William H. Seward came to Quincy. Seward was making ready to attend the Antimasonic Convention as a delegate. The Antimasonic leaders of New York, Pennsylvania, and Ohio were leaning toward Justice John McLean. He seemed most likely to unite the Opposition in the three key states under the banner of the new third party. McLean had come out against Masonry, and gave the Antimasons to understand he would accept their nomination. But the Justice did not go down well with Antimasons in Massachusetts and Rhode Island, who preferred Adams. So Seward made a side trip to those states before he left Albany for Baltimore.[70] His purpose was to reconcile and unite all elements of the new party, if possible, behind McLean.

Seward has left a memorable picture of his first meeting with the ex-President, whom through later years he was to revere and love as "a patron, a guide, a counsellor, and a friend," [71] even as Adams all his life had looked to George Washington.

Adams came down the stairs to meet the visitor. "He was bald, his countenance was staid, sober, almost to gloom or sorrow, and hardly gave indication of his superiority over other men. His eyes were weak and inflamed. He was dressed in an olive frock-coat, a cravat carelessly tied, and old-fashioned, light-colored vest and pantaloons. It was obvious that he was a student, just called from the labors of his closet. Without courtly air or attitude, he paused at the door of the parlor. I walked quite up to him, while he maintained his immovable attitude, and presented my letter of introduction from Tracy. He asked me to sit, read the letter, said he was happy to see me, sat down in the next chair, inquired with the earnestness of a particular friend concerning Tracy's health, my arrival,

[68] "Held a long conversation with Mr. Webster, in which he authorized me to say on all occasions that he was firmly devoted to Mr. Clay." MS. Diary of Edward Everett. August 19 [18], 1831. MHS.

[69] Diary, August 30, 1831.

[70] Blakeslee, op. cit., Chapter VIII, pp. 12–14.

[71] Frederic Bancroft: *The Life of William H. Seward* (2 vols., New York, 1900), I, 201.

etc. . . . Our interview lasted over three hours; he was all the time plain, honest, and free, in his discourse; but with hardly a ray of animation or feeling in the whole of it. In short, he was just exactly what I before supposed he was, a man to be respected for his talents, admired for his learning, honored for his integrity and simplicity, but hardly possessing traits of character to inspire a stranger with affection." [72]

"McLean will accept the nomination," Seward vouchsafed, "but the Antimasons in Boston seemed to favor you."

Adams showed no enthusiasm for the treacherous McLean. "Have you seen Dr. Phelps?" he asked.

Seward, of course, had been conferring with Phelps and the other Antimasonic leaders in Boston. He knew from them that Adams would not decline a nomination. But Adams would leave no doubt in his visitor's mind. He repeated word for word what he had recently told Phelps and Odiorne: if he were to be nominated it must be only because he could get the "most unanimous" vote.[73] He told Seward that he was even then writing something about Freemasonry. He spoke at length of the justice of the Antimasonic movement. Hitherto, he explained, he had not wished to do anything that would injure Mr. Clay's chances for the Presidency and therefore he had been restrained. He regretted that neither Mr. Rush [74] nor himself had advised Clay to abandon the Order, but now the crisis had come.

"I do not desire to be President of the United States again," John Quincy Adams avouched, "even though I had assurance of an unanimous vote. I have had the office. I know its duties, privations, enjoyments, perplexities, and vexations; but if the Antimasons think my nomination would be better than any other I will not decline. I hope they won't mention me except upon the ground that I am the best candidate. . . . I know what the opposing party will say: they will impeach my motives. I don't care about that. I am accustomed to it. I am calloused to it." [75]

"I think we'll be able to agree on a candidate all right," the New York politician assured Adams noncommittally as they parted.

As Seward left the house he felt that he had the answer to the question why "the best President since Washington" had entered and left that high office with so few personal friends.

It was certain that Antimasonic delegates from the Western states would not support the ex-President and that the New England delegates would not line up behind McLean. "Rhode Island and Massachusetts will go to Baltimore in favor of Adams in spite of anything I can do," Seward wrote Weed. "The spirit of New England is jealous of McLean, be-

---

[72] Seward: *Autobiography*, pp. 204–7.

[73] *Memoirs*, VIII, 413. September 14, 1831.

[74] Actually Rush had done so indirectly, through his letter to Edward Ingersoll, a confidential copy of which Adams had. See above, p. 283, n. 41.

[75] Seward: *Autobiography*, pp. 206–7.

cause he is a protégé of Calhoun. I have not erred in believing that this jealousy is grounded upon conversations with Mr. Adams touching Mc-Lean." [76]

Can anyone who reads these characteristic protestations of John Quincy Adams, so similar to those he had expressed to his friends before the election of 1824, can anyone who has read the same kind of declarations and has heard similar ones from Presidential aspirants of our own day, can any sophisticated reader doubt that Adams wanted to be nominated by the Antimasons, hoping that this would also bring him the National Republican nomination over Henry Clay, the two parties then uniting their forces under a Man of the Whole Nation to defeat Andrew Jackson? But that would have to await the events of the month. The Presidential gyroscope, built into his character by John and Abigail Adams, was still holding him to the destiny of his family. Only he must not lift a finger for the office. He must await a Call.

He alerted himself for a Call from Baltimore.

6

Delegates to the Antimasonic Convention arrived at Baltimore mostly divided between Justice John McLean and Adams, with McLean in the ascendant. The latter was willing enough all through his long life to be nominated by any party, be it National Republican, Democratic, Antimasonic, or later Whig, or Republican, any vehicle that afforded a reasonable chance of getting him to the White House before he died. Nevertheless, with Henry Clay coming up for the National Republicans at Baltimore in December 1831, McLean saw no hope for himself. At the last moment he withdrew his name. Chief Justice Marshall, it appeared, would not hear of his own nomination.[77] This left Adams as the only man with substantial support. But it was evident that a majority were unwilling to hand their new standard to a onetime Minority President who had suffered such a defeat in the last election, and against whom Clay's friends might raise the charge of personal disloyalty. In desperation they turned by way of compromise to William Wirt of Maryland, Attorney General during the Administrations of Monroe and Adams—the man with a head like the poet Goethe's, and a lifelong Mason at that! Overnight [78] Weed and others persuaded him to renounce Masonry because of the Morgan murder—even a remote vision of Paris was worth a Mass.

Wirt's statement of acceptance when analyzed was not too greatly different from Clay's position: he had long since ceased to be an active Ma-

[76] Weed: *Memoir*, p. 41.

[77] Samuel Rhea Gammon: *The Presidential Campaign of 1832* (Baltimore: Johns Hopkins University Studies in Historical and Political Science, Series XL, No. 1; 1922), p. 49.

[78] Weed: *Autobiography*, p. 391.

son through lack of interest; he did not believe that those Masons implicated in the Morgan crimes characterized the whole Order. Therefore he
gave the convention an opportunity to change its nomination if they
wished. Of this the Antimasons did not take advantage.[79]

Having learned that Governor Levi Lincoln of Massachusetts would
not accept second place on the ticket, the convention then nominated
Amos Ellmaker, Antimasonic leader of Pennsylvania, for Vice President.
All concerned, Weed, Seward, McLean, Richard Rush, and John Quincy
Adams, professed to be satisfied, but none was really happy about it, not
even Wirt.[80]

Only Charles Francis Adams was perfectly content. "I am very highly
delighted," he wrote in his still unpublished Diary, "with this, and both
from my father's *not* being named, and Mr. Wirt being the man, am almost a disciple." [81]

Adams had already taken his seat in the Twenty-second Congress when
the next news came from Baltimore: the National Republicans in their
first and last national convention had nominated Henry Clay, by acclamation, for President, and John Sergeant for Vice President.

7

In the Presidential campaign of 1832 Adams took no part for Clay or
Wirt, though everybody of course knew that he was opposed to Jackson
and the Democrats.[82] But he did not yet desert the Antimasonic cause. "I
could probably be more useful to their cause," he had told Seward at
Quincy, "if they should not nominate me than if they should." [83] Immediately after the Baltimore Convention of September 1831 he began a
campaign with his pen deliberately designed to bring the defenders of
Masonry out into public discussion by confronting them with a series of
charges.

Again circumstances played into his hands conveniently to set the controversy into motion. Edward Ingersoll of Philadelphia, the confidant of
both Clay and Rush and a long-standing friend of Adams, had written
saying that he had been told that Adams was a zealous Antimason: he
hoped that this did not extend to "political Antimasonry"—that would
only serve to keep alive under the bite of persecution a "silly" institution

[79] Van Deusen: *Clay*, p. 243. Wirt's letter of acceptance, September 28, 1831, is
printed in *Niles' Register*, XLI, 83–5.

[80] Erik McKinley Eriksson, Ph.D., has appraised, for the benefit of twentieth-
century Masons, "William Wirt: Anti-Masonic Presidential Candidate," in *Grand
Lodge Bulletin*, XXVII, No. 4 (Cedar Rapids, Iowa, 1926), 120–5.

[81] CFA Diary, October 2, 1831.

[82] Adams did not leave Quincy for Washington until after election day in Massachusetts; but his MS Diary for that day, November 5, 1832, makes no mention of the
election or of his voting.

[83] *Memoirs*, VIII, 413. September 14, 1831.

that had discredited itself so as to have outlived its usefulness. Political Antimasonry would only divide the Opposition and certainly re-elect Jackson. The whole Masonic Order, containing so many good and patriotic men, ought not to be held responsible for the excesses of a few.[84]

Adams promptly responded in three long letters that found their way into the newspapers. He had no desire, he said, to impugn the honor and integrity of many worthy individuals who were members of the fraternity, but he could no longer remain silent in the face of the Morgan crimes. "I am a zealous Antimason—to this extent— It is my deliberate opinion that from the time of . . . the kidnapping and murder of William Morgan, it became the solemn and sacred, civic and social duty of every Masonic Lodge in the United States, either to dissolve itself, or to discard forever . . . all oaths, all penalties, all secrets, and all fantastic titles, exhibitions and ceremonies hitherto used in the Institution." Only belatedly and reluctantly, notwithstanding the perjury and slanders directed against himself in 1828 and against his father recently, had he just made his stand public in the letter to Stephen Bates.

"Murder" was a plain word, but no Mason dared to sue John Quincy Adams, or Richard Rush, for using it. It would open too dangerous a judicial inquiry. More cautiously Adams went on to list, in the form of an interrogatory, a whole cluster of Masonic crimes in addition to kidnapping and murder: fraudulent abuse, infamous slander, libel, conspiracy, arson, fraud, and false imprisonment.[85]

Ingersoll was helpless to respond to the indictment except for petty technicalities. He suggested that Adams's inquiries be addressed to William Wirt, now the Antimasonic candidate, or to Colonel William L. Stone, editor of the *Weekly Commercial Advertiser*.[86] It was finally agreed that Stone, who was looking for some sort of vehicle for a history of the controversy, should make the response in a series of letters to John Quincy Adams. The New York editor performed the work promptly and conscientiously and published the letters in book form in June 1832 [87] in the middle of the Presidential campaign. It was more of a frank exposé than it was a defense of Freemasonry. So hostile was the reaction of his Masonic friends that Stone finally had to quit the Order altogether. His *Letters to John Quincy Adams on Masonry and Antimasonry* became one of the most copious and reliable of all the documentary supports of Antimasonry. About all that he could say by way of extenuation for the institution was that the words of the oaths, penalties, and obligations didn't really mean what they said, or were not so understood by honorable and intelligent Masons; that the texts varied in different parts of the country; that the real secrets were harmless tokens, symbols, grips, and signals by

[84] Edward Ingersoll to JQA, Philadelphia, September 14, 1831. Adams MSS.
[85] JQA: *Masonic Institution*, pp. 14–24.
[86] Edward Ingersoll to JQA, October 19, 1831. Adams MSS.
[87] William L. Stone to JQA, New York, June 17, 1832. Adams MSS.

which the brethren identified each other in the presence of strangers; that it was unfair to hold honest and fair-minded members of the Order responsible for the misdeeds of a few irresponsible individuals.

In a most friendly manner Adams replied to Stone's remaining defenses of Masonry. In a series of letters, which Stone published in his *Commercial Advertiser* in August and September 1832 and which were widely reprinted throughout the country, Adams gave credit to Stone's honesty and sincerity. It was not the secret tokens, Adams pointed out, but the secret oaths (which Stone had not classified as secret) that were really bad. One could not get away from their literal wording, horrible enough to put to shame a "common cannibal." And it must be remembered that these oaths were taken expressly without reservation of any kind, subject to cruel and unusual punishment, barbaric penalties. That the texts varied from place to place only helped make them worse and worse. Fruit of these oaths, their obligations, and penalties, Adams stated, was nothing less than the whole group of crimes leading to "foul and midnight murder." [88]

There was indeed no effective answer, no plausible palliation that could be marshaled against Adams's formidable indictment, but it did not help one whit to defeat Andrew Jackson.

Jackson's triumph over Antimasons and National Republicans did not dampen Adams's Antimasonic ardor now that he had committed himself so deeply before all the world. In the spring and early summer of 1833 he embarked upon another series of public epistles, this time addressed to Secretary of State Edward Livingston, who was General Grand High Priest of the General Royal Arch Chapter of the United States, highest Masonic office in the land. Adams itched to get this luminary into a public controversy.

Livingston was a most distinguished jurist, humanitarian, and statesman. Adams respected him highly as draftsman of Jackson's famous proclamation against the Nullifiers of South Carolina, as author of the Louisiana code of civil law and of a world-famous treatise on penal law advocating abolition of the death penalty. At the time of installation into his most exalted Masonic office, April 3, 1830, Livingston had delivered an address to the fraternity deploring current "persecution" of the Order. He branded as false the "calumnies" directed against it. "An intelligent and enlightened community will not be deceived by them." [89] Without explicitly denying that individual Masons had kidnapped and murdered William Morgan, Livingston declared that the crimes were not due to any "secret tenets" of Freemasonry. Extolling the patriots who had been members of the fraternity, the pious pastors, and many worthy men who still

[88] JQA: *Masonic Institution*, pp. 47–95.

A long narrative statement on "The Murder of William Morgan," never printed, is to be found in the Adams MSS.

[89] *National Intelligencer* (Washington), XXXI, No. 4475, April 22, 1830.

were in the brotherhood, he exhorted his fellow members not to be tempted by the example of their enemies to the slightest interference in parties nor to any exercise of political intrigue. As for the calumnies against the Order, let them be met with "dignified silence." Under Livingston's grand high priesthood the General Royal Arch Chapter at its next meeting, in November 1832, enjoined the fraternity to adhere to its "ancient landmarks"—that is, to the ritual and degrees of the institution with their oaths, obligations, and penalties, including the death penalty.

Adams, publicly addressing Livingston, rolled the grand high priest's lavish honorifics ridiculously over and over again in long and solemn tautology. If this pompous brotherhood chose to vote in favor of their own members for public office, he asked, if Masonic judges, jurors, and legislators discriminated against Antimasons, how could they object if the latter voted against them? After all there was no compulsion on free voters to vote either way. And how could Livingston as Secretary of State, how could Andrew Jackson as Chief Magistrate of the Union, having taken their Masonic vows, be expected to be impartial in the appointment of public servants, in the administration of the laws of the land? As a humanitarian how could Livingston justify the barbaric oaths, their cruel and unusual penalties, with his own conscientious opposition to the death penalty? How now, Mr. Livingston, was it not Masons who did the kidnapping, who committed the murder? And what had the Order done about it? Nothing but adhere to its *ancient landmarks*.[90]

Livingston's only answer was "dignified silence." It did not meet the charges, but it was probably the most painful reply that could be made to an Adams.

8

During the late summer of 1833 Adams took leave of his polemical labors for a ten days' excursion with Mr. and Mrs. Isaac P. Davis of Boston through New Hampshire and the White Mountains in the hope of improving his health and raising his spirits. Marveling at the sublimity of New England scenery and the majestic face of the Old Man of the Mountains, he experienced momentarily a "cheering influence in the darkness of my declining days." But he came back unwell and discouraged. He felt that the tide of life had turned against him. He worried over the fact that there was no male heir among his son's children to carry on the family name and destiny:

"All is discouraging and gloomy. There is a tide in the Affairs of Men, and when that Tide turns against them in the decline of life, exertion is Vain, Prayer is inefficacious. No blessing of Heaven, no smile of Fortune seconds the purest purposes and most unwearied energies. To lie down and die is a privilege denied. A lingering death tortured with disappointments more and more aggravated, and prospects beyond the grave of no

[90] JQA: *Masonic Institution,* pp. 115–203.

promise for this world, are all that I can see or expect. So it is that prosperous Fortunes go to ruin, and so it is that families are extinguished." [91]

From these depths of gloom and despair and approaching death and dissolution his spirits leapt back as by a miracle with the birth of a fine boy to Charles and Abby Adams on September 23, 1833.[92] The parents gave to their first male child the name of John Quincy Adams. The destiny of the family seemed to rest on this infant. On the day of baptism and christening the grandfather turned over to Charles Francis Adams the family seal: *Piscemur, Venemur ut Olim* [93]—used by John Adams when he signed the final treaty of peace and independence in 1783—to pass on to this child or any other that the young father might elect, to be transmitted in like manner, "so long as it shall please Heaven to continue the family and the name, as an admonitory Memorial of John Adams. And with it I hope and pray," added John Quincy Adams, "that you . . . will ever remember the Motto which the first owner selected for his Seal at Arms: *Fidem, Libertatem, Amicitiam retinebis.*" [94]

The old warrior's spirits and with them his ambition revived. He was ready again for the political fray.

9

John Quincy Adams had been ready and willing to run for President again in 1832 on the Antimasonic ticket, or the National Republican platform, or both, if he had been offered the opportunity. If he could not have that, he was not unwilling, so it proved, to run for Governor of Massachusetts in the same manner. News of the Antimasonic Convention had hardly arrived from Baltimore in 1831 when the Antimasonic Party of Massachusetts nominated him for that office. He declined their nomination that year if only because he would have had to oppose his friend Governor Levi Lincoln, with whose general principles he was in agreement and who had just issued a statement that he was not connected with the Masons in any way, disapproved of their oaths and ritual, although he would not make a party question out of Freemasonry.[95]

This was as far as Adams himself had been willing to go in public in 1831. By September 1833, however, he had committed himself to abolition of Masonic oaths through use of the elective franchise to overthrow opposing Masonic majorities in state legislatures.[96] Levi Lincoln was no longer in the way. After serving nine consecutive terms as Governor he

[91] Diary, August 25–September 9, 1833.

[92] *Memoirs*, IX, 17–18.

[93] See Vol. I, 220.

[94] JQA to CFA, October 27, 1833. Adams MSS. Diary of CFA, October 27, 1833.

[95] *Memoirs*, VII, 414–15. Lincoln's statement of September 13, 1831 is printed in *Boston Press*, I, No. 87, September 30, 1831.

[96] JQA to Benjamin Cowell of Providence, November 28, 1832. JQA: *Masonic Institution*, pp. 107–12.

had now decided to stand for election to the national House of Representatives, with the hope that the state legislature would soon promote him to the Senate. The Antimasonic Convention of Massachusetts, meeting in Boston, finding itself unable to agree upon opposing candidates within the party, turned "unanimously" to Adams. Edward Everett and other National Republican leaders [97] had given Adams to expect the nomination of their party for Governor too if he would but take that of the Antimasons first,[98] thus healing a division in the state among those who looked the same way on the politics of the Union.

Adams therefore accepted the Antimasonic nomination for Governor professedly with a sense of duty in the hope that he might thus reunite the shattered fragments of the National Republican Party that had supported his Administration as President and continued to uphold its principles in Massachusetts until Freemasonry broke it up.[99] He did not consider himself otherwise pledged.[100] In his letter of acceptance he was careful not to speak to the Antimasons as a party, nor did he make any mention of their principles. He addressed merely a "large, respectable, and virtuous portion of the People of the Commonwealth," with whom he would work "to merge all party spirit and feeling in the great interests of the whole Commonwealth," in order *to heal the divisions of Party, to promote the Harmony of the Union,* and to maintain the industry of freedom and the *purity of the Constitution.*" [101]

It was the same pattern of hope that had beckoned to him for a moment on a national scale before the Baltimore Conventions of 1831.

The solid men of Boston and of Essex and Norfolk Counties would have nothing more to do with John Quincy Adams as a candidate for Governor. Already once alienated by his controversy with the Thirteen Confederates, they were furious at his taking up with the Antimasons. When it became apparent that they would not accept him as their candidate too, he offered to withdraw in favor of Edward Everett or any other National Republican acceptable to the Antimasons. But a Masonic and "blue-light" Federalist phalanx [102] within the party put through the name of John Davis of Worcester, another colleague of Adams in the House of Representatives, who had the support also of Governor Lincoln. Adams would not abandon the field to Davis, at least not before the people had

[97] Blakeslee, op. cit., Chapter IX, p. 18, cites the *Boston Daily Advertiser* of August 18, 1833 to suggest that Daniel Webster was one of those who lent themselves to the encouragement of Adams with the hope of expecting the National Republican nomination for him too.

[98] *Memoirs,* VIII, 535.

[99] *Memoirs,* IX, 15; JQA to A. H. Everett, Quincy, September 24, 1833; JQA to Benjamin F. Hallett, Washington, December 16, 1833. Adams MSS.

[100] JQA to CFA, Washington, December 19, 1833. Adams MSS.

[101] JQA to the Anti-Masonic Convention for the Commonwealth of Massachusetts assembled at Boston. Quincy, September 12, 1833. Adams MSS. Italics inserted.

[102] JQA to Richard Rush, Quincy, October 1, 1833. Adams MSS.

spoken at the polls. That he realized his persistence might split the opposition to the Jacksonian Democrats [103] is evident by the fact that he sent word to the "Antimasonics," through his son Charles, that in case the popular election should not give a clear majority to any one candidate, then they should drop his name when the contest came before the Massachusetts legislature, thus allowing the opposition to the Democracy to concentrate its undivided strength upon the two candidates that must, by the terms of the state constitution, be sent up by the state House of Representatives to the Senate for final choice.[104]

Adams was already on his way to the national capital before the election took place. As he was speeding on the new railroad across the neck of New Jersey from Perth Amboy to Bordentown he clocked the train, running in two sections of six or seven cars each to take care of upward of two hundred passengers and baggage. It was going sixty feet per second—over forty miles an hour! Suddenly the car in which he was riding in the second section went off the rails and over on its side, then back upright. The train lurched along two hundred feet to a stop. One car was upset and almost demolished, only one of its sixteen passengers unhurt. Men, women, and children were scattered along the roadbed, bleeding, mangled, and tortured. At Adams's request a coroner's inquest was held on the spot, at which he testified, then proceeded, himself unscratched, on the reconstructed train.[105] He reached Philadelphia safely, finally Washington, before the popular election took place at home.

The vote in Massachusetts for Governor was:

John Davis (National Republican)	25,149
John Quincy Adams (Antimasonic)	18,274
Marcus Morton (Democrat)	15,493
Samuel C. Allen (Workingmen's candidate)	3,495 [106]

The voters had proved that they did not regard John Quincy Adams as the man of the whole people, that he was at best a minority candidate

---

[103] JQA to Pliny Merrick, Antimasonic leader in Worcester. Washington, February 7, 1834. Adams MSS.

[104] *Memoirs*, IX, 58.

The Constitution of Massachusetts (as of 1833) provided, Chapter II, Article 3: ". . . But if no person shall have a majority of votes, the House of Representatives shall, by ballot, elect two out of four who had the highest number of votes, if so many shall have been voted for; and make return to the Senate of the two persons so elected; on which, the Senate shall proceed, by ballot, to elect one, who shall be declared Governor."

By an amendment (No. X) ratified in 1831, the election of state officers was fixed for the second Monday of November every year.

[105] *Memoirs*, IX, 29–32. JQA to CFA, Washington, November 10, 1833. Adams MSS. Only one person was killed.

[106] Arthur B. Darling: *Political Changes in Massachusetts, 1828–1848: A Study of Liberal Movements in Politics* (New Haven, 1925), p. 115.

for Governor of his own state, as once he had been a minority candidate for President of the United States. No candidate having won a majority of popular votes, the election went before the legislature of Massachusetts for decision much the same way that the contested Presidential election of 1824 had gone to the House of Representatives in Washington in 1825. This time, as if admonished by his unfortunate Presidential bargain with Clay [107] and by his unhappy experience as Minority President, Adams refused to make a deal of any kind.[108] He placed in the hands of his son Charles a letter to the speaker of the state House of Representatives withdrawing his name from the contest as soon as the legislature convened.[109] In private letters to Charles and other friends he declared himself in favor of Davis, the man most preferred by the people and Adams's personal preference as well. After the legislature had seated John Davis in the Governor's chair [110] (January 9, 1834), Charles Francis Adams released to the press [111] a long statement by his father: *An Address to the People of Massachusetts.*[112] This *apologia pro sua vita Antimasonica* [113] took occasion once more to repeat all the charges against the oaths, obligations, and penalties of Freemasonry, and justified his withdrawal in favor of the people's preference.

How different was Adams's action in 1833 toward John Davis in Massachusetts from his course vis-à-vis Andrew Jackson, the people's preference for President of the United States in 1825! [114] Then he had made an implicit bargain with Henry Clay—though not a corrupt bargain—for the first office of the nation according to the provisions of the Constitution. He had done this to fulfill the destiny of his family. Now he was nearing the end of his expected span of life. At last the Presidential gyroscope showed signs of running down. He was about through with Destiny. It

[107] "My election [as President in 1825] was effected in the House by the junction of the fourth and excluded Candidate's [Clay's] supporters with mine, and that operation produced the subsequent failure of my reelection, the triumphal elevation of my Successor; and the irretrievable disappointment of him who had as a last resource linked his political fortunes with mine, but who from that hour was deserted and betrayed by his own party." JQA to Robert Walsh, Washington, April 16, 1836. Adams MSS.

[108] JQA to CFA, Boston, December 13, 19, 1833. See also Benjamin F. Hallett to JQA, Boston, December 7, 1833; John Bailey to JQA, Boston, December 10, 1833; JQA to Hallett, December 16, 1833; JQA to John Bailey, December 17, 1833, January 2, 13, 1834. Adams MSS.

[109] JQA to CFA, No. 3, Washington, November 19, 1833. Adams MSS.

[110] Blakeslee, op. cit., Chapter IX, has the best account of the contested election in Massachusetts.

[111] *Boston Press and Daily Advocate,* January 10, 1834.

[112] Reprinted in JQA: *Masonic Institution,* pp. 218–74.

[113] JQA to CFA, No. 12, December 31, 1833. Adams MSS.

[114] John Quincy Adams did not admit any real analogy. See JQA to CFA, No. 7, Washington, December 12, 1833. Adams MSS.

was up to Charles Francis Adams and the precious grandson John Quincy Adams, 2d, to carry on the family's name and fame.

Charles was beginning to realize the heavy responsibilities that were upon him: "The continuance of the family in a male branch renders it more necessary for me not only to support myself by prudence but to guide to the utmost of my feeble abilities the course of the future successors." He didn't really think his abilities were feeble: he felt that he was one of only two or three well-educated men in Boston.[115] Nevertheless he prayed for help in keeping future generations of Adamses up to the standard set by John Adams and John Quincy Adams: "May God in his mercy look with favor upon my efforts." [116]

To the charge of leaving the Antimasons in the lurch John Quincy Adams declared he had never been a real party man anyway. "I have been styled a deserter from all parties," he complained to his confidential political correspondent Benjamin F. Hallett, editor of the Antimasonic *Boston Press and Daily Advocate,* "because I truly never belonged to any party. I have acted with parties, sometimes one, and sometimes another. I never have worn the collar of any. Parties have taken me up and cast me off, just as it suited their caprice or their pleasure; but the true fact is that they have deserted me, and their principles with me. I never deserted them. . . ." [117]

These self-justifications simply do not ring true. The historian and biographer could turn them the other way round just as plausibly. Adams dropped the Antimasonic Party in Massachusetts, just as Richard Rush did in Pennsylvania, because they realized that it was as dead as William Morgan. The only difference between him and Rush was that Rush went over to the Jacksonian Democrats and took his stand against the Bank of the United States.

When the Massachusetts legislature, like the legislatures of Vermont and Rhode Island, finally (1834) passed a law against the administration or the receiving of extrajudicial oaths, Adams could feel that his bout with "the old Handmaiden" was over, for it was the oaths, obligations, and penalties, not the host of worthy individuals who belonged to the Order, that he had made the brunt of his attacks.

Freemasonry was no longer the greatest single political evil besetting the Union, as Adams had declared to Stone in 1832, not even one of the greatest, as he had maintained to Livingston in 1833. It was not as dangerous as Nullification, not so menacing as slavery, not so perilous even as Jacksonian Democracy. And politically there was nothing left in it. So

115 CFA Diary, September 29, 1833.

116 Ibid.

117 JQA to Benjamin F. Hallett, Washington, December 16, 1833; to John S. C. Knowlton, editor of the Worcester *Palladium,* Washington, February 14, 1834; to Henry Sewall, of Augusta, Maine. Quincy, August 25, 1834. Adams MSS.

he took leave of the Antimasons *as a party*,[118] although he continued to write public and private letters against Masonic oaths, obligations, and penalties,[119] and even to consult with Antimasonic members of Congress.

Charles Francis Adams, no longer a political apprentice to his father but a full-fledged and intimate adviser, was now twenty-six years old. With all the maturity of "approaching middle stage of life," [120] Charles was satisfied with the elder statesman's course: Antimasonry was becoming too radical, too opposed to the established order of Society! [121] And John Quincy Adams himself was increasingly dismayed at the general tendency of Antimasons to oppose a recharter of the Bank of the United States.

It remained for Weed and Seward patiently to pick up the shattered pieces of Antimasonry and National Republicanism, beginning in New York, then here, there, and everywhere, and put them together purposefully to form the new Whig Party.

10

One very apparent fruit of the Antimasonic excitement had been its withering effect upon the Order of Freemasonry. The fraternity became so unpopular that a great many lodges ceased to exist. Membership in New York State shrank from 20,000 to 3,000 between 1826 and 1836: of 507 lodges that existed there before 1826, there were only 50 left ten years later. All over the Northern states the Masonic ranks were decimated. In western New York the institution was practically defunct. In Vermont, the one state temporarily captured by the Antimasonic Party,

[118] "It is very clear that if I had been elected Governor the Anti-Masonic Sanhedrin at Boston would have asserted the same controul over me, and that I, not being formed of materials quite so plastic, should have broken down myself and perhaps have broken them down with me. Mr. Bailey writes me that they are now generally satisfied with the course that I have taken and approve the Address—and I have now taken my leave of them as a Party." JQA to CFA, No. 14, Washington, January 18, 1834. Adams MSS.

[119] JQA: *Masonic Institution*, pp. 204–18. JQA to George Bancroft, Washington, October 31, 1834, Quincy, October 25, 1835. *Bulletin of New York Public Library*, X (1906), 234–8.

[120] Diary of CFA, January 1, 1834.

[121] "You say in your Letter of 18 January that you have taken your leave of them as a party. I am on the whole satisfied that you do right because it seems to me pretty clear that your object and the object of the movers here are not exactly the same. There is in connection with the ostensible ground of secession from the principles of National Republicanism, a strong secret cause, a tendency to the errors of radicalism, to the dislike of the established order of Society by which talent does not always maintain the ascendency over wealth. Wealth to be sure is sometimes supercilious and in this case of Masonry has been unfortunately so. . . ." CFA to JQA, No. 15, Boston, February 7, 1834. Adams MSS.

the Order ceased to exist. Lodges in other states were in suspended animation during the years of the excitement, with few or no meetings.[122]

After the absorption of the Antimasonic constituency into the Whig Party the evangelical element transferred its interest to the antislavery crusade. A greatly chastened Freemasonry keeping quietly to its "ancient landmarks" eventually recovered its health and membership—though never so greatly in proportion to the nation's population as in former times—but never again was it to be a factor in politics, not in the United States.

John Quincy Adams had said about all that remained to be said against Freemasonry as practiced during his lifetime.[123] In numerous editions since then his writings on the subject [124] have come down to us as a warning against the influence of secret organizations in American politics.

The Antimasonic crusade had won nothing for him but an outlet for his compulsive genius for political contention. It made him enemies and lost him friends. It interrupted his long intimacy with Governor Levi Lincoln [125] and seriously disturbed his confidence in Richard Rush.[126]

[122] Blakeslee, op. cit., Chapter IX.

[123] In the mass of Antimasonic writings before Stone's *Letters to JQA* there were two outstanding works by seceding Masons that greatly influenced Adams's thought: David Bernard's *Light on Free-Masonry* . . . (Utica, 1829), and Avery Allyn's *Ritual of Free Masonry* . . . (Philadelphia, 1831). They confirmed Morgan's revelation of the first three degrees and made public all the remaining degrees, ritual, and other secrets of the Order. Dr. Erik McKinley Eriksson has published a useful summary with bibliographical notes of "John Quincy Adams: Anti-Masonic Letter Writer," in *Grand Lodge Bulletin*, XXVII, No. 3 (Cedar Rapids, Iowa, 1926), 87–94.

[124] It is the edition of 1847, op. cit., above, p. 273, that has been cited in this chapter. The Preface is by Charles Francis Adams at the request of his father, who was not able to sign his name at this time, much less to write an introduction, as desired by the publisher. JQA to Henry Gappett, Boston. Washington, March 26, 1847. Adams MSS. Other editions appeared during the Ku-Klux activities of Reconstruction days: *Letters of the Honorable John Quincy Adams on the Nature of Masonic Oaths, Obligations, and Penalties, to Colonel William L. Stone, Edward Livingston, and Others* (Philadelphia: William S. Young; 1867). *Letters and Addresses on Freemasonry, by John Quincy Adams, with an Introduction by Charles Francis Adams* . . . (Dayton, Ohio: United Brethren Publishing House; 1875).

[125] For the correspondence see JQA to John Brazer Davis, Philadelphia, April 6, 1832; to Governor Levi Lincoln, private, Philadelphia, April 6, 1832, Quincy, October 10, 1833, and Washington, December 5, 1833, "private, not secret nor confidential"; Levi Lincoln to JQA, October 14, December 9, 21, 1833. A 20,000-word draft letter by JQA to Lincoln, never sent, is also among the Adams MSS. The two men quickly made up with each other as members of the Massachusetts delegation to Congress. Blakeslee, op. cit., Chapter IX, pp. 18–30, has an excellent account of the Massachusetts gubernatorial campaign and election of 1833–4.

[126] "I can never repose confidence in him again. One of the inevitable consequences of his defection will be the ruin of the Anti-Masonic cause in Pennsylvania; and it will go far to abolish it throughout the Union. There is a moral obliquity in his course which proves that his principles sit lightly upon him, and that he cannot stand fire in a minority very long." *Memoirs*, IX, 40. November 29, 1832. Cordial relations

"I subject myself to so much toil and so much enmity," he lamented over the writing table of his chamber in the Quincy Mansion, "with so very little apparent fruit, that I sometimes ask myself whether I do not mistake my own motives. The best actions of my life make me nothing but enemies." [127]

between Rush and Adams were eventually restored in 1842. JQA to Richard Rush, Washington, December 30, 1842. Adams MSS.

[127] *Memoirs,* VIII, 26. October 25, 1833.

CHAPTER XVI
Politics Still Stops at the Water's Edge
(1835 – 1836)

The principle with which I have gone through life,
under every administration of the Government, has
been, in controversies with foreign powers, to sustain the existing authorities of my own Country—
especially and most zealously when the *right* of the
main question was on our side, and the *wrong* on
the side of the foreigner.

JOHN QUINCY ADAMS TO MORTON EDDY,
WASHINGTON, MAY 1, 1836 [1]

JOHN QUINCY ADAMS still looked upon himself as the Man of the Whole
Nation. In December 1834 his constituents had elected him for his third
term in Congress upon nominations by both the Antimasonic and Whig
Parties of his district. He considered this action as a local endorsement
of himself by those parties rather than his endorsement of them. And he
felt that he also had an implied mandate from Democrats of the Plymouth
district, because they put up no candidate to oppose him. So he made it
clear to both Whigs and Antimasons that, although he thought the Jackson Administration more often wrong than right, and the Whigs more
often right than wrong, he would support the Administration when it
brought forth "constitutional" measures for the general welfare.[2] This high
resolve of nonpartisanship met its first test in one of the outstanding issues
of foreign policy during the Jackson era. It concerned the faithful execution of a treaty that Andrew Jackson had finally succeeded in making, for
the settlement of long-standing claims against France.

[1] Adams MSS.
[2] JQA to Solomon Lincoln of Hingham, Massachusetts, accepting the Whig nomination for Congress. Washington, November 8, 1834. See also JQA to secretaries of a
Whig Meeting of the Young Men of Boston, Washington, November 12, 1834; JQA
to Benjamin F. Hallett, Washington, January 30, 1835. Adams MSS.

1

The vexatious claims originated in maritime spoliations on neutral American shipping during the Napoleonic Wars of 1803 to 1815. If one could lay aside the more heinous wrong of impressment, it would be difficult to say which of the two belligerents, Great Britain or France, had been the greater violator of American neutral rights during that conflict. The United States finally submitted its grievances against Great Britain to the arbitrament of war in the hope of conquering Canada, and the Floridas too (from Spain, the ally of Britain). The war yielded precisely nothing: the Peace of Ghent canceled all maritime claims of either party against the other—that was the end of the British issue.

With France peaceful diplomacy merely kept the question alive during and after the wars. Until 1820 that nation was busy paying off a schedule of 700,000,000 francs for reparations imposed by the victorious Allies after Napoleon's final overthrow. Successive French Governments did not deny the American claims but, pleading incapacity, resisted all efforts to settle them. After reparations were fulfilled and the Allied armies evacuated French soil, the Government of Charles X put off the American Minister, Albert Gallatin, with procrastination and counterclaims and showed no real desire to settle. Meanwhile France paid an indemnity of 1,000,000,-000 francs to royalist émigrés returning to their native land.

John Quincy Adams as Secretary of State and President made no headway during eleven years of languid dealing with the French Question. The American claimants themselves reckoned their claims at $7,775,000,[3] doubtless inflated. People other than the claimants showed little interest in the matter. Was it not a problem of wartime traders' risks balanced by compensating insurances? Secretary of State Henry Clay had suggested a message to Congress urging the issue of letters of marque and reprisal if France continued to withhold satisfaction, but the President was unwilling to resort to other than peaceful measures.[4] Sensing this, French Governments held to their easy contumacy. Shortly after Adams left the White House he advised a correspondent that the spoliation claims were not worth ten cents on the dollar.[5] His lack of success in dealing with them was one of the few failures of his justly celebrated career as a diplomatist. The reason for it was that, given public apathy, he had not wished to risk a rupture with a friendly nation over what seemed to so many people such a small matter, of private concern rather than paramount public interest.

Jackson's advent to the Presidency with a broad mandate of popular support put a different accent on a dispute that was slowly sinking unre-

³ *ASPFR*, VI, 384.
⁴ *Memoirs*, VII, 55.
⁵ JQA to James Alden of Philadelphia, Meridian Hill, April 6, 1829. Adams MSS.

solved into history. The new Administration, uncommitted to any previous course of action, or inaction, could tackle the French Question with fresh approach and new vigor. Jackson had a well-known record of challenging boldness in dealing with adversaries personal and political, at home and abroad. He further had the ability to arouse the people's patriotism and put them solidly behind him and the nation.

The claimants—most of them by now heirs or assigns—took heart. They staged mass meetings in New York and other cities, urging a special mission to France. They inspired the mercantile press with sympathetic editorials. They flooded the Department of State with fresh memorials. But Secretary of State Van Buren advised against that time-honored device of American diplomacy, a special mission, as an impressive last recourse for peace. The peace was not yet in danger. The President therefore entrusted the question to William C. Rives of Virginia, whom he sent to France as regular Minister.

Rives met nothing but empty amenities until Jackson in his first annual message to Congress described the unsatisfied claims as a subject of "unpleasant discussion" and "possible collision." Even this allusion provoked from the reactionary Government of Charles X little more than a disposition to argue. Rives advised the President to make the claims a question of national interest and honor if he was to get anywhere with them. Then came the July Revolution of 1830, bringing in the liberal monarchy of Louis-Philippe. The new King had been an exile in the United States. He had warm memories of old friends and kindly treatment. Politically he was liberal-minded, an admirer of American institutions. General Lafayette, as commander of the national guard, the power behind the throne, was a citizen of both countries, long a moderator of Franco-American diplomatic discussions. In deference to "firm and cordial friendship" to be expected from this new French regime, Jackson lowered rather than raised his tone. In his next annual message, of 1830, he expressed a patient expectation of removing an "old and vexatious subject of difference."

So far Jackson and Van Buren had taken no stronger ground than John Quincy Adams and Clay before them. Thanks to the July Revolution, Rives was able after long and patient negotiation to sign the treaty of July 4, 1831. By this instrument, unanimously ratified by the United States Senate, France agreed to pay a lump sum of 25,000,000 francs ($5,000,000) for complete satisfaction of all American claims without discussing further their legal merits, and the United States agreed to pay 1,500,000 francs ($300,000) for full release of counterweighing French claims. Further the United States agreed to lower tariff duties on French wines progressively over a period of ten years, for which concession France agreed to abandon claims for damages arising out of denial of unconditional most-favored-nation treatment for her ships and commerce in the ports of the Louisiana cession. Payment of the 25,000,000 francs (for distribution by the United States among the American claimants) was to be made in six annual installments of 4,166,666.66 francs each plus interest on remaining unpaid installments beginning one year following the exchange of ratifications of the treaty. American payments to France were to be deducted proportionately from each French installment.

Louis-Philippe ratified the treaty promptly, and the United States Congress quickly passed the legislation deemed necessary to put the special tariff reductions into effect. When time for payment of the first installment came round, the Secretary of the Treasury handed to the Bank of the United States for collection a draft on the French Treasury for the scheduled amount. In due time it bounced right back across the Atlantic —and Nicholas Biddle debited the Treasury his usual charge of fifteen per cent on protested drafts! French fiscal authorities had refused payment because the Legislative Chamber, which must initiate all expenditures, had not made the necessary appropriations. It turned out that the Government had not even requested it to do so.[6]

The Old Hero's wrath was now mounting, but still he patiently held his fire. He appointed Edward Livingston, once one of his staff officers at the Battle of New Orleans, to go to France and get payment of the treaty money started. Already the reader has made Livingston's acquaintance as Jackson's Secretary of State as well as Grand High Priest of the Grand General Royal Arch Chapter of Freemasonry in the United States, the dignitary at whose honorifics John Quincy Adams poked such solemn ridicule, but withal a statesman and scholar who knew well the French language, law, and constitution. Livingston labored at the Court of Louis-Philippe until the amiable King affably promised to send to the Chambers the necessary request for a specific appropriation. Jackson continued to be hopeful, but the French Chamber still held back. The members affected dudgeon at the President's presumption in trying to collect a draft before the money was voted. After a five-day debate they turned down a report of their own committee recommending the appropriation.

France, it seemed, would pay foreign indemnities only when alien armies occupied her soil!

Here was a pretty how-de-do. French legislators apparently were convinced that the United States Government and people would not make real trouble over such a small matter, treaty or no treaty. Livingston wrote home that the President should take measures to show he would no longer be trifled with.

The proud Jackson still kept his peace, *suaviter in modo, fortiter in re,* awaiting the effect of further diplomatic remonstrance. After a newly elected Chamber failed to do anything, he referred the matter to Congress in more dynamic terms, in his annual message of December 7, 1834.

---

[6] Richard Aubrey McLemore has published a most helpful précis, from American, French, and British archives, of *Franco-American Diplomatic Relations, 1816–1836* (State, La., 1941), on which I have relied for the diplomatic history of these claims.

The executive branch of the French Government, he said, still gave the most positive assurances of intention to press the appropriation again at the next session of the Chamber, but it was obviously doubtful, given the history of the treaty so far, that the legislative branch would ever respond. "After the delay on the part of France of a quarter of a century in acknowledging these claims by treaty," declared the President, "it is not to be tolerated that another quarter of a century be wasted in negotiating about the payment." He urged Congress to pass a law authorizing reprisals on French property, for the law of nations permitted such means to meet refusal to pay an acknowledged debt. "Such a measure," he explained, "ought not to be considered by France as a menace. *Her pride and power are too well known to expect anything from her fears and preclude the necessity of a declaration that nothing partaking of the character of intimidation is intended by us.*" [7] The President further raised the question whether Congress meanwhile might wish to adopt provisional measures to protect the rights and maintain the honor of the United States.

Jackson's patient but firm handling of the case left little doubt that the *right* was on the side of the United States and the *wrong* on the side of the foreigner.

Each house of Congress referred to its committee on foreign relations the portions of the President's message dealing with France, for report and recommendation. Meanwhile friends of the two countries awaited with more than usual interest the national memorial services in the Capitol at Washington decreed for General Lafayette, who had died on May 24, 1834. The principal feature of the ceremony was to be an oration to a joint meeting of the two houses at the next session of Congress by John Quincy Adams. What would he say about the French Question?

2

The elder statesman of Quincy had of course an unsurpassed reputation in the realm of foreign affairs. He had been personally acquainted with Lafayette for half a century. This is doubtless why Congress at the close of its previous session had chosen him instead of Daniel Webster for the occasion. He worked all summer on his address, restudying the history of the American Revolution, which he had witnessed at first hand in his boyhood; reading up on the Wars of the French Revolution and Napoleon, which he himself had reported from his diplomatic posts in Europe; going over his father's papers; sending inquiries to George Washington Lafayette and receiving materials from the son and heir of the late Marquis.

The eyes of the nation and of the world were on John Quincy Adams at high noon on December 31, 1834 as he was conducted to the Speaker's chair to address the Congress. Before him sat Andrew Jackson, President

[7] Italics inserted.

of the United States; Martin Van Buren, Vice President; Secretary of
State John Forsyth; and all the other members of the Cabinet; the diplo-
matic corps, except for the conspicuous absence of the British and French
Ministers; [8] members of both houses of Congress; and as many visitors,
ladies and gentlemen, as could crowd into the Hall of Representatives.[9]
Behind him on the wall, flanking the rostrum, hung the portraits of the
two inseparable heroes of the American Revolution: George Washington,
Father of His Country, and the Marquis de Lafayette, symbol of Franco-
American friendship.[10]

The eyes of Adams's own state were on him too that winter day, when
the Massachusetts legislature was about to meet to elect a Senator to sit
as colleague with the "god-like" Webster, aspirant now for the Whig nomination for the Presidency in 1836. In the Bay State there was a preponderance of preference among the Whigs in power—notably among those
of Antimasonic heritage—for Adams to fill the Senate seat left vacant by
the resignation of Nathaniel Silsbee. Adams could not hide from himself
the thought that elevation to the Senate would place him more conspicuously before the whole nation as the next Presidential contest came on.
The oration would help. The occasion was an opportunity. But he must
say nothing on controversial matters, nothing that would embarrass the
President in dealing with France.

The orator spoke steadily from his prepared manuscript for nearly three
solid hours. If his distinguished listeners, conscious of an impending diplomatic crisis with France, expected some invocation of traditional Franco-
American amity in the name of Lafayette, they were disappointed. The
address proved to be a long historical essay on the life and times of Lafayette through the period of the American and French Revolutions and
on, on, and on to the July Revolution of 1830.[11] It was an apotheosis of a
gallant soldier and torch-bearer of freedom, carrying American principles
from the New World to the Old, and holding to them in France to the end
of his life. The orator found justest praise for Lafayette in the words of
Tacitus: a leader equal always to the duties of the highest offices that he
attained but never holding himself (like Napoleon) above them. Where,
he asked in his peroration, where was there a benefactor of mankind who
could take precedence over Lafayette?

It was a fitting, an adequate ceremony, but no more. The audience listened dutifully and respectfully and applauded properly if not enthusiastically. Then the President, the Vice President, and the Cabinet officers

---

[8] *Niles' Weekly Register*, 4th Series, XI, No. 19, Baltimore, January 10, 1835, p. 1.

[9] *Register of Debates*, XI, Pt. I, 44, 80, 391. *Memoirs*, IX, 196.

[10] Charles E. Fairman: *Art and Artists of the Capitol of the United States of
America* (Washington: Government Printing Office; 1927), pp. 65, 88.

[11] An anonymous reviewer in the *Southern Literary Messenger*, I (No. 6, February
1835), 307–12, contrasted it unfavorably with Edward Everett's oration on Lafayette
delivered at Faneuil Hall, Boston, September 6, 1834.

quickly withdrew. The Senators filed through the Rotunda to their own chamber, and the House resumed the order of the day.

Congress by joint resolution thanked the speaker for his "appropriate oration" and asked him for a copy for publication. The House expressed its complete satisfaction with its distinguished member's effort, "replete with pure and patriotic sentiments," and resolved that fifty thousand copies be printed. In the Senate, Henry Clay, moving to print the document, gracefully declared that were he guided by the great talents of the author, he would be unable to specify the number of copies. But since the House had ordered fifty thousand, he thought ten thousand would do for the Senate. So it was agreed without a record vote.[12]

John Quincy Adams was proud of his effort that was being distributed so lavishly throughout the land. He felt that the apparent success of the speech, and the marked attentions of the Jackson party to him after it, increased his strength in the senatorial contest, perhaps a prelude to renomination for the Presidency in 1836.[13] Maybe he wasn't through yet. He would make Webster sit up and take notice!

Daniel Webster was already on the *qui vive*. The day after Adams's nationally conspicuous oration he wrote confidentially to his lifelong friend and political confidant in Boston, Jeremiah Mason, that the time had come for Massachusetts to act if she were to seize leadership for the Whig nomination. "Be sure to burn this letter," he warned. Mason asked for specific suggestions: should they elect Governor Davis as Senator; if so, whom should they put in his place as chief executive of the state? Webster answered promptly: he favored Davis for the Senate; as for his successor, Edward Everett as Governor would unite Whigs and Antimasons. On January 22, 1835 he again wrote impatiently from Washington: friends "in other quarters" wanted to know what to expect from Massachusetts.[14]

3

Adams had said nothing in his oration about current difficulties between the United States and France, but that did not mean that he had no opinion on the French Question. Privately he thought that Jackson and his diplomats had sadly mishandled the whole affair.[15] But publicly he would not take a stand against the President on an issue of foreign affairs in which his own country was *right* and the foreign nation *wrong*.

The Whig leaders in the Senate also thought that the President had bun-

---

[12] *Register of Debates*, XI, 113–14, 929.

[13] JQA to CFA, Washington, February 10, March 5, 31, April 8, 1835. Adams MSS.

[14] Daniel Webster to Jeremiah Mason, Washington, January 1, 10, 22, 1835. *Writings and Speeches of Daniel Webster* (New York, 1903), XVI, 245–9.

[15] JQA to Joseph Hopkinson in Philadelphia, Washington, December 22, 1834, January 5, 1835; to Benjamin Pickman in Salem, Washington, January 20, 1835. Adams MSS.

gled the French Question, and they were determined to profit by his supposed mistakes. Henry Clay as chairman of the committee on foreign relations brought in a report on the President's message and the French
Question. Senator Clay now seemed an entirely different statesman from
Secretary of State Clay, who had advised President Adams that a threat
of reprisals was the only way to bring France to terms. The recently organized Whig Party had captured the Senate in the mid-term elections.
Jackson's message presented a red-hot issue of peace or war for the next
Presidential campaign, something to offset his popular success on the newest Bank issue, created by cessation of public deposits. The Whig leaders,
particularly Clay and Webster, were out to make the most of it against
the Administration.

Clay's committee report (January 6, 1835) flatly rejected the President's
proposals. It advised that Congress await final action by the French Chamber before doing anything more: "Nothing should be done to betray sus-
picion of the integrity of the French Government."

"I suppose there is no diversity of opinion in the Senate or the country . . . ," declared Daniel Webster. "It seems to me that our course is
peace, and that determination should be expressed in the fewest words." [16]

Unanimously the Senate adopted the resolution proposed by its committee on foreign relations: "It is inexpedient at present to adopt any legislative measures in regard to the state of affairs between the United
States and France."

Webster, eager candidate for the Whig nomination, had placed himself
before the country as the preserver of peace against the warlike gestures
of a military chieftain. The *National Intelligencer* and other Whig newspapers followed suit in a chorus of editorials praising the Senate and the
great Massachusetts Senator for allaying the war fever caused by the
President's "menacing tone." [17]

4

In the House of Representatives the committee on foreign affairs kept
delaying its report on that part of the President's message which related
to the French Question. It looked as though they might postpone discussion until the end of the session, thus giving silent consent to the Senate's
attitude.

Adams became more and more fearful that the President might be left
to face a foreign crisis bereft of support from either house of Congress. [18]
He brought in resolutions, and the House promptly passed them, requesting from the Executive copies of the most recent correspondence from
Minister Livingston in Paris. These documents the Secretary of State,

[16] *Register of Debates,* XI, Pt. I, 200–6. January 14, 1835. Part II, Appendix,
208–19.
[17] McLemore: *Franco-American Diplomatic Relations,* p. 138.
[18] JQA to CFA, Washington, April 2, 1835. Adams MSS.

John Forsyth, promptly furnished. As weeks passed by without any further action by the House the Plymouth member grew impatient. Finally, February 7, 1835, a month after the Senate committee had made its negative report, Adams introduced a resolution that the committee on foreign affairs make a report *forthwith*. "Let the House be put in possession of the subject," he urged, "and let them say to the nation and to the world, whether they will sustain the President in the spirit of the proposition he has made for maintaining the rights, interests, and honor of the country." [19]

Adams's proposed resolution led to a prolonged debate, in the course of which he became steadily more conspicuous before the country. "It is the duty of the Committee of Foreign Relations to act in some way upon the important subjects referred to it," he told his colleagues; "I have not said whether I am ready to support the President's proposition, or any action of the House, or of the Committee, the effect of which would be to produce a war. I do wish the House to deliberate, and for the very reason that the President's measure, or some other measure which the honor of the country might require, *might possibly eventuate in war. . . .*[20] It does not follow that because the House deliberated, that it must either declare war or authorize reprisals. . . . Possibly, at the end of the discussion, they might come to the same conclusion as has been done in the other branch of the Congress. . . . The Senate too has deliberated, and its deliberations have ended in a determination to dodge the question. Might not the House come to a like conclusion and dodge the question, as the Senate has done?"

In the chair was Speaker John Bell of Tennessee, a Whig supporter of Senator Hugh Lawson White of his state for President. Bell did not want anybody in the House criticizing eminent Senators, particularly those who were contending for the Whig nomination. He called Adams to order: "It is not permitted to speak disrespectfully of any act of the other branch of the Legislature," he reminded the ex-President.

Dodging a question, it seems, was then an expression of a very vulgar vernacular, like "passing the buck" today! Politely Adams withdrew the horrid phrase,[21] to the amusement of many of his hearers.

Adams's reference in the House to the possibility of war caused a mild scare in shipping circles,[22] alarmed the merchant constituencies up and down the coast, and cost him his election as Senator. The legislature was even then engaged in prolonged balloting. John Davis had a bare majority in the lower house; in the state Senate Adams was far ahead; but the two houses had to agree. In the midst of their contest came the news from Washington that the Plymouth member was supporting Jackson's

[19] *Register of Debates*, XI, 1223.
[20] Italics inserted.
[21] *Register of Debates*, XI, 1233, 1359.
[22] JQA to CFA, Washington, March 5, April 4, 1835. Adams MSS.

"war policy" against the Whig Senate.[23] Webster passed the word along
to his friends in Boston that Adams would not do.[24] The state Senate
promptly switched to Davis, and Adams lost out. A Whig caucus then
placated the Antimasonic element by nominating Edward Everett to succeed John Davis as Governor.[25] In return Everett, despite his friendly
relationship with Adams, did everything in his power by secret correspondence to line up the remnants of the Antimasonic Party throughout
the country, particularly in Pennsylvania, behind Webster for President.[26]
Already a convention of 315 Whig members of the legislature had nominated the great constitutionalist for the first office in the Union.

The triple play of Whig politics in Massachusetts—Webster to Davis to
Everett—was a blow to Adams's expectations and to his pride, if not to his
confidence in friends. He knew that Webster was behind the stratagem,
but he did not know of Everett's secret correspondence. He hid his chagrin behind a pardonable rationalization: he had rather be in the House
than the Senate anyway. There he would have at least the undivided support of his constituents of the Plymouth district. There he would not have
to come into collision with a fellow Senator from Massachusetts.[27] But he
nursed a bitter feeling against Webster, not to be eased until national interests of a higher order brought them together again in the next Congress.

5

The House committee on foreign affairs [28] finally brought in a report on
the French Question, Friday, March 1, 1835, only five [29] days before the

[23] P. C. Brooks to Edward Everett, Boston, February 18, 27, 1835. Edward Everett
MSS., II, 1835–6. MHS.

[24] Blakeslee: "Antimasonic Party," Chapter IX, pp. 40–4.

[25] Darling: *Political Changes in Massachusetts*, pp. 184–5.

[26] Private and Confidential Letterbook of Edward Everett. MHS, acquired October 9, 1952. "The difference between Mr. A. and Mr. W. is very unfortunate. As a
friend of both parties, personal and political, I feel it very keenly. It originated in mis-
information and exaggeration; was aggravated by third persons, who had private
griefs to gratify against Mr. Webster; and seized upon as a handle for deserting W. by
Hallett [editor of the Boston *Antimasonic Advocate*], under pretence of espousing Mr.
A's cause, but in reality for the sake of giving the State to Van Buren. If the A.M. in
Mass.ts were polled, 9/10 would go for W., but Mr. A's feelings towards him are, I
fear, irrecoverably alienated." Edward Everett to Hon. H. Denny of Pittsburgh, Pa.
Charlestown, Mass., October 20, 1835. Ibid., pp. 1–3.

[27] JQA to Benjamin F. Hallett, Washington, January 30, March 7, 1835; to CFA,
March 5, 1835. *Memoirs*, IX, 207–8. "My father owes his defeat to himself," noted
Charles Francis Adams, whose father-in-law, Peter Chardon Brooks, insurance broker,
had been greatly alarmed by the war scare. CFA Diary, February 20, 1835.

[28] Such is the proper terminology for the committee, as distinct from the Senate
committee on foreign relations. In our early history the names of House and Senate
committees were often confused. I have used the accepted designations, except as
they vary inside of quotation marks.

[29] Actually the majority members of the committee presented the full content of the

end of the last session of the Twenty-third Congress. Meanwhile, dispatches from our Minister in Paris, just received by the President and transmitted to the Congress, had announced that the French Foreign Office had recalled its Minister from the United States and apprised Livingston that his own passports were ready any time he wished to call for them. Livingston had replied properly that he would await instructions from his own Government before taking leave of the French Court. He explained to the Secretary of State that this near rupture was due professedly to the statement in President Jackson's annual message presumed to reflect upon the French Government for not having assembled the Chambers earlier to consider the treaty. It is more likely that the United States Senate's negative action of January 14, 1835, dividing the nation's Government in the face of an adversary, was responsible for French highhandedness.

The House committee's report supported the President none too firmly in face of the French crisis, notwithstanding an Administration majority in that group, headed by Churchill C. Cambreleng of New York. They advised that the question be left to the next Congress, to meet in December 1835, and presented three resolutions for policy: (1) this House should insist upon execution of the treaty without further negotiations; (2) no reprisals meanwhile; (3) contingent preparations for an emergency vis-à-vis France.

The views of the minority [30] did not vary greatly from those of the majority of the committee. Only they proposed no resolution. After a long disquisition they "concurred" in what they believed to be the "unanimous" opinion of Congress and of the whole country: that execution of the treaty should be insisted on "at all hazards." [31] The minority would insist upon execution of the treaty at all hazards, but they would not recommend with the majority any further necessary preparations to meet the hazards.

Adams had always believed that politics stopped at the water's edge. So he had acted in the days of Thomas Jefferson. So he still stood in the "reign" of Andrew Jackson, no matter how much he disagreed with the President in domestic policy—or in spelling! But he still hoped there might be a peaceful way out. To that end he proposed to the House three resolutions as substitutes for those recommended by the committee on foreign affairs: (1) the treaty rights of American citizens ought not to be *sacrificed, abandoned, or impaired;* (2) the President be requested to

---

report on February 26, 1835, without any final meeting of the committee to agree to disagree. To meet objections to this irregular procedure the House instructed that another full committee meeting be held to present the report on February 27, with majority and minority statements.

[30] Edward Everett, Whig; Robert P. Letcher, Whig; Richard Coulter, Whig.

[31] *Register of Debates,* XI, Appendix, 176–85. February 27, 1835.

undertake any further honorable negotiations with France; (3) no hostile legislative measures at the present time.[32]

The difference between propositions of the committee on foreign affairs (majority) and those of Adams is clear. The committee opposed further negotiation as dishonorable, but Adams was willing for the President to negotiate further if he thought it desirable and honorable. Like a Man of the Whole Nation, John Quincy Adams had sought to combine the views of all—House, Senate, citizens—in a workable formula that would not compromise the President in dealing with France.

Adams closed the debate with what Everett thought a "furious war speech"—on "the existing state of our relations with that mighty and gallant nation who was our earliest ally." [33] What would be the effect on national interests, he asked, of this partisan division of policy among the branches of the Government? "How will the American nation, in its representative magistracy, appear before the nations of the world, and especially before that nation from whom we all claim justice? One branch of the Government declaring that he believes we possess a remedy which we can apply, and another branch of the Government declaring they will not support him in applying it. . . ."

[32] It is easier to understand the two sets of resolutions, the committee's and Adams's, if we put them in parallel columns:

The Committee of Foreign Affairs' proposed resolutions:

1. *Resolved:* That it would be incompatible with the rights and honor of the United States further to negotiate in relation to the treaty entered into with France, on the 4th of July 1831; and that this House will insist upon its execution; as ratified by both governments.

2. *Resolved:* That the Committee on Foreign Affairs be discharged from the further consideration of so much of the President's Message as relates to commercial restrictions, or to reprisals, on the commerce of France.

3. *Resolved:* That preparations ought to be made to meet any emergency growing out of our relations with France.

John Quincy Adams's proposed substitute resolutions:

1. *Resolved:* That the rights of citizens of the United States to indemnity from the Government of France, stipulated by the treaty concluded at Paris on the 4th of July 1831, ought in no event to be *sacrificed, abandoned,* or *impaired,* by any consent or acquiescence of the Government of the United States.

2. *Resolved:* That if it be, in the opinion of the President of the United States, compatible with the honor and interest of the United States, during the interval until the next session of Congress, to resume the negotiations between the United States and France, he be requested so to do.

3. *Resolved:* That no legislative measure of a hostile character or tendency towards the French nation is necessary or expedient at the present time.

Register of Debates, XI, 1507–8. Italics inserted.

[33] Diary of Edward Everett, March 2, 1835. MHS.

The question now before the House was: to maintain and execute the treaty *at all hazards,* or to adopt a do-nothing resolution presented by William Segar Archer, a Virginia Democrat. The House rejected Archer's alternative. The question then came back to that of maintaining and executing the treaty *at all hazards.* Here the Administration Democrat, Churchill C. Cambreleng of New York, moved another amendment that left off the words *at all hazards.* This brought it back to the committee's own first text, except that it omitted reference to national rights and honor: "Resolved; that in the opinion of this House the treaty of the 4th of July 1831 should be maintained, and its execution insisted on."

Adams accepted the newest modification without objection. The House then voted on the much-amended resolution.[34]

Applause broke out in the galleries as the Chair announced 212 ayes and no nays—for "my resolution," as Adams persisted in calling it—and the House adjourned at midnight.[35]

It was, indeed, no longer Adams's resolution, but Cambreleng let him think so. It was a compound product. The applause, of course, was enthusiasm for unanimity finally reached at a late and weary hour, not for Adams. But Adams, thirsty for success, took it for himself.

When all was debated and resolved, the Senate had declared it to be expedient not to do anything at the present time; the House had declared that the treaty should be maintained and its execution insisted on.

There still remained the question of preparations to meet any emergency that might arise before the meeting of the next Congress in December 1835, nine months away. Cambreleng had relegated that to an amendment to the Senate's amendment of the fortification bill, which passed the House the next day, 109 to 77, Adams voting in the affirmative. The amendment appropriated $3,000,000 as a special defense fund to be spent by the President, in the recess of Congress, "if he should deem it expedient, for the military and naval service, including fortifications, ordnance, etc."

This was too big an *et cetera* for Whig opposition Senators to swallow. "It assumes a war with France before Congress meets again," declared Calhoun. It was a proposition to establish a military monarchy, asserted Senator Leigh of Virginia: "We might as well say that the President should be made First Consul for life, or Emperor of the American people." "Preparation for war may lead to war," affirmed Henry Clay, repeating a time-worn fallacy. "It is calculated to keep up the excitement abroad, and may prevent an early settlement of our claims. It partakes of the character of the President's unfortunate message and puts in jeopardy the peace of the country." "I would not hesitate to deny such

[34] *Register of Debates,* XI, 1622–34.

[35] *Memoirs,* IX, 212. The *Memoirs* do not reveal that Cambreleng had changed the resolution at the last moment. Biographers would do well to consult the *Register of Debates* on this point.

power to Washington himself," affirmed Adams's old Secretary of the
Navy, Samuel Southard, now a Senator from New Jersey.

The Senate rejected the House's amendment to the fortification bill.
The House then insisted on its $3,000,000 measure. The Senate adhered
to its disagreement. A committee of conference compromised on $300,000
additional fortification money plus $500,000 more for repairing and equip-
ping ships of war. It was now after midnight, March 3–4, 1835. Many
members of the House, thinking that the session must expire the last hour
of March 3, had gone home, though there had been no adjournment.
Skillfully Webster took advantage of the situation to throw blame for no
more preparedness on the House. He got the Senate to pass a resolution
reminding the House, in effect, that the hour was late: the conference report was in its hands. In vain members called for a quorum. None was
possible. At half past three in the morning of March 4 the Speaker declared the House adjourned *sine die*. The fortifications bill was lost in the
confusion.

Adams got home exhausted and took to his bed at the hour when usually he got up to light his fire and read his Bible. The sun was high above
Capitol Hill when he rose dispirited and anxious. He walked downtown,
reflecting on the loss of the whole fortifications bill in the face of a foreign
crisis, perhaps war. His mind raced back over the debate of the last two
days, and the final vote on "his" resolution. After all, the unanimous vote
had been somewhat forced. It had put him, he thought, in the same position toward his constituents in which he found himself as a Senator back
in 1807–8. Then the Federalists had read him out of the party for refusing to oppose President Jefferson's foreign policy. He belonged to no
party now, but what would his Whig and Antimason friends think? That
he had gone over to Jackson as once he had gone over to Jefferson?

"Standing alone as I do [he soliloquized], disconnected from all parties,
and having at the recent session taken upon the French Question a stand
so conspicuous, so desperately contested, so triumphant in its result, and
so sure to combine against me *all* the candidates for the Presidency, what
can save me from destruction at the next session, if the French quarrel
should continue, but an unseen protecting power? Be thou faithful unto
death." [36]

This initial reaction did not last long. Soon he persuaded himself that
alone and unaided he had won a resounding triumph, the first parliamentary victory of his life. His gloating over this successful battle, in
letters to his close friends and more particularly in his Diary, became so
self-satisfied as to be almost indecent.

"I breasted them all," he boasted to his son and confidant Charles, "and
after thirteen hours of debate closed with a vote of two hundred and ten
ayes for my Resolution and not one solitary *nay*. . . . I obtained in the
House of Representatives of the United States, a triumph unparalleled in

[36] *Memoirs*, IX, 214–17.

the History of the Country, while at the same time, it was the immediate cause of my exclusion from the Senate of the United States." [37]

"Pronounce whether in the whole history of legislative deliberation," he challenged his friend and appointee Judge Hopkinson of Philadelphia, "such debates ever resulted in such a conclusion"—210 to 0.

Were not the "unanimous midnight vote," he asked Benjamin F. Hallett, and the spontaneous burst of applause that followed, sufficient commentary on Webster's maneuver to keep him out of the Senate? [38]

No victory had been so sweet, not even his first election to the House in 1830. " 'The heart knoweth its own bitterness, and a stranger intermeddleth not with its joys.' . . . I would not give [up] the moment of that unanimous vote and that unbought burst of applause, for all the wealth or all the power that man could heap upon me." [39]

At the request of a Boston firm of printers for the text of his recent speeches, he prepared a long autobiographical digest of the debate with a list of illustrating documents, together with hostile editorials in the *National Intelligencer*, for a pamphlet to inform the public fully about his masterful role in the congressional battle.[40] He wrote eight long letters to his son recording for the benefit of his posterity a blow-by-blow account of the debate, with his personal reactions and interpretations.[41] Significantly Charles Francis Adams never chose to print them. He made no reference to them when forty years later he edited the more meager account of the debates contained in his father's Diary.[42]

[37] JQA to CFA, Washington, March 5, April 8, 1835. Adams MSS.

[38] "If the debate of last Monday in the House of Representatives of the United States should ever be reported with any tolerable resemblance to truth, if the midnight vote of two hundred and ten *ayes* and not one *no,* with which it closed, and the spontaneous burst of applause from the crowded galleries *and house,* which followed, if *they* can give you an idea of what I have gone through, and of what yet awaits me you will readily perceive why it is not proper for me at this time to discourse to you upon causes and effects, upon the nomination of Daniel Webster, and the Senatorial greatness thrust upon John Davis, and the wormwood of Edward Everett swallowed by bluelight federalism and Royal Arch Masonry. If you do not understand the debate, and the final vote in which it terminated, it is not for me, certainly at this time to explain them to you." JQA to Benjamin F. Hallett, Washington, March 7, 1835. Adams MSS.

[39] JQA to CFA, Washington, April 6, 1835. Adams MSS.

[40] *Memoirs,* IX, 220. Homer and Palmer to JQA, Boston, March 9, 1835; JQA to Homer and Palmer, March 14, 17, 1835. Adams MSS. See *Public Documents and Congressional Debates, Touching our Relations with France, the Loss of the Fortifications Bill, the Abolition Question, etc.* (Boston: from the Press of Homer and Palmer; 1836). The pamphlet contains only one of Adams's speeches, the principal one, of January 22, 1835.

[41] *Memoirs,* IX, 233. JQA to CFA, Washington, March 31, April 2, 3, 4, 6, 8, 10, 12, 1835. See also JQA to Judge Joseph Hopkinson, March 6, 1835; to Dr. Benjamin Waterhouse of Cambridge, April 26, 1835. Adams MSS.

[42] "This may be noted as the first of the great triumphs of Mr. Adams in the House," notes the editor and son, concerning the midnight vote of 200 to 0 [*sic*], and

Adams asked himself whether he might best end his career by retiring on this great and unanimous triumph. In the next Congress he was certain to meet trouble in the Ohio-Michigan boundary dispute, in which he was deeply involved in special committee work, as well as in the French Question. He would also be bound in duty to take a stand on the patronage bill passed by the Senate in the last session and certain to come up in both houses of the next Congress. He would have to grapple with Webster, Clay, Calhoun, and other Whig Senators on that subject, too. Nemesis would be on the watch for him!

The truth was, and no one knew it better than he did, that he was loath to turn his back on public controversies. He confessed to his son that it contributed to his enjoyment of life.[43] The old gladiator, who believed himself to be on the brink of the grave as he approached threescore and ten, acknowledged to his intimate friend Dr. Benjamin Waterhouse that despite continuous and active attendance through twelve-, thirteen-, and even eighteen-hour sittings of the House, he was not badly off in health. A little haggard in the face perhaps, and sharpened in features, but still going strong.[44] The conflicts of public life seemed as essential to his well-being as they were to Andrew Jackson's.[45]

His son suggested that these quixotic political battles were not worth the struggle. Why did his father not come home and devote himself to literary work?

Adams outdid himself in the self-righteousness of his reply. Charles could get rich, if that would please him, but as for himself he would go on with the purity of his own principles.[46]

6

The French crisis got worse before it got better, but all of a sudden it vanished, during the adjournment of Congress. Public reaction to the

adds: "It is much to be regretted that he [JQA] failed to record it more at large." *Memoirs*, IX, 212.

At the head of one of the letters to Charles, in the father's letterbook, stands this quotation from Psalm xxvii, 3: "Though an host should encamp against me, my heart shall not fear: though war should rise against me, in this will I be confident." In another intimate letter to his son he all but compared himself to Moses, "one of the great Legislators of mankind through all successive ages to the end of time," who conducted his people through forty years of wanderings and sufferings, and calamities and crimes, only to behold the promised land from the summit of a mountain, never to enter it. JQA to CFA, Washington, April 3, 16, 1835. Adams MSS.

[43] JQA to CFA, Washington, April 6, 1835. Adams MSS.

[44] JQA to Dr. Benjamin Waterhouse, Washington, April 26, 1835. Adams MSS.

[45] Edward Everett to Benjamin F. Hallett, private, Charlestown, February 17, 1836. Private and Confidential Letterbook of Edward Everett. MHS.

[46] CFA to JQA, Boston, April 23, 1835; JQA to CFA, Washington, April 28, 1835. Adams MSS.

debate in the House of Representatives made it clear that the people were behind the President. In France the Legislative Chamber and the House of Peers finally passed the required appropriation, albeit with a proviso: no payments to be made until the French Government should receive satisfactory explanations of the "offensive" phrases appearing in the President's message to Congress of December 1, 1834.

"So much for the threat of reprizals," commented John Quincy Adams when the news reached Washington. "It has carried the substance, I trust it will not be lost by the forms and I presume the apology required will be accompanied with a counter-apology quite as courteous and reasonable." [47]

But Jackson vowed he would never taint the honor of the country by making any apology for a communication between himself and Congress; it was not the business of a foreign nation, he declared, to meddle in the Government of the United States. He ordered Livingston to withdraw from France if the Minister of Foreign Affairs refused to name a date when payments would begin. A complete rupture of diplomatic relations took place before the new Congress convened.

In this impasse Europe's distresses again became America's advantage, as so often they had been before. The Spanish Government was requesting armed intervention by Britain and France in the Peninsula on behalf of the Queen. France and England faced possible war with Russia over the Eastern Question. Under these circumstances Louis-Philippe was not sufficiently sure of his throne to risk a war with the United States over an issue of preposterous punctilio. He caused it to be hinted that British mediation would be acceptable. The British were worried lest French forces get tied up in trans-Atlantic hostilities. Already the British Minister in Washington had intimated that Jackson would have to say very little to satisfy France—it would be enough even to repeat what he had already said in his message that had started all the trouble, or only formally confirm personal explanations that Livingston had made in Paris.

Secretary of State Forsyth, Vice President Van Buren, and Livingston (now returned to Washington) contrived an acceptable sentence for Jackson's next annual message, December 7, 1835. In substance, if not exact words, it only repeated what the President had said to Congress the year before: [48] "the conception that it was my intention to menace or insult the Government of France is as unfounded as the attempt to extort from the fears of that nation what her sense of justice may deny would be vain and ridiculous." In a later, separate paragraph of the message he made it clear that these words were not intended as an apology: "The honor of my country shall never be stained by an apology from me for the statement of truth and the performance of duty: nor can I give any ex-

[47] JQA to Benjamin F. Hallett, Philadelphia, May 27, 1835. Adams MSS,
[48] See italicized words on p. 309, above.

planation of my official acts except such as is due to integrity and justice and consistent with the principles on which our institutions were framed." He said as much again in a special message on the subject, January 29, 1836, after the last member of the American mission in France, Thomas P. Barton, had returned.

Apology or no apology, the French Government chose to consider Jackson's latest message to Congress as an apology to France, and it therefore served as such. That ended the dispute. All the British mediation had to do was straighten out the kinks in diplomatic protocol left by a war of words.[49] France began payments on the treaty installments, and full diplomatic relations were restored in the autumn of 1836.

Best commentary on the happy settlement of the French Question is the passage from Shakespeare that John Quincy Adams had quoted in debate on the House resolutions:

> Rashness
> (And praised be rashness for it) lets us know
> Our indiscretion sometimes serves us well
> When our deep plots do fail.

7

Jackson's victory in foreign policy made the Whig Senate look sick. Daniel Webster nearly gave up his political ghost. About all he could do, when Congress convened again, was to attack the House for having caused the whole fortifications bill to fall in the face of possible war.

The new appropriations for national defense came up in the Senate following the President's annual message of December 7, 1835. In a long speech, January 14, 1836, Webster undertook to throw all blame on the House for the failure of the old bill, and to defend his own opposition to it. There had then been no real danger of war, he said. But even if there had been, he would not have voted to place such a large and unrestricted fund in the hands of the President. "The honorable member from Ohio, near me, has said that if the enemy were on our shores he would not have agreed to this vote. And I say, if the proposition were now before us, and the guns of the enemy were battering against the walls of the Capitol, I would not agree to it." [50] The preservation of the Constitution, he added, was worth forty Capitols.

In the House of Representatives, John Quincy Adams rose to cast the blame back where it lay—on the Senate. Immediately the Speaker called

[49] There are two informative articles on the British mediation: William H. Dunham, Jr.: "Thiers and the British Mediation of 1835," *Sewanee Review Quarterly*, XXXIV (No. 4, October–December 1926), 441–50; and Charles K. Webster: "British Mediation between France and the United States in 1834–6," *English Historical Review*, XLII (No. 165, January 1927), 58–78.

[50] *Register of Debates*, XII, 161.

him to order—no allusions to proceedings of the other house! Adams said
he was discussing only reports of some speeches he had seen in the *National Intelligencer.*

Great excitement flared up when it appeared that the Speaker was trying to stop him from criticizing Whig Senators for what they were reported to have said in their own chamber. Members stirred and rose.
They crowded into the aisles. "Order, order," cried some, as Adams tried
to proceed. Others shouted: "Go on, go on!"

After some difficulty he began again, and the audience quieted down
to hear his impassioned and altogether extemporaneous defense of the
House of Representatives and of the President's policy in the French
crisis. The speech, with interruptions, lasted three hours. Very easily he
overthrew Webster's constitutional quibbles. How absurd to say that the
special fund of $3,000,000 would have enabled the President to do any-
thing he wanted with it, such as to make himself a military dictator! The
expenditure was explicitly limited to increasing the military and naval
service, including ordnance and fortification. How else but under direction of the President would such moneys be efficiently expended in the
contingency of an emergency while Congress was not sitting?

Then came the deadly thrust at Webster, not to be parried: "This, Sir,
was the great basis upon which was founded that burst of patriotic indignation and eloquence, which would rather have seen an enemy 'battering
down the walls of this Capitol' than have agreed to this appropriation for
the defence of the Country. Sir, only one more step was necessary, and
an easy step it was, for men who would refuse an appropriation, even in
the terms and under the specifications in which that was proposed, if the
enemy were at the gates of the Capitol—*I say, there was only one step
more, and that a natural and an easy one—to join the enemy in battering
down these walls.*" [51]

A roar of applause burst out from every part of the House, spontaneous,
genuine, patriotic. Thenceforth his countrymen began to call John Quincy
Adams the Old Man Eloquent, though just who it was that started it is
difficult to say.

Enthusiastic members of both parties in the House subscribed to a
special printing of ten thousand copies of Adams's reply to Webster on the
French Question, to send to their constituents.[52] In turn the Whig members of Congress printed a collection of speeches by Webster and his colleagues animadverting upon John Quincy Adams. Webster franked the
publication heavily to a Massachusetts mailing list, concentrating on

[51] *Ibid.,* XI, 2270. January 22, 1836.
[52] JQA to CFA, Washington, January 23, 1836. Adams MSS. *Speech of the Hon.
John Q. Adams, of Massachusetts, on His Resolution for the Appointment of a Select
Committee to Inquire into the Causes of the Failure of the Fortifications Bill at the
Last Session of Congress. Delivered January 22, 1836.* (Washington: Blair and Rives,
Printers; 1836.)

Antimasons and Jackson men,[53] as if to disillusion them, too, about the ex-President. It did Adams no harm. It did Webster no good. In the popular mind there remained little doubt who had won the last round of this congressional battle. The Old Man Eloquent had beat the devil out of Daniel Webster. Adams's victory was so complete that he withheld further blows. He would not "bear down" any more on Webster; the two might need to stand together on great questions of the Union certain to come up in the near future.[54]

Privately each of the two great New Englanders nourished a hearty dislike and contempt for the other.[55]

8

Webster's partisan role in this national issue with a foreign nation was perhaps the greatest mistake of his career as a public man. It ruined his chances for the Presidency. Martin Van Buren, heir apparent to Jacksonian Democracy, won the election of 1836 against the divided opposition of four Whig candidates. Webster carried only his own State of Massachusetts, by less than 8,000 votes.[56]

Adams steered a neutral course [57] during the campaign, but his son supported Van Buren,[58] and there was a falling off in the volume of po-

---

[53] Daniel Webster to Edward Everett, Washington, January 27, 1836. Edward Everett MSS., MHS. JQA to CFA, Washington, April 21, 1836; to Benjamin Waterhouse, April 25, 1836; to Morton Eddy, May 1, 1836; to E. Price Greenleaf of Quincy, May 9, 1836. Adams MSS. Presumably the publication was *Public Documents and Congressional Debates*, cited above, p. 319, n. 40.

[54] JQA to Aaron Hobart of East Bridgewater, Mass. Washington, May 3, 1835; JQA to Alexander H. Everett, Washington, May 10, 1835. Adams MSS.

[55] Daniel Webster to Edward Everett, Washington, January 27, 1836. Edward Everett Papers, MHS, called to my attention by Charles Everett. JQA to Morton Eddy, Esq., Bridgewater, Mass. Washington, May 1, 1836. Adams MSS.

[56] The electoral vote for President in 1836 was:

Martin Van Buren (N.Y., Democrat)	170
William Henry Harrison (O., Whig)	73
Hugh Lawson White (Tenn., Whig)	26
Daniel Webster (Mass., Whig)	14
Willie P. Mangum (N.C., Whig)	11

In Massachusetts the vote was:

Webster	41,287
Van Buren	33,542

[57] JQA to Messrs. Benjamin V. French and Harvey Field, Committee of the Antimasonic Convention held at Hanover on October 18, 1836. Quincy, October 21, 1836. Adams MSS.

"Mr. [A. H.] Everett has got home [from a visit to Washington]. . . . He was disappointed at not finding you quite 'whole hog' for Mr. Van Buren." CFA to JQA, Boston, April 14, 1836. Adams MSS. A. H. Everett broke with his brother Edward Everett on politics (as well as on personal matters). He was defeated in standing for Congress on the Van Buren ticket in the North (Norfolk) district in 1836.

[58] CFA to Benjamin F. Hallett, November 22, 1836. Adams MSS.

litical correspondence between the two during the next few years. Henry Clay also stood aside astutely and let the other Whig candidates vie for defeat. The Whigs had now gone the way of the Federalists—so it looked to John Quincy Adams.[59]

Adams's support of the President on the French Question brought the two no closer politically or personally. These are Adams's bitter one-sided reflections after the Old Hero had retired to the Hermitage:

"Though I had served him more than any living man ever did, and though I supported his Administration at the hazard of my own political destruction, and effected for him, at a moment when his own friends were deserting him, what no other member of Congress ever accomplished for him—an unanimous vote of the House of Representatives to support him in his quarrel with France; though I supported him in other very critical periods of his Administration,[60] my return from him was insult, indignity, and slander."[61]

Adams's other political worries now lifted for a short spell. The Senate patronage bill slept for a year before it reappeared in the House to be killed in Committee of the Whole. The prickly Michigan boundary question was transferred to the judiciary committee, and Congress finally settled it by a compromise that yielded the boundary demanded by the neighboring states to the south but granted to the proposed new State of Michigan territorial compensation in extensive "wild lands" to the northwest. Adams took pride in having been able to help secure this "ample" if shameless "indemnity" for the people of the despoiled territory.[62] It was nothing less than the fabulous Upper Peninsula. What a treasure it would prove to be in lumber, iron, and copper for the needs of industrial twentieth-century America and of the world!

Adams's district re-elected him in November 1836 without a party designation and with only scattering opposition.[63] From then on they would elect and elect and elect him to that post of duty to the end of his life, independent of all parties. He was seventy, and his Presidential gyroscope was running down, but the greatest days of his life were still ahead of him.

[59] ". . . what has become, and what is to become of the *whigs*? Their very name is a fraud, invented by a political swindler, not half so respectable as that of the Federalists of which party the majority of them in New England is composed. The truth is, they are already ashamed of their own name, but they indulge their spite by calling their adversaries Tories. Tory Democracy!" JQA to CFA, December 12, 1836, Adams MSS.

[60] Presumably on the issue of nullification and compromise on the tariff.

[61] *Memoirs*, IX, 436–7. The insult, indignity, and slander are not specified.

[62] JQA to CFA, Washington, April 21, 1836. Adams MSS.

[63] The *Boston Atlas*, V, No. 130, of December 1, 1836 gives the final vote as: John Q. Adams 3,125; scattering 660.

CHAPTER XVII

Slavery and the Gag Rule

(1820 – 1837)

. . . a deep seated disease, preying upon the vitals
of this Union. . . .

JOHN QUINCY ADAMS TO JOHN GREENLEAF WHITTIER
ON SLAVERY [1]

JOHN QUINCY ADAMS towered in ability and prestige and in independence
of mind over his colleagues in the House of Representatives. He was its
hardest-working member, punctual and conscientious in duty whether on
the floor or in committee.[2] Only sheer physical incapacity—and that
rarely—could keep him from his daily post even when work was prolonged far beyond the midnight hour or to early dawn. His name occurs
more often in the official proceedings than that of any other member. He
took part in discussion of nearly all questions great and small, was a stick-
ler for procedure, and a parliamentarian of the highest order. On one celebrated occasion in December 1839, when the House fell into complete
disorganization in an attempt to elect a Speaker, the ex-President rose
and, outcountenancing the Clerk himself, and on the sole authority of his
own prestige, put the question that organized the chamber and saved it
from chaos.[3] No one in this instance trusted his complete impartiality
more than the Southern members: it was on the motion of Robert Barnwell Rhett of South Carolina that he was placed in the chair pending

---

[1] January 26, 1837. Adams MSS.

[2] In addition to much active service on special committees *ad hoc*, John Quincy
Adams served on the following standing committees of the House of Representatives:

Committee on Manufactures (chairman), from the 22d through the 26th Congresses, March 4, 1831 to March 3, 1841.

Committee on Indian Affairs (chairman) in first session of 27th Congress. March
14, 1841 to June 18, 1841, when he was excused upon request.

Committee on Foreign Affairs (chairman) during second and third sessions of
the 27th Congress, December 13, 1841 to March 3, 1843.

Joint Committee on the Library of Congress during first session of the 30th Congress, from March 4, 1847 to his death, February 23, 1848.

[3] Bennett Champ Clark: *John Quincy Adams, "Old Man Eloquent"* (Boston,
1933), pp. 341–50.

election of the Speaker.[4] Hardly a day passed that his voice was not heard. But it would be ungracious to burden the reader with the detailed routine of Adams's legislative career until the end of his life. In this and following chapters we shall focus on those great themes of American history which are also such outstanding features of his biography. They will concern the antislavery impulse and the growing sectional controversy, which came also to involve affairs with Mexico over Texas. They lead us to the most spectacular and the most heartfelt battle of his Second Career—the long constitutional struggle against the rising power of slavery.

1

The reader of the first volume of this work will recall that Adams's inner conviction of the surpassing evil of slavery first began to crystallize in his Diary during the debates in Congress of 1819–20 over the question of admitting Missouri into the Union as a slave state:

"Slavery," he thought to himself at that time, "is the great and foul stain upon the North American Union, and it is a contemplation worthy of the most exalted soul whether its total abolition is or is not practicable: if practicable, by what means it may be effected, and if a choice of means be within the scope of the object, what means would accomplish it at the smallest cost of human sufferance [*sic*]. A dissolution, at least temporary, of the Union, as now constituted, would be certainly necessary, and the dissolution must be upon a point involving the question of slavery, and no other. The Union might then be reorganized on the fundamental principle of emancipation. This object is vast in its compass, awful in its prospects, sublime and beautiful in its issue. A life devoted to it would be nobly spent or sacrificed." [5]

To this heroic role Adams was not yet ready to dedicate himself. He approved the Missouri Compromise as a practical way of putting the slavery question to sleep for a while to let the Union grow in strength and stature. He saw no reason to "obtrude" his opinions upon the public at that time,[6] and was not called upon to do so. Privately he declared to Governor Jonathan Jennings of Indiana that the abolition of slavery where it was established must be left entirely to the people of the state itself.[7] Later, as Secretary of State, he imperturbably performed his official duty in securing indemnity from Great Britain for slaves carried away from Southern posts by departing British forces after the War of 1812,

[4] R. B. Rhett to JQA, Thursday p.m. [December 5, 1839]. John M. Patton to JQA, Richmond, December 27, 1839. Adams MSS.

[5] Vol. I, 418. *Memoirs*, IV, 531.

[6] "Mr. A. has never yet given any opinion on this business and is not at all pleased to be drawn into it as long as he can possibly avoid it." Journal of LCA, written for JA. February 15, 1820. Adams MSS.

[7] JQA to Jonathan Jennings, Quincy, July 17, 1820. *Writings*, VII, 53.

and in seeking the rendition to Southern owners of slaves escaped to Canada or to Mexico. He was only a belated convert to the movement for suppression of the African slave trade by treaties with the maritime powers. As President he succeeded in avoiding any pronouncement on slavery. Thus he arrived at the end of his diplomatic and Presidential service without having given any public expression of his views.

"O the time will come," prophesied an anonymous fellow citizen during the early months of Adams's Presidency, "when reflection on this neglect will blister your very soul as it comes over you. Fatal, fatal deference to proud oppressors!" [8]

Adams's political resistance to an inner voice against slavery is nowhere better illustrated than in a secret sonnet which he wrote, while in the White House in 1827, on the anniversary of John Adams's birth, apotheosizing his father as an immortal spirit of freedom not brooking the tyrant's threat whether by king or slaveholder:

> Day of my father's birth, I hail thee yet.
> 　　What though his body moulders in the grave,
> 　　Yet shall not Death th' immortal soul enslave;
> The sun is not extinct—his orb has set.
> And where on earth's wide ball shall man be met,
> 　　While time shall run, but from thy spirit brave
> 　　Shall learn to grasp the boon his Maker gave,
> And spurn the terror of a tyrant's threat?
> Who but shall learn that freedom is the prize
> 　　Man still is bound to rescue or maintain;
> That nature's God commands the slave to rise,
> 　　And on the oppressor's head to break his chain.
> Roll, years of promise, rapidly roll round,
> Till not a slave shall on this earth be found.

It is the best poem John Quincy Adams ever wrote. One could apply its moral to the political tyrants of his father's day, to American slavemasters of his own day, or to the imperialist slave-drivers behind the Iron Curtain in our tumultuous twentieth century.

The President wrote the sonnet down in shorthand in his Diary. "I record it thus," he explained, "that it may be legible only to myself, or to a reader who will take the trouble to pick it out of the shorthand." Years later in extreme old age, in 1845 or 1846, he wrote out a transcription which somebody tipped in between the pages of the Diary where the cryptic characters stood.[9] Charles Francis Adams first published the lines in 1875 in his father's famous *Memoirs*.

As soon as Adams left the White House he drafted some lines for a memorial tablet to his father and mother to be fixed on the walls of the

[8] "A Son of Massachusetts" to JQA, December 1825. Adams MSS.
[9] VII, 164. Under date of October 30, 1826.

church at Quincy. The tribute to John Adams closed with the last two lines of the secret sonnet:

> Roll, years of promise, rapidly roll round,
> Till not a slave shall on this earth be found.

The ex-President sent the proposed inscription to his friends Robert Walsh and Judge Joseph Hopkinson of Philadelphia for their criticism. Walsh and Hopkinson advised that the last two lines be expunged. Adams accepted their advice and deleted the couplet.[10] Why? He did not say. He did not need to say. Even if he were stepping out of the Presidential picture for good and all, he did not think it prudent to raise an antislavery flag on Meridian Hill, or over the Adams Mansion at Quincy—not yet. The forces of freedom against slavery were too weak, too divided, to be rallied successfully in the spirit of emancipation. On the contrary, the slavery interest was so compact, so built into the Constitution, and so fervent in action as to threaten to overpower the discordant and loosely patched policy of the free.[11] He would wait to make his challenge to slavery.

Adams professed to have entered the House of Representatives in 1831 as a Man of the Whole Nation, with no feeling of discrimination between the interests of the North and South.[12] But he certainly had inner convictions about slavery, and there is a continuing record of them in his Diary and in his private life.

On the eve of his departure for Washington in 1831 two highly intelligent Frenchmen visited Boston on a trip of travel and observation under the ægis of an official study of penology in the United States. They were Alexis de Tocqueville, author later of *Democracy in America,* and his companion Gustave de Beaumont. Alexander Everett gave a dinner for them to meet John Quincy Adams, and Tocqueville found himself seated at the ex-President's right. The young student of American society, finding that his eminent table companion spoke French with facility and eloquence, plied him with questions.

"Do you regard slavery as a great evil for the United States?" asked the French visitor.

"Yes, unquestionably," was the answer. "It's in slavery that are to be found almost all the embarrassments of the present and fears of the future."

"Are the inhabitants of the South aware of this state of things?" pursued the foreign traveler.

[10] JQA to Robert Walsh, Jr., of Philadelphia, Meridian Hill, March 12, 18, 1829, enclosing draft of inscription. Robert Walsh to JQA, Philadelphia, March 29, 1829. Adams MSS. For text as carved on the tablet, see above, p. 125.

[11] *Memoirs,* VIII, 232. Quincy, June 22, 1830.

[12] John Quincy Adams: *Address to His Constituents, at Braintree, September 17, 1842* (Boston: J. H. Eastburn, printer; 1842), p. 42.

"Yes, at the bottom of their hearts,—but it's a truth, concern over which they are not aware that they show. Slavery has modified the whole state of society in the South, but don't deceive yourself. Nowhere is equality among the whites greater than in the South. Here [in New England] we have a great equality before the law, but it ceases absolutely in the habits of life. There are upper classes and working classes. Every white man in the South is a being equally privileged, whose destiny is to make the negroes work without working himself—from this laziness in which the Southern whites live great differences in character result. They devote themselves to bodily exercise, to hunting, to racing; they are vigorously constituted, brave, full of honor: what is called the point of honor is more delicate there than anywhere else; duels are frequent."

"Do you think it is really impossible to get along without blacks in the South?" persisted Tocqueville.

"I am convinced of the contrary," the American statesman replied. "The Europeans work in Greece and in Sicily, why should they not in Virginia and the Carolinas? It's no hotter there."

"Is the number of slaves increasing?"

"It is diminishing in all the states to the east of Delaware,[13] because they cultivate wheat and tobacco, cultures for which the negroes are rather a charge than useful. Therefore one exports them to the provinces [*sic*] where cotton and sugar are cultivated. In those of the western States where they have been introduced, they remain in very small numbers.

"I know of nothing more insolent than a black," added Mr. Adams, "when he is not speaking to his master and is not afraid of being beaten. It is not even rare to see negroes treat their masters very ill when they have to do with a weak man. The negresses especially make frequent abuse of the kindness of their mistresses. They know that it isn't customary to inflict bodily punishment on them." [14]

Adams as member of Congress governed himself by the constitutional bargain with slavery [15] as the issue took stronger sectional shape in Congress from aggressive Southern response to increasing fervor of the anti-slavery crusade. As for the abolition windmill, he tried to keep away from it,[16] as if experience in the rise and fall of Antimasonry had chastened him against participating too readily in another crusade, even in a far more important movement.

[13] I.e., the Northern states.

[14] George Wilson Pierson: *Tocqueville and Beaumont in America* (New York, 1938), pp. 418–20. Copyright by Oxford University Press. Reproduced by permission of the publisher.

[15] JQA to Alexander Hayward, Coventry, Rhode Island; to Friend Isaac Sanborn, Avondale, Pennsylvania; Quincy, October 2, 1835.

[16] "With the Slave and Abolition whirligig I hope to have no concern, but upon the other questions I cannot be silent and must speak my mind." JQA to Dr. Benjamin Waterhouse, Quincy, October 15, 1835. Adams MSS.

2

Contemporaneously with Adams's return to Congress the antislavery impulse began to stir the North. First to respond actively were the Quakers. Their target was the District of Columbia. Congress had full power over it as it did over the territories. Quaker constituents commenced to petition Congress for abolition of slavery and the domestic slave trade within the District. They pitched on the ex-President to present their petitions. Partly it was because some of them could not get their own Congressmen to do it. Partly it was because of Adams's nationally conspicuous position. Perhaps also it was because they sensed or knew his inner abhorrence of slavery.

The first time that Adams rose to address the House, in long unpracticed speech and uncertain voice, it was to present fifteen petitions signed by numerous citizens of Pennsylvania for the abolition of the slave trade and slavery in the nation's capital. Personally, he explained to his colleagues, he did not support that part of the petition that prayed for the abolition of slavery in the District.[17] He read one of the petitions and moved that they all be referred to the committee on the District of Columbia with instructions to report on the expediency of prohibiting the slave trade there. Such petitions had not yet unduly disturbed the Southern members. Nobody objected, and the matter was thus disposed of. The committee soon reported against the proposals.

By implication Adams had registered himself as favoring the abolition of the slave trade, though not of slavery, in the capital district.

Moses Brown, Quaker nonagenarian and philanthropist of Providence, Rhode Island, wrote to the Plymouth member asking him to explain why he could not also support the abolition of slavery. There were three reasons, Adams informed the good Friend, why he could not support emancipation in the District of Columbia: (1) he did not think the inhabitants of one state competent to petition the legislature of another state, or even Congress acting for the District of Columbia, on matters so deeply affecting the interest of that state or the District; (2) he was averse to stirring up ill blood between the Northern and Southern sections of the Union; (3) he believed he was acting in accordance with the opinion of a great majority of his own constituents.[18] None of these reasons, Adams explained, proceeded from any difference of opinion between Moses Brown and himself upon the nature and character of slavery. "I hold the condition of a hereditary slave, as in a moral point of view far above that of an hereditary master. I believe also that the spirit of the age and the course of events is tending to universal emancipation. But bound as I am

[17] *Register of Debates*, VIII, Pt. II, 1426. *Memoirs*, VIII, 434. December 12, 1831.
[18] JQA to Friend Moses Brown of Providence, Rhode Island. Washington, December 9, 1833. Adams MSS.

by the Constitution of the United States I am not at Liberty to take a part in promoting it. The remedy must arise in the seat of the evil."

By the seat of the evil he meant of course the slave states themselves. But there was not much hope that they would take any action to emancipate their slaves. With their manner of life now geared to slavery by the demands of the Industrial Revolution in England for cotton and more cotton, the Southern planters and their spokesmen no longer apologized for their peculiar institution: it was a "positive good," even a "blessing." Their state legislatures enacted special "black codes" to hold the Negroes to servitude without political or even human rights. Other state legislation prohibited all discussion of the slavery question by free men and women whether in church, school, press, or privacy of the study. A white terror backed up the heavy legal censorship with vigilance committees and lynch law. Such was the South's reaction to the antislavery impulse in the North.

3

No economic interpretation of history can adequately explain the agitation of the 1830's against slavery in the United States. It was a deep moral movement that drew its righteousness from wellsprings of Christian ethics in evangelical churches of the Northern states. It received its immediate impulse from the great religious revival of that decade, led by Charles Grandison Finney, which rescued so many congregations from the brimstone heritage of Calvinism. Finney and his followers preached the essential virtue of man and conversion to good works as well as to God. They sought to confirm the new light of their belief by applying Christianity to American life: humanitarian movements such as improvement of education, penal reform, temperance, women's rights, international peace, and social responsibility for the poor, the wayward, the lowly in life, and the slave.[19] John Quincy Adams clearly perceived in his day what a distinguished school of historians [20] has recognized in ours: that all these movements had the same animation of religious fervor.[21]

Finney's most saintly convert, Theodore D. Weld, focused the good works of the Great Revival upon the abolition of slavery. The resulting antislavery movement sprang up in the same Burned-over District that

[19] Nye: *Fettered Freedom*, p. 4.

[20] No one can write of this subject without reading Gilbert Hobbs Barnes's outstanding study of *The Antislavery Impulse, 1830–1844* (New York, 1933), which makes clear the evangelical background; and Russell B. Nye's *Fettered Freedom: Civil Liberties and the Slavery Controversy, 1830–1840* (East Lansing, Mich., 1949), which shows so immitigably how the new aggressive defense of slavery shackled freedom of speech and discussion in the South and threatened to do so in the North. I am indebted to both these scholarly works as well as to the distinguished writings of Whitney Cross and Dwight L. Dumond, loc. cit., for the history of the subject and for leads to sources.

[21] *Memoirs*, IX, 251.

had given root to the Antimasonic excitement [22] and spread out through the same wide area: New York and the states contiguous to it, with Rhode Island, and New Hampshire, Maine, and the Old Northwest. Like Antimasonry it had its isolated disciples in the border states and even in the South. It soon took the place of Antimasonry as the moral issue of the day. Eventually it developed into the greatest political movement of American history in the nineteenth century.[23]

From the countryside antislavery zeal seeped into the cities. The philanthropic Tappan brothers founded the New York City Antislavery Society (1833–40) under Weld's direct inspiration. This organization pledged itself to work for *immediate* abolition of slavery in the whole United States, after the example of the British West Indies, immediate abolition *to be gradually accomplished*. By this statement the leaders meant that gradual abolition would be sufficiently immediate just as soon as some kind of valid start was actually made, such as an amendment to the Constitution enabling a program of legislation for emancipation. This also was the policy of the American Antislavery Society (1833–40) until it fell apart and the fanatical William Lloyd Garrison captured the surviving remnant. At the peak of the movement (1840) there were over 2,000 abolition societies in the Northern states, with a membership of some 200,000 souls.[24] Nowhere is the deep, earnest conviction of these men and women better expressed than in the impassioned poetry of John Greenleaf Whittier:

> Shall outraged Nation cease to feel?
> Shall Mercy's tears no longer flow,
> Shall ruffian threats of cord and steel,
> The dungeon's gloom, th' assassin's blow,
> Turn back the spirit roused to save
> Our Truth, our Country, and the Slave? [25]

Abolitionist leaders such as Theodore Weld, Elijah P. Lovejoy, James G. Birney, Benjamin Lundy, and William Lloyd Garrison were willing to be Christian martyrs for the cause; nay, they even courted martyrdom,[26] and at least one of them, Lovejoy, found it at the hands of a proslavery mob in Illinois.

The enlightened public of the North could not understand such a sole-

---

[22] Cross: *Burned-over District*, pp. 217–26.

[23] Dwight Lowell Dumond has presented the *Antislavery Origins of the Civil War in the United States* in his Commonwealth Foundation Lectures at University College, London (New York and London, 1939).

[24] James Ford Rhodes: *History of the United States from the Compromise of 1850* (New York, 1893), I, 73–5.

[25] *Stanzas for the Times*.

[26] Hazel Catherine Wolf: *On Freedom's Altar: The Martyr Complex in the Abolition Movement* (Madison, 1952).

cism as "immediate emancipation gradually accomplished." They confused it with Garrison's program of immediate revolutionary abolition. To the higher and wealthier classes of society the new crusade to free the slaves was a threat to peace and order, a menace to profitable trade with acceptable Southern customers, a forecast of racial equality and amalgamation. There were even some good people who looked upon abolitionists as infidels because Garrison attacked both Bible and pulpit for refusing to support immediate and unqualified freedom of all slaves.[27] The serious concern of patriotic men of good will was that too much immediate pressure for abolition might break up the Union. They feared that rather than accept abolition of slavery in the nation's capital, some of the Southern states, at least South Carolina, would secede—before the North had grown strong enough to prevent secession. Southern leaders exploited this fear at every turn in order to defend and extend the outworks of their system. To them the District of Columbia was both a citadel and a symbol for the defense of slavery in federal territories and in their own states.

Despite his inner convictions on the evils of slavery Adams did not join any of the antislavery societies or participate in their meetings, because he felt that it was more important to preserve the Union in the long run rather than try to stamp out slavery immediately, and because, as will appear, he had another way of advancing the cause of abolition without loading himself with its political liabilities.

4

The American Antislavery Society, heading up hundreds of local societies all over the North, began agitation in earnest in 1834. A campaign of pamphlet propaganda directed to the South failed to touch the Christian conscience of slaveholders themselves to sweep away their system.[28] If enlightened humanitarian sentiment in the North confused abolition societies with Garrison's revolutionary invective, how could Southern readers look upon antislavery propaganda as other than encouragement to slave insurrection? Southern postmasters, even the postmaster in New York, threw the literature out of the post offices without objection from the Federal Government. A bill to exclude "incendiary" literature from the mails, recommended by President Jackson, failed to pass the Senate by the vote of 19 to 24 (April 1836).

In reporting this bill from the committee on post offices and post roads Calhoun, repeating his arguments for state sovereignty, declaimed against the "blind and criminal zeal" of the abolitionists. They would destroy the

---

[27] Nye: *Fettered Freedom*, p. 157.

[28] W. Sherman Savage has written an exhaustive study of *The Controversy Over the Distribution of Abolition Literature 1830–1860* (Washington: Association for the Study of Negro Life and History; 1938).

peace and prosperity of nearly half the states, burst asunder the bonds of Union, devastate the country, and engulf its institutions in a sea of blood. "It is madness," he declared, "to suppose that the slaveholding states would quietly submit to be sacrificed. Every consideration—interest, duty, and humanity, the love of country, the sense of wrong, hatred of oppressors, and treacherous and faithless confederates, and finally despair— would impel them to the most daring and desperate resistance in defense of property, family, country, liberty, and existence." [29]

After failing to command positive federal interference with the mails, the slaveholding representatives in Congress accomplished their object by state laws prohibiting local acceptance of postal delivery of antislavery literature.[30] Organized antislavery propaganda fell back on the more successful strategy of petitions to Congress for abolition of the slave trade and slavery in the District of Columbia and in the territories of the United States. The very circulation of such petitions was marvelously effective in numberless communities all over the North. So too was the angry expostulation of Southern members. Calhoun again hotly protested: "The peculiar institution of the South—that on the maintenance of which the very existence of the slaveholding States depends, is pronounced to be sinful and odious, in the eyes of God and man; and this with a systematic design of rendering us hateful in the eyes of the world—with a view to a general crusade against us and our institutions. This too, in the legislative halls of the Union. . . . The subject is beyond the jurisdiction of Congress; they have no right to touch it in any shape or form, or to make it the subject of deliberation or discussion." [31]

More and more such petitions came for John Quincy Adams to present to the House of Representatives. They came mostly [32] from other than his own constituents, but he presented them all faithfully. Was he not a Man of the Whole Nation? [33] Did not the people everywhere have a right to send petitions to him to present to their House of Representatives? The memorials gave him a spectacular opportunity of lending himself to the abolitionist urgings of his heart and conscience without alienating his own constituents, divided as they still were on the issue of abolition.

[29] *Register of Debates*, XII, Pt. IV, Appendix, p. 76. February 4, 1836.

[30] Nye: *Fettered Freedom*, pp. 68–9.

[31] *Register of Debates*, XIII, Pt. II, 2184–5. February 6, 1837.

[32] Only one petition of those received and presented before 1836 came from his own constituents. That was from certain inhabitants of Cohasset in the year 1832. JQA to James C. Doane, Cohasset. Washington, January 8, 1836. Adams MSS.

[33] "Mr. Adams belongs to no local district, to no political party, but to the Nation and to the people; he is elected by his district in Massachusetts, comes here with his family during the sessions of Congress, and keeps house by himself. While in the House of Representatives, he consults with no one, takes the advice of no one, and holds himself accountable to no one but the Nation." Diary of Joshua R. Giddings, quoted by Walter Buell: *Joshua R. Giddings, a Sketch* (Cleveland, 1882), pp. 79–80.

So numerous did the petitions become that they threatened to over-whelm the legislative functioning of the House. But it was not their number so much as their content that inflamed the Southern members. "Sir," declared Henry Wise of Accomac, Virginia, polemical successor to John Randolph of Roanoke, "slavery is interwoven in our political existence, is guaranteed by our Constitution, and its consequences must be borne by our Northern brethren as resulting from our system of Government. They cannot attack the institution of slavery without attacking the institutions of our country, our safety and welfare." [34]

The Southern states had successfully nullified the postal laws to prevent delivery of abolitionist literature in their midst. Next their representatives determined to put a stop to abolitionist propaganda by blocking off anti-slavery petitions to Congress, as a threat to the Union. In January 1836 Thomas Glascock of Georgia moved that "any attempt to agitate the question of slavery in this House is calculated to disturb the compromises of the Constitution, to endanger the Union, and if persisted in, to destroy, by a servile war, the peace and prosperity of the country." [35] Debate over Glascock's proposed resolution (never adopted) entered more and more into the general subject of slavery and the Constitution.

With difficulty John Quincy Adams restrained himself. So far the debate had been all on one side. "The voice of Freedom has not yet been heard," he wrote to Charles in Boston, "and I am earnestly urged to speak in her name. She will be trampled under foot if I do not; and I shall be trampled under foot if I do. . . . What can I do?" [36]

He was convinced that the great body of antislavery advocates were not fanatics. Had he yielded to the dictates of his inner voice, the sturdiest of abolitionists would have discovered in him a champion. But not yet did he publicly voice the question in his mind whether by the laws of God and Nature man could hold hereditary property in man. He was keeping back another proposition, portentous in all its implication: Congress did have a power to emancipate the slaves within a state or states, if only under its war powers—in case of insurrection.

Instead of sounding out before the people his long thoughts of civil war, he urged over and over that all antislavery petitions be referred to a select committee for disposal rather than be rejected outright. He voted for a resolution to that effect which Henry Laurens Pinckney of South Carolina presented with instructions to the committee to report that Congress had no constitutional power to interfere in any way with slavery in the states, and *ought not* to interfere in any way with slavery in the District of Columbia. The House adopted it by a vote of 174 to 48.[37] Adams voted for it because it seemed another compromise for the sake of the Union. And it

---

[34] *Register of Debates*, XI, Pt. II, 1399. February 16, 1835.
[35] Ibid., XII, Pt. II, 2137. January 6, 1836.
[36] JQA to CFA, Washington, December 15, 19, 1835. Adams MSS.
[37] *Register of Debates*, XII, Pt. II, 2491–8. February 8, 1836.

preserved the right of petition. Perhaps it meant a truce in the current "servile war" [38] between the sections.

The hollowness of the truce was soon evident when the committee, headed by Pinckney, brought in unanimous recommendations, on May 18, 1836, of three proposed resolutions:

1. Congress had no constitutional power to interfere in any way with slavery in any of the states.

2. Congress *ought not* to interfere in any way with slavery in the District of Columbia.

These two resolutions followed perfectly the instructions by the House, for which Adams had voted. But a third new resolution broke down any suggestion of compromise. The motive for it, reported the committee, was to arrest agitation on the subject of slavery and thus restore tranquillity to the public mind:

"3. All petitions, memorials, resolutions, propositions, or papers, relating in any way, or to any extent whatsoever, to the subject of slavery or the abolition of slavery, shall, without being either printed or referred, be laid on the table, and that no further action whatever shall be had thereon."

The Speaker recognized various Southern members who spoke successively to the three proposed resolutions, opposing particularly the second because it implied that Congress did have the constitutional power to abolish slavery in the nation's capital. The majority made no effort to stop this criticism. Then John Quincy Adams rose. He was not willing now to support any of the three resolutions, and he wanted to tell his constituents and the whole country why. Speaker James K. Polk, staunch Administration man and Tennessee slaveholder, recognized George W. Owens, a Unionist from Savannah, Georgia, who moved the previous question. Promptly the House adopted the motion, 95 to 82, thus shutting off the ex-President, or any other member, from arguing *against* any of the resolutions. [39]

"Am I gagged or am I not?" shrilly cried the elder statesman.

"Order! Order!" Loud calls from majority members of the House.

"The motion [of the previous question] is not debatable," pronounced the Chair.

Adams appealed to the House. It sustained the Speaker's ruling against him, 109 to 89.

They proceeded to vote on each resolution separately.

When the Clerk called Adams's name on the first resolution, he rose politely. "If the House will allow me five minutes in time," he begged, "I pledge myself to prove that resolution false and utterly untrue." He had in mind the terrible argument that in time of insurrection or civil war

[38] JQA to Solomon Lincoln of Hingham, Massachusetts. Washington, April 4, 1836. Adams MSS.

[39] *Register of Debates*, XII, Pt. III, 3758–78. May 18, 19, 1836.

Congress could interfere with slavery even *within the states* by virtue of its war powers.

"Order! Order! Order!" came the cries again, as Adams strove in vain to get the floor.

The Speaker proceeded with the roll-call. The House adopted the first resolution, 182 to 9. Only eight other members, including Edward Everett, dared to vote with Adams against the proposition that Congress had no constitutional power to interfere in *any* way (even with the war power) with slavery in a state of the Union.[40]

Nobody could be more resourceful than Adams in finding technicalities within the *lex parliamentaria* to make an unwilling majority—and the country behind him—listen to him. An opportunity occurred when the House resumed the regular order of the day before voting on the second and third resolutions. It went back to a joint resolution enabling the President to distribute relief rations to refugees from Indian hostilities (the Seminole wars) in Georgia and Alabama. Debate on this subject began within the Committee of the Whole, where the previous question could not apply. Adams got the floor and deftly turned the subject into a discussion of the war powers of Congress for the general welfare. The Administration and its majority of Southern slaveholders and Northern Democrats, he averred, were leading the country into an aggressive war over the Texas Question for the conquest of Mexico and the re-establishment of slavery where it had been abolished. Did they think antislavery England or France would stand by with folded arms? If we grabbed Texas for slavery, England would take Cuba for freedom! The ensuing war might extend to the North American continent itself.

"Mr. Chairman, are you ready for all these wars? A Mexican war? A war with Great Britain, if not with France? A general Indian war? A servile war? And, as an inevitable consequence of them all, a civil war? . . . Do you imagine that while, in the very nature of things, your own Southern and Southwestern States must be the Flanders of these complicated wars, the battlefield upon which the last great conflict must be fought between slavery and emancipation; do you imagine that your Congress will have no constitutional authority to interfere with the institution of slavery in any way in the States of this confederation? . . . From the instant that your slaveholding states become the theatre of war, civil, servile, or foreign, from that instant *the war powers of Congress extend to interference with the institution of slavery in every way by which it can be interfered with,* from a claim of indemnity for slaves taken or destroyed, to the cession of the State burdened with slavery to a foreign power." [41]

[40] *Register of Debates,* XII, Pt. IV, 4027–31. May 25, 1836.

[41] Ibid., XII, Pt. IV, 4046–7. Italics inserted.

For JQA's own intimate account of the proceedings see JQA to S. Sampson of Plymouth, Washington, May 21, 1836; to Benjamin Lundy, June 2, 1836; to Robert Walsh, June 3, 1836; to Nicholas Biddle, June 10, 1836; to Dr. George Parkman, June

John Quincy Adams's speech brought thundering vituperation from the South and West, and shouts of antislavery applause from the North.[42] He had all but said what he really had in mind: not protection of slavery by martial law (as in Nat Turner's rebellion) but total emancipation of slaves in a great civil war for the preservation of the Union. But that day must be put off until the Union was strong enough to win. It would not come during his lifetime. Meanwhile his duty to the Union, and to the cause of antislavery, was to retard rather than hasten the ultimate conflict.[43] His earthly career must soon close—so he continually felt. "To open the way for others is all that I can do. The cause is good and great." [44]

The House, having voted the relief for refugees from Indian hostilities without a record poll, was ready next day (May 26, 1836) to vote on the two other Pinckney resolutions.

On the second resolution (undesirable to interfere with slavery in the District) Adams had nothing to say. Significantly he asked to be excused from voting. He did not attempt to explain why, if only because the majority wouldn't let him. This marked a further crystallization of his antislavery views: he would not yet commit himself publicly to what privately he had been advising his Quaker correspondents: that Congress *ought not* to abolish slavery in the District of Columbia.

The Speaker passed him in the vote on the second resolution. Under the previous question the House proceeded without debate to call the roll on the third resolution (to table all petitions relating to slavery).

When Adams's name was sounded he rose and shouted: "I hold the resolution to be in direct violation of the Constitution of the United States, of the rules of this House, and of the rights of my constituents." [45] He sent

---

22, 1836. Charles Francis Adams, Jr., printed excerpts from these and various other letters to JQA, from the Adams MSS., in *John Quincy Adams and Martial Law*, MHS *Proceedings*, Second Series, XV (January 1902), 436–78, reprinted together with article by Worthington C. Ford on *John Quincy Adams, His Connection with the Monroe Doctrine* (Cambridge, 1902). Hereinafter cited as *Emancipation under Martial Law*. For further remarks on JQA's role in expounding this constitutional theory, which Lincoln pursued in 1863, see Charles Francis Adams, Jr.: *The Sifted Grain and the Grain Sifters*, an address at the dedication of the building of the State Historical Society of Wisconsin, at Madison, October 19, 1900 (privately printed). Copy in MHS.

[42] *Memoirs*, IX, 298.

[43] JQA to Friend E. P. Atlee, Philadelphia. Washington, June 25, 1836. Adams MSS.

[44] *Memoirs*, IX, 298. June 19, 1836.

[45] The first amendment to the Constitution says that Congress shall pass no *law* abridging the right of the people freely to petition the Government for the redress of grievances. It is difficult to accept Adams's argument that a mere *rule* of the House to table in advance a certain class of petitions, by "virtually" denying the right of petition, was unconstitutional. Even he would later propose, in the debates on the much stricter Gag of 1840, that a majority of the members present might vote not even to receive, for a special reason, a petition, provided that, in every case, the reason therefor should be entered in the Journal. *Memoirs*, X, 199–200.

his statement in writing to the Chair to be recorded in the Journal. The Speaker paid no attention to it or him. The roll-call proceeded. The third resolution passed, 117 to 68. Polk kept Adams's caveat from being recorded in the Journal of the House. In vain the ex-President tried next day to get the deliberate omission formally corrected on reading the minutes, but his protest, incorporating the statement, appeared in the stenographic report of the *Register of Debates*.[46]

Passage of the Pinckney resolutions imposed the first form of the notorious "Gag Rule" by which the combination of plain republicans of the North and slavery capitalists of the South attempted to block off all debate over slavery. The House renewed the Gag Rule in more and more stringent form, session by session of each Congress, until 1840, when it voted a standing rule of procedure (the Twenty-first Rule): no abolition petitions, memorials, etc., should be received by the House, nor entertained by it in any way whatever.

5

Gag Rules could nullify the right of petition; they could not destroy it. Abolitionist organizations multiplied the circulation of their petitions a thousandfold. During the year 1837–8 the American Antislavery Society secured from local societies and presented to the House of Representatives 130,200 petitions for the abolition of slavery in the District of Columbia; 32,000 for repeal of the Gag Rule; 21,200 for legislation forbidding slavery in the territories of the United States; 22,160 against admission of any new slave state; 23,160 for abolition of the slave trade between the states. These figures indicate only the number of petitions, not the millions of signatures to them.[47] The House received none of them.

Whom the gods would destroy they first make mad. By successive Gag Rules the Southern slaveholders and their Northern allies had joined the cause of freedom of petition and speech to that of abolition. From then on, more and more white men and women—not necessarily abolitionists—would be increasingly fearful for their own constitutional freedoms as well as concerned over the plight of enslaved Negroes. If the House of Representatives [48] could refuse to consider petitions concerning slavery or abolition, and the Speaker could rule out of order any discussion of that subject, what could prevent the majority from applying similar gags to other subjects obnoxious to them, such as Antimasonry, the dispossessed Indians, the tariff, a national bank, or internal improvements—the whole program of the Opposition?

Much to the indignation of conservative people in the North and slave-

[46] XII, Pt. IV, 4053. *Memoirs*, IX, 287.

[47] Nye: *Fettered Freedom*, p. 37.

[48] The Senate developed a less exceptionable procedure providing for reception of a petition but rejection of its contents, instead of passing a gag rule as Calhoun desired. Ibid., p. 45.

holders in the South, the abolitionists made of women and women's rights an instrument of their propaganda.[49] They stirred the gentler sex to sign the petitions. If John Quincy Adams raised an eyebrow at this radical practice,[50] he did not refuse to present female prayers to Congress. In January 1837 before the House had renewed the Gag Rule for the second session of the Twenty-fourth Congress, he rose to present three petitions identical in language for the abolition of slavery in the District of Columbia: one signed by 150 women of the town of Dorchester, adjacent to his own Plymouth district; the next bearing signatures of 228 women of South Weymouth, wives and daughters of his own immediate constituents; both groups determined to repeat their petitions session by session as long as they should be set aside; and a third sent in by townsmen of Dover in Norfolk County nearby. Other petitions were accumulating in Adams's mail, from groups in Weymouth, Scituate, Hanson, Kingston, Duxbury, all within his Twelfth (Plymouth) District, and from more towns in Massachusetts and in other states.[51]

The antislavery crusade had come home to him at last: one of the petitions was from Braintree, his village birthplace. He still thought the abolitionists a minority in the District;[52] but there was no doubt that the majority—practically everybody within hearing of the historical echoes of Plymouth Rock—believed in the right of petition.

Adams rose on the regular petition day (Monday) to present the memorial from the women of Dorchester. He moved that it be read. Glascock immediately objected to its reception at all. In resisting Glascock's opposing motion Adams managed to get in a good word for the abolitionists and their cause. Already, he said, a class of "pure and virtuous citizens" had to suffer contempt and calumny from a majority of the House for aspiring to "the greatest improvement that can possibly be effected in the condition of the human race—the total abolition of slavery on earth." To refuse even to *receive* their petitions, he warned, would be flying in the face of the Constitution itself. He begged his colleagues to hearken to the petition of these honorable women as they would listen to that of their own mothers.

[49] See *Letters of Theodore Dwight Weld, Angelina Grimké Weld, and Sarah Grimké, 1822–44*, Gilbert H. Barnes and Dwight L. Dumond, editors (2 vols., New York, 1934). Hereinafter cited as *Weld-Grimké Letters*.

[50] JQA to Messrs. Greene and Osborne, editors of the *Quincy Patriot*, U.S.H.R., Washington, January 14, 1837. Adams MSS.

[51] JQA to Messrs. Greene and Osborne, editors of the *Quincy Patriot*, U.S.H.R., Washington, January 14, 23, 1837; to Allen Danforth, editor of the Plymouth *Old Colony Memorial*, January 17, 1837; to Petitioners for the Abolition of Slavery and the Slave Trade in the District of Columbia from the Twelfth Congressional District of Massachusetts, January 31, 1837. Adams MSS.

[52] JQA to the Petitioners for the Abolition of Slavery and the Slave Trade in the District of Columbia, from the Twelfth [Plymouth] Congressional District of Massachusetts, and to the Other Inhabitants of the District, U.S.H.R., Washington, January 31, 1837.

The chivalrous Southerners and their Northern allies would not refuse
to receive the petition, but they voted to lay it on the table without reading it. Adams then presented the other identical petition from the 228
women of South Weymouth. Again Glascock objected to its reception. The
Plymouth member started to read it: " 'impressed with the sinfulness of
slavery, and keenly aggrieved by its existence in a part of our Country
over which'—"

"A point of order!" cried Pinckney. "Has the gentleman from Massachusetts a right under the rule, to read the petition?"

"He has a right to make a statement of the contents," decided Speaker
Polk, not reminding the House that "the rule" had expired with the last
session and had not yet been renewed.

"It is a privilege I shall exercise," declared Adams, "until I am deprived
of it by some positive act—"

"You have a right to make a brief statement of the contents of the petition," vouchsafed the Speaker.

"I am doing so, Sir," asserted Adams.

"Not in the opinion of the Chair," Polk declared.

"I was at the point of the petition," the Plymouth member assured him,
and continued reading: " 'keenly aggrieved by its existence in a part of
our Country over which Congress possesses exclusive jurisdiction in all
cases whatever'—"

"Order! Order!" from all over the House.

" 'Do most earnestly petition your honorable body'—"

"Mr. Speaker," shouted John Chambers of Kentucky, "Mr. Speaker, I
rise to a point of order."

Adams persisted: " 'immediately to abolish slavery in the District of
Columbia.' . . ."

"Mr. Speaker," interrupted Chambers: "a call to order."

"Order! Order!"

"Take your seat," the Speaker bluntly ordered the ex-President.

The friend of freedom sank back slowly toward his chair still reading
loudly and with great rapidity of enunciation: " *'and-to-declare-every-
human-being-free-who-sets-foot-upon-its-soil.'* "

Debate followed whether these words were a brief statement of contents within the Speaker's ruling. He decided in Adams's favor. The native
of Braintree then announced that the petitioners intended to renew their
prayers year by year in the "holy cause of human freedom."

Ratliff Boon of Indiana moved to table the petition. Glascock invoked
the previous question. Instantly they tabled the obnoxious document.
Adams next presented his third petition, from the men of Dover. It served
to produce long debate over slavery in general. They tabled that too.[53] A
few days later, January 18, 1837, the House revived the Pinckney Gag for

[53] *Register of Debates,* XIII, Pt. I, 1314–39. Monday (petition day), January 9,
1837. Italics inserted.

the duration of the session, acting under the previous question without further discussion.

6

Adams choked on the tightening gag.[54] He felt for weak spots in the parliamentary stranglehold. His exasperated opponents in turn watched for opportunities to make a fool of him; and bystanders wouldn't be beyond tripping him up just for the fun of it. Presently someone sent him a petition, not too literally worded and signed, from nine females of Fredericksburg, Virginia, requesting prohibition of the slave trade in the District. He wasn't sure whether the signers were free Negroes or mulattoes, but felt their object was laudable for women of any color or complexion.[55] He resolved to use it to test the Gag Rule: on February 6, 1837 he presented the petition as from "nine ladies of Fredericksburg." He did not read their names, he explained, because he did not know what might happen to them if he did. Further, it was not a petition for the abolition of slavery, only for "prohibition" of the slave trade in the capital. He was careful to tell his colleagues that he could not be absolutely sure it was genuine.

The Speaker ordered the petition to be laid on the table, under "the resolution." There the names of the female signers became available to any member who would take the trouble to look at them.

Adams then announced that he had another paper on which he desired to have a decision of the Speaker before it was presented. It was in an educated handwriting, but signed by scrawls and marks, "purporting to come from slaves." He would send it to the Chair.

In a flash Joab Lawler, a Southern Whig from Tuscaloosa, Alabama, jumped to his feet. "I object to its going to the Chair! I want it to appear on the Journal that I objected."

Speaker Polk was baffled. He couldn't remember a case of slaves ever petitioning Congress. He decided to take the sense of the House. Before he could do so, Charles Eaton Haynes of Georgia was up, expressing his astonishment that the gentleman from Massachusetts "or any other gentleman" should ever make a question of a paper of this kind.

"I call the gentleman from Georgia to order," responded Adams, "on the ground that he is making personal remarks."

Polk cautioned Haynes, who could not trust his feelings to pursue the subject further within the rules of the House.

---

[54] This so-called Hawes Resolution was word for word the same as Pinckney's former gag resolution except that it omitted the word *further* in the last clause of the Pinckney resolution: "and that no [further] action whatever be had thereon." Ibid., XIII, Pt. II, 1411–12.

[55] JQA to the Inhabitants of the Twelfth Congressional District of Massachusetts, U.S.H.R., Washington, March 3, 1837. *Letters from John Quincy Adams to His Constituents*, loc. cit., 4–9.

The paper and the contents remained in Adams's hands, despite wishes of the Speaker to get hold of it.

Waddy Thompson, Jr., a South Carolina Whig, hotly suggested that a grand jury of the District of Columbia might indict the ex-President for the criminal act of inciting slaves to rebellion. Dixon Hall Lewis, huge state-rights Democrat from Alabama, a mountain of a man, called stentoriously on members of the slaveholding states to come forward and demand severe punishment of the gentleman from Massachusetts for disturbance of the House's decorum and infraction of its rules. Southern members got more and more excited. Adams was the willing instrument of "incendiary fanatics." He was offending the South, insulting it, trifling with it, *threatening the Union!* They introduced one by one a whole series of abortive resolutions and amendments to resolutions for formal censure and punishment of the Honorable John Quincy Adams for attempting to introduce a petition from slaves for the abolition of slavery.

During the debate John Mercer Patton of Virginia, a moderate Democrat, remonstrated with Adams for having presented the earlier petition—from the ladies of Fredericksburg. He had been brought up in that town, he said. He could assure the gentleman that there was not one respectable name attached to the paper; they were all free Negroes or mulattoes; he recognized only one of them—she was a mulatto of "infamous" character. (Adams took note to himself of this seeming acquaintance.)

Abijah Mann, a Van Buren supporter from New York, young enough to be John Quincy Adams's son, put on a show of respect and charitable excuse for the old man's recent aberrations. "Sir," he concluded, "it becomes us to respect his gray hairs, his old age, his long public services, and to seek out apologies and excuses in his behalf, if possible, for the obstinacy and ebullitions of temper which on these occasions he so often exhibits, and which is so much opposed to cool deliberation and the dignity of the proceedings of this House. Thus shielded and protected by his age and public character, it had been a matter of surprise to those who are not spectators of our proceedings, that a member of his great learning and experience should so forget his dignity as to presume upon that age and character as to license him to annoy and trifle with the House and its most solemn and satisfactory regulation."

Adams let them continue. No one recognized his age and frailties of health and temperament more than he did. But no one felt more toned up by a good fight for the right. Coolly he reminded his raging adversaries that they had better reshape their resolutions if they expected successfully to censure him. He had only applied respectfully to the Speaker and the House for the Chair's decision whether a petition purporting to be from slaves was in order. He hadn't attempted to present any such petition, much less a petition for abolition of slavery or the slave trade. He hadn't said what was in this one from the slaves. Presently it developed that the paper in question—perhaps originally delivered to John Quincy Adams as a hoax—was actually a prayer *against* abolition lest such a step interfere with the slaves' welfare! [56]

The "Madman of Massachusetts" [57] had hoaxed his hoaxers. It made his assailants more furious than ever. He was a trifler with the South, he was an enemy of the Union! They wanted to drag him to the bar of the House. Some would expel him from their midst. But others began to think twice, lest they themselves some day lose their freedom of speech in Congress, perhaps to speak for Southern rights and slavery. The majority began to cool down. Eventually they agreed to vote on a new set of resolutions designed not so much to curb the freedom of members to express themselves as to fasten slavery tighter on the Union.

"1. *Resolved:* that any member who shall hereafter present any petition from the slaves of the Union ought to be considered as regardless of the feelings of the House, the rights of the Southern States, and unfriendly to the Union."

The slaves of this Union!

"2. *Resolved:* that slaves do not possess the right of petition secured to the people of the United States by the Constitution."

Only the owners and masters of human chattels could speak for the slaves!

"3. *Resolved:* that the Hon. John Q. Adams, having solemnly disclaimed all design of doing anything disrespectful to this House in the inquiry he made of the Speaker as to the petition purporting to be from the slaves, and having avowed his intention not to offer to present the petition if the House was of opinion it ought not to be presented—therefore, all further proceedings in regard to his conduct do now cease."

This made it look as if John Quincy Adams was sorry and had apologized to the House!

The new set of proslavery resolutions now being duly moved and seconded, Aaron Vanderpoel, a New York Democrat from Kinderhook, moved the previous question to cut off all debate. Adams politely asked him to withdraw his motion: "I would like an opportunity for a full hearing in my own defense. I hope you will grant the privilege."

William Kennon, Democrat from Ohio, moved to lay the whole subject, now becoming more and more embarrassing, on the table. Adams opposed this. The House voted against tabling, 50 to 144. For once they voted down the previous question also, thus avoiding a precedent of refusing to listen to one of their members in his own defense—something that might be used against any of them at any time for anything.

The remarkable piece of dialectics that now followed was the most dra-

[56] Buddey Taylowe to JQA, Virginia, February 1, 1837, "On behalf of the petitioners," covering a petition signed by Buddey Taylowe and twenty-one other slaves with crude signatures or marks. Adams MSS.

[57] J. H. Paine to JQA, private, *Daily Advocate* office, Boston, February 6, 1837, enclosing undated clippings from *Albany Argus* and *New York Times.* Adams MSS.

matic and stinging speech of John Quincy Adams's life so far. Posing as
an anti-abolitionist but a champion of freedom of speech, the old master
roamed over the morals of slavery, cracking his whip at the slaveholders
like a Brighton cattle-driver, but always coming dutifully back to the right
of petition.

"What, Sir? Will you put the right of petitioning, of craving for help
and mercy and protection, on the footing of political privileges? It is an
idea which has not even been entertained by the utmost extreme of human despotism; no despot, of any age or clime, has ever denied this humble privilege to the poorest or the meanest of human creatures. . . . That
would be a sad day, Sir, in my opinion, when a vote should pass this
House that would not receive a petition from slaves. What would it lead
to? When the principle is once begun of limiting the right of petition,
where would it stop? . . . The honorable gentleman makes it a crime because I presented a petition which he affirms to be from colored women,
which women were of infamous character, as the honorable gentleman
says—prostitutes, I think the gentleman said."

"I did not say they were prostitutes," Patton hastily explained. "They
are free mulattoes." He said he wished to wipe away the stain placed on
the real ladies of Fredericksburg.

"The word 'woman' is an expression much dearer to my heart than that
of 'lady,'" Adams continued, addressing the Chair. "I thought the honorable gentleman had said they were 'infamous.' I shall forever entertain
the proposition that the sacred right of petition, of begging for mercy,
does not depend on character any more than it does on condition. It is a
right that cannot be denied to the humblest, to the most wretched." He
paused for an instant.

Patton again protested: "I have not said that I know those women."

"I am glad to hear the honorable gentleman disclaim any knowledge of
them," the Plymouth member declared imperturbably, "for I had been
going to ask, if they were infamous women, then who is it that had made
them infamous? Not their color, I believe, but their masters! I have heard
it said in proof of that fact, and I am inclined to believe it is the case,
that in the South there existed great resemblances between the progeny
of the colored people and the white men who claim possession of them.
Thus, perhaps, the charge of infamous might be retorted on those who
made it, as originating from themselves."

"Great agitation in the House!" So comments the *Register of Debates*.
This official record does scant justice to the discomfort of those who had
reviled Adams and his abolitionist friends and said all manner of evil
against them.

In the days of the American Revolution, Mother Abigail had taught her
boy to carry himself modestly and diffidently, to curb his temper, to exercise self-control in the face of provocation. "I do not mean, however,"
she had reminded him, "to have you insensible to real injuries. He who

will never turn when trodden on is deficient in spirit."[58] Abigail Adams, glancing down from near the judgment seat to "U.S.H.R., Washington," would not have found her great son deficient in spirit, even in his old age.

By now his skillful tactics and bold words had so vexed his adversaries that again they tried to table the whole affair, or to adjourn; but both these motions failed. They then decided to vote separately on each of the three new resolutions. The first (branding sponsors of petitions from slaves as unfriendly to the South and to the Union) failed to pass, 92 to 105. That cleared the Old Man Eloquent so decisively in principle that its proponent, Pinckney, expressed the hope that the mover of the third resolution would withdraw it. The Chair ruled it could not be withdrawn. They now passed over the second resolution temporarily in order to vote immediately on the third, in effect pardoning John Quincy Adams.

He asked his colleagues not to vote for the third resolution: to pardon him would be a verdict against him. "I here say, that I have not done one single thing that I would not do over again in like circumstances. Not one thing have I done that I have not done under the highest and most solemn sense of duty."

The third resolution failed to pass, 21 to 105. Only twenty-one members out of the great majority of the House who had been arrayed against him would now vote to censure him even indirectly. Of those twenty-one only three were Northern men—Van Buren Democrats. It was an astounding triumph.

Two days later, February 11, 1837, the House voted by a heavy majority, 163 to 18, in favor of the second resolution (that slaves have no right of petition).[59]

The slaves had lost, but Adams had won.

The Senate followed Calhoun and passed anti-abolitionist resolutions branding any intermeddling with slavery in the states or in the District of Columbia as tending to weaken and destroy the Union.[60] But the House was based on a more direct and popular representation. Despite the handicap of the three-fifths ratio, the increasing population of the North was catching up on the constitutional over-representation of the South. When plain republicans of the North refused to vote with the Southern planters that any man who presented a petition to Congress from slaves was an enemy of the South and unfriendly to the Union, it marked a turning-point in the history of the "slavocracy," to use Adams's word. Van Buren himself would finally give up his formula for national politics; eventually he would become in 1848 the Presidential candidate of the Free-Soil Party, with Charles Francis Adams for his running-mate.

[58] Vol. I, p. 8.
[59] For the debates of February 6 to 11, 1837 on abolition of slavery and on the right of petition, see *Register of Debates*, XIII, Pt. II, 1586–1735; also Benton's *Abridgment of Debates of Congress*, XIII, 265–90, 295–6.
[60] Wiltse: *Calhoun, Nullifier*, pp. 369–73.

All this political controversy gave healthy vent to John Quincy Adams's compulsive character. It made him feel firm and fine, better than he had felt for several years.[61] In the heat of battle he lost sight of those bodily ills and humors that had weighed so heavily upon him.

7

The first Southern threat on John Quincy Adams's life now occurred. It came on a letterhead picturing in red outline a raised bare arm and bowie-knife and the words: "Vengeance is mine, say the South!" Below the upraised blade was a whip and lash with: "Flog and Spare Not!" Under these bloody insignia was the following warning, signed by one dreadful "Dirk Hatteraik":

"Sir, Your conduct during this session of Congress is such as to draw upon you the indignation of the South. Your endeavours to agitate the question of abolition upon each succeeding week shows the blackness of your heart and your ingratitude towards a set of people who supported you in your administration when placed at the head of this Government, but, sir, it will not go unrewarded, depend on it. *The rod is cut and seasoned that will make your old hide smart* for your insidious attempt on the Southern rights.

"I send you this as a caution, as your course will be watched, and if ever you dare attempt to vindicate abolition again you will be *lynched,* if it has to be done by *drawing* you from your *seat* in the *House by force.* So be on your guard. The author of this is now on his way to Washington with *others* able and *determined* to *fulfill their threat.*" [62]

For every Southern threat to lynch him came scores of heartening letters from friends of freedom in the North—many of them abolitionists.

"Respected Man," wrote one anonymous admirer from Boston, expressing gratitude for the Plymouth member's fearless course, "I know you are not an abolitionist in the sense it is generally understood. Still, I believe by what I have read of your writing, speeches, etc., that you will not *fear* to express your views, and if you fully express them it will have a tremendous effect in removing oppression and extending freedom. Go on then, Sage of Quincy! Fear not Southern insolence. Defend our petitions and in turn we will defend and sustain you. You never have been welcomed home with more heartfelt gratitude, and you always will be as long as you possess the courage and patriotism you have lately manifested. Our legislature has sustained you. Yes, and the people will not only sustain you, but love you. I mingle much among my fellow citizens and I *know* that you are more honored for this act than you are aware of. . . ." [63]

"I have always esteemed you," wrote the reformer Gerrit Smith, "But

61 JQA to Peyton Gay, Baltimore. Washington, January 3, 1837.
62 "Dirk Hatteraik" to JQA, P.O., Pittsburgh, February 10, 1837. Adams MSS.
63 "Justice" to JQA, Boston, April 28, 1837. Adams MSS.

now since you have shown the pity of your heart for the enslaved poor—
for the downtrodden millions who are sharers of our common humanity,
and who, as well as ourselves, are made 'in the image of God,' I not only
esteem but love you." [64]

More and more Adams privately associated and corresponded with antislavery people: with those who like William Ellery Channing thought
slavery a great moral evil and called on the South to do away with it; [65]
with William Slade of Vermont, old Antimason who was rapidly becoming an abolitionist; and working abolitionists such as Benjamin Lundy,
John Greenleaf Whittier, Joshua Leavitt, the Grimké sisters, and James
and Lucretia Mott.[66] He described himself to them as a "fellow sufferer
in the same holy cause." [67] He accepted the applause of his abolitionist
friends for his stand on fundamental American freedoms, but was careful to explain that he was opposed to the abolition of slavery in the
District of Columbia as impractical for the present.[68]

The abolitionists felt that his heart was in the right place, even if they
couldn't quite understand his practical politics. The American Antislavery
Society adopted a resolution of thanks to him for having defended "so
wisely and so well" the right of women to be heard in Congress, but they
qualified it with regret that by opposing abolition in the District of Columbia he had not sustained "the cause of Freedom and of God." [69]

Lewis Tappan bluntly asked him why he couldn't champion what he
really believed: "If slavery be a sin, its immediate abandonment is a
duty." [70] Sarah Grimké thanked him for his services to the women of the
United States in defending their right of petition, but regretted his opposition to the abolition of slavery in the nation's capital: "I regretted it because it appeared to me to be a surrender of moral principle to political
expediency." [71]

Adams wrestled night and day with this age-old problem of moral and
political philosophy. "The object is noble," he knew in his heart, "the motive pure—but the undertaking of such tremendous magnitude, difficulty
and danger, that I shrink from the contemplation of it, and much more
from any personal agency in promoting it. I have abstained, sometimes

[64] Gerrit Smith to JQA, Peterboro, Madison County, N.Y., February 3, 1837.
Adams MSS.

[65] William E. Channing: *Slavery* (Boston, 1835).

[66] J. G. Whittier to JQA, Philadelphia, January 23, 1837; JQA to J. G. Whittier,
Washington, January 26, 1837. Adams MSS.

[67] JQA to Reverend William E. Channing, Washington, February 10, 1837. Adams
MSS. *Memoirs*, X, 38–40.

[68] See the letter of JQA to Gerrit Smith, Peterboro, N.Y. Washington, April 5,
1837. Adams MSS.

[69] Barnes: *Antislavery Impulse*, pp. 143, 265.

[70] JQA to Lewis Tappan, New York. Washington, February 9, 1837. Lewis Tappan
to JQA, New York, February 15, 1837. Adams MSS.

[71] Sarah Grimké to JQA, Boston, June 8, 1837. Adams MSS.

perhaps too pertinaciously abstained from all participation in measures *leading* to that conflict for Life and Death between *Freedom* and *Slavery*, through which I have yet not been able to see how this Union could ultimately be preserved from passing." [72]

He had to keep slow pace along the antislavery road with the constituents of his district [73] and the State of Massachusetts. The Massachusetts legislature passed resolutions supporting the right of petition, but said nothing on the abolition of slavery or even the slave trade in the District of Columbia. They praised their representatives in Congress for upholding this freedom, but said nothing about John Quincy Adams individually.[74] "Under these circumstances," Adams explained to Whittier, "you will perceive that great prudence and caution become indispensably necessary to me, with regard to any manifestation on my part giving countenance to the movements of Antislavery Societies. . . ." [75]

His closest friends and own family—Mrs. Adams, son Charles, and Mary (John's widow)—did their utmost to dissuade him from quixotic controversies: [76] sallying forth in search of giants and coming in conflict with every windmill. Particularly they tried to keep him from abolitionism. Heart and mind battled between slavery and abolition as if to destroy him. "I walk on the edge of a precipice in every step that I take." [77]

Anxiously he reported to his constituents,[78] to the newspapers of his home district—the *Quincy Patriot* and Plymouth *Old Colony Memorial*—

[72] JQA to Charles Hammond (editor of the *Cincinnati Gazette*, which had reported fully and accurately Adams's speeches in the House), Washington, March 31, 1837. Adams MSS. See William Henry Smith: *Charles Hammond and His Relations to Henry Clay and John Quincy Adams; or Constitutional Limitations and the Contest for Freedom of Speech and the Press* (Chicago: Chicago Historical Society; 1885), pp. 67–70. This pamphlet is No. LXI in a collection of biographical essays in the Sterling Memorial Library at Yale.

[73] "We are not all practical abolitionists. I presume there is not an individual in New England who does not abhor Slavery in every shape, who does not feel it is a deep stain upon his Country that it is suffered to exist in the very District where our National Government is located. But while we entertain these sentiments, a large portion of your constituents, I believe, concur in the opinions so candidly expressed by you in relation to the manner and the principles on which the removal of this tremendous evil may be accomplished." Jacob H. Loud to JQA, Plymouth, May 10, 1837. Adams MSS.

[74] Joint Resolutions of Massachusetts Legislature, April 11, 1837. Adams MSS.

[75] JQA to J. G. Whittier, Newburyport, Mass. Washington, April 19, 1837. Adams MSS.

[76] JQA to Nicholas Biddle, Washington, June 10, 1836. Adams MSS.

[77] *Memoirs*, IX, 343, 349, 365.

[78] JQA to the Petitioners for the Abolition of Slavery and the Slave Trade in the District of Columbia from the Twelfth Congressional District of Massachusetts, and to the Other Inhabitants of the District, U.S.H.R., Washington, January 31, February 24, 1837. Adams MSS. Other group letters by JQA to constituents, of March 3, 8, 13, [20,] 1837 are printed in *Letters from John Quincy Adams to His Constituents of the Twelfth Congressional District, to which is Added His Speech in Congress Delivered February 9, 1837*. John G. Whittier wrote a stirring Preface for this collection.

and also to the *Boston Daily Advocate* (Hallett's paper, now a Van Buren sheet), explaining his course to members of "all parties," and giving full and accurate accounts of the debates over petitions.[79] When he got home from Congress, he knew that he had divined their feelings accurately. Strong expressions of approval sanctioned his course so far: from the delegates of the Plymouth district in the Massachusetts House of Representatives, who presented him with a gold-headed cane, made by a Braintree man; [80] from the women of South Weymouth; from a mass meeting of citizens in Scituate, and another one in his home town of Quincy.[81]

He had gone just about as far as public opinion would tolerate. Gently he admonished his abolitionist friends to ease up on their impractical petitions for the abolition of the slave trade and slavery in the District of Columbia, while encouraging and reciprocating their hopes for the ultimate freedom of slaves throughout the world.[82] He tried to deflect the antislavery crusade from the District of Columbia to the Rio Grande. There was nothing in the wording of the Gag Rule to prevent consideration of petitions against the annexation of Texas. Here was a new question that stabbed to the heart of the great sectional issue over slavery.

[79] JQA to Messrs. Greene and Osborne, editors of the *Quincy Patriot,* U.S.H.R., Washington, January 14, 23, February 1, March 18, 1837; to Allen Danforth, editor of the *Old Colony Memorial,* January 17, 1837; to James H. Paine of Boston, February 14, 1837. Adams MSS.

[80] Minot Thayer to JQA, April 25, May 1, 1837. Adams MSS.

[81] Resolutions of Citizens of Scituate, May 1, 1837; of Women of South Weymouth, July 29, 1837; Resolutions of a Convention of Citizens Held at Quincy, August 23, 1837; Resolutions of a Convention of Delegates from the Twelfth Congressional District of Massachusetts, August 23, 1837. Adams MSS. See also *Memoirs,* IX, 356–62.

[82] See, for example: JQA to Rowland Johnson at Philadelphia, Washington, January 19, 1837; to John Greenleaf Whittier, Washington, January 26, 1837; to Reverend J. Edwards, President of the Theological Seminary at Andover, Quincy, July 13, 1837; to Benjamin Lundy at Philadelphia, Quincy, August 10, 1837. Adams MSS.

CHAPTER XVIII
Texas and the Right of Petition
(1819 – 1839)

Our country! In her intercourse with foreign nations may she always be in the right; but our country, right or wrong.

TOAST OF CAPTAIN STEPHEN DECATUR,
APRIL 4, 1816

I can never join with my voice in the toast which I see in the papers attributed to one of our gallant naval commanders. I cannot ask of Heaven success, even for my country, in a cause where she should be in the wrong.

JOHN QUINCY ADAMS TO JOHN ADAMS,
AUGUST 1, 1816 [1]

THE ESTABLISHMENT of our Continental Republic—though not on the scale of all of North America that John Quincy Adams had envisioned in the younger years of his First Career—was the most magnificent achievement of American nationality during the nineteenth century. Achieved at what terrible price! In its accomplishment it divided the Republic against itself over the question of free men or slaves in the new states and territories. It cost a great civil war.

[1] *"Fiat justicia, pareat cœlum,"* continued the younger Adams. "My toast would be, may our country be always successful, but whether successful or otherwise always right. I disclaim as unsound all patriotism incompatible with the principles of eternal justice. But the truth is that the American union, while united, *may* be certain of success in every rightful cause, and may if it pleases never have any but a rightful cause to maintain." *Writings*, VI, 58–62. As an old man John Quincy Adams repeated these precise sentiments in the House of Representatives, April 14, 1842, in a speech on *War with Great Britain and Mexico* (Boston: separately published at the *Emancipator* Office; 1842), p. 15.

1

The fervor of abolitionist and of anti-imperialist historians descended from them cast a spell for a long time over the historiography of southwestern expansion. They looked upon it as John Quincy Adams saw it in his old age during the antislavery crusade: a wicked conspiracy secretly plotted by Andrew Jackson and his Tennessee protégé Sam Houston to wrest Texas from the sovereignty and free soil of Mexico in order to bring into the Union a protean covey of slave states that would fortify and perpetuate slavery in this Union against the growing power of freedom.[2] A newer school of historians [3] has shown that the United States Government had nothing to do with the settlement of Texas or the Texas Revolution. Immigration into that vast and empty region between 1823 and 1836 was an uncontrolled movement of Western pioneers attracted thither by the climate and fertility of those expansive prairies and their great rivers, many of them enticed by the lure of Spanish and Mexican land grants and tax exemptions. An unmanageable population of some 30,000 white American settlers, plus 5,000 slaves, flowed across the unguarded frontier, a people alien to the Mexicans in culture, religion, and habits of government. Naturalization and nominal acceptance of the Catholic state religion did not essentially change these frontiersmen. As could have been expected, friction developed between them and the distant Government of Chapultepec.

Mexican attempts to abolish slavery in Texas were not the only cause of trouble with the northern outlanders. A tapering off of tax exemptions, a well-justified introduction of restrictions on further immigration of aliens, the attempt to submerge and Mexicanize the District of Texas in the State of Coahuila across the Rio Grande, with courts of justice six hundred miles away; the chaotic condition of Mexico; all these difficulties stirred the Texans to direct action. The final, real outrage was abolition of the Constitution of Mexico by the Mexican Congress, under the thumb of the dictator Santa Anna. Then the people of Texas did just what the people of New England would have done if the Congress at Washington at the bidding of Andrew Jackson had abolished the Constitution of the United States. They declared their independence. Their fathers had done so before them, and for lesser grievances, in the American Revolution against a distant king and parliament.

[2] William Jay: *A Review of the Causes and Consequences of the Mexican War* (Boston, 1849). Henry Wilson: *History of the Rise and Fall of the Slave Power in America* (3 vols., Boston, 1872–3). Hermann von Holst: *Constitutional and Political History of the United States* (8 vols., Chicago, 1877–92), I, II.

[3] Justin H. Smith: *The Annexation of Texas* (New York, 1911). George Lockhart Rives: *The United States and Mexico, 1821–1848* (2 vols., New York, 1913). Eugene C. Barker: *Mexico and Texas, 1821–1835* (Dallas, 1928). William C. Binkley: *The Texas Revolution* (State, La., 1952).

President Jackson, watching the spectacle from Washington, must have applauded the successful revolution and looked with favor at the "immigrants" recruited in the United States by Texan agents, swarming across the border to help the Texans win their independence and to settle on military land grants from the new Republic. Jackson looked forward, as did the Texans, to the annexation of that country with as broad boundaries as possible. But it has never been established that Jackson plotted the Texan Revolution. He did not have to do so.

2

Hitherto there had been no more enthusiastic exponent of western expansion than John Quincy Adams. He had looked forward to a Union "coextensive with the North American Continent, destined by God and by Nature to be the most populous and most powerful people ever combined under one social compact." [4] Readers of the previous volume will recall that as President he had tried to purchase Texas from Mexico, in 1825 and again in 1827, and had not been too scrupulous about the intrigues of the United States Minister Joel Poinsett, who conveyed the offers. Slavery was then in process of emancipation in Mexico,[5] but the question of slavery, and of its relation to the dormant sectional controversy in the United States, does not seem to have entered the mind of President Adams at all in his approaches to Mexico.

Adams left the White House persuaded that the acquisition of Texas was not far off. His successor continued to work to secure the District from Mexico, and with even less scruple, down to the very time when revolt and independence frustrated his efforts. The last instructions (August 6, 1835) of his Secretary of State John Forsyth on the subject, to the United States Minister in Mexico, were to try to add to the proposed purchase a strip of territory from the Rio Grande to the Pacific Ocean wide enough to include San Francisco Bay.[6] This proposal surpassed John Quincy Adams himself. After the Texan Revolution, Jackson urged the Texans to make their boundaries as expansive as possible against the time when eventually Texas would come into the United States. Both Presidents seem to have been apostles of Manifest Destiny rather than slavery expansionists. Certainly Adams was.

During his retirement from public affairs between 1829 and 1831 Adams, laboring in the midst of family grief and personal controversies to put order into his private affairs, paid scant attention to Texas.[7] What fi-

[4] Vol. I, 82.
[5] Rives: *United States and Mexico*, I, 43–4, 140, 145–7, 184–6.
[6] Ibid., I, 259–61.
[7] JQA to Reverend William E. Channing, Washington, November 21, 1837. Adams MSS.

nally fired his mind and heart with the Texas issue was the writings of the Quaker abolitionist Benjamin Lundy.

Lundy was one of that immortal group of inspired American Christian heroes who pledged their fortunes and their consciences and devoted their lives to the emancipation of the slaves. It was he who had first converted Garrison to the cause, only to split with him as co-editor of the *Genius of Universal Emancipation* over the policy of immediate and revolutionary abolition. An original leader in the abolitionist societies, the Quaker reformer conceived plans for settling liberated slaves in Canada and Haiti and actually conducted several groups of freedmen to the Negro Republic. He also projected a free-labor agricultural station in Texas for sugar, cotton, and rice which would prove that slavery was not necessary for raising these staples in semitropical climates. With this in mind he made two extensive journeys to Texas in 1830–1 and 1834–5, only to find his purpose nullified there by the breakdown of Mexican authority. Finally he secured a grant from the State of Tamaulipas, south of the Rio Grande, of 138,000 acres of land conditional on settling 250 families on it. When he returned to Philadelphia to recruit his settlers, the Texan Revolution had broken out. He abandoned his plans and dedicated himself to exposing what he conceived to be a gigantic plot of the slave power in the United States. His first effort was to contribute, under the pseudonym of "Columbus," a series of nine letters to Robert Walsh's *National Gazette;* next to establish a new antislavery paper in Philadelphia, the *National Enquirer and Constitutional Advocate of Universal Liberty.* The title of this sheet corresponded exactly to Adams's views: the slaves could be emancipated only by constitutional process.[8]

As news was coming from Texas of the victory of San Jacinto (April 21, 1836), Lundy sent to John Quincy Adams at Washington the successive numbers of his "Columbus" articles, published soon in pamphlet form under the title: *The Origin and True Causes of the Texas Revolution Commenced in the Year 1835.*[9] He quoted from an editorial in the New York *Sun:* "Our countrymen . . . in fighting for the union of Texas with the United States, will be fighting for that which at no distant period will in-

[8] *The Life, Travels and Opinions of Benjamin Lundy . . . Compiled under the Direction and on Behalf of His Children* (Philadelphia, 1847). George A. Lawrence: "Benjamin Lundy, Pioneer of Freedom," *Journal of the Illinois State Historical Society,* VI (No. 2, July 1913), 175–205.

[9] Other, expanded, editions appeared in 1836 and 1837 by "a Citizen of the United States": *War in Texas, a Review of the Facts and Circumstances, Showing that this Contest is a Crusade against Mexico, Set on Foot and Supported by Slave Holders, and Speculators, etc., in Order to Re-Establish, Re-Extend, and Perpetuate the System of Slavery in the United States* (Philadelphia: printed for the author by Matthew and Gunther; 1836). A second edition, 1837, still further expanded, contains John Quincy Adams's speech in the House of Representatives, opening up the Texan Question, May 25, 1836.

evitably *dissolve the Union*. The slave states having this eligible addition to their land of bondage, will with its harbors, bays and well-bounded geographical positions, ere long cut asunder the federal tie which they have long held with ungracious and unfraternal fingers, and confederate a new and distant slaveholding republic, in opposition to the whole free republic of the North. Thus early will be fulfilled the prediction of the old politicians of Europe that our Union could not remain one century entire—and then also will the maxim be exemplified in our history, as it is in the slaveholding republics of old, that liberty and slavery cannot inhabit the same soil."

"People of the North!" challenged Lundy, *"Will you permit it?* Will you sanction the abominable outrage; involve yourselves in the deep criminality, and perhaps the horrors of war, *for the establishment of slavery in a land of freedom;* and thus put your necks and the necks of your posterity under the feet of the domineering tyrants of the South, for centuries to come? The great moral and political campaign is now fairly opened." [10]

Lundy's tract speedily became a textbook on Texas for the antislavery cohorts. It remained the prime source for abolitionist historians throughout the century.

These sincere and fervent philippics came out just as the Texas Question, almost by coincidence, injected itself into the abolitionist crusade and John Quincy Adams's campaign for freedom of petition, speech, and debate in Congress. All Lundy's strictures may not stand up against historical criticism in the perspective of our day, but they convinced Adams that the annexation of Texas might mean even the break-up of the Union. Until then the threats of disunion had come from the South against the abolition movement; from now on, more and more antislavery people in the North began to say that they could not stay in the Union if the South succeeded in expanding slavery on the North American continent. It was becoming evident that a house divided against itself could not stand forever. Adams felt this in his bones, but he wanted to put off the inevitable division until the North should have the will and power to mend a severed Union and in doing so to emancipate the slaves by martial law. In the long run the Union would survive. But if the South should annex Texas, there might not be any long run.

Single-handedly Adams manned an anti-Texas battery in Congress, and Lundy passed the ammunition. [11] The first warning shot was Adams's speech of May 25, 1836, already alluded to in the previous chapter. In this and subsequent pronouncements, private and public, the Representative of Plymouth Rock took over Lundy's arguments: that the Texan Revolution was a criminal act set off by slaveholders and land speculators, [12]

[10] *War in Texas*, 1837 edition, pp. 33, 64.

[11] JQA to Benjamin Lundy, Washington, May 12, May 20, 1836. Adams MSS.

[12] Historians have long been aware that there was much speculation by American citizens in Texan land titles and that such material interest may have animated pro-

that the Texan declaration of independence was a dishonest document, that the whole affair resulted from a long-concealed plot of Jackson and the slave power, assisted by Van Buren and Northern men with Southern sentiments, for the double purpose of expanding the dominion of the United States and riveting forever the domination of the slave power upon the Union; [13] above all, that it was a moral wrong.

My country right or wrong? Adams could not subscribe to Decatur's famous toast. He was convinced that this time the foreign country was right and his own country wrong, wrong not because of its destiny under God and Nature, but wrong because of slavery.[14] He would not support Manifest Destiny [15] against Mexico.

3

General Houston's crushing victory over Santa Anna's army at San Jacinto provoked a nationwide burst of applause in the United States. Memorials for the immediate recognition of Texan independence began to pour into Congress without any generally organized effort from various parts of the Union: Tennessee, Ohio, South Carolina, Pennsylvania, Mississippi, Connecticut, North Carolina, Kentucky, New York. None came from Massachusetts, though Webster declared in the Senate that if Texas possessed a working government it was undeniably a duty to recognize it. Calhoun asserted that the United States ought not only to recognize the independence of Texas; it ought also to take that country into the Union.

To prevent precipitate action the committees on foreign affairs in each

ponents of annexation North and South, but it is another thing to say that speculation in land or in bonds of the Republic of Texas brought about the annexation of Texas (just as it is even more doubtful to attribute ratification of the Constitution of the United States to the holders of depreciated state bonds likely to be funded at par by the new United States Government). See the severe reviews of Elgin Williams's recent book: *The Animating Pursuits of Speculation; Land Traffic in the Annexation of Texas* (New York, 1949), reviewed by Eugene C. Barker, *AHR*, LV (No. 1, October 1949), 157–8, and by William C. Binkley in *MVHR*, XXXVI (No. 3, December 1949), 517–19.

13 JQA to CFA, Washington, May 24, 1836. Adams MSS.

14 R. R. Stenberg has argued that Adams became an apostate to his earlier expansionism just as soon as he saw his own district go abolitionist, that like Webster, Calhoun, and other successful Congressmen he was ultimately forced into a sectional attitude for his own political self-preservation. See his "J. Q. Adams: Imperialist and Apostate," *Southwestern Social Science Quarterly*, XVI (No. 4, March 1936), 37–50. It is perhaps sufficient to point out that Adams felt it necessary to hold back on abolition lest he alienate his anti-abolitionist supporters.

15 The phrase Manifest Destiny, used in prolepsis in this work, was not coined until 1845, but the idea and its compulsion, and almost its phraseology, date back to American independence. John C. Parish traced "The Emergence of the Idea of Manifest Destiny" in a lecture printed by the University of California Press (1932), and Julius W. Pratt dated the phrase in an article on "John L. O'Sullivan and Manifest Destiny," in *New York History*, XIV (No. 3, July 1933), 213–34.

house brought forth identical resolutions, less than three months after the Battle of San Jacinto: "that the independence of Texas ought to be acknowledged by the United States whenever satisfactory information shall be received that it has in successful operation a civil Government capable of performing the duties and fulfilling the obligations of an independent power." The Senate passed the resolution unanimously. In the House, Adams moved to table it, but was voted down, 40 to 108; the resolution carried, 128 to 20, together with another one commending the President for taking prompt measures to inquire into the political, civil, and military condition of Texas.[16] Congress then voted to adjourn until December 1836.

Jackson proceeded slowly, cautiously, properly in law, provocatively in fact. He delayed recognizing Texas, but meanwhile nursed along a dispute with Mexico over claims of American citizens for payment for supplies furnished at the time of Mexico's revolution against Spain, and for damages suffered through arbitrary Mexican acts during the Texan war. A secret reason for Jackson's delay was, as Adams suspected,[17] a stratagem to settle the Texas Question by a treaty between the United States and Mexico to be negotiated with General Santa Anna, who had been captured by the Texans at San Jacinto. The dictator President was brought from Texas to Washington for that purpose, but the plan fell through when the Mexican Congress repudiated him and all his acts—as the Mexican people have since repudiated his place in their history.

By the time this hope had vanished, Congress was again in session, and Jackson let it take an eager lead, over Adams's protests in the House. Supported by both houses, the President received the Texan envoys just before he left office on March 4, 1837, and nominated Alcée LaBranche of Louisiana as chargé d'affaires of the United States to the new Republic. Jackson's recognition of Texan independence followed precisely the precedent set by President Monroe under the guidance of Secretary of State John Quincy Adams in 1823 in recognizing the independence of the Latin-American states, including Mexico herself.

To strengthen his arm in dealing with claims against Mexico, Jackson had asked Congress for powers of naval reprisal, while giving "one more opportunity to atone for the past before we take redress into our own hands." [18] It was the same authority that recently he had requested for dealing with France, except in that case the claims of the United States had been acknowledged by treaty. The Twenty-fourth Congress expired on March 4, without acting on Jackson's request. President Van Buren, following Jackson, studiously kept the dispute with Mexico alive during the summer. Meanwhile the people of Texas voted almost unanimously

[16] *Register of Debates*, XII, Pt. IV, 4621, July 4, 1836 (for the House); XII, Pt. II, 1848, 1928, July 1, 1836 (for the Senate).
[17] JQA to Benjamin Lundy, Washington, March 1, 1837. Adams MSS.
[18] Special message of February 6, 1837.

at the polls in favor of annexation to the United States,[19] and the Texan Minister Plenipotentiary at Washington, Memucan Hunt, made a formal proposal to that effect, August 4, 1837.[20]

These movements corresponded with the fears of the abolitionists and of John Quincy Adams that recognition of Texan independence was only a prelude to quick annexation, by hook or by crook. Promptly the American Antislavery Society began the circulation of anti-Texas petitions to present to the next session of Congress. At home in his own district Adams encouraged such protests and accepted the charge of his constituents to fight against a consummation so scarcely to be wished. He could hardly have been prepared for rejection of the proposal by the Red Fox of Kinderhook.

President Van Buren was pledged to the South to be "forbearing" toward slavery: to veto any bill that interfered with slavery in the states or attempted to abolish slavery in the District of Columbia against the wishes of the inhabitants.[21] But he had not taken a stand on the Texas Question. The increasing clamor in the North against Texas, touched off by Adams's warning speech of May 25, 1836, had made it clear that anti-Texas feeling spread far beyond the abolitionists; to challenge it might mean the loss of the Northern wing of the political alliance to which Van Buren owed his success in national politics. So he declined the Texan overture. He considered it inexpedient, it was explained, to raise the question whether the Constitution contemplated the possibility of annexation of a sovereign state and people, or in what manner (treaty, or act of Congress, or constitutional amendment) it might be accomplished. "If the overture of General Hunt were even to be reserved for future consideration," observed the Secretary of State to the Texan plenipotentiary, "it would imply a disposition to espouse the quarrel of Texas with Mexico, something wholly at variance with the spirit of the treaty of amity with Mexico and contrary to the uniform policy and obvious welfare of the United States." [22]

Did the language quoted here dismiss the Texan proposal once and for all? Or was the offer still open to take advantage of in case of war with Mexico over unsettled claims and other paraded grievances? Adams thought that Van Buren's rejection of the Texan offer of annexation was by no means definitive. It was only a cover-up, mysterious double-dealing to lull the North to sleep. The antislavery movement was the only counterbalancing weight to close the door against the pestilence of perpetual slavery and the insupportable burden of a slave-stained Texas.[23]

[19] Rives: *United States and Mexico*, I, 391–2.

[20] Memucan Hunt to Secretary of State John Forsyth, August 4, 1837. H. Ex. Doc. 40, 25th Cong., 1st Sess., pp. 2–11.

[21] Inaugural address, March 4, 1837.

[22] Forsyth to Hunt, August 25, 1837. Loc. cit., pp. 11–13.

[23] JQA to Solomon Lincoln, Hingham. Washington, November 13, 1837. Adams MSS.

Adams's convictions about the sinister significance of the Texas "plot" quickened at the response against it in the North during the summer. Petitions were now piling up everywhere against annexation.[24] Dr. William Ellery Channing wrote a famous public letter to Henry Clay rehearsing in stately prose Lundy's pithy arguments against Texas.[25] It had a powerful effect on public opinion in New England. A group of Adams's Quincy constituents formally requested him to oppose the annexation of Texas as likely to endanger the Union by bringing on a foreign war, "not defensive but a war of aggression [and] conquest, to re-establish slavery where it had been abolished." [26]

In a long letter to Channing, John Quincy Adams poured out his heart and soul, explaining and excusing his own former efforts as President to buy Texas—at that time he would have acquired a country already "purged from that foul infection." Let the real objection be sounded! "There is no valid and permanent objection to the acquisition of Texas, but the indelible stain of slavery. Abolish that, and the geographical accession to the sectional power and influence of the South would be counter-balanced by her purification from the plague of slavery. She would sympathise with the South by geographical neighbourhood, and with the North by her political principles, and the untainted spirit of Freedom."

Deep in this intimate and confidential letter to Massachusetts' great cleric Adams made one of the most surprising statements of his lifetime: if the North did not resist annexation on the ground of slavery, firmly, resolutely, and perseveringly, the American people would be doomed to bear the burden of Texas with her inextinguishable taint of slavery, and not only Texas but Cuba too, whose annexation would follow. And if Britain accomplished her contemporary internal reforms without war, she would before long lead in a war for the express purpose of abolishing slavery in the Western Hemisphere. "Our Confederation then, if not sooner, will fall to pieces; and *our* [i.e., New England's] posterity will I trust be found braving the battle and the breeze in the cause of Human Freedom." [27]

4

The political reins were already slipping from Van Buren's hands amidst the panic of 1837.[28] Beset by these circumstances, he did not wish either

[24] Benjamin Lundy to JQA, Philadelphia, August 5, 1837. Adams MSS.

[25] *A Letter to the Hon. Henry Clay, on the Annexation of Texas to the United States*, Newport, R.I., August 1, 1837 (Boston: James Monroe and Co.; 1837). *Works of William Ellery Channing* (1866 ed., Boston), II, 183–260.

[26] August 23, 1837. Adams MSS.

[27] JQA to Reverend William Ellery Channing, Newport, R.I. Quincy, August 11, Washington, November 21, 1837. Adams MSS.

[28] JQA to Robert Gilmore, Baltimore. Washington, November 28, 1837. Adams MSS.

to alienate too many of the plain republicans of the North or to exasperate the planters of the South. So he postponed action on Texas and dumped the other issues with Mexico into the lap of the Twenty-fifth Congress when it met for the first regular session in December 1837. In doing so he did not explain that during the summer the Mexican Congress, invoking the peaceful procedure laid down in the treaty of 1831,[29] had passed a resolution expressing willingness to arbitrate all issues outstanding between the two countries. Doubtless the President's reticence was due to his belief that Texas would prove to be one of those issues. He now told Congress that he had about given up any hope of being able to bring about a friendly adjustment with Mexico; it was for Congress to decide upon the time, the mode, and the measure of redress.[30]

It seemed to Adams as though the "slavocracy" were all set to press for annexation, that Van Buren would tolerate a war with Mexico if only Congress would propose it. Perhaps it would divert the electorate from embarrassing problems begotten by the Democrats' reckless fiscal policies.

Adams determined to seize the first opportunity to stifle the President's "war-whoop."[31] Peace or war with Mexico presented a welcome issue to add to freedom of petition, freedom of speech, and (after Lovejoy's murder) freedom of the press—fundamental American freedoms of free whites[32] threatened by the underlying evil of slavery itself. If only he could get and keep the floor of the House to speak on them before the country!

At the beginning of the regular session of the Twenty-fifth Congress, Adams, acting for the whole delegation of his state, presented a great batch of anti-Texas petitions from their constituents and others, and moved reference to a select committee with instructions to consider and report on them. Benjamin Chew Howard of Maryland, chairman of the

[29] "If (what can indeed not be expected) any of the articles contained in the present Treaty shall be violated or infracted in any manner whatever, it is stipulated that neither of the contracting parties will order or authorize any acts of reprisal nor declare War against the other on complaints of injuries or damages, untill [sic] the said party considering itself offended, shall first have presented to the other a statement of such injuries or damages verified by competent proofs, and demanded justice and satisfaction and the same shall have been either refused or unreasonably delayed." From Article 34 of the treaty of 1831 between the United States and Mexico.

Jackson and Van Buren had presented statements to the Mexican Government, but the question remained whether they were supported by competent proofs, or whether Mexican requital had been unreasonably delayed.

[30] Message to Congress of December 5, 1837.

[31] JQA to Benjamin Lundy, Philadelphia. Washington, December 29, 1837. Adams MSS.

[32] "I have made up another issue with the administration upon the question of *Peace* with Mexico, intimately connected with and auxiliar[y] to that of the right of Petition." JQA to the Reverend Samuel J. May, Scituate, Mass. Washington, January 7, 1838. See also JQA to Origen Bacheler, secretary of the New York Peace Society. Washington, January 6, 1838. Adams MSS.

committee on foreign affairs, immediately rose to claim them for the province of his committee, with a preponderance (6 to 3) of slaveholding members. A debate then followed on the proper committee for reference, in which Adams managed to discharge a Massachusetts salvo at the South and slavery.

"In the face of this House and the face of Heaven," he declared, "I avow it as my solemn belief that the annexation of an independent foreign power to this government would be *ipso facto* a dissolution of this Union. . . . The question is whether a foreign nation (acknowledged as such in a most unprecedented and extraordinary manner by this Government), a nation 'damned to everlasting fame' by the reinstitution of that detested system of slavery, after it had once been abolished within its borders, should be admitted into union with a nation of freemen. For, Sir, that name, thank God, is still ours!"

Southern members interrupted. Speaker Polk repeatedly called the old fighter to order. Nevertheless he went on, standing up against the Speaker, branding the Texan Revolution as nothing more than a revolt against Mexico's emancipation of slaves.

Hugh S. Legaré of South Carolina tried to correct him, but Adams insisted on his right to continue without interruption. "The time for this discussion is not yet come," muttered Legaré as he sat down, "though it soon may. 'Sufficient unto the day is the evil thereof.'" Legaré's colleague Robert Barnwell Rhett begged the House to let the gentleman continue to the end of this "most extraordinary" speech. The South would have its say at the proper time.

"Whether the question arise now or hereafter," the Plymouth member fired back at the young representatives from the "deep" slave state of South Carolina, "is as immaterial to me as it can be to them: it must come! Though it may be delayed for the present, I do not think it will be forever smothered by the previous question to lay it on the table, and all the other means and arguments by which the institution of slavery is wont to be sustained from this floor—the same means and arguments, in spirit, which in another place have produced murder and arson. Yes, Sir, this same spirit which led to the inhuman murder of Lovejoy at Alton—"

"You are straying widely from the subject of reference," the Speaker admonished him. On this point of order Adam Snyder, a Van Buren Democrat from Illinois, properly requested that the ex-President be required to take his seat. Adams promised to proceed without even a whisper about the Lovejoy tragedy.

"Take your seat!" Polk peremptorily ordered him.

Adams appealed to the House on the Speaker's ruling. Not a whisper to the winds, he repeated, would he let pass his lips on the subject so disturbing to the gentleman from Illinois, if they would only let him continue! Rather than risk the yeas and nays, Snyder withdrew his request, and the "Massachusetts Madman" was allowed to conclude his remarks:

"The annexation of Texas and the proposed war with Mexico are all one and the same thing." [33]

When Adams finally sat down, Henry A. Wise of Accomac, Virginia, moved that both the motions for reference be tabled, on the ground that because of our relations with Mexico the Government had already declined the Texas proposal for annexation. So they were tabled, alongside the big pile of anti-Texas petitions, by a vote of 127 to 68.

At this juncture there came to Adams's hand a new instrument with which to force a discussion of Mexican-American relations and all that they portended. The recently organized New York Peace Society, another manifestation of the religious spirit of reform that had brought forth the abolition movement, memorialized the House for a Congress of Ambassadors to codify the law of nations and establish an international Court of Nations that would give moral sanction to arbitration. It sent resolutions for the former diplomatist to present to the House of Representatives, including a petition that the United States Government accept the readiness of Mexico to arbitrate differences currently outstanding between the two nations. [34] Adams did not believe that an international peace congress or a world court was practical at that time, [35] but he seized upon the petitions, particularly the last-mentioned one, as a means of keeping the subject before the people and letting everybody know that Mexico wanted peace.

Another contest now arose when Adams moved that the petition for arbitration with Mexico be referred to a select committee. Howard immediately moved an amendment to refer all the peace petitions to the committee on foreign affairs, the same committee of six slaveholders and three free-state members over which he presided. To put the arbitration memorial in the hands of that committee, Adams thought, would only serve to entomb it inside the gates of Janus. But it was hopeless to stand out against the ostensible propriety of such a reference. The Plymouth member therefore moved an amendment to Howard's amendment: that the committee on foreign affairs be instructed to consider the memorial and *report* upon it. In a three-hour debate [36] he forced Howard to concede what he had at first denied: that the Mexican Government had expressed a willingness to arbitrate.

Adams's agitation with the peace petitions stirred the whole country.

[33] Adams's speech of December 13 and the debate are printed in *National Intelligencer*, XXXVIII, No. 5533, December 16, 1837. They are much abbreviated in the *Congressional Globe*, VI, 24, where Adams's speech is barely mentioned.

[34] For the petition as presented at length by Adams in the House of Representatives, see *National Intelligencer*, XXXIX, No. 5539, January 2, 1838. *Journal of House of Representatives*, December 18, 1837.

[35] JQA to J. Edwards, president of the Theological Seminary at Andover. Quincy, August 23, 1838. Adams MSS.

[36] Reported in *National Intelligencer*, XXXVIII, No. 5538, XXXIX, No. 5539, December 30, 1837, January 2, 1838.

"Will the nation go to war for this?" asked the *National Intelligencer.*[37] It was evident that public opinion would not stand for a refusal to arbitrate debatable claims. Van Buren's Government, prodded by Adams, was obliged to accept the Mexican offer (with reservations excluding the Texas Question from arbitration). Prolonged negotiations led to the treaty of April 11, 1839, submitting all outstanding claims of the United States against Mexico to a mixed commission, with a provision for the King of Prussia to appoint an umpire.

"If the petitioners of the Peace Societies had never rendered to their country any other service," wrote John Quincy Adams to the secretary of the New York Peace Society, "they would have deserved the thanks of the whole Nation for this." [38] On the project of a congress of ambassadors and a world court of arbitration the committee on foreign affairs made a decent and sympathetic, if noncommittal report, and the House in due course ordered ten thousand copies to be printed.[39] Nothing further came of it then, but at the end of the century the New York Peace Society's proposal served as a blueprint for the Hague Conferences and Hague Court of International Arbitration.

5

John Quincy Adams, assisted by the logic of circumstances, had made it certain that there would be no immediate war with Mexico to annex Texas; but what about the possibility of annexation by treaty with the new Republic? Van Buren had declined the Texan proposal; on the surface it looked as though there were little danger that he would take it up again during the session of Congress; but the Texan Government had not yet withdrawn its offer. Its envoys at Washington were reporting the President still to be inclined toward annexation. Secretary of State Forsyth had given them to believe that all would go well if the Texans conducted themselves properly. Joel Poinsett, Secretary of War, onetime Minister to Mexico under President Adams, had assured them that the Washington Government was merely proceeding with diplomatic caution out of deference to the prejudices of the North.[40] Adams suspected some-

[37] XXXVIII, No. 5534, December 19, 1837.

[38] JQA to Origen Bacheler, secretary of the New York Peace Society, Washington, June 13, 1838. JQA to Silas Livermore, Newton Theological Institution, Washington, June 1, 1838. Adams MSS. See also: *Prize Essays on a Congress of Nations, for the Adjustment of International Disputes, and for the Promotion of Universal Peace without Recourse to Arms* (Boston, 1840), p. 593. John Quincy Adams and Daniel Webster served on one of the committees to judge the essays, but it could not agree that any merited the prize. Upon Adams's advice the society nevertheless printed the best ones.

[39] June 13, 1838. H.R. Rept., 979, 25th Cong. 2d Sess. *Congressional Globe,* VI, 449.

[40] Rives: *United States and Mexico,* I, 410.

thing like this, if only from covert information.[41] He got through the House a call for more documents on Texas,[42] not hitherto communicated, only to be told by the Secretary of State that there were none: the Texans had made their proposal and it had been "disposed of." [43]

Proceedings in the Senate did not give any impression that Southern spokesmen had abandoned their hopes of taking Texas speedily into the Union. Calhoun and his rival colleague from South Carolina, William C. Preston, were demanding annexation as a Southern and Western right.[44] Meanwhile members of Congress in either house could talk all they wanted about defending slavery and expanding slave territory while the Gag Rule hermetically sealed off all adverse discussion of that institution in the House.[45]

Among the flood of petitions against the annexation of Texas that had continued to flow into the House from various groups, signed by individuals in tens of thousands, came now resolutions from state legislatures, documents of more deliberate significance than memorials privately circulated for signatures. Thus Rhode Island protested against any degradation of the United States in the eyes of the world by the annexation of foreign territories of immense and unknown extent for the purpose of encouraging the propagation of slavery—promoting the raising of slaves within the very bosom of freedom, to be exported and sold in those unhallowed regions. Immediately the Administration majority in the House tabled the document (December 27, 1837) as if it had been an abolition petition, without reading it or even extending to it the courtesy, customary with a state resolution, of being printed. It treated in the same way similar resolutions of the State of Vermont (February 14, 1838), but by a strange quirk of inconsistency allowed them to be printed in the *Journal*. Other protests followed from the legislatures of Michigan, Ohio, and Massachusetts. As if to meet the challenge, the legislatures of Tennessee and Alabama presented energetic memorials *for* the annexation of Texas, backed by proslavery arguments.

The Tennessee appeal extolled the gallant and chivalrous bravery of the Texans as entitling them to American brotherhood and citizenship. It declared that the annexation to these United States—by treaty or purchase —at such time as may be deemed most expedient was a consummation de-

[41] "I yesterday wrote you on a subject in which my friends and relations who reside at the North are deeply interested. My husband is a clerk in the State Department and repeats to me that the proposition of annexation has been rejected by Mr. Forsyth but that it is not given up. He states too there is a great deal of Texas influence about the President." Anonymous to JQA, received September 14, 1837. Adams MSS. The "yesterday" letter does not seem to be preserved.

[42] *Congressional Globe*, VI, 414, 425.

[43] Smith, op. cit., p. 66, citing H.R. Ex. Doc. 409, 25th Cong., 2d Sess.

[44] Wiltse: *John C. Calhoun, Nullifier*, p. 387. *Congressional Globe*, VI, 55.

[45] JQA to Reverend Samuel J. May, Scituate, Massachusetts. Washington, January 7, 1838. Adams MSS.

voutly to be wished. The Alabama document deprecated the introduction of the slavery issue as an argument against annexation. It was due to the disturbed and distempered imagination of "many well-meaning but mis-informed females of some of our sister states," whose hopes and reveries of universal emancipation would be frustrated by the admission of Texas into the Union. Actually, declared the Alabama legislature, Texas would counterbalance the existing overbalance of the extreme Northeast. It prayed that the Texan overture be accepted as soon as it could be done without violation of national honor or international law. All of these res-olutions instructed the state delegations to press the subject upon the consideration of Congress and the Government.

Now a curious political phenomenon showed itself. The House voted to table the Tennessee pro-Texas resolutions by the same majority, 122 to 74, that it had voted for renewal of the Gag Rule and for tabling the anti-Texas resolutions of the Northern state legislatures. This move signalized a decided weakening of the Democratic coalition North and South. The majority for the suppression of freedom of debate seemed to be dwin-dling toward a minority so far as the annexation of Texas was concerned.[46] To the Plymouth member it meant the dawn of a new day. It was evident that henceforth members from states whose legislatures had adopted res-olutions *favoring* annexation would vote against blocking any discussion of it, and it was equally clear that once the Texas Question was opened to discussion the Gag Rule could not prevent members from talking about slavery in a debate on Texas.[47]

The sectional strain on Van Buren's formula invited a new parliamen-tary strategy from Adams. When George N. Briggs of Massachusetts pre-sented the resolutions of his state against annexation, Adams himself moved their reference to the committee of foreign affairs with its six-to-three majority of slaveholders, expecting an opportunity to debate Texas, and, with Texas, slavery, when the committee should bring in its report. As if to meet his expectations, the Administration majority then took all the Texas petitions from the table and put them in the hands of the same committee.[48]

Waiting for a chance to debate Texas and slavery before the whole country, Adams appealed to his friend Lundy for more material. He never got it. Lundy was about to turn over the editorship of the *National En-quirer* in Philadelphia to Whittier and to transfer his antislavery opera-tions to Illinois. On the eve of his departure for the West he had gathered together his papers and personal belongings and placed them for safety

[46] JQA to the Inhabitants of the Twelfth Congressional District of the Common-wealth of Massachusetts. Quincy, August 13, 1838. Printed in *Quincy Patriot*, August 13, 1838.
[47] The above is based on JQA's published comments on the debate. See note 56 below. The *Congressional Globe*, VI, gives only meager traces.
[48] May 21, 25, 1838. Ibid.

in a room in Pennsylvania Hall, the splendid new edifice that the abolitionists had just built as a forum for freedom of speech in Philadelphia. He was there when a mob of "gentlemen" descended on the building and set fire to it as the police stood by with folded arms. Mournfully Lundy watched his papers, books, and clothes being sacrificed upon the altar of universal emancipation. "Methought I could read, on this mighty scroll," he wrote his friend in Washington, "the woful destiny of this nation of oppressors. God grant that this may prove to have been only the workings of my imagination!"

In the hour of tragic disappointment Texas was still uppermost in the mind of this valorous man. "I fear that I shall not succeed in procuring the papers which thee requested, but I will try further. I am *almost* inclined to hope that Texas will yet *back out*. But we must not trust to the professions of such unprincipled pirates. They must be watched, with a jealous eye, and beaten off, with the voice of power. Let every American patriot be on the alert, until the desperadoes shall have withdrawn from our threshold." [49]

Arrived in Illinois, Lundy quickly identified himself with local antislavery societies and re-established the *Genius of Universal Emancipation*. But he died soon after of natural causes, in August 1839. Adams mourned him like a brother.[50]

6

The opportunity for which Adams was preparing came one day in June 1838, with Congress scheduled for adjournment early the following month. George C. Dromgoole of Virginia had presented the report of the committee on foreign affairs on the Texas resolutions of seven states, pro and con, and the other petitions, memorials, and remonstrances against annexation signed by more than one hundred thousand people in the North.

No proposition, declared the majority of the committee, was pending in the House, either for the admission of the Republic of Texas as a state into the Union or for its territorial annexation to the United States. Therefore it was not advisable to recommend any action on the part of the House of Representatives calculated to prejudge any such proposition, should it hereafter be formally submitted for decision, or to "forestall" public sentiment on it. Accordingly they recommended that the committee be discharged from further consideration of the whole subject, and that all the Texas memorials be laid back on the table.

The whole thing was quite obvious. The committee had not even read, much less considered, the petitions. They did not want to make a report.

[49] Benjamin Lundy to JQA, Philadelphia, May 18, 1838. JQA to Lundy, May 22, 1838. Adams MSS.

[50] JQA to J. G. Whittier, Philadelphia, Quincy, October 28, 1839. Adams MSS. Adams never found time to write the biography of Lundy, as the deceased friend's family begged him to do.

They were afraid that Adams would ventilate the Texan business unfavorably if they should report on it, that he would rally public opinion to forestall future annexation, and that in doing so he would roam over the whole subject of slavery itself. So they were locking it up in a dark Administration closet.

"I cannot anticipate a single good result from the prolongation of a general debate upon the subject of Texas," declared Howard in the confused debate that followed the report of his committee. Many of the anti-Texas petitions, he pointed out, were *signed by women.* "I think that these females could have a sufficient field for the exercise of their influence in the discharge of their duties to their fathers, their husbands, or their children, cheering the domestic circle and shedding over it the mild radiance of the social virtues, instead of rushing into the fierce struggles of political life. I feel sorry at this departure from their proper sphere, in which there is abundant room for the practice of the most extensive benevolence and philanthropy, because I consider it discreditable, not only to their own particular section of the country, but also to the national character, and thus giving me a right to express this opinion."

After complicated maneuvering Adams succeeded in moving an amendment (to an amendment) to recommit the negative report with instructions to the committee to report resolutions declaring that it would be unconstitutional to annex the people of any foreign independent state to this Union.[51]

At last the issue was joined in Congress: for or against the annexation of Texas. This meant a debate for or against slavery, despite the Gag Rule. In the Senate, John Caldwell Calhoun, Nullifier, was calling upon his colleagues to declare that refusal to annex Texas as a slave territory or state would be a violation of rights reserved to the states under the Constitution; it threatened to destroy the Union.[52] In the House of Representatives, John Quincy Adams, Nationalist, was actually proposing to his fellow members that they brand any annexation of Texas as unconstitutional, null, and void, because it would be a violation of the rights reserved to the people.

Union versus disunion, freedom versus slavery, right against wrong! So the great question stood in Adams's mind and conscience. In taking this stand he was utterly oblivious of its inconsistency with his former support of the Louisiana Purchase by treaty in 1803 [53] and of his own treaty

[51] "Resolved: That the power of annexing the People of any independent foreign State to this Union would be an usurpation of power, unlawful and void, and which it would be the right and duty of the free People of the Union to resist and annul."

[52] See sixth and last of the state-rights resolutions that Calhoun presented to the Senate, December 27, 1837. *Congressional Globe,* VI, 55.

[53] In 1803 Adams declared that he would have voted for the Louisiana Purchase Treaty had he been present when the vote was taken. But he refused to vote for the act of Congress extending government over the people of Louisiana without first amending the Constitution. See Vol. I, 119–22.

with Spain of 1819 which annexed the foreign territory of Florida and its foreign people, in both instances including slaves.

By adroit parliamentary strategy Adams finally got the floor of the House during the morning hour for committee business and succeeded in holding it each day until Congress adjourned three weeks later. His famous anti-Texas speech on the freedom of petition and debate was not so much a filibuster against annexation as a long indictment of slavery. In daily dialectics the Old Man Eloquent rang all the changes on slavery and its political, social, and moral evils. He challenged the Administration members to cut him short by the previous question. They couldn't get the votes to do it. By clever tactics he forced an admission from one of the majority of the committee on foreign affairs that they had never read the anti-Texas memorials and never had any intention of doing so. This in itself, he averred, was a deliberate nullification of the right of petition, which, together with the suppression of freedom of debate, was bringing the House into obloquy with free men throughout the world. He scored the "plot" to get Texas for slavery. He accused the Executive of withholding important documents from the correspondence with Mexico sent up to the House—notably the instructions of Jackson's Secretaries of State to their Ministers in Mexico. He showed that Texas had not yet withdrawn its annexation offer. He defended his own effort as President to procure the annexation of Texas as free territory—though in his heart he recognized it to be one of his great political mistakes, an apple of discord cast between two free and friendly nations.[54]

On four successive mornings he had veritable field days, at Howard's expense, on the seemliness of females petitioning Congress for the prevention of great moral wrongs. What a vicious principle, declared this son of Abigail Adams, to bind women exclusively into the social sphere! What a reproach to the 238 women of his district who signed the first anti-Texas petition that he had presented to the House!

"Why does it follow," he asked, "that women are fitted for nothing but the cares of domestic life, for bearing children, and cooking the food of a family, devoting all their time to the domestic circle—to promoting the immediate personal comfort of their husbands, brothers, and sons? . . . The mere departure of woman from the duties of the domestic circle, far from being a reproach to her, is a virtue of the highest order, when it is done from purity of motive, by appropriate means, and the purpose good." He read the words of the Plymouth women: "Thoroughly aware of the sinfulness of slavery, and the consequent impolicy and disastrous tendency of its extension in our country, we do most respectfully remonstrate, with all our souls, against the annexation of Texas to the United States."

Was this discreditable? "I do believe slavery to be a sin before the sight

[54] Unprinted holograph notes for speech on the Texas issue and the right of petition. June [15], 1838. Adams MSS: "JQA, Controversial, 1829–1844," II.

of God," he testified for his part, "and that is the reason and the only insurmountable reason why we should not annex Texas to this Union." [55]

The old warrior still held the floor on this unfinished business of the morning hour when Congress adjourned July 9, 1838, and was therefore entitled to it when that body should reconvene in December. Southern spokesmen promised to reply to him then. But by the time Congress met again, the Texas Question had been shelved. Adams and the anti-Texas petitions had scared the Administration out of any schemes it might have nursed for annexation. Impressed by the situation, the Texan plenipotentiaries in Washington backed out, as Lundy had hoped they might. Acting on behalf of their Government, they formally withdrew their proposal (October 12, 1838).

7

Adams put together the daily fragments of his long speech and caused it to be printed, with explanatory remarks, making a pamphlet of 131 pages of small print. [56] In a long and eloquent public letter to his constituents the Plymouth member, who would be up for re-election in the autumn, justified his course in the House. [57] Although he did not say so in this open statement, he considered himself an abolitionist at heart. In private memoranda that he had written while preparing for his speech he had noted that the South took him for an abolitionist. Very well, he said to himself, let any man who pleased so take him. "For, if the most ardent desire, and a most vivid hope of the total extinction of Slavery on Earth, and especially at no distant day throughout this North American Union, constitutes an abolitionist, I am one, to the extent of readiness to lay down my life in the cause, and to go forth with it as my credential before the tribunal of posterity, and before the tribunal of God." [58] In similar vein he wrote to the Garrisonian abolitionist Edmund Quincy of Boston a letter promptly published in the *Liberator:* [59] "I live in the Faith and Hope

[55] See following note 56.

[56] *Speech of John Quincy Adams, of Massachusetts, upon the Right of the People, Men and Women, to Petition: on the Freedom of Speech and of Debate in the House of Representatives . . . : on the Resolutions of Seven State Legislatures, and the Petitions of More than One Hundred Thousand Petitioners, Relating to the Annexation of Texas to this Union.* Delivered in the House of Representatives in fragments of the morning hour, from the 16th of June to the 7th of July 1838 (Washington: printed by Gales and Seaton; 1838). My account of the debate and parliamentary situation is taken largely from this source. The pertinent volume of the *Congressional Globe* (VI) gives only sketches of the debates and proceedings, and makes only the most meager mention of Adams's speech.

[57] JQA to the Inhabitants of the Twelfth Congressional District of Massachusetts, Quincy, August 13, 1838, published in *Quincy Patriot*, August 13, 1838. See also *Memoirs*, X, 129.

[58] Holograph notes for speech on Texas and the right of petition. Adams MSS.

[59] Vol. VIII, No. 31, August 3, 1838.

of the progressive advancement of Christian Liberty, and expect to abide by the same in death." [60]

Such expressions did not yet mean that he would have anything publicly to do with the abolitionists [61] or that he would vote for the abolition of slavery (as distinct from the slave trade) in the District of Columbia,[62] or in the Territory of Florida, where he considered the United States pledged by treaty to preserve existing institutions even when admitted to the Union as a state, or in any district or territory of the United States, until this could be accomplished without injustice to the white inhabitants —that is, with indemnity to slaveholders.[63]

So John Quincy Adams continued to champion the right of petition and freedom of speech, of press, and of debate, making use of such contests to indict slavery and to oppose its expansion, thus holding the evil in check—until the people of this Union should be ready to abolish slavery by constitutional process, or perhaps ultimately through emancipation by martial law in a great civil war. In accepting, without commitment to the party, the Whig nomination of his district for re-election in 1838, he spoke in such a way as to please abolitionists without coming out openly with them. He did not subscribe, he said, to the axiom that freedom lived only from sucking the blood of slaves. He was inexpressibly pleased to see that "all" his constituents stood with him for four essential American freedoms: freedom of thought, freedom of the press, freedom of speech for themselves, and freedom of speech for their representatives in Congress. He congratulated his fellow citizens that the danger of war with Mexico and the iniquitous and pernicious project of annexing the slave-ridden Republic of Texas had both disappeared. But he warned them that Northern subservience to Southern dictation gave less hope for revival of the right of petition and freedom of speech.

"The spirit of true Freedom is not yet sufficiently awake, and while she slumbers, all the vigils of the watchman will be vain. . . . The suspension

---

[60] Quincy, July 28, 1838. Adams MSS.

[61] JQA to the committee that invited him to participate in the dedication of Pennsylvania Hall, Washington, January 19, 1838. Adams MSS. *Quincy Patriot*, May 26, 1838. JQA to A. Bronson, Fall River, Mass. Quincy, July 30, 1838; to Committee of Antislavery Society of Utica; Quincy, July 30, 1838. Adams MSS.

[62] "At the time of the first gag resolution of twenty-sixth of May, 1836, I had been five years a Member of the House, and your Representative. I had deprecated all discussion of slavery or its abolition in the House, and gave no countenance to petitions for the abolition of slavery in the District of Columbia or the Territories. But I presented all such petitions which were committed to my charge, and moved their reference to appropriate Committees, which was accordingly done without opposition." JQA to the Inhabitants of the Twelfth Congressional District of the Commonwealth of Massachusetts, Quincy, August 13, 1838. *Quincy Patriot*, August 18, 1838.

[63] JQA to J. Edwards, president of the Theological Seminary at Andover, Quincy, August 23, 1838; to Charles P. Kirkland, Utica, N.Y. Quincy, October 15, 1838; to Benjamin Silliman, at Brooklyn, Quincy, August 21, 1839. Adams MSS.

of the right of petition, the suppression of the freedom of debate, the thirst for the annexation of Texas, the war whoop of two successive Presidents of the United States against Mexico, are all but varied symptoms of a deadly disease seated in the marrow of our bones, and that deadly disease is Slavery. The Union will fall before it; or it will fall before the Union. The abolition of Slavery in the District of Columbia, or in the Territory of Florida, the prohibition of the internal piracy between the States, the refusal to admit another Slave contaminated State into the Union are all partial ineffective plaisters for the great elemental evil.

> " 'They will but skin and film the ulcerous part
> 'While rank corruption, mining all within
> 'Infects unseen.' " [64]

Adams certainly had the people of his own district overwhelmingly behind him, particularly the women, on the Texas Question and on the four freedoms of the day. He received touching testimonials of gratitude, from his home town, from his state, from all over New England and the North. "True and honest hearts love you," wrote the abolitionist Lydia Maria Child from Northampton, "bold and strong hearts venerate you, pious hearts pray for you, and breaking hearts murmur a blessing on your name." [65]

It must be said that his acknowledgments of such affecting compliments were moderate and restrained. For instance, when Miss Anna Quincy Thaxter of Hingham thanked him for his "just, generous, and Christian defence of the character and claims of her sex," he replied that he was only doing his duty by the memory of his own mother. "My intercourse with the sex," he wrote to Miss Thaxter, "since that time has not left me ignorant of the imperfections in which they participate as a portion of the human race nor of the frailties incidental to their physical and intellectual nature. My attachment to them is not enthusiastic, nor have I ever been remarkably exemplary in the observance of those delicate attentions which men who esteem them less deem indispensable. . . . I have throughout my Life reverenced the Sex, and treated them individually with coldness and reserve, believing in all the younger portion of my Life, that *one* of the duties of man to woman is to abstain from the attempt to engage her affections, more than may be suited to promote her own happiness. It is not from a man of my years that the gallantry genial to a champion of the sex is to be expected, nor is it among my purposes to aspire to that title. I look to the women of the present age with the feelings of a father." [66]

[64] JQA to Messrs. Isaac L. Hedge, Seth Sprague, and Elihu Hobart. Quincy, October 27, 1838. See also JQA to Oliver Johnson, corresponding secretary of the Rhode Island Anti-Slavery Society, Washington, December 13, 1838. Adams MSS.

[65] August 15, 1838. Adams MSS.

[66] Anna Quincy Thaxter to JQA, Hingham, July 24, 1838. JQA to Miss Anna Quincy Thaxter, Quincy, July 31, 1838. Adams MSS.

Undismayed by this heavy graciousness, the women of Quincy honored Mr. and Mrs. Adams at a picnic on the Hancock lot.

There the Plymouth Representative extolled the ladies after Mr. Whitney, the minister, had made some devoted remarks. "I felt myself called upon," Adams told them righteously, "to repel the violent outrage upon the petitioners by Howard and his insult upon their sex, to defend the rights and fair fame of women." He assured the Quincy females that it was quite proper for them to take a part in public affairs up to the point of their own discretion. "There is not the least danger of your obtruding your wishes upon any of the ordinary subjects of legislation—banks, currency, exchange, Sub-Treasuries, internal improvements, all of which so profoundly agitate the men of the country. Women, so far from intermeddling with them, could scarcely be prevailed upon to bestow a thought upon them. . . . But, for objects of kindness, of benevolence, of compassion, women, so far from being debarred by any rule of delicacy from exercising the right of petition or remonstrance, are, by the law of their nature, fitted above all others for that exercise. I hope your right will never again be questioned. . . . I hope no member of the House of Representatives will ever again be found to treat with disrespect the sex of his mother." [67]

The women of Quincy were still undaunted—so far as the record reveals—and a collation followed, with dancing afterward. And from near and far began to come gifts of gloves and stockings knitted by women crusaders to warm his aging limbs. [68]

In the election of November 1838 the Democrats tried to turn the abolitionists against Adams in his district. At the last moment they ran a "highly charged" abolitionist as a write-in candidate in the expectation that many of the ex-President's supporters, knowing that no one had been formally nominated to oppose him, would not bother to go to the polls. As a result he won by only a few hundred votes. [69]

8

Before Adams left for Washington to attend the short session of the Twenty-fifth Congress in December 1839, he had some earnest talks with William Ellery Channing and a company of antislavery sympathizers in Boston.

"Let me ask your opinions on two points," begged Channing: "one, the present test question of the abolitionists—the immediate abolition of

[67] *Memoirs*, X, 36–7.

[68] "They fit my limbs as if they had been measured to receive them." JQA to Miss Louisa Price of Shelbyville, Ky., acknowledging the gift of a pair of stockings made with her own hands, Washington, March 20, 1843. Adams MSS.

[69] Diary, November 13, 15, 1838. JQA to Origen Bacheler, New York. Boston, November 19, 1838. Adams MSS.

slavery in the District of Columbia and the Territory of Florida; and the other, whether in the event of the adoption of those measures, the Southern States would secede from the Union?"

"On the first point," Adams pronounced, "it is absurd to make a test question upon *immediate* abolition. There is something captious about it, because it is notoriously impracticable. There is in the present House of Representatives a majority of nearly two to one opposed to the consideration or discussion of the subject; and if the proposition should be made they would refuse to consider it. . . . As to the second question, I do not believe the South would dissolve the Union if slavery should be abolished in the District of Columbia and in Florida. Perhaps South Carolina might secede, but she could not carry the South with her."

Channing had preached and lived in Maryland and Virginia. He was smarting under attacks of Garrisonian abolitionists and fearful that their extreme demands would bring about an insurrection of slaves. "The Southern slaveholders would dissolve the Union," he kept telling Adams. "Caleb Cushing has been saying that there is a growing coldness on the part of the Southern members towards those of the North. How do they treat you?"

"They all treat me as gentlemen," Adams declared, "and most of them with kindness and courtesy. Mr. Cushing has been desirous of a very intimate personal intercourse with the Southern members and perhaps has seen some change in their deportment towards him. I have thought it apparent that they generally hold in contempt the Northern members who truckle to them, such as John Randolph has called 'dough-faces.' But there is so marked a difference between the manners of the South and the North that their members could never be very intimate personally together."

"I distrust the political action of the abolitionists," Channing averred. "I fear they will ruin their own cause and its friends."

"I wish you would take some method of publishing your opinion," Jonathan Phillips, one of Channing's company, had already suggested to Adams.

"I have already written to C. P. Kirkland," Adams disclosed, "and I shall probably take some occasion to express similar opinions at the approaching session of Congress." [70]

Charles P. Kirkland of Utica, New York, was a Whig candidate for Congress whom the abolitionists were quizzing about slavery and the slave trade in the District of Columbia and the admission of Florida into the Union as a slave state. In desperation he had appealed to Adams for confidential advice on what answers *he* would give.[71] Adams replied that he would vote for immediate prohibition of the interstate slave trade but not for immediate abolition of slavery in the District of Columbia or the

[70] *Memoirs*, X, 39–44. November 10, 12, 24, 1838.
[71] Charles P. Kirkland to JQA, Utica, N.Y., October 6, 1838. Adams MSS.

Territory of Florida. He declared that he stood for abolition of slavery throughout the globe, including the United States, "with all practical diligence and speed," but only with indemnity to the slaveowners. Abolition in the District or the territories was still impractical, he implied: no more than thirty votes could be mustered in Congress to wipe out slavery in the nation's capital. The abolitionists were still a small persecuted minority who were retarding instead of advancing their cause by their extreme principles: "As yet their vote counts for nothing in the Elections." [72] Kirkland had declared he would not make public Adams's views as expressed to him, and apparently he did not do so.

If Southern gentlemen in Congress were correct in their personal attitude toward Adams, it was not so with all their constituents. Frustration of the annexation of Texas was impelling some of the latter to desperate devices. When he got back to the last session of the Twenty-fifth Congress, his mail began to swell with threats to assassinate him if he did not change his course. So numerous were they as to seem concerted, though there is no proof of this.

"Congress cannot get on with its business of the American people owing to your d–d abolition petitions . . ." wrote a Virginian who had once voted for Adams for President. "Some Gentlemen in this section of the country are ready and anxious to pay a large premium for the head of J. Q. Adams. I have prevailed on them to desist, daily expecting that your better judgment would lead you to better doings. But if you do not desist I will in company with them let loose the reign of my Vengeance and the consequence will be that the life of our once beloved President will be no more." [73]

"My dear and venerable old fellow . . ." wrote a citizen of Montgomery, Alabama, protesting against petitions presented by the ex-President for recognition of the Republic of Haiti: "beware how you proceed, Sir, beware, or something will come over you as a thief in the night, which may not be so agreeable." [74]

"You (Jno. Q. Adams) should be ashamed (but a modern Whig has no shame) of yourself to try to disgrace our country," advised a fellow American from Augusta, Georgia, "as to wish a Big Black, Thick lipped, Cracked Heeled, Woolly headed, Skunk smelling, damned Negro, alias whig, to be seated in Congress hall, and to be considered an equal to a white man in law and in justice. For this act alone I demand that satisfaction which nothing but your life can satisfy. . . . If you don't you will when least expected, be shot down in the street, or your damned guts will be cut out in the dark." [75]

[72] JQA to Charles P. Kirkland, Utica, N.Y. Quincy, October 15, 1838. Adams MSS.

[73] Thomas Jones to JQA, Westmoreland, Va., January 8, 1839. Adams MSS.

[74] C. N. Stonington to JQA, Montgomery, Ala., January 12, 1839. Adams MSS.

[75] Richard Rinald to JQA, Augusta, Ga., January 15, February 15, 1839. Adams MSS.

"Rather than have an insurrection among us . . ." wrote a disturbed individual from Frankfort, Kentucky, bordering on the free states of Indiana and Ohio, "we are determined to put an end to your existence." He named the day when he would take the elder statesman's life: February 10, 1839.[76] Another person preferred to do the business a little later: "I shall be in Washington next March and shall shoot you. *Remember!!!*" [77]

"On the first Day of May next I promise to cut your throat from ear to Ear," announced a sharp-mannered gent from 'way down in Alabama.[78]

"I would not write this without I saw it was necessary both for the safety of my family and the Union," wrote a more euphemistic "Friend of Slavery" from Richmond: "Unless you do something to stop the flood of Abolition Petitions now pouring in Congress I shall be constrained to put you out of the way." [79]

These are only samples of many similar letters, nearly all of them bearing Southern postmarks—the deeper from the South, the more crude and menacing the tone. Never before or since, one would believe, had such letters been written to an illustrious patriot and ex-President. But again for every irresponsible Southern threat to shoot or stab him to death in cold blood came more than one prayer from some Northern man or woman that his life be spared to his country to carry on the struggle for free men.

Some of the menacing letters [80] he had attracted by proposing a congressional investigation (immediately voted down) into the provocative conduct in London of Minister Andrew Stevenson in a public newspaper controversy with Daniel O'Connell, the Irish nationalist leader in the British Parliament, whom Stevenson challenged to a duel over charges of slave-breeding for sale and profit in the United States.[81]

Adams regarded these threats as vulgar reflections of that aggressive sensitivity by which Southern leaders on a higher level tried to frighten Northern members of Congress from saying anything too severe about slavery, lest it be taken as a reflection on some Southern Representative's honor and provoke a personal challenge.

[76] Shylock Shelton to JQA, Lawrenceburg, Ky., January 31, 1839. Adams MSS.

[77] Henry de la Vigne to JQA, Philadelphia, January 23, 1839. Adams MSS.

[78] Peter Longate to JQA, Carter's Hill, Ala., February 27, 1839. Adams MSS.

[79] A Friend of Slavery to JQA, Richmond, Va., January 25, 1839. Adams MSS.

[80] "B. I. Convuld" to JQA, Cumberland, January 7, 1839; Sam'l Gibbons to JQA, Fredericksburg, January 9, 1839; Thomas I. McKing to JQA, Cumberland, January 18, 1839; John H. P. Smith and nine others to JQA, Montgomery, Ala., January 19, 1839. Adams MSS.

[81] *H.R. Journal, 1838–39*, pp. 17–18. December 4, 1838. Francis Fry Wayland: *Andrew Stevenson, Democrat and Diplomat, 1785–1857* (Philadelphia, 1949), pp. 183–9.

9

A spectacular exhibition of Southern "chivalry" had shocked the nation earlier in the year 1838. William G. Graves, an amiable young member of Congress from Kentucky, had considered himself obliged to challenge Jonathan Cilley of Maine. Each man was serving his first term in the House of Representatives. Cilley had done nothing to offend Graves personally. He had refused to satisfy a demand for personal explanations brought to him by the hand of Graves from James Watson Webb, a New York journalist. What Graves took exception to was not the Maine member's reason for declining to meet Webb: refusal to be held personally responsible outside of the House of Representatives for remarks made on the floor. Rather it was that Cilley in declining had refused to state unequivocally whether he considered Webb to be a gentleman; therefore he had reflected on Graves's own honor, for how could it be supposed that Graves would bring a card from other than a gentleman? Cilley, who was said to be able to put ten balls in succession into a man's hat at one hundred yards, accepted the challenge, naming rifles at that range! Graves had never touched his hand to a dueling weapon and only knew rifles because he had lived in Kentucky. He stood up to Cilley unhurt and on the third exchange of fire shot him dead, through the stomach.

Both duelists had professed the most cordial respect and friendship for each other. It was said that the survivor suffered more anguish than the fallen and his young family, including three children. Outraged public opinion directed itself not so much to principals of the tragic affair as to their seconds, notably Henry A. Wise of Virginia, the dueling enthusiast, who represented Graves and seemed to have egged him on. After the first round had satisfied all requirements of personal courage the seconds had insisted that they keep up the shooting—Wise had even suggested that if both men remained unharmed after the third exchange then they should shorten the distance.[82]

Petitions to Congress flooded in, mostly from Northern groups praying for the abolition of dueling in the District of Columbia. Even Andrew Jackson was shocked at the "murderous death of poor Cilley," and thought that Congress must do something to quench the flame of indignation arising in the public mind.

Hitherto John Quincy Adams had refused to crusade for laws to prohibit dueling, as he had hesitated to take up so many other reform movements. He abhorred the practice as barbarous and un-Christian; it had threatened his own Administration when President;[83] but, given human

[82] Don Seitz: *Famous American Duels* (New York, 1929), pp. 251–83. Myra L. Spaulding: "Dueling in the District of Columbia," *Records of the Columbia Historical Society*, XXIX–XXX (Washington, 1928), 186–210.

[83] See above, p. 99.

nature and social sanction and his own feeble influence in Congress on such an issue, he had felt it quixotic to try to put an end to it by legislation.[84] He opposed any effort by the outraged House to try Graves or Wise for a capital crime: that was only for the proper courts. Encouraged now by the revolt of public opinion, particularly in the North, Adams supported a resolution for a congressional inquiry, and himself introduced into the House and sponsored the anti-dueling bill [85] originated by Senator Samuel Prentiss of Vermont in the upper chamber. The threats of Southern ruffians to assassinate Adams, plus persistent defense of dueling by Southern members of Congress, convinced him that the murderous institution was an "appendage to slavery."

As finally enacted, the Prentiss-Adams law (February 20, 1839) prohibited within the District of Columbia the giving, delivering, or acceptance of a challenge to a duel, under penalty of ten years' imprisonment at hard labor if any of the parties should be killed or mortally wounded in or outside the District, five years in case of no such casualty, and three years for assaulting a person who refused to accept a challenge.[86]

Adams championed the bill through the House. Henry A. Wise did not speak to it or vote on it. "The anti-dueling law is producing its bitter results," the disappointed Virginian later bemoaned on the occasion of some angry exchanges in the House in February 1841. "Here, with the permission of the Chair and Committee and without a call to order from anybody, we see and hear one member say to another that he has been branded as a coward on this floor. The other says back that 'he is a liar!' And, Sir, there the matter will drop. *There will be no fight.*"

Southern duelists clapped their hands. From the gallery came hisses.

"I maintain the contrary," Adams flung back. "I maintain it for the independence of this House, for my own independence, for the independence of those with whom I act, for the independence of the members of the Northern section of this country, who not only abhor dueling in theory, but in practice; in consequence of which members from other sections are perpetually insulting them on this floor, under the impression that the insult will not be resented."

"Order! Order!" The House was in such an uproar that the official reporter could scarcely hear the presiding chairman or the member speaking.

"I say there is no more important subject," continued Adams, "that can go forth, North and South, East and West; and I therefore take my issue upon it. I have come here determined to do so between the different portions of this House, in order to see whether this practice is to be continued; whether the members from that section of the Union whose prin-

[84] *Memoirs*, IX, 500.

[85] *Congressional Globe*, VII, 50, 143, 191–3.

[86] *Laws of the U.S., March 4, 1833–March 3, 1839* (Washington, 1839), pp. 957–8.

ciples are against dueling are to be insulted, upon every topic of discussion, because it is supposed that the insult will not be resented, and that 'there will be no fight.' . . . I am not willing to sit any longer here, and see other members from my own section of the country, or those who may be my successors here, made subject to any such law as the law of the duelist. . . . I do not want to hear perpetual intimations, when a man from one part of the country means to insult another coming from other parts of the country, as, 'I am ready to answer here or elsewhere'; and 'The gentleman knows where I am to be found.' " [87]

Silence reigned when he finished. The swashbuckling Wise would hear still more from the old Quincy gladiator on this matter.

10

Adams methodically filed the "bullying letters" and kept on presenting the hundreds of petitions—abolitionist or otherwise—that came to him from all over the North: more remonstrances against the annexation of Texas; memorials for the abolition of slavery and the slave trade in the District of Columbia; for the same in the territories of the United States; opposing the admission of another slave state (Florida) into the Union; for prohibition of the domestic slave trade between the states; for recognition of Haiti; for rescinding the Gag Rule, and so forth. Other petitions were designed to make him look foolish, such as petitions to expel him from the House of Representatives as a public nuisance. As long as they were made in good faith he presented them, by the hundreds, by stacks and by bushels, and kept an indexed register of them prepared in his own hand, together with a file of covering letters by which they were communicated.[88] But he did not change the existing temper of Congress; the petitions only goaded the defiant Southerners to a more and more aggressive attitude.

Their spectacular attacks on the four freedoms that Adams was defending—outrages such as the murder of Elijah Lovejoy, "first American martyr to the freedom of the press, and the slave" [89]—could make any man feel that these Southern threats of assassination were more than idle

[87] *Congressional Globe*, IX, 320–2. February 4, 1841. Cited by Josiah Quincy: *Memoir of the Life of John Quincy Adams* (Boston, 1858), pp. 322–5. *Memoirs*, X, 413.

[88] In the third session (December 1838–March 4, 1839) of the Twenty-fifth Congress alone he presented 841 petitions. They are summarized and classified in *National Intelligencer*, XXVII, No. 8171, April 23, 1839. JQA's register of petitions is in Adams MSS., "JQA Congressional, 1840–1846." There are three bound volumes of "Petition Letters," 1836–44.

[89] JQA so characterized him in an Introduction to the *Memoir of the Rev. Elijah P. Lovejoy; Who Was Murdered in Defence of the Liberty of the Press, at Alton, Illinois, November 7, 1837*. By Joseph C. and Owen Lovejoy (New York, 1838), p. 12.

foam and fury. Even in the North there was a frenzy of public feeling against abolition and abolitionists: witness the destruction of Pennsylvania Hall.[90] Adams kept admonishing his antislavery friends to reduce their petitions, at the same time reciprocating their hopes for the ultimate abolition of slavery throughout the universe. But he could not dam the stream. Dutifully he presented them in the face of mounting indignation North as well as South.

Adams rose on January 21, 1839 to address the Speaker of the House. Stating that he had a large number of abolition petitions to present, he asked leave to explain the position that he personally held on the subject. "I further ask the courtesy of the House, because I have received a mass of letters threatening to assassinate me for my course. My real position has never been understood by the Country."

Various members immediately objected, whereupon George Grennell, Jr., of Greenfield, Massachusetts, moved a suspension of rules to let Adams proceed. William Key Bond of Chillicothe, Ohio, called for the yeas and nays. The motion carried by a vote of 117 to 58 without any clear party or sectional division.

"I wish distinctly to aver," Adams then stated to his colleagues, "that though I have earnestly advocated the right of persons to petition for the abolition of slavery in the District of Columbia, I myself am not prepared to grant their prayer. On the contrary, if the question were presented at once, I should vote against it. What change a fair and full discussion might make upon my mind I do not know, but so far I see no reason to change my opinion, though I have read all that the abolitionists themselves have written and published on the subject."

Having said as much, he presented a bundle of recent petitions, including some that prayed for censure of whoever had moved to censure him for introducing such papers. Other New England colleagues, Edward Everett and Heman Allen of Vermont, unloaded themselves of similar bundles of memorials. The Speaker as usual ordered them all to be tabled, and the House took up other business.[91]

William Slade stood aghast when he read his friend's statement to the House. Respectfully he asked Adams whether an explanation was not due to the country, particularly to those who were supporting the cause of abolition in the District of Columbia. What were the reasons that satisfied him that the prayers of the petitioners should not be granted? "Must we wait until the 'Northern men with Southern principles' shall consent to *ungag* us, for an exposition of those reasons?" Adams replied rather curtly that if a suitable occasion should present itself during the current session, he would expose his views on the floor of the House; otherwise

[90] JQA to Samuel Webb, Philadelphia. Washington, April 23, 1839. Adams MSS. This passage not printed by CFA, Jr., in *Emancipation by Martial Law*.

[91] *Congressional Globe*, VII, 137. JQA's statement was published in the *National Intelligencer* of next morning, January 24, 1839, Vol. XL, No. 5690.

he would make a statement to his constituents at the close of the session of Congress.[92]

To make his position absolutely clear before the whole Union, Adams now offered a plan for abolition of slavery by constitutional amendment, somewhat in the manner that Jefferson had once privately suggested.[93] On February 25, 1839 he asked leave of the Speaker to present the resolutions for the following three amendments to the Constitution of the United States, which he succeeded in reading for the information of the House:

1st. From and after the 4th day of July, 1842, there shall be, throughout the United States, no hereditary slavery; but on and after that day every child born within the United States, their Territories or jurisdiction, shall be born free.

2d. With the exception of the Territory of Florida, there shall henceforth never be admitted into this Union any State, the constitution of which shall tolerate within the same the existence of slavery.

3d. From and after the 4th of July, 1845, there shall be neither slavery nor slave trade at the seat of Government of the United States.[94]

To the Administration majority these proposals for amending the Constitution were so many more abolition petitions. Somebody immediately objected.

"Order! Order!"

The Speaker decided that a motion to suspend the rules was necessary to receive the resolutions. Adams did not press his motion further. He knew there was no chance for such amendments to the Constitution.[95] He had put himself on record before the country and before the abolitionists to show the only conceivable way in which, in his opinion, slavery could be abolished without violence and without injustice [96]—namely, by constitutional amendment.

[92] William Slade to JQA, Washington, January 23, 1839. JQA to William Slade, Washington, January 25, 1839. Adams MSS.

[93] Jefferson to Edward Coles, Monticello, August 25, 1814. P. L. Ford: *Writings of Jefferson*, IX (1899), 478.

[94] *Congressional Globe*, VII, 218.

[95] "I had no expectation that my resolutions would be *received* by the House. I knew they would not be discussed. I presented them rather to the *petitioners*, as comprising the only mode by which I believe the abolition of slavery could possibly be effected without violence and without injustice." JQA to the Citizens of the United States. . . . Quincy, May 21, 1839. *Daily National Intelligencer*, post cit., XXVII, No. 8201, May 28, 1839.

[96] ". . . I adopted the principle of the States of Pennsylvania and New York, when their legislatures abolished Slavery within themselves, by declaring all children free born after a given day. If Slavery is ever to be abolished in the United States *peaceably*, I am persuaded it must be in this manner. And as to undertaking to abolish it by law, enacted by the votes of Representatives from the Free States against the Will of the Slaveholders themselves, it would be in my opinion neither practicable nor

Following the adjournment of the Twenty-fifth Congress, Adams sternly advised his abolitionist friends that immediate abolition even in the District of Columbia was for the present a moral and physical impossibility, "utterly impracticable." Their "senseless and overbearing clamor" [97] was hardening the resolution of the slaveholders to resist at any cost. The antislavery societies were weakening rather than promoting the cause of ultimate emancipation. [98]

This cold counsel from the principal advocate of constitutional emancipation, almost the hero of an antislavery host throughout most of the North, doomed the antislavery societies to early dissolution. [99] Their remnants now fell into the control of the revolutionary and uncompromising Garrison, who convinced them that the Constitution was a covenant with death and an agreement with hell.

"If you had been as explicit in your declarations at the time your election was pending, as you now are," the implacable Garrison charged Adams, "a majority of your constituents would have cast their votes for some other candidate." [100]

Adams's attitude stunned the antislavery leaders. To some of them it looked like another chapter in a lifelong personal history of apostasy, first from the Federalists to the Republicans (to support Jefferson's Embargo), then from the Republicans to the Democrats (upholding President Jackson in the French crisis), and now a desertion from the antislavery cohorts whose course he had accepted as his own:

---

just." JQA to Samuel Webb, Philadelphia. Washington, April 23, 1839. Adams MSS. This portion of the letter was not printed in *Emancipation by Martial Law*.

[97] *Memoirs*, X, 132.

[98] JQA "to the Citizens of the United States, whose Petitions, Memorials, and Remonstrances have been intrusted to me." This long public statement, reviewing the legal basis of the right of petition and the whole slavery controversy, appeared in two installments in the *National Intelligencer*, XXVII, Nos. 8171 and 8201 of April 23 and May 28, 1839, and reprinted in numerous other papers all over the country.

For further private letters of JQA to individual abolitionist friends see JQA to Samuel Webb of Philadelphia, Washington, April 23, 1839; to Joshua Leavitt and H. B. Stanton of the Committee of Arrangements of the American Antislavery Society of New York, Quincy, July 11, 1839; to Gerrit Smith of Petersborough, N.Y., Quincy, July 31, 1839; to Benjamin D. Silliman of Brooklyn, N.Y., Quincy, August 21, 1839. Adams MSS. Except for the last, these letters are only partially printed by CFA, Jr., in *Emancipation by Martial Law*.

[99] Barnes: *Antislavery Impulse*, pp. 165–6. There is a significant change at this time in the tone of Adams's public addresses. The "antislavery sermon" in his *Oration Delivered before the Inhabitants of the Town of Newburyport, at their Request, on the Sixty-First Anniversary of the Declaration of Independence, July 4, 1837* (Newburyport, Mass.: printed by Morse and Brewster; 1837) is softened to strictures against state rights in his *Jubilee of the Constitution* (New York: Samuel Coleman; 1839), delivered before the New York Historical Society, April 1839, on the occasion of the fiftieth anniversary of President George Washington's inauguration.

[100] Henry Wilson, op. cit., I, 436. J. G. Birney expressed, before the election, this distrust of Adams as a *political* supporter of abolition.

He that played Sir Pander
　　While wages were to be had,
And saved slave-trading Andrew
　　Now rails at them like mad;
And turning to us says modestly,
　　'Your language is too bad.' [101]

One abolitionist in Ohio accused Adams of retracting in principle under threats of assassination and threatened to make way with him if he said anything more that sounded like a denunciation of abolitionism.[102]

A new and dramatic incident now appeared to take the place of Texas in keeping the slavery issue alive before the country and to redeem John Quincy Adams once more in the hearts of his abolitionist friends.

[101] *Emancipator*, September 26, 1839. Quoted by Barnes: *Antislavery Impulse*, pp. 167, 278. I have (perhaps) slightly improved the fifth line.
[102] Sawies Silvey to JQA, Chillicothe, February 9, 1839. Adams MSS.

CHAPTER XIX
The Africans of the *Amistad*
(1839 – 1841)

The world to me is but the lions' den.

JOHN QUINCY ADAMS, 1839 [1]

IN the eyes of the world what was the national character of this Union half slave and half free? On a diplomatic issue involving the slave trade or slavery how would the Government at Washington speak to other governments—with the voice of a free nation or that of a slaveholding nation? So far no President, no party, had been able to come to power and stay in power without the sympathy of the South and some tenderness toward its peculiar institution. From the Administration of George Washington down to that of Martin Van Buren, including John Quincy Adams's, the executive branch had spoken as for a slaveholding nation.

Adams was now an old man and the antislavery impulse had begun to stir the country—and his conscience. No longer need he heed a behest of the slave power. If he could not by his experience halt that power over the Executive in the existing Administration, or by his parliamentary prowess subdue it in Congress, he might yet in his vast knowledge of the law serve to check it in the courts. *A cause célèbre* was at hand which it is now necessary to review before it reached the pleadings of the compulsive defender of freedom.

1

The case of the *Amistad* is a challenge to the novelist [2] as it has been to the courts and should be to the historian. In April 1839 a Portuguese pirate slave-trader purchased a cargo of kidnapped natives of the Dark

---

[1] From sonnet written for Miss Sidney Peirce, printed in *Memoirs*, X, 133. September 28, 1839.

[2] William A. Owens has made it the basis for his exciting book, a dramatic evocation of verisimilitude in action and dialogue: *Slave Mutiny: The Revolt on the Schooner Amistad* (New York, 1953). He deposited in the New Haven Colony Historical Society typescripts of newspaper comments and editorials on the case, and of letters from collections of personal papers (not always identified) which are useful to the historian.

Continent from a Spaniard involved in the nefarious business on the Guinea coast and transported them to Havana in the abominable hold of the slave ship *Teçora*. At that time the slave trade had been prohibited by treaties between Great Britain and Portugal (1817), Great Britain and Spain (1817, 1835), and Great Britain and the Netherlands (1818). An Anglo-Spanish mixed commission sat at Havana to deal with violations of the treaty and take care of Negroes liberated from slave-trading vessels— the few that were caught. Both the United States and Great Britain had branded the slave trade as piracy and forbidden their citizens and subjects to engage in it under penalty of death. The King of Spain had issued ordinances (December 17, 1817 and November 2, 1838) declaring that every African slave imported into a Spanish colony in violation of the British treaty should be considered free in the first port to which he came, but such decrees were practically dead letters.

The unfortunate captives on the *Teçora*, then, were not slaves but free men illegally enslaved whom Spanish law had not caught up with and liberated. Among the survivors of the terrible Middle Passage in that faithless ship were fifty-two Negroes, including three female children between the ages of seven and nine, most of them members of the Mendi tribe on the northern borders of Nigeria. Their natural leader was Singbe-Piéh, rendered Cinqué in Spanish and English, a splendid specimen of savage manhood who became the hero of their captivity.

The *Teçora* landed her outlawed cargo at night near Havana with practiced skill and the complicity of Spanish authorities. The victims were marched in coffles to the city's slave market, where they could be bought and sold as openly as in Washington itself. Two Cubans by the names of Ruiz and Montes purchased the captives: Ruiz forty-nine of them, Montes three, including two of the little girls. They planned to take them as slaves to the province of Puerto Principe (Camagüey). In order to transport Negroes from place to place in Cuba a license was necessary. Accordingly Ruiz and Montes procured papers from the Havana authorities for clearance in the coastal schooner *Amistad*, and for passage of two separate parcels of "black *ladinos*" enumerated under Spanish names—Francisco, Julian, Hipolito y Ramón, and so on.

Ladino was a Spanish word (corrupted from *latino*) widely used to describe a person who had been in the country long enough to know the customs and speak the language. The Africans of the *Amistad* were not *ladinos;* [3] they could not even recognize the Spanish names so hastily bestowed upon them. Their obvious youthful appearance made it impossible for any of them to be old enough to have been imported before the Anglo-Spanish treaty of 1817 had abolished the slave trade. They were *bozales*, meaning new and green to the country, but to call them such would reveal their real identity; so they were put down as *ladinos*. Spanish offi-

---

[3] The usage of this word went back to Moorish times and occurs both in *The Cid* and in *Don Quixote*.

cials grew rich, at rates of ten to seventeen dollars a head,[4] for permitting importation of thousands of African Negroes and allowing them to be transported illegally out of the Havana market to the Cuban sugar plantations. They were perhaps no worse than American consuls suspected of issuing false papers to slavers who wanted to fly the American flag for protection against British patrol cruisers.

The *Amistad,* so cleared, put out to sea for the port of Granaja, Puerto Principe, on June 28, 1839.

"What are the white men going to do with us?" one of the captives asked the ship's cook, in sign language, as they stood on deck for a little fresh air and sunlight.

The grinning creature who tended the ship's rice boilers passed a forefinger across his throat. "The white men will eat you," he added with another sign.

On the fourth night out, being then about three or four leagues from the coast of Cuba and about forty from Havana, the Africans managed to get free of their irons by breaking the padlock of a common chain that ran through their individual collars. In the ship's hold they laid hands on heavy knives for cutting sugar cane. In the morning they rushed the captain, one Ramón Ferrer, and his crew of three men plus his mulatto slave, the cabin boy Antonio. Cinqué split the captain's head with one mighty machete-stroke. They fell upon the cook and killed him too. The two remaining members of the crew got away in the ship's boat and spread the alarm along the Atlantic littoral. Antonio, a real *ladino,* remained unharmed. The self-liberated Negroes spared the lives of their white "owners" on promises by them to steer the ship eastward toward the rising sun, back to Africa and to home.

Ruiz and Montes kept the schooner's prow pointed east—by day; but by night they turned her toward the United States, doubtless hoping to make some Southern port. Already the collectors of customs at the various seaports had detailed revenue cutters to search out the pirates,[5] meaning by that not the Spaniards who were taking the kidnapped people into slavery, but the Africans who had restored themselves to freedom. Eventually the *Amistad* reached Long Island, near Montauk Point. There Lieu-

[4] See testimony of Dr. Richard R. Madden in *Amistad* trial, 15 Peters *U.S. Reports* 537. Charles P. Butler to JQA, Mobile, December 23, 25, 1840. Adams MSS.

[5] See Introductory Narrative to *The African Captives: Trial of the Prisoners of the Amistad on the Writ of Habeas Corpus, before the Circuit Court of the United States, for the District of Connecticut, at Hartford: Judges Thompson and Judson. September Term, 1839.* (New York: 143 Nassau St.; 1839.) Published by the Committee for the Defense of the Africans. Hereinafter cited as *Trial of the Prisoners of the Amistad.* More colorful is John W. Barber: *A History of the Amistad Captives: being a Circumstantial Account of the Capture of the Spanish Schooner Amistad, by the Africans on Board; Their Voyage, and Capture near Long Island, New York; with Biographical Sketches of Each of the Surviving Africans. Also an Account af the Trials Had on Their Case, before the District and Circuit Courts of the United States, for the District of Connecticut.* (New Haven: Published by E. L. and J. W. Barber; 1840.)

tenant Thomas R. Gedney, commander of the United States coastal survey brig *Washington,* came upon them, August 26, and took ship and
people into custody, including several of the Africans who had gone
ashore for food and water. He brought the vessel and all on board into the
nearest port, New London.

The two Cuban slave-traders immediately denounced Cinqué and his
companions as revolted slaves, pirates, and murderers, and claimed them
as their lawful property. Judge Andrew T. Judson of the Federal District
Court of Connecticut held an inquiry on board the *Washington.* Upon
representation of United States District Attorney William S. Holabird he
committed Cinqué and thirty-eight other survivors on a charge of piracy
and murder at the next session of the United States Circuit Court, to convene at Hartford on September 17. At the same time Lieutenant Gedney
and a fellow officer, Lieutenant Meade, filed suit in admiralty libeling the
Amistad and her cargo, including the "slaves," for salvage on behalf of
themselves and the crew of the *Washington.* A federal marshal took the
Africans and their ship into custody, sending the people to New Haven to
be incarcerated in the county jail pending trial. He detained the three
children and the cabin boy Antonio as witnesses, committed for lack of
bail. Trial of this suit was set for September 19 in the Federal District
Court sitting also at Hartford coincidentally with the Circuit Court.

Ruiz and Montes set forth for New York and Washington to see the
Spanish Consul and Minister. Before they left New London they inserted
in the local *Gazette* a card, composed with the help of the editor, expressing their gratitude and appreciation on behalf of the Queen of Spain to
Lieutenant Gedney and the officers and crew of the *Washington* for their
unexpected and providential rescue from an awful death at the hands of a
"ruthless gang of African buccaneers," for their unremitting kindness and
hospitality, and for protection of the Spaniards' "property." This did not
prevent them later from contesting the salvage suit on the ground that the
gallant seamen had only done their duty to their country, pledged as it
was to protect all Spanish subjects in distress in American waters, together with all that belonged to them. When the District Court met at
Hartford, September 18, 1839, they filed an attachment against the Africans as their slaves and property.

"I suppose it will be my duty to bring them to trial," District Attorney
Holabird suggested to the Secretary of State, "unless they are in some
other way disposed of." He asked for instructions. "Are there no treaty
stipulations," he inquired, "that would authorize our Government to deliver them up to the Spanish authorities; and if so, could it be done before
our court sits?" [6]

[6] Holabird to Forsyth, September 5, 9, 1839. H.R. Ex. Doc. 185, 26th Cong., 1st
Sess., pp. 38–9. The abolitionist press published a reprint of this congressional docu-
ment with notes of commentary under the title of *Africans Taken in the Amistad*
(New York: Antislavery Depositary; 1840).

Forsyth submitted the question to the President. "In the meantime," he ordered Holabird, "take care that no proceeding of your circuit court, or of any other judicial tribunal, places the vessel, cargo, or slaves beyond the control of the Federal Executive." [7]

The case of the *Amistad* was already lodged in the courts when the Spanish Minister to the United States, Angel Calderón de la Barca, then about to return home, learned of the events at New London. Immediately he demanded the release of the ship and captives and their restoration to their true owners as shipwrecked property according to the treaty of 1795 between the United States and Spain. He further desired a declaration by the Executive that no tribunal in the United States had a right to institute proceedings against or impose penalties upon Spanish subjects for crimes committed on board a Spanish vessel and in Spanish territorial waters. The revolted slaves, he asserted, should be conveyed by the United States to Havana, there to be tried by Spanish law.

"The crime in question," declared Señor Calderón, "is one of those which if permitted to pass unpunished would endanger the internal tranquillity and safety of the island of Cuba, where the citizens of the United States not only carry on a considerable trade but where they possess territorial properties which they cultivate with the labor of African slaves." He felt that it would not be enough to have capital punishment inflicted on them by an "incompetent" American court, even with indemnification to the owners: "The satisfaction due to the [Cuban] public would not be accorded." He assured the Secretary of State that the Spanish Government would immediately allow extradition of any American slaves that might seek refuge in Cuba from the Southern states.[8] Having delivered himself of this charge, he left the issue in the hands of his successor, the Chevalier Pedro Alcántara de Argaiz.

As will appear presently, legal counsel came to the aid of the Africans. The first thing they did was to address President Van Buren to request him not to allow any executive order for delivery of the captives to the Spanish Minister until facts justifying it should be established by judicial authority in the courts.[9] The President gave them no satisfaction. He was, it seems, a little miffed that these American citizens should presume to address him directly, rather than the Secretary of State, upon such a subject.[10]

Secretary John Forsyth, who had been Minister at Madrid when John Quincy Adams was Secretary of State, did not deny the Spanish pretensions. To him, a Georgia slaveholder, they appeared to correspond too

[7] Forsyth to Holabird, Department of State, Washington, September 11, 1839. Ibid., pp. 39–40.

[8] Calderón to Forsyth, New York, September 6, 1839. Ibid., pp. 3–12.

[9] Seth P. Staples and Theodore Sedgwick, Jr., to Martin Van Buren, Esq., President of the United States, New York, September 13, 1839. Ibid., pp. 62–4.

[10] Lewis Tappan to Roger S. Baldwin, New York, April 27, 1840. Roger Baldwin MSS. in Sterling Memorial Library, Yale University. Hereinafter cited as Baldwin MSS.

well (as Señor Calderón had intimated) with the position which the Van Buren Government was then taking under the comity of nations, without support of treaty, toward Great Britain in the contemporary cases of the *Enterprise* and *Hermosa*.[11] Treaty or no treaty, Forsyth would have turned the Africans over to the tender mercies of Spanish justice and public vengeance if it had not been for the fact that they had been so firmly placed under court jurisdiction.

If only Holabird, an Administration appointee, had first sought instructions from Washington *before* he got the Africans and the *Amistad* so tied up with the judges! Then how simple it would have been, how seemingly consistent with the American position toward Great Britain, how altogether satisfactory, to turn the "slaves" over to the Spanish Minister and thus to be done with them! As it was, all that the Government could do was to libel the Negroes before the District Court, when it convened at Hartford, upon representation of the Spanish Government that they be restored as the property of Spanish subjects.

2

The captives found themselves in the New Haven county jail without a friend in the world, completely ignorant of the language and life of the country in which perforce they found themselves, with the President of the United States and all the executive machinery of the Government set against their freedom and their lives. But soon friends came to their prison door in this strange land of the white man. The moment the news reached New York, Lewis Tappan organized a meeting of abolitionists, which raised funds and appointed a committee headed by himself to defend them. With him on the committee were the Reverend Joshua Leavitt, that sturdy Puritan reformer and son of Massachusetts, a graduate of the Yale Divinity School, editor of the New York antislavery journal *Emancipator;* and Simeon S. Jocelyn, a native of New Haven and formerly pastor of a colored congregation there, best known for his unsuccessful effort to establish a Negro college in that city. All three were closely identified with the humanitarian and antislavery élite of New Haven and Yale College. All three were friends and correspondents of John Quincy Adams; Tappan had tried in vain to enlist him openly in the abolitionist cause.

---

[11] These ships were American coastwise vessels engaged in carrying real slaves from one Southern port to another, which were wrecked in the Bahama Islands, where British colonial authorities liberated the slaves. The British Government paid indemnity for slaves freed from the *Comet* and *Encomium* before domestic slavery was abolished (with compensation) in the islands, but refused to in the cases of the *Enterprise* and *Hermosa*, where the castaways were liberated after colonial emancipation. The United States Government demanded and eventually recovered compensation to the Southern slaveowners. For the correspondence see Sen. Doc. 174, 24th Cong., 2d Sess.; Sen. Doc. 216, 25th Cong., 3d Sess.; and J. B. Moore: *Digest of International Arbitrations*, I, 408–19.

Their first task, after engaging legal counsel, was to break down the language barrier between them and their protégés in order to bring forth the Africans' side of the story and to establish the facts of their freedom. No one in New Haven, not even the learned members of the Yale faculty, could tell what tongue they spoke or to what tribe they belonged. Reverend Thomas Hopkins Gallaudet of Hartford, the celebrated teacher of the deaf and dumb, had not been able to get very far with them in his sign language. But Professor Josiah Willard Gibbs (the elder) of the Divinity School, visiting the captives in jail day after day, soon learned their word sounds for the first ten numerals. And Tappan brought to New Haven four African seamen picked up in New York. One of these, John Ferry, spoke a kindred native dialect, recognized the numerals, and identified the people as Mendi. Through him a limited communication was possible with the captives before the court met at Hartford—enough to establish the fact that they were native Africans who knew neither Spanish nor Portuguese, had been in Cuba only a day or two, and therefore obviously were not legal slaves. This little was helpful but not enough; the worthy professor would have to search farther for a satisfactory interpreter.

In a few days the defendants were taken on a canal boat to Farmington, amazing the country folk along the way by their outlandish appearance; from there they went by stage to Hartford for hearings before the grand jury of the Circuit Court and to meet the libels filed against them in the Federal District Court. Judge Smith Thompson, from the Supreme Court at Washington, presided over the Circuit Court. Present also on the bench was Judge Judson of the District Court. He was a Van Buren appointee and anti-abolitionist. Before his appointment he had taken a prominent part in getting a law passed by the state legislature to prohibit the teaching of colored girls from out of Connecticut without the consent of the local selectmen. The legislation was aimed at Miss Prudence Crandall's famous school for Negro girls in Judson's home town of Canterbury. As state attorney Judson had prosecuted Miss Crandall for violation of the act, but she won out on appeal to a higher state court from a jury conviction. A mob of his fellow townsmen later sacked and wrecked the school. Judge Judson seemed a safe man for the Administration's case.

Counsel for the defense were Seth P. Staples and Theodore Sedgwick, Jr., of New York; and Roger Sherman Baldwin of New Haven, grandson of the Revolutionary patriot.[12] Ralph I. Ingersoll and William Hungerford,

[12] Joseph A. Howland treated the episode of the *Amistad* and the court trials as the "first broken link in the chain that held so many millions in bondage as chattel slaves in our land" in a paper, "The Captives of the *Amistad*," read before the Worcester Society of Antiquity on April 6, 1886. *Proceedings,* 1886 (Worcester, 1887), pp. 61–75. By a curious coincidence Judge Simeon E. Baldwin (1840–1927), Governor of Connecticut (1910–14) and well-known jurist, Roger Sherman Baldwin's son, who had access to his father's papers, delivered an address along the same lines, "The Captives of the *Amistad*," before the New Haven Colony Historical Society on May 17,

well-known Connecticut attorneys, appeared for the Spanish Crown. District Attorney Holabird had asked the court to try the principal issue on the claim of the Spanish Minister, put forward by the United States: if it should appear that the captives should be delivered up, he asked that a mandate be issued accordingly; but if on the other hand it should be found that they had been imported illegally into the country, then he requested an order to enable the President to send them back to Africa in accordance with the law of March 3, 1819 providing for the disposition of Africans captured from slaveholders.

Immediately the trial opened, Staples, for the defense, moved a writ of habeas corpus to release the children held as witnesses to the charge of piracy and murder against the adult Africans. He explained that bail was available for them. Hungerford opposed the motion, claiming the children as the slave property of two "Spanish gentlemen." He reminded the court that there were several salvage claims also pending against these persons. Judge Thompson immediately granted the writ of habeas corpus and said that all the contested matters could come up on that point when the writ was returned next day. First arguments therefore turned about the justice of detaining the Negro children as slave property claimed by would-be owners or libeled for salvage by alleged rescuers.

Counsel for the Africans argued that they were all free persons. Suppose the color of the case were reversed, suggested Baldwin. Suppose that Pedro Montes, a white man, had been captured by dark-skinned Algerine corsairs and escaped ashore in the United States.[13] Suppose his captors had then libeled him in court as their property and demanded his return because by the laws of Algiers white men could be treated as property. Algiers like Spain had a treaty with the United States providing for the return of shipwrecked property.[14] Yet no court in the United States, he asserted, no court in all Christendom, would entertain a claim for the restoration of a white man as property. "It is only when men come here with a black skin that we look upon them in a condition in which they may by any means be made slaves. But when we find them here from the coast of Africa the same rule must apply to the black man as to the white man." So spoke the descendant of a Connecticut signer of the Declaration of Independence, which had declared all men free and equal, endowed with inalienable rights to life, liberty, and the pursuit of happiness.

Holabird coolly answered that however one looked upon them in Connecticut, the Africans were foreign property: "We are under obligation by the treaty with Spain," said he, "to return these slaves to the Spanish

1886, printed in the society's *Papers*, IV (New Haven, 1888), 331–70. Both addresses rest primarily on the government documents printed in H. Ex. Doc. No. 185, 26th Cong., 1st Sess., cited throughout this chapter.

[13] This argument, an old one in antislavery literature, was suggested by William Jay in his letter to the *Emancipator* of September 7, 1839.

[14] Actually this treaty lapsed in 1830 when Algiers became a French colony.

claimants. That obligation must be discharged, and we cannot plead our treaty [15] with Great Britain against it." [16]

While the arguments were proceeding, the grand jury entered the courtroom with a statement of facts and asked Judge Thompson for a charge. He decided that the Circuit Court had no jurisdiction over the case because the alleged crime of piracy and murder had been committed on a Spanish ship; American laws against piracy covered only such crimes in American territorial waters or on an American ship on the high seas. It followed that he had no power to hold the children as witnesses to a crime over which his court had no jurisdiction. But he could not release either children or adults because they were all libeled in admiralty before the District Court. It would be for the several claimants [17] to show in that court why the captives should be held further.

Upon this pronouncement Judge Judson instantly convened the District Court. He had already intimated to counsel for the libelants that the District Court could not sell the Negroes like a ship to secure libel claims, but that did not settle the problem whether they could be returned to the Spanish claimants as property. This question would require more investigation. He set a trial for the coming session of the District Court in November (later postponed to January 7, 1840). Meanwhile he was willing to release the Africans on bail, but this would require an appraisal of their value. Their counsel would not think of recognizance on such a condition, because they could not yet admit that free men could be appraised as property. So the unfortunate captives went back to jail in New Haven.

In Washington the newly arrived Spanish Minister gave the Department of State no rest. "The public vengeance has not been satisfied," he complained, "for be it recollected the legation of Spain does not demand the delivery of slaves, but of assassins." [18] He desired the Government to turn them over to him by executive action (*gubernativemente*) and thus relieve their Spanish owners of the vexations of "fanaticism." For such a claim—extradition of fugitive criminals rather than return of property—

[15] Article X of the Treaty of Ghent read: "Whereas, the Traffic in Slaves is irreconcilable with the principles of humanity and Justice, and whereas both His Majesty and the United States are desirous of continuing their efforts to promote its entire abolition, it is hereby agreed that the contracting parties shall use their best efforts to accomplish so desirable an object."

[16] *Trial of the Prisoners of the Amistad.* This was an abolitionist report of the trial, but it gives the arguments more at length than the summary of the case in the lower courts when it was later argued in the Supreme Court of the United States as reported in 15 Peters *U.S. Reports* 523–38.

[17] Meanwhile another libel had been entered against the Africans by two bystanders who claimed they had assisted in Lieutenant Gedney's capture of the Negroes who had been found on shore at Long Island when their ship was taken offshore. Governor William Wolcott Ellsworth of the State of Connecticut stooped to take the case of these characters in private practice.

[18] H. Ex. Doc. No. 185, 26th Cong., 1st Sess., p. 21.

there was no basis in the treaty of 1795; all that he could fall back on was extradition under the comity of nations.

The President directed the Secretary of State to consult the Attorney General, Felix Grundy, a slaveholder from Tennessee. In a long opinion Grundy declared that in the intercourse and transactions between nations due faith and credit must be given by each to the official acts and functionaries of other governments—hence the United States could not go behind the *Amistad's* papers evidencing that the Negroes were *ladinos* and slaves. He advised that they should be surrendered to the public officers of the Spanish Government to the end "that if the laws of Spain have been violated they may not escape punishment." [19] Obviously Grundy was more anxious that the Africans be punished than that they be freed.

Van Buren on his part could not desert his alliance with the Southern slavery capitalists by which he had reached the White House, where he still hoped to stay after the election of 1840. He joined his Southern Cabinet of officers in speaking—behind his hand—with the voice of slavery for this Union half slave and half free. He allowed the Attorney General's opinion to be communicated confidentially to the Spanish Minister as that of a "learned lawyer" which had been adopted by the Cabinet.[20] But he did not dare defy the courts, certainly not in an election year when he needed Northern as well as Southern votes. After a consultation with Holabird at Albany, he gave orders to send a public ship, the *Grampus,* to New Haven, there to be ready to transport the Negroes back to Havana for delivery to Spanish authorities in case the District Court should, as anticipated, give an order to that effect at the end of the forthcoming trial. And Lieutenants Gedney and Meade received orders to hold themselves ready to proceed to Havana in the same vessel with copies of the *Amistad's* papers and the court record to testify in a Spanish trial of the Negroes.

The Government made no preparation to take the captives back to their homeland if the District Court decided the other way. In that event the District Attorney had orders to appeal the decision to the Circuit Court, allowing things to remain as they were until the appeal should be decided.[21] Thus did the President mobilize every executive power at his disposition in favor of the Spanish Government's demand and against the freedom of the Africans of the *Amistad.*[22]

[19] Ibid., pp. 57–62.

[20] Argaiz to Forsyth, Washington, December 25, 1839. Ibid., p. 34.

[21] Holabird to Forsyth, November 14, 1839, January 11, 1840; Forsyth to Holabird, January 6, 12, 17, 1840. Ibid., pp. 54–7. Department of State to Secretary of the Navy, January 2, 7, 1840; Secretary of the Navy to the Department of State, January 3, 1840. Ibid., pp. 67–9. Van Buren's *Autobiography* does not allude to the *Amistad* case.

[22] The Defense Committee in the name of Cinqué and another of the Africans brought suit against Ruiz and Montes before the New York courts in an action for damages for false imprisonment, and Ruiz lay in jail six weeks for lack of bond. On

8

News of the *Amistad* interrupted the murmur of John Quincy Adams's Indian-summer leisure amidst his seedbeds, his nursery, his garden, and fruit trees, preceding his return to the winter session of Congress. His first notice of the affair was a suggestion in the pro-Administration Washington *Globe* that the Government might turn the Negroes over to slave-trading justice and mercy. Then he read in Joshua Leavitt's *Emancipator* [23] a letter from William Jay, son of the famous Chief Justice who had once been Adams's diplomatic mentor at Paris and London in 1783 and 1794.

William Jay was one of the most eminent exponents of evangelistic reform that followed the Great Revival—a Sabbatarian, a temperance advocate, an antiduelist, a passionate proponent of Sunday schools and Bible societies, an enthusiastic agrarian experimenter, and of course an abolitionist. Commenting on the heroism of the Africans in rising to free themselves from the slave-traders, Jay recoiled from the idea of their being handed back to a Spanish doom. His righteous indignation inspired a sympathetic private reply to him from Adams: no grand jury of free men, the latter hoped, could be found to indict the Africans for vindicating their own liberty against slave-traders and pirates. Could anybody imagine, he asked, that an executive officer of the United States Government could be found daring enough to lay his hand upon them to deliver them to the mockery of a Cuban tribunal of slave-smugglers? [24]

It may be presumed that William Jay told Joshua Leavitt and Lewis Tappan how John Quincy Adams, the friend of them all, felt about the Africans; they had long been working on him to join the abolitionists and were disappointed at his recent advice to reduce antislavery petitions to Congress. After the decision of the Circuit Court, Tappan's Defense Committee, facing a long-drawn-out legal battle, were casting about for some champion of national eminence and personal integrity who could muster public respect as well as marshal the law on their side. They approached Adams indirectly through Ellis Gray Loring, well-known Massachusetts lawyer and antislavery advocate, Adams's host at many a fishing excursion and chowder party down the Bay from Boston. If the Plymouth Representative was not generally acknowledged as a Man of the Whole Nation, he was certainly a friend of freedom, an exponent of the inalienable rights of the Declaration of Independence, and a constitutional foe of the slave power. They sought to draw him into the contest.

---

orders from Washington the United States District Attorney for New York went out of his way to give them legal guidance toward their release.

[23] Vol. IV, No. 20, Whole No. 176, p. 79, for September 12, 1839. William Jay's letter is dated Bedford, September 7, 1839.

[24] JQA to Williams Jay, Bedford, N.Y. Quincy, September 17, 1839. Adams MSS.

Adams pondered. Was this another trap-door like the tariff question that had closed on his head a few years ago? Was it another windmill similar to that briefly blown around by the Antimasonic excitement? Was it another abolition whirligig? Ought he to pay any attention to the behests of his family, the counsel of his precocious son, to sidestep political pitfalls that could only bring contention and unnecessary trouble to himself and his dependents? Or should he be Mr. Greatheart in a continuing pilgrim's progress through the American scene?

Loring pressed him for an opinion. Could President Van Buren turn the Africans over to the Spanish Minister as persons charged with high crimes against the laws of Spain not recognizable within the jurisdiction of American courts? Were the Negroes *property* or *merchandise* or *effects* within the meaning of Articles VI and IX of the Spanish treaty of 1795, to be libeled as such in the federal courts? Was the Government of the United States estopped from denying such persons to be property by its position persistently taken in deference to the slave states vis-à-vis Great Britain? [25] Loring challengingly reminded him that these were questions of deep moral interest and important political principle as well as knotty legal problems.[26]

"The time has not come," Adams told himself after a conference at Loring's office in Boston, "when it would be proper for me to give an opinion for publication. Prudence would forbid my giving an opinion upon it at any time; and if I ever do, it must be with great consideration and self-controul." [27]

He thought back to his younger years. Once more he remembered the words his father, John Adams, had written to him at the beginning of his diplomatic career when he was in London arranging for exchange of ratifications of the unpopular Jay Treaty of 1794: "I hope you have not flinched." [28] "*I did not flinch*," the son had been able to write back.[29] Should he shrink from an unpopular duty now because he was an old man? He laid fresh hold on his soul before the *Amistad* challenge. "May I walk humbly and uprightly, on this and all other occasions, *flinching from no duty*, obtruding no officious interposition of opinions, and prepared to meet with firmness whatever obloquy may follow the free expression of my thoughts." [30]

Once more John Quincy Adams's inner compulsions were impelling him into a battle that his outer direction rejected. He began to consult his lawbooks, to reach for every scrap of information. With increasing absorption [31] he read the papers that Loring set before him. At first he

[25] See note 11, above.
[26] Ellis Gray Loring to JQA, Boston, September 23, 1839. Adams MSS.
[27] Diary, September 26, 1839.
[28] Vol. I, 69.
[29] JQA to JA, London, February 10, 1796. Adams MSS.
[30] Diary, September 26, 1839. Italics inserted.
[31] *Memoirs*, X, 133–5. October 1, 2, 1839. Diary, October 7, 8, 1839.

shrank from giving an outright responsible opinion: he answered Loring's questions by questioning him in turn.[32] But at the end of his questionnaire he declared that he would cheerfully offer his services to the defense, like Governor Ellsworth of Connecticut, if he thought they could be of any real help.[33] Loring agreed that there was great force to Adams's statement that the Africans should have gone completely free of both Circuit and District Courts on the writ of habeas corpus, but questioned other points. Loring's practiced sparring incited Adams to write back a long and eloquent letter showing that it was contrary to American treaty practice and the law of the land and to all the moral dictates of sympathy, compassion, and justice to turn these free men over to Spain.[34]

Passages from Adams's letters got into the press through Loring and Tappan.[35] It became public knowledge that Adams thought the Africans should go free on habeas corpus, and that he was willing to offer his services for their defense. This brought immense moral weight to their cause in the Northern states if not in the South.

"Gracious heavens, my dear Sir," wrote a disgusted Virginian, once an Adams supporter, "your mind is diseased on the subject of slavery. Pray what had you to do with the captured ship? 'Out of the abundance of the heart the mind will speak.' You are great in everything else, but here you show your weakness. Your name will descend to the latest posterity with this blot on it: Mr. Adams loves the negroes too much, *unconstitutionally.*" [36]

Tappan did not immediately avail himself of Adams's offer to help. Relations between the Old Man Eloquent and the abolitionists had cooled down, following the public dampers he had put upon them earlier in the year for their "senseless and overbearing clamor for the immediate, total, uncompensated abolition of slavery in the District of Columbia." [37]

. . .

[32] *Memoirs,* X, 134. JQA to E. G. Loring, October 3, 1839; E. G. Loring to JQA of November 14, 1839. Adams MSS.

[33] JQA to E. G. Loring, Quincy, October 3, 1839. Adams MSS.
Actually, Governor Ellsworth was apparently looking for private clients to supplement his official income. He had offered his services to the Defense Committee, but when they were declined he accepted the job of presenting the salvage claims of the Long Island claimants against the Negroes as property. Either way, as long as there was a fee!

[34] JQA to E. G. Loring, Quincy, November 19, 1839. Adams MSS.

[35] *Boston Courier,* XIII, No. 1636, December 26, 1839. *New York Journal of Commerce,* XXIII, No. 4699, December 25, 1839. JQA to E. G. Loring, Washington, December 11, 1839. E. G. Loring to JQA, Boston, December 4, 27, 1839. Adams MSS.

[36] "A Virginian" to JQA, Alexandria, Va., December 31, 1839. Adams MSS.

[37] *Memoirs,* X, 132. September 28, 1839.

4

The trial before the District Court came on in the first week of January 1840 at New Haven, with the U.S.S. *Grampus* waiting in the harbor to take the Africans to Cuba as soon as Judge Judson should issue the expected order. It was rumored that the abolitionists of the city, determined to frustrate such a disposition, were organized to snatch the prisoners from the custody of the law and ship them by the "underground railway" to Canada before Marshal Willcox could embark them for Havana.[38] Certain it is that people of New Haven—except perhaps the contingent of Southern students at Yale College—were most sympathetic to the captive Negroes. A local committee headed by the Reverend Mr. Henry Ludlow looked after their presumed spiritual needs. George E. Day, then an assistant instructor at the Divinity School, took over the task of imparting to them some knowledge of Christian morals and teaching them to read and write English; and Professor Gibbs proceeded missionary-wise to compile a dictionary of their language. With his small store of Mendi vocables he haunted the waterfronts of New Haven and New York looking for an English-speaking Mendi sailor who might serve as a fully competent interpreter.

The trial lasted a full week in a tense and crowded courtroom. The Administration must have been sorely disappointed at the result.[39] Judge Judson decided, January 23, 1840, that Lieutenant Gedney and his fellow officer and crew were entitled to salvage money on the vessel and its material cargo, but not on the Negroes, who *even if* they were slaves had no value in Connecticut; that Antonio, the cabin boy, was a real slave and must be returned to Spanish authority to be delivered over to his owner.[40] The Government thus established, in the instance of this one person, the major principle for which it contended: that castaway slaves were property and must therefore be returned, under the Spanish treaty, to their true owners. But people lost sight of this important point as the court

[38] Many years later it was recalled that the brother of Simeon Jocelyn, Nathaniel Jocelyn, who painted the superb portrait of Cinqué now hanging in the gallery of the New Haven Colony Historical Society, had a private vessel ready to take them to some friendly shore. Baldwin, op. cit., p. 349, citing the New Haven *Daily Morning Journal and Courier*, XLIX, January 15, 1881. It is difficult to believe this *ex-post facto* gossip if only because no private ship could have prevailed against the *Grampus* and the United States Navy.

[39] "A gentleman this morning informed me that John Van Buren, the President's son, expressed to him great dissatisfaction at Judson's opinion, and said that the question had a great and important political bearing of which Judson had taken no notice. He spoke of the opinion in terms of great disapprobation. My informant was well convinced that the President would be greatly dissatisfied with the opinion." Seth P. Staples to Roger S. Baldwin, Albany, January 21, 1840. Baldwin MSS.

[40] Presumably the heir of the deceased Captain Ferrer of the *Amistad*, killed by the Negroes in the uprising.

pronounced the other prisoners to be free men illegally kidnapped in
Africa and transported to Cuba—free by the law of Spain itself; that
therefore they should be delivered to the President of the United States
to be transported back to Africa in accordance with the Act of March 3,
1819.[41] As for the slave Antonio, he took the law into his own hands and
walked away to freedom. Once arrived in New York, a vigilance committee of abolitionists got him safely out of the way.[42]

District Attorney Holabird, acting under orders from Washington, appealed the decision to the Circuit Court. So did the other libelants who
lost salvage for the persons of the Negroes. The Circuit Court affirmed
(April 1840) the judgment of the District Court. Thereupon the District
Attorney and the other litigants appealed to the Supreme Court of the
United States, scheduled to convene in January 1841 after the Presidential
election. The Africans, now reduced to thirty-nine in number,[43] lingered
on in jail in New Haven, but under easier conditions, with fresh air and
exercise. Professor Gibbs had at last found an interpreter, James Covey,
a kidnapped Mendi who had been liberated from a slave ship captured
by a British patrol cruiser. With his aid the prisoners were now picking
up English and learning to read the Bible. Meanwhile they shivered in
the New England winter. Another year must pass before the Supreme
Court at Washington could review their case.

In the House that winter Adams put through a resolution calling upon
the President for the diplomatic correspondence and other official papers
connected with the case of the *Amistad*, in so far as it was compatible
with the public interest to make them known.[44] The Secretary of State
presented all the papers on file in the Department except a most recent
correspondence with the Chevalier de Argaiz in regard to testimony to be
furnished to the federal courts. Included were originals and translations
of the ship's papers in which the word *ladino* appeared in English as
"sound Negroes," an obvious effort to twist the meaning away from any
suggestion that they could not be real Cuban slaves. Adams immediately
called for a congressional investigation into this trick. The Speaker appointed a committee, including Adams, but no chicanery could be absolutely established: a government proofreader took the blame for ordering
this "correction." [45]

The committee hearings served to keep the affair before the public
during the months while the case was awaiting the next term of the Supreme Court. Southern proslavery leaders became nervously conscious of

[41] 15 Peters *U.S. Reports*, 523–31.

[42] Joshua Leavitt to JQA, New York, March 31, 1841. Adams MSS. Lewis Tappan to Roger S. Baldwin, New York, April 1, 1841. Baldwin MSS.

[43] *Memoirs*, X, 360.

[44] Resolution of March 23, 1840. See 26th Cong., 1st Sess., H.R. Ex. Doc. 185.
Memoirs, X, 216, 233, 241.

[45] December 10, 1840. 26th Cong., 2d Sess., *House Journal*, p. 28. *Congressional
Globe*, IX, 13. *Memoirs*, X, 377, 379, 381–2, 385–6.

the significance of the *Amistad*. In the Senate, Calhoun proposed two resolutions, carefully worded so as not to alienate Northern patriotic support in an election year for the position taken by the Administration. As unanimously adopted, April 15, 1840, they declared:

[1.] *Resolved*—That a ship or vessel on the high seas, in time of peace, engaged in a lawful voyage, is according to the laws of nations under the exclusive jurisdiction of the state to which her flag belongs as much so as if constituting a part of its own domain.

[2.] *Resolved*—That if such ship or vessel should be forced, by stress of weather, or other unavoidable cause into the port, and under the jurisdiction of a friendly power, she and her cargo, and persons on board, with their property, *and all the rights belonging to their personal relations, as established by the laws of the state to which they belong*, would be placed under the protection which the laws of nations extend to the unfortunate under such circumstances.[46]

Adams countered by bringing forward four resolutions in the lower chamber denouncing as unlawful the detention and imprisonment of the Africans of the *Amistad*, but the House would not even receive his motion, though he succeeded in reading it.[47]

5

At length the time approached for the trial before the Supreme Court. Meanwhile some of the defense counsel were apparently getting nervous about their fees. Staples had quit after the Circuit Court decision on appeal. Sedgwick was none too energetic. Only Roger Baldwin stayed on, accepting what Lewis Tappan was able to raise from his abolitionist friends.[48] Tappan looked about for an eminent lawyer of greater moral weight to appear with Baldwin before the court of last appeal, somebody who perhaps would be willing to contribute his services. He went to Boston and talked with Ellis Gray Loring. They approached Rufus Choate, who then rivaled Daniel Webster as the leading trial lawyer of New England. Choate declined the case. He had no sympathy for the abolitionist cause. He wanted to keep the Whigs united. Tappan then fell back on John Quincy Adams. With Loring he rode out to Quincy and urged the Old Man Eloquent to accept the assignment as a moral duty. Adams tried to excuse himself. "I am too old," he protested, "too oppressed by my duties in the House of Representatives, too inexperienced after a lapse of thirty years in the forms and technicalities of arguments

---

[46] *Congressional Globe*, VIII, 267, 328. Italics inserted.

[47] *Congressional Globe*, VIII, 416. May 25, 1840. *Memoirs*, X, 296. May 25, 1840.

[48] Lewis Tappan to Roger S. Baldwin, New York, October 16, 1840, April 1, 1841. Baldwin MSS.

Baldwin received from the Committee a total of $700 for his services.

before the Supreme Court. But I will cheerfully do what I have hitherto offered, that is, to give any assistance with counsel and advice to Mr. Baldwin."

The abolitionist leaders wanted him to do more, to appear before the Court: "It is a case of life and death for these unfortunate men," they persisted.

The aging contender yielded to their plea. "By the blessing of God," he declared, "I will argue the case before the Supreme Court."

Tappan and Loring promised that Baldwin would supply him with a brief of the case, and Tappan turned over two copious scrapbooks, containing clippings from the newspapers and pamphlets relating to the *Amistad*.[49] There was no mention of a fee, nor did Adams ever think of one. His only concern was to hold in check his own contentious spirit, to measure up in every way to this last great challenge.

"I implore the mercy of God," he prayed that night, "so to control my temper, to enlighten my soul, and to give me utterance, that I may prove myself in every respect equal to the task." [50]

Son Charles eyed his father's two visitors with misgivings. "This will be productive of results unpleasant to myself," he mused after he heard what they wanted, "for it must greatly embarrass the political party with which I have undertaken to act." [51]

The Boston Whigs had just nominated young Charles Francis Adams as candidate from his ward for the Massachusetts House of Representatives. He won easily in the general Whig triumph of that year—his first elective office. That same day the Twelfth Congressional District of Massachusetts once more re-elected John Quincy Adams to Congress, by a two-to-one majority.

In the white-paneled study at Quincy father and son debated long and tenaciously the merits of the *Amistad* case and the bearing of habeas corpus on the Africans in prison at New Haven. The older man's memory flashed back in the heat of argument to youthful days in Europe when after the treaty of peace and independence he first visited London in the year 1783. One day he had strolled into the British Museum and gazed upon the Magna Charta. Among the signatures and seals appended to the historic document was that of one Saer de Quincy.[52] John Quincy Adams of Quincy, Massachusetts, was content in his time to pledge himself to the principle of habeas corpus, the greatest constitutional defense of free men in England and the United States whatever their color. What a satisfaction to be a lawyer! What a blessing to be a friend of human freedom!

[49] Lewis Tappan to Roger S. Baldwin, Boston, October 28, 1840. Owens Transcripts in New Haven Colony Historical Society.

[50] *Memoirs*, X, 358.

[51] Diary of CFA. Monday, October 27, 1840.

[52] JQA to CFA, Washington, April 14, 1841. Adams MSS. Adams was excessively fond of seals, signatures, and heraldry.

Let his family think of him what they would. His country would remember.

As once again he set out for Washington that November in the seventy-fourth year of his life, it seemed that this would be his final term in Congress. To defend the Africans of the *Amistad* would be his last great service to the nation. It was well to have it so.

"The life I lead," he noted in his Diary on the eve of this new adventure, "is trying to my constitution, and cannot be long continued with impunity. Repose and regularity of hours and occupations, are essential to my health and to what remains of my capacity for useful labour. I live in continual bustle; a succession of Chinese Shadows, successive banqueting, late and early hours and political excitement and conflict, which stretches my old machine upon the rack. My eyes are threatening to fail me. My hands tremble like an aspen-leaf. My memory daily deserts me. My imagination is fallen into the sear and yellow leaf and my judgment sinking into dotage. . . . Should my life and health be spared to perform this service, I shall have been the only Representative of the District during the ten years of its existence. I had represented in one Congress the preceding District of Plymouth. Before the next Election for Congress the Districts will be re-organized and new modelled, and then will be a proper time for me to withdraw, and take my last leave of the public service." [53]

He proceeded to Washington by way of Hartford and New Haven, in order to lecture in the newly founded public lyceums of those towns and to confer with Roger Baldwin in New Haven. It was a much quicker trip than in the old days when he had gone across country by carriage and stage to call on his friend Ward Boylston at Princeton. Now there was a railroad from Boston to Springfield; from Hartford it took him only two hours and a half to speed in the steam cars to New Haven.

What a busy day he had in the college town! First thing in the morning Roger Baldwin called at the old Tontine Hotel. This devoted lawyer had cheerfully accepted Adams as senior counsel,[54] and had already furnished him with a carefully prepared brief.[55] He had long since been trying, anonymously, to get Adams stirred up publicly over the *Amistad*.[56] The

[53] Diary, November 11, 1840.

[54] Lewis Tappan to Roger S. Baldwin, Boston, October 28, 1840. Owens Transcripts in New Haven Colony Historical Society.

[55] Roger S. Baldwin to JQA, November 2, 1840, enclosing a fifty-two page "Narrative of the Case of the Amistad." JQA to Roger S. Baldwin, Boston, November 11, 1840. Adams MSS. Baldwin MSS.

[56] On December 4, 1839 Baldwin sent a long letter to Adams in Washington, dated at New Haven, and signed "One of the People," suggesting arguments in favor of the Africans (doubtless designed for any speech in Congress the Plymouth member might care to make). Baldwin sent another version of the same to Gales and Seaton, editors of the *National Intelligencer* at Washington. Adams MSS. Baldwin MSS. *Memoirs*, X, 287.

two men rehearsed the history of the case. Baldwin laid out his own strategy, including an initial motion to the Supreme Court to dismiss the appeal. Then they went to visit the prisoners, who had been moved from the county jail to a more liberal confinement out in the country two miles from the New Haven Green at Westville.

The new counsel did not see the girls, who were quartered in a separate building under supervision of Mrs. Pendleton, the marshal's wife. Pendleton showed them the men, thirty-six in number, in one chamber about thirty feet long by twenty wide, with two rows of eighteen crib beds. They were all under thirty years of age, small in stature, not quite so tall as Adams himself, with characteristic Negro bodies, features, and hair, and complexion from ebony black to light mulatto. Cinqué and Grabow, the two principal defendants, stood out among the others for their remarkable countenances. Three of the Africans showed how well young Mr. Day had taught them to read the New Testament. One of the boys already could write a tolerable hand. It seemed to Adams that, huddled together as they were with nobody to talk to but themselves, their learning must be very slow.[57] He thought their clothing and bedding were not what they ought to be.[58]

That afternoon Adams dined with Mr. and Mrs. Baldwin and family, including Baldwin's step-mother, a daughter of the patriot Roger Sherman, and the Reverend Mr. Ludlow. President Jeremiah Day of Yale College, Professor James Luce Kingsley, the classicist, and Benjamin Silliman (the elder) came in. The last-named savant had accumulated a title longer than that of the future New York, New Haven, and Hartford Railroad: he was Professor of Chemistry, Mineralogy, Pharmacy, and Geology. These good people were all friends of human freedom. After dinner Adams walked with Professor Silliman and took tea with his family at his home on Hillhouse Avenue. He saw Silliman's aged uncle John Trumbull, painter of the Revolution, whom he had known in London back in 1795. Professor Silliman also took him to visit the widow of Vice President Elbridge Gerry. Adams had experienced Gerry as a troublesome diplomat in Europe during the X Y Z affair; Mrs. Gerry was the last surviving widow of any signer of the Declaration of Independence. Then they proceeded past the Green and down Church Street to Mr. Ludlow's meeting-house, where Adams delivered to a full and attentive audience his lecture on "Society and Civilization."

Next morning he was up three hours before breakfast, busy at a writing-table in his chamber. About sunrise a rather "over-officious" student appeared to escort him to the New York boat, where he turned the visiting celebrity over to the offices of another student, a "well-bred" youth, who later proved to be nephew of a colleague in the House of Representatives,

[57] *Memoirs*, X, 360. November 17, 1840.
[58] Lewis Tappan to Roger S. Baldwin, New York, November 21, 1840. Baldwin MSS.

Josiah Ogden Hoffman.[59] Many a visiting dignitary thus slipped quietly out of New Haven of an early morning in those days when the professors were busy with their seven-o'clock classes.

After Adams reached Washington he received two letters from George Day's precocious pupils at Westville. "Dear Friend Mr. Adams," began Ka-le, one of the youngest of the adult prisoners: "I want to write a letter to you because you love Mendi people and you talk to the Great Court. We want to tell you one thing. Jose Ruiz say we born in havanna, he tell lie. . . . we all born in Mendi—we no understand Spanish language. . . . we want you to ask the court what we have done wrong. What for Americans keep us in prison. Some people say Mendi people crazy dolts because we no talk American language. Americans no talk Mendi. Americans people crazy dolts? They tell bad things about Mendi people and we no understand. . . . Bad men say Mendi people no have souls. Why we feel bad we no have no souls. . . . Dear friend Mr. Adams you have children and friends you love them you feel very sorry if Mendi people come and take all to Africa. Cook say he kill, he eat Mendi people—we afraid—we kill cook. . . . We never kill captain, if he no kill us. If court ask who bring Mendi people we bring ourselves. . . . All we want is make us free." [60]

Another young captive, Kinna, wrote in curious English phraseology: "I want to write you open lines, my dear friend, because you love us, and because you talk to the great court, and tell American people to make us free. We want to go home to Mendi and see our fathers, and mothers, and brothers and sisters. . . . American people say we have no slaves, we make you free. . . . Judge Judson say you be free, but Government say No. . . . If man have knife and come to America people and say I kill I eat what America people do? Mendi people no kill captain and cook, they no kill us. Mendi people no hurt anybody. Dear friend Mr. Adams we love you very much we ask we beg you to tell court let Mendi people be free. . . ." [61]

As the trial neared, the British Minister in Washington, Henry S. Fox, privately called on Adams by appointment. His Government had instructed him to use his good offices in behalf of the freedom of the cap-

[59] Diary, Tuesday, November 17, and Wednesday, November 18, 1840. W. E. Robertson to JQA, Yale College, June 23, 1841. Adams MSS.

[60] Ka-le to JQA, Westville, January 4, 1841. Adams MSS. "You may rely that this letter was wholly composed by the Africans." Lewis Tappan to S. D. Hastings, Philadelphia. New Haven, March 15, 1841. Lewis Tappan MSS., LC.

[61] Kinna to JQA, Westville, January 4, 1841.

"Have the goodness to inform Kale and Kinna, that I received their Letters with great satisfaction. Let them know that I think of them, hope for them, and pray for them, night and day. They have made so great progress in their studies that I exhort them to persevere in them with unabating assiduity." JQA to Roger Baldwin, Washington, January 25, 1841. Adams MSS.

tured Africans, without interfering in the judicial procedure. He very much wanted Adams's advice on what to do if the Supreme Court should decide against them.[62] He had heard that this would happen. Adams advised him to direct a note to the Secretary of State at once. Next evening Fox called again and left some parliamentary papers recently published on abuse of the American flag for protection of the slave trade. It seems likely that Adams talked with him about the note under preparation, but apparently he did not see its text before it was delivered to Secretary Forsyth on January 20, 1841.[63]

Fox's note invoked the Treaty of Ghent and the firm intention of both the United States and Great Britain, declared therein, to do their best to abolish the slave trade.[64] This pledge, he suggested, entitled Great Britain to call serious attention to the Africans whose case was about to be tried before the Supreme Court. He observed that these newly imported Negroes could not in fact possibly be slaves according to the treaties between Spain and Great Britain, and Spanish enforcing ordinances. "It is under these circumstances that Her Majesty's Government earnestly hope that the President of the United States will find himself empowered to take such measures in behalf of the aforesaid Africans as shall secure to them the possession of their liberty, to which, without doubt, they are by law entitled." Forsyth politely acknowledged the note as merely an expression of Her Majesty's benevolence. He reminded Fox that the Spanish Government did not agree with the facts as presented. The United States Government would with great reluctance erect itself into a tribunal to investigate such questions between two friendly sovereigns. If these facts were established, they could not be without their force in the proper time and place: that would be before a Spanish tribunal in the islands and Cuba.[65] Forsyth released this exchange of notes to the press while the *Amistad* case was being argued before the Supreme Court. It was obviously a reminder to the judges of that august tribunal of the diplomatic implications of the case.

6

Adams worried about the coming trial, fretted about his temperamental unfitness for such responsibility. In anguish of heart he searched for the means to expose and defeat the "abominable conspiracy, Executive and Judicial, of this Government" against the lives of the Africans. His mother, Abigail, had warned him as a youth to curb his temper, to be cool in the face of provocation. All his long life he had fought unsuccessfully

[62] H. S. Fox to JQA, private, January 17, 1841. Adams MSS.

[63] *Memoirs*, X, 400–1. H. S. Fox to JQA, January 20, 1841. Adams MSS.

[64] See note 15, above.

[65] H. S. Fox to John Forsyth, Washington, January 20, 1841; John Forsyth to H. S. Fox, February 1, 1841. *National Intelligencer* of Washington, XXIX, No. 5987, February 18, 1841. The printed correspondence concerning the *Amistad* of course made good abolitionist propaganda.

against his weakness. Could he now hold himself with calmness, with moderation, with firmness, in argument? It was one thing to pitch his scorn against an unscrupulous adversary on the floor of Congress; it was something else to argue reasonably and unheatedly before the Supreme Court. "Of all the dangers before me," he acknowledged, "that of losing my self possession is the most formidable." [66]

His continued attendance in the House and participation in daily proceedings, committee hearings, his many visitors, his arrears of correspondence, and journalizing left little time to concentrate on the case before him. Even after the trial had been postponed repeatedly—until February 20, 1841—he found himself arranging and rearranging documents, with no clear outline for oral argument after the defense's brief was filed. Then a distressing accident intervened. On the eve of the trial his coach horses took fright at an exhibition of firearms in front of the Capitol and fatally injured his coachman and friend of long standing, Jeremy Leary. The Court obligingly suspended the trial until the following Monday while Adams spent the week-end at the deathbed and obsequies of his devoted old servant.

The 22nd of February was historically a day of good omen for Adams. It was the birthday of his great patron and exemplar, George Washington. On that day, too, he had signed the Transcontinental Treaty with Don Luis de Onís in 1819—the greatest diplomatic victory ever won by a single individual in the history of the United States. On the same day two years later the Senate had finally ratified the treaty and it went into force. But this Monday, February 22, 1841, he walked from his house on F Street to the Capitol with a thoroughly bewildered mind to listen to the Attorney General open the argument for the Government.[67]

The Supreme Court room was then in the east wing of the Capitol building beneath the Senate chamber. A sedate elegance of furnishings lent quiet dignity to the apartment, but the space was so limited that the judges had to put on their robes after they came in. The Hall of Justice was shaped somewhat like a piece of pie, with windows at the circumference letting light down upon the raised mahogany bench. Below was the attorneys' bar. Behind and above the Court was a colonnade with rows of seats for visitors; ladies dressed in the height of fashion lent a cheerful color to the balcony there whenever Daniel Webster appeared to argue an important case.[68]

The tribunal comprised nine judges by 1841. Before Andrew Jackson left the White House, Congress had added two members, if only for the purpose of furnishing much needed judges for circuit work. Only the two oldest members, Thompson and Story, had been appointed before Jack-

---

[66] *Memoirs*, X, 373, 383, 387, 410.

[67] *Memoirs*, X, 429.

[68] Charles Warren: *The Supreme Court in United States History* (3 vols., Boston, 1923), I, 456–63.

son's Presidency. Joseph Story of Marblehead and Salem, Massachusetts, the senior in years of service, had been a Justice of the Supreme Court since Madison appointed him in 1811. A professor at the Harvard Law School and author of celebrated *Commentaries* and other treatises on the Constitution and the law, he was the most learned member of the tribunal. Round-faced and bespectacled, alert and benevolent in appearance, he was an old Federalist and nationalist. Story was almost a disciple of John Quincy Adams on the theory of the Union. Smith Thompson of New York, who had handed down on appeal the decision in the Circuit Court for the District of Connecticut in the case of the *Amistad,* aged seventy-three, was the oldest on the bench. He had been a colleague of Adams in Monroe's Cabinet. He was a follower of John Marshall's nationalist school of judicial thought. Like Adams he had been alarmed for the fate of the judiciary and the Bank of the United States in the hands of the Democrats, fearful that the Government of the Union would fall into the imbecility of the old Confederation.[69] The rest were Jacksonians. Adams knew them all personally and had little respect for their ability or that of the other members of the Court except Story.[70]

The Chief Justice, Roger B. Taney of Maryland, former Attorney General and Secretary of the Treasury under Jackson, was an old Federalist who like Adams had broken with the party over the War of 1812. His long black hair fell heavily over his ears and collar to frame a melancholy face deeply furrowed and compassionate. A kindhearted slaveholder, who emancipated his own slaves, he was a product of Southern agrarian life who felt that slavery would be necessary as long as there was any great mass of Negroes left in the United States. Adams looked upon him as one of a group of "supple and submissive assentators"[71] to Jackson's war on the Bank. Despite forebodings of the Whig Party as to Taney's partisanship, he was proving to be an able and even-handed Justice.

John McLean of Ohio had been the efficient but treacherous and double-dealing Postmaster General in Adams's Administration; he received his reward when the Old Hero came into office and appointed him to the Court. In his own conscience McLean believed that slavery had its origin in force, was contrary to right, and was sustained only by local law.

Justice Henry Baldwin of Pennsylvania, born in New Haven, Connecticut, was a character who had a reputation as a practical joker in his youth, smoked constantly small, black Spanish cigars, and carried candy in his pockets to give to children in the streets. He gave his brother justices cause for concern because he had periods when he was a little touched

[69] *Memoirs,* VIII, 304.

[70] "The Associate Judges from the time of his [Marshall's] appointment have generally been taken from the Democratic, or Jeffersonian party. Not one of them, excepting Story, has been a man of great ability. Several of them have been men of strong prejudices, warm passions, and contracted minds; one of them [Baldwin], occasionally insane." *Memoirs,* IX, 243. July 10, 1835.

[71] *Memoirs,* X, 115.

in the head.[72] He had privately argued with Adams in defense of slavery at the time of the Missouri Compromise. He did not want to see the controversy reopened.

James Moore Wayne was a Georgian slaveholder and Princeton graduate who had studied law under Judge Chauncey in New Haven, a Jacksonian wheel-horse who had received his due recognition before Old Hickory went back to the Hermitage. Philip P. Barbour of Virginia, another Jackson appointee, had been an uncompromising state-rights leader in Congress. We have already seen how John Quincy Adams had feared that "some shallow-pated wild cat like Philip P. Barbour fit for nothing but to tear the Union to rags and tatters" might become successor to John Marshall. Justice John Catron of Tennessee had been a soldier under Jackson in the War of 1812. He had been an astute politician and accomplished chancery lawyer. Adams must have had some respect for him as a pronounced antiduelist. Catron was one of the two men recently appointed by President Van Buren; the other was John McKinley, an Alabama planter and lawyer with whom Adams had exchanged dialectical blows in the House of Representatives on the bank question and the national deposit. McKinley did not sit at all on the *Amistad* case.

On a case involving slavery Adams had felt that there was not much hope in this court with its majority of Southern slaveholders and Northern men with Southern principles.

Attorney General Henry D. Gilpin, a Philadelphia lawyer, successor to the deceased Felix Grundy, opened for the Government. He took two hours: the Court could not go behind the regularly documented ship's papers; it must deliver over the slave property as demanded by the Spanish Minister and required by the comity of nations and the articles of the treaty of 1795, renewed in the treaty of 1819 with Spain.[73] Roger Baldwin followed for the defendants. Painstakingly he rehearsed all the arguments in fact and law that had been advanced for the prisoners in the lower courts. "The American people," he affirmed, "have never imposed it as a duty upon the Government of the United States to become actors in an attempt to reduce to slavery men found in a state of freedom, by giving extraterritorial force to a foreign slave law. . . . The United States as a nation is to be regarded as a free state." [74]

Gilpin replied at length. He referred to Calhoun's resolutions of the Senate. He cited the contemporary demands of the United States Government for restitution or reparation for American shipwrecked slaves liberated in British islands. "In what respect," he asked, "were these slaves, if such by the laws of Spain, released from slavery by acts of aggression

[72] Warren: *Supreme Court*, II, 277 and note.
[73] 15 Peters *U.S. Reports*, 539–49.
[74] *Argument of Roger S. Baldwin, of New Haven, before the Supreme Court of the United States, in the case of the United States, Appellants, vs. Cinque, and Others, Africans of the Amistad* (New York: S. W. Benedict, 128 Fulton St.; 1841).

upon their owners, any more than a slave becomes free in Pennsylvania who forcibly escapes from Virginia?"

Next day Adams rose to close for the defense. Word had got about the city that he would speak then. He noticed that the courtroom was full, if not crowded, but there were few ladies in the gallery.[75] He had been deeply distressed and agitated up to the moment of addressing the Court. Once he was on his feet, his spirit did not sink within him. With grateful heart for strength to go on he began his argument, steadily gaining confidence as his points fell into order.

If the Africans were slaves by the laws of Spain! That was the very issue. Adams showed they were free men of an illegal cargo in *continuous voyage* in time of war—the perpetual war of civilized nations upon pirates and slave-traders outlawed by Spain's treaties with Great Britain—free men by Spain's own enforcement ordinances. It was absurd, he declared, to argue that the fugitive-slave laws of the United States had any force or example for the outlawed transatlantic slave trade!

As the old man spoke, his years seemed to drop away. Infirmities fell from him as always they did in combat. His aged voice took on the spirit of youth. His watery eyes grew strong with a blaze of righteous scorn. He was bitter in his sarcasm at those who would make slaves out of resolute free men, damning in his strictures on an executive power that would deliver them over to the vengeance of foreign slaveholders—expanding his arguments to general principles of human morality. From the bench the Justices fixed their eyes on him hour after hour.

"Extraordinary," marveled Judge Story. "Extraordinary for its power and its bitter sarcasm, and its dealing with topics far beyond the record and points of discussion." [76]

After four hours and a half the Court adjourned; Adams was to conclude his argument the following day.

That night Judge Philip Barbour died in his sleep. "A wise dispensation of Providence," wrote a Quaker to Adams after the trial.[77] The Court suspended again to do homage to the departed brother. Adams attended the funeral in the same courtroom where the deceased Justice had looked down upon him only two days before. He rode with the official cortege to the Eastern Branch Cemetery.

The Court convened again on March 1. After paying his respects to the dead, Adams recapitulated his argument and continued, speaking extemporaneously for three hours more. Only the principal points of his re-

[75] *Memoirs*, X, 431. February 24, 1841.

[76] Warren: *Supreme Court*, II, 350, citing letter from Joseph Story to his wife in William Wetmore Story's *Life and Letters of Joseph Story* (2 vols., Boston, 1851).

[77] "It is not for me to say what effect the death of the judge had upon the cause. To me it seems likely it had some." Jesse Kersey to JQA, Fallowfield Township, Chester County, 15th day, 3rd month, 1841. Adams MSS.

marks, what later came to be called his "speech," can be presented here. He ridiculed the opinion of the late Attorney General Felix Grundy and the argument of his successor, that the Court could not go behind the regularly attested but fraudulent documents of the *Amistad*. He reasserted the doctrine of continuous voyage as applied to the slave trade. Even if the Africans were agreed to be slaves, he demonstrated by his complete knowledge of treaty law and practice, slaves could not be included as property unless specifically so denominated. He showed that Calhoun's resolutions could be interpreted as much in favor of the free Africans and *their* property, the *Amistad*, as against them. He arraigned the Secretary of State for not repelling instanter the demands of the Spanish Minister. He excoriated the executive power for assisting those demands. Above all he dwelt upon the ancient principle of habeas corpus. Suppose the President had followed the advice of the Attorney General and delivered the Africans over to Spain *gubernativemente:* "What would have been the tenure by which every human being in this Union, man, woman, or child, would have held the blessing of freedom? Would it not have been by the tenure of executive discretion, caprice, or tyranny . . . at the dictate of a foreign minister? Would it not have disabled forever the effective power of *habeas corpus*?"

At length the old advocate closed his argument. He paused and looked up benevolently at the seven old men on the bench above the bar, all of them younger than he. Then he addressed a last word, as if they all were soon to present themselves after him to a still Higher Court:

"May it please your Honors: On the 7th of February, 1804, now more than thirty-seven years past, my name was entered, and yet stands recorded, on both the rolls, as one of the Attorneys and Counsellors of this Court. . . . Very shortly afterwards, I was called to the discharge of other duties—first in distant lands, and in later years, within our own country, but in different departments of her Government. Little did I imagine that I should ever again be required to claim the right of appearing in the capacity of an officer of this Court; yet such has been the dictate of my destiny—and I appear again to plead the cause of justice, and now of liberty and life, in behalf of many of my fellow men, before that same Court, which in a former age I had addressed in support of rights of property. . . . I stand before the *same* Court, but not before the same judges—nor aided by the same associates—nor resisted by the same opponents. As I cast my eyes along those seats of honor and of public trust, now occupied by you, they seek in vain for one of those honored and honorable persons whose indulgence listened then to my voice. Marshall—Cushing—Chase—Washington—Johnson—Livingston—Todd— Where are they? . . . Alas! where is one of the very judges of the Court, arbiters of life and death, before whom I commenced this anxious argument, even now prematurely closed? Where are they all? Gone! Gone! All gone!

Gone from the services which, in their day and generation, they faithfully rendered to their country . . . gone to receive the rewards of blessedness on high. In taking, then, my final leave of this Bar, and of this Honorable Court, I can only ejaculate a fervent petition to Heaven, that every member of it may go to his final account with as little of earthly frailty to answer for as those illustrious dead, and that you may, every one, after the close of a long and virtuous career in this world, be received at the portals of the next with the approving sentence—'Well done, good and faithful servant; enter thou into the joy of thy Lord.'"

The audience sat silent, then stirred as the Justices rose, put off their robes, and filed out.

Next day Adams went back to hear the Attorney General close for the Government. Gilpin spent three hours dutifully reviewing, with great moderation of manner, the technical points of Roger S. Baldwin's argument. Only slightly did he notice the general subjects raised by the senior counsel for the defense.[78] But the Court had noticed them.

Announcement of the decision was set for March 9. Adams arrived ahead of time, eager as a young candidate for the civil service to hear the results of his examination. For half an hour he sat on tenterhooks waiting for the Court to convene. Then he patiently presented a young lawyer for admission as an attorney. This done, he took his seat. The Justices' eyes turned to Story. They had assigned to their senior member the duty of delivering the opinion. That was a good sign. The old man's heart beat hard and fast as his friend Story, speaking slowly and at great length, reviewed the facts and the law. Would he never get on to the real judgment?

The learned Justice finally came to the merits of the case. "There does not seem to us to be any ground for doubt," he concluded, "that these Negroes ought to be deemed free: and that the Spanish treaty interposes no obstacle to the just assertion of their rights." Since the Government had not asked, on final appeal, for an order to return the Negroes to Africa if found free, the Court revised that decree of the District Court. It reaffirmed the lower courts' award of salvage to Lieutenant Gedney against the ship itself.[79]

Only Justice Baldwin dissented. Adams had already left the courtroom without waiting to hear what that singular character might have to say.[80]

"The captives are free!" he wrote jubilantly to Lewis Tappan in New York. " 'Not unto us! Not unto us!' but thanks, thanks, in the name of humanity and justice to *you*." [81] Free after eighteen months of false imprisonment! "Praise be to the God of *Justice*," Joshua Leavitt wrote back. "May the blessing of many ready to perish fall upon you!" echoed Simeon Jocelyn. "Glorious!" congratulated Baldwin from New Haven; "Glorious

---

[78] *Memoirs*, X, 436–7. March 2, 1841.
[79] 15 Peters *U.S. Reports*, 587–98.
[80] *Memoirs*, X, 441–2.
[81] JQA to Lewis Tappan, New York. Washington, March 9, 1841. Adams MSS.

not only as a triumph of humanity and justice, but as a vindication of our national character from reproach and dishonor." [82]

Tappan was less impulsive. He waited a decent interval, perhaps for Adams to present a bill. None came. A month later he joined with the two other members of the Defense Committee in a formal expression of thanks for "valuable services, gratuitously rendered, in rescuing the lives and liberties of our humble clients from the imminent peril to which they were exposed." [83]

Adams's championship of the Africans restored him to the good graces of all but the most inveterate abolitionists. "Some of us," wrote Whittier, "may have at times done thee injustice in our regret and disappointment at thy expressed sentiments in regard to the District of Columbia, but, I believe we now all appreciate thy motives, and while we regret that there should be any difference of opinion between us, we feel that thou art entitled to our warmest gratitude as abolitionists." [84]

Another voice was heard from. "It is a great relief to me that your cause is settled and well settled," wrote Charles Francis Adams from Boston.[85]

For the first time since George's death the parent let slip a not unmerited reproach to his only surviving son: "The agony of soul that I suffered from the day that I pledged my faith, to argue the cause of the Africans, before the Supreme Court, till that when I heard Judge Story deliver the opinion and decree of the Court, was chiefly occasioned by the reprobation of my own family, both of my opinions and my conduct, and their terror at the calamities which they anticipated they would bring upon *them*. The Signature and Seal of Saer de Quincy to the old parchment were with a clear conscience almost my only support and encouragement, under the pressure of a burden upon my thought that I was to plead for more, much more than my own life. . . ." [86]

[82] Joshua Leavitt to JQA, New York, March 11, 1841. Simeon S. Jocelyn, Joshua Leavitt, and Lewis Tappan to JQA, New York, March 11, 1841. Roger S. Baldwin to JQA, New Haven, March 12, 1841. Adams MSS.

[83] Simeon S. Jocelyn, Joshua Leavitt, and Lewis Tappan, the Committee acting on behalf of the *Amistad* captives, to JQA, New York, April 15, 1841. Adams MSS.

[84] J. G. Whittier to JQA, 10th day, 2d month, 1841. Adams MSS.

[85] CFA to JQA, March 18, 1841. Adams MSS.

[86] JQA to CFA, Washington, April 14, 1841. Adams MSS. It was a pretty fancy, but no more, that John Quincy Adams, pleader for the Africans of the *Amistad* on habeas corpus before the Supreme Court of the United States, was a descendant of the Saer de Quincy who signed the Magna Charta. A privately printed *Memoranda Respecting the Families of Quincy and Adams* (Havana, April 1841) notes that there was no known male posterity of the second Saer de Quincy, who received his earldom from King John in 1210.

7

Many were the problems and questions of law and policy left in the wake of the Supreme Court's decision. For example, what was to be done with the former captives? Even Daniel Webster, the new Whig Secretary of State under President Harrison, hesitated when Adams importuned him to send them back to Africa in a public ship. The succession of John Tyler, the Southern state-rights proslavery Whig, following Harrison's death a few weeks after inauguration, offered no hope for such a step: it could be pointed out too easily that these Negroes had not been illegally imported into the United States; therefore there was no obligation to send them back under the law of March 2, 1819. Eventually Tappan and his abolitionist friends took care of the situation; by exhibitions of the Africans and various appeals they raised money enough to keep them on an agricultural establishment in Farmington, Connecticut, until a missionary ship was fitted out to take them—thirty-five survivors—back to the Gold Coast, where, once released, they reverted to their natural state.

The Southern Democrats, in session after session of Congress until just before the Civil War, brought forth bills for the indemnification of the Cuban "owners" of the "slaves" liberated by the Court. Needless to say, Adams fought such proposals as long as he lived, and they never passed Congress.[87]

To fearful slaveholders all the oratory of Adams's championship of the Africans was nothing less than an invitation to American slaves to rebel, kill their masters, and free themselves. It brought more bullying letters to him.

"Is your pride of abolition oratory not yet glutted?" anonymously wrote a pious Virginian. "Are you to spend the remainder of your days endeavoring to produce a civil and servile War? Do you like Aaron Burr wish to ruin your Country because you failed in your election to the Presidency?

[87] On April 11, 1844, the committee on foreign affairs of the House of Representatives, consisting of five members from the free states and four members from the slave-holding states, brought in a majority report recommending indemnification of the "owners" of the *Amistad* "for the unlawful seizure, detention, and salvage allowed of that vessel and her cargo, and liberation of the slaves on board her in the year one thousand eight hundred and forty, and afterwards, during their detention and by their liberation." The committee also reported a bill appropriating $70,000 for that purpose, which was referred to the Committee of the Whole, where it remained unacted upon. The report studiously changed the date of capture of the *Amistad* from August 26, 1839 to August 26, 1840, as if to give the Negroes the character of *ladinos* instead of *bozales*. Adams was all primed with a really unanswerable speech denouncing the report as "a coarse, glaring, stupid, shameless, unmitigated falsehood," but the report was never allowed to come up for consideration. He published his speech anyway, April 3, 1845, in the form of an *Address of the Hon. John Quincy Adams to His Constituents*. Copy in Sterling Memorial Library at Yale University. No place of publication given.

May the lightning of heaven blast you, and may the great Eternal God in his wrath curse you at the last day and direct you to depart from his presence to the lowest regions of Hell! . . . Your craven spirit would quail before the menace of the outraged Southern man and nothing but a good horsewhip will serve you and you must and shall have it. You detested vindictive villain. . . . The Devil will have his own when he gets your rascally soul." [88]

The old statesman continued to walk the streets of Washington unattended and unmolested by day and by night.

Soon a slave rebellion after the example of the Africans of the *Amistad* did occur. One hundred and thirty-five undeniable slaves mutinied (November 7, 1841) in the coastwise vessel *Creole* bound from Hampton Roads to New Orleans. The mutineers killed one of the owners and forced the white crew to take the ship into Nassau. British authorities seized and hanged those identified as the murderers, and freed the others. Southerners, clamoring against Great Britain for another act of interference with an American ship and slaves, demanded compensation for the liberated slaves. The *Creole* case added to the grating complex of Anglo-American issues which Daniel Webster and Lord Ashburton had to deal with in their celebrated negotiation of 1842. It also produced a long train of sectional debate in Congress. Both call for attention in later chapters.

Tappan and the Defense Committee were anxious to make the most of the *Amistad* decision in a further drive against the slave trade abroad and at home. They suggested that Adams might deem it his duty as a citizen and a man to address a sympathetic note to Lord Palmerston on the subject.[89] Adams pondered over the documents they sent him, and studied the voluminous parliamentary bluebooks that Fox, the British Minister, put in his hands to show connivance of American citizens and ships in the traffic, but he drew back from any communication of his own to the British Foreign Minister, if only for fear of falling afoul of the Logan Act of 1798.[90]

The *Amistad* case led Adams to long and sober thoughts about the internal slave trade in the United States, and the rendition to Southern owners of fugitive slaves escaped to Northern free states, both sanctioned by the Constitution, and to all the dreadful problems of slavery in this Union. "The world, the flesh, and all the devils in hell," he lamented, "are arrayed against any man who now in this North American Union shall dare to join the standard of Almighty God to put down the African slave trade, and what can I, upon the verge of my seventy-fourth birthday, with a

[88] Anonymous to JQA, postmarked Dumfries, Virginia, June 15, 1841. Adams MSS. *Emancipation under Martial Law,* p. 109.

[89] Simeon S. Jocelyn, Joshua Leavitt, and Lewis Tappan to JQA, New York, March 24, 1841. Adams MSS.

[90] Diary, March 28, 1841. *Memoirs,* X, 453–5. Jocelyn, Leavitt, and Tappan to JQA, New York, March 24, 1841. JQA to Jocelyn, Leavitt, and Tappan, Washington, April 3, 1841. Adams MSS.

shaking hand, a darkening eye, a drowsy brain, and with all my faculties dropping from me one by one, as the teeth are dropping from my head— what can I do for the cause of God and man, for the progress of human emancipation, for the suppression of the African slave trade? Yet my conscience presses me on; let me die upon the breach." [91]

This from a man who at seventy-five read ordinary print morning and evening by lamp or candlelight without glasses! [92] The teeth began to drop from his head only when he had no good fight on his hands.

"Be not weary in well-doing," urged Tappan, beseeching the triumphant advocate to come out openly and join the cause of God and man, to let the world see that he favored the great objects of the antislavery petitions as well as the right of petition itself.[93]

Adams wrote out his oral argument before the Supreme Court and gave it to Tappan and his *Amistad* committee to publish as propaganda for their cause,[94] and he franked hundreds of copies to his own friends and prominent people, including every member of Congress, the American foreign service abroad, and the foreign diplomatic corps at Washington. But he refused to come right out and join the abolitionist crusade.

Resting at Quincy during the summer, he sagged back to the worldly directions of sensible politics. It was too early to risk the supreme issue, and he was too old. Given the existing complexion of Congress, he felt that no action of his could contribute successfully to the extinction of slavery in the District of Columbia or to its abolition in general. A younger

[91] *Memoirs*, X, 453–4. March 29, 1841.

[92] JQA to Reverend Henry Jackson, New Bedford. Quincy, October 4, 1843. Adams MSS.

[93] Tappan to JQA, New York, July 10, 1841. Adams MSS.

[94] *Argument of John Quincy Adams, before the Supreme Court of the United States, in the Case of the United States, Appellants vs. Cinque, and Others, Africans, Captured in the Schooner Amistad, by Lieut. Gedney, Delivered on the 24th of February and 1st of March, 1841. With a Review of the Case of the Antelope, Reported in the 10th, 11th, and 12th Volumes of Wheaton's Reports* (New York: S. W. Benedict; 1841).

Such passages as newspaper reporters could take down at the trial were promptly published at the time. Richard Peters, the Supreme Court reporter, besought Adams to provide him with a text of his "excellent and eloquent argument," as the other counsel had furnished theirs, but would not wait to take it from the forthcoming pamphlet. In his report Peters (15 Peters *U.S. Reports* 566), referring to the fact that he had not received Adams's "able and interesting argument," observed officiously and cavalierly: "As many of the points presented by Mr. Adams were not considered by the Court essential to its decision, and were not taken notice of in the opinion of the Court, delivered by Mr. Justice Story, the necessary omission of the argument is submitted to with less regret."

Tappan's committee printed Adams's "speech" to the Supreme Court not later than July 9, 1841, certainly not an unreasonable time for Peters to wait. See Richard Peters to JQA, Philadelphia, April 18, May 7, 1841; JQA to Richard Peters, Boston, May 3; Quincy, May 19, 1841. Lewis Tappan to JQA, Philadelphia, July 10, 1841. Adams MSS.

man, perhaps his son,[95] must follow through in riper, more propitious days, when the North would be more cemented in the cause of Union and freedom, strong enough to emancipate the slaves by martial law in any war to prevent secession.

"When I find my opinions, in the formation of which my will has no dispensing power, conflicting with the deliberate judgment and purposes of both parties in this great controversy, I feel the finger of Heaven pressing upon my lips, and dooming me to silence and inaction. I consult the *sortes biblicæ*, and read that when David promised to build a temple to the Lord, the prophet, speaking from the inspiration of his own mind, approved his design and exhorted him to carry it into execution. But when reposing upon his pillow, the Lord appeared to him in visions, and commanded him to go to David and tell him that he did *well*, in that it was in his heart, to build a temple to the Lord but that *he* was not the chosen instrument to accomplish that great undertaking, but that it was to await the halcyon age reserved for the wisest of mankind, Solomon his Son." [96]

Nunc dimittis? Was it not a good time, after this splendid triumph before the Supreme Court, to take leave of public life? An impertinent anonymous correspondent begged him to do so straightway. Adams refused to comply. "I cannot afford it," he confessed to himself. "There is another [reason] which I should have much trouble to overcome, but which I would encounter; that is, the vacuity of occupation in which I could take an interest. More than sixty years of incessant active intercourse with the world has made political movement to me as much a necessary of life as atmospheric air. This is the weakness of my nature, which I have intellect enough left to perceive, but not energy to control. And thus, while a remnant of physical power is left to me to write and speak, the world will retire from me before I shall retire from the world." [97]

John Quincy Adams's life battle was not yet over. Another great struggle for the freedom of petition was in the offing, one which would be a public trial before the whole nation for vindication of his Second Career, an ordeal that would bring him closer than ever to the cause of abolition.

---

[95] "Keep up your courage and go ahead!" JQA to CFA, after the latter's election to the Massachusetts legislature, Washington, November 28, 1840.

"My father wishes me to follow in the same path, but the idea gives me a choking feeling whenever I recur to it." CFA Diary, February 24, 1841.

[96] JQA to Lewis Tappan, New York. Washington, July 15, 1841. Adams MSS.

[97] *Memoirs*, X, 450–1. March 23, 1841.

"Conversation in the afternoon with my father upon various points connected with the future policy of the country. He has about as feeble hopes as I have and yet he keeps on in his zeal for a career that can now bring him nothing but vexation." Diary of CFA, Quincy, April 24, 1841.

CHAPTER XX

Trial for Censure

(1841 – 1844)

Stop the music of John Quincy Adams.

THOMAS W. GILMER
IN THE HOUSE OF REPRESENTATIVES,
JANUARY 25, 1842 [1]

THE SLAVE power has been repeatedly mentioned in preceding chapters. The antislavery propaganda of the forties, and the historiography of the slavery controversy for a long time after the Civil War, took it for fact that there was a vast organized conspiracy constantly plotting either to enthrall the Union or to break it up.[2] More recent scholarship denies that the South was ever sufficiently unified, before the election of 1860, to produce a definite *conspiracy,* even on such issues as the annexation of Texas, the War with Mexico, the Wilmot Proviso, the Compromise of 1850, or the Kansas Question.[3] But despite intrasectional divergences political and economic, the slaveholding aristocracy—that is to say, the slavery capitalists, the "slavocracy"—constituted what Abraham Lincoln later called a "peculiar and powerful interest." This interest, bolstered in Congress by an additional exclusive representation for three slaves to every five white inhabitants of their states,[4] controlled the politics of that section on slavery. It made all the subsections act together to support slavery as basis of the Southern way of life. That is what John Quincy Adams meant by the slave power, the "slavocracy." The more the abolitionists attacked slavery, the more the Southern representatives in Congress moved together in aggressive defense of the institution.[5] They would have no Union without slavery.

---

[1] *Congressional Globe,* XI, 168.

[2] The classic example of this historiography is, of course, Henry Wilson: *History of the Rise and Fall of the Slave Power in America* (3 vols., Boston, 1872–7).

[3] Nye: *Fettered Freedom,* p. 249. See also Chauncey S. Boucher: "*In re* that Aggressive Slavocracy," MVHR, VIII (Nos. 1–2, June–September 1921), 13–80.

[4] Albert F. Stimson has explained "The Political Significance of Slave Representation, 1787–1821," *Journal of Southern History,* VII (No. 3, August 1941), 314–42. The three-fifths ratio still awaits its historian, particularly for the period 1825–67.

[5] Charles S. Sydnor: *The Development of Southern Sectionalism, 1819–1848* (State, La., 1948).

A whole row of historical exhibits since Adams left the White House had confirmed his feelings. The defeat of national internal improvements; the attempt to withhold protection from the manufacturing industries of the North while demanding it for the "Southern machinery" of slavery; nullification in South Carolina, and in Georgia (by successfully ignoring Indian treaties); the war against the Bank; the cutting off from free territory of a rich alluvial triangle north of the compromise line of 1820, as big as the State of Rhode Island, and adding it to the slave state of Missouri; [6] Jackson's frustrated "plot" to take the free territory of Texas from Mexico in order to fashion more slave states for the Union; the long-drawn-out Seminole War against the Indians and escaped slaves in the Territory of Florida, including the use of bloodhounds by the army to run them down; Presidential apathy in suppressing the foreign slave trade from Africa; the efforts of the Executive to defend slavery in international relations, and to protect American slavery on the high seas; the scarcely disguised hope of Van Buren to dragoon the federal courts in the *Amistad* case; the predominance of slaveholders in executive offices, in federal courts, in the army and navy; the impunity with which South Carolina denied the treaty rights of British free Negroes in her ports, and even sold into slavery free Negro citizens of Massachusetts who touched there on Northern ships; the ever growing menace of war with England over problems of the slave trade and the expansion of slavery—all these facts seemed to prove a deliberate concerted effort of the owners of twelve hundred millions of dollars of wealth in human flesh and blood, possessed through the constitutional three-fifths ratio of twenty-five additional members in the House of Representatives, to fasten slavery irretrievably upon the Union.[7]

Nothing signalized the conspiracy in Adams's mind so notably as the Gag Rule against reception, not to mention discussion, of petitions to Congress for the abolition of slavery and the slave trade in the District of Columbia and the territories of the United States where it still existed.

[6] This piece of territory, included between the Missouri River and the old western boundary of the original State of Missouri, was added to the state by act of Congress approved June 7, 1836 conditional upon ratification of a contract with the Sac and Fox Indians.

[7] JQA to Thomas Kempshall et al., officers of a Meeting of Citizens of Rochester, N.Y., held February 8, 1842. Washington, February 16, 1842. Adams MSS. For indictments of conspiracy of the slave power see: JQA to Thomas Loring of Hingham, Mass., Washington, August 8, 1842. Adams MSS. JQA to his Constituents in the 12th Congressional District of Massachusetts, September 17, 1842. *Boston Atlas*, XI, No. 69, of September 20, 1842. JQA to H. I. Bowditch and William F. [*sic*] Channing of Boston, Washington, March [no other date] 1843; to Asa Walker, Charles A. Stackpole, and F. M. Sabine, Committee of Correspondence of a Meeting of the Citizens of Bangor, Maine, held on May 27, 1843 (to celebrate the ninth anniversary of emancipation of slaves in the British colonies on August 1, 1843), Quincy, July 4, 1843. Adams MSS., printed in *Boston Courier*, XX, No. 5960, August 12, 1843; JQA to William H. Seward at Auburn, N.Y., Washington, May 10, 1844. Adams MSS.

Together with the black codes of the Southern states, the Gag showed that
the slavocracy was willing to suppress fundamental constitutional rights
of free white Americans in order to enforce the perpetual slavery of black
Americans. The pity of it all, thought Adams, was that there were always
enough Northern members of Congress who were willing to give in to
Southern demands in order to keep the Union from disruption. It seemed
to make no difference whether the Democrats were in power or the
Whigs.

1

Inauguration of the first Whig President, William Henry Harrison, took
place March 4, 1841 while John Quincy Adams was waiting for the Supreme Court's decision in the *Amistad* case. A special place in the inaugural parade had been reserved for ex-Presidents, but Adams had not
joined it. He and Joshua Leavitt were in the upstairs front chamber of
Adams's house sorting over legal papers when they heard the bands coming down F Street on the way to the Capitol.

Again Washington was swarming with thousands of visitors from far
and near, this time to witness ceremonies that would throw the Democrats
out of office—so everybody certainly believed. None gave a second thought
to the new Vice President, John Tyler. The vast crowd, the largest yet to
descend on the city, bigger than the Jackson turnout of 1829, was good-
natured and orderly. Once more observers marveled at the tranquillity
with which a republic could experience such a political change-over.

The Whigs had taken a page from Martin Van Buren's primer for national politics. They had made their own alliance of Southern planters
and plain republicans of the North. Not having a first-class military hero
like Andrew Jackson, they had dressed one up and nominated him, and
elected him with a plea for change and reform but without a platform or
even a statement to the people. During the campaign Harrison had promised like Van Buren not to interfere with slavery in the states or territories where it existed or in the District of Columbia without the consent of
the people there. And he had let it be known that he was not friendly to
abolitionist petitions. As if to make the election doubly sure, the party had
nominated for Vice President John Tyler of Virginia, a former Democrat
and a slaveholder, and a Nullifier—at least he had voted in the Senate
against the Force Bill of 1833.

The old ex-President and his abolitionist companion peered down discreetly upon the "showy-shabby" procession two miles long that passed
beneath his windows. Military cavalcades alternated with marching civil-
ian bodies, students and schoolboys, Tippecanoe clubs from various states,
floats of log cabins, with ungainly banners and hastily lettered mottoes.
There was little of pomp and circumstance. It was a spectacle for plain
people. Adams saw General Harrison riding on a "mean-looking white

horse" in a company of seven, including two former military aides who had fought at the battles of Tippecanoe and the Thames.

The President-elect wore no overcoat in the chilling fatal air despite his sixty-seven years. Except that the General bowed and waved his top hat to the crowd,[8] the lookers-on from behind the F Street windows could hardly distinguish him from any other personage in the parade.

Already in the Senate chamber John Tyler had taken his oath of office when Harrison appeared on the east steps of the Capitol to be sworn in. Thus there was a second in command ready to step in and take full charge of the Republic if anything happened to the President-elect before he took the oath of office—or after. The inaugural speech was mostly patriotic rhetoric, full of classical allusions, despite cuts that Clay and Webster had made in the first draft (Webster privately boasted that he alone had knocked out fourteen Roman proconsuls). There was scarcely a mention of the vexing current issues of the day—the national bank, currency, an independent sub-Treasury, public lands, bankruptcy law, tariff, and foreign relations, notably with Great Britain. Having listened respectfully for an hour, the crowd applauded heartily and dispersed. The first Whig Administration had begun.

John Quincy Adams had kept strictly aloof from the Presidential campaign of 1840.[9] The victorious "Harrison hurricane" brought him into a somewhat more compatible relationship with the executive authority, but without patronage or political influence. During the campaign various Democratic newspapers had published a plausible quotation, never denied by Adams: "The greatest beggar and the most troublesome of all the office seekers during my Administration was General Harrison."[10] The record of such a statement did not put the ex-President in any position to beg offices from the political beggar who had now become President.

A somewhat more hopeful situation in Washington did not altogether compensate Adams's disappointment that the Massachusetts Legislature had again refused to elect him to the United States Senate, to take the place of John Davis, who resigned at the end of the Twenty-sixth Congress; or that once more it passed him by when electing another Senator to succeed Daniel Webster in the Twenty-seventh Congress after March 4.[11] It would do so a fourth time in 1843.

[8] Freeman Cleaves: *Old Tippecanoe: William Henry Harrison and His Time* (New York, 1939), p. 336. *Memoirs*, X, 439.

[9] JQA to Samuel Lawrence, Quincy, August 18, 1840; to Committee of the Pawtucket Union Tippecanoe Club, Quincy, September 30, 1840; to Messrs. Solomon Lincoln, Josiah Brigham, and Joseph Richards, Quincy, October 19, 1840. Adams MSS. *Memoirs*, X, 347–51, 357.

[10] E. P. Walton, editor of the *Vermont Watchman and State Journal*, to JQA, Montpelier, March 27, 1840; Aaron B. Howell to JQA, Trenton, New Jersey, April 17, 1840. Adams MSS. *Memoirs*, VII, 530; VIII, 4–6; IX, 312; X, 256, 366.

[11] "The Old State has now three times passed over her oldest servant whose name

With Webster as Secretary of State and Henry Clay in the Senate,[12] the Whig Administration would seem to have been endowed with united and competent leadership as well as a conciliatory disposition in international affairs. But it did not survive long enough to enjoy these advantages. The whole front crumpled upon the death of Harrison one month after he had taken office. In Adams's mind John Tyler, the successor, was a "political sectarian of the slave-driving Virginian, Jeffersonian school." He had "all the interests and passions and vices of slavery rooted in his moral and political constitution." [13] He had usurped the title of President and taken the oath of office as such, instead of moving into constitutional authority as Acting President.[14] The Whigs soon read Tyler out of their party as an unregenerate Democrat in Whig clothing. The Harrison Cabinet resigned, all except Daniel Webster, who at the urging of Adams [15] and others stayed on as Secretary of State, at least long enough to conciliate Anglo-American affairs.[16]

2

Adams still held to his political strategy of subordinating antislavery agitation to four fundamental freedoms of the Constitution: freedom of speech, freedom of petition for the redress of grievances, freedom of debate in Congress, freedom of the press. The wisdom of this course was slowly demonstrating itself. Each successive session of the House had imposed the Gag Rule in increasingly rigid form by a steady majority of 48 or 49 votes, but the proportion of members from *free* states (out of the total voting in favor of the Gag) was shrinking: 82 out of 117 in 1836; 49 out of 126 in 1839.[17] On January 28, 1840, following a reiteration of state-rights proslavery principles, the House adopted the tightest gag yet voted

---

and story will only reflect the more strongly in future history the darkness of her dishonour." Diary of CFA, February 18, 1841.

"In this evolution of partizan positions I have been little more than a looker on. . . .

"There was indeed but one thing in which it would have been possible for the successful party to have manifested personal regard for me, by an apparent testimonial of their confidence, which would have consisted in transferring me from the House to the Senate, for which two opportunities were presented. . . ." JQA to CFA, Washington, March 9, 1841. Adams MSS.

12 Freeman Cleaves, op. cit., pp. 339–40, reveals, however, a foretaste of trouble between Clay and Harrison.

13 *Memoirs*, X, 458, 463. Diary of CFA, Quincy, April 24, 1841.

14 Tyler thereby established an unchallenged precedent for Millard Fillmore, Andrew Johnson, Chester A. Arthur, Theodore Roosevelt, Calvin Coolidge, and Harry S. Truman.

15 *Memoirs*, XI, 13, 36.

16 See below, Chapters XXI, XXII.

17 Von Holst: *Constitutional History*, II, 289. Nye: *Fettered Freedom*, p. 53, note 90.

as a standing rule (the Twenty-first, later numbered the Twenty-fifth Rule) to govern all future sessions: "No petition, memorial, resolution or other paper, praying for the abolition of slavery in the District of Columbia, or any state or territory, or the slave trade between the states and territories of the United States in which it now exists, shall be received by this House, or entertained in any way whatsoever."

To Adams, at least, the difference between the standing rule and the previous gags as successively renewed and tightened was nothing less than that between highway robbery and petty larceny.[18] As a conciliatory substitute he proposed a device that would keep the mass of petitions from clogging business of the House and at the same time preserve the right of petition. Misnamed by some historians the "Adams Gag," it would have provided for the reception of every petition and memorial *unless* objection should be made for special reason (that is, abolition); in that case the name of the objecting member would be recorded, with the reasons for objection, and a vote taken on whether it should be rejected or not.[19] Immediately the Chair sustained an objection to Adams's proposal and the House quickly passed (January 28, 1840) its perfected gag by a majority of six votes (114 to 108). But this time only 26 of the 128 members responding from the free states voted aye.[20]

Petitions, memorials, and remonstrances of all kinds kept coming in to "Father Adams." [21] With the State of Massachusetts [22] ranged behind antislavery memorials and instructions to its representatives in Congress to work for them and against the Gag, Adams could scarcely escape the self-imposed duty of presenting petitions even if he wanted to. He again moved to rescind the Gag Rule at the opening of the special session of Congress which Harrison had called for the summer of 1841. This time the House at first supported him, 112 to 104, but upon reconsideration of the vote reversed itself.[23] Three times the House by a small majority supported Adams, but three times upon motions of members from Pennsylvania it voted to reconsider. Upon the third vote the House again closed its doors upon the prayers of the people,[24] thanks to thirty Northerners who voted for the Gag. The latter included the whole delegation of New Hampshire and half that of Maine. The vote was very close: 110 to 106.

[18] *Memoirs*, X, 200.

[19] *Memoirs*, X, 194–206. Barnes: *Antislavery Impulse*, pp. 119, 256.

[20] Compare tabulation of ayes and nays in *Congressional Globe*, VIII, 151 (January 28, 1840) with membership of the Twenty-sixth Congress in *Biographical Dictionary of the American Congress* (Washington: Government Printing Office; 1928), pp. 184–90.

[21] *Weld-Grimké Letters*, II, 963.

[22] See resolutions passed by the House of Representatives of the State of Massachusetts on March 21, and by the Senate on March 23, 1840. *Acts and Resolves Passed by the Legislature of Massachusetts, 1840* (Boston, 1840), pp. 263–4.

[23] *Memoirs*, X, 475. June 7, 1841.

[24] JQA to R. F. Paine, Esq., Washington, March 22, 1845. Adams MSS.

During the course of the debate Henry Wise delivered a six-hour speech attacking Adams as the friend, inspirer, leader, and general hellhound of abolition.[25]

Once more, at the beginning of the regular session of the Twenty-seventh Congress in December 1841, the Plymouth member tried to open the door to antislavery petitions and discussion of them; the House voted him down by only two votes, 97 to 95.[26] The Northern votes necessary to maintain this bare majority had dropped to twenty-one. (All New Hampshire still stood for it.)

"You seem to feel sore upon the vote adopting the Gag Rule excluding petitions," remarked Edward Stanly of North Carolina, lingering a moment at Adams's seat. "I do," acknowledged the old man, "but the mortification that I feel is not of mere defeat: it is the disgrace and degradation of my country, trampling in the dust the first principle of human liberty. This is the iron that enters into my soul." [27]

Like a bayonet the Gag was jabbing his conscience, driving him ever closer to the ranks of the abolitionists.

In these slender margins for the Gag the Southern members, both Democrat and Whig, saw freedom's writing plainly on the walls of Congress. It was in the unmistakable hand of John Quincy Adams. He was identifying the cause of antislavery with the cause of white freedom. He was undermining their Northern sympathizers. He was breaking down party lines on sectional issues. A further shift of only a few Northern votes in either party would loosen the Gag. They must get rid of that "mischievous bad old man" [28] before he crystallized freedom of petition and debate into a positive antislavery movement in Congress. Their alarm quickened as they observed the old contender hobnobbing with a new abolitionist group that had appeared in Congress.

3

In the election of 1840 the abolitionists had tried to organize a third party after the example of the Antimasons. They had put up James G. Birney as candidate of the Liberty Party on an out-and-out abolition platform. The paltry total of 7,059 votes cast for Birney throughout the whole

[25] *Memoirs*, X, 478–9. *Congressional Globe*, X (1st Sess., 27th Cong.), 27–53. June 7, 8, 14, 15, 1841.

"Mr. Adams has thrown a firebrand among the combustibles of the South, and Mr. Wise, the most inflammable among them, blazes away. . . . It would be happy for the country, and I doubt not agreeable to their colleagues, if the fox of Massachusetts and the wild-cat of Virginia were both tied up in some menagerie for the remainder of the session." *Diary of Philip Hone*, II, 547–8. June 15, 1841.

[26] *Congressional Globe*, XI, 1–9. December 7–8, 1841.

[27] *Memoirs*, XI, 33–5. December 6–8, 1841.

[28] Calhoun to Mrs. T. G. Clemson, Washington, April 22, 1842. *Annual Report 1899 AHA*, II (Washington, 1900), 513.

country convinced the leaders that they must work within the existing parties if they wanted to make headway. So they sent Joshua Leavitt to Washington, ostensibly to report the proceedings of Congress for his paper, really to be advance agent for an abolitionist lobby.

Leavitt found a small but devout group of Whig members of the House who were willing to make opposition to slavery, rather than classical Whig measures (national bank, protective tariff, internal improvements), the leading object of public policy. Their long-range program was to work within the forms of the Constitution to secure legislation for prohibition of slavery and the slave trade within the District of Columbia and all the territories of the United States; effective suppression of the African slave trade on the high seas by genuine co-operation with Great Britain; outlawing of the slave trade between the states of the Union; and, eventually, an amendment to the Constitution—like that proposed by John Quincy Adams in 1839 to abolish slavery within the states.

Political chieftain of this insurgent Whig group was Joshua R. Giddings of Ohio, a man personally beloved by Adams:

> And here, from regions wide apart,
>   We came, one purpose to pursue,
> Each with a warm and honest heart,
>   Each with a spirit firm and true.
>
> And here, with scrutinizing eye,
>   A kindred soul with mine to see
> And longing bosom to descry,
>   I sought, and found at last—in thee.[29]

At Giddings's side were William Slade of Vermont, Seth M. Gates of New York, and Sherlock J. Andrews of Ohio. All these zealots were former "professors of religion," old "revival men" from the Burned-over District and its fringes. Giddings, Gates, and Andrews were Theodore Weld's personal converts to abolition. They attached a handful of earnest fellow travelers and constituted a "Select Committee on Slavery." Leavitt closeted himself with this conventicle unsanctioned by any congressional sanction. Their immediate strategy was to concert an aggressive program of bills, resolutions, and speeches designed to open discussion of the subject of slavery by ingenious circumlocution of the Gag Rule, proceedings that would be printed and franked all over the nation. To assist them with research and ghost writing they brought to Washington their old teacher and master. Weld established himself along with the abolitionist members of Congress in Mrs. Sprigg's boarding-house across the park from the Capitol—thenceforth known as Abolition House.

[29] From a poem by John Quincy Adams addressed to Joshua Giddings. June 17, 1844. Adams MSS.

As soon as Weld arrived in Washington, Leavitt took him to call on Mr. and Mrs. Adams. It was New Year's Day 1842, and the house was choked with callers, for it had become the custom in Washington to drop in to present the season's compliments. Over five hundred people were coming in and out: [30] members of Congress, foreign diplomats, army and navy officers, literary and scientific personalities, clergymen—and now abolitionists.

"Found him and his wife living in a plain house," Weld wrote home, "plainly furnished, and themselves plainly dressed—the old gentleman very plainly. When Mr. Leavitt introduced me, Mr. A. asked: 'Is this Mr. Theodore Weld?' Yes. 'I know you well, Sir, by your writings.'" They fell into talk about slavery and abolition, and the *Creole* case. Then Adams took Weld by the hand and led him across the room to introduce him to his wife. "In doing so I was glad to hear him call her '*my dear*,' as I think you told me they lived unhappily together." [31]

A week later Weld dined with the Adamses. "It was a genuine abolition gathering and the old patriarch talked with as much energy and zeal as a Methodist at a camp meeting. Remarkable man! " [32] All teetotalers, noted the winebibber host: "Rechabites who drink no wine." Weld announced himself also a Grahamite who ate no animal food.[33] It was plain enough that these good religionists were little short of fanatics—fanatics for freedom. They must be handled with care. The best way to manage them might be to join them or at least seem to join them.

Adams straightway claimed for himself a place on the "Select Committee," [34] only he called it a "Committee of Friends of the Right of Petition." He tried to take it under his wing. Assuming the initiative, he called them into meeting in a room of the House during January 1842 to concert a plan of action. He even formulated a six-point program calculated to regain the right of petition, and presented it to the group. It met no dissent, but elicited little real enthusiasm.[35] We may guess that the original organizers of the "Select Committee" wanted to make abolition rather than the right of petition the immediate issue and spearhead of their campaign, and that they did not relish the readiness with which the ex-President was taking the lead from them.

[30] *Memoirs*, XI, 48. January 1, 1842.

[31] *Weld-Grimké Letters*, II, p. 886.

[32] Theodore Weld to Angelina G. Weld and Sarah Grimké, Washington, January 9, 1842. Ibid., 888–91.

[33] Diary, January 8, 1842.

[34] Joshua Giddings to his wife, February 18, 1842, included Adams in the committee and indicated that the association had occurred some time before (*Weld-Grimké Letters*, II, 889–90, note 3). Barnes (*Antislavery Impulse*, p. 184) suggests that it was at the dinner at Adams's home on January 8, 1842 that the ex-President enlisted in the insurgent group.

[35] *Memoirs*, XI, 61–2, 68. January 15, 22, 1842.

The first opening for abolitionist tactics appeared in the *Creole* case. Weld worked up a set of resolutions to be presented by one of the group, with arguments all prepared. They declared that the laws of the United States (as distinct from those of the Southern slave states) gave no protection to slavery in ships flying the Stars and Stripes on the high seas. But before Weld's paper could be presented, Adams himself opened up the antislavery campaign in the House with an assault much bolder than anything hitherto ventured.

Students of the abolition movement have wanted to believe, but have not been quite sure, that Adams planned this new attack with Abolition House. The fact is that he had worked on the abolitionists more successfully than they had worked on him. He had enlisted himself with the insurgent group and seized the initiative in order to keep the antislavery movement still cloaked with the right of petition and the other fundamental freedoms of the Constitution. Only in that way could he cover in more support for the antislavery cause from Northern Whig members of Congress who did not want to be listed as abolitionists—and Democratic members too. Thus could he more quickly break down the slight but disciplined majority by which the Whig Party leaders were still able to gag the discussion of slavery. In this strategy he was remarkably successful. It was to bring him the greatest triumph of his political career.

4

The occasion for John Quincy Adams's new drive against the slave power was another factitious memorial irresponsibly concocted by certain citizens of Georgia to embarrass him in championing the right of petition. It asked that he be removed from his appointment as chairman of the committee on foreign affairs on the ground that he was "possessed of a species of monomania on all subjects connected with people as dark as a Mexican," and therefore was not fit to be entrusted with the business of relations with Mexico.

Adams pounced on this paper as an opportunity to get around the Gag Rule. With an air of conscientious duty he presented the petition, following the tabling of several others, obnoxious to the South, that he had brought forward. He then claimed the floor, as a matter of personal privilege, to defend himself against the imputations contained in the document. Several members jumped up to raise a point of order. Speaker John White of Kentucky referred the question to the House itself. In a short debate James Cresap Sprigg of Shelbyville, Kentucky, suggested it would be better to sue out a writ that would give Adams a fair trial before a court of lunacy!

"Order! Order!"

The House tabled Adams's request for privilege, 94 to 92. Next day he explained that he had intended (after being heard in his own defense) to move reference of the petition to the committee on foreign affairs with instructions to elect another chairman, *if they thought proper.*[36] Thereupon the House voted to reconsider the question of privilege.

"I believe the paper to be a hoax," declared Richard Wylly Habersham of Clarksville, Georgia. "Whether it is genuine or whether it is a forgery," answered the Plymouth member, "it is equally an outrage on me and the House."

Amidst cries of "Order! Order!" "Stop him!" "Let him go on!" Adams proceeded with his remarks. "There is an alliance," he shouted, "between Southern slave traders and Northern democrats." That was why they wanted to get rid of him as chairman of the committee on foreign affairs. By a vote of 91 to 76 the House refused to let him proceed.[37]

Theodore Weld has left a description of Adams's remarks less restrained than that of the partisan reporters of the *Congressional Globe*, who rarely did him full justice.

"Old Nestor lifted up his voice like a trumpet," wrote Weld to his wife, Angelina Grimké, "till slaveholding, slave trading, and slave breeding absolutely quailed and howled under his dissecting knife. Mr. Adams had said the day before that he should present some petitions that would set them in a blaze, so I took care to be in the house at the time, and such a scene I never witnessed. Lord Morpeth, the English abolitionist of whom you have heard, was present and sat within a few feet of Mr. A., his fine intelligent face beaming with delight as the old man breasted the storm and dealt his blows upon the head of the monster. Wise of Va., Raynor [Rayner] of N.C., W. C. Johnson of Md., and scores more of slaveholders, striving constantly to stop him by starting question of order and by every now and then screaming at the top of their voices: 'That is false.' 'I *demand* Mr. Speaker that you *put him down.*' 'I demand that you shut the mouth of that old harlequin.' 'What are we to sit here and endure such insults.' A perfect uproar like Babel would burst forth every two or three minutes as Mr. A. with his bold surgery would smite his cleaver into the very bones. At least half of the slaveholding members of the house left their seats and gathered in the quarter of the Hall where Mr. Adams stood. Whenever any of them broke out upon him, Mr. Adams would say 'I see where the shoe pinches, Mr. Speaker, it will pinch *more* yet.' 'I'll deal out to the gentlemen a diet that they'll find it hard to digest.' 'If before I get through every slaveholder, slave trader and slave breeder on this floor does not get materials for better reflection it shall be no fault of mine.' "[38]

. . .

[36] *Congressional Globe*, XI, 157–9, 161–4. January 21, 1842.

[37] *Congressional Globe*, XI, 161–7. *Memoirs*, XI, 69–70. January 22, 24, 1842.

[38] Theodore Weld to Angelina G. Weld and Sarah Grimké, Washington, January 23, 1842. *Weld-Grimké Letters*, II, 899–1000.

Following the failure to remove Adams from chairmanship of the committee on foreign affairs, five Southern members of the committee resigned rather than serve under him.[39] Speaker White appointed five other Southerners to take their place.[40] Three of these [41] refused to serve, but three other Southern members [42] were found who were willing to go on with Adams. So the committee kept functioning without too much interruption.

The Whig leaders were beside themselves with vexation. They laid their plans to get him, to make an example of him. If Adams could be crushed it would be a long while before anyone else could raise his head successfully to challenge their power. A caucus of Southern Whigs decided to bring the formal censure of the House upon him at the first opportunity. Northern Whig leaders silently acquiesced.[43] The majority of the Democratic opposition were of course quite pleased at any plan to get rid of him.

As if to suit the convenience of his sworn adversaries Adams on January 25, 1842 stood up and read a memorial so enormous in its implications that no one had even thought of gagging in advance such a request. It was a petition from Benjamin Emerson and forty-five other citizens of Haverhill, Massachusetts, praying that Congress immediately adopt "measures peaceably to dissolve the Union of these States." [44] Imperturbably the age-honored champion of the Union and of freedom of petition moved that the document be referred to a select committee with instructions to report an answer to the petitioners showing the reasons why their prayer ought not to be granted.

The Haverhill petition brought all the Southern hotspurs snapping at

[39] Thomas W. Gilmer of Virginia, R. M. T. Hunter of Virginia, Richard Barnwell Rhett of South Carolina, George H. Proffit of Louisiana, William Cort Johnson of Maryland.

[40] Edward D. White of Louisiana, Augustine L. Shepperd of North Carolina, Isaac E. Holmes of South Carolina, Reuben Chapman of Alabama, and Mark A. Cooper of Georgia.

[41] Chapman, Holmes, and Cooper.

[42] James A. Meriwether of Georgia, Robert L. Carruthers of Tennessee, and Alexander H. H. Stuart of Virginia. See *Memoirs*, XI, 89–94.

[43] Barnes: *Antislavery Impulse*, pp. 185, 285.

[44] The petitioners adduced the following reasons for peaceable dissolution of the Union:

"First. Because no union can be agreeable or permanent which does not present prospects of reciprocal benefits.

"Second. Because a vast proportion of the resources of one section of the Union is annually drained to sustain the views and course of another section without any adequate return.

"Third. Because (judging from the history of past nations) that Union, if persisted in the present course of things, will certainly overwhelm the whole nation in utter destruction." *Congressional Globe*, XI, 168.

the member who presented it.[45] So the Madman of Massachusetts was on the rampage again! He would go so far as to present petitions for the dissolution of the Union!

George Washington Hopkins of Goochland County, Virginia, rose and addressed the Speaker. "Is it in order," he asked, "to burn the petition in the presence of the House?"

"I move," said Hopkins L. Turney of Winchester, Tennessee, "that the petition be laid on the table and printed, that the country may understand what its character is."

Henry A. Wise got the Speaker's nod. "Is it in order," he inquired, "to move to censure any member presenting such a petition?"

"Good!" exclaimed Adams from his seat.

A Babel of Southern inquiries and objections filled the House.

"I am surprised," professed the Plymouth member, "that such an objection should come from a quarter where there have been so many calculations of the value of the Union."

Someone moved to adjourn.

"I hope the House will not adjourn," declared Adams. "If there is to be a vote of censure, the House might as well settle the question now as adjourn."

The House refused to adjourn, 49 to 87.

Thomas Walker Gilmer of Albemarle County, Virginia, then submitted, as a question of privilege, the following motion:

"*Resolved,* That in presenting to the consideration of this House a petition for the dissolution of the Union the member from Massachusetts has justly incurred the censure of this House."

Was such a motion in order?

"I do not feel at liberty to arrest the proceeding," decided Speaker White. He cited the precedent of 1836, the immediate action on Patton's resolution that Adams be brought before the bar of the House and censured for offering a petition purporting to come from certain slaves in Virginia. Members must have recalled how that first attempt to censure the Plymouth member had failed.

"I hope this resolution will be received and debated," averred Adams, "and that I shall have the privilege of again addressing the House in my own defence, especially as the gentleman from Virginia [Gilmer] has thought proper to play second fiddle to his colleague from Accomac [Henry Wise]."

"Order! Order!" from the House in deafening roars.

"I play second fiddle to no man," Gilmer shouted amidst the din. "I am endeavoring to stop the music of one

> 'Who, in the course of one revolving moon,
> 'Was poet, fiddler, statesman, and buffoon.' "

[45] *Diary of Philip Hone,* II, 582–5.

Stop the music of John Quincy Adams! Put an end to his eternal trumpeting for freedom! So demanded the Southern slaveholders, inside and outside of Congress.

Eventually a longer and more eloquent resolution of indictment prevailed as presented by Thomas F. Marshall of Kentucky, chosen as the Southern whip to beat down the aged challenger: that while John Quincy Adams might well merit expulsion from the national councils, the House in its grace and mercy would inflict upon him only its severest censure "for conduct so utterly unworthy of his past position to the State, and his present position." The proposed resolution read:

"Whereas, the Federal Constitution is a permanent form of Government and of perpetual obligation, until altered or modified in the mode pointed out by that instrument, and the members of this House, deriving their political character and powers from the same, are sworn to support it, and the dissolution of the Union necessarily implies the destruction of that instrument, the overthrow of the American Republic, and the extinction of our national existence: A proposition, therefore, to the Representatives of the people, to dissolve the organic law framed by their constituents, and to support which they are commanded by those constituents to be sworn, before they can enter upon the execution of the political powers created by it, and entrusted to them, is a high breach of privilege, a contempt offered to this House, a direct proposition to the Legislature and each member of it, to commit perjury; and involves, necessarily, in its execution and its consequences, the destruction of our country and the crime of high treason.

"*Resolved, therefore,* That the Hon. JOHN Q. ADAMS, a member from Massachusetts, in presenting for the consideration of the House of Representatives of the United States, a petition praying the dissolution of the Union, has offered the deepest indignity to the House of which he is a member; an insult to the people of the United States, of which that House is the Legislative organ; and will, if this outrage be permitted to pass unrebuked and unpunished, have disgraced his country, through their Representatives, in the eyes of the whole world.

"*Resolved, further,* That the aforesaid JOHN Q. ADAMS, for this insult, the first of the kind ever offered to the Government, and for the wound which he has permitted to be aimed, through his instrumentality, at the Constitution and existence of his country, the peace, the security, and liberty of the people of these States, might well be held to merit expulsion from the national councils; and the House deem it an act of grace and mercy, when they only inflict upon him their severest censure for conduct so utterly unworthy of his past relations to the State, and his present position. This they hereby do

for the maintenance of their own purity and dignity; for the rest,
they turn him over to his own conscience and the indignation of all
true *American* citizens." [46]

Marshall, a magnificent figure of a man in youthful prime, nephew of
the late Chief Justice, was a new white hope of the slaveholding South,
if only he would keep sober. For the moment he was carrying himself
with unusual steadiness.

"May I accompany my resolution with a few remarks?" he asked the
Speaker deferentially.

"Certainly, certainly," volunteered orderly voices from the floor.

Speaker White replied in the affirmative.

"I am aware to what I expose myself in submitting these resolutions,"
Marshall declared gravely. He explained that he had never manifested
any hostility toward the North, nor any personal feelings against the
gentleman from Massachusetts to whose past career he paid deserved
tribute. But in recent days that gentleman had excited discreditable
scenes in the House. "I give him this opportunity of defending himself
against the charges contained in the petition he has presented." The gentleman from Massachusetts, said Marshall, had done nothing less than
invite members of the House to commit high treason when he submitted
a petition for the dissolution of the Union! [47]

"Sir," Adams responded, "what is high treason? The Constitution of the
United States says what high treason is. . . . It is not for the gentleman
from Kentucky, or his puny mind, to define what high treason is, and
confound it with what I have done."

He called upon the Clerk to read the first paragraph of the Declaration
of Independence. "The first paragraph," raising his voice, "of the Declaration of Independence. The first paragraph"—the old man pitched his voice
still higher—"of the Declaration of Independence!"

The Clerk droned out the immortal lines: "When, in the course of human events, it becomes necessary for one people to dissolve the political
bands which have connected them with another, and to assume among
the powers of the Earth the separate and equal station to which the laws
of Nature and of Nature's God entitle them, a decent respect to the
opinions of mankind require that they should declare the causes which
impel them to the separation—"

"Proceed, proceed," Adams shouted shrilly, "proceed, down to the 'right
and duty.'"

The Clerk read on to describe the inalienable rights of life, liberty, and

[46] *Congressional Globe,* XI, 168–70. January 25, 1840. *Memoirs,* XI, 72–3.

[47] I have taken these excerpts from the *Congressional Globe.* Marshall's speech
was later edited for publication in *Speeches and Writings of Thomas F. Marshall,*
edited by W. L. Barre (Cincinnati, 1858).

the pursuit of happiness, and the right and duty of free men after a long train of abuses to provide new safeguards for their future security.

"Now, Sir," continued this son of the American Revolution whose father had helped to draft the undying Declaration, "if there is a principle sacred on earth and established by the instrument just read, it is the right of the people to alter, to change, to destroy, the Government if it becomes oppressive to them. There would be no such right existing if the people had not the power in pursuance of that right, to petition for it. . . . I rest that petition on the Declaration of Independence."

Certainly, argued Adams, whatever his own unquestionable attachment to the Constitution and the Union despite all slanders against him, certainly these fellow citizens of Haverhill had as much right as their forefathers to petition for a redress of grievances. "If the right of habeas corpus, and the right of trial by jury are to be taken away by this coalition of Southern slaveholders and Northern Democracy, it is time for the Northern people to see if they can't shake it off, and it is time to present such petitions as this. I can say it is *not yet time* to do this, the other means have not been tried. I say that if the petition is referred and answered, it will satisfy the petitioners. They will see that there are other measures to be pursued; and, first of all to restore the right of petition."

Several members observed that if the gentleman from Massachusetts were to be heard in his own defense he would have to speak right away to the resolution before it was adopted and the matter disposed of.

"If it is the intention of the House to proceed now at once—" began Adams.

"Now! Now!" came cries from the House.

"—then I must submit. Was it ever known," he asked his colleagues, "that, to a man on whom charges of this kind were started of a sudden, and totally unexpected, no time was to be allowed for his defence?"

"You can submit a motion for further time for defence, by yourself or by a friend," the Speaker declared curtly.

Horace Everett of Windsor, Vermont, moved for a week's time, but the House would not hear of it.

Henry Wise rose and had the Clerk read a paragraph from George Washington's Farewell Address, on the necessity for unity in government. He insisted on debating the main question then and there. " 'Come on Macduff,' " he cried, "and damned be he who first cries, 'Hold, enough!' I am at all times prepared to meet gentlemen. The gentleman from Massachusetts, after treading on the graves of members of the old English party [the Massachusetts Federalists], the early friends of his father, and then going to Ghent and incorporating in our treaty with England a provision for the payment of slaves which has stood the severest test of the British Government—for the payment not for assassins and murderers, like those on board the *Creole*, but for runaways, who had forsaken their master's [*sic*] plantations and gone on board the British fleet. The same authority now comes forward and tells this House that we cannot consent to go to war with England [48] for the support and maintenance of slavery, and this under flagrant circumstances of violence done to the national flag in behalf of mutineers and murderers."

Wise defended slavery against the "British-abolitionist-dissolutionist" party in the House. "The principle of slavery," he insisted, and these are his very words, "is a leveling principle; it is friendly to equality. Break down slavery, and you would with the same blow destroy the great democratic principle of equality among men." [49]

At this, admits the official report, a laugh arose from "one portion of the House."

Wise closed with a sad lament on John Quincy Adams's fall from such an illustrious place in the nation's history. "That one should so have outlived his fame! . . . To think of the veneration, the honor, the reverence with which his person might have been loved and cherished—the weight that would have been attached to every word he uttered, so that the moment he rose to speak every breath should be hushed, and that vast Hall be silent as the tomb—to think how he would have been looked upon with awe approaching to dread, as the last link that bound this age to the Revolutionary Fathers. . . . I thank God that the gentleman, great as he was, neither has, nor is likely, to have sufficient influence to excite a spirit of disunion throughout the land. . . . The gentleman is politically dead; dead as Burr—dead as Arnold. The people will look upon him with wonder, will shudder, and retire."

Adams, smothering ejaculations, listened to Wise. One by one the Virginian rehearsed the South's grievances and the multiplying threats to slavery and to the Southern way of life. Most recent was defeat of the annexation of Texas at the hands of the abolitionists, he averred, in cooperation with their English brethren. Texas, he all but declared, was necessary to balance and offset the new free states that would someday come into the Union from the vast expanses of territory north of the Missouri Compromise line. Adams had been the man who frustrated annexation, and it was on him that Wise poured the vials of Southern wrath hour after hour.[50] It took two days for the member from Accomac to empty himself of his "filthy invective." [51] That gave Adams time to plan his own defense.

At the end of Wise's diatribe Theodore Weld came and offered to help Adams with research in documents, books, and papers. "The temper of people here," he assured the alleged suborner of high treason, "is highly

---

[48] JQA's earlier speech of September 4, 1841. See below, p. 458, n. 26.
[49] *Congressional Globe*, XI, 170–2.
[50] Wiltse: *Calhoun, Sectionalist*, p. 150.
[51] *Memoirs*, XI, 73. *Congressional Globe*, XI, 173–7. January 25, 26, 1842.

excited by these motions of censure on you and the inflammatory harangues of Marshall and Wise against you, but I think the tide is turning in your favor." [52]

"I thank you. I accept your offer gratefully." [53]

Adams could not have found a more devout or able helper. Together they worked incessantly day and night to prepare the defense. They quickly became intimate friends. Often the older man would stop in their conferences and recall scenes of his boyhood and college days, which Weld later handed down to his children.[54]

The old man was now in his element. He had left Quincy for the regular session of Congress in poor health, beset with pimples, boils, eruptions, and other bodily miseries. His head had felt as if stung all over by a swarm of bees. A catarrhal cough was fixing itself in his lungs. His only relief seemed to be a shifting of pain from one place to another.[55] But as the session opened, with its controversies, he began to feel better. Now that the battle was on, his health returned magnificently. Weld marveled at his energy and strength of voice as he practiced his speeches at F Street.

"When they talk about his old age and venerableness and nearness to the grave," remarked Ralph Waldo Emerson about John Quincy Adams, "he knows better. He is like one of those old cardinals, who, as quick as he is chosen Pope, throws away his crutches and his crookedness, and is as straight as a boy. He is an old roué, who cannot live on slops, but must have sulphuric acid in his tea." [56]

"I am afraid you are tiring yourself out," Weld ventured to advise Adams after a six-hour rehearsal. "No, no, not at all, I am all ready for another heat." The old crusader then went through the main points of the next day's speech with rapidity and energy of utterance and gesture as if he were addressing the House itself. "Stop," cautioned Weld in vain. "You will need all your strength for the next day." Adams went on for another hour, in a voice loud enough to be heard by a large audience. "Wonderful man!" [57]

The actual speeches in the House, stimulated by extemporaneous exchanges, of course exceeded the rehearsals in power and expression.[58] The

---

[52] *Memoirs,* XI, 75.

[53] Theodore Weld to Angelina Grimké Weld, Washington, January 30, 1842. *Weld-Grimké Letters,* II, 905.

[54] Barnes: *Antislavery Impulse,* p. 286.

[55] Diary, November–January 1841–2.

[56] *Journals,* XI, 344.

[57] Theodore Weld to Angelina Grimké Weld, Washington, January 30, 1842. *Weld-Grimké Letters,* II, 905–6.

[58] A bundle of miscellaneous papers in the Adams MSS. contains a hurried holograph outline of the defense that he began on February 2, 1842. The texts are only meagerly preserved in the official reports in the *Congressional Globe.*

Old Man Eloquent more than made good the title that the public had long since bestowed upon him. The Haverhill petition proved to be a greater opportunity to defend human freedom than it was for those who were trying to ruin him in order to defend slavery and hold the Whig Party together.

Facing his accusers, he challenged them to come on against him. "I am still in the power of the majority. If they say they will try me, they must try me. If they say that they will punish me, they must punish me. If they say that in grace and mercy, they will spare me expulsion, I disdain and cast their mercy away; and I ask them if they will come to such a trial and expel me. I defy them. I have constituents to go to who will have something to say if this House expels me. Nor will it be long before gentlemen will see me here again!"

Adams did not neglect Henry Wise. Once, when some members of the House had wanted to try Wise for his participation in the Cilley-Graves duel, Adams had protested against such action as a violation of the Constitution because it might have condemned a man without due process of law, just as the House was now, by Wise's definition of law, trying Adams himself for alleged subornation of treason. Wise had spoken, in reference to the *Creole* case, of assassins and murderers! He, the very man who had been far more guilty in the Cilley-Graves affair than the duelist who actually pressed the trigger that leveled to the ground a member of this House! "That far more guilty man," Adams cried in Ciceronian tones that chilled the House with horror, "came into this House with his hands and face dripping—when the blood spots were yet visible upon him. . . . It is very possible that *I* saved this blood-stained man from the censure of the House . . . although his hands were reeking with the blood of murder."

Wise rose to a point of order: "Is it my character or conduct which is involved in the issue before the House? Is it in order for the member from Massachusetts to charge me with the crime of murder, and with being stained with innocent blood? . . . I now pronounce the charge made by the gentleman from Massachusetts as base and black a lie as the *traitor* was black and base who uttered it."

The veteran ignored the insult and turned more briefly to Marshall. He had nothing but the kindest feelings for him personally. He respected his talents. He hoped he would succeed in rescuing himself with the help of his friends from the vice of drunkenness. But where did he learn his law? Certainly not from his distinguished uncle! "Nor did you learn yours from your illustrious father," the Kentuckian retorted. "Let him go home," responded Adams tolerantly, "let him go to some law school, and learn a little of the rights of the citizens of these states and the members of this House."

Marshall, and later Gilmer, attempted to score by pointing out that Adams as a young Senator had wanted the Senate to try one of its members, John Smith, for treason by implication in Aaron Burr's projects.[59] As if John Quincy Adams were now being tried for treason!

More threats of assassination came to Adams as the trial continued. "Stop the music of John Quincy Adams, sixth President of the United States," suggested one of them postmarked Norfolk, Virginia. It showed a picture of the ex-President with a bullet mark in his forehead, written over by the word *abolition*. On the margin were the words *Mene, tekel, upharsin*. Another letter reminded him that the South was watching his villainous course in Congress. The writer repeated Gilmer's quotation applied on the floor of the House to John Quincy Adams: "poet, statesman, and buffoon," substituting "babbler" for "fiddler." It was clear he had got his cue from reading Gilmer's remarks in the House. "Unless you very soon change your course," the anonymous Virginian continued, "death will be your portion. Prepare, prepare, by the —— of —— you will unexpectedly be hurled into Eternity where you ought to have been long since."[60] Adams exhibited the document to the House. Of such stripe, he declared, were Gilmer's "auxiliaries."

The majority shifted back and forth in their indictment, now trying to use Gilmer's original resolution, now Marshall's. Finally Gilmer offered to withdraw his resolution if Adams would withdraw his petition.

"No! No! I cannot do that," declared Adams. "That proposition comes to the point and issue of this whole question,—that is to say, to the total suppression of the right of petition to the whole people of this Union. . . . If I withdrew the petition I would consider myself as having sacrificed the right of petition; as having sacrificed the right of habeas corpus; as having sacrificed the right of trial by jury; as having sacrificed the sacred confidence of the post office; as having sacrificed the freedom of the press; as having sacrificed the freedom of speech; as having sacrificed every element of liberty that was enjoyed by my fellow citizens; because if I should prove craven to my trust under intimidation of the charges of the gentleman from Albemarle and the gentleman from Kentucky, never more would the House see a petition presented from the people of the Union, expressing their grievances in a manner that might not be pleasing to the members of the 'peculiar institution' until at length the people should teach them the lesson that, however their representatives might be intimidated from the discharge of their duty, they the people would be their own champions and the defenders of their own rights. *There* is the deadly character of the attempt to put me down."[61]

As the debate went on day after day, with suspensions for indispensable

---

[59] Bennett Champ Clark's own experience in the Senate and in parliamentary practice helped him to give a vivid description of the personal passages in this famous Senate trial in his *John Quincy Adams, "Old Man Eloquent,"* pp. 304–7.

[60] —— to John Quincy Adams, Jackson, N.C., January 20, 1842. Postmarked Norfolk, Virginia. Adams MSS.

[61] *Congressional Globe*, XI, 208.

business, it became evident to the slaveholders that they had made a mistake. Petitions were now pouring in from all over the North against the attempt to censure Adams. It had become a famous case for constitutional rights. The newspapers of the North were up in arms. Northern Whigs were weakening, even border Whigs, even some Southerners. The Whig leaders were ready to give up the fight. Adams still had the floor for his defense. The old man seemed very fit, too, enjoying himself. His dialectical resources and his personal energy seemed inexhaustible. The more he talked, the worse things looked for the party. On February 7, 1842 he declared that he would need at least a week more to complete his defense, but if anybody wished to put the whole matter on the table never to be taken up again, he would be satisfied. Thereupon John Minor Botts, a Whig from Henrico, Virginia, promptly made the motion to table. It passed 106 to 93.

The day's session was not yet over. Before adjournment Adams presented nearly two hundred more petitions! Most of them were outlawed under the Gag Rule, but he was content for the time being. Young Tom Marshall was left "sprawling in his own compost," [62] while the sound of *Io Triumphe* rang exultantly in the old gladiator's ears.

A few weeks later Daniel D. Barnard, Representative from the Rochester, New York, district, presented a document from his constituents similar to the Haverhill petition, and the House simply refused to receive it, with no further fuss.[63]

Marshall was beaten and he knew it, and respected John Quincy Adams for it. At the end of the session he went back to Kentucky, never to return to Congress. The two antagonists, the elderly constitutional lawyer and the defeated young hopeful, came to exchange friendly letters during the following year [64] and lived in happy relations toward each other ever after.

Wise and Adams also resumed their personal correspondence. Later in life, after John Quincy Adams's death, the Virginian boasted at the hustings of the very severe training he had received in combat with the "acutest, the astutest, the archest enemy of Southern slavery that ever existed. I mean the 'Old Man Eloquent,' John Quincy Adams."

It would be difficult to find an appraisal to the contrary from anyone young or old who had ever crossed swords in the House with that terrible adversary. "I must have been a dull boy indeed," added Wise, "if I had not learned my lessons thoroughly on that subject. And let me tell you that again and again I had reason to know and to feel the wisdom and sagacity of that departed man. Again and again, in the lobby, on the floor,

[62] *Memoirs*, XI, 86–8.

[63] Willis Fletcher Johnson: "John Quincy Adams and Secession," *Magazine of History*, XXV (No. 1, July 1917), 76–9.

[64] T. F. Marshall to JQA, Lexington, Ky., November 16, 1843. JQA to Thomas F. Marshall, Lexington, Ky. Washington, December 2, 1843.

he told me vauntingly that the pulpit would preach, and the school would teach, and the press would print, among the people who had no tie and no association with slavery, until, would not only be reached the slave-trade between the States, the slave-trade in the District of Columbia, slavery in the District, slavery in the Territories, but slavery in the States. Again and again he said that he would not abolish slavery in the District of Columbia if he could; for he would retain it as a bone of contention,— a fulcrum of the lever for agitation, agitation, agitation, until slavery in the States was shaken from its base. And his prophecies have been fulfilled—fulfilled far faster and more fearfully, certainly, than ever he anticipated, before he died." [65]

The spectacular "trial" of John Quincy Adams for censure by the House served as nothing else could do to publicize the danger to the rights of free men and women, even in the North, who dared to raise their voices against slavery. It made anti-abolitionists search their consciences more and more as to the evils of slavery and its portent for the Union. It put Adams before the nation as the greatest champion of constitutional rights and defender of human freedom. It warmed the abolitionists to praise his stand even though he would not join their formal ranks. A mammoth antislavery meeting (January 28, 1842) in Faneuil Hall, the Cradle of Liberty, pressing for the abolition of slavery in the District of Columbia, included in its twelve resolutions one of praise and thanks from the friends of liberty everywhere to John Quincy Adams for his "bold, faithful, and indefatigable advocacy of the right of petition under circumstances of great difficulty and peril," and pledged to sustain him in whatever "constitutional" efforts he might make in favor of the rights of man, "irrespective of complexional differences." [66]

The stirring of Northern opinion during the trial enraged the defenders of slavery. In Congress they closed their ranks the more tightly to defend the Gag Rule. Outside of Congress some Southern sympathizers, to be sure, continued patiently to reason with Adams that his course was threatening the Union.[67] But the extremists—overseers, slave-drivers, slave-traders, as Adams labeled them in the files of his correspondence— renewed their ugly protests against his course and multiplied their threats on his life. Here are some new samples: [68]

[65] Statement made by Henry A. Wise as candidate for Governor of Virginia in 1855. Barton H. Wise: *The Life of Henry A. Wise of Virginia 1806–1876* (New York, 1899), pp. 61–2. The quotation is from the book *verbatim et literatim.*

[66] Handbill printed copy of the resolutions of January 28, 1842. Adams MSS. *Liberator,* XII, No. 5, February 1, 1842.

[67] "An Humble American Citizen" to JQA, February 1842. Anonymous to JQA, Baltimore [no date]. John R. Kellogg to JQA, Allegan, Mich., March 2, 1842. Jno. A. Watkins to JQA, Rodney, Miss., March 3, 1842. Robert Study to JQA, Augusta, Ga., April 22, 1842. Adams MSS.

[68] Adams MSS.

Resolved: that John Quincy Adams is a "purged man," purged before his country and before the world, that he "shall be expelled from the House of Representatives and drumd through the streets of Washington." [69] "You are perfectly insane and should apply for admission to the Lunatic Asylum. You have cost the Government more than half your state is worth. You are a curse to the Whig Party and to the nation." [70] "Ages hence your name will be pronounced with curses and jeers. . . . 'Oh, for a whip in every hand to lash the rascal through the land.'" [71] ". . . be prepared for you know not the hour when we will have your head upon a pole. . . ." [72]

But again—as when the slave-drivers had threatened to murder Adams because he had frustrated the annexation of Texas—for every irresponsible expression of Southern abuse and threat of assassination there came, and continued to come in the years that followed, hundreds of letters with heartfelt thanks from religious men and women and humanitarian societies all over the North to the brave old man who had successfully confronted the slave power, and prayers that his life might be spared to carry forward the fight for freedom. His mail swelled with requests for copies of his speech of defense, with odes in his praise, with quotations from the Bible supporting his stand. Expressions such as the following fortified his spirit:

"Stand your ground like a man and a Christian, and the North will sustain you." [73] "Go on, Sir. The hearts of free men are with you." [74] "Stand by the Northern man's Rights. The North will defend you, and go to the death for the firm support of their principles." [75] "The voice of the Green Mountain Boys is with you in your late manful defense of the Right of Petition." [76] "You are honored, old man,—the hearts of a hundred thousand voters in Pennsylvania are with you." [77] ". . . the only public man in the land who possesses the union of courage with virtue." [78] "Old Man, there is a reverence round thy name." [79] "God bless thee, and preserve thee!" wrote John Greenleaf Whittier, the poet of the abolitionist crusade, at the

[69] Thomas Merryweather, secretary for a Public Meeting at Charlotte, Virginia, to JQA, January 14, 1842. Adams MSS.

[70] Isaac T. Milne to JQA, Highland County, O., February 15, 1842. Adams MSS.

[71] "Justice" to JQA [no place or date]. Adams MSS.

[72] Solomon Thompson and nine others to JQA, Spartansburgh Court House, S.C., March 3, 1842. Adams MSS.

[73] "Equal Rights" to JQA, New York, January 27, 1842. Adams MSS.

[74] A. Brown to JQA, January 27, 1842. Adams MSS.

[75] "Ten thousand Freemen but not 'Abolitionists Instanter'" to JQA, New York, January 27, 1842. Adams MSS.

[76] G. L. Knapp to JQA, Montpelier, February 1, 1842. Adams MSS.

[77] Isaac Fisher to JQA, Lewiston, Pa., February 15, 1842. Adams MSS.

[78] William Shinn to JQA, Pittsburgh, March 4, 1842. Adams MSS.

[79] R. Patterson to JQA, Pittsburgh, March 14, 1842. Adams MSS.

height of Adams's trial.[80] And Theodore Weld, who returned to his home in New Jersey when the trial was over, sent Adams his constant prayer to God that he might be long preserved as "a terror to all who plot against liberty." [81]

The mass meeting of antislavery people in Faneuil Hall, unmolested and wildly cheering, presided over by William Lloyd Garrison, who only a few years before had been attacked by a mob of "gentlemen of property and standing," was only one evidence of the change in the climate of Boston opinion, inspired in large part by John Quincy Adams's stand in Congress toward slavery and slaveholders.[82] Adams's eloquent defense in the House of Representatives had moved one anti-abolitionist after another throughout the Northern states to write him his new feelings about the threat of slavery to the Union.

"I am no abolitionist yet I am in favor of the emancipation of the colored race whenever it can be done without injury to master or slave." [83] "I am no abolitionist yet I cannot consent to be an apologist for slavery." [84] "The course pursued by the South toward us of the North cannot fail to bring about speedily a crisis. Either the rights guaranteed to us by the Constitution must be restored or the dissolution of the Union is inevitable." [85] "You have awoke a spirit in the North which I trust will prevent them hereafter from unworthily quailing before the slave dictation." [86]

After letting the Old Man Eloquent go, the Whig leaders took revenge on Joshua Giddings when the Ohio Representative brought up the resolutions that Theodore Weld had framed on the case of the *Creole*. These expressed the doctrine that by the Constitution the states had surrendered to the Federal Government all jurisdiction over commerce and navigation on the high seas; Virginia ceased to have jurisdiction over the *Creole* and the persons on board once she left the territorial waters of that state; only the laws of the United States applied, and these did not sanction slavery

[80] John Greenleaf Whittier to JQA, Amesbury [Mass.], January 31, 1842. Adams MSS.

[81] "My special object, in this line, is to say that, if, before the close of the session, or during the recess, or at any time hereafter, in the discharge of those vast responsibilities to human freedom, which press upon you, any services of mine, can at all relieve you from any *drudgery* or lessen any tax upon your invaluable time, or lighten any care or toil of yours, in your almost solitary struggle against the 'principalities and powers' of slaveholding aggression, it will be more than my *joy* to render them, at all times, and *to any extent*." Theodore C. Weld to JQA, Belleville, N.J., March 13, 1842. Adams MSS.

[82] Edmund Quincy to JQA, Dedham, January 31, 1842. Adams MSS.

[83] T. H. Brower to JQA, Troy, N.Y., February 8, 1842. Adams MSS.

[84] William John Hawke to JQA, Rochester, N.Y., February 5, 1842. Adams MSS.

[85] Silas M. Martine, Castine (Me.) to JQA, February 17, 1842. Adams MSS.

[86] J. Whittelsey to JQA, Rochester, N.Y., July 24, 1842. Adams MSS.

or the coastwise slave trade. The people on the *Creole* therefore had resumed their natural freedom.[87]

This may have been plausible law, but it was not yet court law, and it
was anathema to the slaveholding states as an intimation of what was to
come when they should lose their control over Congress. Under pressure
of the previous question they immediately tabled the resolutions by a
voice vote. Botts then brought in a resolution holding Giddings's conduct in presenting these resolutions to be "altogether unwarrantable and
deserving the severe condemnation of the people of this country and of
this House in particular." Adams did his best to get a hearing for Giddings
in his own defense, but the majority, again under the previous question,
quickly jammed through the resolution by a vote of 125 to 69.

Giddings immediately resigned his seat and went home to his district
to stand for re-election. The older man barely mustered voice to say as he
shook the hand of his departing friend: "I hope we shall soon have you
back again." [88] It looked like a successful resurgence of the slave power.
But within six weeks the voters of the Western Reserve returned their
Whig abolitionist by the biggest majority, so it was said, ever given to a
member of the House of Representatives.

5

During all the excitement attending the "trials" of Adams and Giddings
for defying the slave power in the House, Congress was agitated by the
spectacular contest of the Whig Party with their repudiated President,
John Tyler. Tyler's series of vetoes of the bank and tariff bills, presented
under the leadership of Henry Clay as the party program, resulted in the
political prostration of both the party and the renegade President, as well
as Clay himself.

The Compromise Tariff of 1833 was approaching the end of its ten-
year term with graduated decrease of imposts to a twenty-per-cent maxi-
mum. As the rates dropped so did the national revenue, until the government faced bankruptcy. Meanwhile an act of September 4, 1841 had
fortified the Compromise of 1833 by stipulating for distribution among
the several states of the proceeds of future sale of public lands, with a
provision that if the tariff rates were ever raised above twenty per cent
the distribution should cease. In this way the champions of tariff for
revenue only hoped to ensure continuance of the compromise rates after
1842. But Congress in passing the tariff bills of 1842, raising some schedules above the twenty-per-cent level, expressly provided for continuation
of the distribution. President Tyler, who wanted to get hold of the public-
lands money in order to lessen Treasury deficits, vetoed these bills,

[87] *Congressional Globe*, XI, 342. March 21, 1842.
[88] *Memoirs*, XI, 114. March 22, 1842.

thereby leaving the revenue of the country in a still more precarious situation, for it was uncertain whether the twenty-per-cent compromise rates would continue in effect after the ten years without further express legislation.

Adams had supported the principle of distribution as well as protection—reasonable protection. But he looked upon the public lands as a national treasure—God's gift to the American people—to be devoted to projects of internal improvement, physical and moral, and not to be frittered away in meeting current expenses of government. Now that his program of Liberty with Power had gone with the wind, he looked to the states as sponsors of education and improvement, to be paid for out of the proceeds of distribution. He also had in mind the Smithsonian Institution, to be noticed more particularly in a later chapter.[89] At his instance Congress had attached a clause to the act of September 4, 1841 withholding from distribution to any defaulting state an amount to cover defaulted interest on its bonds held by the Federal Government; this was to protect the funds of the Smithson bequest "for the increase and diffusion of knowledge among men," which had been invested in Arkansas bonds and other shaky state stocks. If only because of this provision for the better security of that national trust of the Smithson fund he disapproved Tyler's veto of the tariff bill. But most of all he resented the "Acting President's" unprecedented use of his office to defy steadily a majority of Congress with his veto power, thereby assuming in effect for the Executive an inordinate share in the legislative process. It was Adams, triumphant after his recent trial for censure, who moved a resolution that Tyler's most recent veto, returning to Congress the tariff bill of August 5, 1842, be referred to a select committee of thirteen with instructions to report on it.

The House immediately voted the resolution, and Speaker John White appointed Adams chairman. He brought in the majority report, a blistering indictment of Tyler's alleged abuse of the veto power, accompanied by a proposed amendment to the Constitution which would have practically abolished that power by giving Congress authority to override the Chief Executive by a bare majority rather than a two-thirds majority of each house.

"The public lands are the noble and inappreciable inheritance of the whole nation . . ." Adams declared in this Report. "To appropriate the proceeds of sales to defray the ordinary expenses of Government is to waste and destroy the property . . . held by Congress in trust. . . . The whole legislative power of the Union," continued the Report, "has been for the last fifteen months, with regard to the action of Congress upon measures of vital importance, in a state of suspended animation, strangled by the five times repeated stricture of the Executive cord. . . . The

[89] See Chapter XXIII.

power of Congress to enact laws essential to the welfare of the people has been struck with apoplexy by the Executive hand." [90]

Adams's Report openly pointed to the possibility of impeachment of Tyler for depriving the people of self-government, but recognized that the House might not be ready to follow this suggestion.[91]

The Whigs could not command the two-thirds majority necessary to submit such a constitutional amendment to the states.[92] Finally Congress passed the tariff of 1842, raising some schedules above twenty per cent in the direction of protection, without continuing distribution. Adams voted against the bill, not because it raised the tariff protectively, but because it killed distribution. So far as the tariff feature was concerned he found the act acceptable enough. Actually the schedules were not much different from those of the Adams Tariff of 1832. Whether because of the new tariff or coincidentally with it, the economy of the country began to pick up following the mad fiscal antics of Jacksonian Democracy and the prostrating depression of 1837–42.[93]

Tyler won his point, the solvency of the Treasury was assured, the Whig Party was left badly compromised, while the Democrats girded for the election of 1844 with a determination to write off the new protection when they should come again into power.

Clay seemed to have given up, at least for the time being, and left the fight to Adams. Upon the defeat of his Whig program by Tyler's vetoes he had resigned his seat in the Senate (March 31, 1842) and gone home to Kentucky. "Looking back upon the gloomy state of things, now existing in Washington," he wrote to Adams from Ashland, "my hopes concentrate more upon you than on any other man. In the dispensations of an all wise Providence it has hitherto so happened in our Country, that, upon every great emergency, some man appeared who was adequate to the service of conducting us in safety through the impending danger. Upon the present occasion that noble office is yours." [94]

Adams did not raise the banner that Clay would have thrust into his hands in this moment of despair. At seventy-four he was at last too old. His Presidential gyroscope had run down. He knew that the Whigs would not adopt his antislavery views and leadership. He declined invitations,

---

[90] H. R. Report No. 998, 27th Congress, 2d Session, "Respecting the Veto on the Tariff."

[91] "The majority of the committee believe," said the Report, "that the case has occurred, in the annals of our Union, contemplated by the founders of the Constitution by the grant to the House of Representatives of the power to impeach the President of the United States; but they are aware that the resort to that expedient might, in the present condition of public affairs, prove abortive." See Leonard B. White: *The Jacksonians: a Study in Administrative History, 1829–1861* (New York, 1954), pp. 28–33.

[92] Ames: *Proposed Amendments to the Constitution,* pp. 131–3, 295.

[93] Stanwood: *American Tariff Controversies,* II, 1–37.

[94] Henry Clay to JQA, Ashland, July 24, 1842. Adams MSS.

prompted by Clay, to address huge Whig political meetings and barbe-
cues in the West. "I am aware it would no longer become me to take the
lead in the councils of the Nation," he replied cordially to Clay, stressing
their old policy of trying to promote the general welfare of the Union by
application of its resources to the improvement of its condition, physical,
moral, intellectual, and political: "Internal improvements," he mournfully
recalled, "was at once my conscience and my treasure." [95]

The containment of slavery had more lately become his conscience and
his crusade. From now on he stuck to his task of resisting, from his seat
in the House of Representatives, the expansion of the slave power, of
holding the way open for ultimate emancipation of all the slaves in this
Union.

6

When Adams got home from Washington at the end of that trying
summer of 1842 his constituents expressed their thanks in a grand reception. It was the last time that he could appear before them as Representative of the Twelfth Congressional District, for Massachusetts had been
redistricted following the census of 1840. A great procession of citizens
formed in Weymouth and marched to the church in Braintree village,
crowding every nook and corner of the old meeting-house of Adams's
boyhood. Around and about the pulpit appeared great white banners
with inscriptions. One above it read: "Let there be light!" On one side:
"Shame on a nation that fosters and sustains an institution which dares
assail and would destroy the sacred right of petition." On the other:
"Welcome, defender of the right of petition."

Everybody rose as old John Quincy Adams entered and walked up
front to take his seat behind the pulpit. After a prayer by the pastor, Mr.
Perkins, the president of the reception committee, Nathaniel M. Davis of
Plymouth, referred to Adams's valiant role in the struggle against the
annexation of Texas and in defense of the right of petition under the Constitution.[96] "Let us not suffer that Union," he said on behalf of the gathering, "to become the instrument by which slavery is to be perpetuated, at
the expense of the rights and interests of the North." He reviewed the
half-century of Adams's services to his country after those of his illustrious father: as diplomatist, as Secretary of State, as President. As he sat
there in front of his friends and neighbors, the honored townsman's heart
must have swelled, despite his self-deprecation,[97] at the apotheosis: "Your
proudest honors are your last. Advancing years have but advanced your
usefulness and fame. The course of your life is like that of the unclouded
sun—bright in its dawn—splendid at the meridian—going down in glory!"

[95] JQA to Henry Clay, Quincy, September 30, 1842. Adams MSS.

[96] "They were intended in kindness; but in fulsome praise I can take no pleasure,
and it always covers me with humiliation." *Memoirs*, XI, 252. September 17, 1842.

[97] *Memoirs*, XI, 252.

For three hours and a half the people listened without a moment's flagging of attention, as their Representative justified his long contest with the slave power. A large part of the discourse was devoted to an explanation of why he voted against the tariff of 1842 with its slightly increased protection over the final rates of the Compromise Tariff of 1833: it was because of the incongruous rider that stopped the distribution to the states of the proceeds from sales of public lands and turned them into the federal Treasury, thus depriving Massachusetts of a valuable revenue that could be used for public improvements of all kinds. With the new tariff itself he professed to be tolerably satisfied as at least a measure of protection to manufacturing interests.

"Among the animadversions upon my public conduct . . ." he declared toward the close of his indictment of the slavocracy, "is the charge that . . . I have manifested a harsh and acrimonious temper and have used violent and abusive language." Admitting that perhaps there might be some foundation for it, he asked his friends, or any impartial person, to consider the virulence and rancor of his adversaries whom he had to meet face to face in Congress. These men had nothing against him personally, he declared; avowedly they wanted, like Thomas F. Marshall, to put him down *in order to remove him from the councils of the nation,* to silence the cause of freedom for which he spoke, and thus to establish a parliamentary terror to browbeat all other representatives from the free states who might speak against slavery and the slave power in this Union.

When applause subsided at the end of the long harangue, the audience adopted by acclamation a series of resolutions: upholding their aged representative's conduct in thwarting the annexation of Texas, and in watchful defense of their constitutional rights; condemning the attempt to censure and degrade him; extolling his masterly defense; and congratulating him upon his victorious and complete triumph over his enemies. Then they rose and sang an ode specially written for the ceremony by the Reverend Mr. John Pierpont, minister of Hollis Street Church, Boston, to the tune of "My Country, 'Tis of Thee":

> Time shall touch the page
> That tells how Quincy's sage
> Has dared to live. . . .[98]

There was no doubt that Adams's own constituents were solidly, even affectionately, behind him in the great sectional contest that was developing over slavery. Not only the Plymouth district but all Massachusetts, all New England, Boston itself, were recovering their respect and admiration

[98] The ceremonies are described and Adams's speech is printed, revised by himself after delivery from outline heads, in: *Address of John Quincy Adams to his Constituents of the Twelfth Congressional District,* at Braintree, September 17, 1842 (Boston: J. H. Eastman, Printer; 1842). Reported originally in the *Boston Atlas,* XI, No. 69. September 20, 1842. See also *Memoirs,* XI, 251–3.

for the old crusader from Quincy. Even Harrison Gray Otis, meeting Adams on the street the previous November, had invited him to Thanksgiving dinner! To be sure, it was late in the season, and the ex-President had already accepted an invitation to dine with Peter Chardon Brooks and his family,[99] but it was a notable gesture, an accolade from the most proper Bostonian, leading survivor of New England Federalism, guiding spirit of the Thirteen Confederates of 1829.

Strictly speaking, Adams ceased to be the representative of Plymouth after 1842, though it may be permissible to continue to refer to him as the Plymouth member. It was a new district, the Eighth Congressional, refashioned from fewer Plymouth County towns and more of Norfolk, nearer Boston, that elected him to the Twenty-eighth Congress in November 1842. This time he accepted the Whig nomination, declaring that his heart was with the party, and that the welfare of the country depended upon their harmony.[100] Even so he did not consider himself a party man.[101] He declined, on one pretext or another, to attend any Whig dinners or local assemblies, or any political meetings of any kind, even a local rally in Quincy on the eve of election. He did make a statement directed to the Irish-Americans who had become an appreciable element in his new district. What candidate for public office in eastern Massachusetts has ever failed to do so when necessary? "With regard to the relations between Great Britain and Ireland," declared the author of *Dermot MacMorrogh,* the epic poem on the struggle for Irish freedom in the twelfth century, "my sympathies have always been in favour of the Irish people, and are so still." [102]

This politician's appeal to the recent "alien infusion" in Massachusetts

[99] Diary, November 24, 1841.

[100] JQA to Hon. Thomas Kinnicutt, Boston. Quincy, September 12, 1842. Adams MSS.

[101] "Were I permitted to select a name for the party to which I should wish to belong, it would be that of Constitutionalist; meaning thereby faithful adhesion to the two Constitutions, of the United States and of the Commonwealth [of Massachusetts]. . . . But after and above all, let us never forget, in the most fervent heat of our party conflicts, that there is a *cause,* embracing and transcending all others— . . . the cause of *our Country.*" John Quincy Adams: *The Social Compact, Exemplified in the Constitution of the Commonwealth of Massachusetts; with Remarks on the Theories of Divine Right of Hobbes and of Filmer, and the Counter Theories of Sidney, Locke, Montesquieu, and Rousseau, concerning the Origin and Nature of Government: A Lecture, delivered before the Franklin Lyceum, at Providence, R.I., November 25, 1842* (Providence: Knowles and Vose, Printers; 1842).

[102] JQA to John A. Green, Quincy, November 7, 1842. Adams MSS.

In declining on grounds of ill health and recent domestic affliction (death of his grandson, Arthur, son of Charles Francis and Abigail Brooks Adams) to attend a St. Patrick's Day dinner in Washington in 1846, Adams sent his good wishes to the chairman in the shape of a couplet from his *Dermot MacMorrogh:* "Soon, soon may dawn the day as dawn it must/When Erin's falchion shall be Erin's trust."

JQA to E. Robinson *et al.,* at Coleman's Hotel, Washington, March 16, 1846. Adams MSS.

may have meant all the difference between victory and defeat, for he won by only three or four hundred votes over Ezra Wilkinson of Dedham, and his own town of Quincy went against him by three votes.[103] The state elections that year left the Whigs overwhelmed and the Democracy altogether in the ascendant,[104] in Massachusetts and in the nation. Consequently when the Twenty-eighth Congress convened in December 1843, Adams lost his chairmanship of the committee on foreign affairs.

7

Under the impulse of his spectacular victory in the Twenty-seventh Congress, and with his own district and the State of Massachusetts behind him on the slavery question, Adams now felt free to encourage instead of discouraging abolitionist petitions. In the lame-duck session that began in December 1842 the Whig antislavery insurgents issued a signed appeal to the nation to send in petitions and more petitions to pile up against the Gag Rule, clearing them through Abolition House. They would keep the fundamental issue alive as the antislavery forces consolidated their position and extended their influence. When the names of the signers of the appeal were printed, that of John Quincy Adams led all the rest.[105]

In 1843 the legislature of Massachusetts passed a resolution drafted by Charles Francis Adams which his father introduced into the House of Representatives: to amend the Constitution by doing away with the right of slaveholding states to count every five slaves as equal to three white men in establishing representation in the lower house of Congress.[106] In his early years as Senator he had supported a similar amendment which his colleague Timothy Pickering had brought forward, also under instructions from the Massachusetts legislature.[107] All his life he had chafed against this provision, "that fatal drop of Prussic acid in the Constitution of the United States," which gave the South such an over-representation in Congress because of its human chattels, which enabled the slave power to keep its grip on the nation.[108] After a long and acrimonious disputation—"the most memorable debate ever entertained in the House," Adams thought at the moment [109]—the House buried the proposal in a select committee under his own chairmanship but carefully packed

---

[103] Charles Francis Adams [Jr.]: *Three Episodes of Massachusetts History* (New York, 1903), II, Chapter XXI, "The Alien Infusion."

[104] *Memoirs*, XI, 268–9.

[105] Barnes: *Antislavery Impulse*, p. 195.

[106] *Acts and Resolves of Massachusetts*, 1843, p. 79.

[107] Vol. I, 126.

[108] JQA to William H. Seward, Auburn, N.Y. Washington, May 10, 1844. Seward had written, May 4, 1844: "I regard this Report [of the minority, on the Massachusetts Resolves] as the crown of your fame." Adams MSS.

[109] *Memoirs*, XI, 455, 495, 511. *Congressional Globe*, XIII, 62–6, 179–80, 194–6, 229.

so as to bring in a majority report against the amendment.[110] The House then adopted the report 156 to 13 and discharged the committee.[111] Three times in the next year, 1844, the House refused to receive such a resolution as repeatedly presented from the State of Massachusetts. Southern Senators stigmatized it as the "Hartford Convention Amendment" and refused to print the resolutions.[112] The "federal ratio" remained firmly implanted in the Constitution.

Such a constitutional amendment could not count on the necessary two-thirds majority of both houses of Congress, much less the required three-fourths of the states of the Union. It was otherwise with the Gag Rule. That restriction rested on a simple majority of the House of Representatives. At the second session of the Twenty-eighth Congress, Adams introduced a resolution to rescind the 25th Standing Rule (as the Gag Rule was then numbered). The House adopted it that same day, by a vote of 105 to 80. The great battle for the freedom of petition and of debate in Congress was over. "The antislavery impulse had consolidated its victory." [113] It was a turning-point in American history, from slavery toward freedom.

"Blessed, ever blessed be the name of God," John Quincy Adams wrote that night in his Diary.[114]

In South Carolina the state senate declared that the action of the House of Representatives in Washington was a "flagrant outrage" upon Southern rights, and that Congress had no right to legislate upon the slave question: "such legislation would in fact be a dissolution of the Union." [115]

Adams's mail swelled with scores of communications from friends of freedom all over the North—individuals and organizations—congratulating him on his great victory and extolling his crusade. During the long struggle against the Gag the firm of Julius Pratt and Company of Meriden, Connecticut, through the courtesy of Henry L. Ellsworth, United States

---

[110] JQA to CFA, Washington, January 15, 1844. Adams MSS. For the majority report see 28th Cong., 1st Sess., H. Rept. No. 404.

[111] Adams's minority report was privately printed: *Minority Report on the Resolutions of the Legislature of Massachusetts of March 23, 1844* . . . (Washington, 1844).

[112] Herman V. Ames: *The Proposed Amendments to the Constitution of the United States during the First Century of its History* (*Annual Report 1896 AHA*, II), pp. 45–9.

[113] Barnes: *Antislavery Impulse*, p. 193.

[114] *Memoirs*, XII, 116.

A pleasing by-product of repeal of the Gag Rule by the House of Representatives was the resolves of the two houses of the legislature of the State of Ohio expunging a vote of censure on Adams passed in February 1842. See R. F. Paine to JQA, Columbus, O., February 21, 1845, and JQA's long answer of March 22, 1845. Also JQA to Hon. Benjamin S. Cowen, Columbus, O. Washington, January 3, 1845. Adams MSS.

[115] Wiltse: *Calhoun, Sectionalist*, p. 195.

Commissioner of Patents, had presented the ex-President with an ivory cane tipped with silver, an eagle inlaid in gold on the top, bearing a scroll and the motto: "Right of Petition Triumphant." On a gold ring immediately below the pommel were the words: "To John Quincy Adams," followed by the familiar quotation from Horace: *"Justum et tenacem propositi virum."* The donors requested that when the Gag Rule should be rescinded he would add to the motto the date of the act. Adams deposited the cane in the Patent Office awaiting that day. In March 1845 Ellsworth sent the present to F Street to have the date added: December 3, 1844. The veteran legislator obeyed the behest with pardonable pride and returned the cane to remain in the Patent Office until his death. In his will he declared his desire that this memento should be still kept there as before. His son and executor, Charles Francis Adams, would have the exquisite pleasure of conveying an official copy of this proud bequest to his father's old political opponent, President James K. Polk.[116]

In vindicating the right of petition against the Gag Rule, Adams had won the first clean-cut victory over the slave power in the United States.[117] He had won it by keeping the newly formed abolitionist front in Congress directed to the inalienable rights of man as proclaimed in the Declaration of Independence and embedded (at least for white men and women) in the Constitution of the United States, rather than to the abolition of slavery and the slave trade in the District of Columbia and the territories of the United States. That was the only practical course then possible. Adams now considered himself the leader of the antislavery movement,[118] even though the abolitionists would not accept him as such because he would not go far enough fast enough. To have pressed further at this time might have provoked secession of the South before bands of steel had bonded the new Northwestern states to the Northeast, and before millions of young men from Massachusetts Bay to the broad Missouri would be ready to lay down their lives to save this one and indivisible Union.

Could the setback to the slave power be retrieved by the annexation of Texas? Could a new combination between the slavery capitalists and Western expansionists be fashioned to take the place of the broken-down alliances between Southern planters and plain Republicans of the North?

[116] For the cane see *Memoirs*, XI, 543; XII, 15, 182. Henry L. Ellsworth to JQA, [Washington] March 26, 1844. JQA to H. L. Ellsworth, Washington, April 23, 1844. Adams MSS.

[117] JQA to R. F. Paine, Esq., Washington, March 22, 1845. Adams MSS.

[118] *Memoirs*, XII, 135.

CHAPTER XXI
Tyler and Texas
(1841 – 1845)

The Tiger only "crouches," in order to spring with certainty at the proper time. He must still be watched, with the eye of a Lynx, or he will be in the fold.

BENJAMIN LUNDY TO JOHN QUINCY ADAMS,
DECEMBER 13, 1838 [1]

HISTORIANS of the almost fatal sectional controversy in the United States have attributed the annexation of Texas to a general desire on the part of the South to add more slaveholding territory to the Union in order to balance potential free states north of the Missouri Compromise line with the certainty of at least an equal number of new slave states and thus protect itself against the growing antislavery impulse in the Union and throughout the civilized world. That many Southern leaders—most notably John C. Calhoun—wanted Texas for this reason cannot be successfully denied. That antislavery leaders—most eminently John Quincy Adams—opposed it for the same reason no one would dispute. But how could one seriously contend that if the Republic of Texas had abolished slavery after the achievement of its independence, as British diplomacy preferred, it would not have been added to the Union, and all the sooner? Texas, we repeat, was a major manifestation of the Western Movement, a vast magnetic field for continental expansion dynamically pulling on the whole nation. The slavery issue had served only temporarily to demagnetize the field, to postpone annexation.

1

John Tyler, the Virginia state-rights Whig of Democratic principles, sought to gain political luster for his repudiated leadership by making a great national objective out of the Lone Star Republic.[2] In November and

---

[1] Adams MSS.

[2] "I gave you a hint as to the probability of acquiring Texas by treaty. I verily believe it could be done. Could the North be reconciled to it, could anything throw so

December 1841, articles again began to appear in Democratic newspapers favoring the "re-annexation" of that Texas which—so the Democrats kept saying—John Quincy Adams had ceded away to Spain in 1819. A long article in James Watson Webb's _Morning Courier and New York Enquirer_ (December 16, 1841) appealed to abolitionists themselves, as well as to national interests. With Texas under the American flag, the argument ran, United States authorities would be more able and willing to cut off the African slave trade to that state. And slaveholders in Maryland, Virginia, Kentucky, Missouri, and North Carolina would sell so many of their slaves to the Texas market, where they would be happier and better off in that "genial" clime, that these states, finally sold out of slaves, would themselves abolish slavery. Thus there might be five new free states out of the Old South to offset five new slave states to be anticipated from the annexation of Texas! Abolitionist friends—Ellis Gray Loring in Boston, and Joshua Leavitt [3] and Seth Gates in Washington—warned Adams that the old project was on foot.[4] The Texan tiger, to use Benjamin Lundy's old metaphor, was again crouching for its spring.

There was little likelihood of a Texan _Anschluss_ as long as Daniel Webster remained Secretary of State. He had voiced in no uncertain terms his unwillingness to do anything that should extend slavery on this continent or add more slaveholding states to the Union.[5] Nevertheless a majority of Tyler's Cabinet seemed to favor annexation, though some feared a Texan treaty might not get the necessary two-thirds majority in the Senate.[6]

There was also the possibility of acquiring Texas by treaty with Mexico as part of a general settlement of that Republic's external debts and obligations. Mexico's borrowings abroad to purchase munitions and supplies during her own revolution against Spain, and the arbitrary actions of her unstable Government since then, had given rise to claims of foreigners for the satisfaction of debts and reparations for despoilments. France had resorted to the bombardment of Fort San Juan de Ulloa, with heavy loss of life, and the occupation of Vera Cruz to force Mexico to pay a cash indemnity of $600,000 and guaranties for the future. Great Britain in the role of mediator between Mexico and France had undertaken a powerful naval demonstration to oblige Mexico to refund a defaulted debt of some $50,000,000 to British bondholders.

---

bright a lustre around us?" John Tyler to Daniel Webster, Secretary of State, Washington, October 11, 1841. Rives: _United States and Mexico, 1821–1848_, I, 505–6, citing _Letters and Times of the Tylers_, II, 126. See also Oliver Perry Chitwood: _John Tyler, Champion of the Old South_ (New York, 1939), pp. 342–66.

[3] Diary, July 20, 1842.

[4] _Memoirs_, XI, 29, 41. November 20, December 18, 1841.

[5] Speech of March 15, 1837, delivered by him at a reception in New York City. _Works of Daniel Webster_ (Boston, 1851), I, 355–6.

[6] Rives: _U.S. and Mexico_, I, 506.

Jackson and his successor had favored similar measures by the United States to secure claims of American citizens. John Quincy Adams had used the petitions of the peace societies to bring the Van Buren Administration to an arbitration.[7] A Mexican-American mixed claims commission, the Prussian Minister to the United States serving as umpire, awarded $2,026,339.68 to American claimants out of a total of $8,542,710.16 presented.[8] But it proved one thing to get the Mexican Government to arbitrate, still another to make it pay the awards, particularly when it seemed not unlikely that the United States and Great Britain might go to war over a complex of controversies of their own. And there were some remaining claims that the Mexicans would not yet even agree to arbitrate. Relations were further complicated by imprisonment of American citizens taken among the Texan expedition captured at Santa Fe (September 1841). Perhaps a treaty could be forced on Mexico that would wipe the slate clean by the annexation of Texas to the United States.

2

Adams was convinced that the design he had attributed to Jackson and Van Buren—to use these lingering issues with Mexico to keep open a running sore in order to breed a war for Texas and slavery—was in the mind of President Tyler. He would have to scotch it again before the world as he had done at the close of Jackson's Administration. An opportunity to do so appeared when Archibald L. Linn, a New York abolitionist, moved in the House to cut down that item in the annual appropriation for civil and diplomatic expenses which paid for the regular mission to Mexico. William Slade supported him. It was not so much the mission that they objected to: it was the individual—Waddy Thompson of South Carolina—appointed to it, and the ulterior object, the annexation of Texas.

Henry Wise, Adams's dashing young adversary from Virginia, rose in Committee of the Whole to defend the appropriation and also the idea of annexing Texas. Annexation, he averred, would be a means of checkmating British policy in North America. Were not the English newspapers openly saying that Britain should make insolvent nations pay their debts with territory: Mexico with California and Texas, and Spain with Cuba? "Let her obtain Cuba, and she will command the Gulf of Mexico and the Mississippi, and nothing will prevent her from making that sea a *mare clausum* to the people of the West. Let her obtain California and establish a naval base there, and she at once controls the whole trade of the Pacific Ocean."

Wise cited the old instructions of President Adams's Secretary of State Henry Clay to Joel Poinsett to purchase Texas up to the Rio Grande—"twice as large a territory as is now included [in that Republic]"—by a treaty that would provide for bringing its inhabitants into the Union

[7] Above, p. 363.   [8] Moore: *International Arbitrations*, II, 1209–32.

with the full privileges of citizens, as in the case of the Louisiana Purchase. If President Adams had thought annexation desirable in 1825 and again in 1827, why did he not think it so now? As for Northern abolitionists, Wise declared, with tongue in cheek, they could not do anything about freeing slaves in Texas so long as it remained foreign country; once it was a part of the Union, they could work on slavery there for all they were worth.

Thousands of volunteers from the great valley of the Mississippi, Wise declared, were ready to go to the aid of Texas if Mexico persisted in attempts to reconquer her. They would speedily conquer all of Mexico. They would then extend the boundaries of slavery to the shores of the Western Ocean. The Virginia planter and slaveholder declaimed against Mexican imprisonment of the American citizens captured near Santa Fe. "I am for sending a Minister to preserve peace," he asserted. "But unless she treats our citizens on an equal footing with those of England [General Santa Anna had released a British subject from captivity], then I am for war and that soon. . . . Let a war come, with France, the United States and Texas on one side, and England and Mexico on the other. I would ask for nothing better.

"The majority of the people of the United States are in favor of annexation," he concluded. "At all events I would risk it with the democracy of the North. . . . Remember the fate of those who opposed the last war."

Charles J. Ingersoll, former National Republican and now a Democrat from Pennsylvania, added his voice to that of the Southern warmongers. He turned spitefully on Great Britain, whose envoy extraordinary, Lord Ashburton, had just arrived in Washington to settle peaceably outstanding issues with the United States. The Philadelphia politician professed to want no war. As if by contrast with his own peaceful feelings he referred to the aggressive attitude of Great Britain on all the points in controversy: the northeast boundary; the invasion of New York (McLeod and the *Caroline* affair); Oregon; her pretensions against American "property" in the case of the *Creole;* her insufferable demands that we should submit our commerce on the great oceans, even our coastwise traffic, to the visit and search of her naval captains—this must be abandoned. War with Britain would not be too bad, he declared, if, alas, it should come. It would rid us of some $200,000,000 of public debts of various states in the Union. Gentlemen reminded us that the British might burn New York; well, we could burn London, five times as big! And think of Canada, of Ireland, even of India, all of which hung to British suzerainty only by the thinnest of threads. We would have the sympathies of France, Prussia, Russia, Sweden, Denmark, every maritime nation in the world—Texas too.

Laughter, records the official reporter, at this point in the record.

Suddenly the House was still. All eyes turned to John Quincy Adams. The silence called upon him with a voice of thunder. He waited a moment to give any other member a chance to take the floor. No one stirred.

Up then rose the Old Man Eloquent. If we did go to war, he observed, the gentleman from Pennsylvania would disarm us in advance, by renouncing our most powerful weapon, the right of visit and search. To take away this right would throw a shield over the entire mass of British commerce.

"I said no such thing . . ." declared Ingersoll, equivocating, "although as usual the gentleman chooses to indulge his passions and play the termagant whenever anything is said that does not happen to suit his own *senile* notions."

John Quincy Adams was now approaching his seventy-fifth birthday. "For a rebuker of a little transient intemperate feeling," he gently admonished, "I think the gentleman himself seems a little excited." They laughed again at Ingersoll, who was already in his sixtieth year.

"That what I said," continued Adams, "and that what I shall yet say is 'senile' I admit; for I am much older than the honorable gentleman and am very conscious of the infirmities which that advanced age has brought upon me. I refer to the gentleman's conscience to decide whether such allusions are made in a moderate and kind temper, or are very likely to restore good feeling if for a moment it has been lost." [9]

The ex-diplomatist proceeded to review the whole historic question of visit and search and the part he had played in it. The gentlemen who had just risen would deny to the United States its most powerful belligerent right at the very time they were uniting to involve us in war with Mexico and Great Britain. But Southern Senators and their Northern middlemen, he suggested, were not really worried about British interference with free Americans on the high seas. What they really wanted was to perpetuate slavery and the slave trade.[10] That is what had animated Minister Andrew Stevenson in his recent remonstrances at the Court of St. James's against interference with slave-traders flying the American flag.[11] That is what had led our Minister to France, Lewis Cass, to protest—on his own personal authority, to be sure—against the principles of the Quintuple Treaty of 1841 (Great Britain, France, Russia, Austria, Prussia), which would have all but codified into international law a mutual right of visit and search for suppression of the African slave trade; and to publish the famous pamphlet that had induced the French Chamber to reject the treaty.[12] For the sake of Southern support these party politicians would

[9] "Oh for restraining grace, for inflexible firmness, for untiring perseverance, for suavity of manner, and for self-control!" *Memoirs*, XI, 51, January 4, 1842.

[10] Vol. I, 409–35.

[11] Hugh G. Soulsby: *The Right of Search and the Slave Trade in Anglo-American Relations 1841–1862* (Johns Hopkins University Studies in Historical and Political Science, LI, No. 2, Baltimore, 1933), pp. 48–77.

[12] St. George L. Sioussat: "Duff Green's 'England and the United States'; with an Introductory Study of American Opposition to the Quintuple Treaty of 1841" (American Antiquarian Society *Proceedings*, New Series, XL, October 1930), pp. 175–276.

protect a nefarious traffic in human beings under the guise of freedom—freedom of the seas!

Adams made fun of Ingersoll's suggested entangling alliance with an ally like France, where the Opposition in the Chambers were urging war with England, not to protect Texas, not to uphold the freedom of the seas, but rather to make an issue by which they could overthrow the July Monarchy of King Louis-Philippe and put the Duke of Orléans on the throne. He professed to have no time to go into that feature of European politics. Someone took him at his word and moved that the Committee of the Whole rise. Others protested: "No! No! Go on! Go on!"

On and on the old man spoke for two solid days. The real purpose of the proposed war, he repeated, was not to collect unpaid awards or unarbitrated claims: it was to annex Texas. He frankly admitted that he himself as Secretary of State had tried to include Texas during the negotiations with Spain, and as President to purchase it from Mexico. *But there had been no slaves or slavery in Texas then.* It would have been added as free territory. He would still welcome it as a free state; but never as a slave territory, to perpetuate slavery in this Union.

Adams had now got to the subject of slavery despite the Gag Rule, still in existence. So far, he said, Congress had no power to meddle with slavery in those states where it existed. "So long as the slave States are able to sustain their institutions without going abroad or calling upon other parts of the Union to aid them or act upon the subject, so long will I consent never to interfere. I have said this, and I will repeat it; but if they come to the free States and say to them you must help us to keep down our slaves, you must aid us in [case of] an insurrection and a civil war, then I say that with that call comes a full and plenary power to this House and to the Senate over the whole subject. It is the war power."

He repeated what he had broadcast to the South ever since 1833: emancipation from slavery could come by martial law. The warning stung the South to the quick.[13]

Finally he turned back to Wise's arguments. As for American citizens captured by Mexico in company with Texan troops, he considered them as he had looked on Arbuthnot and Ambrister, the British subjects who had instigated the Florida Indians to make war on the United States. General Andrew Jackson had court-martialed and executed those individuals in 1818, and Adams as Secretary of State had successfully defended his action vis-à-vis the British Government.[14] He went on to heap ridicule on the member from Accomac and all his big talk about the conquest of Mexico by thousands of brave spirits from the valley of the Mississippi, robbing priests and pillaging churches. "But I am inclined," he suggested as he lowered himself sidewise into his seat, "to consider all this rather as approaching to what is sometimes called rhodomontade, than a thing in the serious contemplation of the gentleman from Virginia; and I look

[13] *Memoirs*, XI, 136. April 15, 1842.   [14] Vol. I, 315–16, 325–8.

forward to the time when, in the records of history, the gentleman's name shall be placed side by side, not with the names of Ghengis Khan or Tamerlane, but with that of a still more glorious conqueror by the name of TOM THUMB."

Roars of laughter rose and recurred long and loud.

The House approved the diplomatic appropriations as budgeted, including those for the mission to Mexico. It also passed by overwhelming votes, before the end of the session, two resolutions introduced by Adams calling upon the President for the diplomatic correspondence with Mexico and Texas over claims and imprisonments.[15] Before Waddy Thompson reached Mexico, that Government had liberated the American citizens. After protracted negotiations he signed a new treaty (January 30, 1843), duly ratified, by which Mexico began payment in five annual installments of the neglected awards of the mixed claims commission. Further negotiations were begun on another treaty to provide for a mixed commission to settle claims still unadjusted.[16]

The thanks of a foreign government, particularly by a provisional executive—not to mention one like General Santa Anna—for supporting its cause in the United States Congress in an issue between that government and the United States, are not necessarily a measure of the justice of that cause. In December 1843 the Mexican Minister in Washington, Don Juan N. Almonte, acting under instructions from his Government, made a formal call on Adams to express officially to "that worthy personage" the gratitude of the Supreme Magistrate for upholding in the public councils at Washington "the cause of Mexico in the Texas Question, in respect to slavery, humanity, and the principles of justice." [17] Adams, an experienced diplomatist, took satisfaction in receiving such expressions in an instance in which he believed his own country to be *wrong* and the foreign country *right*.

For a second time he had single-handed frustrated the annexation of Texas. The abolitionist press distributed Adams's latest Texas speech [18] far and wide. Once more the Texan tiger crouched back in Southern savannas the better to gauge his final spring. Meanwhile Secretary of State Daniel Webster began the famous negotiations with Lord Ashburton, head of the house of Baring, British Minister Plenipotentiary on Special Mission to the United States.

[15] *Congressional Globe*, XI, 745, 751; *Memoirs*, XI, 204–7. July 12–13, 1842.

[16] Rives: *United States and Mexico*, I, 508–10.

[17] Bocanegra to Don Juan N. Almonte, March 18, 1843. Copy in Adams MSS. *Memoirs*, XI, 442. December 2, 1843.

[18] *Mr. Adams's Speech, on War with Great Britain, with the Speeches of Messrs. Wise and Ingersoll, to which it is in Reply* (Boston: Emancipator Office, 32 Washington Street; [1842]).

3

It is difficult for the twentieth-century historian to realize that the United States and Great Britain were on the verge of a third war in 1841. Yet such was the case. A group of issues was heading up which made responsible statesmen on both sides fear the worst.[19] Let us take more note of the five principal disputes that Ingersoll in his burn-London speech had told the House of Representatives could be settled so easily if Great Britain would but accept the American position on all of them.

First and oldest was the boundary question or rather series of boundary controversies stretching along the line described in the treaty of peace and independence from the Bay of Fundy to the Lake of the Woods. Of these the so-called northeast boundary dispute was most serious in 1841. It involved nearly half the State of Maine. British diplomacy had kept alive a historic controversy in the hope of securing an all-British military road from Montreal to the ice-free port of St. John. The forces of both countries confronted each other on the border in an uneasy state of armed truce. Subsidiary disputes had developed at the head of Connecticut River and at the outlet of Lake Champlain. And there was disagreement about a larger tract of territory—one that would prove to be fabulously valuable in the twentieth century—at the head of Lake Superior between that body of water and the Lake of the Woods.[20]

The second controversy was the Oregon Question west of the Rocky Mountains: it had narrowed down to a contest between the United States and Great Britain. According to the terms of the British-American treaty of 1818, signed under Adams's regime as Secretary of State and renewed in 1827 without term during his Presidency, but subject to termination by either party on one year's notice, the whole Oregon country was to be "free and open . . . to the citizens and subjects of the two powers," thus leaving ultimate settlement and sovereignty to the march of time. Here was another potential controversy big with future significance, not yet quite acute.[21]

The third issue was the *Creole* case, already noticed in previous chapters.

Fourth was the question of visit and search of suspected slavers falsely flying the American flag. It was one of the scandals of the civilized world that the Stars and Stripes could be used to protect such an abomination.

[19] "What is more probable," the Duke of Wellington asked the Prime Minister, Sir Robert Peel, in May 1841, "than we shall have a war before we can settle our difficulties with the United States?" Wilbur D. Jones and J. Chal Vinson: "British Preparedness and the Oregon Settlement," *Pacific Historical Review*, XXII (No. 4, November 1953), 354.

[20] Vol. I, 469–81.

[21] Ibid., 468–533.

Fifth in dispute was the celebrated case of the *Caroline* and Alexander McLeod. During the Canadian insurrection of 1837 some sympathizers in New York had prepared a hostile expedition intended to cross in the ship *Caroline* with men and arms into Ontario. The United States authorities did not act promptly to suppress it, and a group of armed Canadians invaded New York, seized the hostile ship, and cut it adrift above Niagara Falls.[22] In the mêlée a citizen of New York named Durfee was killed. Later one of the boarding party, Alexander McLeod, crossed over to New York, was arrested and indicted for the murder of Durfee, and his trial was set for the fourth Monday in March 1842. The British Government formally protested. Explaining that McLeod was acting under the Queen's orders, it assumed full responsibility for the incident and demanded his release. Lord Palmerston let it be known to Minister Andrew Stevenson that if the British subject McLeod were convicted *and executed,* war would follow.[23]

Fortunately a change of governments brought in more irenic statesmen in both the United States and Great Britain. Webster had taken over the Department of State from the aggressive Georgian John Forsyth; the conciliatory Lord Aberdeen relieved the truculent Palmerston as Secretary for Foreign Affairs. Both believed in peace and fair play.

For more reasons than one Webster strove for peace with Britain. In the first place he was a broad-minded statesman who, like John Quincy Adams, saw nothing but disaster in an Anglo-American conflict. In the second place there were less high-minded considerations: Webster as a lawyer had been receiving, while serving in the United States Senate, a steady retainer from the London banking firm of Baring Brothers, who had heavy investments in the United States as well as in Mexico. Senator Webster, also under retainer from the Bank of the United States, had been a powerful defender of sound banking, sound money, and Anglo-American amity.

Very astutely for the cause of peace and fair play, Lord Aberdeen sent Alexander Baring, Lord Ashburton, to Washington to settle Anglo-American difficulties before they drifted into war. It was an ideal appointment for the purpose. Ashburton had an American wife, had long been engaged in land speculations in southern Maine (between the St. Croix and Penobscot Rivers), and knew the disputed northern area from his youth, by canoe and portage.[24] As head of the house of Baring he had close and

---

[22] Actually it hit a rock and sank before it reached the Falls.

[23] C. A. Duniway: "Daniel Webster," *American Secretaries of State and Their Diplomacy,* V, 15–17.

[24] This appears in a description of the Baring Papers in a paper read by Frederick S. Allis, Jr., to the Colonial Society of Massachusetts, December 17, 1953. See also typescript "Calendar of the Letters of Alexander Baring, 1795–1801," prepared for the Library of Congress by Ruth Anna Fisher, 1954. LC.

extensive trans-Atlantic connections with the United States—and with Daniel Webster.[25] If anybody had a stake in peace, and an instrument for achieving it, it was Lord Ashburton.

Adams looked hopefully upon the special British mission. His bouts with British foreign policy in the days of Castlereagh and Canning had made him none the less an exponent of Anglo-American friendship. To be sure, as Secretary of State and President, he had insisted on an equality of temper and exchange in diplomatic encounter that had been a bit difficult for British diplomats to get used to, but he had long since accommodated his inveteracy on visit and search to humanitarian sentiment in Britain and the United States which demanded suppression of the slave trade. Emancipation of slaves in the British colonies—at a cost of $100,000,000 (£20,000,000)—had impressed Adams greatly. He had come to view the British people, if not their actual Government, as leaders of the antislavery movement throughout the world, even as he felt himself to be leader of the American people against expansion of slavery in the United States.

Only in the matter of national boundaries would Adams have advised a determined stand on the several issues that threatened war. It seemed to him that our boundaries tended to contract in the north and east and expand toward the southwest, that the various governments of the United States since his Administration had been too willing to make territorial concessions to Great Britain along the northern frontier as if in return for a free hand in the direction of Texas and Mexico.

Adams's sympathies for Great Britain soon manifested themselves. During the special session of 1841 he made an impromptu speech in the House, on September 4, defending the British position on McLeod. We had one major issue on our hands with Great Britain, he reminded his colleagues, in which we were right: the northeast boundary. How inept it would be to involve that issue in another controversy in which we were wrong![26]

The next conspicuous pro-British expression was a lecture that John Quincy Adams, LL.D. (New Jersey College, 1806), delivered to the Massachusetts Historical Society on November 22, 1841, after the outbreak of the "Opium War" between Great Britain and China. To many people it seemed strangely incongruous and even hypocritical that a great power which worked for suppression of the traffic in slaves should be fighting a war to enslave the Chinese people to the opium habit for the profit of its East Indian traders. Not so to Adams. The true ground for the war, he concluded after assiduous study of American consular corre-

[25] Ralph W. Hidy depicted The House of Baring in American Trade and Finance . . . (Harvard University Press, 1949). See pp. 100, 283–4, 293, 316, 320–1, 327, 423.

[26] Speech of Mr. John Quincy Adams on the case of Alexander McLeod delivered in the House of Representatives, September 4, 1841 (Washington: Gales and Seaton; 1841). Memoirs, XI, 4–5.

spondence and British blue books, was the assertion of Chinese superiority over foreign subjects and their governments that called upon Englishmen or Americans to submit their lives and property unreservedly to an insufferable Oriental despotism. It was time, he told the learned members, that this enormous outrage upon the rights of human nature and upon the first principle of nations should cease: "The cause of the war is the *kotow!*"

Such a point of view rather shocked the select audience. Adams's friend Dr. John G. Palfrey, editor of the *North American Review,* wouldn't even print the lecture.[27]

One of those who shared and expressed the popular feeling against Britain was Caleb Cushing. He had been chairman of the committee on foreign affairs during the special session of 1841 until supplanted by Adams in December. Cushing, a Whig who was now going over to Tyler politically, intimated that appointment of a new chairman looked like hostility to himself. Adams frankly told his Newburyport colleague that he would have no confidence in him as chairman of the committee because of his rancorous hostility to England, "not only with reference to the Northeastern Boundary question, but upon numerous other points, on which I believe England more sinned against then sinning." [28]

After accepting his new committee assignment Adams had a three-hour conference with Webster at the Department of State and reviewed the whole field of foreign problems. He found that he and the Secretary agreed fully at least on the right of search.

"My own disposition with regard to all questions in negotiation with Great Britain," Adams vouchsafed, "is essentially pacific. I am especially averse to everything irritating in form or offensive in language, and against everything of war tendency, *excepting the Boundary question,* upon which we should be inflexible."

It was fair warning that the man who had worsted Webster in Congress on the French Question in 1836 might oppose any boundary concession to Great Britain. To this point Webster made no reply.

"It is my most earnest desire," added the new committee chairman, "to move in perfect harmony with the Executive Administration and to give to its measures my cordial support."

To this "overture" Webster returned only "cold-hearted thanks."

Adams the diarist noted that Webster's great difficulties were not in

[27] *Memoirs,* XI, 31. The lecture was published in full (including some passages Adams had omitted in delivering it) in the Boston *Quarto Notions,* I, No. 9, December 4, 1841, to whose editors the author had loaned it merely for the purpose of making short abstracts for publication. The manuscript lay in Palfrey's possession, unused by him, until his death. In 1910 his daughter found it and gave it to Charles Francis Adams, Jr., who printed it in full, with explanatory notes of its provenance, under the running head, "J. Q. Adams and the Opium War," in MHS *Proceedings,* XLIII (February 1010), 295–325.

[28] *Memoirs,* XI, 36. December 9, 1841.

foreign affairs, or anything in the Department: "Money, public and private, is the insuperable obstacle to his successful progress." [29]

Webster made use of public money, out of the secret-service contingent fund, to prepare opinion in the State of Maine to yield title to the disputed territory in a new "conventional line"—that is, treaty line—in return for a cash indemnity of $150,000 from the Federal Government for the territory thus given up in the interest of peaceful settlement.[30] It has already been suggested that Webster as Secretary of State connived at use of other money, British money from Lord Ashburton—£2,998 1s., to be exact—in the hands of Professor Jared Sparks, to exhibit spurious maps to the Maine legislature to convince it of the reasonableness of the new treaty line in the northeast (Sparks presumably also collected expense money from the United States Government). For the sake of peace Webster yielded an area of 3,207,680 acres that subsequent historical and cartographical research, in sources even then not unavailable, has shown to have been perfectly titled American territory.[31]

Once agreed on a new boundary for Maine, Webster and Ashburton quickly compromised the subsidiary boundary questions along the Canadian frontier. The McLeod case vanished when a New York jury acquitted the defendant on a not very plausible alibi. (In case of a conviction Governor Seward had secretly pledged to Webster that a pardon would be forthcoming.[32]) The two negotiators disposed of the *Caroline* affair by an exchange of notes. In a classic statement Webster conceded the British Government could justify armed intervention by showing "a necessity for self-defense, instant, overwhelming, leaving no choice of means, no moment for deliberation." Lord Ashburton replied that this had been exactly the case, but softly regretted that some explanation or apology had not been made.

---

[29] *Memoirs,* XI, 47–8. December 31, 1841.

[30] Webster's principal agent in this domestic propaganda was Francis O. J. Smith of Portland, Me., who credited himself with proposing to Webster the solution by a new conventional boundary to be agreed on independently of past diplomatic disputations. See H. Rept. 684, 29th Cong., 1st Sess., June 9, 1846. *Journal of the House of Representatives,* 29th Cong., 1st Sess., pp. 649–54, 690–9. April 9, 20, 1846.

These congressional documents furnish such of the testimony as was made public in the report of a congressional committee inquiring into the alleged misappropriation of public funds by Daniel Webster. The testimony of ex-President Tyler before the committee played a major part in exonerating Webster from charges made by Charles J. Ingersoll.

[31] Vol. I, Chapter XXIII. In a more recent review of "Lord Ashburton and the Maine Boundary Negotiations," *MVHR,* XL (No. 3, December 1953), 427–90, Wilbur Devereux Jones, taking his cue principally from the Aberdeen Papers, feels that to the British the Webster-Ashburton Treaty boundary seemed a considerable concession on their part.

[32] Duniway, op. cit., V, 16. Webster was ready to have the case appealed to the federal courts if Seward did not grant a pardon in the contingency of McLeod's conviction by the New York courts.

As to the *Creole*, Webster contended that international law should protect persons and "property" on ships in distress entering foreign ports. To satisfy the South he tried to secure a more explicit provision to cover slave mutineers under a treaty formula of extradition for "mutiny on board ship." Here Ashburton held back, suggesting that this question be referred to London for settlement. Meanwhile he took it upon himself personally to give assurances that there would be "no officious interference with American vessels driven by accident or violence" into British colonial ports near the southern coast of the United States. Webster thereupon agreed to postpone settlement of the *Creole* case.[33]

It remained to do something about the slave trade. Webster did not dare acknowledge a reciprocal right of visit and search for fear that Southern Senators would block the treaty, as they had done with John Quincy Adams in 1824.[34] He contented himself with a unilateral statement, which Ashburton merely acknowledged politely: "In every *regularly documented* [35] American merchant ship the crew who navigate it will find their protection in the flag which is over them." It was at once a declaration, which could not but appeal to Adams, against the traditionally hateful British practice of impressment, and at the same time a warning to England that might soothe Southern sensitivity about the interstate coastal slave trade. But it was also necessary to mollify Northern feeling that not enough was being done by the United States for the suppression at least of the overseas traffic in human beings. So the two parties agreed jointly to remonstrate with other powers that allowed the importation of slaves into their dominions. They provided for British and American cruising squadrons on the African coast, separately commanded but acting in co-operation against the outlawed trade. Whether they would really work together depended on what people were in power in Washington. Actually the Democratic Administrations of Polk, Pierce, and Buchanan would reef their sails in suppressing the shameful traffic.

On the Oregon Question the plenipotentiaries of 1842 reached no agreement, though they talked it over, as will be seen in the following chapter.

The Webster-Ashburton Treaty, with accompanying exchanges and declarations, may not have been an ingenuous piece of diplomacy or of domestic politics, but it was certainly a consummately clever device for securing Anglo-American peace. The antislavery element in the North supported it because it meant peace with England, and England was the hope of the abolitionists. If the treaty did not gain all that the South wanted, neither did it abandon any Southern interest. Calhoun upheld the settlement in the Senate with an able speech that helped pile up a

[33] It was finally referred to the Anglo-American mixed-claims commission set up by the convention of 1853, the umpire of which awarded $110,330 on behalf of the *Creole* claimants.

[34] Vol. I, 433–5.

[35] Italics inserted.

majority of 39 to 9 in advising and consenting to ratification. Finally it was a triumph for the ways and means of British diplomacy.

Despite the boundary concession, Adams did not say anything against the treaty. He voted for the necessary appropriations to carry out its provisions.[36] He wanted peace with Britain as much as anybody. Of course he did not know about the Secretary of State's skullduggery with Lord Ashburton and Jared Sparks.

4

Ratification of the Webster-Ashburton Treaty, by removing the danger of war between the United States and Great Britain, reopened to the Tyler Administration a vista across the immense plains of Texas to the Rio Grande. The President immediately began to send up trial balloons. One that confirmed the suspicions of Adams and his abolitionist friends was a letter from Tyler's close Virginia friend and spokesman in the House of Representatives, Thomas W. Gilmer, published in Tyler's new Washington organ, the *Madisonian,* January 23, 1843. Gilmer advanced what was to be a standard Southern argument for the annexation of Texas: the United States must have that country before British diplomacy abolished slavery there and acquired an overweening influence. Then came resolutions of the states of Mississippi and Alabama in favor of annexation, and of Massachusetts, Connecticut, Vermont, Ohio, and sundry private groups against it.

Behind the scenes Andrew Jackson was still working for annexation. In a letter, reserved for future timely publication, to Aaron Venable Brown, Polk's former law partner in Nashville, Tennessee, and now a Democratic whip in Congress, the Old Hero approved Gilmer's letter and declared that the acquisition of Texas was necessary to protect the western flank of New Orleans in case of another war with Great Britain. It had been carelessly abandoned to Spain, he asserted, in the negotiation (by John Quincy Adams) at Washington in 1818–19, just as the American Minister in Madrid, George W. Erving, was laying the foundations of a treaty to secure our boundary at the Rio Grande.[37] Hence the need for "re-annexing" Texas!

Jackson's memory was playing him a mean trick in his old age. There was, of course, nothing to his charge of carelessness on Adams's part. As

---

[36] It was necessary to appropriate money to pay the salaries of American members of joint commissions to mark the boundary; and there was also a gratuitous provision by which the United States Government agreed to indemnify the states of Maine and Massachusetts with $150,000 each for any loss of territory they might have suffered. (Upon the separation of Maine from Massachusetts, the latter state had reserved title to certain tracts of land in the area disputed by Great Britain and the United States.)

[37] Jackson to Aaron V. Brown, Hermitage, February 9, 12, 1843. This letter was not printed until a year later in the *Richmond Enquirer* of March 22, 1844. A draft in Jackson's spelling is in *Correspondence of Jackson,* VI, 201–2. See Wiltse: *Calhoun, Sectionalist,* pp. 150–2, 506.

to Erving's diplomacy in Spain, about all that can be said historically is that, though authorized [38] to accept the line of the Sabine River in return for the cession of the Floridas to the United States, he had never fallen back to that American *sine qua non* but had insisted instead on the more western Colorado of Texas. Thereupon the Spanish Secretary of State had transferred the negotiation to Washington. There Adams held out for a boundary farther to the west in Texas, at first the Rio Grande, then the Colorado, but finally accepted the Sabine [39] at the positive direction of President Monroe. Before he signed the treaty with Spain, Adams, upon Monroe's suggestion, showed the Sabine boundary to General Andrew Jackson on Melish's Map and Jackson without reservation approved it. [40]

Adams in 1843 tried unsuccessfully to block the annexation of Texas by proposing to the committee of foreign affairs of the House that they bring forward his propositions of 1838: [41] (1) a denial of the power of Congress or any department or departments of the Government to annex any foreign *state* or *people*; (2) a declaration that any attempt by act of Congress or by treaty to annex Texas would be a violation of the Constitution, null and void, to which the free states of the Union and their people *ought not* to submit. [42]

Shades of Thomas Jefferson and the Virginia and Kentucky Resolutions! Ghosts of the Hartford Convention! Presence of Harrison Gray Otis, still living, and of John C. Calhoun, Nullifier! Did John Quincy Adams realize how close he was to nullification himself?

Failing in an attempt to put the House of Representatives on record against the constitutionality of annexation, Adams and twelve other antislavery members at the close of that session of Congress, March 3, 1843, signed a public circular of protest to the free states of the Union which he had drafted. They quoted Daniel Webster's statement of 1837 against the expansion of slavery, as if to hold him to his word. They reviewed the history of our relations with Mexico and Texas, citing Wise's speech of January 25–6, 1842 and Gilmer's more recent public letter. The real issue, they declared, as Adams kept telling them, was whether slavery was to be extended or put in the way of ultimate extinction. Texas would be the test. Annexation, they averred, would be contrary to the fundamental purpose of the Union: "to secure the blessings of liberty to ourselves and our posterity." It would be "identical with dissolution" of the Union. [43]

The Massachusetts legislature echoed with a solemn resolve—not approved by the Democratic Governor, Marcus Morton—that the proposi-

[38] Under powers granted by President Madison and never revoked before Erving's recall in 1818.

[39] The present western boundary of the State of Louisiana.

[40] *Memoirs*, IV, 238–9. February 1, 2, 3, 1819. See Vol. I, 332.

[41] Above, p. 368.

[42] *Memoirs*, XI, 330. February 28, 1843.

[43] Wiltse: *Calhoun, Sectionalist*, p. 152, citing *Niles' Register*, LXIV, 173–5.

tion to admit Texas into the Union could be regarded by the people of that commonwealth in no other light than as "dangerous to its continuance in peace, in prosperity, and in the enjoyment of those blessings which it is the object of a free government to secure." [44]

Southern spokesmen had long since threatened that any further legislative check on slavery would mean the break-up of the Union. Now the antislavery leaders in Congress, Adams at their head, were saying that the annexation of Texas as a slave state would be identical with a dissolution of the Union. They would not have accepted an amendment of the Constitution guaranteeing slavery in all parts of the Union any more than the defenders of slavery, Calhoun in their lead, would have accepted an amendment abolishing slavery throughout the United States. The house of the Union was rapidly dividing against itself. Could the national urge for western expansion hold it together North and South, East and West, with a slaveholding Texas balanced by a free-soil Oregon—Oregon, say, only to the Columbia?

Webster, unequivocally committed against annexation of Texas, had finally resigned as Secretary of State (May 8, 1842). Tyler now looked exclusively to his own section for the direction of foreign affairs. Attorney General Hugh S. Legaré of South Carolina served as Secretary ad interim for a month in the interval between the Twenty-seventh (Whig) and Twenty-eighth (Democratic) Congresses, until his death, June 20, 1843. Tyler then moved his Secretary of the Navy, Abel P. Upshur of Virginia, to the Department of State. [45] Upshur thought like Calhoun, and Tyler too, on Texas and on Oregon and on commercial reciprocity with England; he had corresponded freely with the President and other friends of annexation. [46] There was no doubt that Upshur like Tyler would favor the annexation of Texas, but it was doubtful whether he would stand firm for Oregon at least to 49° N. Lat., as Adams had stood for that boundary throughout his diplomatic career.

5

When the weary Adams returned to Quincy for the summer of 1843, he found Lewis Tappan and Stephen P. Andrews on his doorstep. Andrews was a native of Massachusetts who had emigrated to Texas and had been mobbed there for favoring the abolition of slavery. These resolute friends of human freedom were about to leave Boston to attend the World Antislavery Convention in London. They wanted Adams's opin-

[44] *Acts and Resolves of Massachusetts*, 1843, Chap. 19, p. 69. Not dated, but printed between dates of March 16 and 17, 1843.

[45] Attorney General John Nelson, a Maryland Democrat, served as Secretary of State ad interim from Upshur's death, February 28, 1844, until Calhoun entered on his duties as Secretary of State, April 1, 1844.

[46] Wiltse: *Calhoun, Sectionalist*, pp. 153–5.

ion on what to do there to advance the cause. The latter withheld advice, but bade them Godspeed: "I believe the freedom of this country and of all mankind depends upon the direct, formal, open, and avowed interference of Great Britain to accomplish the abolition of slavery in Texas; but I distrust the sincerity of the present British Administration in the anti-slavery cause." [47] Tappan and Andrews took this word personally to Lord Aberdeen without Adams's authority, but not against his wishes.[48] It may have induced Aberdeen later in the year to make a very famous statement on slavery in Texas and the United States and throughout the whole wide world.

6

Adams, noting the renewed trend toward annexation, brooded all that spring and summer of 1843 in Washington and Quincy over another address to his constituents on the slave power in this Union. If favorably received at home, he planned to carry the message farther afield, beginning in western New York.[49] It would be the last of his public labors in the cause. He worked long and hard at the first draft of a two-hour philippic, but was far from satisfied with its form and content.[50] Finally he compressed his thoughts into an open letter to a committee of abolitionists at Bangor, Maine, who had invited him to deliver at that place on August 1, 1843 an address in celebration of the ninth anniversary of the emancipation of slaves in the British colonies. He wrote the Bangor letter as a blast against slavery and the slave trade, intended to raise a controversy that he could take to the whole country before his lamp of life burned out.

"The extinction of *Slavery* from the face of the earth," he began under date of the Fourth of July 1843, "is a problem, moral, political, religious, which at this moment rocks the foundations of human society. . . . It is indeed nothing more nor less than the consummation of the Christian Re-

---

[47] *Memoirs*, XI, 380. May 31, 1843.

[48] *Memoirs*, XI, 406. August 7, 1843. *Memoirs*, XII, 66. July 1, 1844.

"I have been, from the first, received and treated with the utmost courtesy and my suggestions seem to have made all proper impression upon the Ministry. They have recently informed me that they have already commenced acting upon them at Mexico, and intend opening negotiations directly with Texas also. I am fully satisfied of their honest intentions to use their influence in the matter as far as practicable. Their first effort will be to endeavor to induce Santa Anna (who *is* Mexico) to propose abolition to Texas as the terms of a peace. To effect this it is highly important to show him the true channels and *locality* of the machinations that have been carried on in the U.S. to wrest Texas from his hands, and to show him that he could by no possibility inflict so righteous and in their view terrific a retribution upon the Virginia politicians, who, and not alone the 'tumultuary population of the Valley of the Mississippi,' as he has styled them, have been participating so largely in these nefarious transactions. The old population of Texas was made in a great degree the passive instruments of their political juggling." Stephen Pearl Andrews to JQA, London, July 18, 1843. Adams MSS.

[49] JQA to Seth M. Gates, Washington, April 22, 1843. Adams MSS.

[50] *Memoirs*, XI, 371.

ligion." He followed with another implacable indictment of the slave power.

"Oh! my friends!" he declaimed to the Bangor abolitionists, "I have not the heart to join in the festivity on the first of August, the *British* Anniversary of disenthralled humanity, while all this and infinitely more that I could tell, but that I would spare the blushes of my Country, weighs down my Spirits, with the uncertainty, sinking into my grave as I am, whether she is doomed to be numbered among the first Liberators or the last oppressors of the race of immortal man." [51]

These passionate words fell quite flat on the general public ear. Publication of the letter caused so little comment that Adams found himself exasperatingly bereft of contention. Failure to raise an adversary worthy of being answered was the worst thing that could have happened to him,[52] or to any Adams. It is noteworthy that after experiencing the ineffectiveness of the Bangor blast he made no significant allusions to the slave power in the nonpolitical speeches that he delivered during an excursion to Canada and Niagara Falls in the summer with his daughter-in-law, Mrs. Charles Francis Adams, and his eldest grandson, all guests of Abby's father, Peter Chardon Brooks.[53]

7

The Brooks and Adams party "sped" westward on the "cars" through Massachusetts, blooming in those days like an Eden, a land fruitful with meadow, garden, and orchard, the countrymen busy with scythe and pitchfork, a region of peace, plenty, and contentment. Then came the "dark forests" and "stupendous rocks" of the Berkshires. Once across the divide between Massachusetts and New York, the tourists looked down upon the rich valley of the Hudson, and went sightseeing at Lebanon Springs, where the surrounding mountains were crowned with oak and beech, birch and black walnut, sugar maples on the slopes, willows and sycamores in the lowlands, the common sumac and locust trees lush and heavy along the carriage roads—all pleasantly recorded by the longtime student of forestry. They took the stage from Saratoga Springs and its fashionable hotels to the storied and scenic wonders of Lake George and Lake Champlain, by lake, river, and rail to the historic sites of Montreal

[51] JQA to Asa Walker, Charles A. Stackpole, and F. M. Sabine, Committee of Correspondence of a Meeting of the Citizens of Bangor. Quincy, July 4, 1843. Adams MSS. The letter was printed in the *Bangor Courier*, XI, No. 6, August 8, 1843, and the *Boston Courier*, XIX, No. 5960, August 12, 1843. Separately printed, Quincy, 1843.

[52] *Memoirs*, XI, 407–8. August 12, 1843.

[53] Mr. and Mrs. Joseph Grinnell, with their niece and adopted daughter Cornelia, accompanied the Brooks-Adams party from Boston to Lebanon Springs, and from Saratoga to Niagara Falls (via Montreal and Quebec) and return. With them as "literary and social companion" was Miss Elise Charlotte Otté, a young Englishwoman, of Danish background, whose interesting diary of the trip is now among the Adams MSS. in MHS

and Quebec, and the falls of Montmorency, then doubling back up the St. Lawrence and by steamer and stage to the Thousand Islands and into Lake Ontario. From Toronto they crossed the lake to Lewiston and made their way toward Niagara Falls. En route they visited with General Peter B. Porter the Tuscarora Indian reservation and heard a sermon being translated into the Indian language to an audience as somnolent as any white Christian congregation. But the Indians listened with alert respect to Adams's extemporaneous remarks.[54] Doubtless some of them took him for the Great White Father.

At Niagara the tourist and his namesake grandson gazed speechless from above and below upon the snowy foam of the cataract, reflected in an ever shifting rainbow, and marveled at the unspoiled beauty of nature around the awful grandeur of the falling flood. Then they crossed the river into Canada again, to inspect the field of Lundy's Lane on the anniversary of that battle, under the personal guidance of General Porter.

At Fort Schlosser, scene of the *Caroline* affair, the visiting statesman accepted an official invitation to be guest of the city of Buffalo. Escorted by old colleagues from the House of Representatives, Millard Fillmore and Thomas Cutting, the party took passage on a chartered steam launch to the new city on Lake Erie. Flags and bunting were flying from a hundred masts as they entered the harbor.[55] Fillmore, who seven years later would be President of the United States, introduced the distinguished visitor to an enormous crowd massed in the public park. Adams responded extemporaneously, with some embarrassment for lack of preparation.[56] From the park they rode with the mayor and Mr. Fillmore about the city in an open barouche, accepting the plaudits of the people. That evening a firemen's procession with torchlights paraded before the distinguished visitor.[57]

Adams marveled at the warmth of his reception. Nothing like this had ever happened to him before. It was the same at Batavia, William Morgan's old stamping-ground; at Rochester,[58] hard by Lake Ontario's prosperous shore; before the "beauty and fashion" of locust-shaded Canandaigua,[59] overlooking the outlet of that long and mirrored water, where

[54] *Rochester Daily Democrat*, August 11, 1843. "John Quincy Adams at Rochester," MS. by John C. Chumasero, Rochester, August 7, 1843. Adams MSS.

[55] *Buffalo Daily Courier and Economist*, II, No. 458, July 27, 1843. I am indebted to Mr. William T. O'Rourke of the Buffalo Public Library for newspaper references on Adams's visit to Buffalo.

[56] Dictated at five o'clock next morning to the editor of the *Buffalo Commercial Advertiser* and published that afternoon, July 27, 1843, in Vol. IX, No. 2727. See *Memoirs*, XI, 396–7.

[57] Adams MSS.

[58] *Rochester Daily Democrat*, XI, Nos. 176, 177, 189; *Rochester Daily Advertiser*, II, No. 386, July 27, 28, 1843. I am indebted to Miss Emma Swift of the Rochester Public Library for local newspaper references on Adams's visit to Rochester and other New York communities.

[59] Perhaps the only discordant note was sounded by the *Ontario County Messen-*

his friend Governor Seward met him; at Auburn,[60] home of the Governor; at Utica in the valley of the quiet Mohawk, where he spent six active [61] days as guest of his kinsmen by marriage A. B. Johnson and family, and received among others a group of colored people grateful for his devotion to the cause of human rights.

It was at Utica, while attending an assembly of the Female Seminary, that he broke into uncontrollable sobs upon listening to the reading of some of his mother's recently published letters to his father and himself back in the days of the American Revolution. From Utica he traveled on in the railway cars to the brisk towns of Little Falls and Herkimer, to the city of Schenectady, to Albany, where he spoke from a house porch overlooking the great park, with the people listening to him under the elms before the State Capitol, and later he received three times three at a reception within that edifice.

What a triumphal journey! Invitations to visit and speak, from towns and cities all along the way; [62] deputations of prominent citizens coming to escort him, guns booming, church bells ringing, torchlight processions, great crowds of people shouting, all to greet and honor the Old Man Eloquent.[63] He was traversing the Burned-over District, that nursery of humanitarian reform, the home of Antimasonry, the hothouse of antislavery. Everywhere among these goodly folk he met with veneration and affection. He slaked his thirsty heart with the flattering salutations and applause of the people, blush though he tried to in his Diary.[64]

In one part of this Union, at least, John Quincy Adams was on the way to becoming a national hero.

---

ger (weekly) of Canandaigua, Vol. XLI, No. 2, Whole No. 2082, August 2, 1843. This Van Buren paper complained that Adams had violated the spirit of the strictly nonpartisan character of his public reception by eulogizing several of his political friends whom he met in the course of his journey. "In other respects, his speech was not remarkable for anything except its source."

[60] *Auburn Journal*, August 1, 1843.

[61] On Sunday, July 30, he attended services at three different churches, Episcopalian, Dutch Reformed, and Presbyterian. On Monday, July 31, he visited the scenic falls at Trenton. On Tuesday, August 1, this was his schedule: 9 a.m., inspection of the Female Seminary; 10 a.m., a three-quarters-of-an-hour speech on the front steps of the Bleeker House; then a visit to Bishop and Gray's Daguerreotype Rooms to have portraits taken for presentation to friends in Utica; next a visit to the Museum to view the celebrated dwarf Charles S. Stratton; a visit to the State Lunatic Asylum; later an excursion to the New York Mills and other villages on the Saquoit; in the evening a reception to shake hands with townsmen. *Utica Democrat*, VII, No. 375, and *Utica Daily Gazette*, August 8, 1843. See also *Memoirs*, XI, 399–401.

[62] See Adams MSS., incoming general correspondence of JQA.

[63] *Utica Democrat*, August 8, 1843; Albany *Evening Journal*, XIV, No. 4063, August 3, 1843. Diary of Elise C. Otté. MHS.

[64] "To myself it was but the crowning proof how unfit I am for such occasions, and a lesson at once of profound gratitude and humility." *Memoirs*, XI, 402. Albany, August 3, 1843. For portions of the trip see *Memoirs*, XI, 389–408, and behind that the MS. Diary in detail.

8

President Tyler spoke out sharply on Mexican-American relations in his message at the opening of the Twenty-eighth Congress in December 1843. With unmistakable implication he stressed the mutual interests of Texas and the United States. Senator Robert J. Walker of Mississippi followed with a lengthy article in the Washington *Globe* of February 3, 1844 stating the case for immediate annexation. It attempted by argumentative legerdemain to take in antislavery feelings by asserting that the addition of Texas to the Union would bring about the ultimate extinction of slavery in the United States by a process of "diffusion" [65]—shaky reasoning that would be much developed by slavery apologists in the years ahead. Following Walker's publication Andrew Jackson's letter to Aaron V. Brown of the previous year [66] was released to the *Richmond Enquirer*. Tyler's Texan tiger at last had made his spring into the open arena of American politics.

Secretary of State Upshur was secretly negotiating a treaty for the annexation of Texas as a territory of the United States when he was accidentally killed, together with Thomas W. Gilmer, recently appointed Secretary of the Navy, in the tragic explosion of a big naval gun on board the U.S.S. *Princeton* on a Presidential excursion on the Potomac, February 28, 1844—*dies iræ*, Adams allowed himself to note in his Diary.[67] Tyler immediately appointed Calhoun Secretary of State to conclude the Texas business on the line of the Rio Grande; next to settle the Oregon Question, on the line of the Columbia.[68] Calhoun, the defender of slavery, promptly signed the Texan annexation treaty, April 12, 1844.

. . .

[65] "It [slavery] *will certainly disappear if Texas is reannexed to the Union;* not by abolition, but against and in spite of all its frenzy, slowly and gradually, by diffusion, as it has already thus nearly receded from several of the more northern of the slaveholding States, and as it will continue thus more rapidly to recede by the reannexation of Texas, and finally, in the distant future, without a shock, without abolition, without a convulsion, disappear into and through Texas, into Mexico and Central and South America." Published in pamphlet form by the *Globe* printing office under title of *Letter of Mr. Walker of Mississippi relative to the Annexation of Texas; in Reply to the Call of the People of Carroll County, Kentucky, to Communicate his Views on that Subject* (Washington, 1844). See pp. 14–15. Charles Francis Adams replied in a series of eight articles in the *Boston Courier,* expanded and reprinted in pamphlet form under the title of *Texas and the Massachusetts Resolutions* [of 1843] (Boston; Eastburn's Press; 1843).

[66] See above, p. 462.

[67] *Memoirs,* XI, 521. Adams himself had been guest in the *Princeton* only a few days before, and had seen the big gun, named "The Peacemaker," successfully fired off three times. He and his ladies had then been invited to attend the Presidential party, with other members of Congress, but he had declined under pressure of work. *Memoirs,* XI, 516.

[68] See p. 486, below.

Calhoun made the mistake of presenting the Texan treaty to the Senate as an instrument necessary to prevent the interference of Great Britain with slavery in the Union rather than as a healthy step in inevitable national expansion. On this issue he hoped to unite the Democratic Party behind a Southern leader in the election of 1844.[69]

For this deliberate purpose he found a dubious expedient ready to hand. A great deal of information had been coming in to the President and to the Department of State from correspondents abroad, both official and private,[70] to the effect that the British Government, under the influence of abolitionists [71] in Old England and New England—signalized by the World Antislavery Convention of June 1843 in London, which adopted a resolution in honor of John Quincy Adams [72]—was using all its diplomatic arts to bring about abolition in Texas. To quiet official American apprehensions Lord Aberdeen had sent an instruction to Richard Pakenham, the new British Minister in Washington, dated December 23, 1843, for communication to the United States Government. It lay on the deceased Upshur's desk still unanswered when Calhoun took over.

The British Foreign Secretary had frankly acknowledged diplomatic intervention to bring about Mexican recognition of Texan independence—valuable to Great Britain only in a commercial way—and implied that abolition of slavery there would be an acceptable equivalent. "It must be

---

[69] James C. N. Paul: *Rift in the Democracy* (Philadelphia, 1951), p. 112.

[70] Tyler sent Duff Green to consort with the Opposition in England, and supplement the information sent by the regular Minister, Edward Everett, a Whig and antislavery man.

[71] Lewis Tappan accompanied a six-man committee of the British and Foreign Antislavery Society (under whose auspices the World Antislavery Convention was held) which waited upon Lord Aberdeen, July 7, 1843, urging that an opportunity such as never before had existed was now at hand to press for the extinction of slavery in Texas. "With respect to the annexation of Texas the committee would deprecate it as one of the greatest evils that could befall the human race, inasmuch as it would serve to insure the extension and perpetuation of slavery in both countries. But they are not without hope that this catastrophe might be prevented by the timely interposition of the British Government." Thomas Clarkson to JQA, August 11, 1843, enclosing resolutions of the convention; transmitted by Lewis Tappan to JQA, New York, August 8, 1843. Adams MSS.

[72] "That this Convention views with eager interest the important position relative to the cause of human freedom now held by the venerable John Quincy Adams, formerly President of the United States; and while admitting the moral heroism with which he had thrown himself into the breach, we will not cease our prayers to the Giver of all good gifts, that his hands may be strengthened for the great work to which he has given himself, and that his valuable life may be mercifully prolonged until he shall witness the abolition of slavery, not only in his own country, but throughout the world."

This resolution, introduced by Lord Morpeth, chairman of the convention, who refered to the "cause" in the United States as "still inspired by the aged but untiring energies of John Quincy Adams," was adopted by acclamation. *Liberator*, XIII, No. 31, Whole No. 656, August 4, 1843.

and is well known," continued Aberdeen, in the famous note to Pakenham, "both to the United States and to the whole world, that Great Britain desires, and is constantly exerting herself to procure, the general abolition of slavery throughout the world." At the same time he perfunctorily disavowed any intention of disturbing the domestic tranquillity of the Southern states of the Union.[73]

Really, as Adams divined, the British Government [74] of the day was interested more in preserving the independence of Texas in order to offset the power in North America of the expanding Union than it was in the abolition of slavery there.[75] This was a strong part, indeed, of the Southern argument for annexation. An independent Texas would be the Uruguay of North America, a creature of the British balance of power in the New World. Aberdeen had doubtless thrown in the honest admission of a desire to see slavery abolished everywhere, including Texas, in order to please public opinion in England and perhaps to reassure mistrustful antislavery sympathizers like Adams in America.

Calhoun seized on the Foreign Secretary's avowal as a justification for annexation: it was, he stated, precisely to put an end to such a danger that he had signed the annexation treaty. It might be wise and humane, he acknowledged, for Great Britain to abolish slavery in her own colonies, but it would be neither wise nor humane to abolish slavery in the Southern states, where, asserted Calhoun, the slaves were better off than wage workers in England. "What is called slavery is in reality a political institution, essential to the peace, safety, and prosperity of those states in the Union in which it exists." All this the Secretary of State set forth for public consumption [76] in an answer to Pakenham's note made public contemporaneously with the treaty itself.[77]

[73] Aberdeen to Pakenham, No. 9, December 26, 1843, and Pakenham to Upshur, January 26, 1844. Sen. Doc. 341, 28th Cong., 1st Sess., pp. 48–9.

[74] "The policy of the British Government is to cherish, sustain, and protect the institution of slavery in our Southern States and Texas, and their task is to do it by humbugging the abolitionists in England into the belief that they intend directly the reverse. . . . I perceive nothing, as yet, to relieve the deep distrust, which I would fain discard if I could, of the British ministerial policy with regard to slavery in Texas and in our Southern States." *Memoirs,* XI, 406–7. Quincy, August 7, 11, 1843.

[75] St. George L. Sioussat's sketch of John C. Calhoun in *American Secretaries of State,* V, 148.

[76] Wiltse, op. cit., p. 171, thinks that Calhoun never intended the letter for publication. If so, why did he write it? St. George L. Sioussat, op. cit., V, 140–55, shows that Calhoun had urged Upshur to make such an explanation to the British Government, "calculated to make a deep impression on the public mind generally." Furthermore, Tyler wrote confidentially to Andrew Jackson that the treaty had been held back from the Senate a few days so as to include a copy of Calhoun's reply to Pakenham, which it took some time to prepare.

[77] Calhoun to Pakenham, April 18, 1844. Sen. Doc. 341, 28th Cong., 1st Sess., pp. 50–3.

The newspapers published the treaty and accompanying documents on the eve of the nominating conventions of the Whig, Democratic, and Liberty Parties. This forced prominent candidates to declare how they stood on the question. To plump for admission of Texas as a slave state was now a political liability in the North, thanks to the success of the antislavery impulse and Adams's campaign against annexation. To declare against the Texan treaty was likely to antagonize the South.

Henry Clay, obvious candidate of the Whig Party, came out strongly against the treaty. Annexation and war with Mexico were identical, he declared; even if Mexico should assent to our acquiring Texas, a large portion of the American people would oppose it—that was enough. The unanimous nomination of Clay shortly after this statement practically pledged Whig Senators North and South against the treaty even though the party platform studiously avoided any mention of Texas. It was the last time that the Southern Whigs could be rallied to the old national issues of currency and banking, internal improvements and public land policy over and above the sectional issue of slavery.[78]

Van Buren, leading contender for the Democratic nomination (a two-thirds majority of the party convention had become necessary), now faced a rising tide of antislavery feeling in the North, notably in his own State of New York. In a courageous public letter in reply to W. H. Hammett, a member of Congress from Mississippi, he came out against annexation but in such a way as to leave a door open later: it was incompatible with friendly relations with Mexico; he would have to await the final judgment of Congress, a "large portion" of which would be chosen in the next election.[79] Van Buren's painful decision alienated enough of the Southern wing of the party to lose him the nomination. It marked the end of his democratic alliance of planters of the South and plain republicans of the North; the Little Magician now turned to the Free-Soil movement for the resurrection of his political fortunes.

President Tyler, nominated by an independent convention sitting at Baltimore simultaneously with the Democrats,[80] could not command a two-thirds majority in the Democratic Convention. So the Democracy named a dark horse out of the political paddocks of Andrew Jackson: former Speaker James K. Polk of Tennessee, as ardent a Texas man as his great patron. The principal plank of the party platform called for the "re-occupation of Oregon and the re-annexation of Texas at the earliest possible period." By the re-occupation of Oregon was meant, of course, a

---

[78] Charles Grier Sellers: "Who Were the Southern Whigs?" *AHR*, LIX (No. 2, January 1954), puts forward some corrective suggestions as to the preponderating strength of these issues before the annexation of Texas.

[79] Justin H. Smith: *Annexation of Texas* (New York, 1913), pp. 243–4, analyzes the Hammett letter.

[80] Later Tyler withdrew from the race so as not to split the Democratic Party.

termination of the so-called "joint occupation." The Democratic slogan during the ensuing campaign was to be "Fifty-four Forty or Fight"—a demand for the extreme American claim to the whole Oregon country, calculated by balancing all of Oregon against all of Texas to appeal to men of all parties, even to a Man of the Whole Nation such as John Quincy Adams believed himself to be. But all this was a future, a near future chapter of diplomatic history; John Tyler was still President until March 4, 1845. What he preferred was Texas for future slave states, not Oregon for more free states in the Union.

The Liberty Party nominated James G. Birney, opposed to the annexation of Texas in any shape, manner, form, or shadow, and adopted a thoroughgoing antislavery platform within the limits of the Constitution.

The Senate deliberated on Tyler's Texas treaty, as Calhoun had colored the issue, on the eve of the Presidential campaign. Thomas Hart Benton, Adams's old political enemy and Calhoun's rival for command of a new Democratic alliance between the South and the West, turned the vote against Texas; that is to say, against the expansion of slavery. His tremendous speech divided the Democratic vote on the treaty by swinging nine out of twenty Southern Senators present against it in a total vote of 16 ayes to 35 nays,[81] June 9, 1844, just before the adjournment of Congress.[82]

"I record this vote," noted Adams in his Diary, "as a deliverance, I trust, by the special interposition of Almighty God, of my country and of human liberty from a conspiracy comparable to that of Lucius Sergius Catalina. May it prove not a mere temporary deliverance, like that, only preliminary to the fatally successful conspiracy of Julius Cæsar! The annexation of Texas to this Union is the first step to the conquest of all Mexico, of the West India Islands, of a maritime, colonizing, slave-tainted monarchy, and of extinguished freedom." [83]

9

Ex-President Adams as usual declined to take sides publicly in the national election of 1844, though he personally favored Clay. Clay's election, he told intimate friends, would restore confidence in the Government: money would then pour from capitalists into a new national bank.[84] The

---

[81] Elbert H. Smith: "Thomas Hart Benton: Southern Realist," *AHR*, LVIII (No. 4, July 1953), 795–807.

[82] W. Stull Holt: *Treaties Defeated by the Senate* (Baltimore, 1933) has shown how the Texan annexation treaty became an important victim of politics. Fifteen Democrats (out of 22 present) and 1 Whig voted for the treaty; 28 Whigs (out of 29 present) and 7 Democrats voted against it.

[83] *Memoirs*, XII, 49.

[84] Diary of Elise C. Otté, recounting a conversation between JQA and his fellow grandfather Peter C. Brooks in the stage en route from Saratoga to Glens Falls, New York. Adams MSS.

most he did was to advise an anxious Quaker correspondent, who had been worried about Clay's tergiversations [85] during the campaign, that annexation would be less likely under Henry Clay as President than if Polk were elected.[86] His immediate concern was to defend himself against the warmed-up Democratic propaganda that he had carelessly ceded Texas to Spain in 1819, and to strengthen his new political fences in the Eighth Congressional District of Massachusetts, jeopardized by a double opposition of Democrats and Liberty Party people.[87] This time he definitely accepted a local Whig nomination, ran on the Massachusetts Whig ticket, and spoke to a rally of the Young Men's Whig Club, Charles Francis Adams president, in Tremont Temple, Boston. In a lengthy address he used his own Diary and Minister George W. Erving's published diplomatic correspondence to refute savagely the "bold, dashing, and utterly baseless lies of Andrew Jackson" and his political "bloodhounds" Brown and Ingersoll, who accused him of carelessly ceding away Texas.

"Your trial is approaching," he said in peroration. "The spirit of freedom and the spirit of slavery are drawing together for the deadly conflict of arms. The annexation of Texas to this union is the blast of the trumpet for a foreign, civil, servile, and Indian war, of which the government of your country, fallen into faithless hands, have already twice given the signal—first by a shameless treaty, rejected by a virtuous senate; and again by the glove of defiance, hurled by the apostle of nullification, at the avowed policy of the British empire peacefully to promote the extinction of slavery throughout the world. Young men of Boston: burnish your armor, prepare for the conflict, and I say to you, in the language of Galgacus to the ancient Britons, think of your forefathers! Think of your posterity!"

This bold appeal [88] furnished a fiery anti-Texas campaign document all over the North and border states on the eve of the national election.

Jackson dismissed Adams's Boston oratory as a "barefaced falsehood" resting upon nothing but the testimony of his own Diary for the statement that the Secretary of State had shown him the treaty of 1819 with Spain before it was signed and that he, Jackson, had fully approved. "Who but a traitor to his country," he asked, "can appeal as Mr. Adams

[85] During the campaign Clay became impressed with the strength of Polk's stand on the Texas issue and wrote a statement that he would be glad to see Texas annexed "without dishonor, without war, with the common consent of the Union, and upon just and fair terms." He now thought it would be "unwise to refuse a permanent acquisition, which will exist as long as the globe remains, on account of a temporary institution" and intimated that, if elected, he would be guided by public opinion and existing circumstances. Justin H. Smith, op. cit., pp. 307–8.

[86] JQA to Daniel L. Miller, Jr., of Philadelphia. Quincy, October 29, 1844. Adams MSS.

[87] *Memoirs*, XII, 92, 97, 103.

[88] Printed in *Niles' Register*, LXVII, or, 5th Series, XVII, 105–11. October 19, 1844.

does to the youth of Boston, in the close of his address: 'Your trial is approaching.' ?" [89]

Adams's Diary, so trustworthy in fact if not in opinion, is not the only proof that Jackson had personally assented to the Sabine boundary. In a letter to President Monroe in 1820 the General had approved the territorial arrangements of the Transcontinental Treaty before final ratification of that instrument.[90]

Adams elaborated his defense against Jackson, and further developed the Texas issue, in another long address to his constituents at Weymouth and North Bridgewater. When a deputation from the Liberty Party of his district quizzed him as to his views on the abolition of slavery in the District of Columbia and the federal territories, and on prohibition of the slave trade between the states, he answered that he opposed immediate abolition in the District and in the territories (of which position they voiced their disapproval), but said he would vote "tomorrow" for any bill to abolish the interstate slave trade. He warned them that internal divisions within the Opposition might only serve to bring in the "worst party." [91]

The Whigs won a sweeping victory in Massachusetts. Adams's big lead over his two opponents exceeded his fondest hopes.[92] But the nation elected James K. Polk over Henry Clay, thanks to the Liberty Party can-

[89] Andrew Jackson to General Armstrong, Hermitage, October 22, 1844. Ibid., p. 171, November 16, 1844.

[90] Compare, once and for all, Jackson's assertion with this letter to President James Monroe of June 20, 1820:

"I am clearly of your opinion, that for the present, we ought to be content with the Floridas—fortify them, concentrate our population, confine our frontier to proper limits, until our country, to those limits, is filled with a dense population; it is the denseness of our population that gives strength and security to our frontier. With the Floridas in our possession, our fortifications completed, Orleans, the great emporium of the west, is secure. The Floridas in possession of a foreign power, you can be invaded; your fortifications burned, the Mississippi reached, and the lower country reduced. From Texas, an invading enemy will never attempt such an enterprise; if he does, notwithstanding all that has been said and asserted on the floor of Congress on this subject, I will vouch that the invader will pay for his temerity." General Andrew Jackson to President James Monroe, June 20, 1820. *Correspondence of Andrew Jackson*, III, 28.

See Vol. I, 217–40, and Philip Coolidge Brooks: *Diplomacy and the Borderlands; the Adams-Onís Treaty of 1819* (Berkeley, 1941). Erving's diplomatic correspondence was published in 1834, in *ASPFR*, IV, 433–524. See immediately below for JQA's savage review of it, in the light of Jackson's allegations of 1842–3, in his campaign addresses to the Young Men's Whig Club at Boston, October 7, 1844, and North Bridgewater, November 6, 1844, reprinted in *Niles' National Register*, LXVII or, 5th Series, XVII, 105–11, 154–9, 188–9, November 9, 23, 1844.

[91] *Memoirs*, XII, 79–80.

[92] The vote in the eighth district was: John Quincy Adams, Whig, 8,041; Isaac H. Wright, Democrat, 5,322; Appleton Howe, Liberty, 850. *Memoirs*, XII, 104–6.

didate having deflected enough votes in the Burned-over District in New York to throw that decisive state into the Democratic fold. As Adams had feared, the abolitionists helped to divide the Opposition and elect another unequivocal slaveholder to the Presidency on a platform calling unreservedly for the immediate "re-annexation" of Texas.

10

Even before the Senate acted on the Texan treaty, President Tyler and Secretary of State Calhoun had determined, in case of an adverse vote, to submit annexation to the next session of Congress, perhaps even to a special session, for action by joint resolution. After the election Tyler was quick to interpret Polk's substantial victory in the electoral colleges [93] as a mandate for annexation. All the states west of the Alleghenies had voted for Polk. And Polk's patron, the dying Jackson, labored for annexation to the last, with both his friends in Washington and those, including Sam Houston, in Texas. "You might as well attempt to turn the current of the Mississippi," Old Hickory had declared, "as to turn the democracy from the annexation of Texas to the United States . . . obtain it the U. States must—peaceably if we can, but forcibly if we must." Three fourths of "all the people," he declared, were for the measure. "The perpetuation of our republican system, and of our glorious Union," was involved.[94]

Tyler acted quickly. As soon as the last session of the Twenty-eighth Congress assembled following the election, he recommended immediate annexation by legislative act—that is, by joint resolution. A majority had been lacking in the Senate for annexation by treaty the previous spring. There was little doubt that there would be a simple majority now in favor of it in each house of Congress.

Calhoun and South Carolina were in the ascendant. "The prospect," noted Adams, "is death-like." [95]

With increasing bitterness and dismay Adams watched the rapid progress of the annexation resolution. He hesitated whether to sit and witness in silence the perpetration of a wrong that he saw all too clearly was not

---

[93] Although Polk lacked a majority of popular votes cast, he had 38,300 more votes than Clay, and carried the electoral colleges by the substantial majority of 170 to 105.

The popular vote, in so far as it could be registered (in several states the legislatures still chose the Presidential electors), was almost evenly divided for or against annexation in terms of declaration of the candidates, viz:

For Clay (against immediate annexation)	1,299,062
For Birney (against annexation)	62,300
Against immediate annexation	1,361,362
For Polk (for immediate annexation)	1,337,243

Edward Stanwood: *A History of the Presidency* (New York, 1898), p. 223.

[94] Smith: *Annexation of Texas*, pp. 252, 263–4, 304, 360, 439.

[95] *Memoirs*, XII, 128. December 20, 1844.

to be avoided.[96] But when did John Quincy Adams ever remain silent under the compulsion of his being? On January 24, 1844 he spoke up in Committee of the Whole under a debate limit of one hour.

Gentlemen had argued, he said, that Texas was ours by natural right. Well, that simply wasn't so. Nor had it belonged to us as a part of the Louisiana Purchase. He himself as President had tried to buy Texas from Mexico, yes, but only with the consent of the owners and when there had been no slavery there. He had never opposed the annexation of foreign territory, though he had taken exception (in the case of Louisiana) to incorporating a foreign *people* into the Union without a constitutional amendment.[97] "I am still willing to take Texas without slavery," he finally admitted, "and with the assent of Mexico. . . . Under these conditions I would go for Texas tomorrow." [98]

Adams's final protest against Texan annexation did not turn the tide that had set in after the election. The joint resolution was finally accepted by both houses of Congress [99] (February 27, 1845). It provided that when there should be sufficient population, additional states, not exceeding four in number and always with the consent of Texas, might be fashioned out of its territory for admission into the Union; if any of those states should lie north of 36° 30′ N. Lat., the established line of the Missouri Compromise, slavery should be prohibited therein. Since the portion of Texas north of the line of 36° 30′ constituted only a narrow slice off the top of the Panhandle, for long afterward an absolutely barren area, it was not likely that any new free state would soon be possible there.

Tyler quickly signed the joint resolution, March 1, 1845, three days before turning the Government over to Polk. With equal promptness, before he vacated the White House, he forwarded the final offer of annexation to Texas for quick acceptance. Even to wait a few days for Polk to take over might jeopardize the affair—he feared that at any moment the Texans might accept a treaty of peace and independence already initialed, at the hands of Anglo-French mediation, thus blocking annexation altogether.[100]

As the joint resolution was advancing to a final vote in Congress, the

[96] *Memoirs,* XII, 150–1. January 22, 24, 1845.

[97] Vol. I, 120–1.

[98] *Congressional Globe,* XIV, 188–90, January 24, 25, 1845, gives a meager summary of Adams's speech as compared with the pro-Texas speeches. See also *Memoirs,* XII, 152–3.

[99] In the Senate the margin was very close: 27 to 25. Two New York Democratic Senators elected in 1844, John A. Dix and Daniel S. Dickinson, voted for annexation. Even so, there would have been a tie, to be decided by the Speaker in favor of annexation, if Benton had not voted aye, trusting to Polk, the new President, to execute the resolution without war with Mexico. Elbert B. Smith, op. cit., p. 800. See also H. Donaldson Jordan: "A Politician of Expansion: Robert J. Walker," *MVHR,* XIX (No. 3, December 1932), 362–79.

[100] Richard R. Stenberg: "President Polk and the Annexation of Texas," *Southwestern Social Science Quarterly,* XIV (No. 4, March 1934), 13–15.

legislature of the Old Bay State, as if under the inspiration of John Quincy Adams, resolved that there was no precedent for admitting by legislation a foreign state into the Union, that Massachusetts in ratifying the Constitution had never delegated such powers to the Federal Government, and that the people of the state would never consent to delegate such powers as long as slavery or slave representation was a condition of admission.[101] After the President approved the joint resolution, the legislature "solemnly and strenuously protested" the act because it was a violation of the Constitution, because it would perpetuate the slavery of a portion of mankind in America, and because it extended the unequal federal ratio of representation over a new region never within the contemplation of those who ratified the Constitution. Massachusetts therefore refused to acknowledge the act of annexation and pledged herself to co-operate with other states "by every lawful and constitutional measure, to annul its conditions and defeat its accomplishment." No future state should be admitted to the Union, affirmed this resolution of the legislature, except upon condition of abolishing slavery therein.[102]

Massachusetts, there she stood, on the edge of nullification!

11

"A signal triumph of the slave representation in the Constitution of the United States . . ." was Adams's comment when the annexation resolution passed Congress, "the heaviest calamity that ever befell myself and my country was this day consummated." [103] Texas would be but a stepping-stone to all of Mexico. Canada would follow next, then the whole continent of North America. The Union could not stand the shock of an oligarchy of slave-traders "hell-bent" on military conquest of a continent.[104]

"Now you may Rant and Rave," wrote one of the anonymous illiterate Southern bullies to the old legislator. "In spite of you and all your Black-hearted and Blackskinned Friends or that Notorious old Whore Abby Folsom [105] let me advise you and Honest Dan Webster to go and hang on the first Tree." [106]

Adams must have felt almost like hanging himself on the nearest tree

[101] *Acts and Resolves of Massachusetts, 1845,* pp. 598–9. Approved February 22, 1845.

[102] Ibid., 651–3. Approved March 26, 1845.

[103] *Memoirs,* XII, 173. February 27, 28, 1845.

[104] JQA to Mrs. Abby B. [Charles Francis] Adams, Washington, April 2, 1845. Adams MSS.

[105] Mrs. Abby Folsom, born in England in 1792, emigrated to the United States in 1837, married and settled down in Massachusetts, became a conspicuous friend of the Negro race and speaker at abolitionist meetings, or any other meetings that would permit her to speak.

[106] "More Annon" to JQA, New Orleans, April 1, [1845]. Adams MSS.

as he watched annexation proceed under the new President's management. The Texan Senate unanimously rejected the Anglo-French mediation treaty, and the Texan Congress unanimously accepted the joint resolution of the United States Congress. A special ratifying convention in
Texas, elected by what amounted to a plebiscite to pass on the issue of
annexation, confirmed the act with only one dissenting vote.[107]

For months following the consummation of Texan annexation Adams's
mail continued heavy with remonstrances and memorials against the accomplished fact. "Go on, good old man!" [108] was the essence of many of
them.

"If the voice of the people is the voice of God," was the old fighter's
gloomy commentary, "this measure has now the sanction of Almighty
God. I have opposed it for ten long years, firmly believing it tainted with
two deadly crimes: 1, the leprous contamination of slavery; and, 2, robbery of Mexico. *Victrix causa Deo placuit.*[109] The sequel is in the hand of
Providence. . . ." [110]

"Our Country, if we have a country is no longer the same . . . ," he
wrote to Richard Rush acknowledging the latter's published memoir on
his mission to England back in 1817–25; [111] ". . . the polar Star of our
Foreign Relations at that time was Justice it is now Conquest. Their vital
Spirit was then Liberty it is now Slavery. As our Dominion swells she becomes dropsical and by the time when our Empire shall extend over the
whole Continent of North America we shall be ready for a race of Cæ-
sars to subdue the South[ern continent] or to fall at the feet of Pompey's
Statue. Liberty has yet her greatest warfare to wage in this Hemisphere.
May your posterity and mine be armed in Celestial Panoply for the conflict." [112]

Soon the old crusader began to hear resolutions brought forth on the
floor of the House, reflecting similar proposals in the Senate, for negotiations with Spain to acquire the island of Cuba—where slavery prospered
legally and the African slave trade flourished illegally. "These are mere
explosive effusions," he commented dubiously in his Diary, "of the spirit
of aggrandisement which has taken possession of this people, and which
will hereafter characterize their history. The North American continent
and the archipelago of islands separating it from the Southern continent
must, and will in no great distance of time, form component parts of this
great confederated Anglo-Saxon republic." [113]

[107] For final stages of annexation see J. Smith: *Annexation of Texas,* pp. 432–61.
[108] H. H. to JQA, February 11, 1846. Adams MSS.
[109] God is on the side of the winning cause.
[110] *Memoirs,* XII, 202. July 7, 1845.
[111] *Memoranda of a Residence at the Court of London . . . from 1817–1825,* by
Richard Rush, Envoy Extraordinary and Minister Plenipotentiary from the United
States (Philadelphia: Carey, Lea and Blanchard; 1845).
[112] JQA to Richard Rush, Quincy, October 16, 1845. Adams MSS.
[113] *Memoirs,* XII, 247. February 14, 1846.

The veteran champion for freedom had won his great fight for the repeal of the Gag Rule only to witness the "hell-born spirit of slavery" rise again over the Union in the shape of Texas.[114] He had broken down Van Buren's old combination only to see the political heir of Andrew Jackson ride into power with a new alliance, of Southern planters and Western expansionists. He felt too old now to stop the mighty current of evil that had seized upon the nation. It was for younger men, it was for the next generation, it was for another Adams to carry on the struggle. His hopes centered on his son Charles Francis, rapidly rising to leadership in his father's image [115] within the Whig Party in Massachusetts, to lead the final fight for the glorious triumph of Freedom and Truth.[116] All that could be done for the time being was to float with the irresistible tide, watching the times for an opportunity to recover the rights of the Northern states and vindicate their authority in this Union.[117]

James K. Polk was in the saddle, and his steed was Manifest Destiny.

[114] JQA to William H. Seward and Christopher Morgan, Auburn, New York. Quincy, August 8, 1844. Adams MSS.

[115] "Mr. Lincoln embarrassed me much by pointing me out to the attention of many as the 'facsimile,' to use his phrase, of my father. This of late has become a matter of very common remark, although I do not myself perceive it." Diary of CFA, January 18, 1844.

[116] "I have noticed with inexpressible pleasure your firm unwavering adherence to honest principle, and feeling as I do that my own career of exertion for the cause of my country and of human liberty, is at its close, at the approach of the most portentous crisis that it ever encountered, it is a consolation to me that you have engaged in it, with all your faculties, and such is my faith in the Justice and Mercy of God, that I will die in humble hope, that however severe your trial may be, your strength will be found equal to it, and will finally result in the glorious triumph of Freedom and of Truth." JQA to CFA, Washington, April 15, 1844. Adams MSS.

[117] JQA to CFA, Washington, March 27, 1845. Adams MSS.

CHAPTER XXII
Manifest Destiny
(1845–1846)

❁

Away, away with all those cobweb tissues of rights

of discovery, exploration, settlement, continuity, etc.

[Even without them] our claim to Oregon would

still be best and strongest. And that claim is by the

right of our *manifest destiny* to overspread and to

possess the whole of the continent which Providence

has given us for the development of the great ex-

periment of liberty and federative self-government

entrusted to us.

JOHN L. O'SULLIVAN'S ARGUMENT FOR THE
ANNEXATION OF OREGON AND CALIFORNIA.[1]

JOHN QUINCY ADAMS could have written the words at the head of this chapter. He had all but coined the magic-making phrase "Manifest Destiny." The negotiator of the Transcontinental Treaty with Spain, the President who had held the line of forty-nine against George Canning in the Pacific North West,[2] now an old man in Congress, could not blind himself to the fact that Jackson, Tyler, and Polk had something more than slavery behind them. Texas, he realized, reflected a popular "passion for national aggrandizement, influencing the feelings of multitudes. . . ."[3] Oregon too. For fuller continental measure the expansionists had coupled the "re-occupation" of Oregon with the "re-annexation" of Texas.

---

[1] *New York Morning News*, December 27, 1845. Cited in Julius W. Pratt's article on "John L. O'Sullivan and Manifest Destiny," *New York History*, XIV (No. 3, July 1933), 223–4.

[2] Vol. I, 482–536.

[3] JQA to Robert Walsh, Washington, June 3, 1836; JQA to Benjamin Lundy, Washington, March 11, 1838; JQA's holograph review of the diplomatic history of the Texas Question, [June 15] 1838. Adams MSS.

1

The Governments of both the United States and Great Britain were desirous to improve upon the Webster-Ashburton Treaty with another treaty to settle the Oregon Question. The British Government had reason to believe that the United States might be willing under certain conditions to accept the Columbia River as a boundary, that Tyler and Webster were more interested in all of Texas than all of Oregon, or even very much of Oregon. No sooner had Ashburton returned to London than his chief, Lord Aberdeen, suggested to President Tyler, through the British Minister in Washington, Henry M. Fox, that they follow up the Webster-Ashburton Treaty with a return mission to London like that of Lord Ashburton to Washington.[4] Taking his cue from Fox, Tyler looked toward another broad and comprehensive treaty with Great Britain that would combine a settlement of the Oregon Question—perhaps on the line of the Columbia—with a relaxation of tariff restrictions on both sides. In this way he might unite behind himself the two diverging wings of the Democracy: the Calhoun planter faction, which constantly clamored for free trade with England, and the Benton and Van Buren or Locofoco succession to Jackson, which sought for its western constituents larger markets for surplus wheat, and assured American land titles to covered-wagon emigrants setting forth to the new settlements south of the Columbia River. Such a treaty might win for the President without a party a larger measure of support from both parties in all sections of the Union before the next election.

"Money, public, and private!" Daniel Webster had conjured up a further political and diplomatic deal with Great Britain. He would settle the remaining claims against Mexico and at the same time appease the expansionist appetite with the free territory of California instead of the slave Republic of Texas. For this purpose Webster had his eye on the Bay of San Francisco, so coveted by Andrew Jackson in the later phases of his Mexican negotiations, and the harbor of Monterey: all the territory, six degrees wide in latitude, between the Pacific Ocean and the Rocky Mountains below the line of John Quincy Adams's Transcontinental Treaty. He had something in mind that would please his British banker friends too.

Webster planned a characteristic negotiation in London, to be undertaken by himself as a special envoy. As Secretary of State he had already sacrificed 3,207,680 acres of indubitable American territory in the Atlantic Northeast in order to seal a peace with Lord Ashburton in 1842. Now he was prepared to let go 21,523,840 more acres of American claims in

---

[4] I am indebted for this point to an unpublished thesis by Mr. Jarvis O. McCabe of Glasgow, Scotland, who used the records of the British Foreign Office and the personal papers of Lord Aberdeen in the British Museum.

the Pacific North West south of the line of forty-nine in order to settle the Oregon Question with Great Britain—at the expense of Mexico!

The United States claimed the Oregon country as far north as the latitude of 54° 40', but had been not unwilling ever since the days of John Quincy Adams's diplomacy to compromise at the line of 49° North Latitude. Great Britain claimed the same territory, but had been ready to settle for the boundary of the Columbia River, yielding the Olympic Peninsula (west of Puget Sound) to the United States. Mexico owed the United States over $2,000,000 of arbitral awards; there was more than that in outstanding claims of American citizens still unadjudicated. Mexico was also indebted to British creditors through loans made from the house of Baring, for $50,000,000 of bonds refunded in 1838. Such financial burdens were more than that unstable Republic was likely to prove able to carry. Webster had conceived the following tripartite settlement: the United States would yield all its pretensions to Oregon north of the Columbia and east of a line dropped south from Puget Sound to the river. It would compensate itself by purchasing, for millions still untold, a strip of territory six degrees wide—between 36° and 42° N. Lat.—across the northern provinces of Mexico, wide enough safely to take in at least San Francisco Bay—approximately 110,000,000 acres! Any purchase money not absorbed by the American awards and claims would be paid not to Mexico but to Great Britain for credit upon Mexico's bonded debt to Baring Brothers.

All was to be signed and sealed in London by Honest Dan himself in a treaty between the United States, Mexico, and Great Britain. Why should Mexico not be willing to pay off her responsible foreign debts with empty territory in remote northern regions, at the same time drawing the lightning of Manifest Destiny away from Texas? And how could Great Britain object to such a treaty?

Webster had talked over the outlines of the proposed arrangement with Lord Ashburton before the head of the house of Baring left Washington in 1842. Needless to say, the British envoy had approved, so far as he was personally concerned. The Secretary of State next intimated to Edward Everett, the regular Minister in England, appointed by the deceased Harrison, that a special mission to London, similar to the mission of Lord Ashburton to the United States, was in the making. He was also sounding out the Mexican Government when Captain Thomas ap Catesby Jones, U.S.N., momentarily occupied Monterey, California, under a mistaken impression that war had broken out, and thereby dampened the prospect of immediate friendly negotiations with that country.[5]

[5] Rives: *United States and Mexico*, I, 516–23; II, 47.

Adams offered (January 30, 1843) the following resolutions, but the House refused to receive them:
"Resolved,
"That the President of the US be requested to inform this house, by what authority and under whose instructions, Captain Thomas ap Catesby Jones, Commander of the squadron of the United States in the PACIFIC Ocean, did on or about the 19th of

Tyler readily gave his sanction to Webster's project. The President communicated to the committee on foreign affairs of the House, through Caleb Cushing, his wishes for an appropriation to cover the expenses of such a mission. At that moment Adams did not sense the whole purview of the negotiation. He joined with Cushing and John Holmes of Maine in favoring the appropriation, but the committee voted it down six to three.[6]

Thus rebuffed, Tyler gave up the idea of a special mission, but Webster did not abandon his own plans nor did Tyler cease to countenance them, even after the President made clear his intentions to annex Texas, which led Webster finally to resign. He hoped that the Chief Executive would bless his resignation by appointing him as regular Minister to the Court of St. James's in place of Edward Everett. It would gratify a lifelong ambition, and he could there negotiate in congenial company his proposed tripartite treaty. A place might be found for Everett if the President would appoint him as American Commissioner to China.[7]

2

Nobody was interested in events in China more than Adams. Many of his old friends, such as Thomas Handasyd Perkins, the firm of Bryant and Sturgis, the Cabots, the Lymans, the Cushings, had for many years been venturing trading voyages to China out of Boston, Salem, and Newburyport. The China trade, by way of the North West Coast and the Sandwich (Hawaiian) Islands, was the most spectacular feature of the maritime history of Massachusetts.[8] Adams had read everything on China on which he could lay his hands. His constant resolutions calling upon the President for papers relating to all phases of our relations with China had helped to provide a documentary history of the subject.[9] All this material

October last invade in warlike array the territories of the Mexican Republic; take possession of the town of Monterey, and declare himself commander of the naval and military expedition for the occupation of the Californias.

"Resolved,

"That the President of the United States be requested to communicate to this house, copies of *all* instructions given by him or under his authority to the said Captain Jones, from the time of his appointment to the command of the said squadron. Also copies of all communications received from him, relating to the expedition for the occupation of the Californias. And also to inform the house, whether orders have been despatched to the said Captain Jones recalling him from his command."

Adams MSS. *Memoirs*, XI, 304.

[6] *Memoirs*, XI, 327–30. February 25, 28, 1843.

[7] This abortive sport of American diplomacy under Webster is set forth in Robert Glass Cleland's chapters on "The Early Sentiment for the Annexation of California: an Account of the Growth of American Interest in California, 1835–1846," *Southwestern Historical Quarterly*, XVII (Nos. 1, 2, 3, July 1914–January 1915), 1–41, 121–61, 231–60. See pp. 27–40.

[8] Samuel Eliot Morison has described this trade and those who pursued it in his *Maritime History of Massachusetts* (Boston, 1921).

[9] Tyler Dennett: *Americans in Eastern Asia* (New York, 1922), p. 105.

he had studied for his lecture to the Massachusetts Historical Society. He became the friend of Peter Parker, first medical missionary to China of the American Board of Foreign Missions of Boston, who returned to Boston in 1841 to urge mediation of the United States in the Anglo-Chinese War. But Adams did not favor such a move. He sympathized too strongly with Great Britain as an abolitionist Christian power opening up Western trade with China.[10]

By the end of 1842 the Anglo-Chinese War had ended with the Peace of Nanking, and the time was ripe for the United States to send out an official mission to China. Tyler so recommended on December 31, in a special message to Congress, written by Webster. Adams drafted the ensuing report of the committee on foreign affairs, which recommended that the House appropriate $40,000 to open up diplomatic relations with that distant country. It was one of his last acts as chairman of that committee, for the Democrats had captured the House of Representatives in the previous November election. Congress passed the bill and President Tyler approved it, March 3, 1843.[11]

Already Webster had written Edward Everett in London a glowing letter about the new appointment that was coming his way—the $40,000 appropriation [12] (of which $5,000 was for Fletcher Webster, the Secretary's own son, as Everett's secretary), a first-class frigate to convey the Commissioner and his staff, and all the glory of opening up China to American trade. The President now followed up with a more dignified letter appealing to Everett's patriotism in urging the distinguished Bostonian to take the appointment.[13]

Adams did not yet see through the stratagem behind the proposed appointment. He did not suspect that Webster would sell Oregon short in London, while Tyler in Washington was annexing Texas. He presumed it was merely the back door by which Webster was securing to himself a safe retreat from the Tyler Cabinet.[14] Innocently he helped to abet the artifice before he tumbled to the truth.

[10] "The war of Great Britain with China, is a branch of that against *Slavery,* which she has undertaken, and is now waging throughout the globe. It is the war of her Democracy, most reluctantly waged by her rulers, but stimulated and impelled by that public opinion which combines the power of the thunderbolt and the hurricane. Her people have made it the hinge upon which the whole system of her intercourse with the other nations of the earth revolves. It is the cause of human freedom, a glorious and a blessed cause." JQA to Richard Rush, Washington, December 30, 1842. Adams MSS.

[11] Kenneth Scott Latourette: *The History of Early Relations between the United States and China, 1784–1844 (Transactions* of the Connecticut Academy of Arts and Sciences, XXII [August 1917], (New Haven, 1917), pp. 131–2.

[12] The British Government allowed £ 92,792 17s. 5d. for a similar mission of Lord Amherst to China!

[13] Charles Everett: MS. biography of Edward Everett.

[14] "If Everett declines the Chinese mission, Webster can take it himself." *Memoirs,* XI, 335. March 4, 1843.

"I have been much gratified," he told the Secretary of State, "with the appointment of Edward Everett as Minister to China, a mission of transcendant importance. I deem him by his character and attainments peculiarly well suited for it."

Webster was delighted. Apparently he had not expected Adams to react so favorably. He warmed up to the old gentleman at once. "I will be greatly obliged," he said immediately, "if you will write as much to Edward Everett himself." Adams wrote a letter that very night to Everett, via the Department of State, urging him to accept: he had the needed qualities more than any other man in the United States. "And if you go out to China," he added to his friend, "you will find time to let me hear from you directly of your progress and success?" [15]

Everett, for whatever reason of his own,[16] did not lend himself to the arrangement. He was properly willing to resign the London post to make way for a new appointment there, but he declined the mission to China. Tyler did not accept his offer of resignation. It was therefore Caleb Cushing, certainly no private correspondent of John Quincy Adams, who had the honor of concluding in Canton the celebrated Treaty of Wanghia, of 1844, opening up diplomatic relations between the United States and China.

So Daniel Webster did not go to London to cede away so great an area of Oregon. But Tyler did not give up the idea. Once he had taken Texas for the South, he and his new Secretary of State Upshur didn't care so much for Oregon—only enough of it to keep Northern Democrats united with the Southern wing, if possible. He sent to Edward Everett very full powers to negotiate a settlement of the Oregon boundary question "and of all matter and subjects concerned therewith which may be interesting to the two nations." Privately he intimated to that Minister that the line of the Columbia could be made acceptable to the Senate, and to pub-

---

[15] *Memoirs*, XI, 337. March 14, 1843.

"Temper, Selfpossession, Candour, fairdealing, firmness and conciliation, an utter detestation of all trickery and indirection with patience and discretion are of stronger prevailment in diplomatic bargaining than all the subtleties of the old Serpent himself. . . . I have staked much personal responsibility on the opinion that Great Britain was justifiable in her recent war with China. And now in the triumph of her success, I want the crown of my argument in the power to point the observation of my countrymen to the disinterestedness and magnanimity of her Peace."

JQA to Edward Everett, Envoy Extraordinary and Minister Plenipotentiary, London. Washington, March 13, 1843. Adams MSS.

[16] Professor Charles Everett of Columbia University, in his still unpublished biography of his collateral ancestor Edward Everett, thinks it was because Everett could not personally afford the China mission, and also regarded it as a demotion. "If I were at the bottom of the class," he wrote to Webster, "the mission to China would arouse my ambition." Charles Everett further suggests that Everett was disgusted at Webster's willful refusal in 1842 during the negotiations with Ashburton to let him look further for maps in London that would have established American title to the disputed Northeast boundary.

lic opinion in the United States, if accompanied by a separate commercial treaty radically lowering tariffs on both sides.[17] The President also sent Duff Green back to London in order to help informally.

Tyler and Upshur missed their low aim on Oregon if only because the British did not know that these Southern statesmen had let down their sights from the forty-ninth parallel to the Columbia. The Foreign Office— for once apparently not aware of the President's private letter to Everett— thought that diplomat too stiff an American to deal with on territorial questions; for one thing, he knew too much about maps! So Lord Aberdeen informed him that a new British Minister already had been assigned to the United States to negotiate an Oregon settlement in Washington.[18] The British Government thus lost a rare chance to stay on the Columbia. By the time the new plenipotentiary, Richard Pakenham, presented himself at the White House, in February 1844, the "Oregon fever" had begun to infect the country. The Democracy was already clamoring for "Fifty-four Forty or Fight." After the defeat of his Texas treaty Secretary of State Calhoun did not want to risk a shrunken Oregon treaty with the Senate.[19] Fortunately the Oregon Question went over to the new Administration of James K. Polk.

3

Polk planned to acquire California from Mexico, but without sacrificing Oregon to Britain south of forty-nine or making any deal for the comfort of the house of Baring and its British holders of Mexican bonds, not to mention its onetime American lawyer, Daniel Webster. Texas having been annexed, Oregon stood first upon the new President's calendar of foreign affairs: Oregon, and free trade with England.

The Great Emigration of 1843, which poured a preponderance of American settlers into the Willamette Valley south of the Columbia, had made the Oregon Question acute by 1844. The pioneers, and their friends back home, were petitioning Congress for land grants within the United States. They had much support across the whole country from St. Louis to Boston. What they wanted required either a settlement with Great

[17] Everett's full powers are in National Archives, State Department Records, Credences, III, 54. For the President's private instructions, see John Tyler to Edward Everett, confidential, Washington, April 27, 1843. Everett Papers, MHS. Miller: *Treaties*, V, 22–3 prints essential parts of Upshur's instructions to Everett of October 9, 1843. While contending for the line of 49° straight through to the sea and across Vancouver Island, the instructions allowed him to refer home any plausible offer of compromise.

[18] Journal of Edward Everett, October 31, 1843. Everett Papers, MHS. Courtesy of Charles Everett. At that moment Henry Fox had not yet been informed of his impending recall. Miller: *Treaties*, V, 24. Miller gives a helpful précis of Everett's diplomatic dispatches and instructions, and of the British diplomatic correspondence.

[19] Pakenham to Aberdeen, private and confidential, Washington, September 28, 1844. Miller: *Treaties*, V, 27.

Britain or an end of the treaty of 1818 (renewed indefinitely by President Adams in 1827, subject to termination by either party on a year's notice, which made all the territory between 42° and 54° 40′ N. Lat. free and open to the citizens and subjects of *both* countries. To ignore their demands would have repudiated the new alliance of the West and South that had revived the Democratic Party in the name of Manifest Destiny. But Southern leaders, while "re-annexing" all of Texas, were none too keen to "re-occupy" all of Oregon. They opposed giving the termination notice.[20]

Adams, for his part, believed the time had come for action on Oregon, but not too abruptly, not without giving the one year's notice required for terminating the so-called "joint occupation." He offered a resolution calling upon the President for the diplomatic correspondence with Great Britain over Oregon, which was adopted, 166 to 4.[21] But the Twenty-eighth Congress expired March 4, 1845 without any resolution on Oregon.

Polk did not really want to fight Great Britain for Fifty-four Forty, if only because he expected any moment to have a war with Mexico on his hands following the "re-annexation" of Texas. He also knew that the South did not want all of Oregon as it had wanted all of Texas. When the newly elected Twenty-ninth Congress convened in December 1845, he explained that, although we had good right to all of Oregon, his predecessors (James Monroe and John Quincy Adams) had prejudiced our case by offering repeatedly to take the boundary of 49°. So he caused the former offer to be presented once more, only to have the new British Minister, Pakenham, turn it down out of hand without even consulting the Foreign Office. The British Government, disconcerted at Pakenham's officious action, then offered to arbitrate. The President refused. He believed a bold and freer course the only pacific one, that if Congress faltered or hesitated, Great Britain immediately would become more arrogant and grasping. "The only way to treat John Bull," he declared, "is to look him straight in the eye." [22]

That is just what Adams thought too. Despite his own willingness when President to accept the line of 49°, he believed our title perfectly good up to Fifty-four Forty. The day for compromise was over.

Polk called on Congress to back him with a resolution giving the necessary one year's notice to Great Britain. "Oregon," he confidently affirmed in his first annual message, "is a part of the North American Continent to which the title of the United States is the best now in existence." The United States could not in silence permit any European interference on this continent. " 'The American continents,' he continued, quoting from

[20] Avery O. Craven: *The Growth of Southern Nationalism, 1848–1861,* in *History of the South* Series, VI (State, La., 1953), 31.

[21] *Congressional Globe,* XIV, 197–209. January 27, 29, 1845.

[22] *The Diary of James K. Polk during his Presidency, 1845–1849,* Milo Milton Quaife, editor (4 vols., Chicago, 1910), I, 154–5.

President Monroe's famous message of 1823, 'by the free and independent condition which they have assumed and maintain, are henceforth not to be considered as subjects for future colonization by any European power.' " [23] It was this dictum that Adams himself had drafted as Monroe's Secretary of State; he freely acknowledged its real authorship when the historian George Bancroft of Massachusetts, Secretary of the Navy in Polk's Administration, questioned him on that point.[24]

He quite approved the President's position on Oregon, if only he would stick to it. He was sure that British refusal to accept 49° had strengthened American adherence to the claim of all Oregon. But he expected the President would finally "flinch" from 50° 40'.[25]

The old diplomatist listened restlessly to the long discussion in Committee of the Whole on the resolution for termination of the "free and open" treaty. He resolved to vote for it, but wanted to keep out of the debate if only to save himself physically. Robert Barnwell Rhett of South Carolina opposed the motion, as did Calhoun's supporters generally. They would risk war for Texas, but not for Oregon. Rhett was all for peace and free trade with England, even as the gentleman across the way (looking at Adams), who voted against the War of 1812, had once been for peace with that country.

Adams tartly reminded Rhett that he had been Minister to Russia in 1812, not a member of Congress. "I apprehend no war," he told his colleagues, "because I believe the present Administration will finally back down from their own ground."

William Lowndes Yancey of Alabama called Adams to order for reflecting upon the Administration, and Speaker John W. Davis, of Indiana, made the old man take his seat, for the "irrelevancy" of his remarks.[26]

Giddings and the abolitionists supported the proposed resolution. They were contending for all of Oregon in order to balance Texas with three or four future free states in the North West. Various members kept urging Adams to speak up. Finally Thomas Butler King of Georgia challenged him directly: was the learned and venerable member from Massachusetts ready to declare that the title of the United States to Oregon up to latitude 54° 40' was "clear and unquestionable" (the words of the Democratic platform of 1844)?

Adams rose undaunted. He had devoted a lifetime to the expansion of our sovereign title, republican institutions, and free people throughout the whole continent of North America. He had plowed through the recent correspondence with Great Britain which President Polk had just communicated to Congress in response to Adams's own resolution. He had

[23] First annual message of President Polk, December 2, 1845.

[24] Vol. I, 391; *Memoirs*, XII, 218.

[25] *Memoirs*, XII, 219, 221, 234.

[26] *Memoirs*, XII, 234, 242. January 7, 1846. *Congressional Globe*, [XV], 29th Cong., 1st Sess., 1845–6, p. 157.

read everything he could get hold of on the subject, more recently Robert Greenhow's *History of Oregon and California,*[27] which Senator Lewis F. Linn of Missouri had induced that scholar to write to prove the superior right of the United States to the whole of Oregon.[28]

What did the gentleman from Georgia mean, Adams asked, by "unquestionable"? Did he mean right or wrong, or did he refer to fact? "On the question of right I do hold the title of the United States to be clear and unquestionable."

King threw up his hands. "Then why," he asked the Speaker, "had the gentleman not given that definition when he was Secretary of State?"

Adams asked them to defer for a moment all technical arguments. He called upon the Clerk to open the Bible that lay on his table, the well-worn Book on which so many members had taken the oath of office. Would he please to read the 26th, 27th, and 28th verses of the first chapter of Genesis? They would show our title.

The Clerk intoned the ancient Word:

"26. And God said, Let us make man in our image, after our likeness; and let them have dominion over the fish of the sea, and over the fowl of the air, and over the cattle, and over all the earth.

"27. So God created man in his own image, in the image of God created he him: male and female created he them.

"28. And God blessed them, and God said unto them, Be fruitful and multiply, and replenish the earth and subdue it; and have dominion over the fish of the sea, and over the fowl of the air, and over every living thing that moveth upon the earth."

"There, Sir," uttered the old Puritan prophet of Manifest Destiny, "there in my judgment is the foundation not only of our title to Oregon, but the foundation of all human title to all human possessions."

Clearly Adams believed that though the United States had no natural right to Texas, claimed by Mexico, it did have a natural right, under God, to Oregon, claimed by Great Britain! But the treaty must first be terminated, with all proper notice, before proceeding to the rightful occupation.

27 London, 1844; Boston, 1845.

28 On the motion of Stephen A. Douglas, chairman of the House committee on territories, Congress had appropriated $3,000 for the purchase of Greenhow's book. Other books of the time on Oregon, in addition to the correspondence communicated by Polk with his annual message of December 2, 1845, were: Thomas J. Farnham: *History of Oregon Territory, it being a Demonstration of the Title of these United States to the Same* (New York, 1844); George Wilkes: *The History of Oregon, Geographical and Political* (New York, 1845); Thomas Falconer: *The Oregon Question; or a Statement of the British Claims to the Oregon Territory* (London, 1845); *Documents Accompanying the President's Message of December 2, 1845,* 29th Cong., 1st Sess., Sen. Doc. 1, pp. 138–92.

Albert Gallatin's *Oregon Question* (New York, 1846), advocating renewal of the "free and open occupation treaty," did not appear until after JQA's Oregon speech in the House of Representatives.

He called again upon the Clerk. "Read the 8th verse of the second book of Psalms." The Clerk proceeded:

"8. Ask of me, and I shall give thee the heathen for thine inheritance, and the uttermost parts of the earth for thy possession."

"Turn back a verse or two," directed Adams, "and you will see to whom it is said He would give them." He knew the text by heart, chapter and verse.

The Clerk read again:

"6. Yet have I set my King upon my holy hill of Zion.

"7. I will declare the decree: the Lord hath said unto me, Thou art my son: this day have I begotten thee.

"8. Ask of me, and I shall give thee the heathen for thine inheritance, and the uttermost parts of the earth for thy possession."

Oregon was for the asking of a chosen people. The Bible said so!

Adams then went on to develop out of his own experience and vast learning the historical and juridical title of the United States to all of Oregon, from the time of the papal bulls of 1493 to the present: by Spanish discovery, by treaties of the United States with Spain, by treaties of Spain and of the United States with Great Britain; by colonial charters from the King of England, and from the King of France; by discovery, occupation, prescription, treaties, contiguity—in short, by everything except the final act of complete possession—"that is the only thing we now want to have a perfect, clear, indisputable, and undoubted right to the territory of Oregon."

Why had he not protested as Secretary of State in 1818 or as President in 1827 against the British claim as he did now? Because at that time it was in our interest to leave the territory free and open without prejudice to our own claims. Now it was no longer so. "I am for putting an end to that state of things. *I want the country for our western pioneers*, to afford scope for the exercise of that quality in man which is most signally exemplified in the population of our western territory, for them to go out and make a great nation that is to arise there, and which must come from us as a fountain comes from its source, of free, independent sovereign republics, instead of hunting grounds for the buffaloes, braves, and savages of the desert."

The Speaker's gavel fell sharply. Adams's hour was up.[29]

That afternoon the House passed by a vote of 163 to 54 (Adams in the affirmative) a joint resolution, with a conciliatory proviso attached, requesting the President to give the twelve months' notice necessary for abrogating and annulling the Convention of August 6, 1827,[30] which Adams himself had once ratified as President. The Senate amended the resolution still more in the path of conciliation, so that the joint resolu-

[29] *Congressional Globe*, [XV], 29th Cong., 1st Sess., 1845–6, pp. 338–42. See also *Memoirs*, XII, 242–5. Italics inserted.

[30] *Congressional Globe*, loc. cit., 341–50.

tion, as finally passed, April 23, 1846 by both houses, contained a long preamble stating the purpose of the notice: to settle definitively the respective claims of both countries, so that the Oregon territory "be no longer subject to the divided allegiance of its American and British population, and to the confusion and conflict of national jurisdictions, dangerous to the cherished peace and good understanding of both countries." [31]

Immediately the President gave the notice, April 27, 1846.

4

Adams's Oregon speech brought protests and remonstrances from his pacifist friends in the United States; it elicited more in England. Already the debates in Congress had been heard across the Atlantic. Lord George Bentinck, opposing any precipitate repeal of the Corn Laws, declared in the House of Commons: "Surely, Sir, this is not the time—when America is arming her seaboard, and Mr. John Quincy Adams impiously and blasphemously calls to his aid the Word of God as a justification for lighting up the firebrand and unleashing the hell-dogs of war. . . . If, Sir, all honourable means have been used in vain, I shall meekly and humbly appeal, in confidence, to the All-powerful God of battles, and not address America in the language of purchase, but the thundering broadsides of line-of-battle ships. . . ." [32]

"Hear, hear!" echoed Adams sarcastically when he read in a Baltimore newspaper the noble lord's bellicose words.[33]

The British Government correctly appraised the President's notice, and the congressional resolution behind it, as an invitation for a negotiated settlement rather than a threat of war for 54° 40'. But some good people in England were frightened. Joseph Sturge, prominent Quaker of Birmingham, a leading member of the English Abolition Society whom John Greenleaf Whittier had introduced to Adams in 1841, wrote to say how grieved he and a large proportion of his countrymen were at Adams's remarks in the House, and charged him, in effect, with inflaming his countrymen to war. Sturge implored the recent champion of Anglo-American amity to throw his influence on the side of peace in any future discussions on Oregon. The working classes of England, said the good Quaker, the very people who filled the ranks of the army, were decided for peace, and it would not be difficult to maintain if only there were a moderate forbearance by the United States.[34]

Adams made it clear to Sturge and his friends that the American people

[31] Ibid., 715–20.

[32] *Hansard's Parliamentary Debates*, LXXXIV, 1321–2. March 20, 1846.

[33] *Memoirs*, XII, 259, citing the Baltimore *Sun* of April 23, 1846.

[34] Joseph Sturge to JQA, Birmingham, March 3, 1846. Adams MSS. *Memoirs*, XII, 256.

stood behind the President in demanding a settlement, once and for all, of the Oregon Question. He abhorred aggression, he said, but highly approved defensive warfare. "Heaven forbid that war should now come between the United States and Great Britain." If it did, the blood of all its victims would be on Britain's head. He went on to extol the mission, under God, of the American people on the North American continent:

"The Atlantic Ocean rolls, and the North American Continent stands between her [the Queen of Great Britain], and the shores which her advisers demand for subjection to her eminent domain. Those shores are the natural boundaries of our contiguous lands. We want to fulfil the commands of Almighty God, to increase and multiply, and replenish, and *subdue* the Earth. Britain wants them for no honest purpose of her own. She wants them to check, and control and defeat the progress of our prosperity, to stunt our natural growth, and put off the evil day of our aggrandizement. She wants them to prevent the conversion of them from a wilderness of savage hunters to a cultivated land of civilized Christian men. She wants them to prolong the dominion of the buffalo and the bear, and she claims accession from *us* of 700 miles of sea shore on the Northwest Coast of our own Continent, to give her a perfect title to a territory, to not one inch of which she has any title whatever. To this compromise subscribe who will it can never be yielded with my consent." [35]

Notice of termination had the desired effect. Great Britain did not want to fight a war with the United States for Oregon south of 49° any more than the United States wanted to fight for Oregon north of that line.[36] For one reason the Hudson's Bay Company had trapped most of the valuable furs out of that region. Overawed by the new preponderance of American settlers, its directors had prepared to move their Pacific trading post from Fort Vancouver, on the lower Columbia, to Fort Victoria, on Vancouver Island.[37] For another reason, the British Navy was distractingly involved in a joint Anglo-French intervention in the distant estuary of the Plate River in South America, during which the *entente cordiale* with France was coming to an end.[38] Again, the American market, soon to be opened still wider for British manufactures by a new Democratic tariff for revenue

[35] JQA to Joseph Sturge, Birmingham, England. Washington, April 1846. Adams MSS.
". . . be assured I never intended to make an invidious comparison [between] England and America in reference to the martial spirit being more rife in your country than mine. No one can more lament than I do the war spirit which pervades the councils of those who rule over us and I believe there are few who have done more to try to alter it and I rejoice in knowing that the great body of the people who have no voice in the selection of those who make the laws they are bound to obey are opposed to war." Joseph Sturge to JQA, Birmingham, June 3, 1846.

[36] "The interests involved are of no great moment." Foreign Minister Aberdeen to Prime Minister Peel, October 17, 1845. Miller: *Treaties*, V, 29.

[37] Frederick Merk: "The Oregon Pioneers and the Boundary," *AHR*, XXIX (No. 4, July 1924), 681–99. Vol. I, 534–6.

[38] John F. Cady: *Foreign Intervention in the Rio de la Plata* (Philadelphia, 1929).

only, was far more valuable for England in full tide of the Industrial Revolution than all of Oregon. And there was always the vulnerability of Canada to consider in case of a war with the United States.[39] The Peel Government resolved to offer the boundary of 49° continued west from the Rocky Mountains to salt water, if the United States would now accept it, and the Queen's loyal Opposition agreed not to contest such a settlement.[40]

Polk's glance—deflected by impending war with Mexico—now wavered in the eye of John Bull. He flinched, as Adams thought he would. Publicly the President declared he was still for 54° 40', but actually he allowed the State Department to say that if the British Government offered a treaty boundary at 49° he would not refuse to submit it for the advice and consent of the Senate.[41] Accordingly Lord Aberdeen presented a treaty draft. Polk submitted the document to the Senate, word for word as the British Foreign Secretary had spelled it out, including the boundary of 49° to salt water, and the free navigation of the Columbia River for members of the Hudson's Bay Company and British subjects trading with it. The Senate quickly advised the President (June 12), by a vote of 37 to 12, to accept the treaty as it stood. Secretary of State Buchanan then promptly signed the instrument, June 15, 1846.

Most historians [42] now agree that the Oregon "compromise" boundary really was no compromise at all. It was a diplomatic victory for the United States. British claims to the territory essentially in dispute, the "triangle" south of 49° and north of the Columbia River, were stronger than those of the United States, Adams to the contrary notwithstanding. In a historical sense the new treaty with Great Britain was handsome compensation for the really unquestionably American territory in the State of Maine that Daniel Webster had so readily abandoned in his "compromise" of 1842.

The impending Walker Tariff of 1846—a tariff for revenue only—in Washington and repeal of the British Corn Laws in London had created an atmosphere of Anglo-American free trade [43] that buoyed up the final Oregon negotiation. What induced the Senate to accept the Oregon Treaty so eagerly after all the recent blustering campaign for Fifty-four Forty or Fight, and what moved President Polk to follow the advice so

[39] Wilbur D. Jones and J. Chal Vinson: "British Preparedness and the Oregon Settlement," *Pacific Historical Review*, XXII (No. 4, November 1953), 353–64.

[40] Frederick Merk: "British Party Politics and the Oregon Treaty," *AHR*, XXXVII (No. 4, July 1932), 653–77, and "British Government Propaganda and the Oregon Treaty," *AHR*, XL (No. 1, October 1934), 38–62.

[41] St. George L. Sioussat: "James Buchanan," in *American Secretaries of State*, V, 244–64.

[42] Not so Jones and Vinson, op. cit.

[43] T. C. Martin: "Free Trade and the Oregon Question, 1842–1846," in *Facts and Factors of Economic History*, E. F. Gay Memorial Volume (Cambridge, 1932), pp. 470–91.

promptly, was that war had just broken out between the United States and Mexico. To renew negotiations would only enable the British Government to take advantage of the altered situation and insist again on the line of the Columbia.[44] Polk had signed the treaty in the nick of time.

If the Oregon Treaty did not meet Adams's express approval, he nevertheless voiced no objection. Grumble though he might in his Diary, he could scarce come out against a treaty that secured the boundary he had been willing to take when Secretary of State and President. But he didn't like the free-trade tariff bargain with England that sealed the Oregon settlement, to the threatened disadvantage of New England manufactures.[45] Of course he voted against the Walker Tariff.[46]

5

The full grasp of Polk's determined hold on Manifest Destiny, as revealed by modern historians [47] after the study of his extraordinary *Diary*, was, after Texas, to take California, either by diplomatic purchase from Mexico, or as Texas had been taken, or by war. Mexico played into the President's hand to assist his designs. Her Minister in Washington gave formal notice that his Government would regard the annexation of Texas as an act of war, and withdrew from the country when Congress passed the joint resolution of March 2, 1844. Much less would Mexico sell California and intervening territory: the great Southwest of the present day, including what now comprises the states of Arizona, New Mexico, Nevada, Utah, the western slope of Colorado, and the southwestern corner of Wyoming. Her successive revolutionary governments refused to receive the American Minister, John Slidell of Louisiana, whom the President dispatched to Mexico City loaded with peace offers and territorial proposals.

Meanwhile Polk had moved American troops under General Taylor into the area in dispute between the United States and Texas: stationed at first on the coast at Corpus Christi on the west bank of the Nueces River; later, following Mexican refusal to receive Slidell, he moved them

[44] Out of a vast literature see Hunter Miller: *Treaties*, V, 55–96, and Wiltse: *Calhoun, Sectionalist*, Chapter XVIII, "Oregon and Free Trade," pp. 247–72.

[45] "It is evident that the Oregon question will be settled by the repeal of the corn laws and the sacrifice of the American [protective] tariff; a bargain, both sides of which will be for the benefit of England, and to our disadvantage; a purchase of peace, the value of which can only be tested by the lapse of time." *Memoirs*, XII, 248. February 20, 1846.

[46] *Congressional Globe*, [XV], 29th Cong., 1st Sess., 1845–6, p. 1053. July 3, 1846.

[47] In addition to authorities already cited (G. L. Rives, J. H. Smith, St. George L. Sioussat, and C. M. Wiltse), see also Jesse S. Reeves: *American Diplomacy under Tyler and Polk* (Baltimore, 1907); Ephraim Douglass Adams: *British Interests and Activities in Texas, 1838–1846* (Baltimore, 1910); Eugene Irving McCormac: *James K. Polk, a Political Biography* (Berkeley, 1922); William Campbell Binkley: *The Expansionist Movement in Texas, 1836–1850* (Berkeley, 1925), and entries in Bemis and Griffin: *Guide*, pp. 241–71.

to the east bank of the Rio Grande. Thereupon a *de facto* Mexican President, General Mariano Paredes, proclaimed a "defensive war" against the United States, April 23, 1846. The next day, after giving local notice that hostilities had commenced, Mexican forces crossed the Rio Grande and attacked General Taylor's forces.

The news reached Washington on the afternoon of May 9, after the impatient Polk had been discussing with his Cabinet that day the expediency of asking Congress for an immediate declaration of war without waiting for an overt act of hostility on the part of Mexico. We had ample cause for war, he said.[48] By that, of course, he meant Mexico's refusal to pay the arbitral awards as pledged by treaty, or to recognize the annexation of Texas. Only the historian George Bancroft, Secretary of the Navy, had demurred.

The arrival of Taylor's dispatches telling of hostilities brought the Cabinet to unanimous support of the President in a second meeting held the evening of the same May 9.[49] On May 11, Polk sent in his famous message to Congress: "Mexico has passed the boundary of the United States, has invaded our territory, and shed American blood on American soil. She has proclaimed that hostilities have commenced, and the two nations are now at war." He appealed to Congress to recognize at once the existence of the war and to place adequate means at his disposal to prosecute it with vigor.

James K. Polk was a slaveholder like Andrew Jackson, and he came from the same slaveholding State of Tennessee. But his *Diary* shows that his mind was not fixed first and foremost on the expansion of slavery into the Far West. Rather did he have his eye on the fine harbor of San Francisco. Like Adams in the case of Oregon, Polk wanted California for our Western pioneers. He would be dismayed to have the issue of slavery come into the political picture as a result of the War with Mexico and the new territorial acquisitions. With Polk the territory came first; the slavery question could be settled later.

Not so with John Quincy Adams. To him the President's war message was the climax of a long festering plot against Mexico for the advancement and perpetuation of slavery in this Union. Worst of all, Polk had overridden that provision of the Constitution which gave to Congress the power to declare war—in Adams's opinion, the "exclusive" [50] power to declare war, without which a state of war could not constitutionally exist.[51]

[48] *Diary of James K. Polk*, I, 384–7.
[49] Ibid.
[50] JQA to Albert Gallatin, Washington, December 26, 1847. Adams MSS. Quoted below, pp. 499–500.
[51] Adams's opinion was at least a dubious one. The Constitution says merely that Congress shall have the right "to declare War, grant Letters of Marque and Reprisal, and make Rules concerning Captures on land and water." It does not say that there can be no war unless Congress "declares" it. How can a state of war be denied in fact, if not in law, when another power declares it and attacks the United States? Of course

Polk's action disturbed other eminent members of Congress who would not, however, vote against supporting him. It bothered Senator Benton: he was ready to vote men and money to defend American soil, but no more than that, no farther than the Nueces. He did not believe that American territory in the State of Texas extended beyond that stream; like John Quincy Adams [52] he did not approve of the President's moving Taylor's army to the Rio Grande. It bothered Senator Calhoun too. Like Adams the South Carolinian believed there could be no war until Congress declared one. Like his Western rival Benton, he conceived that the President was empowered to repel invasion but not empowered to make war. But the party leaders, Lewis Cass of Michigan in the Senate and Hugh A. Haraldson of Georgia in the lower chamber, bore down with their majority. They presented a bill with a preamble: "Whereas by the act of Mexico a state of War exists between the United States and that Republic." It authorized the President to prosecute the conflict to a successful termination. After a quick debate the bill passed the House that same day, 174 to 14.

Hesitant members of both parties bowed before the fact of war. Half the Massachusetts delegation, which had been anti-Texas to a man, voted for what Adams called a "most unrighteous war." [53] Next day, May 12, the Senate passed the measure, 40 to 2, Benton finally voting aye, Calhoun not voting. Calhoun feared the war because it would damage the slave interest in the South by tying it to a war of aggression. Like Adams he felt that ordering Taylor into the disputed area was a deliberate provocation, that the vote of Congress to support Polk would set a precedent whereby any President could in future make war on his own initiative [54] and Congress would have to ratify the accomplished fact.

Adams's name, if only because of the alphabet, led the list [55] of fourteen

---

the President as Commander in Chief may station, rightly or wrongly, the armed forces of the United States where some foreign power may declare war and attack them, foolishly or otherwise. That is what Polk did. It was up to Congress then to approve or disapprove the war, to support it in resources, men, and money, or to withhold that support.

[52] "That we had a shadow of right beyond the Sabine I have never believed since the conclusion of the Florida [Transcontinental] Treaty and it is from the date of that treaty that Great Britain had not a shadow of right upon the Oregon Territory until we have been pleased to confer it upon her.

"The Mexican War rests, however, upon other questions of right or wrong, with which France and Spain have no concern. But there is no aspect of right and wrong of which we can claim the benefit in the controversy." JQA to B. Mayer of Baltimore. Quincy, July 6, 1847. Adams MSS.

[53] *Memoirs*, XII, 263. May 11, 1846.

[54] See Wiltse: *Calhoun, Sectionalist*, p. 284.

[55] The list of those in addition to Adams voting against the war resolution of May 11, 1846 in the House of Representatives was as follows: George Ashmun, of Springfield, Mass.; Henry Young Cranston, of Newport, R.I.; Charles Vernon Culver, of Venango County, Pa. (born in Logan, Hocking County, O.); Columbus Delano, of Mt. Vernon, Ohio (born in Shoreham, Vt.); Joshua Reed Giddings, abolitionist of the

antislavery Whigs in the House of Representatives who voted against the
war resolution. They were the famous "Conscience Whigs." They came
from that well-harvested swath of territory, from Massachusetts out
through the Burned-over District of New York and Ohio and adjacent
Pennsylvania, which had nourished so many reform causes in the last
two decades. In the Senate only two Whigs voted against war: the veteran
John M. Clayton, of New Castle, Delaware, and John Davis of Worcester, Massachusetts.

The overwhelming majority for war in both parties in Congress, North
and South and East and West, gave little heed to the danger of a great
sectional conflict to be precipitated by acquisition of the new territory
from Mexico. As Charles M. Wiltse has recently said in two fine sentences: "The young men who left the city offices, the farms, the colleges,
to storm the enchanted gateways to the west cared nothing for slavery
one way or another. They were wooed and won by adventure, empire,
the boundless freedom of an unsettled land, the sheer magnetism of the
setting sun." [56]

6

Now that Congress had accepted the war, Adams voted for the necessary military appropriations,[57] but not for frills, decorations, or thanks
and reward to participants; and on every occasion he threw his vote in
favor of resolutions for peace without indemnity and without territorial
cessions.[58] He did not speak inside the House or beyond its walls on the
issue of peace or war, neither on that fateful May 11 nor on any occasion
afterward. He was too old, too spent, too weary in heart and mind. His
fires of life were burning low. He was approaching his eightieth year. All
he could do now was to point the way to younger men: to Seward, to
Charles Sumner,[59] to his own son. "Proceed—Persevere—never despair,"

Western Reserve, O. (born Bradford County, Pa.); Joseph Grinnell, of New Bedford,
Mass.; Charles Hudson, Universalist minister from Marlboro, Mass.; D. P. King, of
Danvers, Mass.; Joseph Mosley Root, of Huron County, O. (born in Brutus, N.Y.);
Luther Severance, of Augusta, Me. (born in Montague, Mass.); John Strohm, of
Providence, R.I. (born in Lancaster County, Pa.); Daniel Rose Tilden, of Portage
County, O. (born in Lebanon, Conn.); Joseph Vance, of Urbana, O. (born in
Washington County, Pa.). *Congressional Globe* [XV], 29th Cong., 1st Sess., 1845–6,
p. 795. May 11, 1846.

[56] Wiltse: *Calhoun, Sectionalist*, p. 286. See also Bernard De Voto's colorful rendering of the spirit of the *Year of Decision, 1846* (Boston, 1943).

[57] For example, he voted in favor of the act supplementary to the act of war
passed by the House on May 11. *Congressional Globe*, XV, 923–4. June 4, 1846.

[58] See below, pp. 534–5.

[59] "It belongs to you to lead the way. There are enough to follow as fast as time
and circumstances will permit." Seward to JQA, Auburn, May 4, 1844.

"I see you have a mission to perform. I look from Pisgah to the promised Land.
You must enter upon it, but you will be compelled to modify your theory of non-
resistance and resort to the Labarum of Constantine." JQA to Charles Sumner, Quincy,
August 29, 1846. Adams MSS.

he wrote to Charles, "don't give up the ship! The Mexican War and the free trade Tariff will in time give you topics to handle, not yet disclosed." [60]

It remained for another man to put forward, unsuccessfully, the famous proposal that might have been a fitting climax to John Quincy Adams's Second Career: the Wilmot Proviso,[61] to prohibit slavery in any territory to be purchased by treaty from the Republic of Mexico. Adams's overthrow of the Gag Rule had opened the first sectional crack in the new South-and-West alliance of the Democratic Party. The Wilmot Proviso was signal of the still deeper rift in the Democracy developed by the Texas Question and the War with Mexico.[62]

Adams voted for the Proviso when it passed the House, August 8, 1846,[63] only to see it filibustered to death in the Senate. He voted for it again during the next session in the roll-call of March 3, 1847, when the Three-Million Bill came back from the Senate and the Proviso failed, 97 to 102, to pass the House; then he voted against the bill which would have appropriated that much money to purchase peace with a conquered Mexico—stripped of the Proviso.[64]

Adams's considered view of the right or wrong of the war was contained in a letter to the aged Albert Gallatin acknowledging a newspaper article which controverted Polk's statement in his war message that Mexico's refusal to pay the arbitral awards was in itself a justifiable reason for war:

"I do not so consider it. Without considering the course of the Mexican Government as entirely justifiable, it was never such, as to have justified War on our part. But the design and the purpose to dismember Mexico, and to annex to the United States not only Texas, but several of her adjoining Provinces on this side the Continent, and the Californias on the other side, has in my opinion been what my old Colleague Caleb Cushing calls a 'fixed fact,' at least from the year 1830, and has been pursued by means, which gave to Mexico from that time ample cause of War in self-defense against the United States.

"The annexation of Texas, to the United States was but one fact in that series of transactions. The march of General Taylor from Corpus Christi to the Rio Del Norte was another, and his position at Corpus Christi itself was an act of flagrant War. It was War unproclaimed, and the War has never to this day been declared by the Congress of the United States, according to the Constitution. It has been recognized as existing by the Act of Mexico, in direct and notorious violation of the truth.

[60] JQA to CFA, Washington, June 29, 1846. Adams MSS.

[61] See Charles Buxton Going: *David Wilmot, Free-Soiler, a Biography of the Great Advocate of the Wilmot Proviso* (New York, 1924), pp. 285–6.

[62] Paul: *Rift in the Democracy*, p. 178.

[63] *Journal of House of Representatives*, 1st Sess., 29th Cong., pp. 1285–7; *Congressional Globe*, XV, 1217.

[64] *Congressional Globe*, [XVI], 29th Cong., 2d Sess., p. 573. March 3, 1847.

"The most important conclusion from all this, in my mind, is the failure of that provision in the Constitution of the United States, that the power of declaring War, is given exclusively to Congress. It is now established as an irreversible precedent that the President of the United States has but to declare that War exists, with any Nation upon Earth, by the act of that Nation's Government, and the War is essentially declared.

"The most remarkable circumstance of these transactions is, that the War thus made has been sanctioned by an overwhelming majority of both Houses of Congress, and is now sustained by similar majorities, professing to disapprove its existence, and pronouncing it unnecessary and unjust.

"It is not difficult to foresee what its ultimate issue will be to the people of Mexico, but what it will be to the People of the United States, is beyond my foresight, and I turn my eyes away from it." [65]

Through old, sad eyes John Quincy Adams looked upon the war as a victory for the United States that might be fatal to liberty and to all that the Union meant, physically and morally. Before we note his last dying protest at the War with Mexico, it is appropriate to describe his long campaign for a scientific institution which, by increasing and diffusing knowledge among men, would be an instrument of the Union for the improvement of mankind upon this planet.

[65] JQA to Albert Gallatin, Washington, December 26, 1847. Adams MSS.

CHAPTER XXIII
Lighthouses of the Skies
(1825–1846)

❁

The heavens declare the glory of God: and the firmament sheweth his handywork.

PSALM XIX, 1

A SCHOLAR in the White House is a pleasing image, if not too frequent a
fact of American history. There have been some conspicuous examples,
of course, both among the founding fathers and in our own twentieth
century. The realistic John Adams, the versatile Thomas Jefferson, the
constructive James Madison, presented a succession of scholarly Presidents who were ornaments to the young nation. In the twentieth century
Theodore Roosevelt and Woodrow Wilson lent luster to the Presidency as
rival men of letters in history and politics. But between the intellectual
monuments of the Revolution and the beginning decades of the present
century there was a long stretch barren of literary or scientific distinction
in that highest office. To be sure, Abraham Lincoln wrote a few words
that may live longer than those of any other statesman of his day, but like
Washington he was not a scholar and certainly had only the most rudi-
mentary understanding of science and its meaning for mankind. During
the nineteenth century, after the passing of the talents of the Revolution,
there was only one American President who was a notable sponsor of
learning: that was John Quincy Adams. He continued the role even more
strongly during his public service after he left the White House.

The second Adams was not an original thinker like his father, not a
scientist, not the historian that the quality of his mind entitled him to be,
not an artist, not a poet for all his reams of scribbled verse and hymns, not
even a great orator despite his sobriquet of Old Man Eloquent. But he
was a prodigiously studious and generally erudite man, a defender of
learning and a contender for the physical and moral improvement of man
by the diffusion of knowledge and its application to government. During
the years of his congressional career no one was in greater demand as a
lecturer at lyceums and institutes—mostly unpaid.[1] There was scarcely a

---

[1] So numerous were such invitations to speak that he could not even answer them
all and had to put "cards" in the public press declining them generally.

learned society in the land to which he did not belong, or a college students' literary group of which he was not made an honorary member. No one was better known throughout the republic of letters. First and foremost of his activities in this realm, during his Second Career, was his steady and disinterested patronage and promotion of the wondrous science of astronomy.

1

Adams had a consuming interest in order and in numbers, expressed among other ways in his notation of thermometers and chronometers and the careful numeration of his Diary and correspondence. He partly sublimated this immitigable passion in a study of the movement of matter and the measurement of time and space and their practical relation to human affairs and government. During his lengthy diplomatic sojourns in Europe he had perforce to deal with different measures of money and distance and weight. The more he compared these vexatious variations the more content he became with the new decimal dollar of the United States and enthusiastic for the whole metric system. He began to collect information on weights and measures, an inquiry which developed into formidable researches presented in his celebrated *Report* of 1821.[2]

From weights and measures of the earthly globe his mind turned to the universe around him. The long winter nights of four years at the Court of St. Petersburg sharpened an interest in the mysteries of the firmament that sparkled so mightily over the vast realm of Russia, and he began to study astronomy. His curiosity about the movements of the heavenly bodies continued during the peaceful years of his London mission in the idyllic residence at Ealing, hard by the Meridian of Greenwich. He made himself familiar with the works of Newton, Schubert, Lalande, Biot, and Lacroix and other standard treatises of the day. Astronomy and mathematics appeared to him as the keys that would somehow unlock illimitable reaches of science and its application to human welfare.

Before Adams's Presidency no opposition had been voiced on constitutional grounds to the sponsorship of learning by Government, whether state or Federal. There had simply been no real interest in it except for a few distinguished individuals. Washington had advocated a national university at the nation's capital. Jefferson had made amateur astronomical observations and at one time had a plan for a national observatory. During his Presidency, Congress passed a law providing for a coastal survey of the United States, a task that proved difficult for lack of precise astronomical observations and calculations. A handful of scientists and professors, including such lights as the Swiss-born Ferdinand Rudolph Hassler, early a professor at West Point and at Union College, later the first United States coastal surveyor; and William Lambert, of Virginia and the

[2] Vol. I, 258-9.

District of Columbia, kept urging the establishment of an observatory and
the precise fixing of a prime meridian, perhaps through the city of Washington, as essential to any accurate survey and consequently to the protection of navigation. The House of Representatives referred the subject
to President Madison's Secretary of State, James Monroe, who declared
that the United States, like the principal countries of Europe, ought to
have an observatory. In 1813 a special committee of the House, headed by
Dr. Samuel L. Mitchill of New York, with John C. Calhoun a prominent
member, brought in a report and bill for the establishment of a national
observatory and creation of the office of national astronomer. Preoccupation with the war with Great Britain prevented the bill from ever coming
up for a vote, and afterwards widespread public apathy rather than any
expressed opposition to federal powers held back the project.[3]

From these earlier urgings President John Quincy Adams, with his developing interest in science, tried to take the lead in his program for
Liberty with Power—paternalistic action by the Federal Government for
the physical and moral improvement of mankind, including advancement
of knowledge and learning. For such a program a national university and
a national observatory seemed like noble and shining instruments, already
advocated by some of the country's most illustrious personages. Again a
special committee of the House reported favorably on the establishment
of an observatory in the District of Columbia and offered another bill to
that effect. But by 1826 the reaction to National Republicanism was setting in against the Minority President, and the Opposition made successful sport of Adams's metaphor for astronomical observatories—"lighthouses of the skies" [4]—by misquoting it as "lighthouses *in* the skies." Then
followed the Opposition's appeal to Old Republicans, Van Buren's political alliance between planters of the South and plain republicans of
the North, the triumph of Andrew Jackson, the rise of the state-rights
school, the concept of the least government possible, and the complete
frustration of Adams's national program. The defeated scholar in politics
moved from the White House to retirement, appropriately enough, on
Meridian Hill. A decade passed before he had another opportunity to
advocate his favorite project.

2

The unusual bequest of a singular Englishman, in the year 1835, resulted in the first foundation for the general advancement of science in
America, and that under the direct control of the United States Government. James Smithson, a natural son of the Duke of Northumberland, was
half-brother to that Hugh, Lord Percy, "the handsomest man of his day,"

[3] Charles O. Paullin has described the "Early Movements for a National Observatory, 1802–1842," in *Records of the Columbia Historical Society*, XXV (Washington, D.C., 1923), 36–56.

[4] See JQA's first annual message to the Congress, December 6, 1825.

who had commanded the British troops at the Battle of Lexington. A graduate of Pembroke College, Oxford, Smithson was an experimenter in natural science and a writer of numerous papers on chemistry and mineralogy. Like his American contemporary John Quincy Adams, he was greatly interested in expanding the mental horizon of mankind. Because of the circumstances of his birth he could not inherit the title, a fact that may help to explain the unusual provisions of his will, made at the age of sixty-one.

After providing one hundred pounds annuity for a faithful servant, Smithson bequeathed the remaining income of his entire estate to a nephew, Henry James Hungerford, for his lifetime. Should the heir marry, the testator Smithson empowered him to make a jointure. At Hungerford's death the whole property was to go to any child or children, legitimate or illegitimate, which he might leave. But if the nephew should die without leaving any child or children, then the entire property was bequeathed to the United States of America, "to found at Washington, under the name of the Smithsonian Institution, an Establishment for the increase and diffusion of knowledge among men." [5]

The contingent provision was that sort of stipulation which a man puts in his will only to take care of a remote chance. In this instance the chance that there should be no marriage, no jointure, no children legitimate or illegitimate, seemed very small, but it was interesting and perhaps significant that this scion sinister of one of England's leading noble families should pitch upon the United States and the Government of a trans-Atlantic Republic far from the cultural centers of the enlightened world, the sarcastic butt of English writers of the day, as a trustee to carry out his contingent preference, "the increase and diffusion of knowledge among men." Perhaps he had read the injunction of John Quincy Adams's great patron George Washington, in the Farewell Address: "Promote, then, as an object of primary importance, institutions for the general diffusion of knowledge."

The remote contingency came to pass. Five years after Smithson's decease Hungerford died unmarried and childless. Jackson, in a special message of December 17, 1835, notified Congress of the surprising bequest—amounting to half a million dollars. He asserted that the Executive had no authority to accept the trust and obtain the funds; therefore

[5] Copy of the will in *Documents Relating to the Origin and History of the Smithsonian Institution*, edited by William J. Rhees, in *Smithsonian Miscellaneous Collections*, XVII (Washington: Smithsonian Institution; 1880), 1–2. This convenient volume, hereinafter referred to as *Smithsonian Documents*, reprints proceedings of House and Senate, diplomatic correspondence connected with the bequest, together with those passages from JQA's *Memoirs* which relate to the bequest and the establishment of the Smithsonian Institution. These documents, except for the reprints of passages from JQA's *Memoirs*, are largely duplicated in Vol. I of *Smithsonian Miscellaneous Collections*, XLII (Washington: Smithsonian Institution; 1901), prepared by the same editor.

he left it to Congress to initiate such measures as it should deem necessary.

To Adams, now a member of Congress, it seemed that the finger of Providence by incomprehensible means had guided the will of the brother of Lord Percy of Lexington memory to the capital of the independent United States to encompass great results. He determined to see that this wonderful gift should not be frittered away by political joinery and jobbery, that it should be secured and used for the highest type of research. During the remainder of his life, amidst all the bitter controversies and debates on sectional and other issues, he stuck to this task through thick and thin, with such success as we shall see.

The first concern was to see that the bequest was actually accepted and the money secured. Each house of Congress referred the President's message to a committee: the Senate to its judiciary committee, the House of Representatives to a special committee of nine members. Adams was chairman of the House committee. The Senate committee, Benjamin Watkins Leigh of Virginia chairman, acted first. It brought in a matter-of-fact report accompanied by a proposed joint resolution authorizing the President to assert the claim of the United States to the legacy. The House committee gave Adams the lead, and he took pains in composing its report, unanimously presented, to expand eloquently on the historical background of the testator, the exalted nature of the trust, the moral example of leaving it to a republic such as the United States, and the high responsibility of the trustee before all mankind.

"The attainment of knowledge," declared Adams in this report, "is the high and exclusive attribute of man, among the numberless myriads of animated beings, inhabitants of the terrestrial globe. . . . It is by this attribute that man discovers his own nature as the link between earth and heaven; as the partaker of an immortal spirit; as created for a higher and more durable end. . . . To furnish the means of acquiring knowledge is therefore the greatest benefit that can be conferred upon mankind. It prolongs life itself and enlarges the sphere of existence. The earth was given to man for cultivation to the improvement of his own condition. Whoever increases his knowledge multiplies the uses to which he is enabled to turn the gift of his Creator to his own benefit and partakes in some degree of that goodness which is the highest attribute of Omnipotence itself . . . to what higher or nobler object could this generous and splendid donation have been devoted?" [6]

The House approved the report by ordering five thousand copies to be printed. It had its effect on the debates in the Senate.

The two Senators from South Carolina immediately attacked the joint resolution as an ominous expression of national power against the reserved rights of the states!

John C. Calhoun declared that it was not in the power of Congress to

[6] *Smithsonian Documents*, pp. 149–51.

establish a national university. (The Constitutional Convention of 1787 had twice rejected specific power for that purpose, though it was generally conceded that it could set up a university for the District of Columbia.) The same principle, he decided, would apply to an institution for the increase and diffusion of knowledge—what was that but a university? But, quibbled Calhoun, Smithson had not said anything in his will about the District of Columbia; he had designated the city of Washington! Besides, added the great Nullifier and Sectionalist, it should be beneath the dignity of the United States to receive gifts like this from anyone.

"I am against the power," affirmed Calhoun's colleague, William C. Preston, "and would be against the policy, if they [the Congress] had the power." [7]

Nevertheless the joint resolution passed the Senate 31 to 7.[8] But the House substituted Adams's bill for the joint resolution, which the Congress then accepted without a record vote. It enabled the President to present the claim in the English chancery courts, appropriated $10,000 for expenses, and, what was most important in Adams's bill, pledged the faith of the United States to apply all money received from the bequest to the founding and endowment of the Smithsonian Institution at Washington.[9] In due time Richard Rush, acting as special agent of the President, brought home from England £104,960 8s. 6d., after expenses, in gold sovereigns (except for change), and deposited them in the Mint at Philadelphia, where they produced the sum of $508,318.46,[10] which was transferred to the Treasury of the United States and then, by an enabling act of Congress,[11] invested in bonds of certain Western states, most of it in those of Arkansas. There were those who complained that Rush had not advertised with sufficient zeal in England for the discovery of illegitimate heirs to Smithson! [12]

3

What now should be done with this great fund, big enough in those days to found a university, scarcely sufficient in our times to build a dormitory for a junior college? Just what kind of institution should be established by Congress at Washington best to carry out James Smithson's purpose of increasing and diffusing knowledge among men?

Some people seemed to think it naturally meant a national university.

[7] Ibid., pp. 143–6.
[8] Ibid., pp. 147, 156.
[9] Act of July 1, 1836. *U.S. Statutes at Large*, V, 64.
[10] *Smithsonian Documents*, p. 120, and pp. 6–122.
[11] Section 6 of the act of July 7, 1838, for the maintenance of the Military Academy at West Point, also provided that all the money coming from the Smithson bequest should be invested by the Secretary of the Treasury, with the approval of the President, in stocks of the states bearing interest at not less than five per cent per annum.
[12] *Memoirs*, X, 93–4.

Dr. Stephen Chapin, president of Columbian College, to which Adams had lent over $13,000, including arrears of interest, went to see the college's benefactor and creditor. "If this money should be applied to the foundation of a college or university," he represented, "it must necessarily effect the total destruction of my college."

"I have not permitted myself to think upon the subject till the money should be in the Treasury," Adams straightway told him. "I hope, however, that no disposal of the fund will be made which will in any manner injure the Columbian College. I do not think the Smithsonian Institution should be a college, or a university, or a school of education for children, but altogether of a different character. . . . I hope the President will in his next message propose some plan. . . . I advise you to see the President and converse with him on the subject." [13]

Adams revealed his own ideas to President Van Buren in a long talk at the White House the next Sunday evening. Referring to his report on the Smithson bequest, he urged the Chief Executive to recommend some plan at the coming session of Congress. He suggested first the establishment of an astronomical observatory, then an annual course of lectures on the natural, moral, and political sciences. "Above all, no jobbing," he told Van Buren, "no sinecures—no monkish stalls for lazy idlers." [14]

The President seemed to concur, and asked Adams to name any persons who might usefully be consulted.

Before the opening of Congress, Adams called again at the White House to urge that something be done. Van Buren declared he would leave the matter entirely to Congress. He said noncommittally that he had found the idea of an astronomical observatory favorably received by all to whom he had mentioned it. [15] Meanwhile the Secretary of State, John Forsyth, had sent out a letter to a list of learned men, including Adams, asking for their ideas. Most of the suggestions advanced then and thereafter were for a university of some kind, with professional graduate schools and lectureships. That was what Dr. Chapin recommended too; he felt that it met Adams's requirements for the promotion of original research—and obviously it would not compete with the undergraduate activities of his own Columbian College; perhaps it might help them. Others were for a national library, with lectureships attached, a normal school, or an agricultural college. There were also those who favored a national museum and botanical garden. [16]

In two long communications to the Secretary of State, Adams further developed his own thoughts. He rested them on three principles, which he brought forth on every occasion in discussions thereafter: (1) keep

13 *Memoirs*, X, 23. June 22, 1838.
14 *Memoirs*, X, 25. June 24, 1838.
15 *Memoirs*, X, 44. November 29, 1838.
16 For the different plans sent in response to Forsyth's circular letter, see *Smithsonian Documents*, pp. 838–90.

the principal of the fund intact, spend only the interest, not entrust it to any bank, nor loan it on any pledge of state stocks; (2) no application of it to any school for the education of youth, or any religious establishment—such would be more likely to diffuse than to increase knowledge among men; (3) the first appropriations of accruing interest to go to erect an astronomical observatory along the lines of the Greenwich Observatory in London and the Bureau des Longitudes in France. "But the great object of my solicitude," he said, "would be to guard against the canker of almost all charitable foundations—jobbing for parasites, and sops for hungry incapacity. . . . Not so easy will it be to secure, as from a rattlesnake's fang, the fund and its income, forever, from being wasted and dilapidated in bounties to feed the hunger or fatten the leaden idleness of mountebank projectors, and shallow and worthless pretenders to science." [17]

Van Buren contented himself with laying all these suggestions before Congress.[18]

Dr. Chapin was more and more alarmed. The Columbian College was practically insolvent. For several years it had been trying without success to get money from its sponsors, the Baptists. The good doctor went to Adams again to inquire if any assistance could be had from the Smithson Fund. He wanted the Government to take charge of the college as an appendage to the intended Smithsonian Institution.

"Without knowing what the views of others are," replied Adams, "mine are that no part of the Smithson Fund shall be applied to any school, college, university, or seminary of education; but that equal care should be taken to avoid doing any injury whatever to any such institution."

"The condition of the College at present," Chapin mournfully declared, "is such that unless it can receive assistance from some quarter it must go down and its concerns must be closed."

"If the Faculty thinks there is any prospect of their obtaining anything from the Smithson Fund," declared Adams, "they might apply to the President of the United States, or to any other member of the committee [the joint committee on the Smithson Fund]; and if there should be any disposition in Congress to aid the college from the fund, I will immediately withdraw from the committee and leave the whole arrangement to be made by others. As I deprecate above all things the application of the funds to purposes for the benefit of individuals, I am determined at least to be disinterested myself, and *will in no shape or form receive one dollar of the fund myself.* And as the principal debt of the Columbian College is to me, I can be instrumental to no arrangement which would result in the payment of the college debt from the Smithson Fund."

[17] JQA to John Forsyth, Secretary of State, Quincy, October 8, 11, 1838. Ibid., pp. 842–9.

[18] Message of President Van Buren, December 6, 1838, with accompanying documents. H. Ex. Doc. No. 11, 25th Cong., 3d Sess.

"We are aware there is some delicacy in your position in regard to the college debt," suggested Dr. Chapin, "but we have ample means for the payment of our debt—as preliminary to the receiving of any assistance from the Government."

"At all events," declared Adams, "it is a subject in which I can have no agency, though if you obtain encouragement to your wishes from the President, I will cheerfully withdraw from the committee." [19]

Dr. Chapin talked with Van Buren, who asked him to put his ideas in writing. Needless to say, Chapin got nowhere with Adams even though the latter was in debt to his former valet. Adams in the House of Representatives continued to insist—and the select committee consistently backed him up—that none of the Smithson money should go to any college or university. The Columbian College struggled on and survived, thanks in part to Adams, who in 1842 compounded its mortgage to him for $8,776.23, at about fifty-two cents on the dollar.[20] Today the George Washington University, twentieth-century incarnation of the Columbian College, proclaims with proper pride that John Quincy Adams was one of its early benefactors.[21]

The movement in favor of a university rather than a research institution threatened to deny Adams's basic principles and set aside all his efforts to keep the Smithson bequest out of politics. He was very suspicious of any member of Congress who brought up a suggestion that might feather a nest for himself. While Adams's committee was studying the bundle of documents that Van Buren had transmitted to Congress, Asher Robbins of Rhode Island rose in the Senate and delivered an elegant speech, flowery with Latin quotations. The United States, he said, should emulate the example of ancient Greece and her schools, that gave to Rome her eloquence and her literature: *Græcia capta ferum victorem cepit, et artis intulit agresti Latio.*

"I could wish, if all were agreed to it," said Robbins, referring to George Washington's Farewell Address, "that this institution should make one of a number of colleges to constitute a university to be established here, and to be endowed in a manner worthy of this great nation and their immense resources."

This suggestion would have greatly helped the Columbian College.

Senator Preston, who had denied the constitutionality and opposed the idea of a national university, now chimed in: "Surely, Mr. President," he said, "the establishment of the Smithsonian Institute could not commence under more favorable auspices than to have attracted the care of

---

[19] *Memoirs*, X, 89–90. January 5, 1839. Italics inserted. I have inserted a dash between "payment of our debt" and "as preliminary to" in the next to the last paragraph above.

[20] See above, p. 197, n. 83.

[21] *A University in the Nation's Capital, 1821–1947* (Washington, D.C.: George Washington University; 1947), p. 8.

the honorable Senator, who in every way is so eminently qualified to take charge of whatever concerns the interest of learning or of charity. . . . Nor can I forbear, also, to thank him for introducing those elegant and elevated topics which carry us for a moment into regions of calm and serene air, above the smoke and din of our accustomed and more strenuous efforts on this floor." [22]

It was evident that Preston and those who opposed all that Adams stood for in the nation, yet could no longer hope to decline the Smithson bequest, would be willing to water it down into some species of educational authority in the District of Columbia under Robbins's innocuous chancellorship.[23] And what delight they took in giving an accolade to the Senator from Rhode Island as the country's foremost friend of learning, rather than to John Quincy Adams!

Robbins sat down much pleased with himself, particularly when the Senate passed his resolution to set up a joint committee to bring in plans for providing an "institution of learning" to which to apply the Smithson legacy. And even more so when the House of Representatives concurred in the resolution, thus seeming to set aside the deliberations of Adams's special committee.

The joint committee as established consisted of seven members of the Senate, Robbins chairman, together with the members of the old House committee, Adams chairman. Its meetings proved to be no more than a brief bout between the Senate group and the House group. Adams held his colleagues unanimously in line with their previous commitments to his three principles. The conferences therefore ended in a deadlock. All that could be agreed upon was that the leader of each group should prepare a separate bill conforming to its views, the two bills to be reported to both houses for consideration. Adams drafted a bill for an astronomical observatory; Robbins presented resolutions in favor of a "scientific and literary institution," denying that the erection and support of an astronomical observatory would fulfill in good faith the intentions of Smithson. The last session of the Twenty-fifth Congress ended a few days later (March 3, 1839) without any action being taken by either house on either set of resolutions or either bill.[24]

[22] *Smithsonian Documents*, pp. 159–66.

[23] ". . . I spoke also to Mr. Woodbury [Secretary of the Treasury] also of the Smithsonian fund . . . how Asher Robbins, a Senator from Rhode Island, being laid politically on the shelf by his constituents, had taken a fancy to this fund for the comfort and support of his old age, and projected a University, of which he was to be the Rector Magnificus." *Memoirs*, X, 109. March 23, 1839.

[24] *Smithsonian Documents*, pp. 158–99. As a testimony to his constituents Adams set forth his views on the "sluggish" response of the National Government to the memory of a "munificent stranger" who had manifested such confidence in our institutions, in two lectures on the Smithson bequest, to the Quincy Lyceum and to the Mechanics Apprentices and Library Association in Boston, in November 1839.

JQA delivered the first part of the Quincy lecture in person the evening of November 13, 1839, repeated in Boston, November 14. The death at Quincy of his little

The opposition of Calhoun, Preston, Waddy Thompson, and their cohorts, and the desultory attitude of the Senate in general, all but discouraged Adams. "It is hard to toil through life for a great purpose," he lamented to himself, "with a conviction that it will be in vain; but, possibly, seed now sown will bring forth good fruit hereafter." [25]

The deadlock between House and Senate developed into a long contest between a national observatory and a national museum, as one President after another, not to mention the Corporation of the City of Washington, urged Congress to do something about the Smithson bequest. Meanwhile advocates of the new projects steadily petitioned Congress, often presenting their prayers through Adams himself. As champion of the right of petition he faithfully presented their memorials whether he agreed with them or not. There were proponents of a national university of higher education, of a national agricultural institution, a professorship of the German language, a national library, a fund for the award of big prizes in literary and scientific competition, and other proposals. Most plausible contender for the bequest was the National Institution (soon renamed Institute) for the Promotion of Science and Literature. The controlling mind behind this movement was Adams's old diplomatist friend the South Carolina Unionist Joel R. Poinsett. It seemed as though the Institute (incorporated by act of Congress, June 27, 1842) had been organized for the sole purpose of capturing and absorbing the Smithson money. Its roster listed many of the most prominent members of Congress, including Adams himself, and friends of science from all sections of the country. It looked to the establishment of a national museum, with lectureships and publications. [26]

Preston and some of Adams's Southern opponents fell in with the idea of such an Institute as the best way to dispose of Smithson's legacy. At one time Adams himself was almost willing to go along with the National Institute as the most practical nonpolitical solution, particularly when Poinsett agreed with him on his basic tenets of no expenditure of anything but interest on the principal of the fund, and an astronomical observatory to come first. [27] Adams's principal objection to such a merger was that the National Institute might overshadow the Smithsonian Institution and thus defeat the testator's trust in the United States Government to make it a real monument to his memory and philanthropy; he also wanted

---

granddaughter Georgiana Frances Adams, second daughter of John Adams, 2d, and Mary Hellen Adams, prevented him from giving the second part. *Boston Daily Evening Transcript*, X, No. 2861, November 23. His pastor, Mr. Lunt, read it in his absence, in Quincy, November 20, and in Boston, November 21, 1839. Diary. The lectures are printed in the *Christian Register and Boston Observer*, XIX, Nos. 11 and 15, April 6 and 11, 1840.

[25] *Memoirs*, X, 139.

[26] *The Smithsonian Institution, 1846–1896: The History of its First Half Century*, edited by George Brown Goode (City of Washington, 1897), pp. 33–49.

[27] *Memoirs*, X, 462. April 14, 1841.

to keep it separate from any national establishment requiring appropriations of money.[28] And the fact that the State of Arkansas, through a process of default, held back the interest on its own bonds, served to delay action on the fund. This default made it impossible to secure the greater part of even the income accrued until Congress should take measures to make good the national pledge to apply the money to the Smithsonian Institution, whatever it should be. A large part of Adams's energy in this crusade for the promotion of research had to be devoted to a campaign for such legislation. Before he could obtain passage of the necessary laws,[29] the National Institute had faded from the picture, though not without effect on the ultimate character of the Smithsonian Institution.

For ten years Adams served as chairman of the special Smithsonian committees of the House of Representatives through consecutive sessions until the end of the Twenty-eighth Congress. As such he continued to present committee reports and bills—in 1840, 1841, 1842, and 1845—embodying his three principles and pressing for an observatory as the first and best means of increasing knowledge among mankind. The Democratic victory of 1844 resulted in loss of his chairmanship at the opening of the Twenty-ninth Congress in December 1845.

"The increase and diffusion of knowledge among MEN," he declared in his report of March 5, 1840, "present neither the idea of knowledge already acquired to be *taught,* nor of childhood or youth to be instructed; but of new discovery, of *progress* in the march of the human mind—of *accession* to the moral, intellectual, and physical powers of the human race—of dissemination throughout the inhabitable globe." Seldom does one find in a congressional document such passages as adorn some of his invocations of the duty of the National Government to use the Smithson bequest as an instrument for advancing the frontiers of knowledge

---

[28] *Memoirs,* XI, 173. June 11, 1842.

[29] The act of September 4, 1841 (*U.S. Statutes at Large,* V, 454) appropriating the proceeds of the sale of public lands to all the states pro-rata contained a section, introduced by Adams, whereby the portion coming to any state should first be applied to the payment of any debt, principal, or interest (like that on state stocks in which the Smithson Fund had been invested) from that state to the United States Treasury.

The act of September 11, 1841 (ibid., V, 465) repealed the law of July 7, 1838, which had required the Smithson Fund and all accruing interest to be invested in state stocks, and stipulated that in future all accruing interest of the Smithson Fund and all other funds held in trust by the United States Government be invested in stocks (i.e., bonds) of the United States Government.

The passage of these laws did not bring about any real recovery of defaulted interest on the state bonds. Distribution of proceeds of the sales of public lands among the several states was soon made inoperative by the tariff of 1842, which Adams voted against on that ground, despite the modicum of increased protection. Not until Congress passed the Smithsonian Act of August 10, 1846, advancing interest and principal of the fund, could a tangible program be proceeded with.

through a program of research rather than by a pedagogical process of education:

"The express object of an observatory [continued this same Report] is the *increase* of knowledge by *new discovery*. The physical relations between the firmament of heaven, and the globe allotted by the Creator of all to be the abode of man, are discoverable only by the organ of the eye. Many of these relations are indispensable to the existence of human life, and, perhaps, of the earth itself. Who can conceive the idea of a world without a sun, but must connect it with the extinction of light and heat, of all animal life, of all vegetation and production; leaving the lifeless clod of matter to return to the primitive state of chaos, or to be consumed by elemental fire? The influence of the moon—of the planets, our next door neighbors of the solar system—of the fixed stars, scattered over the blue expanse in multitudes exceeding the power of human computation, and at distances of which imagination herself can form no distinct conception; the influence of all these upon the globe which we inhabit, and upon the condition of man, its dying and deathless inhabitant, is great and mysterious, and, in the search for final causes, to a great degree inscrutable to his finite and limited faculties. The extent to which they are discoverable is, and must remain unknown; but, to the vigilance of a sleepless eye, to the toil of a tireless hand, and to the meditations of a thinking, combining, and analyzing mind, secrets are successively revealed, not only of the deepest import to the welfare of man in his earthly career, but which seem to lift him from the earth to the threshold of his eternal abode; to lead him blindfold up to the council chamber of Omnipotence; and there stripping the bandage from his eyes, bid him look undazzled at the throne of God." [30]

Once the astronomical observatory was set up, he was willing to concede that other expenditures might be made out of the interest of the fund, as available, for the improvement of *all* the arts and sciences: a botanical garden, a cabinet of natural history, a museum of mineralogy, conchology, and geology, and a general accumulating library: let not any branch of knowledge, "the source of all human wisdom, and of all beneficent power," be excluded from its equitable share of the benefaction.[31]

4

The debates in Congress year after year over what to do with the Smithson bequest stimulated widespread interest in astronomy. There had been temporary or makeshift observatories in the United States as early as 1769, but it was literally true, as Adams had said in his first

---

[30] Report of the Select Committee on the Smithson Bequest, John Quincy Adams Chairman, House of Representatives, March 5, 1840. *Smithsonian Document*, pp. 202–36.

[31] Ibid., p. 214.

Presidential message to Congress, that the country could not boast a single one in 1825. The University of North Carolina established a small observatory in 1831, but it burned down seven years later and was not rebuilt. Williams College dedicated the Hopkins Observatory early in 1838—the oldest extant observatory in the United States. Later in the same year Western Reserve College put one into service at Hudson, Ohio; and student vandals tore down a crude structure covering a mounted telescope at Miami College, Ohio (1838–40). In 1839 the United States Military Academy at West Point constructed an observatory, and the next year the Philadelphia High School Observatory made it possible for curiously inclined citizens of the City of Brotherly Love to scan the heavens.[32]

Adams had wanted Harvard to have the honor of establishing the first permanent astronomical observatory in the United States. He gave one thousand dollars to the university in 1823—contingent on an adequate fund being raised by other gifts—for the establishment of a professorship of astronomy and an observatory, with a plan for periodical publication of observations; but the necessary further donations were not forthcoming, so the money was returned.[33] Later his name led the list of donors that made possible the Harvard Observatory, opened in 1839, and he served diligently on the committee of the Board of Overseers for its supervision.[34]

The Navy Department had created at Washington a Depot of Charts and Instruments as far back as 1830. Young Lieutenant James M. Gilliss was detailed to duty there. He began to make observations with transit instruments and a forty-two-inch telescope from a small observatory set up in a frame building on Capitol Hill, and in 1846 published his volume of meteorological and magnetic data.[35] The increasing interest stirred up

[32] Willis I. Milham: *Early American Observatories: Which Was the First Astronomical Observatory in America?* (Williamstown, Mass.: published by Williams College; 1938). Professor Milham credits the David Rittenhouse observatories, set up first at Norriton, Pa., about 1769–74, later at Philadelphia, about 1786–96, as the first such institutions to be established in America, and lists the various temporary or makeshift observatories existing in the United States between then and 1838.

[33] JQA to Rev. John T. Kirkland, president of Harvard University, Washington, December 15, 1823. Adams MSS. *Memoirs*, X, 142.

[34] JQA to President Josiah Quincy, president of Harvard University, Boston, May 19, 1845. JQA to Edward Everett, president of Harvard University, October 27, 1847, with long report of the committee of the Board of Overseers for the visitation of the observatory: "There is yet one instrument of extraordinary power for astronomical observation, long since ordered, but still to be received before the apparatus of observation will be complete." Adams MSS.

[35] *Astronomical Observations Made at the Naval Observatory,* Washington . . . dated August 13, 1838. By Lieutenant J. M. Gilliss, U.S.N. (Washington: Gales and Seaton; 1846). See also: *Astronomical Observations made during the Year 1845 at the National Observatory, Washington,* under the direction of M. F. Maury, M.A., U.S.N. (Washington: Gales and Seaton; 1846).

by the widespread publication of Adams's reports on the Smithson bequest bore fruit for Gilliss's separate efforts to secure a naval observatory. In 1842 Congress appropriated funds for the construction of a building for the Depot of Charts and Instruments, soon changed in name to the United States Naval and Hydrographical Office, then to the United States Naval Observatory,[36] finally to be called the National Observatory. Establishment of this official observatory greatly weakened Adams's recommendations to use the first fruits of the Smithson Fund for such an institution.

5

Nowhere else was the new passion for astronomy so strong as in Ohio. When Adams reached Niagara Falls on his pleasure trip in the summer of 1843, he found there awaiting him Professor Ormsby M. Mitchel with a formal invitation to deliver an address at the laying of the cornerstone of an observatory to be erected by the recently established Cincinnati Astronomical Society. Previously he had not thought much of Mitchel's unrepressed enthusiasm when the professor from the West had appeared at Washington and begged letters of introduction to scientific friends abroad.[37] Now he welcomed the Cincinnati invitation [38] as a heaven-sent opportunity to exploit the new popular interest and thus to build up support in the next session of Congress for his Smithsonian bill. Upon his return to Quincy from Niagara Falls he set to work to prepare a paper embodying his long thoughts on the relation of science and research, particularly in the realm of astronomy, to the progress and leadership and improvement moral and physical of a democratic republic such as the United States. "My task is to turn this transient gust of enthusiasm for the science of astronomy at Cincinnati into a permanent and persevering national pursuit, which may extend the bounds of human knowledge and make my country instrumental in elevating the character and improving the condition of man upon earth. The hand of God Himself has furnished me this opportunity to do good." [39]

The prospect of another, longer trip west for the seventy-six-year-old man in a more dubious season of the year dismayed his friends and appalled his family. Two nights before he started, the last week in October, he sat up till half past one writing out passages of a speech to his constituents on the slave power and the inherent iniquity of the constitu-

---

[36] Paullin: "Early Movements for a National Observatory," loc. cit., pp. 50–5.

[37] "There is an obtrusiveness of braggart vanity in the man, which he passes off for scientific enthusiasm, and which is very annoying." *Memoirs*, XI, 183. Washington, June 2, 1842. "Scant praise for Mitchel," added Charles Francis Adams in one of his rare editorial notes, "but Mr. Adams knew him better afterwards,—though he did not live to appreciate his patriotic services during the war."

[38] JQA to Professor O. M. Mitchel, Cincinnati, O. Niagara Falls, July 25, 1843. Adams MSS.

[39] *Memoirs*, XI, 409.

tional three-fifths ratio on representation in Congress, which was still gagging the right of petition; [40] he was up at half past four in the morning to go to Dedham to deliver it to a throng of worshipping fellow citizens. The following day, tired out already, he started from Boston on the Western Railroad in company with Mr. and Mrs. Joseph Grinnell of New Bedford, who had been with him on a part of his summer tour, and Mrs. Grinnell's brother-in-law, Mr. Dalton; W. C. Johnson, a kinsman by marriage, later joined them at Geneva, New York.

The first stop was at Springfield to deliver that evening his much repeated lecture on Society and Civilization. Still fatigued, he started next day for the West. At Albany he rested overnight in a hotel. A rattle of hail awakened him in the morning before it turned to snow. He sallied forth for a shave. As he was leaving the barbershop, another customer was seated on the "anxious stool."

"Who is that stranger?" he asked, looking sharply at the ex-President.

"My name is John Quincy Adams, if you have never heard it."

"I thought so," said the local worthy, springing up from the chair, "My name is Weeks."

The two citizens shook hands.

After breakfast Adams climbed into the train, only to find it frozen to the rails. It took a team of horses an hour and a half to pull it loose, then the locomotive required another half hour to get up steam, all this on the 26th day of October.

The distinguished traveler and his party proceeded to Buffalo almost incognito, "silent and unnoticed," greeted only by a few informed friends, quite in contrast with the flattering public attentions of a few weeks earlier. Once embarked on Lake Erie, their steamer, the *General Wayne*, ran into a raging snowstorm that delayed them a day and a half in a sheltered cove under Point Albion on the Canadian side, "cold as Nova Zembla." Adams spent the time reading a Bible placed on the boat by the Young Men's Bible Society (he didn't approve of leaving out the Apocrypha) and perusing the *Memoirs of the Life of Aaron Burr* (he didn't approve of this either). At Erie, Pennsylvania, he went on shore for a reception, a short address, a military escort back to the boat, and a firemen's torchlight procession. At Cleveland someone recognized him early in the morning, again in a barbershop, and a public reception was hastily organized. He made some highly acceptable remarks about the tremendous growth of the Western states during his lifetime, and the mighty commerce of the inland seas.

It was not what he said so much as his venerable presence that made a lasting impression in Ohio. People connected him with the American Revolution and the whole history of the United States since then. The Old Northwest owed much to the Adamses, father and son. There were

[40] Transcript of notes of speech at Dedham, October 24, 1843. Adams MSS. *Memoirs*, XI, 410.

those who remembered how his father and his colleagues at Paris resisted all efforts of the enemy negotiators of the peace treaty to bring the boundary line down to the Ohio River and leave the Great Lakes to Great Britain. Again they recalled how in 1814 the younger Adams and his fellow negotiators at Ghent stood out against the same stratagem in the shape of a neutral Indian barrier state.[41]

"Blessings on thee, Patriot, Statesman, and Sage! . . ." apostrophized the *Cleveland Herald*. "No two men have ever lived and filled so large a space in our public life, whose names will be transmitted to future ages with more true greatness and patriotism than John Adams, and his illustrious son." [42]

From the thriving port of the old Western Reserve the famous visitor proceeded southwestward for four days on the Ohio Canal to Columbus in the center of the state. The efforts of the journey had already nearly prostrated him, racked as he was by a constant old man's cough and now beset by a sore throat and fever. The "canal packet" *Rob Roy* was a slow floating pillory eighty feet long and fifteen feet wide that cramped twenty passengers, crew, and four tow horses into overheated "rooms" with windows sealed against the driving snow. The ailing ex-President spent the nights as one of four men sleeping fitfully feet to feet on two opposite settees of a small compartment next to a "bulging stable." There is no record of the sanitary facilities, if any. During the daytime, as the cumbersome craft staggered along like an old nag, two and a half miles an hour, thumping heavily through the locks, he tried now to write, now to play cards with the other uncomfortable passengers.

At Akron a pleasant respite occurred. Friends appeared to take Adams and his party for a good breakfast, then to a public reception, where he made a short speech. A very pretty young woman came forward with others to greet him. As he took her by the hand, she kissed him on the cheek. He returned the salute to her lips and then kissed every woman who followed her. Some made faces at the elderly man's osculations, but none refused. He felt better as the boat plodded on through more snow squalls and he tried to make up arrears of his Diary. They stopped for friendly exchanges at Newark and at Hebron.[43] The publicity and prestige of his recent trip to New York State had only served to increase his popularity among the people of the Old Northwest.

At Columbus, Governor Shannon greeted him attentively. That evening he spoke at another public meeting. "The subject of astronomy," he told the townsmen, "I regard as one of the most important that can engage the attention of the human race." [44] Next morning two German

---

[41] Vol. I, 202–5.

[42] *Cleveland Herald*, November 1, 2, 1843. *Annals of Cleveland* (Cleveland: Works Progress Administration, Project 16823; 1938), XXVI, 206–7.

[43] *Weekly Ohio State Journal*, XXXIV, No. 11, November 15, 1843.

[44] Ibid., No. 10, November 8, 1843.

military companies with a brass band escorted his stagecoach across the
Scioto River. At Jefferson, at Springfield, more greetings; at Dayton a triumphal procession taking him into the city,[45] and a speech to a great
crowd from an open barouche; at Lebanon another one, where his old
colleague and friend Thomas Corwin welcomed him eloquently. All these
testimonials of veneration and affection, after years of obloquy from so
many sources, touched the old man tremendously, much as he professed
to himself to be annoyed: "the only comfort I have is that they are intended to manifest respect, and not hatred." [46]

Everywhere people greeted him as an authentically great American, a
friend of human liberty. He responded, more and more moved on each
occasion, often with reminiscences of the Revolution.

Finally the stage approached Cincinnati. A large cavalcade, headed by
Mayor Henry E. Spencer and Professor Mitchel, came out to meet him at
Mount Auburn, as the booming of cannon announced the long-awaited
arrival to the people. The day was fine and the sun shone down on
the city nestled in its circle of steep hills. An immense crowd followed the
procession to the Henrie House. There the Mayor formally welcomed the
distinguished visitor, and he responded to the multitude which answered
with deafening shouts of applause.[47]

To his surprise he found that his formal oration would take place later,
in the Wesleyan Methodist Chapel, and that he was expected first to give
a preliminary address at the actual laying of the cornerstone of the observatory. Worn down with fatigue and anxiety, and self-professed shame
at his inability to respond properly to the eloquent welcomes of practiced orators, he sat up until one o'clock composing this new speech. It
was still unfinished when he retired exhausted to a sleepless bed. In the
morning a large procession turned out despite the bad weather, and proceeded to the site. On the way they passed under a long banner hung
across Sixth Street: "John Quincy Adams, the Defender of the Rights of
Man." [48]

The speaker looked out over a sea of mud and an audience of umbrel-
las as he began his address, lamenting the lack of public support for
lighthouses of the sky, in contrast to public works such as bridges, turn-
pikes, canals, aqueducts, and railways. "Fellow citizens!" he declaimed.
"The Astronomical Society of the city of Cincinnati have determined to
wipe the reproach from the fair fame of our beloved country." The rain
blotted his manuscript so that he could hardly read it; but he finished,
and the audience quickly dispersed.

[45] Ibid., No. 11, November 15, 1843. *Memoirs,* XI, 425.

[46] *Memoirs,* XI, 423.

[47] *Memoirs,* XI, 425, November 8, 1843. *Cincinnati Gazette,* November 9, 1843.
Weekly Ohio State Journal, XXXIV, No. 11, November 15, 1843. Transcript of JQA's
remarks in Adams MSS.

[48] *Weekly Ohio State Journal,* XXXIV, No. 11, November 15, 1843.

JOHN QUINCY ADAMS, NOVEMBER 7, 1843

FROM A DRAWING FROM LIFE MADE AT LEBANON, OHIO, BY THE
QUAKER ARTIST, MARCUS MOTE. NOW IN THE GOLDEN LAMB
HOTEL, LEBANON, OHIO. COURTESY OF MR. ROBERT H. JONES,
THE HISTORICAL AND PHILOSOPHICAL SOCIETY OF OHIO, AND THE
UNIVERSITY OF CINCINNATI.

That evening he spoke to two thousand people at a temperance tea party given by the ladies of Cincinnati in a local theater. He walked there from his hotel through double lines of torchlights, in company with Judge Jacob Burnet, president of the Astronomical Society. (Soon after he learned that Burnet produced over a thousand barrels of wine a year from his local presses.) Adams all his life had been dead set against prohibition but always strong for temperance. "The cause of temperance," he soberly told the ladies, "is the emanation of a female mind. . . . I cannot but hope that it is one of the steps in the progress of man towards perfection, so far as it can be attained upon this planet." [49]

Adams's oration, delivered the next day, was really a long and learned lecture on the history of astronomy from the days of mythology and antiquity to the foundation of the Cincinnati Astronomical Observatory, interspersed with reflections on man's awesome response to the heavens through the ages: "The music of the spheres is the chorus of Angels conveying to man the inspiration of the Almighty, which giveth him understanding." It was, says his distinguished grandson Brooks Adams, "a gem," which might well compare in the history of science with his celebrated *Report on Weights and Measures,* if only he had had the time to polish it a little more. As printed it consisted of sixty-three pages, some twenty-five thousand words. Fortunately he delivered only half of it. As it was, they heard him for nearly two hours "without a symptom of impatience or inattention." [50] It is doubtful whether a modern audience, or indeed any congregation at that time other than the one in Cincinnati, would have listened without restiveness for that long.

"But what, in the meantime, have *we* been doing?" he asked the illuminati of Cincinnati after reviewing the notable discoveries from Anaxagoras to Herschel and the current progress of astronomy in Europe. Had we carried out the duties of that separate and equal station among nations which we had claimed under the Declaration of Independence, according to the laws of Nature and of Nature's God? "The God in whose name they [the men of 1776] spoke, had taught them, in the revelation of his gospel, that the only way in which man can discharge his duty to him, is, by loving his neighbor as himself, and doing with him, as he would be done by,—respecting his rights, while enjoying his own, and applying all his emancipated powers of body, and of mind, to self improvement, and improvement of the race." [51]

[49] Transcript of JQA's remarks at the Ladies' Temperance Tea Party at Cincinnati, on the evening of November 9, 1843. Adams MSS. See also *Weekly Ohio State Journal,* XXXIV, No. 11, November 15, 1843.

[50] *Memoirs,* XI, 427.

[51] *An Oration Delivered before the Cincinnati Astronomical Society on the Occasion of Laying the Corner Stone of an Astronomical Observatory on the 10th of November, 1843.* By John Quincy Adams (Cincinnati: printed by Shepard and Co.; 1843), pp. 61–2. This print also contains the earlier address of November 9, 1843. A pleasing description of the ceremonies, with selected letters from the Adams MSS.,

Thus, on that memorable day of his life, did John Quincy Adams reconcile science and religion. Who has done it better?

The citizens of Cincinnati regaled Adams with four more days of their city's hospitality and all that it could show of the good life. He accepted greetings from a deputation of colored people, and he spoke reminiscently to the bar association of Hamilton County.[52] Invitations came to extend his trip farther west and south: to Louisville, to Lexington, to Frankfort, in Kentucky; to St. Louis, Missouri; and to the State of Indiana. It was not within his physical powers to attempt such an itinerary and get back to Washington with time and strength to carry on in the approaching session of Congress. But he did cross the river with former Governor Morehead of Kentucky to speak at Covington, where a great concourse of people greeted him with bands and processions, as enthusiastically as any he had experienced in Ohio. He went out of his way to pay tribute to "that great man, your own citizen . . . my associate and friend, Henry Clay," [53] who was then entering his last campaign for the Presidency.

"The first kiss in Kentucky!" whispered a very pretty young woman as after his speech he shook hands with men, women, and children of Covington. Of course, he did not refuse.

After a final farewell to Cincinnati the steamboat stopped sixty-five miles up the river at Maysville, Kentucky, where again he paid his respects to Clay. "And here I solemnly declare," he privately recorded in his Diary, "that the charges of corrupt bargaining which had been trumped up against him and me are utterly without foundation." [54]

The personal triumph of his progress from Cincinnati to Washington helped to compensate for the weariness and utter exhaustion of the journey. People overwhelmed him with friendly welcomes at Portsmouth, at Marietta, where he went on shore to inspect the remarkable Indian mounds, and in Pennsylvania at Pittsburgh,[55] where he enjoyed four days of tumultuous ovations and speechmaking. It was the same at Centerville, Pennsylvania, and at Canonsburg (Jefferson College) and Washington (Washington College) and Brownsville; and at Cumberland, Maryland, and Harper's Ferry, Virginia. At towns along the Baltimore and

and twentieth-century reflections, may be found, with illustrations, in *The Centenary of the Cincinnati Observatory, November 5, 1843, Including the Addresses and Miscellany Relating to the Centennial Celebration of the First Large Astronomical Observatory in America* (Cincinnati: The Historical and Philosophical Society of Ohio and the University of Cincinnati; 1944).

[52] *Memoirs*, XI, 428–9. November 11, 1843. Transcript of "Mr. Adams's Meeting with the Bar of Cincinnati, November 11, 1843." Adams MSS.

[53] Transcript of "Mr. Adams's Remarks at Covington, Ky., November 13, 1843." Adams MSS.

[54] *Memoirs*, XI, 431.

[55] *Weekly Ohio State Journal* (Columbus), XXXIV, No. 13, November 29, 1843, quoting the Pittsburgh *Gazette*.

Ohio Railroad appeared deputations to greet him, with speeches of welcome before enthusiastic crowds cheering his responses.

Finally he reached his home in Washington, by way of Baltimore, on November 23, 1843, almost a month from the day he had left Quincy, his strength prostrated beyond anything he had ever experienced. But he was satisfied that he had done something to advance scientific research, particularly the study of astronomy. "I have little life left in me," he wrote in his Diary, "but it is my duty to cherish that which God has given me, till it be His pleasure to take it back." [56]

However much he had overtaxed his strength and alarmed his family by this long trip, there was still much life left in the old crusader, as the next session of Congress, which repealed the Gag Rule, would show, and as the events of five more fruitful years were to testify.

6

Perhaps to Adams's personal chagrin, but certainly not to his disapproval, the creation of the Naval Observatory brought to nothing all his efforts on behalf of a national observatory of any other kind. "I am delighted," he told the House in 1846 during debate on the final Smithsonian bill, "that an astronomical observatory—not perhaps so great as it should have been—has been smuggled into the number of institutions of the country, under the mask of a small depot for charts, etc.[57] There is not one word about it in the law. I would like to ask the gentleman from South Carolina [Alexander D. Sims, who had opposed the constitutionality of a National Observatory, and wanted to turn the bequest back to the English chancery courts] [58] where is the power under the Constitution to make this appropriation?"

"I do not know," chaffed Mr. Sims, "but since the doctrine promulgated by a distinguished President of the United States, of erecting lighthouses in the skies, has grown into popular favor, I presume that the gentleman would find no difficulty in the question of power!"

"I am very glad to hear that it has grown in popular favor . . ." Ad-

[56] *Memoirs*, XI, 441. Except where indicated in citations above to other sources, I have followed JQA's own account of his western trip as printed in *Memoirs*, XI, October 24 to November 24, 1843, with numerous quotations therefrom. So also did Brooks Adams in his notable Introduction to Henry Adams: *The Degradation of the Democratic Dogma* (New York, 1919), pp. 64–76.

[57] "Your efforts to advance in America the cause of practical Astronomy, are known to the world. The lively interest you manifest in all that concerns the [Naval] Observatory causes you to be considered as one of its most active and zealous friends," wrote Lieutenant M. F. Maury to JQA, transmitting at the latter's request a detailed description of the Observatory, its staff, and current work: "The Observatory is, literally, also, a 'Depot of Charts and Instruments for the Navy.'" M. F. Maury to JQA, National Observatory, Washington, November 17, 1847. Adams MSS.

[58] *Smithsonian Documents*, p. 439.

ams temperately responded. "I claim no merit for the erection of the astronomical observatory, but in the course of my whole life, no conferring of honor, or of interest, or of office, has given me more delight than the belief that I have contributed, in some small degree, to produce these astronomical observatories, both here and elsewhere. I no longer wish any portion of this fund to be applied to an astronomical observatory." [59]

In the final debates on the Smithsonian bill he directed his efforts to the establishment of his two surviving principles: no expenditures for any college, university, or other institution for the teaching of youth, and only interest on the fund to be spent as it became available. He opposed the use of any of the taxpayers' money for the Smithsonian Institution: he would rather wait until the interest on the defaulted bonds should be recovered and the principal finally paid when due and reinvested in United States Government securities. This last stand was perhaps a little inconsistent with his earlier demand that the faith of the United States be pledged to the conservation of the fund and execution of the trust.[60] It was certainly contrary to the provisions of the act of August 10, 1846, which advanced a sum of money equal to the back interest, paid and unpaid, for the erection of suitable buildings for the Smithsonian Institution and other current expenses, and further guaranteed for future expenses a continuing income of six per cent on the net principal of the fund ($501,169) originally received into the Treasury from the British chancery court.[61]

Adams nevertheless voted for the final bill. As enacted it embodied two of his essential principles. But the Smithsonian Institution took the shape rather of a national museum or treasure house for the Federal Government's scientific curiosities,[62] controlled by a nonpolitical board of regents, than of a carefully organized research institution; this character closely resembled the plans that Poinsett and the National Institute had advanced rather than what Adams had conceived. As time went on, the Federal Government gradually made the Smithsonian a catchall for its heterogeneous scientific activities as they developed in a sprawling way throughout the nineteenth century.[63] There still remained a need for advanced research institutions in Washington, as attested by the foundation of the Carnegie Institution of Washington (1902) and the National Research Council (1916).

[59] Ibid., p. 443.

[60] Ibid.

[61] Ibid., pp. 121, 429–34. *U.S. Statutes at Large*, IX, 102–6. The net principal was the original $508,318.46 paid into the Treasury minus certain expenses.

[62] The first important collection was the scientific specimens in many fields of knowledge gathered by the United States Exploring Expedition under command of Lieutenant Charles Wilkes, 1838–42.

[63] Goode: *Smithsonian Institution, 1846–1896, passim*. Webster B. True: *First Hundred Years of the Smithsonian Institution, 1846–1946* (Washington, August 10, 1946).

Of all these foundations the Smithsonian Institution with its variegated programs, however imperfectly co-ordinated, was a not unworthy prototype. No one did more than John Quincy Adams to keep it out of politics. And no statesman since Franklin had done so much to advance the cause of science in America.

CHAPTER XXIV

The Last of Earth

(1846 – 1848)

This is the end of Earth, but I am composed.

LAST WORDS OF JOHN QUINCY ADAMS

IT was nearly half a century since John Quincy Adams and his wife, Louisa, had been united in marriage at the Church of All Hallows, Barking, in London on July 26, 1797. At best only a few years of life remained for them. At Quincy on July 26, 1845, he looked back over the years to review once more his marriage and their life together during his career as a public man.

Their life had been a checkered one. They had enjoyed much. They had suffered not a little. Good and evil had followed them alternately toward the end of their days. Now he was the last of his generation of Adamses. His brother Charles had gone long ago. His dear sister Abigail had followed. Then his adored mother. Then the old patriot himself, John Adams, the President who had lived to see his son President; then his remaining brother, Thomas; and then his eldest son, George Washington Adams; next the second son, John; and more recently two beloved little grandchildren.[1] Only Charles Francis and his surviving sons [2] were left to carry on the destiny of a family.

Since George's tragic death John Quincy and the sorrowing Louisa had grown closer together. On the whole he judged his lot on earth had been a happy one and thought that every feeling of his heart ought to be of gratitude to Him who is the disposer of events.

---

[1] Georgiana Frances Adams (1830–9), second daughter of John Adams, 2d, and Mary Hellen Adams, died at Quincy, November 20, 1839.

Arthur Adams (1841–6), son of Charles Francis Adams and Abigail Brooks Adams, died in Boston, February 9, 1846.

[2] Charles Francis Adams's other children were:
Louisa Catherine Adams (1831–70), married Charles Kuhn
John Quincy Adams (1833–94)
Charles Francis Adams (1835–1915)
Henry Adams (1838–1918)
Mary Adams (1846–1928), married Henry Parker Quincy
Brooks Adams (1848–1927).

As for his own career, here are his reflections on the wheel of fortune, now spinning for him toward the end:

"My career in life has been, with severe vicissitudes, on the whole highly auspicious. With advantages of education perhaps unparalleled, with principles of integrity, of benevolence, of industry and frugality, and the lofty spirit of patriotism and independence taught me from the cradle, with the love of letters and the arts, useful and ornamental, and with aspirations of science, limited only by the scanty spark of ethereal fire in my soul, my intercourse with my contemporaries has in all its fluctuations been more successful than I deserved. My life has been spent in the public service. Washington, Madison, Monroe, were my friends and benefactors; Jefferson, a hollow and treacherous friend; Jackson, Charles J. Ingersoll, George W. Erving, Jonathan Russell, base, malignant, and lying enemies—a list to which I might, but will not, add other names. I have enjoyed a portion of the favor of my country at least equal to my desert, but have suffered, and yet suffer, much from that slander which outvenoms all the worms of Nile. But I am wandering from my wedding-day." [3]

1

With thanksgiving in his heart Adams entered his eightieth year, in Washington July 11, 1846, during the sweltering debates on the Mexican War and the Oregon Question. How well he knew the Potomac scene! Every nook and pillar of the Capitol building from pedestal to pediment. Every street, every corner of the city, every vista of sunrise, of tree bud, of garden, and accustomed flight of bird. Two days after his birthday he rose at dawn as usual and set out alone for a stroll through the scantily peopled streets. It was a still, hot morning, 84° Fahrenheit. Suddenly, drawn by an irresistible impulse, he walked across the lower Tiber (Goose Creek) bridge over toward the river. There under shelter of the bluff he found his old bathing-place where he used to go swimming when President. Some young men were already disporting themselves in the water. He saw their clothes loosely dropped on his favorite diving-rock. One of them said: "There is John Quincy Adams."

The water was warm, the surface calm, the rising sun clear above the sluggishly flowing river. Leaving the young fellows undisturbed, he went a few steps along the riverbank toward the Potomac bridge to another place. There he peeled off his apparel. Each man to his own rock. The tide was low, so he had to wade in slowly, as if to sample the bath he craved. Adams swam about for half an hour before coming out and mounting his rock again, like the old pelican he was, to dry and dress in the morning sun.

Two more mornings he repeated the baths, from his familiar rock, despite a ten-degree drop in temperature that made him shiver as he drew

[3] *Memoirs*, XII, 206. July 26, 1845.

on his clothes. Apparently he suffered no inconveniences from the ventures, or from the walks to and from his F Street house, which now took him half an hour each way,[4] as compared with eighteen minutes in the days of his prime.

These were his last swims in the Potomac. From then on, the feebling veteran bathed at sunrise in his bedchamber, rubbing his ancient body to what glow he could get with the aid of a horsehair strap and mitten.[5]

What a lot we know about John Quincy Adams, without and within, thanks to his unequaled Diary! [6]

"If my intellectual powers had been such as have been sometimes committed by the Creator of man to single individuals of the species," he wrote in October 1846, "my diary would have been, next to the Holy Scriptures, the most precious and valuable book ever written by human hands, and I should have been one of the greatest benefactors of my country and of mankind. I would, by the irresistible power of genius and the irrepressible energy of will and the favor of Almighty God, have banished war and slavery from the face of the earth forever. But the conceptive power of mind was not conferred upon me by my Maker, and I have not improved the scanty portion of His gifts as I might and ought to have done." [7]

2

Mr. and Mrs. Adams got back to Quincy in August 1846, worn out from the exciting session that had lasted late into the hot Washington summer. His only public activity that autumn was at the request of Charles Sumner and Dr. Samuel Gridley Howe to rise from a bed of fatigue and with declining faculties [8] (as he sensed them) preside in Faneuil Hall, Boston, over a civic meeting of protest against rendition of a stowaway fugitive slave from Boston harbor back to his master in New Orleans. An audience estimated at five thousand persons greeted him rapturously with continued cheering as he made his way to the speakers' rostrum. Yielding the chair for a few moments to Stephen C. Phillips, he joined the remarks of his son Charles Francis Adams with a few words of his own.[9] He compared the occasion with that famous meeting he had attended in the same hall thirty-eight years before when an outraged citizenry had protested the impressment of American seamen in the *Chesa-*

[4] *Memoirs*, XII, 269.

[5] *Memoirs*, XII, 279.

[6] "There has perhaps not been another individual of the human race, of whose daily existence from early childhood to fourscore years has been noted down with his own hand so minutely as mine." *Memoirs*, XII, 276–7.

[7] *Memoirs*, XII, 277. October 31, 1846.

[8] ". . . my faculties are now declining from day to day into mere helpless impotence." *Memoirs*, XII, 271. August 16, 1846.

[9] *Memoirs*, XII, 272–5. August 27, 1846.

peake-Leopard affair.[10] "It is a question," he declared, most solemnly and impressively, "whether your and my native Commonwealth is to maintain its independence or not. It is a question whether my native Commonwealth is capable of protecting the men who act under its laws or not." [11]

His voice was so old and thin and tired that only a few people on the platform could hear him, but that did not matter; his presence was enough, his look was testimony to the antislavery cause.[12]

That autumn Adams accepted the unanimous nomination of the Whig Convention of the Eighth District of Massachusetts, voting by ballot. A no-party man in general principle, he was now proud of being a Conscience Whig.[13] He reminded the committee of notification that he had favored the notice to Great Britain over Oregon and had voted against the War with Mexico. They expressed themselves as satisfied. He made no campaign, not even the usual report to his constituents in the local press or a speech by the village green—only a few words to the committee that came to his home. Again his fellow citizens of the Eighth District returned him to Congress with a generous majority of 1,600 votes.[14]

After the election he left Quincy to pass the remainder of the month at his son's home in Boston, at 57 Mount Vernon Street, in accord with what by now had become an annual custom. Mrs. Adams and Mary Hellen Adams, John's widow, and her surviving daughter, Mary Louisa, with two servants went on ahead to Washington. Charles Francis accompanied them as far as Philadelphia. A few days later, on November 20, 1846, the old statesman rose as usual between four and five in the morning. After bathing in his room and rubbing down with strap and mitten, he breakfasted with the family and started out for a morning walk with his old friend Dr. George Parkman to visit the new Harvard medical college. Suddenly his knees buckled under him and he could go no farther. With the help of his companion he staggered back to his son's house. They summoned his own doctor, John Bigelow. Also came Dr. Jackson, who had happened to be in consultation with Bigelow. The physicians put him to bed, where he stayed for several days and nights without pain but with little power of thought. "From that hour," he later wrote in a curious "posthumous memoir" attached to his Diary, "I date my decease,

[10] Vol. I, 140–1.

[11] Wilson: *Rise and Fall of the Slave Power in America*, II, 54–5.

[12] *Emancipator*, X, No. 22, September 30, 1846. *Liberator*, XVI, No. 40, October 2, 1846. CFA Diary, September 24, 1846.

[13] *Memoirs*, XII, 276.

"The Slave power and the puritan spirit are coming to close quarters. The slave power sneers at *Conscience*, as in the days of yore our pilgrim forefathers were called *puritans* in derision. Let us not be ashamed of the name of Conscience Whigs but inscribe it on our banners and deserve it if need be with martyrdom in the cause of human Liberty. What say the Sons of the Pilgrims? Will they answer *Conscience* with a sneer?" JQA to the Hon. John G. Palfrey of Boston. Quincy, November 4, 1846. Adams MSS.

[14] *Boston Daily Evening Transcript*, XVII, No. 4999, November 10, 1846.

and consider myself, for every useful purpose to myself or to my fellow-creatures, dead." [15]

It was undoubtedly a light cerebral hemorrhage. The frail Louisa hurried back to him from Washington, anxiously making the trip alone and unattended in the record time of thirty-six hours by rail and steamer.[16] Her husband recovered rapidly.[17] By the first of the new year he was able to go out again for daily carriage rides.

It was after recovery from shock that Adams carefully drew up his final last will and testament, thirty-three detailed articles in ten long pages of foolscap. The care and precision bestowed on the instrument shows that he was by no means so "dead" as he fancied. After appointing his son Charles Francis Adams his executor, administrator, trustee, and residuary legatee, he divided the bulk of his estate, real and personal (after debts), among his wife, Louisa; his daughter-in-law Mary Catherine (Hellen) Adams and granddaughter Mary Louisa Adams (daughter of the deceased John and Mary Hellen Adams); and his surviving son, Charles Francis. To his son he applied the same stipulation that his own father, John Adams, had placed upon him in regard to the paternal mansion and adjacent acres: a right to full title in them by paying $20,000 into the estate.[18] Very meticulously he left small portions to his other grandchildren, to his various nephews and nieces; and a small annuity to his cousin Louisa Catherine Smith (niece of his mother, Abigail), a familiar at various periods in the Adams household at Quincy. Item by item he distributed tokens and mementos among relatives and close friends. To the people of the United States he bequeathed the gold-headed ivory cane that certain grateful countrymen had presented to him on the occasion of the repeal of the Gag Rule in 1844, to remain in the custody of the Patent Office at Washington. His fine library of some 8,450 volumes, perhaps the best personal collection in the country at the time, together with his pictures, manuscripts, and papers, including those of his father in his possession, he gave to Charles, recommending that the latter cause a fireproof building to be constructed at some convenient time to house them, the whole to be transmitted in turn to his eldest son as one property, "to remain in the family as long as might be practicable," always confided "to the faithful custody of the person holding the legal property in the same." [19]

[15] *Memoirs*, XII, 279. The entry is dated Washington, Sunday, March 14, 1847.

[16] Mrs. Adams traveled up Long Island Sound from New York to the railhead at Allyn's Point (Stonington, Conn.) on the ill-fated *Atlantic*, which on the return trip to New York was driven ashore and dashed to pieces with heavy loss of life on November 27, 1846. See *Boston Daily Evening Transcript*, XVII, No. 5014, November 28, 1846.

[17] Statement of Dr. George Parkman, December 24, 1846. Adams MSS.

[18] John Quincy Adams had had by his father's will the privilege of buying from John Adams's estate the paternal seat for $12,000. See above, p. 191.

[19] Last Will and Testament of John Quincy Adams, January 18, 1847. Proved

JOHN QUINCY ADAMS, 1843

LITHOGRAPH BY P. HAAS, AFTER A DAGUERREOTYPE BY SAME. FROM THE
COLLECTIONS OF THE LIBRARY OF CONGRESS

JOHN QUINCY ADAMS, 1847

(AFTER HIS FIRST STROKE)

DAGUERREOTYPE BY MATTHEW BRADY.

FROM THE COLLECTIONS OF THE LIBRARY OF CONGRESS

The old gentleman was on his feet again, in the Boston streets, by the end of January 1847. He walked to divine services morning and afternoon on the 7th of February and took communion from the Reverend Dr. N. L. Frothingham. The following day he and his wife left for Washington in company with Charles and a nurse. They reached the F Street home comfortably on February 12, 1847, Mrs. Adams's seventy-second birthday.[20] Next morning he was back in his seat in the House of Representatives.

3

When the ancient Plymouth member walked into the House for the first time after his illness, the members rose as one man to greet him. Proceedings were interrupted as two of his colleagues informally conducted him to his place. His adversaries no longer attacked him and baited him as a firebrand and a madman. No one else now enjoyed as much prestige and respect in either house of Congress. He had become a patriarch, personifying the nation's history, venerated on both sides of the aisle by members from all sections, North, South, East, and West, a last personal link between George Washington and their own day, a son of the American Revolution mingling, as it were, among his posterity.

The old gentleman dutifully attended this and the next session, re-

---

March 18, 1848, in Probate Office, Norfolk County Court, at Dedham, Mass. Docket No. 121, Probate Records, LXXXI, 73–85.

Soon after his father's death in 1848 Charles Francis Adams presented to the Boston Athenæum between 6,000 and 7,000 pamphlets drawn from the library, apparently deeming it not "practicable" to keep them any longer in it. In 1870 he built a stone library building in the garden of the paternal estate at Quincy, now a National Historic Site. There the main portion of the library remains to this day. Worthington Chauncey Ford described the history and content of "The John Quincy Adams Library" in his Introduction to *A Catalogue of the Books of John Quincy Adams Deposited in the Boston Athenæum, with Notes on Books, Adams Seals and Book-Plates* by Henry Adams (Boston: printed for The Athenæum; 1938). (During John Quincy Adams's sojourns abroad and for some time thereafter his books had been deposited in the Athenæum.)

The Adams Manuscripts, papers of John Adams and John Quincy Adams, and later of Charles Francis Adams, remained in the stone building at Quincy until 1905, when the heirs created a fifty-year trust for control of the papers and placed them in the custody of the Massachusetts Historical Society, where they now repose. The first trustees were the three surviving sons of Charles Francis Adams (1807–86), all distinguished historians: Charles Francis Adams, Jr. (1835–1915), Henry Adams (1838–1918), and Brooks Adams (1848–1927); and Charles Francis Adams (1866–1954), son of their brother John Quincy Adams (1833–94). In 1955 the trustees considered turning over the family archive to the Massachusetts Historical Society after having had the documents microfilmed and distributed to a number of subscribing libraries throughout the United States for use of history students. Plans for publishing and editing the papers of John Adams, John Quincy Adams, and Charles Francis Adams were announced in 1954.

[20] All this Adams recorded with details in his "posthumous memoir." *Memoirs,* XII, 279–81. March 17, 1847. CFA Diary, February 7–12, 1847.

lieved of all committee duties except that of the Library of Congress, to which he clung devotedly. He would die, he told his wife, the minute he gave up his public life.[21] Regularly he responded to the roll-calls. For example, he voted in favor of the resolution (defeated 4 to 137) introduced by his colleague Charles Hudson of Marlboro, Massachusetts: that the committee on military affairs be directed to inquire into the expediency of withdrawing American forces to the east bank of the Rio Grande, and proposing peace to Mexico without indemnities and without territorial cessions, but payment of all "just" claims of American citizens due at the beginning of the war. Even Abraham Lincoln, who believed the war unnecessary and unconstitutional, and that it had been wrong for President Polk to send General Taylor's division into the disputed area on the Rio Grande, would not vote for such a peace resolution.[22]

One subject only brought Adams to his feet that session for anything like a speech. This was a proposal, in the shape of an amendment to the civil and diplomatic appropriation, to provide $50,000 indemnity to the owners of the *Amistad* for the libel adjudged against their ship and its self-liberated cargo of mutinied slaves. As he rose to speak, members from more distant seats moved in about him the better to hear his feeble voice.

With clear mind and memory the old champion of human rights summarized the history of that *cause célèbre*. He reminded the House that the Spanish Minister had demanded the rendition of the Africans not as slaves but as assassins. "He wanted to have them tried and executed for liberating themselves."

"There is not even the shadow of a pretense for the Spanish demand of indemnity . . ." insisted the man who had defended the Africans before the Supreme Court. "God forbid that any claim should ever be allowed by Congress which rested on such a false foundation! . . . The demand, if successful, would be a perfect robbery committed on the people of the United States. Neither these slave dealers, nor the Spanish government on their behalf, has any claim to this money whatever."

The House followed Adams and defeated the amendment, 28 to 94.[23] It continued to vote down the proposal as brought up again from time to time in later years until the Civil War put an end to the issue forever.

After the adjournment of Congress that spring the ex-President and his wife set out again for home the first of June. On July 27, 1847 they took

[21] LCA to Harriet Boyd, Washington, February 23, 1848. Dorothie Bobbé: *Mr. and Mrs. John Quincy Adams* (New York, 1930), p. 301. LCA to Abigail B. Adams, Washington, February 3, 1848. Adams MSS.

[22] *Congressional Globe*, [XVII], 30th Cong., 1st Sess., pp. 93–4. January 3, 1848.

One is disappointed to find nothing in JQA's Diary or papers to indicate any personal contact between him and Lincoln, then a Whig member from Illinois serving his only term in Congress.

[23] *Congressional Globe*, [XVI], *Appendix*, pp. 437–8. March 2, 1847.

great enjoyment in a modest celebration of their fiftieth wedding anniversary in the paternal Adams home. A quiet summer followed at Quincy before they returned in November to the capital.

Of the numerous good wishes and plaudits that greeted the venerable friend of freedom that year was the following resolution (November 3, 1847) of the executive committee of the American and Foreign Antislavery Society, transmitted to him as he passed through New York on his last journey from Quincy to Washington:

> *Resolved:* that Messrs. Arthur Tappan, Rev. Christopher Rush, Arnold Buffum, Lewis Tappan, and Rev. Luther Lee be a committee to wait upon the Hon. John Quincy Adams, now in this city on his way to Washington, and express to him the thanks of this committee for all that he has done in Congress and elsewhere on behalf of the Anti-Slavery cause; with their most respectful wishes for his health and usefulness during the approaching session of Congress and while his valuable life shall be preserved.[24]

Once more the veteran took his seat and responded dutifully to rollcalls in the House. But his correspondence languished. His lifelong Diary began to flicker out. "I had a long conversation of speculative politics with Mr. Walker [Robert J. Walker, Secretary of the Treasury]," he recorded in his crippled handwriting, December 1, 1847, "and I consider every word henceforth issuing from my lips as my last words and dying speech." Then followed irregular entries and scraps of verse, scattered listings of names of visitors. The last entry would be of February 20, 1848, apparently intended to be transcribed into some young lady's album:

> Fair Lady, thou of human life
> Hast yet but little seen,
> Thy days of sorrow and of strife
> Are few and far between.

One of his last letters, written in his own hand [25] on New Year's Day 1848, was to his only remaining son, his hope for the nation, Charles Francis Adams. Full of praise and thanksgiving and paternal affection, it ended: "A stout heart and a clear conscience, and never despair." [26]

Every action of the old statesman in his faithful attendance upon Congress now assumes a final interest. On December 10, 1847 he declined,

[24] Adams MSS. Actually, Adams had already left New York for Washington when the committee called at his lodgings, and Lewis Tappan mailed the resolution to him.

[25] Actually his correspondence continued scantily until February 4. The last letter recorded in his letterbook, dated Washington, February 4, 1848, was to Lord Ashburton in England, introducing a Miss Porter, daughter of General Peter B. Porter of Niagara Falls, New York. Adams MSS.

[26] *Memoirs*, XII, 281.

on the grounds of precarious health, an invitation to deliver the ceremonial address at the laying of the cornerstone of the Washington Monument.[27] On December 20 he presented several petitions, including two for peace with Mexico, which after some small debate were referred to the committee of foreign affairs.[28] On February 1 he refused unanimous consent to dispense with a reading of the Journal in order to give more time for a debate scheduled to close at two o'clock on assigning to appropriate committees the various sections of President Polk's annual message. Not to read the minutes of the previous day, he said, would set an evil precedent. Presently a more important question arose.

The House had presented a resolution (Adams voted aye in a tally of 145 to 15) requesting the President to communicate instructions to army officers or to Minister John Slidell relating to the return of the exiled Santa Anna to Mexico, with American assistance, at the time of the march of General Taylor's army from the Nueces to the Rio Grande. The resolution did not contain the customary words "providing that it be not incompatible with the public interest." Obviously the purpose was to air the question whether Polk had conspired with Santa Anna to overthrow the *de facto* Mexican Government on the eve of the war, whether the President had not helped the dictator to get back to Mexico in return for an assurance he would make a satisfactory territorial arrangement with the United States.

Polk responded by conveying reports from the Secretaries of State, War, and Navy with accompanying documents which contained all the information in the possession of the Executive which he deemed it compatible with the public interest to deliver; he also referred to his recent annual message on the state of the Union and other documents attached to it.[29] To go further, he explained, would break down the secrecy essential to diplomatic negotiations of a delicate nature. To justify his position Polk cited President Washington's refusal in 1796 to hand over the diplomatic instructions and correspondence relating to Jay's Treaty.[30]

Adams as a member of Congress thought that the House had the right to demand and receive *all* the papers unless it had explicitly excepted such as were incompatible with the public interest to disclose. He stuck to this position in the rather sharp debate that followed. His persistence showed the degree to which his opposition to Polk's Mexican policy had carried him.

"I think this House ought to sustain, in the strongest manner," he declared, "their right to call for information upon questions in which war

[27] JQA to Committee of the Washington Monument, Washington, December 10, 1847. Adams MSS.

[28] *Congressional Globe*, [XVII], pp. 56–7.

[29] Special message of President Polk to the House of Representatives, January 12, 1848.

[30] *Congressional Globe*, [XVII], pp. 103–4, 166.

and peace are concerned. They ought to maintain their right, and maintain it in a very distinct manner, against this assertion on the part of the President of the United States. . . .

"I should say more, sir, if I had the power." [31]

There is no question who had the better of the argument. George Washington and James K. Polk were right and John Quincy Adams was wrong.

Perhaps the brief debate on the President's powers stimulated the veteran to a last resurgence of strength and vivacity. On Thursday the 17th of February he was seen at a reception of the Mayor of Washington, in company with Justice John McLean, Henry Clay, and several other Senators. Observers noticed that he seemed in good health and spirits. On Friday he sat on the library committee, and on the floor he participated in action on a bill for relief of the heirs of the naval hero of the Revolution, John Paul Jones. On Saturday he spent three hours on his feet inspecting the collections of the bibliophile and ventriloquist Nicholas M. A. Vattemare. An engraving of the death of Queen Elizabeth led the old scholar to give a fifteen-minute informal lecture to a circle of listeners who quickly gathered around. Then he set about preparing a memorial to present next day in the House in support of Vattemare's system for the exchange of duplicate books among libraries and museums in America and Europe.

That evening Mr. and Mrs. Adams held open house for a throng of visitors. [32] Although he appeared in famous health, he is said to have remarked to one of his friends that he did not expect to live out the session. [33] Alone with Louisa, he had kept telling her just where to find his will when the time came. The next day, Sunday, he attended church twice, rising at each accustomed call of worship. At some hour during the day he found time to copy some stanzas of agedly playful verse for Miss Caroline Edwards, a young lady of Springfield, Massachusetts, who had asked for his autograph. [34] In the evening his wife read to him Bishop

[31] *Congressional Globe*, [XVII], pp. 167, 168. January 13, 1848. For the debates of 1796 see *Annals of Congress*, 4th Cong., 1st Sess., pp. 764–82, 971–4, 1280–93, *et passim*.

[32] Correspondent of *New York Journal of Commerce*, Washington, February 21, 1848. Ibid., XXXVII, No. 7227.

[33] Washington correspondent of the *New York Express* under date of February 21 and 24, 1848. Ibid., February 22 and 25, 1848. Boston *Christian Register*, XXVII, No. 10, March 4, 1848.

[34]
    In days of yore, the poet's pen
       From wing of bird was plundered,
    Perhaps of goose, but now and then
       From Jove's own eagle sundered.
    But now, metallic pens disclose
       Alone the poet's numbers;
    In iron inspiration glows,
       Or with the poet slumbers.

Wilberforce's sermon on Time.[35] They both planned to attend the grand ball for Washington's Birthday, at which Mrs. Adams was to be a patroness.

On Monday, February 21, 1848 he rode in his carriage, as usual in these last years, to the Capitol, was early in his seat, and conversed freely with various members before the day's session began,[36] the last being Henry Washington Hilliard of Alabama. The official proceedings had already started when he autographed some stanzas to the Muse of History perched on her wheeled and winged car over the front door of the Hall of Representatives.[37]

When the business of the day got under way, he voted against suspension of the rules to interrupt the calendar in order that resolutions might be considered tendering the thanks of Congress and decorations to various generals for gallant actions in the campaigns of 1847 in Mexico. The Speaker then called for ayes and noes on whether to put the main question. Adams responded with a clear and resolute voice *No* against the motion, which carried overwhelmingly.

Even if it cost him his last breath he would vote against decorating generals, however brave and gallant, for fighting in a "most unrighteous war"!

The onetime expansionist and negotiator of the Transcontinental

---

Fair damsel could my pen impart,
In prose or lofty rhyme,
The pure emotions of my heart,
To speed the flight of time,
What metal from the womb of earth
Could worth intrinsic bear,
To stamp with corresponding worth
The blessings thou shouldst share?

Boston *Christian Register*, XXVII, No. 10, March 4, 1848. Washington correspondence of *New York Express*, February 21, 1848. *National Intelligencer*, February–March 1848.

[35] William H. Seward: *Life and Services of John Quincy Adams* (Auburn, N.Y., 1849), p. 332.

[36] Correspondent of the *New York Express* under date of February 24, 1848, Washington. *New York Express*, February 25, 1848. *National Intelligencer*, February 24, 1848.

[37]

Muse! quit thy car! come down upon the floor,
And with thee bring that volume in thy hand;
Rap with thy marble knuckles at the door,
And take at a reporter's desk thy stand.

Send round thy album, and collect a store
Of autographs from rulers of the land;
Invite each Solon to inscribe his name,
A self-recorded candidate for fame.

Washington correspondent of the *New York Express*, February 28, 1848. Ibid., March 1, 1848.

Treaty of 1819 with Spain did not know, as he voiced this his final protest at the Mexican War, that at that very moment Manifest Destiny had reached its high-water mark: President Polk had just received a treaty of peace and was making ready to send it to the Senate the next day.[38] Much less could Adams know, nor could anybody then in Washington or in Mexico know, that four weeks before signature of the Treaty of Guadalupe Hidalgo one of Johann A. Sutter's workmen had made the momentous discovery of heavy yellow particles in tailings of his millrace in distant California, within the territory newly ceded to the United States. James K. Polk had gathered in the Golden West and the Great Southwest, and a momentous sectional struggle over slavery was sure to follow.

The ringing *No* was the Old Man Eloquent's last word on the floor of Congress. The Speaker now put the main question: should the resolutions of thanks to the generals and their troops be engrossed for a third reading? [39] The Clerk began to read the texts so that everybody might have them clear before the vote. So noisy was the House that it was difficult to hear him. Adams, whose name would come third on the roll-call, was waiting most excitedly to cast his vote against the measure. The Clerk proceeded: ". . . gallantry and military skill . . . splendid victories achieved by our armies in the Valley and before the City of Mexico . . . scattering the armies of Mexico like chaff before the wind . . . crowned by possession of the far-famed 'Halls of Montezuma' . . ." [40]

Suddenly a deep touch of color tinged John Quincy Adams's temples. Nobody seemed to notice it except an abolitionist reporter seated at the press table fifteen feet away who was watching him closely, wondering if he would vote for such a string of rhodomontade. The old man's lips were moving, seemingly trying to shape some words, perhaps "Mr. Speaker." His right hand clutched convulsively at the corner of his desk as if for support in rising. Then he slumped over to the left.[41]

"Mr. Adams is dying!" cried Washington Hunt, a member from New York, who sat near him.

The hubbub stopped. All eyes turned to the spot. David Fisher of Ohio, who sat next to the venerable Representative, had caught him in his arms to prevent his falling to the floor.[42]

---

[38] Nicholas Trist, the repudiated envoy, had signed the treaty at Guadalupe Hidalgo, in the outskirts of Mexico City, on February 2, 1848. The news reached the White House on February 18, 1848; the treaty arrived the following day. Polk held it confidentially in Cabinet discussion until February 22, 1848, when he sent it to the Senate for advice and consent as to ratification. Wiltse: *Calhoun, Sectionalist*, p. 329.

[39] *Congressional Globe*, 30th Cong., 1st Sess., 1847–8, pp. 380–1. Monday, February 21, 1848.

[40] Ibid.

[41] Account of H. B. Stanton, reported for the Boston *Emancipator and Republican*, dated Washington, February 21, 1848. Ibid., XII, No. 45, March 1, 1848.

[42] *Biographical Directory of the American Congress, 1774–1927* (Washington, 1928), p. 968.

"Mr. Adams is dying! Mr. Adams is dying!" swept in hushed tones through the quickly quieted House.

Members crowded about to help the fallen statesman. Several of them tenderly lifted him forward into the area in front of the Speaker's table. Speaker Winthrop suggested that someone move an adjournment, which was promptly done; the Senate also rose as soon as the news reached that chamber; so did the Supreme Court.

Colleagues brought in a sofa and laid the dying man on it. In this way they carried him first into the Rotunda, then on the advice of four physician members [43] to the east Portico. There the air proved too damp and chilly. At the suggestion of Winthrop they bore the sofa and its burden into the Speaker's room, where everybody was excluded except physicians and close friends. Lying there, the stricken man revived slightly. He called for Henry Clay. His old rival and associate came in and, weeping, clasped his hand,[44] then departed to fulfill political engagements in Philadelphia and New York. After trying to express his thanks to the "officers of the House," Adams said: "This is the end of earth, but I am composed." [45] Soon afterward Mrs. Adams with her intimate friend Miss Mary

[43] Dr. William Newell of New Jersey, Dr. Thomas O. Edwards of Ohio, Dr. George Fries of Ohio, and Dr. Samuel Oldham Peyton of Kentucky. A local physician, Dr. Harvey Lindsley, was also called in.

[44] *New York Journal of Commerce*, XXXVII, No. 7228, February 24, 1848. Epes Sargent: *The Life and Public Services of Henry Clay* (New York, 1848), p. 113.

[45] "Dr. Payton [*sic*] tells me he [JQA] has just said: 'This is the end of earth, but I am compozed [*sic*].' " John G. Palfrey to CFA, Speaker's Room, House of Representatives, 21st [February 1848], 1 1/2 p.m. Adams MSS. Palfrey, the well-known Boston Unitarian clergyman, Harvard professor, writer, lecturer, editor and publisher (proprietor of the *North American Review*, 1835–43), member of the House of Representatives, 1847–9, was a close friend of both John Quincy Adams and his son Charles Francis Adams.

The *National Intelligencer*, XLIX, No. 7045, February 22, 1848, whose reporter was in the House at the time, but probably not in the Speaker's Room, as was Palfrey, quoted Adams's last words similarly, except for the word *but*. The resolutions of a meeting of citizens of Washington recited that Adams was heard to say: "This is the last of earth. I am content," and these words immediately received wide circulation in the press. This more classical and literary version suited William H. Seward better in the notable eulogy he delivered to the New York legislature, April 6, 1848, when he used the words as a text to illustrate John Quincy Adams's general contentment with life's offerings and acceptance of the will of God. William H. Seward: *Life and Public Services of John Quincy Adams, Sixth President of the United States, with the Eulogy Delivered before the Legislature of New York* (Auburn, 1849).

To me "This is the end of earth, but I am composed" seems more characteristic of John Quincy Adams than the more lyrical line: "This is the last of earth—I am content."

One of the physicians who attended John Quincy Adams was Dr. William A. Newell, member from New Jersey who sat directly in front of him. Fifty years later in an undated excerpt of a letter to George S. Boutwell and another written from Hartford, Conn., to Charles Francis Adams, Jr., December 29, 1898, Dr. Newell declared that

Elizabeth Cutts arrived at his bedside. As Louisa bent over her husband he gave no sign of recognition.[46] The attending physicians and male friends then prevailed upon the anguished women to withdraw.[47]

The ex-President lay in a coma, half paralyzed, throughout the 22d of February 1848, anniversary of his great patron. That day the Senate met briefly in executive session to receive the treaty of peace and order it printed with accompanying documents. The House met only to adjourn after perfunctory routine. In the city the ball and all festivities were canceled.

On the evening of the 23d of February 1848 at twenty minutes past seven the old contender breathed his last, in the Capitol building, forum and symbol of the Union he had labored to expand in sovereign strength, to preserve, and to make free for all men.

Next day the Speaker officially announced to the assembled House the death of their venerated fellow member. Charles Hudson, surviving senior member of the delegation in the House from Massachusetts, rose to review his beloved colleague's sixty years of public service: "but the crowning glory of his character was his devotion to the cause of his Redeemer." Hudson then moved the customary expressions of mourning, with a committee of thirty to superintend the funeral ceremonies in the Hall of the House of Representatives. Before the motion was voted, Isaac E. Holmes, Democrat from Charleston, South Carolina, rose to speak in gifted tones of sorrow: "When a great man falls, the nation mourns; when a patriarch is removed, the people weep." Samuel Finley Vinton, Ohio Whig born in New England, added his tribute to the famous son of Massachusetts: "His fame, his wisdom, and his works, were all his country's." Vinton moved and the House unanimously agreed to an additional resolution: that a committee of one member from each state and territory of the Union be appointed to escort the remains of

---

he was with the stricken man "until he died" (Newell to Boutwell) or "until he was comatose" (Newell to CFA, Jr.): "I had my ear, as had others, frequently in place to catch his last utterance, but he never uttered an intelligible sound . . ." (Newell to Boutwell). Adams MSS.

Dr. Newell's two accounts are so different from each other and from the letter of Palfrey written within the hour of the dying man's stroke, and from other contemporary records, that they afford a notable illustration of how an old man's memory can trick him fifty years after even a vivid event when details are not supported by his contemporary diary or letters.

[46] J. G. Palfrey to CFA, February 21, 1848. Adams MSS.

[47] LCA to Harriet Boyd, Washington, February 23, 1848. Bobbé: *Mr. and Mrs. John Q. Adams*, p. 301. Mary Estelle Elizabeth Cutts was the daughter of Mr. and Mrs. Richard Cutts, both deceased. Richard Cutts, 1770–1845, was a native of Maine who served in the House of Representatives, 1801–13, later as Superintendent General of Military Supplies, 1813–17, and Assistant Comptroller of the Treasury, 1817–29. Noting Cutts's death in his Diary, April 7, 1845, Adams mentioned "his one unmarried daughter Mary Estelle Elizabeth who lived with him and kept his house, and who for the last seven years has been almost an inmate of ours."

their venerable friend, the Honorable John Quincy Adams, to the place designated by his friends for his interment.

In the Senate, John Davis of Worcester, Massachusetts, former National Republican Governor of the Commonwealth in Antimasonic days, now a leading Whig, reviewed his fallen associate's long career: "Let not the grave of the Old Man Eloquent be desecrated by unfriendly remembrances, but let us yield our homage to his many virtues." But it was Thomas Hart Benton, Adams's ancient political enemy, in recent years reconciled over the Texas Question, who delivered a notable tribute to him and his devotion to public duties on all occasions great or small: "Wherever his presence could give aid and countenance to what was useful and honorable to man, there he was. . . . Where could death have found him but at the post of duty?" [48]

Amid all this spread of proper oratory no one mentioned Adams's greatest battle and finest victory, his winning of the bitter sectional contest for freedom of petition to Congress.

They laid his body in a committee room of the House of Representatives. During the next two days thousands of people filed by for a last view of the sage's features,[49] serene in their final stillness. The procession was interrupted on Friday the 25th to allow Charles Francis Adams, arrived from Boston too late to see his father alive, to be alone for a few moments at the bier. "I am alone in the generation," he thought as he stood and looked upon all that was left of the "great landmark" of his own life. Then the long row again began to move by the casket, spread with evergreens and early flowers of spring, so loved by the vanished spirit.[50]

"A Patriarch has gone to his rest—a link between the past and the present generation is broken—a Sage has fallen at his post!" So read a call for a public meeting of mourning by the citizens of Washington. On Friday the 24th they assembled—and passed a series of resolutions testifying to the long public service and Christian virtues of John Quincy Adams, and suspending all public business during the period of the obsequies.[51]

The funeral ceremonies in Washington and elsewhere assumed the proportions and significance of a national pageant, and as such they may be recorded in some detail.

A cannon salute greeted the sun as it rose over the Potomac that Saturday morning. From then until high noon gunfire rolled over the District

[48] *Token of a Nation's Sorrow: Addresses in the Congress of the United States and Funeral Solemnities on the Death of John Quincy Adams who died in the Capitol at Washington on Wednesday Evening, February 23, 1848* (Washington, 1848).

[49] Washington correspondence of *New York Journal of Commerce*, Washington, February 25, 1848. Ibid., XXXVII, No. 7231, February 28, 1848. *Hingham Patriot*, X, No. 36, March 3, 1848.

[50] Diary of CFA. February 22, 23, 24, 25, 1848.

[51] *National Intelligencer*, XLIX, Nos. 7046 and 7047, February 24 and 26, 1848.

anecdotes, reminiscences, and editorials in praise of the venerable patriot and public servant. Newspapers printed selections from his verse, quotations from his letters, wise sayings, illustrations of his steady habits, statements of his religious opinions.[59] The obsequies developed into what amounted to a country-wide ceremony, as if of emotional release at the end of a conscience-troubling war, not so much of formal grief as of rejoicing that in those dubious years the Republic should have produced such a great and honorable man and so notable a Christian.

Proud Boston, which would not make John Quincy Adams wholly her own while living, now took him to herself in death. Upon news of his passing, the Massachusetts legislature, which four times had declined to elevate him from the House of Representatives to the Senate in Washington, had listened to eulogies and passed resolutions extolling his republican simplicity of manners, his elevated morals, his Christian virtues, his reverence for religion and its institutions: "With melancholy pleasure, we behold such a public servant, when summoned to his final account, falling at the post of his duty." [60]

Citizens thronged the streets when the funeral train arrived. A distinguished local committee received the escort and amid more tolling bells and minute salutes took the corpse to Fanueil Hall, where many men and women of Massachusetts were waiting in mourning. Conspicuously placed inscriptions listed the state and national posts that Adams had held from boyhood through old age. Over the entrance to the hall, grasped in the eagle's beak, was a placard: "This is the last of Earth—I am content." Beneath: "John Quincy Adams, aged 81. Born a citizen of Massachusetts. 'Died a citizen of the United States.'" Between the galleries above the auditorium were these words of George Washington in 1797: "John Quincy Adams is the most valuable character we have abroad and the ablest of all our diplomatic corps."

Adams's onetime enemy and later friend Joseph T. Buckingham, state senator from Middlesex County, who had delivered a eulogy in the legislature, received the body from the Congressional Committee and consigned it to Mayor Josiah Quincy of Boston for delivery to the fellow townsmen of Quincy.

"This is no mere pageant," responded Adams's lifetime friend. "The spots on which this bier rests on its journey to the grave will not be marked by visible tokens . . . but associations and recollections shall cluster there, inspiring the living with the spirit of the dead; and, should

[59] A collection of such accounts, with newspaper clippings, is preserved in the Adams MSS. These are largely published in *The Adams Memorial* (Boston, 1848), with which are bound together (in the copy at the Sterling Memorial Library at Yale) thirteen addresses, orations, and discourses on John Quincy Adams, with a copy of *Token of a Nation's Sorrow,* op. cit.

[60] Resolutions unanimously adopted by the Massachusetts House of Representatives, February 26, 1848. *Testimonials of Respect to the Memory of John Quincy Adams by the Legislature of Massachusetts* (Boston, 1848).

minute by minute as public groups and civic societies took shape and moved down Pennsylvania Avenue, between private buildings heavy with crepe, toward the Capitol.

At ten minutes before noon the Speaker called the House of Representatives to order. The bell on Capitol Hill commenced to toll. The President of the United States entered the Hall and took his place at the right hand of the Speaker. Then came the Justices of the Supreme Court, the high officers of the army and navy in full uniform, the diplomatic corps in formal costume, taking their seats in proper order right and left of the aisle in front of the rostrum. The Senate followed, the Vice President stepping to his place at the Speaker's left. Finally Charles Francis Adams, striking in personal resemblance to his deceased father, and others of the family [52] and close friends, came in and seated themselves in a row reserved for them. Then, after a prayer, entered Senators Webster and Davis of Massachusetts, preceding the coffin.[53]

On a catafalque in the space directly in front of the Speaker rested the mortal remains of the patriarch. A silver-mounted coffin, decorated with a spread-eagle, bore a plate with an inscription written, at the request of the Massachusetts delegation to Congress, by Daniel Webster:

JOHN QUINCY ADAMS
BORN
An inhabitant of Massachusetts
July 11, 1767
DIED
A citizen of the United States, in the
Capitol, at Washington, February 23, 1848,
Having served his country for half a century,
And enjoyed its highest honors.

Could the deceased have looked down from Olympus, he must have been content with the inscription, if not with the hand that wrote it. He and Webster had concurred in one greatest goal: Liberty and Union, now and forever, one and inseparable!

From above the Speaker's dark-shrouded chair the portraits of Washington and Lafayette, hung with black, looked down upon the Son of the American Revolution.

The Chaplain of the House, the Reverend R. R. Gurley, opened the service with prayer. A choir in the ladies' gallery sang a dirge. The Chaplain followed with a funeral discourse, memorable not so much for its pious content and patriotic length as for its fitting text from Job xi, 17—

[52] They included Mrs. John (Mary Hellen) Adams and daughter Mary Louisa, and Isaac Hull Adams, nephew of John Quincy Adams. The widow was too bereaved to be able to attend. Diary of CFA, February 26, 1848.

[53] Correspondent of the *New York Journal of Commerce,* Washington, February 25, 26, 1848. Ibid., XXXVII, No. 3271, February 28, 1848.

18: "And thine age shall be clearer than the noonday; thou shalt shine forth, thou shalt be as the morning. And thou shalt be secure, because there is hope."

John Quincy Adams had lived his life deep in the Book of Job in all its despair and all its hope.

The choir sang a closing hymn. Then the cortege moved out of the hall through the east front of the Capitol. A civic funeral procession formed at the Portico, with the statue of George Washington standing singularly and with striking effect in the distance.[54]

Not since Philadelphia paid similar homage to the dead Franklin had there been such public testimony to a deceased American statesman. The various groups of citizens and officers of the Republic and of the District of Columbia embodied Adams's associations during sixty years of public service from the American Revolution to the end of the War with Mexico. They started slowly through the north gate, around the western portion of the public park, on the way to the congressional burying ground, whither Adams in his lifetime had accompanied so many friends and colleagues.

First marched the military companies of Washington with a funeral band. Many a time had Adams reviewed them in the District.

Then came the Chaplains of the House and Senate, and clergy of the District and attending physicians. In his day Adams had worshipped at all the churches of Washington and had been personally acquainted with their pastors and priests.

Next followed the Committee of Arrangements, composed of one member of the House from each state and territory. Young Abraham Lincoln represented the State of Illinois, the only association between the two men which history records.

There followed a Committee of Escort similarly representing the states and territories, then the funeral carriage, flanked by twelve honorary pallbearers, including John C. Calhoun.[55] Adams had known Calhoun as a friend and colleague during his Administration, and had argued with him in tractates on the Constitution; each had thought ill-natured things about the other in the heat of political controversy; each had respected the other as a man and statesman.

The family, represented by Charles Francis Adams and Mary Hellen Adams, followed in carriages after the hearse; after them selected Senators and Representatives as mourners; the Sergeant at Arms of the House; the members of the House, preceded by the Speaker and the Clerk. Behind the House were the Senate and its officers in corresponding order. Adams had been a Senator, and had resigned in 1808, forty years before, when the legislature of Massachusetts in effect recalled him for having

[54] Diary of CFA, February 26, 1848.

[55] He is so listed in the order of the funeral procession as drawn up by the committee on arrangements. See *Token of a Nation's Sorrow*, op. cit., p. 39.

stood behind the President in Embargo days. He had devoted the last seventeen years of his life to service in the lower house of Congress.

After the Congress marched the President of the United States. John Quincy Adams had held that office in a strange interlude between his two careers.

The Justices of the Supreme Court then followed. President Madison had appointed Adams to that tribunal, but he had declined the office while serving as Minister to Russia.

Next came the foreign diplomatic corps. Adams had been America's greatest diplomatist, during the first half-century of our independence when the foundations of American foreign policy were set in classic form.

Finally followed a procession of minor government dignitaries, military and naval officers, members of state legislatures, and the Corporation of Washington, ending with the Columbian Typographical Society, the faculty and students of Georgetown College and of the Columbian College, and members of literary institutions, fire companies, and other organizations and societies of the District of Columbia.[56] With all these groups Adams had had close and friendly relationships during his many years in the nation's capital.

Following these national honors the body rested temporarily in the tomb of the congressional cemetery pending conveyance to Quincy. A week after the ceremonies at Washington the Committee of Escort entrained to take all that was left of the Old Man Eloquent back to Massachusetts.

John Quincy Adams's timely end at his post of duty touched the imagination of his countrymen as nothing had since the deaths of John Adams and Thomas Jefferson on the 4th of July 1826, fiftieth anniversary of American independence. People sensed in a dramatic way the breaking of the last personal link between the founding fathers and the men of a new and uncertain era. All along the route flags were at half-mast; business was suspended in the towns where the funeral party stopped for local obsequies and tributes. Along the countryside people stood with bowed heads as the train passed by with its black-draped car. The nation experienced an outpouring of eulogies,[57] elegies, obituaries, requiems, odes, poems, orations, sermons, resolutions,[58] biographical sketches,

[56] *Token of a Nation's Sorrow,* op. cit. Washington, correspondent of the *New York Journal of Commerce,* under date of February 26, 29, 1848. Ibid., XXXVII, Nos. 7231, 7236, February 28, March 4, 1848.

[57] For a list of these funeral discourses see *Bibliography of John and John Quincy Adams,* op. cit. (in Preface to this volume).

[58] Many of these testimonials are preserved, methodically filed by his family and found at the end of the last volume of JQA's incoming General Correspondence.

A sour note prevailed in the Virginia legislature, where the Senate voted on strict party lines to lay on the table appropriate resolutions unanimously passed by the lower house. Louisville, Ky., *Journal,* XVIII, No. 82, March 11, 1848.

minute by minute as public groups and civic societies took shape and moved down Pennsylvania Avenue, between private buildings heavy with crepe, toward the Capitol.

At ten minutes before noon the Speaker called the House of Representatives to order. The bell on Capitol Hill commenced to toll. The President of the United States entered the Hall and took his place at the right hand of the Speaker. Then came the Justices of the Supreme Court, the high officers of the army and navy in full uniform, the diplomatic corps in formal costume, taking their seats in proper order right and left of the aisle in front of the rostrum. The Senate followed, the Vice President stepping to his place at the Speaker's left. Finally Charles Francis Adams, striking in personal resemblance to his deceased father, and others of the family [52] and close friends, came in and seated themselves in a row reserved for them. Then, after a prayer, entered Senators Webster and Davis of Massachusetts, preceding the coffin.[53]

On a catafalque in the space directly in front of the Speaker rested the mortal remains of the patriarch. A silver-mounted coffin, decorated with a spread-eagle, bore a plate with an inscription written, at the request of the Massachusetts delegation to Congress, by Daniel Webster:

JOHN QUINCY ADAMS
BORN
An inhabitant of Massachusetts
July 11, 1767
DIED
A citizen of the United States, in the
Capitol, at Washington, February 23, 1848,
Having served his country for half a century,
And enjoyed its highest honors.

Could the deceased have looked down from Olympus, he must have been content with the inscription, if not with the hand that wrote it. He and Webster had concurred in one greatest goal: Liberty and Union, now and forever, one and inseparable!

From above the Speaker's dark-shrouded chair the portraits of Washington and Lafayette, hung with black, looked down upon the Son of the American Revolution.

The Chaplain of the House, the Reverend R. R. Gurley, opened the service with prayer. A choir in the ladies' gallery sang a dirge. The Chaplain followed with a funeral discourse, memorable not so much for its pious content and patriotic length as for its fitting text from Job xi, 17–

---

[52] They included Mrs. John (Mary Hellen) Adams and daughter Mary Louisa, and Isaac Hull Adams, nephew of John Quincy Adams. The widow was too bereaved to be able to attend. Diary of CFA, February 26, 1848.

[53] Correspondent of the *New York Journal of Commerce*, Washington, February 25, 26, 1848. Ibid., XXXVII, No. 3271, February 28, 1848.

18: "And thine age shall be clearer than the noonday; thou shalt shine forth, thou shalt be as the morning. And thou shalt be secure, because there is hope."

John Quincy Adams had lived his life deep in the Book of Job in all its despair and all its hope.

The choir sang a closing hymn. Then the cortege moved out of the hall through the east front of the Capitol. A civic funeral procession formed at the Portico, with the statue of George Washington standing singularly and with striking effect in the distance.[54]

Not since Philadelphia paid similar homage to the dead Franklin had there been such public testimony to a deceased American statesman. The various groups of citizens and officers of the Republic and of the District of Columbia embodied Adams's associations during sixty years of public service from the American Revolution to the end of the War with Mexico. They started slowly through the north gate, around the western portion of the public park, on the way to the congressional burying ground, whither Adams in his lifetime had accompanied so many friends and colleagues.

First marched the military companies of Washington with a funeral band. Many a time had Adams reviewed them in the District.

Then came the Chaplains of the House and Senate, and clergy of the District and attending physicians. In his day Adams had worshipped at all the churches of Washington and had been personally acquainted with their pastors and priests.

Next followed the Committee of Arrangements, composed of one member of the House from each state and territory. Young Abraham Lincoln represented the State of Illinois, the only association between the two men which history records.

There followed a Committee of Escort similarly representing the states and territories, then the funeral carriage, flanked by twelve honorary pallbearers, including John C. Calhoun.[55] Adams had known Calhoun as a friend and colleague during his Administration, and had argued with him in tractates on the Constitution; each had thought ill-natured things about the other in the heat of political controversy; each had respected the other as a man and statesman.

The family, represented by Charles Francis Adams and Mary Hellen Adams, followed in carriages after the hearse; after them selected Senators and Representatives as mourners; the Sergeant at Arms of the House; the members of the House, preceded by the Speaker and the Clerk. Behind the House were the Senate and its officers in corresponding order. Adams had been a Senator, and had resigned in 1808, forty years before, when the legislature of Massachusetts in effect recalled him for having

[54] Diary of CFA, February 26, 1848.

[55] He is so listed in the order of the funeral procession as drawn up by the committee on arrangements. See *Token of a Nation's Sorrow*, op. cit., p. 39.

stood behind the President in Embargo days. He had devoted the last seventeen years of his life to service in the lower house of Congress.

After the Congress marched the President of the United States. John Quincy Adams had held that office in a strange interlude between his two careers.

The Justices of the Supreme Court then followed. President Madison had appointed Adams to that tribunal, but he had declined the office while serving as Minister to Russia.

Next came the foreign diplomatic corps. Adams had been America's greatest diplomatist, during the first half-century of our independence when the foundations of American foreign policy were set in classic form.

Finally followed a procession of minor government dignitaries, military and naval officers, members of state legislatures, and the Corporation of Washington, ending with the Columbian Typographical Society, the faculty and students of Georgetown College and of the Columbian College, and members of literary institutions, fire companies, and other organizations and societies of the District of Columbia.[56] With all these groups Adams had had close and friendly relationships during his many years in the nation's capital.

Following these national honors the body rested temporarily in the tomb of the congressional cemetery pending conveyance to Quincy. A week after the ceremonies at Washington the Committee of Escort entrained to take all that was left of the Old Man Eloquent back to Massachusetts.

John Quincy Adams's timely end at his post of duty touched the imagination of his countrymen as nothing had since the deaths of John Adams and Thomas Jefferson on the 4th of July 1826, fiftieth anniversary of American independence. People sensed in a dramatic way the breaking of the last personal link between the founding fathers and the men of a new and uncertain era. All along the route flags were at half-mast; business was suspended in the towns where the funeral party stopped for local obsequies and tributes. Along the countryside people stood with bowed heads as the train passed by with its black-draped car. The nation experienced an outpouring of eulogies,[57] elegies, obituaries, requiems, odes, poems, orations, sermons, resolutions,[58] biographical sketches,

[56] *Token of a Nation's Sorrow,* op. cit. Washington, correspondent of the *New York Journal of Commerce,* under date of February 26, 29, 1848. Ibid., XXXVII, Nos. 7231, 7236, February 28, March 4, 1848.

[57] For a list of these funeral discourses see *Bibliography of John and John Quincy Adams,* op. cit. (in Preface to this volume).

[58] Many of these testimonials are preserved, methodically filed by his family and found at the end of the last volume of JQA's incoming General Correspondence.

A sour note prevailed in the Virginia legislature, where the Senate voted on strict party lines to lay on the table appropriate resolutions unanimously passed by the lower house. Louisville, Ky., *Journal,* XVIII, No. 82, March 11, 1848.

anecdotes, reminiscences, and editorials in praise of the venerable patriot and public servant. Newspapers printed selections from his verse, quotations from his letters, wise sayings, illustrations of his steady habits, statements of his religious opinions.[59] The obsequies developed into what amounted to a country-wide ceremony, as if of emotional release at the end of a conscience-troubling war, not so much of formal grief as of rejoicing that in those dubious years the Republic should have produced such a great and honorable man and so notable a Christian.

Proud Boston, which would not make John Quincy Adams wholly her own while living, now took him to herself in death. Upon news of his passing, the Massachusetts legislature, which four times had declined to elevate him from the House of Representatives to the Senate in Washington, had listened to eulogies and passed resolutions extolling his republican simplicity of manners, his elevated morals, his Christian virtues, his reverence for religion and its institutions: "With melancholy pleasure, we behold such a public servant, when summoned to his final account, falling at the post of his duty." [60]

Citizens thronged the streets when the funeral train arrived. A distinguished local committee received the escort and amid more tolling bells and minute salutes took the corpse to Fanueil Hall, where many men and women of Massachusetts were waiting in mourning. Conspicuously placed inscriptions listed the state and national posts that Adams had held from boyhood through old age. Over the entrance to the hall, grasped in the eagle's beak, was a placard: "This is the last of Earth—I am content." Beneath: "John Quincy Adams, aged 81. Born a citizen of Massachusetts. 'Died a citizen of the United States.'" Between the galleries above the auditorium were these words of George Washington in 1797: "John Quincy Adams is the most valuable character we have abroad and the ablest of all our diplomatic corps."

Adams's onetime enemy and later friend Joseph T. Buckingham, state senator from Middlesex County, who had delivered a eulogy in the legislature, received the body from the Congressional Committee and consigned it to Mayor Josiah Quincy of Boston for delivery to the fellow townsmen of Quincy.

"This is no mere pageant," responded Adams's lifetime friend. "The spots on which this bier rests on its journey to the grave will not be marked by visible tokens . . . but associations and recollections shall cluster there, inspiring the living with the spirit of the dead; and, should

---

[59] A collection of such accounts, with newspaper clippings, is preserved in the Adams MSS. These are largely published in *The Adams Memorial* (Boston, 1848), with which are bound together (in the copy at the Sterling Memorial Library at Yale) thirteen addresses, orations, and discourses on John Quincy Adams, with a copy of *Token of a Nation's Sorrow,* op. cit.

[60] Resolutions unanimously adopted by the Massachusetts House of Representatives, February 26, 1848. *Testimonials of Respect to the Memory of John Quincy Adams by the Legislature of Massachusetts* (Boston, 1848).